Handbook of Microprocessors, Microcomputers, and Minicomputers

JOHN D. LENK

Consulting Technical Writer

Prentice-Hall, Inc., *Englewood Cliffs, New Jersey 07632*

Library of Congress Cataloging in Publication Data

Lenk, John D.
Handbook of microprocessors, microcomputers, and minicomputers.

Includes index.
1. Microprocessors. 2. Microcomputers.
3. Minicomputers. I. Title.
QA76.5.L455 001.6'4'04 78-24307
ISBN 0-13-380378-3

Editorial/production supervision and interior design
by Barbara A. Cassel
Jacket design by George Alon Jaediker
Manufacturing buyer: Gordon Osbourne

Printed in the United States of America

10 9 8 7 6 5 4

PRENTICE-HALL INTERNATIONAL, INC., *London*
PRENTICE-HALL OF AUSTRALIA PTY. LIMITED, *Sydney*
PRENTICE-HALL OF CANADA, LTD., *Toronto*
PRENTICE-HALL OF INDIA PRIVATE LIMITED, *New Delhi*
PRENTICE-HALL OF JAPAN, INC., *Tokyo*
PRENTICE-HALL OF SOUTHEAST ASIA PTE. LTD., *Singapore*
WHITEHALL BOOKS LIMITED, *Wellington, New Zealand*

To

IRENE, the "Sandpiper Lady,"

and to

MR. LAMB, the "Magic Bunny"

Contents

Preface

This book is a "crash course" in microprocessor-based devices, written with five classes of readers in mind. First, there is the engineer who must design with (and program) microprocessors. Next is the technician who must service microprocessor-based equipment. Then there is the programmer/systems analyst who must adapt programs of larger, conventional computers to those of microprocessors. Finally, but not of least importance, are students and hobbyists who want an introduction to microprocessors as well as information they can put to immediate use in experiments and projects.

These various classes of readers start from a different learning point. Obviously, the engineers and technicians understand electronics, but they may have little knowledge of programmed devices and no knowledge of microprocessors. Programmers may be expert in computer language and systems but not know the differences between conventional computers and microcomputers. The student/hobbyist may have only an elementary knowledge of electronics and no understanding of computers or programmed equipment.

This book starts by bringing all these readers up to the same point of understanding. This is done in a unique manner. The descriptions of how microprocessors operate are technically complete (to satisfy the technicians and engineers) but are written in simple, nontechnical terms (for the benefit of programmers/students hobbyists).

The book also bridges another gap. Unlike other electronic devices (such as transistors) that are universal in nature and can operate in many different circuits, microprocessors operate in response to a specific set of instructions applied in the form of electrical signals. Each microprocessor has its own set of instructions and will respond to no other. Thus, you must read the user literature of the particular microprocessor. Some of this literature is comprehensive and well written. However, all microprocessor literature is written on the assumption that the reader has previous knowledge of electronics and/or programmed devices. This book assumes no such previous knowledge and thus fills in the missing gaps.

In addition to providing an understanding of microprocessor literature, this book shows a cross section of present-day microprocessor-based equipment and microcomputers. Throughout the book, there is heavy emphasis on the interrelationships between microprocessors and peripheral equipment (which connects microprocessors to the outer world).

Chapter 1 is an introduction to microprocessors, and covers such subjects as number systems used with microprocessors, alphanumeric codes, relationships between number systems and electrical signals that control microprocessors, basic circuit functions, hardware (memory and input/output), basic microcomputer systems, system timing and synchronization, system operation, machine and assembly languages, development of a microprocessor-based system, and the basic microprocessor troubleshooting approach.

Chapter 2 concentrates on peripheral and support equipment and covers the need for peripheral equipment, electric typewriter terminals, video terminals, paper-tape readers and punches, printers, magnetic recording basics, tape recording basics, diskette (floppy disk) recording basics, and data communications terminals.

Chapters 3 through 7 describe specific microprocessor systems of RCA Corporation Solid State Division, Motorola Semiconductor Products, Intel Corporation, Mostek Corporation, and Texas Instruments. The details presented in these chapters represent only a small fraction of the data taken from the manufacturers' literature (manuals and data sheets). However, the information presented in these chapters is sufficient for readers of any level to evaluate the system. The chapters also provide the reader with a realistic view of actual state-of-the-art microprocessor-based systems. This supplements the theoretical and "typical" descriptions of Chapters 1 and 2.

Chapter 8 is devoted entirely to the 8002 Microprocessor Lab manufactured by Tektronix, Inc., and provides an introduction to microprocessor development aids.

A glossary is included following Chapter 8.

Many professionals have contributed their talent and knowledge to the preparation of this book. The author willingly acknowledges that the tremendous effort to make this book so comprehensive is impossible for one person, and wishes to thank all who have contributed directly and indirectly.

The author gives special thanks to the following persons: Walter B. Dennen of RCA Corporation, Solid State Division; Lothar Stern of Motorola Semiconductor Products, Inc.; J. C. Carsten and Rob Walker of Intel Corporation; Stanley F. Victor, Jr., of Mostek Corporation; E. S. Huber, Jr., of Texas Instruments, Incorporated; Pat Whitty and Wyn Giluck of Tektronix, Inc.; and Joseph A Labok of Los Angeles Valley College.

JOHN D. LENK

1 Introduction to Microprocessors and Microcomputers

The purpose of this chapter is to bring all readers up to the same point. The first sections of the chapter are written on the assumption that some readers may not be familiar with such basics as the number systems used in digital computers, the functions of a computer, and the elements of computer programming. These subjects are discussed here to provide the necessary background for such readers to understand microprocessors and microcomputers. Those readers already familiar with these subjects can skip the first sections at their option.

With basics out of the way, we proceed directly to microprocessors and cover operation, hardware, support equipment, peripheral equipment, programming, and design of microprocessor-based systems. Although specific examples are given, this chapter describes microprocessors in general terms. The microprocessor-based systems of specific manufacturers are given in the remaining chapters of this book.

1-1 MICROPROCESSORS, MICROCOMPUTERS, MICROCONTROLLERS, AND MINICOMPUTERS

A *microprocessor* is an integrated circuit (IC) that performs many of the functions found in a digital computer. A single microprocessor IC is capable of performing all the arithmetic and control functions of a computer. By itself, a typical microprocessor IC does not contain the memories and input/output (I/O) functions of a computer. However, when these functions are provided by additional ICs, a *microcomputer* is formed.

Typically, a basic microcomputer requires a read-only memory (ROM) to store the computer program or instructions, a random-access memory (RAM) to store temporary data (the information to be acted upon by the computer program), and an I/O IC to make the system compatible with outside or (peripheral) equipment such as an interactive video computer terminal, teletype, or line printer. There are some ICs that contain some, or all, of these functions. In effect, when an IC contains all of the basic functions, the IC is a "computer on a chip." However, this is not the typical case.

Microprocessors are sometimes referred to as *microprocessor units* (MPU) or *control processor units* (CPU) (CPU can sometimes mean *central processor unit*). It should also be noted that a microprocessor is not always used in digital computer applications. Instead, the microprocessor is used as a controller. As a matter of interest, the microprocessor was originally developed as the control element for those applications where digital computer functions (the ability to store and execute a complete program automatically) were required, but where a computer (even a simple minicomputer) was too large or expensive. Sometimes, the microprocessor is called a *microcontroller* when used in these control applications. The various terms are discussed further throughout the remainder of this chapter.

The term *minicomputer* can be applied to many relatively small and relatively simple computers. A minicomputer often contains many ICs, but not necessarily a microprocessor IC. In this book, we are concerned primarily with microprocessor-based systems, whether they be computers, controllers, or whatever.

1-2 NUMBER SYSTEMS IN MICROPROCESSORS/ MICROCOMPUTERS

The decimal number system is generally used in the world outside the microprocessor. Inside a microprocessor-based system, the *binary* number system is used most often. This is because binary numbers are compatible with the electrical *pulses* used in digital or logic systems. Binary numbers use only two digits, 0 or 1. The zero can be represented by the absence of a pulse, with the 1 being represented by the presence of a pulse (vice versa in some systems). The pulses [typically about 5 V in amplitude, and a few microseconds (μs) or nanoseconds (ns) in duration] can be positive or negative without affecting the binary number system (as long as only two states exist). In any event, to understand the language of microprocessor-based systems (generally referred to as *machine language*), it becomes necessary to examine number systems in general and the binary number system in particular.

Although microprocessors use binary numbers in the form of pulses, most microcomputer systems use some other form of number system for assembly of computer programs (generally referred to as *assembly language*). This is because binary numbers (although compatible with pulses) are cumbersome when the values are beyond a few digits. Shorthand number systems are used to enter and read out programs and data in a microcomputer system. The most common shorthand number systems used for microcomputer programming are the *octal, hexidecimal* (or hex), *binary-coded decimal* (or BCD), and *alphanumeric* systems. We discuss each of these systems in the following paragraphs.

1-3 BINARY NUMBER SYSTEM

The binary number system uses only two digits, 0 and 1. The *positional weights* of the digits increase from right to left as in the familiar decimal system. In all number systems, digits are assigned positional weights, or values, so that numbers can be written to express all quantities, no matter how large or small. The real value of a digit depends on its position in the number. With binary, the increase of value is in ascending powers of 2. Thus, the digit at the extreme right (the least significant digit, or LSD) has a weight or value of 2^0, or decimal 1. A digit in the position immediately to the left has a weight of 2^1, or decimal 2. The next digit to the left is equivalent to decimal 4, and so on. This can be shown as follows:

2^7	2^6	2^5	2^4	2^3	2^2	2^1	2^0
128	64	32	16	8	4	2	1
MSD							LSD

When all of these decimal values are added, the total is 255. Thus, an eight-digit binary number can represent decimal numbers from 0 to 255.

1-3-1 Words, bits, bytes, and nibbles

Note that the extreme left-hand digit (the most significant digit, or MSD) has a value of 128. Also, note that this combination of eight binary digits is commonly used in microprocessors to form a binary *word.* In computer work, binary digits are referred to as *bits* (a contraction of *bi*nary digi*ts*). The LSD bit is bit zero, or b_0, whereas the MSD bit is seven, or b_7. When eight binary digits are used to form words, the arrangement is known as an 8-bit system. When all eight bits are used at once, the combination is referred to as a *byte.* Any number less than 8 bits is called a *nibble,* although in an 8-bit system, a nibble is generally considered to be four bits. Likewise, some computer systems use 4-bit or 16-bit binary words or bytes. In fact, many of the newer microcomputer systems are designed for 16-bit words, but will also accept 8-bit words so as to be compatible with the majority of present-day microcomputer systems.

1-3-2 Binary number values

In binary, if the digit is zero, its value is zero. If the digit is 1, its value is determined by its position from the right. For example, to represent the decimal number 73 in binary form, the following combination of 0s and 1s can be used:

b_7	b_6	b_5	b_4	b_3	b_2	b_1	b_0		
b_7	b_6	b_5	b_4	b_3	b_2	b_1	b_0		(bit number)
0	1	0	0	1	0	0	1		(binary number)
128	64	32	16	8	4	2	1		(weight or value)
0	+ 64	+ 0	+ 0	+ 8	+ 0	+ 0	+ 1	= 73	(decimal)

which means that 01001001 in 8-bit binary form = 73.

Note that it is not always necessary to use the full 8 bits to write a binary number. For example, decimal 15 requires only four binary digits 1111, and need not be written as 00001111 on paper. However, in an 8-bit microprocessor system, all 8 bits must be included by adding the 0s.

1-3-3 Number identification

Note also that binary number 1011 (which may be interpreted as 8 + 0 + 2 + 1, or decimal 11) is not read as "one thousand eleven" but as "one, zero, one, one." In some computer literature where binary and decimal numbers are mixed, a number subscript (as 2 for binary, a 10 for decimal) is added to minimize confusion. For example, 101_{10} is decimal "one hundred and one," whereas 101_2 is binary "one zero one," or decimal 5_{10}. In other literature, a letter is added to the number (D for decimal, B for binary) for identification. Two other commonly used number systems, octal and hexidecimal (described in the following paragraphs), are identified by number subscripts (8 for octal, 16 for hexidecimal) in some literature.

1-3-4 Counting in binary

The counting method for binary numbers is the same as for the decimal system except that we use only two digits, 0 and 1. Thus, starting with 0, if we add one count, we get 1. Adding another count, we go back to 0 again, and a carry is added to the next position at the left, producing 10 (decimal 2).

Adding another count produces 11 (decimal 3); and if another count is added, we get 100 (decimal 4). The next count produces 101 (decimal 5); and so on.

1-3-5 Binary fractions

When we come to binary fractions, we use the same rules that we apply to decimal fractions. A binary point (similar to the decimal point) is used to separate the integers (whole numbers) from the fraction. The weight of the digit to the right of the binary point is 2^{-1}, or decimal $\frac{1}{2}$. The next position to the right has a weight of 2^{-2}, or decimal $\frac{1}{4}$; the next position to the right has a weight of 2^{-3}, or decimal $\frac{1}{8}$; and so on. A partial table of binary fractions showing their decimal equivalents is as follows:

Fraction	*Decimal*	*Power of 2*	*Binary Equivalent*
$\frac{1}{2}$	0.5	2^{-1}	0.1
$\frac{1}{4}$	0.25	2^{-2}	0.01
$\frac{1}{8}$	0.125	2^{-3}	0.001
$\frac{1}{16}$	0.0625	2^{-4}	0.0001
$\frac{1}{32}$	0.03125	2^{-5}	0.00001
$\frac{1}{64}$	0.015625	2^{-6}	0.000001
$\frac{1}{128}$	0.0078125	2^{-7}	0.0000001
$\frac{1}{256}$	0.00390625	2^{-8}	0.00000001
$\frac{1}{512}$	0.001953125	2^{-9}	0.000000001

The binary fraction 0.101 may be interpreted as $0 + \frac{1}{2} + \frac{0}{4} + \frac{1}{8}$, or as $0 + 0.5 + 0 + 0.125$, which is equal to the decimal fraction 0.625. If we have a mixed binary number containing integers and fractions, such as 101.101, we may find the decimal equivalent by means of the following tabulation:

Binary Digit	*Positional Weight*	*Decimal Equivalent*
1	$\times\ 2^{2}$	= 4
0	$\times\ 2^{1}$	= 0
1	$\times\ 2^{0}$	= 1
1	$\times\ 2^{-1}$	= 0.5
0	$\times\ 2^{-2}$	= 0
1	$\times\ 2^{-3}$	= 0.125
		5.625

1-3-6 Signed binary numbers

Thus far, we have assumed that all binary numbers are positive. This is the case for *true, natural,* or *pure binary* numbers. However, the *signed binary* system may be used to represent both positive and negative numbers. With signed binary, the extreme left bit of a binary number or word is used to indicate the *sign* of the number, and the remaining bits give the magnitude. The number is positive (+) if the leftmost bit is 0; the number is negative (−) when the leftmost bit is 1.

Using signed binary, when the sign bit is changed from 0 to 1, the whole number is negated and its magnitude is not changed. For example:

01101001 = +105 (decimal)
11101001 = −105 (decimal)

1-3-7 Conversion from binary to decimal numbers

To convert binary numbers to decimal numbers, multiply each binary digit by its positional weight and add all the products, as is done in Sec. 1-3-2. There are other methods for conversion, but they are generally not any simpler.

1-3-8 Conversion from decimal to binary numbers

A decimal number can be converted into a binary number in two ways. The obvious way is to make up a chart showing the power of 2, as has been done in previous paragraphs, and to then count the necessary number of 1s and 0s to make up the desired decimal number.

For example, assume that the decimal number 33 is to be converted. The number 33 is more than 32 (sixth position from the right) but less than 64 (seventh position from the right). This means that you need a combination of six digits (1s or 0s, probably both).

Start with the sixth position, or 32. Since you want number 32, write a 1 in the sixth position. Then move to the fifth position, or 16. Thirty-two plus 16 is greater than the desired 33, so use a zero for the fifth position. The fourth position is 8, and 8 plus 32 is more than 33, so you use a 0 for the fourth position. The same is true of the third position, or 4, and the second position, or 2, so both these positions use a 0. The first (right-hand, or LSD) position is 1, and 1 plus the sixth position (or 32) makes the desired 33, so both of these positions require a 1. Thus, the pure binary equivalent of decimal 33 is 100001. If the 8-bit system is used, the binary number will read 00100001 for a decimal 33. This is shown in the following table, along with some other examples for tabular conversion of decimal and binary numbers.

An alternative method for converting from decimal to binary is to divide the decimal number by 2 as many times as is necessary to lower the quotient to a number less than 2 (1 or 0), using the *remainders* for each step of division as the binary numbers. This is shown on page 7.

For example, again assume that 33 is to be converted. Thirty-three divided by 2 is 16, with a remainder of 1. This 1 is the right-hand or LSD.

	2^7	2^6	2^5	2^4	2^3	2^2	2^1	2^0
Decimal	*128*	*64*	*32*	*16*	*8*	*4*	*2*	*1*
0	0	0	0	0	0	0	0	0
1	0	0	0	0	0	0	0	1
2	0	0	0	0	0	0	1	0
3	0	0	0	0	0	0	1	1
4	0	0	0	0	0	1	0	0
5	0	0	0	0	0	1	0	1
6	0	0	0	0	0	1	1	0
7	0	0	0	0	0	1	1	1
8	0	0	0	0	1	0	0	0
9	0	0	0	0	1	0	0	1
10	0	0	0	0	1	0	1	0
20	0	0	0	1	0	1	0	0
30	0	0	0	1	1	1	1	0
→ 33	0	0	1	0	0	0	0	1
40	0	0	1	0	1	0	0	0
47	0	0	1	0	1	1	1	1
50	0	0	1	1	0	0	1	0

33 = 0 0 1 0 0 0 0 1

Successive Dividers	*Original Number and Dividends*	*Remainder (Binary Number)*
2	33	1
2	16	0
2	8	0
2	4	0
2	2	0
2	1	1

1 0 0 0 0 1

33 = 1 0 0 0 0 1

Sixteen divided by 2 is 8, with a remainder of 0. This 0 is the second-position digit.

Eight divided by 2 is 4 with a remainder of 0. This 0 is the third-position digit. Two divided by 2 is 1 with a remainder of 0. This 0 is the fourth-position digit.

One divided by 2 is considered as 0 (since the whole number 1 cannot be divided by 2), and there is a remainder of 1. This 1 is the sixth position. The 1 is also the left-hand or MSD.

Thus, the binary count for the decimal number 33 is 100001.

1-3-9 Binary addition

As in the case of decimal addition, binary addition is essentially a counting process. However, binary addition is simpler than decimal addition. There are only four simple rules for binary addition:

$0 + 0 = 0$	with no carry
$0 + 1 = 1$	with no carry
$1 + 0 = 1$	with no carry
$1 + 1 = 0$	with a carry of 1

For example, suppose that we wish to add binary numbers 11101 and 1011:

Binary							*Decimal Equivalent*	
	+1	+1	+1	+1			(carry)	
		1	1	1	0	1	(augend)	29
+			1	0	1	1	(addend)	+ 11
	1	0	1	0	0	0	(sum)	40

The same rules apply to the addition of binary fractions and the addition of binary mixed numbers. Care must be taken so that the binary points of the augend and the addend are lined up one below the other, for example:

Binary		*Decimal Equivalent*
101.101	(augend)	5.625
+ 1.001	(addend)	1.125
110.110	(sum)	6.750

1-3-10 Binary subtraction

There are also four simple rules for binary subtraction:

$0 - 0 = 0$	with no borrow
$1 - 1 = 0$	with no borrow
$1 - 0 = 1$	with no borrow
$0 - 1 = 1$	with a borrow of 1

For example, suppose that we wish to subtract binary 0111 from binary 1001:

Binary						*Decimal Equivalent*	
	−1	−1				(borrow)	
	1	0	0	1		(minuend)	9
−	0	1	1	1		(subtrahend)	− 7
	0	0	1	0		(difference)	2

Note that when the first borrow is subtracted from the 0 of the minuend, it leaves a 1 with a borrow from the digit at the left. When the 1 of the subtrahend is subtracted from the resulting 1 of the minuend, the difference is 0 with no borrow.

Binary fractions and binary mixed numbers are subtracted in the same way, taking care to place binary points below each other. For example:

Binary									*Decimal Equivalent*				
−1	−1	−1	•	−1			(borrow)		−1	•	−1		
1	0	1	•	0	0	1	(minuend)		5	•	1	2	5
−	1	1	•	1	1	1	(subtrahend)	−	3	•	8	7	5
0	0	1	•	0	1	0	(difference)		1	•	2	5	0

1-3-11 Binary complements

As in the decimal system, binary subtraction can be performed as an addition process using the complement method. There are two types of binary complements, the *one's complement* and the *two's complement.*

One's complement. The one's complement of a binary number is found by subtracting each digit of the number from 1 or, more simply, by *reversing the digits of the number.* For example, to find the one's complement of 10101:

```
  11111                                    10101  (binary)
                              or           ↕↕↕↕↕
- 10101  (pure binary)                     01010  (one's complement)
  01010  (one's complement)
```

Although simple, the one's-complement system has certain problems and is not generally used for microprocessor-based systems. However, the one's-complement number must be found as the first step in finding a two's-complement number.

Two's complement. The two's-complement system is in general use for microcomputer arithmetic systems. To convert a pure binary number (which is considered to be positive) to its positive equivalent in two's complement, simply add a zero (or sign bit, as discussed in Sec. 1-3-6) as the next-higher significant-bit position. For example:

b_7	b_6	b_5	b_4	b_3	b_2	b_1	b_0	
	1	1	1	1	1	1	1	(pure binary 127)
0	1	1	1	1	1	1	1	(+127 in two's complement)
	0	0	0	0	0	0	1	(binary 1)
0	0	0	0	0	0	0	1	(+1 in two's complement)

To convert a pure binary number (considered to be positive) to its negative equivalent in two's complement, invert all the bits (that is, find the one's complement) and then add 1 to the LSD. For example, to convert decimal +37 to negative two's complement:

	00100101	=	+37
invert	11011010		
add	1		
	11011011	=	−37 in two's complement

Since the positive form of two's complement is the same as pure binary with a positive sign bit added, the same procedure can be used for conversion. That is, when the negative of a positive two's-complement number is required, the negative is formed by complementing each bit position of the positive representation and then adding 1, as follows:

b_7	b_6	b_5	b_4	b_3	b_2	b_1	b_0	
0	1	1	1	1	1	1	1	(+127 in two's complement)
1	0	0	0	0	0	0	0	(one's complement)
							1	(add 1)
1	0	0	0	0	0	0	1	(−127 in two's complement)
0	0	0	0	0	0	0	0	(0 is two's complement)
1	1	1	1	1	1	1	1	(one's complement)
							1	(add 1)
0	0	0	0	0	0	0	0	(0 is same in either notation)
0	0	0	0	0	0	0	1	(+1 in two's complement)
1	1	1	1	1	1	1	0	(one's complement)
							1	(add 1)
1	1	1	1	1	1	1	1	(−1 in two's complement)

Note that while + 127 is the largest positive two's-complement number that can be formed with eight digits, the largest negative two's-complement number is 10000000, or −128. Thus, with two's complement, an 8-bit byte can represent whole numbers between −128 and +127. Bit 7 can be regarded as a sign bit (if b_7 is 0, the number is +; if b_7 is 1, the number is −):

10000000	//	11111111	00000000	00000001	//	01111111
−128		−1	0	+1		+127

1-3-12 Relationship between two's complement and signed binary

Since much of the literature on arithmetic operations in microcomputers presents the information in terms of signed binary numbers (Sec. 1-3-6), the difference between two's complement and signed binary is of interest. As discussed in Sec. 1-3-6, signed-binary-number notation also uses the most-significant bit as a sign bit (0 for positive, 1 for negative). The remaining bits represent the magnitude as a binary number. For example:

±	64	32	16	8	4	2	1	
b_7	b_6	b_5	b_4	b_3	b_2	b_1	b_0	
1	1	1	1	1	1	1	1	(−127 in signed binary)
1	0	0	0	0	0	0	1	(−1 in signed binary)
0	0	0	0	0	0	0	0	(0 in signed binary)
0	0	0	0	0	0	0	1	(+1 in signed binary)
0	1	1	1	1	1	1	1	(+127 in signed binary)

An 8-bit byte in signed binary represents whole numbers between −127 and +127:

11111111	//	10000001	00000000	00000001	//	01111111
−127		−1	0	+1		+127

Comparing this to the two's-complement representation, the positive numbers are identical and the negative numbers are reversed (−127 in two's complement is −1 in signed binary, and vice versa). In microcomputers, the difference between the two number systems causes no particular problem since numerical data are usually converted (automatically) to the correct format when the microcomputer is programmed. That is, the program should provide for the conversion. This is done as follows:

±	64	32	16	8	4	2	1	
b_7	b_6	b_5	b_4	b_3	b_2	b_1	b_0	
1	1	1	1	1	1	1	1	(−127 in signed binary)
1	0	0	0	0	0	0	0	(one's complement except for sign bit)
							1	(add 1)
1	0	0	0	0	0	0	1	(−127 in two's complement)

1-3-13 Binary subtraction using two's complement

Section 1-3-10 describes how binary numbers are subtracted on paper. In most microcomputer systems, binary numbers are subtracted by adding the two's complement of the subtrahend to the minuend and ignoring the carry bit. This arrangement simplifies circuits in the *arithmetic logic unit* (ALU) of the microprocessor. For example, assume that decimal 3 is to be subtracted from decimal 10:

On Paper			*In Microcomputer*	
00001010	(decimal 10)		00001010	
	=	=		
−00000011	(decimal 3)		+11111101	(two's complement)
00000111	(decimal 7)		00000111	

The final carry bit (ninth bit) that results from adding these two binary numbers is not needed. Thus, the bit is not carried, but is ignored and lost. In an 8-bit microcomputer, the circuits are simply not capable of carrying more than 8 bits, so the ninth bit disappears.

1-3-14 Binary multiplication

There are three rules for binary multiplication:

$$0 \times 0 = 0$$
$$0 \times 1 = 0$$
$$1 \times 1 = 1$$

The binary multiplication process is simple. If the digit of the multiplier is 0, the partial product is 0. If the multiplier digit is 1, the partial product is the same as the multiplicand. Then the partial products are summed as follows:

Binary		*Decimal*
1 0 1 0 1	(multiplicand)	21
× 1 0	(multiplier)	× 2
0 0 0 0 0	(first partial product)	42
1 0 1 0 1	(second partial product)	
1 0 1 0 1 0	(final product)	

From this it will be seen that multiplication in binary numbers is a form of addition and shifting (the partial product is shifted to the left for each digit in the multiplier; then the products are added). In a microcomputer system, the addition is done by means of *adder circuits* within the microprocessor, and shifting is done with *shift registers* also in the microprocessor.

Keep in mind that shift operations are used to multiply binary numbers by powers of 2 (not multiples of 2). A left shift of one position multiplies by 2; a left shift of two bit positions multiplies by 4; three bit positions multiplies by 8, and so on. Similarly, as discussed in Sec. 1-3-14, a right shift of one position divides by 2 (that is, multiplies by ½); a right shift of two positions divides by 4; and so on.

The same process applies to multiplication of fractions, or mixed numbers, for example:

Binary		*Decimal*
10.01	(multiplicand)	2.25
× 1.01	(multiplier)	× 1.25
10 01		11 25
0 00 0	(partial products)	450
10 01		2 25
10.1101	(final product)	2.8125

1-3-15 Binary division

Binary division is performed in much the same way as decimal long division. The process is much simpler, since there are only two rules in binary division:

$$0 \div 1 = 0$$
$$1 \div 1 = 1$$

Generally, a microcomputer system does division in the reverse way as multiplication. That is, division is a series of subtractions and right shifts to provide partial dividends (as opposed to a series of additions and left shifts to provide partial products for multiplication). The following examples illustrate the binary division process:

```
        Binary                  Decimal

           3
     11 ) 1001                  3 ) 9
          11                        9
          ---                       -
          011
           11
           --

           111                        7
    100 ) 11100                 4 ) 28
          100                       28
          ---                       --
          110
          100
          ---
           100
           100
          ----

            1100                     12
  1011 ) 10000100              11 ) 132
         1011                       11
         --------                   --
          1011                      22
          1011                      22
         --------                   ---
```

1-4 OCTAL NUMBER SYSTEM

The octal number system uses eight digits from 0 to 7 in ascending order. Conventional (non-microprocessor-based) computers often use octal numbers in their circuits since octal can provide a shorthand method for bridging the gap between decimal and binary. Microcomputers rarely use octal directly. However, you should have an understanding of octal numbers since 8 is a power of the binary 2, and the octal number system can be used as an aid in programming and number conversion.

In octal, when a count is added to the largest digit, 7, the count goes back to the start, 0, and a carry is added to the next position to the left. Thus, decimal 8 appears as octal 10 (pronounced "one, zero," not "ten"). The following list shows the octal equivalents of the 10 digits of the decimal system.

Octal	*Decimal*
0	0
1	1
2	2
3	3
4	4
5	5
6	6
7	7
10	8
11	9

As in other systems, the digits of an octal number are arranged in positions of ascending powers, from right to left. The following shows the position weights of the octal system.

Digital Position							
8^3	8^2	8^1	8^0	8^{-1}	8^{-2}	8^{-3}	powers of 8
512	64	8	1	$1/8$	$1/64$	$1/512$	decimal equivalents

Thus, octal number 1305.1 really means $(1 \times 512) + (3 \times 64) + (0 \times 8) + (5 \times 1) + (1 \times 0.125)$, which is equal to 709.125 in the decimal system.

1-4-1 Conversion from decimal to octal numbers

To convert a decimal number to its octal equivalent, divide the decimal number by 8 and record the remainder, even if it is 0, which becomes the LSD of the octal number. Divide the quotient by 8 again and record the remainder of this division, which becomes the next-significant octal digit. Continue this process until the quotient becomes 0. The remainder from this division process is the MSD of the octal number. For example, to convert 759_{10} to its octal equivalent:

$759 \div 8 = 94$	with remainder 7 (LSD)
$94 \div 8 = 11$	with remainder 6
$11 \div 8 = 1$	with remainder 3
$1 \div 8 = 0$	with remainder 1 (MSD)

Thus, $759_{10} = 1367_8$.

1-4-2 Conversion from octal to decimal numbers

To convert an octal number to its decimal equivalent, multiply each digit by its positional weight expressed in decimal equivalents and add the products. For example,

$$\begin{aligned} 123_8 &= (1 \times 8^2) + (2 \times 8^1) + (3 \times 8^0) \\ &= (1 \times 64) + (2 \times 8) + (3 \times 1) \\ &= 83_{10} \end{aligned}$$

1-4-3 Conversion from octal to binary numbers

To convert an octal number to its binary equivalent, convert each digit of the octal number the binary equivalent *using three binary digits per octal digit.* Then combine these binary groups in proper order. For example to convert 377_8 to its binary equivalent,

3	7	7	(octal digits)
011	111	111	(binary equivalents)

Thus, $377_8 = 011111111_2$. As you can see, this grouping of three binary digits will not work for an octal 10 or 11 (decimals 8 and 9, respectively). Also, for three octal digits, it is necessary to use nine binary digits. For these reasons, the octal number system is generally not compatible with the typical 8-bit byte used in microprocessor-based equipment.

1-4-4 Conversion from binary to octal numbers

To convert a binary number to its octal equivalent, divide the digits of the binary number into groups of three, starting from the right. If necessary, fill out the last group (at the left) by placing 0s in front. Then convert each binary group to its octal digit equivalent and combine these digits in proper order. For example, to convert 10110110_2 to its octal equivalent:

	010	110	110	(binary)
added → (0 added)	2	6	6	(octal)

Thus, $10110110_2 = 266_8$.

1-4-5 Conversion of decimal–binary numbers using octal numbers

One way to convert decimal numbers to their binary equivalents, or vice versa, is to use an octal conversion as an intermediary step. This is often done in nonmicroprocessor computers. Using this system, to change a decimal number to binary, first convert the decimal number to its octal equivalent and then change this octal number to its binary equivalent. The same procedure may be applied in going from binary to decimal numbers. For example, binary 10101 can be handled as

```
                      1   0  1  0  1           (binary)
added ————————> 0   1   0  1  0  1           (octal)
                     16          5      = 21    (decimal)
```

1-5 HEXADECIMAL NUMBER SYSTEM

One problem with binary numbers is that they are difficult to manipulate, particularly when large values are involved. The length of a large binary number makes it tedious to write and thus more vulnerable to error. This problem is overcome by use of the octal number system, described in Sec. 1-4, where three binary digits are represented by one octal digit. The *hexadecimal* number system goes one step further; *each digit represents four binary digits.*

Unlike the base 10 of decimal numbers, base 2 of binary numbers or base 8 of octal numbers, *the hexadecimal number system* uses a base of 16. Since the familiar decimal system has only 10 digits or characters (0, 1, . . . , 9), six additional characters are required for the hexadecimal system. The first six letters of the English alphabet (A, B, C, D, E, and F) are used. Letter A represents a value of 10, letter B a decimal value of 11, and so on, with letter F representing decimal 15. The math on page 17 shows the relationship among the decimal, binary, octal, and hexadecimal number systems.

Note that the carry occurs at 16 in hexadecimal numbers. Additional digits are required when the count goes beyond 16. For example, a decimal 16 is hexadecimal 10 (one, zero), decimal 17 is hexadecimal 11 (one, one), and so on. Thus, it is possible to represent a large decimal number with a hexadecimal number of fewer digits. For example, $FF_{16} = 255_{10}$ and $FFFF_{16} = 65{,}535_{10}$.

1-5-1 Conversion from hexadecimal to decimal numbers

To convert a hexadecimal number to its decimal equivalent (beyond those numbers in the previous table), use the following rules:

1. Multiply the most-significant hexadecimal digit by 16.
2. Add the next-most-significant hexadecimal digit to the product and multiply the sum by 16.
3. Continue the process (adding, then multiplying) until the least-significant hexadecimal digit has been added to the last product.

For example, to find the decimal equivalent of hexadecimal 3C7:

Decimal	*Pure Binary*	*Octal*	*Hexadecimal*
0	0	0	0
1	1	1	1
2	10	2	2
3	11	3	3
4	100	4	4
5	101	5	5
6	110	6	6
7	111	7	7
8	1000	10	8
9	1001	11	9
10	1010	12	A
11	1011	13	B
12	1100	14	C
13	1101	15	D
14	1110	16	E
15	1111	17	F
16	10000	20	10
17	10001	21	11
18	10010	22	12
.	.	.	.
.	.	.	.
.	.	.	.
25	11001	31	19
26	11010	32	1A
27	11011	33	1B
.	.	.	.
.	.	.	.
.	.	.	.
32	100000	40	20
33	100001	41	21

```
               3        C        7
Multiply:     16        |        |
             ---        |        |
              48        |        |
Add:          12 <------+        |
             ---                 |
              60                 |
Multiply:     16                 |
             ---                 |
             960                 |
Add:           7 <---------------+
             ---
             967
```

Thus, $3C7_{16} = 967_{10}$.

This conversion process can be somewhat simplified by means of the table that appears in Fig. 1-1. Note that there are four columns in the table. Column 4 represents the LSD of a four-digit hex number, column 3 is the next-higher-order digit, column 2 the next-higher digit, and column 1 is the MSD of the four-digit hex number.

1		2		3		4	
Hex	Dec	Hex	Dec	Hex	Dec	Hex	Dec
0	0	0	0	0	0	0	0
1	4,096	1	256	1	16	1	1
2	8,192	2	512	2	32	2	2
3	12,288	3	768	3	48	3	3
4	16,384	4	1,024	4	64	4	4
5	20,480	5	1,280	5	80	5	5
6	24,576	6	1,536	6	96	6	6
7	28,672	7	1,792	7	112	7	7
8	32,768	8	2,048	8	128	8	8
9	36,864	9	2,304	9	144	9	9
A	40,960	A	2,560	A	160	A	10
B	45,056	B	2,816	B	176	B	11
C	49,152	C	3,072	C	192	C	12
D	53,248	D	3,328	D	208	D	13
E	57,344	E	3,584	E	224	E	14
F	61,440	F	3,840	F	240	F	15

Figure 1-1 Basic hexadecimal-decimal conversion table.

To convert from hex to decimal, simply add the decimal equivalents for each of the hex digits. Using the same number, $3C7_{16}$, find the decimal equivalent of hex 3 in column 2, or 768_{10}. Add this to the decimal equivalents of hex C (in column 3, or 192_{10}) and hex 7 (in column 4, or 7_{10}). Thus, $3C7_{16} = 768 + 192 + 7 = 967_{10}$.

1-5-2 Conversion from decimal to hexadecimal numbers

To convert a decimal number to its hexadecimal equivalent, divide the decimal number by 16, and use the remainder of each division as the hexadecimal number. For example, to find the hex equivalent of decimal 967,

967 16 = 60 with remainder 7 (LSD)
60 16 = 3 with remainder 12 (or C)
3 16 = 0 with remainder 3 (MSD)

3 C 7

Thus, $967_{10} = 3C7_{16}$.

Again, this conversion can be somewhat simplified by means of Fig. 1-1. To convert from decimal to hex, first find the next-lowest decimal number in one of the columns, and note the corresponding hex digit. Then move to the nearest column to the right and find a decimal number that, when added to the previous decimal number, will come nearest to the desired decimal number. Note the corresponding hex digit in this column. Repeat the procedure until the decimal numbers, when added, are equal to the desired decimal number. Note all the corresponding hex digits.

For example, to convert from decimal 4011 to hex using Fig. 1-1, note that 3840_{10} in column 2 is the next-lowest decimal number and that F is the corresponding hex digit. Thus, F is the MSD for our hex equivalent number, and the number will have two more digits. Moving to column 3 (the next column to the right), note that 160_{10}, when added to the 3840_{10} (for a total of 4000), will come nearest to the desired 4011. (If 176_{10} in column 3 were chosen, the total is 4016 and thus higher than the desired 4011.) The hex equivalent digit for 160 in column 3 is A. Moving to column 4, note that 11_{10}, when added to the previous 3840 + 160 (which equals 4000), will equal the desired 4011 exactly and that the hex equivalent digit is B. Thus, $4011_{10} = FAB_{16}$.

1-5-3 Conversion from hexadecimal to binary numbers

To convert a hexadecimal number to its binary equivalent, convert each digit of the hex number to its binary equivalent *using four binary digits per hex digit.* Then combine these binary groups in proper order.

For example, to convert $3C7_{16}$ to its binary equivalent,

3	C	7	(hex)
0011	1100	0111	(binary)

Thus, $3C7_{16} = 001111000111_2$.

From this, it can be seen that hex is a very convenient shorthand notation which can be substituted for binary. Most microcomputers use 8-bit bytes and thus only require two hex digits. That is, the 8-bit byte can be divided into two 4-bit nibbles. The left nibble represents the left (MSD) hex digit, and the right nibble represents the right (LSD) hex digit. For example, 115_{10} or 01110011_2 can be written

0111	0011
7	3

When an 8-bit byte is involved, the smallest hex number is 00_{16} (00000000_2) and the largest is FF_{16} (11111111_2). Keep in mind that the microcomputer still reads binary numbers only. Hexadecimal is the user's shorthand, not the microcomputer's.

1-5-4 Conversion from binary to hexadecimal

To convert a binary number to its hex equivalent, divide the digits of the *binary number into groups of four,* starting from the right. If necessary, fill out the last group (at the left) by placing 0s in front. Then convert each binary group to its hex-digit equivalent and combine these digits in proper order. For example, to convert 11011001011_2 to its hex equivalent,

added ⟶	0110	1100	1011	(binary)
	6	C	B	(hexadecimal)

1-5-5 Manipulating hexadecimal numbers

Hexadecimal addition is a form of counting, as in other number systems. However, since the carry function occurs at 16, the carry must be added when the sum of digits is greater than F (decimal 15). For example, to add hex 7 (decimal 7) and hex A (decimal 10), the sum is hex 11 (decimal 17).

Hexadecimal subtraction is similar to other number systems, except that the borrow occurs at 16. Hexadecimal multiplication is similar to decimal multiplication. However, since the base is 16, this must be included when the final product is greater than F (decimal 15). For example, 3 multiplied by 8 is 24 in decimal, but this is represented as 18 in hex. When there is more than one digit in either the multiplier or multiplicand of a hex number, the digits must be handled one at a time, with a shift for each digit. Then the product of the two digits is added. Hexadecimal division is accomplished by means of subtraction and shifting, as in other number systems.

From this, it can be seen that manipulating hex numbers on paper is a difficult task, especially for those familiar with decimal. Manipulating hex numbers in a microprocessor is equally complex, but fortunately it never occurs. In microprocessors, all nonbinary numbers (including hex numbers) are converted to binary before they are added, subtracted, multiplied, divided, and so on. Then the number is converted back from binary as necessary. For example, assume that a microcomputer is operated with a terminal that has a hex keyboard and a decimal readout. When a hex key is pressed, the number is generated in hex form, then converted to binary. The binary number is then manipulated (added, subtracted, etc.) and the result is obtained in binary. This binary result is then converted to decimal for display on the readout.

1-6 BINARY CODES

There are a number of codes based on the binary number system. The simplest form of such coding is where decimal numbers (0–9) are converted into binary form using four binary digits or bits. This *4-bit* system is one of the original codes used in early computers and is still used by some business-oriented systems. With this system, generally known as *binary-coded-decimal* or BCD, decimal 1 is represented by 0001, decimal 2 by 0010, and so on.

When the decimal number has more than one digit, 4 binary bits are used for each decimal digit. For example, the decimal number 3738 is represented by 16 binary bits, in groups of 4, as follows:

3	7	3	8	(decimal)
0011	0111	0011	1000	(BCD)

In a typical 8-bit byte microcomputer, each byte can be thought of as containing two 4-bit BCD numbers. With this interpretation, each byte can represent numbers in the range from 0 to 99 (decimal). This is shown as follows:

2^3	2^2	2^1	2^0	2^3	2^2	2^1	2^0	
b_7	b_6	b_5	b_4	b_3	b_2	b_1	b_0	
0	0	0	0	0	0	0	0	(decimal 0)
0	0	1	1	1	0	0	0	(decimal 38)
1	0	0	1	1	0	0	1	(decimal 99)

There are also many other codes using the binary system, including the 2421, 5421, XS3, reflected gray, 2 out of 5, and biquinary. However, only the BCD is used to any extent. Going further, in present-day systems, the trend is to use *only hexadecimal outside* the microcomputer, and *binary inside* the system. This is because binary is most compatible with the signal pulses used in microcomputer circuits, and conversion between binary and hex is relatively simple. Also, it is possible to have as many as 256 coded characters with only two hex digits (since each hex digit represents up to 16 possibilities).

1-7 ALPHANUMERIC CODES

While the 4-bit system is adequate to represent any decimal digit from 0 to 9, additional bits are necessary to represent letters of the alphabet and special characters (such as dollar signs, percent symbols, etc.) that are often required for microcomputer applications. Most microcomputer manufacturers have settled on the United States American Standard Code for Information Interchange, or USASCII, which is now generally written ASCII (pronounced "askey"). Although microprocessor circuits are not designed to accommodate ASCII directly, there are adapter circuits (decoders) that convert the microprocessor's binary code into ASCII (and vice versa) for interchange of information with the world outside the microcomputer.

ASCII is an 8-bit code and is thus ideally suited for hexadecimal representation. Also, since hex–binary conversion is relatively simple, both on paper and in the electrical circuits, ASCII can be adapted to any micro-

Least-significant hex digit	Most-significant hex digit 0	1	2	3	4	5	6	7
0	NUL	DLE	SP	0	@	P	\	P
1	SOH	DC1	!	1	A	Q	a	q
2	STX	DC2	"	2	B	R	b	r
3	ETX	DC3	#	3	C	S	c	s
4	EOT	DC4	$	4	D	T	d	t
5	ENQ	NAK	%	5	E	U	e	u
6	ACK	SYN	&	6	F	V	f	v
7	BEL	ETB	/	7	G	W	g	w
8	BS	CAN	(	8	H	X	h	x
9	HT	EM	)	9	I	Y	i	y
A	LF	SUB	*	:	J	Z	j	z
B	VT	ESC	+	;	K	[	k	{
C	FF	FS	,	<	L	\	l	¦
D	CR	GS	–	=	M	]	m	}
E	SO	RS	.	>	N	↑	n	~
F	SI	US	/	?	O	←	o	DEL

Notes:

(1) Parity bit in most-significant hex digit not included.

(2) Characters in columns 0 and 1 (as well as SP and DEL) are non printing.

(3) Model 33 teletype prints codes in columns 6 and 7 as if they were column 4 and 5 codes.

Figure 1-2 ASCII–hexadecimal conversion table.

processor-based system. Figure 1-2 shows the conversion between ASCII and hex. To convert from ASCII to hex, select the desired letter, symbol, or number, then move up vertically to find the hex MSD. Then move horizontally to the left and find the hex LSD. For example, to find the hex code for the letter I, note that I appears in the "4" column of the hex MSD, and in the "9" column of the hex LSD. Thus, hex 49 equals the letter I in ASCII. Going further, the hex 49 can be converted to 0100 1001 in binary, as is generally done inside the microprocessor circuits. The process can be reversed to convert from binary to ASCII. For example, binary 0010 0100 is 24 in hex and $ in ASCII. As an exercise, find the ASCII letters for binary 0100–1100 0100–0101 0100–1110 0100–1011.

Keep in mind that all microprocessor terminals do not use ASCII keyboards or printouts. Thus, although any 8-bit byte in binary can be converted to hex for convenience, the result does not necessarily mean anything in ASCII. Also, when ASCII is used, the ASCII characters are converted to binary for use by the microprocessor and then converted back to ASCII for use by the terminal. Also, as shown in Fig. 1-2, there are some variations in ASCII-coded devices but not in the basic format. For example, a Model 33 teletype prints codes in MSD columns 6 and 7 as if they were column 4 and 5 codes. Such factors must be considered when interfacing an ASCII terminal with a microprocessor-based system.

1-8 RELATIONSHIP BETWEEN BINARY NUMBERS AND ELECTRICAL SIGNALS

Thus far, we have discussed how binary numbers and words are used on paper. A microprocessor operates with electrical signals (generally pulses) *arranged in binary form.* For example, a microprocessor performs its functions (program counting, addition, subtraction, etc.) in response to *instructions.* Usually, these instructions come from a memory within the system, but they can also come from the outside world via a terminal. A typical microprocessor can perform from 70 to 100 functions (or possibly many more), with each function being determined by a specific instruction.

The instructions are applied to the microprocessor as electrical pulses, arranged to form a binary word. Each pulse is applied on a separate electrical line (or wire) as shown in Fig. 1-3, where a basic microprocessor has eight lines to accommodate an 8-bit binary word or data byte. In this system,

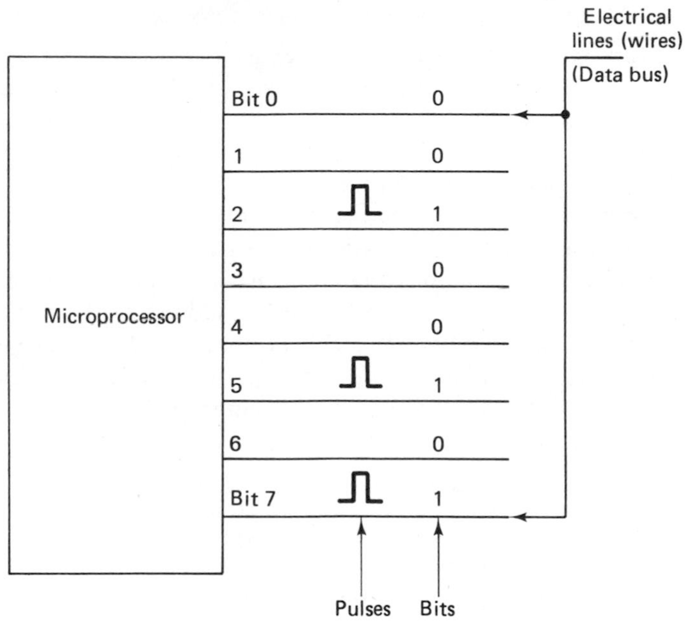

Figure 1-3 Relationship between binary numbers and electrical signals.

which is typical for the great majority of microprocessors, the pulses are +5 V in amplitude and a few ns or μs in duration. The presence of a pulse indicates a binary 1; the absence of a pulse or zero volts indicates a binary 0. Thus, in Fig. 1-3, the microprocessor is receiving a binary 10100100, which can be converted to hex A4 for convenience.

For one microprocessor, this word may be an instruction to perform addition. For another microprocessor, the same word may mean perform subtraction. For still another microprocessor, the word may be meaningless. Thus, one of the first things you must do to understand and use a microprocessor is to *learn all its instructions* (known as the *instruction set*), including the corresponding binary code, hex code, and what is accomplished by the microprocessor when the instruction is received. Microprocessor manufacturers provide information on the instruction set in their user manuals. This is fortunate since it is a nearly impossible task to remember the entire instruction set of even a simple microprocessor.

1-8-1 Microprocessor memories and addresses

Microprocessors also use electrical signals arranged in binary form to communicate with other elements in the systems. Most microprocessors are used with memories (RAMs or ROMs, typically both) which hold data bytes to be manipulated by the microprocessor and instructions to be followed by the microprocessor during the program. (Data bytes are usually stored or held in the RAM; instructions are usually stored in the ROM.)

Memories are divided into locations called *addresses.* Each address is identified by a number (usually decimal). During a typical microprocessor program, the microprocessor will select each address in a certain order (determined by the program) and "read" the contents of the address. Such contents can be an instruction, data, or a combination of both. Likewise, it is possible to "write" information into memory using electrical signals arranged in binary form.

1-8-2 Buses and ports

A typical microprocessor/memory arrangement is shown in Fig. 1-4, where a microprocessor is connected to a RAM and a ROM by data and address *buses.* The term *bus* is applied when several electrical lines are used for a common purpose. In our example, the data bus has eight lines (which is typical) and the address bus has eight lines (which is not typical) Generally, the address bus will have as many as 16 lines. The eight-line system is used here for simplicity. The term *highway* is sometimes used when a bus is used to interconnect many system components. Also, the term *handshake bus* is sometimes used to indicate a bus that interconnects a microprocessor system with the outside world.

The term *port* is often applied to the point or terminals at which the

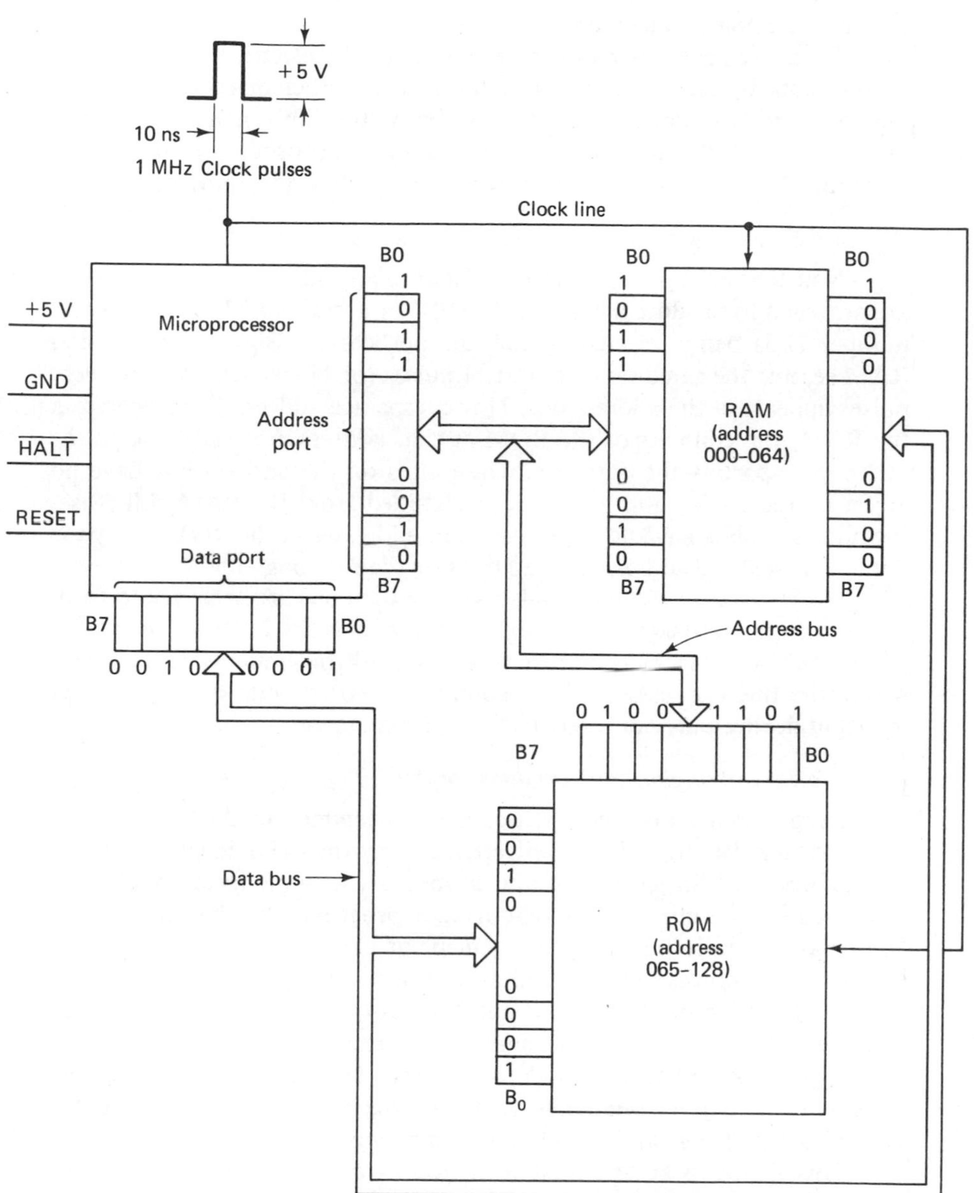

Figure 1-4 Typical microprocessor memory arrangement, including data and address buses.

bus enters the microprocessor or other IC element. Thus, in Fig. 1-4, there is an address port and a data port.

Buses are generally *bidirectional.* That is, the electrical pulses (representing data bytes, addresses, etc.) can pass in either direction along the bus lines. For example, data bytes can be written into memory from the microprocessor, or read from memory into the microprocessor on the same data bus. Ports may or may not be bidirectional, depending upon design.

1-8-3 Address and data buses

Note that in Fig. 1-4, the electrical pulses appearing on the address bus are arranged to produce a binary 01001101, or a decimal 77. Thus, address number 77 is being selected by the microprocessor. Both the ROM and RAM receive the same set of electrical pulses (or binary word) since these pulses appear on the address bus. However, since address 77 is located in the ROM, the contents of the ROM at that address are read back to the microprocessor via the data bus. The pulses on the address bus have no effect on the RAM, and no data are obtained from the RAM. Likewise, the address pulses have no effect on other addresses in the ROM. Only the data at the selected address are read back on the data bus.

In Fig. 1-4, the electrical pulses on the data bus are arranged to form the binary word 00100001, which can be converted to hex 21. In our particular microprocessor, hex 21 is an instruction to add the contents of a register within the microprocessor to the contents at some address in the RAM (read out during a previous step in the program).

1-8-4 Debugging and troubleshooting

Keep in mind that the microprocessor responds to the *arrangement* of electrical pulses. It makes no difference where the pulses originate. Thus, if an undesired instruction is stored in memory at some location which is addressed by the microprocessor during a program, that instruction will appear as the corresponding arrangement of electrical pulses on the data bus. The microprocessor will follow the instructions when received and will thus produce an erroneous result. Probably the program will come to a complete halt or jump to an undesired address. Under these conditions, the program is said to have a *bug* or *bugs.* The process of finding the undesired instruction, removing it, or placing it at the correct address is known as *debugging,* which applies to finding any fault in a program.

This is not to be confused with *troubleshooting,* which is the term used to find electrical or mechanical faults in a microprocessor system. Troubleshooting implies that the system once performed the program properly. For example, referring to Fig. 1-4, assume that the electrical line labeled B0 on the data bus becomes broken (after weeks of operation) at the microprocessor terminal. The B0 pulse from the ROM still appears on the data bus but does not reach the microprocessor. Thus, the microprocessor sees zero volts, or binary 0, on terminal B0. This produces binary word

00100000, or hex 20, instead of the desired binary 00100001, or hex 21. The hex 20 might be meaningless or might be an erroneous instruction. In any event, the microprocessor will not perform the correct function.

1-8-5 Nature of pulses

The pulses used by microprocessors are instantaneous electrical signals. Typically, pulses start at zero volts, rise to 5 V, and then drop back to 0 V, all within a few ns or μs. All the pulses in a given binary word or data byte must arrive at the same time. Thus, all the pulses are said to be transmitted in *parallel* on the bus. All binary information within a microprocessor system is transmitted in parallel form.

This is not always true in the world outside the microprocessor system, where information can also be transmitted in *serial* form. In serial transmission of an 8-bit binary word, eight pulses (for binary 1) or spaces (for binary 0) are transmitted at regular intervals on a single electrical line (or pair of lines). This is followed by a long space before the next 8-bit byte is transmitted. Obviously, serial is slower but requires only one or two lines, compared to one line for each bit in parallel. Since microprocessors use only parallel within the system, serial data bytes must be converted before they are used with a microprocessor system (and vice versa). This is one of the functions of an I/O device.

1-8-6 Clock and timer pulses

The electrical pulses used by the microprocessor, ROM, and RAM are generated by a *clock* or *timer,* which may be part of the microprocessor or can be external. In Fig. 1-4, the clock is external and is a +5-V pulse of 10-ns duration, at a frequency of 1 MHz. The clock circuit is an oscillator that produces pulses of fixed amplitude and duration at regular intervals. One to 3 million pulses per second (or 1–3 MHz) is a typical clock frequency.

The microprocessor, ROM, and RAM do not actually generate the binary pulses, but produce their binary word pulses on the address and data lines *when they receive clock pulses.* It may take many clock pulses to form a binary word. In some cases, the microprocessor, ROM, and RAM must also receive other signals before they will produce the binary word pulses or data bytes. For example, a RAM usually requires a "read" signal, plus the clock pulses, before the contents of an address is read onto the data bus from the RAM. Such control signals are discussed in later paragraphs.

1-8-7 Power supply and other signals

Not all electrical voltages and signals applied to a microprocessor, ROM, or RAM are in pulse form. For example, referring to Fig. 1-4, note that there are two lines into the microprocessor, labeled +5 V and GND. These are the power supply lines connected to an external 5-V power supply.

There are also two lines labeled $\overline{\text{HALT}}$ and RESET, respectively.

The RESET and $\overline{\text{HALT}}$ lines receive a +5-V signal from various circuits in the system. This signal may be a momentary pulse identical to those on the address and data buses, or may be a fixed +5 V which remains on the line for some time. When a fixed signal (sometimes called a *level*) is applied, the line is said to be "high" and the function is "turned on."

For example, if a +5 V is applied to the RESET line, the RESET line is high, and all circuits within the microprocessor are reset to zero, regardless of their condition before the line goes high. When the fixed voltage is removed, the RESET line goes low (is at zero volts) and the RESET function is no longer in effect. In most microprocessors, when a reset signal is received, all circuits return to zero and then resume their normal function (counting, etc.). Note that in some literature, the terms *true* and *false* are used instead of high and low, respectively. Likewise, the binary 1 and 0 are used for high and low in some literature. However, the terms "high" and "low" are generally preferred.

An overbar is used on the word $\overline{\text{HALT}}$. This indicates that the $\overline{\text{HALT}}$ operates on the reverse of all other lines. That is, the $\overline{\text{HALT}}$ function is in effect when the line is at 0 V (the normal low condition). When the line is at +5 V (normal high), the HALT function is removed.

In our microprocessor, when the $\overline{\text{HALT}}$ line is at 0 V, all functions within the microprocessor (counting through the program, etc.) are stopped and remain stopped as long as the $\overline{\text{HALT}}$ line remains low. All functions resume normal operation when the $\overline{\text{HALT}}$ line is made high by a +5-V level. If the microprocessor is in the middle of some operation when $\overline{\text{HALT}}$ is applied (by 0 V on the line), the operation will stop, but will continue from the same point when the +5 V is reapplied.

This illustrates the need to understand *all instructions and control signals* applied to a particular microprocessor. A thorough knowledge of microprocessor functions and controls is essential for writing and debugging programs as well as troubleshooting. For example, should the program inadvertently issue an instruction that removes +5 V from the $\overline{\text{HALT}}$ line, the microprocessor will stop in the middle of a program, possibly in the middle of an instruction. The same condition can be caused if the $\overline{\text{HALT}}$ line is accidently disconnected from the $\overline{\text{HALT}}$ terminal on the microprocessor, if the $\overline{\text{HALT}}$ line is shorted to ground, or if the $\overline{\text{HALT}}$ line is broken.

1-8-8 Parity-bit signals

The notes in Fig. 1-2 refer to a *parity bit.* Although the ASCII code is considered as an 8-bit code, note that the most significant bit is always 0. For example, the highest number required for ASCII is 0111–1111 in binary or 7F in hex. Thus, the MSB can be 0, or simply omitted, whichever is convenient. This permits the MSB to be used for a parity check. The parity system is one of the many codes that have been developed to detect errors that might occur in electronic equipment using binary numbers and signal pulses.

Any complex equipment that operates with the binary counting system is subject to counting errors due to circuit failure, electrical noise, or some similar occurrence. For example, a defect can reduce the amplitude of a pulse (representing a binary 1) so that it appears as a binary 0 on the line or bus. Likewise, noise on the line or bus can be of equal amplitude to a normal binary 1 pulse. If the noise occurs at a time when a port is being opened to pass what is supposed to be a binary 0, the circuit will react as if a binary 1 is present.

One method for error detecting is known as *parity check. Parity* refers to the quality of being equal, and a parity check is actually an equality-checking code. The coding consists of introducing additional bits or pulses into the binary number. The addition bit is known as the *parity bit,* and may be either a 0 or a 1. The parity bit is chosen to make the number of all bits in the binary group even or odd. If a system is chosen in which the bits in the binary number, *plus the parity bit,* are even, the system is known as *even parity.* Even parity is in general use. However, odd parity can be used.

As an example of even parity, 7F in hex or 0111-1111 in binary requires a 1 as the parity bit. Thus, in the total of 8 bits (7 binary bits, plus the one parity bit, or 1111–1111), there will be an even number of 1s.

Error-detection circuits based on the parity system use both *parity generators* and *parity detectors* or *checkers.* The function of a parity generator is to examine the word (or group of binary bits) and calculate the information required for the added parity bit. For example, if there are three 1s in the binary group and even parity is used, a 1 must be used for the parity bit to make an even number in the "parity word."

Once the parity bit has been included (a pulse has been added on the appropriate line of the bus), the parity word (binary bits, plus parity bit) can be examined after any transmission, or at any point in the system, to determine if a failure or error has occurred. A parity detection circuit or parity checker examines the parity word to see if the desired odd or even parity still exists (say, after passing through several ICs in a microcomputer system). If an error has occurred, the system control can be informed that the system is not functioning properly by means of a signal. Parity circuits are often used with peripheral equipment such as tape recorders and magnetic disks. For that reason, parity circuits are discussed further in Chapter 2.

1-9 BASIC MICROPROCESSOR/MICROCOMPUTER CIRCUIT FUNCTIONS

All circuit elements of a microcomputer system are in integrated circuit (IC) form. Possible exceptions are the interconnecting buses, wiring, and a few external switches, gates, readouts, keyboards, and so on. In any event, the microprocessor, ROM, RAM, and I/O device are all IC. Thus, you do not have access to the circuit elements, nor can you change them in the way they function. Also, it is not necessary that you understand every detail of the internal circuits to effectively use and understand microprocessors. That is, you do not need to know that diodes are interconnected to form flip-flops, and that flip-flops are interconnected to form registers and counters. However, you must know what registers and counters are, and how (in the simplest terms) they operate.

As an example, a typical microprocessor instruction (found in the user manual) might say that a hex 33, or binary 00110011, applied to the data bus will cause the microprocessor to "add the contents of register A to register B, and increment (advance) the program counter by 1." All basic circuits found in microprocessor literature are described in the following paragraphs of this section.

1-9-1 Counters, registers, accumulators, and pointers

For our purposes, counters, registers, accumulators, and pointers are all circuits used to hold and manipulate binary numbers in electrical (pulse or level) form. As such, these circuits have one stage for each binary bit to be held or manipulated. Thus, an 8-bit counter/register has eight stages. Generally, flip-flop (or FF) stages are used. An FF stage can be in only one of two electrical states, 1 or 0. If you measured the instantaneous state of a particular stage, you would find it at +5 V if the stage is to represent a 1 and at 0 V for binary 0. (Except in certain troubleshooting situations, it is not necessary to actually measure the states of counter/register stages. However, this concept may help you to understand operation of counters/registers.)

In a microprocessor, the purpose of a counter is to count events (such as steps of a program, a sequence of addresses selected, etc.). This is usually done by counting pulses. Counters are sometimes used as *pointers,* in that they point to another event or location. For example, a typical program counter counts each step of the program and then advances to the next address to be used in the program. Thus, the counter "points" to the next step of the program. Note that when a counter, register, or another circuit in a microprocessor system is used solely or primarily for one purpose, it is said to be *dedicated.* For example, a microprocessor counter used only to count program steps is referred to as a *dedicated counter.*

A microprocessor register is similar to a counter except that the primary function of a register is to hold the binary numbers (or words) so that they can be manipulated. Registers are often used to hold some binary number taken from a particular address in memory so that number may be added to another number in memory. Likewise, one register can hold a binary number that is to be added to another binary number in another register. When a register is used primarily for arithmetic operations, the word *accumulator* is often applied.

Serial operation. Microprocessor manufacturers use many methods or symbols to represent counters and registers. One of the most common methods is shown in Fig. 1-5, which illustrates operation of a typical counter used to count serial pulses. Assume that the circuit is used as a program counter and that it receives one pulse for each step in the program; that is, the counter is to be incremented (or advanced) for each pulse representing a step. (When each step or pulse *removes* one count, the counter is said to be *decremented.*)

Initially, all stages are *reset* or *cleared* to low, binary 0, or 0 V by a reset signal. In serial operation, the first or LSB stage operates on the pulses

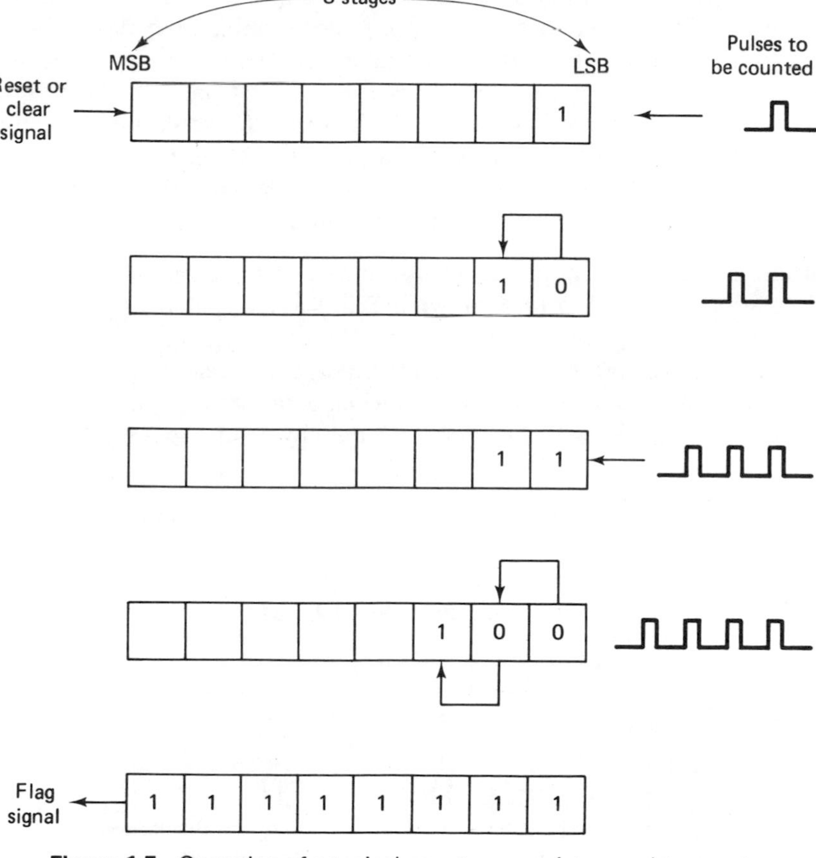

Figure 1-5 Operation of a typical counter or register used to count serial pulses.

to be counted. All other stages receive a pulse from the stage ahead. As each pulse to be counted is applied, the stage representing the LSB is changed from 0 to 1 (0 V to +5 V). When the next pulse arrives, the first stage returns back to 0 V (binary 0) and sends a signal to the next stage, which moves to binary 1. This process continues until all pulses are counted.

If there are four pulses, as shown in Fig. 1-5, the third stage moves to 1 and the first two stages are at 0. All remaining stages are at 0. The counter indicates a binary 00000100 (decimal 4), which corresponds to the number of pulses applied and, in turn, to the number of steps in the program accomplished thus far. In this way the instantaneous count corresponds to the program step just accomplished, or to be accomplished next, depending upon design.

When all stages are moved by sufficient pulses to 1 (the binary count is 11111111, decimal 127) the counter is full. Generally, the counter then sends a *flag* or *signal* to other circuits, indicating the full count. This flag can be used for any number of functions. For example, the flag could be used to halt or reset operation of the microprocessor if the program had only 127 steps. Or, the flag can be used as the first pulse to the LSB of another counter (to accommodate a 16-bit word). It should be noted that flag signals do not always indicate a full count. The term "flag" can be applied to any signal which indicates that a particular condition has occurred (full count, error, request for further information, etc.).

Parallel operation. Counters and registers can also be designed to receive information in parallel form as shown in Fig. 1-6. Here, all the stages are set simultaneously by pulses in binary word 01100100 (decimal 100). That is, bits 2, 5, and 6 receive +5-V pulses, and all other bits remain at 0 V. Sometimes, the terms *load* or *dump* are used when data bytes are so applied to a register. Typically, a register will hold the data byte (all stages remain at the

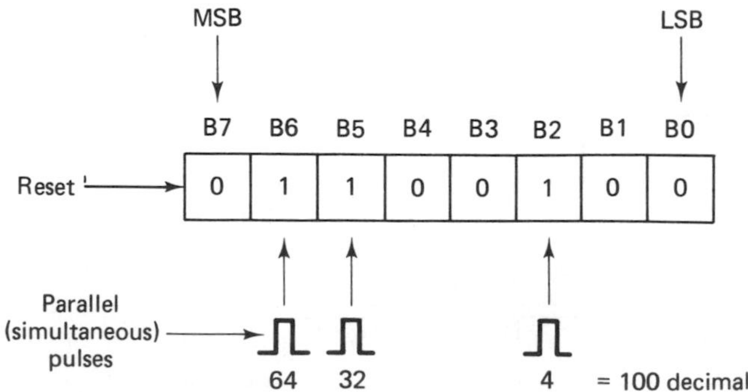

Figure 1-6 Operation of a typical counter or register used to count (or receive) parallel pulses.

selected stage) until the register is cleared (reset to zero), or until another set of pulses forming a data byte is applied (or the power is removed).

Initializing. This ability to set by both serial and parallel pulses makes it possible to *initialize* counters and registers (although the term "initialize" is usually applied to counters). It is not always desired to start all counts from zero, or that all counts go through every step in the count. For example, assume that the count is to start at the seventh step in a program. This could be accomplished by applying +5-V pulses to bits 1, 2, and 3 simultaneously, as shown in Fig. 1-7. Then the first serial pulse to be counted moves bit 1 to 0, which in turn moves bit 2 to 0, bit 3 to 0, and bit 4 to 1.

Shifting. The contents of counters and registers can also be shifted by an appropriate signal. That is, the contents of each stage in the counter or register are shifted by one position to the right or left by a shift signal applied to all stages simultaneously. The effects of a left shift are shown in Fig. 1-8, where a register is holding the binary word 00001000 (decimal 8). Bit 3 is at binary 1, and all remaining bits are at 0.

During the shift, the contents of bit 0 move to bit 1, bit 1 to bit 2, and so on. After the shift, bit 0 remains at binary 0, since there is no new pulse entering bit 0. Bit 4 is at binary 1, since this was the state of bit 3 before thc shift. All other bits are at 0, since 0 was the state of corresponding stages to the right (before the shift).

As a result of the shift, the binary number is changed from 00001000

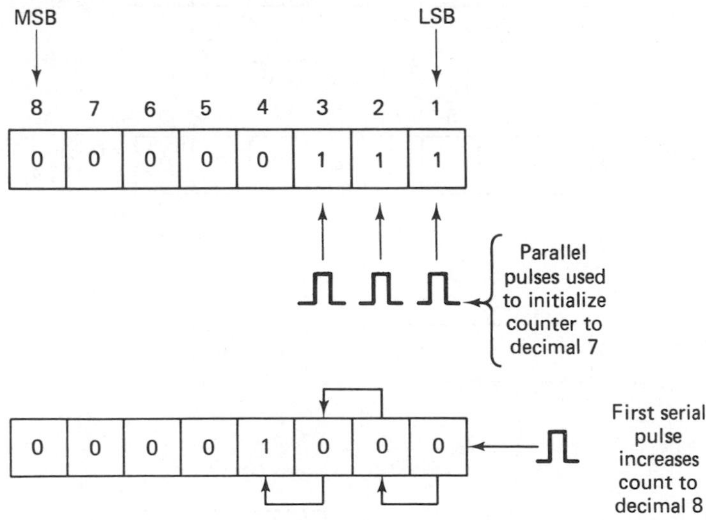

Figure 1-7 Operation of a typical counter or register initialized to decimal 7 by parallel pulses, and increased to decimal 8 by first serial pulse.

to 00010000 or from decimal 8 to decimal 16. Thus, *one left shift multiplies the number by the power of 2.* If there are two shifts to the left, the binary number is changed to 00100000, decimal 32 (or the same as multiplying by 4). Three left shifts produce 01000000, decimal 64 (multiplication by 8). Registers can also be shifted to the right, which *results in division by the powers of 2.* This is also shown in Fig. 1-8, where a register is shifted four places to the right for a division by 16. That is, binary 01000000 (decimal 64) is shifted to binary 00000100 (decimal 4); 64 divided by 16 is 4.

1-9-2 Decoders and multiplexers

The terms "decoder" and "multiplexer" are often interchanged in microprocessor literature. In a strict sense, a *decoder* converts from one code or numbering system to another, such as from hex to decimal, and so on. Equally strict, a *multiplexer* (or MUX) is a data selector and/or

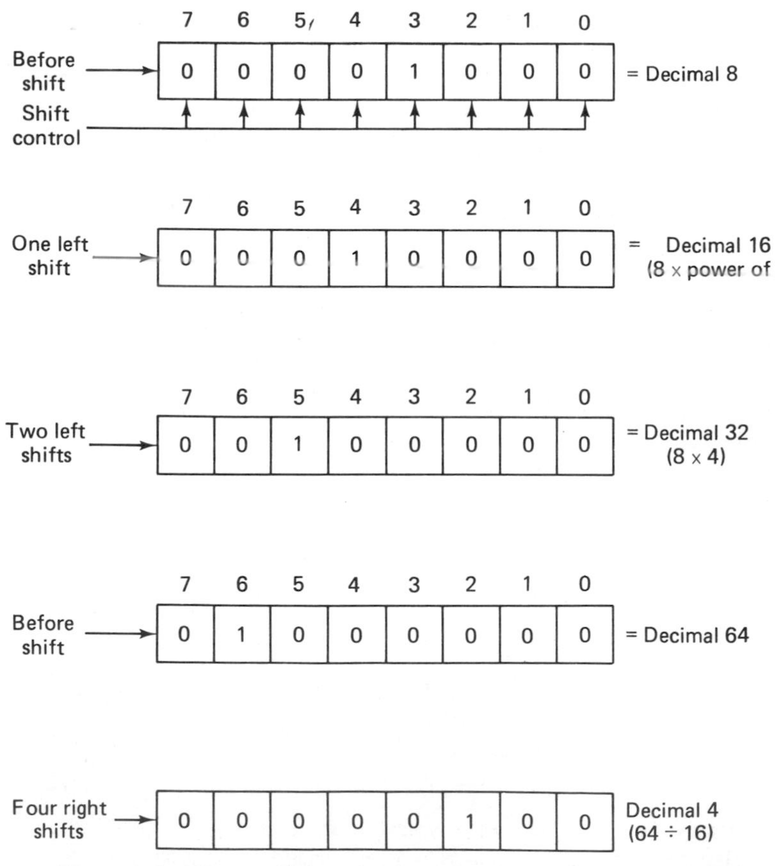

Figure 1-8 Effects of left and right shifts on counters and registers.

distributor. However, in microprocessor literature, the terms are generally applied to any circuit that converts data from one form to another.

For example, one microprocessor contains a circuit (designated by the manufacturer as a multiplexer) that converts 16 lines of information from a register into eight lines suitable for an eight-line address bus. Another microcomputer system contains a decoder in each ROM which makes it possible to select one of 128 memory addresses with an 8-bit word supplied on an 8-bit address bus.

The symbol for such decoders and multiplexers is usually a box with the appropriate number of lines in and out, as shown in Fig. 1-9.

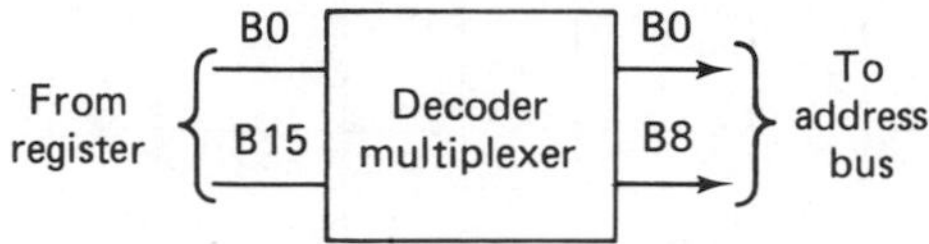

Figure 1-9 Basic decoder/multiplexer symbol.

1-9-3 Buffers, drivers, and latches

Buffers, drivers, and latches are also terms often interchanged in microprocessor literature. A buffer can be considered any circuit between two other circuits that serves to isolate the circuits under certain conditions and to connect the circuits under other conditions. A buffer circuit between an internal register and the data bus (at the data port) is a classic example, as shown in Fig. 1-10. Here, the buffer can be switched on or off by a *bus enable* signal or pulse. (This same signal can also be known as an *enable, select,* or *strobe* signal.)

When the enable signal is present, the buffer will pass data, instructions, or whatever combination is on the data bus to the register within the microprocessor. When the enable signal is removed, the buffer will prevent passage of data. This feature is necessary, for example, when the register is holding old data not yet processed but there are new data on the bus. The buffer closes the data port until the register is ready to accept new data. This raises the obvious problem of what happens when the new data are momentary. In such cases, the buffer has a "latch" function which permits each bit in the buffer to be latched to 1 or 0 by the data pulses. The latched data word is held in the buffer until the register is ready to accept new data.

Three-state buffers. Typically, buffers are three-state devices, with one stage for each bit to be handled. The stages can be in one of three states: *in, out,* or at a *high-impedance* level. This high-impedance level or state makes it appear that the circuit is closed to the passage of data. Some buffers also include a *driver* function, particularly where the buffer is going

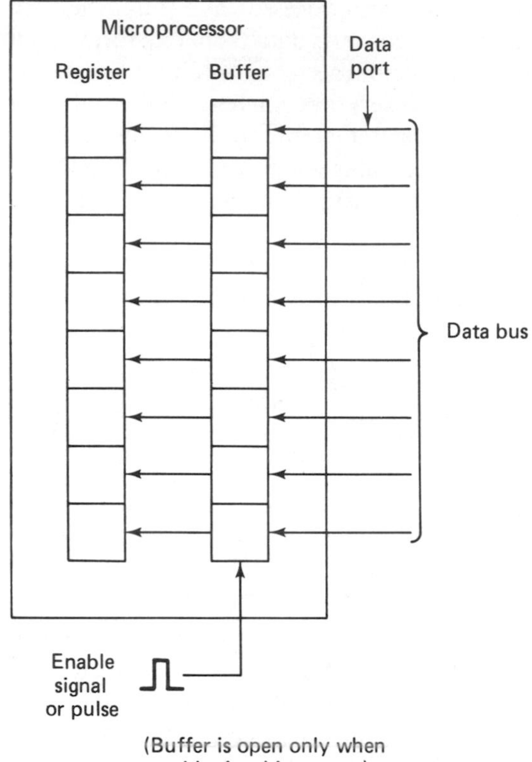

Figure 1-10 Buffer circuit between an internal register and the data bus.

to feed many devices simultaneously via a bus. The output of a register or counter may be sufficient to drive one other register, but not many registers or devices. Thus, the buffer includes a driver function which amplifies the drive capability.

1-9-4 Matrix

The term *matrix* is generally applied to the memory circuits within the RAM or ROM, but it is also applied by some manufacturers to a group of registers in the microprocessor. A typical memory matrix is divided into sections or locations, with each section identified by an *address,* as shown in Fig. 1-11. In turn, the addresses are divided into a number of stages, with one stage for each bit to be held in memory. Thus, each address in an 8-bit memory will have 8 bits. The number of addresses in a memory matrix depends on use. Generally, the number is based on the powers of 2, since the addresses are selected by a number system based on binary (such as hex). A typical ROM matrix will have 128 addresses, each with 8 bits, and will

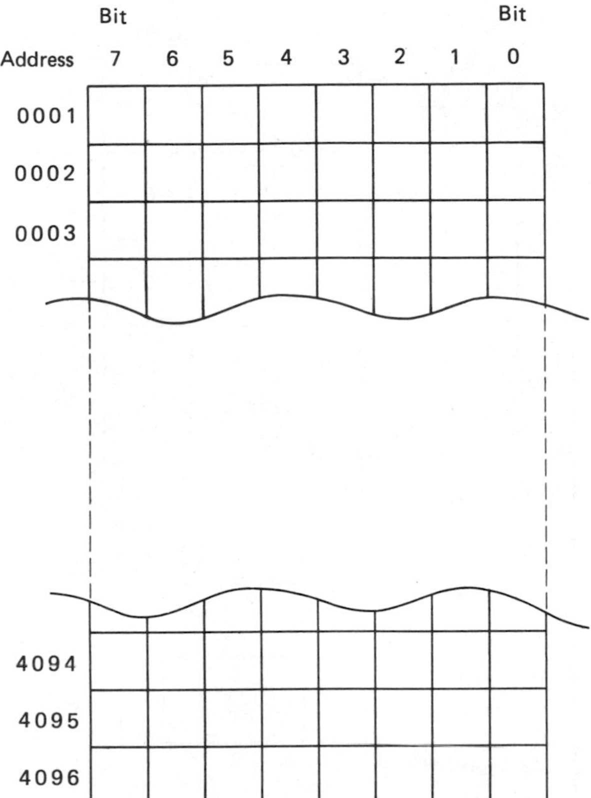

Figure 1-11 Typical 4096 × 8 memory matrix.

be described as a 128 × 8 matrix. A typical RAM matrix can have 512, 1024, or 4096 addresses (or possibly more). Sometimes a 1024 × 8 memory matrix will be described as a *IK memory* since there are approximately 1000 addresses available. A 4096 × 8 memory matrix will likewise be called a *4K memory.*

Matrix vectors. The addresses within a matrix are selected by some form of *vector* or *intersect* system, as shown in Fig. 1-12. The memory address to be read in or read out is selected when a *combination of two* appropriate bit lines have a +5-V pulse present (are at binary 1). Only one of the X lines and one of the Y lines can be binary 1 at any given time. All other lines are at binary 0. This action is controlled by some form of decoder or multiplexer as discussed in Sec. 1-9-2.

As an example, assume that address 8 is to be selected. The desired decimal 8 is converted to hex 22 (0010 0010) by a decoder/multiplexer. This causes bits b_1 and b_5 to receive pulses (+5 V or binary 1). All remaining bit

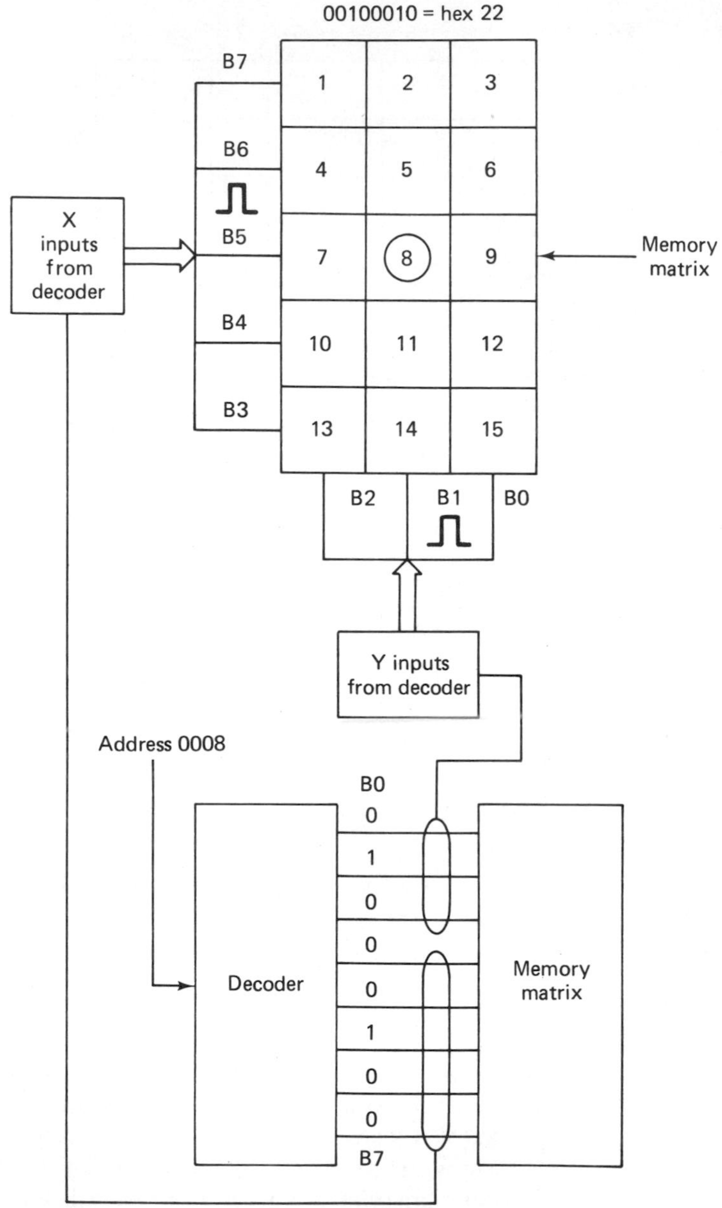

Figure 1-12 Vector system for selecting one address in a 15-address memory matrix.

lines are at binary 0 (zero volts). Thus, the address (number 8) at the intersection or vector of the two lines is selected. Keep in mind that there are 8-bits *in each address,* and that each of the 8 bits is fed back to the microprocessor or other destination on a bus (usually the data bus).

1-9-5 Arithmetic logic unit

Virtually all microprocessors have an arithmetic logic unit or ALU (although it may not be called an ALU). The ALU performs the arithmetic and logic operation on the data bytes. The symbol for an ALU is generally a simple box with lines or arrows leading in or out. Sometimes, the box will contain some hint as to the functions capable of being performed by the ALU. However, these functions are usually described only in the microprocessor's instruction set.

As a minimum, the ALU will have an *adder* circuit which is capable of combining the contents of two registers in accordance with the logic of binary arithmetic (Sec. 1-3-9). This adder-register combination permits the microprocessor to perform arithmetic manipulations on the data obtained from memory and other inputs. Using only the basic adder, a skilled programmer can write routines that will subtract, multiply, and divide, giving the microprocessor system complete arithmetic capabilities. However, most ALUs provide other built-in functions, including Boolean algebra, logic operations, and shift capabilities.

The ALU is generally capable of producing flag bits (as described in Sec. 1-9-1) that specify certain conditions arising in the course of arithmetic and logic operations. It is possible to program *jumps* that are conditionally dependent on the status of one or more flags. For example, the program may be designed to jump to a special routine if the carry bit is set following an addition instruction.

1-9-6 Control circuitry or logic

All microprocessors have some form of control or logic circuit (or circuits). As in the case of the ALU, the symbol for the control circuit is usually a simple box with lines and arrows leading in and out. Generally, the halt, reset, interrupt, initialize, start, and similar lines are shown going into the control logic box symbol. This is because the control logic is the primary functional circuit or unit within the microprocessor. Using clock inputs, the control logic maintains the proper sequence of events required for any processing task.

For example, after a microprocessor instruction is taken from memory (or "fetched") and decoded, the control logic issues the appropriate signals (to the microprocessor, and to such external units as the ROM, RAM, and I/O) for initiating the proper processing action (such as a "write" signal to write data into memory, a "read" signal to read data from memory, and so on).

One function found in most microprocessor control logic circuits is the capability of responding to an *interrupt* signal or *service request* (say from an external video terminal, disk, tape reader, etc.). An interrupt request causes the control logic to temporarily interrupt the program execution, jump to a special routine to service the interrupting device, and then automatically return to the main program.

1-10 MICROPROCESSOR HARDWARE

The term *hardware* applied to a microprocessor or any other element in a microcomputer system refers to the physical components, wiring, and so on. This contrasts with the term *software,* which applies to programs, instructions, and the like. Some microprocessor manufacturers also use the term *firmware* to describe something between hardware and software. For example, when instructions (software) are permanently programmed into a ROM (hardware), the result is firmware.

The microprocessor of one manufacturer will have little in common with the microprocessor of another manufacturer, with the possible exception of outward physical appearance. Compare the two microprocessors shown in Fig. 1-13. Both are 40-lead, dual-in-line (DIP) IC packages. Both are about 2 in long and ½ in wide. Now compare this to the terminal assignment diagrams of Fig. 1-14. Although both have 40 leads (also known as *pins* or *terminals*), the terminals are used for entirely different purposes.

For example, the RCA microprocessor has eight data lines to a data bus, and eight memory lines to an address bus, whereas the Motorola unit has eight data lines (D) and 16 address lines (PA and PB). From this, it can be seen that *you must have all available data on a particular micro-*

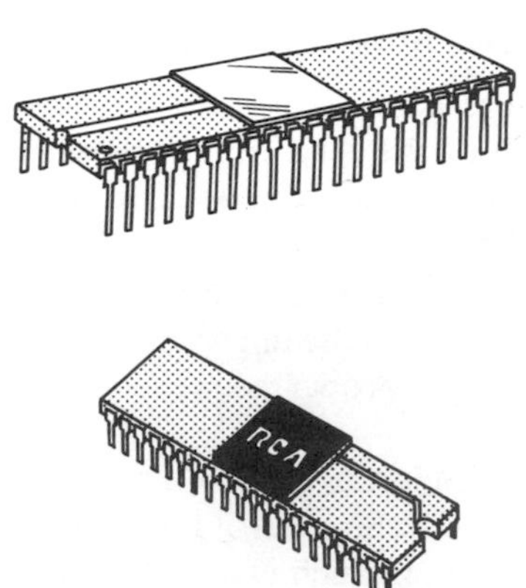

Figure 1-13 RCA and Motorola microprocessors in 40-lead dual-in-line (DIP) IC packages.

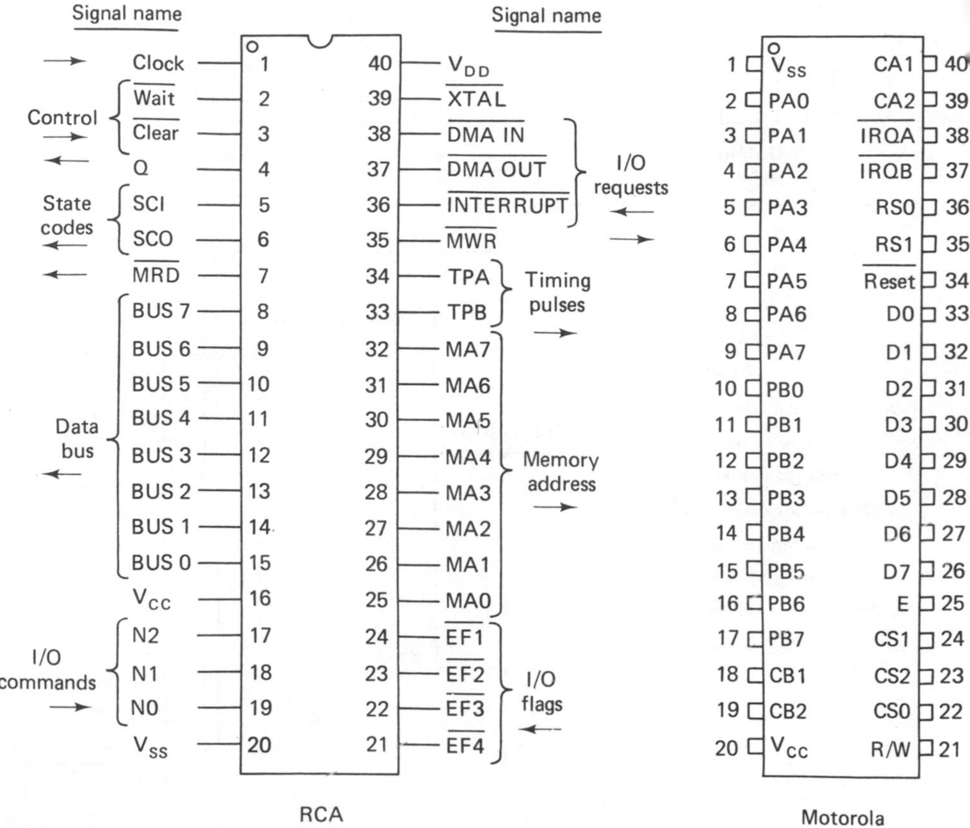

Figure 1-14 Typical microprocessor terminal assignment diagrams.

processor to use the unit effectively. Fortunately, such information is available (samples of manufacturers' data are described in appropriate chapters). However, the format used to show the internal arrangement of microprocessors will vary from manufacturer to manufacturer. The following paragraphs of this section deal with these differences in format and introduce you to the internal functions of typical microprocessors.

1-10-1 Microprocessor architecture

The term *architecture* is most accurately applied to the arrangement of counters, registers, ALUs, and so on, within the microprocessor. However, some manufacturers apply the term "architecture" to the entire system arrangement.

There are two commonly used methods to show architecture. The *block diagram* of Fig. 1-15 shows all the internal registers, counters, and so on, of the Motorola M6800 microprocessor of Figs. 1-13 and 1-14.

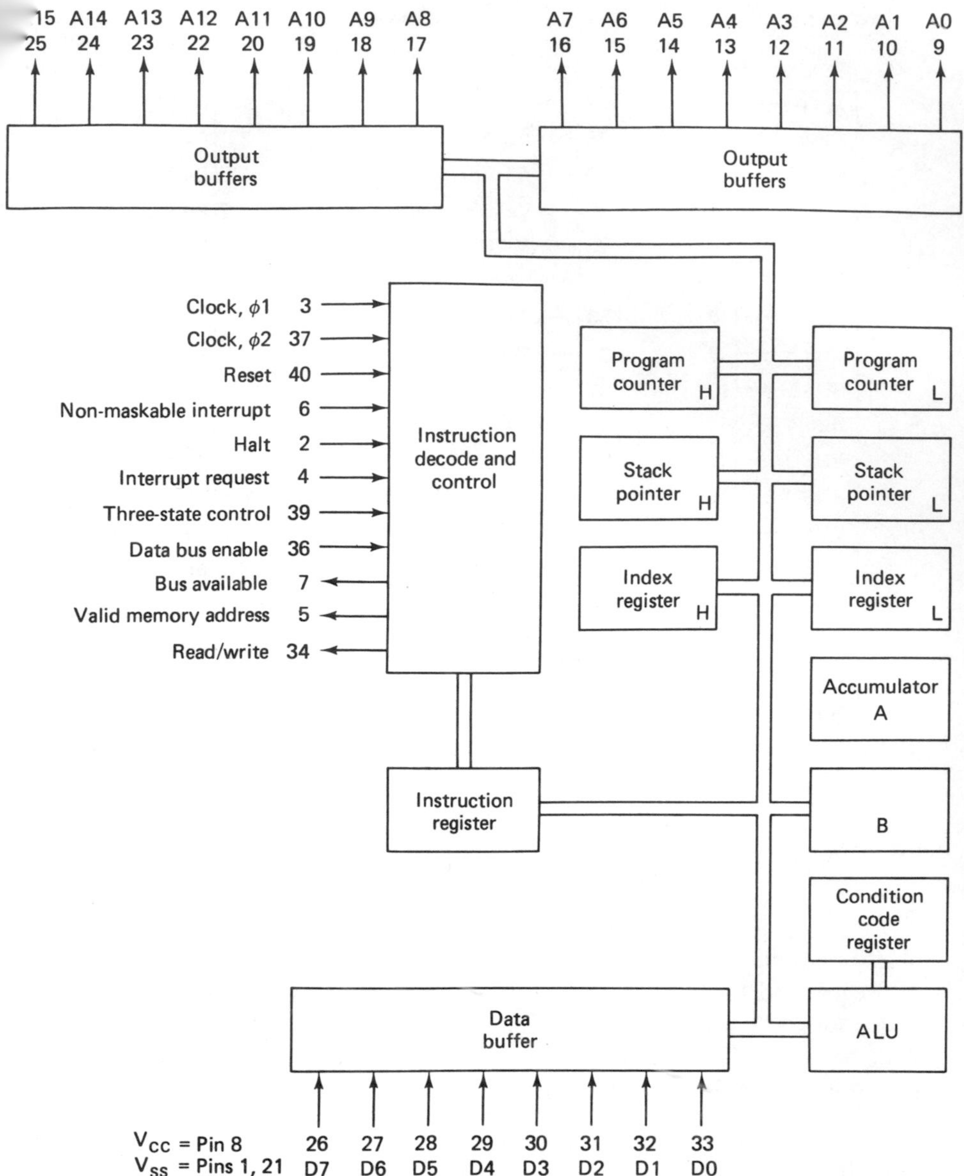

Figure 1-15 Motorola M6800 microprocessor, block diagram.

Compare this to the *program model* of Fig. 1-16, which shows only accumulator, register, counter, and pointers. Obviously, the information shown in Fig. 1-16 is suitable for programming only. The information in Fig. 1-15 is required for design and service, since each line to and from the microprocessor is identified by function (or destination) and pin number. For

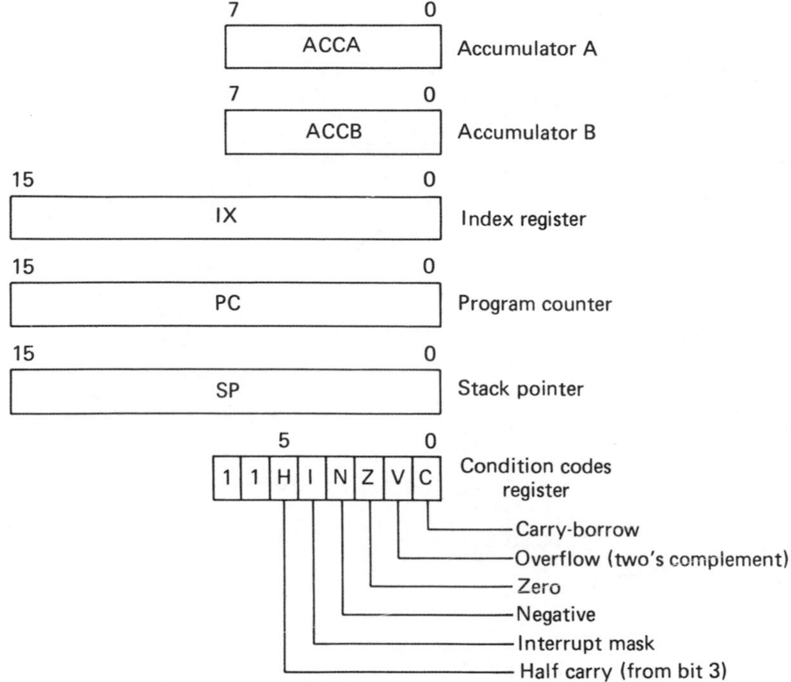

Figure 1-16 Motorola M6800 microprocessor, programming model.

example, address line A_{15} is connected at terminal 25, and so on. Compare this to the block diagram of Fig. 1-17, which shows the architecture of the RCA CDP1802 microprocessor, also shown in Figs. 1-13 and 1-14.

Note that none of these diagrams show how the microprocessor accomplished its functions (in the same sense that a TV set block diagram shows the functions of the set's circuits). This is typical for microprocessor design and user literature. You must consult the instruction set to find out what the microprocessor will do in response to commands. You will probably never know how the microprocessor accomplishes this response.

We will not go into any detail here concerning operation of the microprocessors shown in Figs. 1-13 through 1-17. Operation of these units is covered in the appropriate chapters (Chapter 3 for RCA and Chapter 4 for Motorola).

1-11 MEMORY HARDWARE

There are two types of memory units used in microprocessor-based systems: the RAM and ROM. Generally, each of these memories is contained in a separate IC package. However, there are systems where one of the memories, or both, are contained in the same IC package as the microprocessor. Such

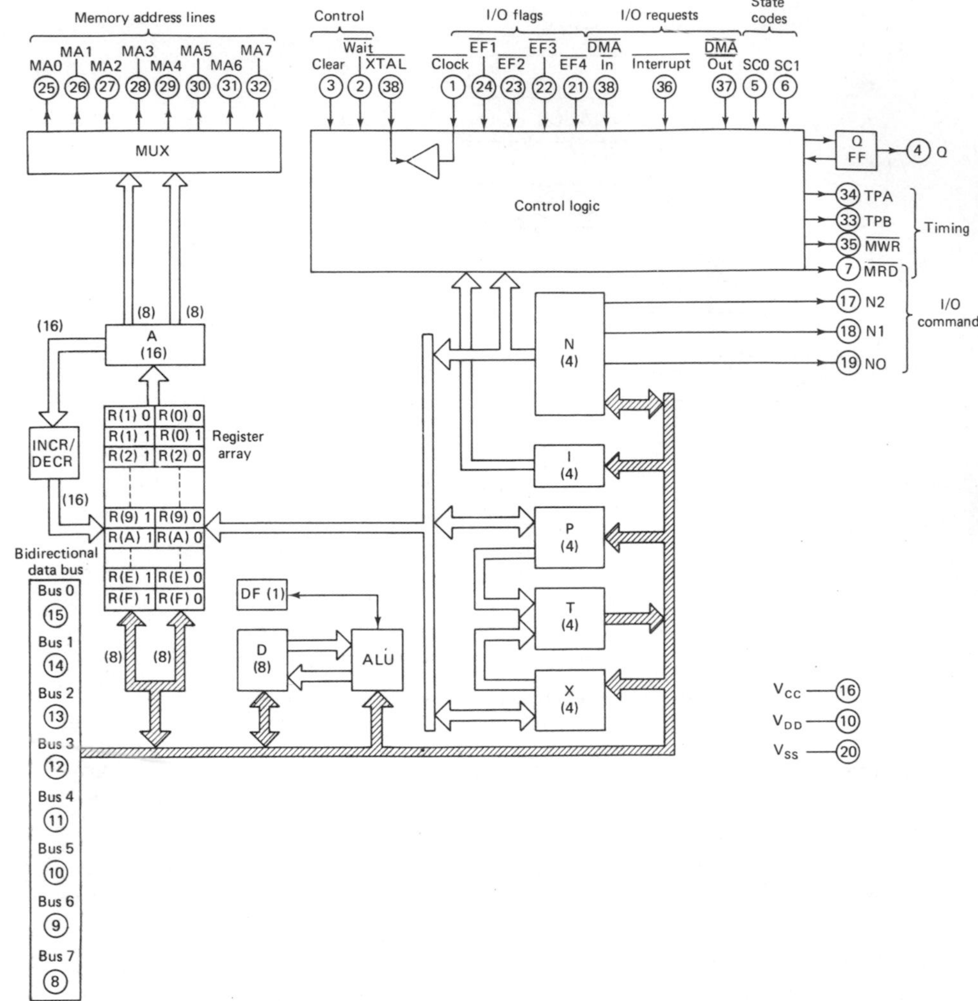

Figure 1-17 RCA CDP1802 microprocessor, block diagram.

arrangements are discussed in appropriate chapters. For now, we will consider the more typical case where there is a separate ROM and RAM in individual IC packages (or several ROMs and RAMs in separate packages).

1-11-1 RAM circuits

Figure 1-18 shows the package, pin assignment diagram, and functional block diagram of a typical RAM. This unit is described by the manufacturer as a 128 × 8 static RAM. This means that the matrix has 128 addresses, each with 8 bits. Thus, 8-bit bytes can be read into, or out of, 128 locations. The data bytes appear on the data lines D0 through

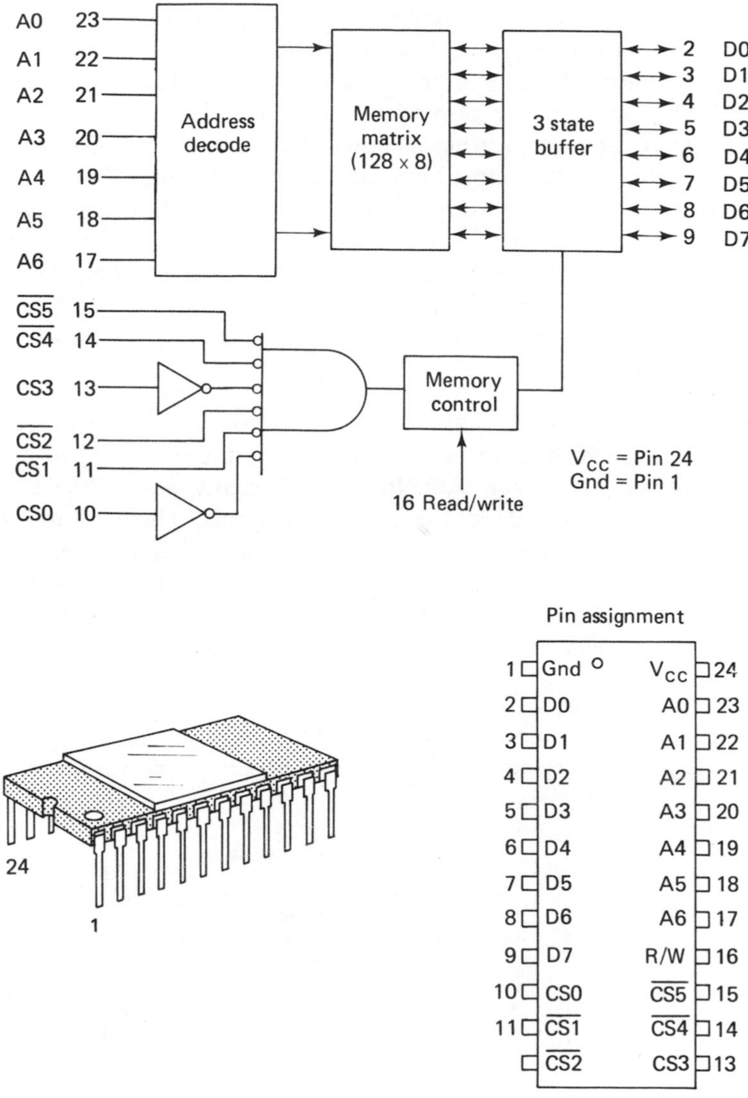

Figure 1-18 Motorola 128 × 8 static RAM.

D7, usually connected to a data bus. The data byte is read into the matrix if the buffer is in the "in" state, and is read out when the buffer is in the "out" state. The data lines are disconnected from the matrix if the buffer is in the "high-impedance" state.

Buffer-state control. The buffer state is controlled by two factors; the read/write signal at pin 16, and the control signals at pins 10 through 15. If any one of the control signals (called "chip select inputs") is absent, the buffer remains in the high-impedance state, and no data pass between the matrix and the data lines. Thus, it is possible to shut off the memory from the microprocessor system by controlling only one of six lines or inputs.

Note that some of the chip select inputs are *active high* (turned on when the line is at binary 1), whereas others are *active low* (turned on when the line is at binary 0). Active lows are indicated by the overbars. This arrangement permits one memory IC to be turned on, with other memories to be turned off, by the same signal on the same address line.

When all the chip select inputs are present (all active highs are at 1, all active lows are at 0), the buffer can be placed in the read (data into the matrix) or write (data from the matrix to the data line) condition by a signal on the read/write line.

Address selection. The address to be read in or out is selected by an address decoder, which is, in turn, controlled by the binary word on the address bus (lines A0 through A6). In certain systems, part of the address lines are connected to some of the chip select inputs. This is done where there may be several memories, all connected to the address and data buses. For example, assume that a 128 × 8 RAM is used on the same data and address buses with a 1024 × 8 ROM, as shown in Fig. 1-19. Usually, the RAM will be assigned to lower number addresses (say from 0000 to 0127,

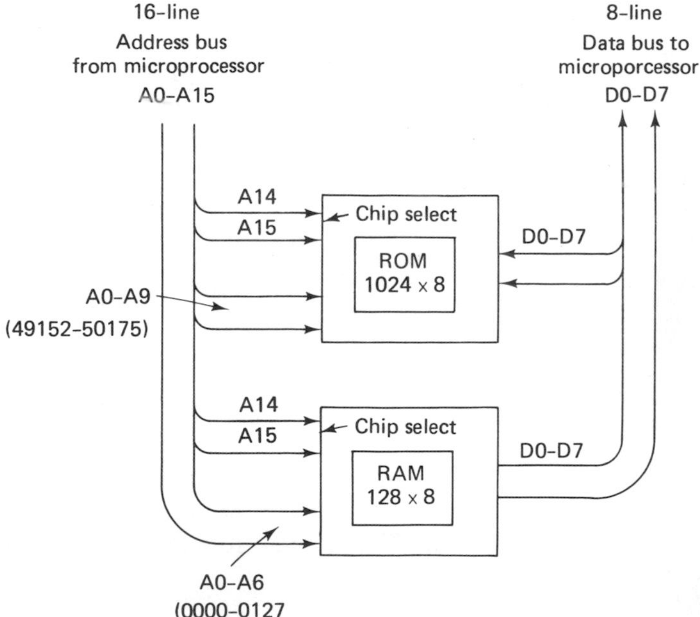

Figure 1-19 Typical address and data bus arrangement where one address line (A15) is used for chip select.

in decimal) with the ROM containing the higher-number addresses (say from 49152 to 50175, in decimal). When the highest address line A_{15} is at 1, the ROM is made active; when A_{15} is at 0, the RAM is active.

Keep in mind that the use of address line signals to control memory ICs is not used in all systems. For example, Fig. 1-20 shows the block diagram of a 32-word by 8-bit static RAM, together with the operational

Operational modes

Function	$\overline{CS}$	$\overline{MRD}$	$\overline{MWR}$	Data pins status
Read	0	0	X	Output: high/ low dependent on data
Write	0	1	0	Input, output disabled
Not selected	1	X	X	Output disabled High-impedance state
Standby	0	1	1	

Logic 1 = high Logic 0 = low X = don't care

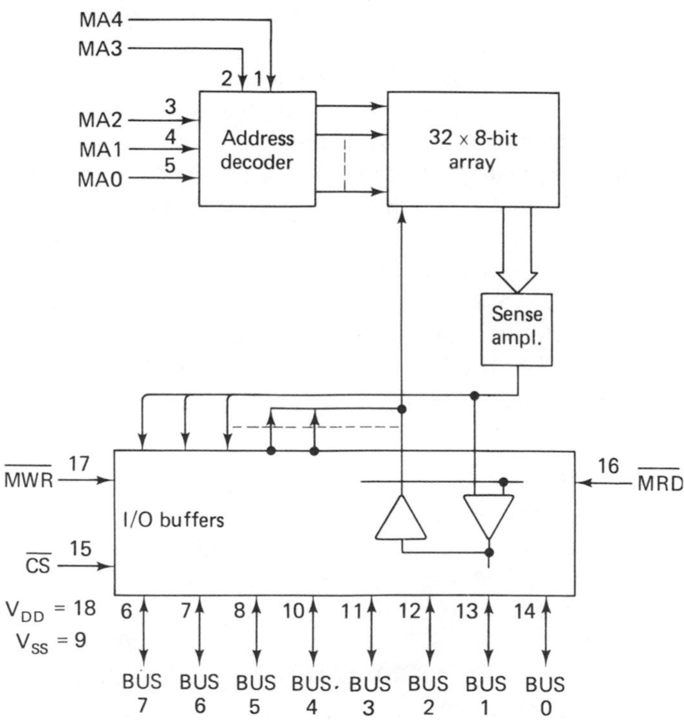

Figure 1-20 RCA 32 × 8 static RAM, functional diagram.

modes of the buffer. The buffer between the matrix (shown as an *array*) and the data bus is controlled by the $\overline{\text{MWR}}$, $\overline{\text{MRD}}$, and $\overline{\text{CS}}$ lines. Since all these lines are identified with an overbar, they are active-low, as indicated by the operational mode table.

As an example, assume that the $\overline{\text{CS}}$ and $\overline{\text{MRD}}$ lines are at binary 0 and the state of the $\overline{\text{MWR}}$ line is undetermined (the "don't-care" state). Under these conditions, the output of each bit in the selected address is passed through the buffer to the data bus. If the bit is high, the corresponding data line is high, and vice versa. If the $\overline{\text{CS}}$ and $\overline{\text{MWR}}$ lines are 0 and the $\overline{\text{MRW}}$ line is 1, the state of each line in the data bus is read into the corresponding bit of the selected address. If the $\overline{\text{CS}}$ line is 1, the buffer is in the high-impedance state, and no data pass between the array and data bus, no matter what the state of the $\overline{\text{MRD}}$ and $\overline{\text{MWR}}$ lines. This same high-impedance condition (no input, no output) can be produced when the $\overline{\text{MRD}}$ and $\overline{\text{MWR}}$ lines are both at 1 simultaneously.

From this, it can be seen that there is no common method to control RAM hardware during the read/write function.

1-11-2 Static versus dynamic RAMs

In a typical *dynamic RAM,* information is stored as an electrical charge on the gate capacitance of a MOS (metal oxide semiconductor) transistor. Since these transistors have some leakage, the charge is removed in time, even with the power applied. Thus, the information (binary 0 or 1 for each bit at each address) is lost in time if the charge is not periodically *refreshed.* There are many ways to refresh a dynamic RAM. However, the circuitry is complex and usually involves circuits outside the RAM IC. The main advantages of a dynamic RAM are high-speed operation and low power consumption.

In a typical *static RAM,* each bit of information is stored on a flip-flop or latch. Static RAMs do not require refreshing and are thus far less complex than dynamic RAMs of the same capacity. However, static RAMs are slower and consume more power.

1-11-3 Volatile RAMs

Most present-day semiconductor RAMs are *volatile.* That is, all information is lost when the power is removed. This problem can be avoided by using a battery-maintained power supply during standby operating conditions. Dynamic RAMs are often used for battery operation since they draw less power than static RAMs. Also, there is a form of static RAM, the CMOS (complementary MOS) RAM, which draws lower power and is suitable for battery operation.

1-11-4 ROM circuits

The term *ROM* is applied to a wide range of devices in which fixed two-state information is stored for later use. Usually, the ROM is housed in a separate IC package containing a matrix of addressed locations. In a ROM, each bit in each address is *permanently set* to binary 1 or 0. ROMs are generally used to hold the program of microprocessor instructions and possibly other data constants, such as routines, tables, and so on. Unlike the RAM, the ROM is nonvolatile (the memory remains after power is removed), and the write function does not exist for a ROM.

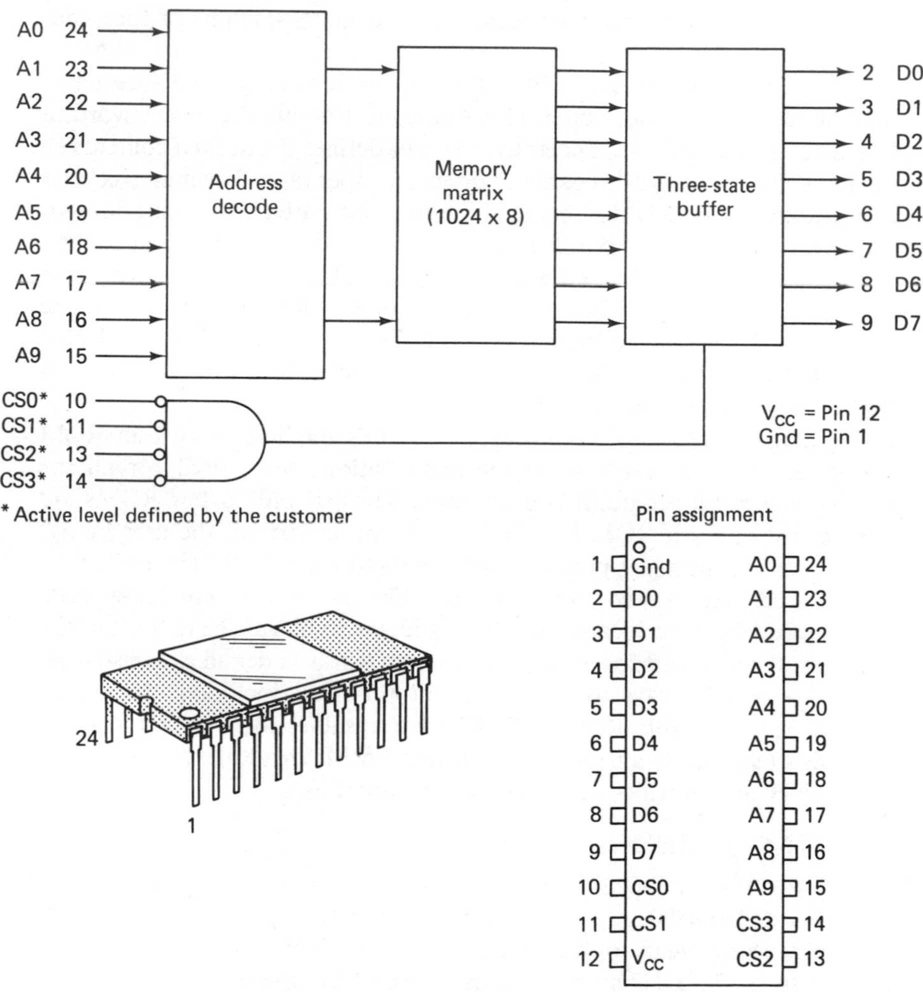

Figure 1-21 Motorola 1024 × 8 ROM.

Figure 1-21 shows the functional block diagram of a typical ROM. This unit is described by the manufacturer as a 1024 × 8 ROM. This means that the matrix has 1024 addresses, each with 8 bits. Thus, 8-bit binary words or bytes can be read out of 1024 locations. The bytes appear on the data lines D_0 through D_7, connected to the data bus. Although the buffer is three-state, only the high impedance and output states are used. When all chip select (CS) inputs are available, the permanent information stored at the selected address is passed to the data bus. When one or more of the chip select inputs are absent, the buffer remains in the high-impedance state and no data pass from the matrix to the data bus. Thus, it is possible to shut off the ROM from the system by controlling only one of four lines or inputs.

Note that the user can define whether the chip select inputs are active high or active low. Also, note that the user must define the binary word to be stored at each address. Generally, the user defines the desired contents of the ROM by means of IBM cards or punched paper tape. The manufacturer then programs the ROMs (sets in the binary bit pattern at each address), usually by means of a mask for the final metalization step in IC manufacture. This process is generally used where a large number of ROMs are required (typically 300 or more), but can be used for smaller numbers. As in the case of the RAM, the address to be read in or out of the ROM is selected by an address decoder, which, in turn, is controlled by the binary word on the address bus (lines A0 through A9).

There are two obvious problems for this method of custom ROM manufacture. First, the cost of the metalization mask (used for all the ROMs of a given program) is quite high. Thus, if only a few ROMs are needed, the cost per ROM is quite high. More important, the user rarely, if ever, knows the exact programming required for a ROM until after the program has been tested and debugged. That is, you do not know what binary word is to be located at which address until you have written the program, tested it, and found that the program works under all circumstances. There are several ways to overcome this problem, including the use of PROMs (programable ROMs), EPROMs (erasable, ultraviolet PROMs), EAROMs (electrically alterable ROMs), and RMMs (read mostly memories), all of which are described in the following paragraphs.

1-11-5 PROM circuit

A PROM is shipped by the manufacturer with all bits at each address blank (or at binary 0, in most cases). The user then programs each bit at each address by means of an electrical current. Typically, when current is applied to a bit, a Nichrome wire is "fused" or opened by the current, making that bit assume the electrical characteristics of a binary 1. Bits to be at binary 0 are left untouched. The program in the PROM is then permanent and irreversible.

The programming can be used with simple switches and a voltage source, as shown in Fig. 1-22. In this circuit, the address switches are set to produce the binary word at the address terminals of the PROM (switches closed to provide 5 V for each binary 1, switches open for a 0). With the proper address selected, the rotary programming switch is set to each bit requiring a binary 1, in turn, and the fusing switch is pressed for about 1 s to fuse the Nichrome wire within the PROM. This process is very time consuming and tedious. Also, if a mistake is made on even one bit in one address, the entire PROM is made useless for that program. There are automatic and semiautomatic PROM programming devices available to overcome this problem, as discussed in Chapters 3 through 7.

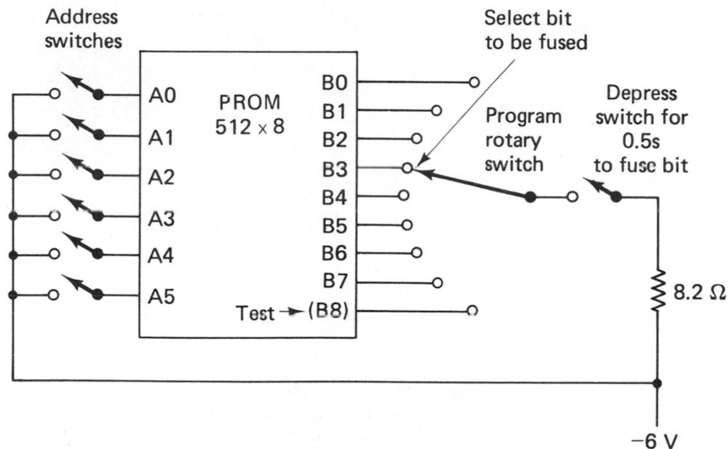

Figure 1-22 Basic PROM programming circuit.

1-11-6 EPROM circuit

Even though it is possible to program a large number of PROMs with automatic equipment rather quickly, there is still the problem of testing and debugging before a final program is obtained for ROM. This problem is overcome by means of an EPROM in which information is stored as a charge in a MOSFET (metal oxide semiconductor field-effect transistor). Such EPROMs can be erased by flooding the IC with ultraviolet radiation. Once erased, new information can be programmed into the PROM in the normal manner. The erasure and reprogramming process can be repeated as many times as required.

As shown in Fig. 1-23, an EPROM package is provided with a transparent lid which allows the memory content to be erased with ultraviolet (UV) light. For proper erasure, the semiconductor chip within the IC package must be exposed to strong UV light for a few minutes. Exposure

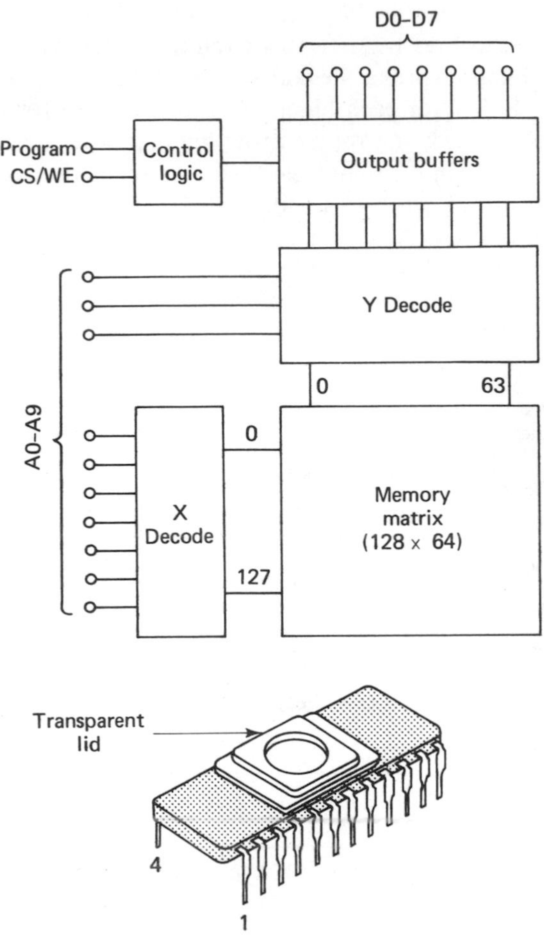

Figure 1-23 Motorola 1024 × 8 alterable (ultraviolet) ROM.

to ordinary room light will take years to produce erasure; thus, there is no danger of the program being erased accidentally. Even exposure to direct sunlight will not produce erasure for several days.

Except for the erasure feature, a typical EPROM is similar to a ROM in function, as shown by the block diagram of Fig. 1-23. In addition to the usual address inputs, data outputs, decoders, and buffers, an EPROM usually has a "program" input line. An appropriate signal on the program line permits information to be programmed into the selected address.

1-11-7 EAROM and RMM circuits

These devices are a form of erasable PROM, but use electrical currents instead of UV light for erasure. The programming is similar to that of the EPROM, but the erasure is a slow process and requires special circuits.

For that reason, EPROMs are generally used for microprocessor-based systems rather than for EAROMs and RMMs. However, this trend can change in the future.

1-12 INPUT/OUTPUT HARDWARE

The microprocessor and memories described in Secs. 1-10 and 1-11 can be connected to form a simple and almost complete microcomputer system. The missing element is an input/output device between the microcomputer hardware and the outside world, or peripherals. Without some I/O hardware, the transfer of data between the outside world and the microcomputer would be impossible.

Assume, for example, that a basic microcomputer (microprocessor, ROM, and RAM) is used with a conventional video terminal (keyboard and CRT video display), and that the data lines of the video terminal are connected to the microcomputer data buses. Information to be processed is typed on the keyboard and transmitted directly to the microcomputer data lines. After processing, the data bytes are returned directly to the video display. There are three basic problems with such an arrangement.

First, data bytes from the keyboard can easily appear simultaneously with data from the selected memory. Second, the video terminal and microcomputer would have no way of telling each other that they are ready to transmit or receive data. Third, there is no synchronization of timing between the microcomputer and the video terminal. That is, the microcomputer and video terminal clocks may be operating at different frequencies, phase relationships, and so on.

A further problem is created if the peripheral operates with serial data rather than the parallel data required for the microcomputer. Also, there is always the problem of *interfacing* electronic devices (different operating voltage levels, impedances, etc.). These and other problems are overcome by means of an input/output IC. Most microprocessor manufacturers supply one or more I/O ICs for their systems. Typically, there is one I/O device for interfacing with parallel peripherals, and another for serial peripherals.

1-12-1 Typical parallel I/O IC

Figure 1-24 is the block diagram of a basic parallel I/O IC. The circuit is described as an 8-bit input/output port by the manufacturer, and consists essentially of an 8-bit register and 8-bit buffers, together with the control elements. The MODE control is used to program the device as an input port or output port. The MODE control is 0 for input and 1 for output.

Input port. When used as an input port, information is passed into the 8-bit register when pulses on the clock line are high. The clock also sets the

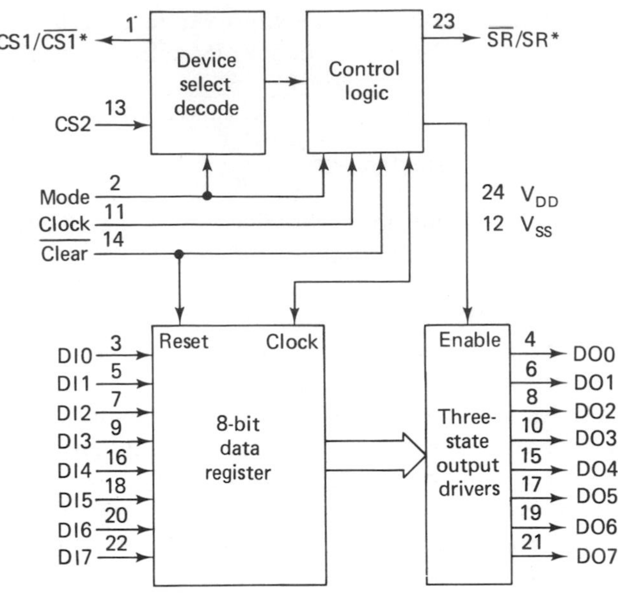

Figure 1-24 RCA COSMAC 8-bit I/O port.

service request (SR/SE) circuit and latches the data in the register. The SR output can be used to signal or flag the microprocessor that the data from the peripheral are ready for processing. The CS1 and CS2 inputs are used to control the three-state buffers. The buffers are enabled when the CS1 and CS2 lines are high. This also resets the SR circuits (to flag the microprocessor that the data bytes have been passed).

Output port. When used as an output port, the buffers are enabled at all times, and information is passed into the 8-bit register (if CS1, CS2, and the clock are all high). The service request SR signal is generated when CS1 and CS2 are swinging low, and remains until the clock swings low. Stated another way, SR is generated when CS1 and CS2 go from 1 to 0, and remains until the clock line goes to 0.

Clear signal. A CLEAR signal is provided for resetting the register and the service request circuit. The CLEAR function operates in both the input and output port modes.

From these descriptions, it can be seen that the circuit of Fig. 1-24 provides the basic I/O functions. Using the video terminal example, a data byte from the keyboard can be held in the register until the microprocessor is ready to accept new data. This condition is signaled or flagged to the microprocessor by the SR line. Then the buffers are enabled by the microprocessor, and the data byte is passed to the microcomputer system. The buffers are set to the high-impedance state, and the registers are reset. After processing in the microcomputer system, the data byte is placed in the registers, and this condition is flagged to the video terminal by the SR line. When the video terminal is ready to accept data for display on the CRT, the buffers are enabled by the video terminal, the byte is passed to the CRT display, the buffers are again returned to the high-impedance state, and the registers and SR line are reset.

1-12-2 Serial I/O IC

Operation of a serial I/O circuit is generally far more complex than that of the basic parallel I/O circuit just described. In addition to all the control, timing, and data-transfer functions, a serial I/O must also convert from parallel to serial and vice versa for each exchange of information between the peripheral and microcomputer system. Because of this complexity, and because each manufacturer uses a somewhat different system for their I/O devices, the discussions of serial I/O ICs are covered in the related Chapters 3 through 7, and in Chapter 2.

1-13 BASIC MICROCOMPUTER SYSTEM

Now that we have covered basic microcomputer hardware (microprocessor, ROM, RAM, and I/O ICs) and the circuits within these ICs, we are now ready to describe a simple, yet complete microcomputer system.

Figure 1-25 is the block diagram of an elementary microcomputer system. This is the basic RCA system described more fully in Chapter 3. The circuits shown in Fig. 1-25 provide for control of the I/O devices, transfer of data or control information between I/O and memory, movement of data bytes between different memory locations, and interpretation of data bytes stored in memory. The system consists of a microprocessor, ROM, RAM, and I/O. All these devices can be interfaced directly without external components. The only external component required (besides a power supply and wiring) is a crystal for frequency control of the clock signal pulses.

1-13-1 System functions

The major functions performed by the system of Fig. 1-25 include:

1. Control of peripheral devices such as video terminals, tape/card readers, printers, etc.).
2. Transfer of data and/or control information between the peripheral devices and memory.

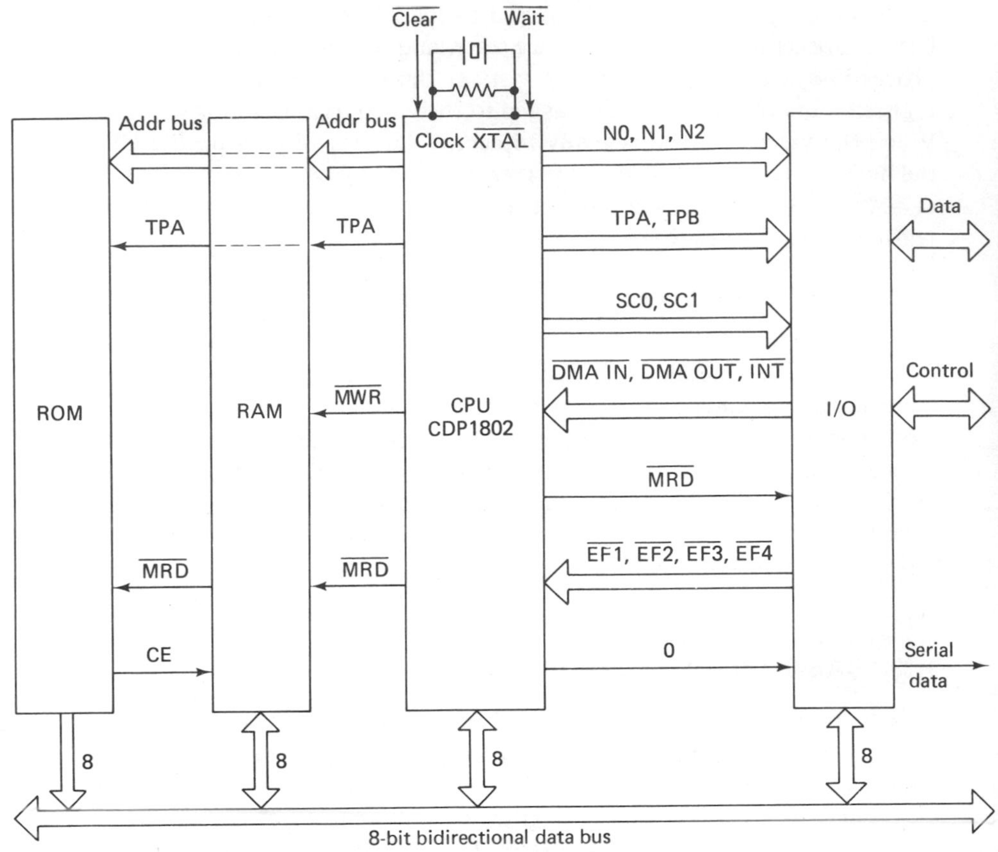

FIGURE 1-25 Basic RCS COSMAC Microcomputer System.

3. Movement of data bytes between different memory locations.
4. Interpretation or modification of bytes stored in memory.

In such a system, the microprocessor can, for example, control the entry of data bytes from an input keyboard and store them in predetermined memory locations. The microprocessor can then perform specified arithmetic operations using the stored bytes and transfer the results to an output display or printing device.

1-13-2 Typical peripherals

Typical system input peripheral devices may include simple switches, paper-tape/card readers, magnetic-tape/disk devices, relays, modems, analog-to-digital (A/D) converters, photodetectors, and other computers. Output peripherals may include lights, relays, CRT, light-emitting diode (LED) and liquid crystal devices (LCD), digital-to-analog (D/A) converters, modems, printers, and other computers. Typical peripherals are discussed in Chapter 2.

1-13-3 System memory and data bus

The system memory can be any combination of RAM and ROM up to a maximum of 65,535 bytes. ROM is used for permanent storage or programs, tables, and other types of fixed data. RAM is required for general-purpose computer systems that have frequent program changes. RAM is also required for temporary storage of variable data. The type of memory and required storage capacity is determined by the specific application of the system. Bytes are transferred between peripheral devices, memory, and the microprocessor by means of a common, bidirectional, 8-bit data bus.

1-13-4 I/O (peripheral) control signals

Fifteen I/O signal lines are provided for control between the system and peripherals. Systems can use some or all of these signals, depending on required I/O or peripheral sophistication.

N-code signals. A 3-bit, N-code (N0, N1, N2) is generated by the I/O instruction. The N-code can be used to specify whether an I/O byte on the bus is meant to represent data, an I/O device selection code, an I/O status code, an I/O control code, and so on. Use of the N-code to specify an I/O peripheral device directly permits simple, inexpensive control of a small number of peripheral devices or I/O modes. Use of the N-code to specify the meaning of the word on the data bus facilitates systems incorporating a large number of peripheral or I/O devices.

I/O flag signals. Four I/O flag inputs (EF1–EF4) are provided. Peripheral or I/O devices can control these inputs at any time to signal the microprocessor that a byte transfer is required (a "service request"), that an error condition has occurred (such as when an abnormal parity condition is detected by the peripheral), and so on. These flags can also be used as binary input lines, if desired. The flags can be tested or sampled to determine whether or not they are active. For example, one of the flags can be used by a peripheral to indicate to the microprocessor that the peripheral needs servicing (the peripheral has data to be entered into the system). Use of the flag input must be coordinated with programs that test them.

Output line (Q). An output line Q is provided from the microprocessor to peripherals. The Q line is controlled by the microprocessor and can be used to activate or signal peripheral or I/O devices. The Q line can also be used in connection with one of the flag inputs to form a serial I/O interface.

Interrupt signals. A program interrupt line ($\overline{\text{INT}}$) can be activated at any time by peripherals or I/O circuits to obtain an immediate microprocessor response. The interrupt signal causes the microprocessor to suspend the current program sequence and execute a predetermined sequence of operations designed to respond to the interrupt condition. After servicing the interrupt, the microprocessor assumes execution of the interrupted program. The microprocessor can be made to ignore the interrupt line by resetting an interrupt enable flip-flop.

Direct memory access (DMA). Many microcomputer systems use some form of DMA, which allows data to be transferred between peripherals and memory without interference to the microprocessor. DMA is often referred to as a method for speeding up data movement between elements of the microcomputer system. DMA allows fast peripherals (or perhaps another microprocessor) access to the system memory without taking up microprocessor time. In actual practice, however, DMA does use some microprocessor program time. How much time depends on the DMA system in use. DMA systems are discussed further in Chapters 3 through 7.

In the system of Fig. 1-25, two DMA lines ($\overline{\text{DMA-IN}}$ and $\overline{\text{DMA-OUT}}$) are provided for special types of byte transfer between memory and I/O devices or peripherals. Activating the $\overline{\text{DMA-IN}}$ line causes an input byte to be immediately stored in a memory location without intervention by the program being executed. Activating the $\overline{\text{DMA-OUT}}$ line causes a byte to be immediately transferred from memory to the requesting peripheral or I/O circuit.

A register within the microprocessor is used as a DMA *pointer.* This built-in DMA memory pointer register is used to indicate the memory location for the DMA cycles. The program initially sets the DMA pointer to a beginning memory location. Each DMA byte transfer *automatically increments the pointer* to the next-higher memory location. Repeated activation of a DMA line can cause the transfer of any number of consecutive bytes to and from memory independent of concurrent program execution.

Note that the DMA lines, as well as the $\overline{\text{INT}}$ (interrupt) line, are shown with an overbar in Fig. 1-25. This means that these lines are active when at zero volts (or binary 0, or low), and that a +5 V (or binary 1, or high) signal must be applied to these lines when they are not in use.

Data transfer. Peripherals and I/O device circuits can cause data transfer by activating a flag line, the interrupt line, or a DMA line. The flag lines must be sampled by the program to determine when they become active (a request for service by the peripheral or I/O) and are used for relatively slow changing signals. Activating the interrupt line causes an immediate microprocessor response, regardless of the program currently in progress, suspending operation of that program and allowing real-time access. Use of DMA provides the quickest response with the least disturbance of the program.

State code and timing lines. A 2-bit state code (SC0, SC1) and two timing lines (TPA, TPB) are provided for use by peripherals and I/O device circuits. These four signals permit synchronization of peripheral and I/O circuits with internal microprocessor operating cycles. The state code indicate whether the microprocessor is responding to a DMA request, responding to an interrupt request, fetching an instruction, or executing an instruction. The timing signals are used by the memory and I/O systems to signal a new microprocessor state code, to latch memory address bits, to take memory data from the bus, and to set and reset peripheral or I/O control flip-flops.

1-13-5 Control of memory read/write cycles

Data bytes are transmitted to and from memory by means of the common data bus. The microprocessor provides two lines to control memory read/write cycles.

Memory write. During a memory-write cycle, the byte to be written appears on the data bus, either from the microprocessor or from a peripheral or I/O device, and a memory-write signal ($\overline{\text{MWR}}$) is generated by the microprocessor at the appropriate time.

Memory read. During a memory-read cycle, a memory-read ($\overline{\text{MRD}}$) level is generated. The read signal or level is used by the system to pass the memory output byte onto the common data bus for use by the microprocessor or by a peripheral or I/O device.

1-13-6 Memory address control signals

The microprocessor provides eight memory address lines. These eight lines can supply 16-bit memory addresses in the form of *two successive* 8-bit bytes. (Note that some microprocessors have 16 address lines, making it possible to address memory in one byte. This arrangement makes for a faster system, but requires more wiring to accommodate the 16 lines.) In the system of Fig. 1-25, the more significant (high-order) address byte appears on the eight address lines first, followed by the less-significant (low-order) address byte. The number of high-order bits required to select a unique memory byte location depends upon the size of the memory.

As an example, a 4096-byte memory requires a 12-bit address. This 12-bit address is obtained by combining 4 bits from the high-order address byte with 8 bits from the low-order address byte. One of the two microprocessor timing pulses (TPA, TPB) may be used to strobe the required high-order bits into an address latch (or register) when they appear on the eight address lines. Latch circuits are not required if address registers are incorporated in the memory ICs, as is the case in the RCA ROM of Fig. 1-25. An internal register holds the 8 low-order address bits on the address lines for the remainder of the memory cycle.

1-13-7 Wait and clear control signals

The WAIT and CLEAR lines are, in effect, the start–stop and reset or initialize control lines, respectively.

When the WAIT line is active (0 V), microprocessor operation is halted. Microprocessor operation can start when the WAIT line is at 5 V.

When the CLEAR line is at 0 V, the microprocessor is initialized (all registers set to zero or to the desired starting value). When 5 V is applied to the CLEAR line, the microprocessor starts the program.

When both the CLEAR and WAIT lines are active (0 V), the microprocessor is stopped and is in the *program load mode,* ready to accept a program. With both CLEAR and WAIT at 5 V (inactive) the microprocessor is turned on and is processing the program loaded into the memory and registers.

1-13-8 Clock and crystal control signals

Clock pulses are applied to the microprocessor and the entire system through the CLOCK line. The clock pulses can be from an external source, such as a peripheral or an external oscillator, or can be generated internally when a *quartz crystal* is connected between the CLOCK and XTAL lines. If a crystal is used, the frequency of the clock pulses is determined directly by the crystal. For example, a 1-MHz crystal produces a clock frequency of 1 MHz, and the duration of each clock pulse cycle is 1 μs. When an external clock pulse is used, the system operating frequency is determined by the external source. The maximum operating frequency for the system of Fig. 1-25 is 6.4 MHz, when a 10-V power supply is used for the microprocessor. With the more common 5-V supply, the maximum clock frequency is 3.2 MHz. A further discussion of timing and clock frequencies is provided in Sec. 1-14.

1-14 SYSTEM TIMING AND SYNCHRONIZATION

It is obvious that all the system functions described in Sec. 1-13 and shown in Fig. 1-25 must be synchronized as to time. For example, if a data byte is to be entered into memory at a particular address, that (and only that) data byte must be on the data bus when the desired address byte is on the address bus. If the two bytes (data and address) are not synchronized exactly, the data byte will be entered at the wrong address (or at no address). This problem is overcome by timing within the microprocessor. Registers are opened and closed at exact time intervals to accomplish the desired results.

System timing is primarily a function of the microprocessor. As in the case of microprocessor instructions, you *cannot change* the time relationships or operating cycles of the microprocessor. However, you can change system speed. As discussed in Sec. 1-13, the system speed or operating frequency is determined by the crystal or other clock pulses. If a 1-MHz crystal is used, the clock pulses will be approximately 1 μs; with a 3-MHz crystal, the clock pulses will be about one-third of this, or about 333 ns; and so on. However, if it takes eight clock pulses to complete a certain function or instruction at one speed, it will take eight clock pulses to complete the same function at any other speed.

The time relationships and synchronization are shown by *timing diagrams* such as Fig. 1-26. The clock pulses are shown at the top and bottom of the diagram. There are two sets of eight clock pulses. Thus, each

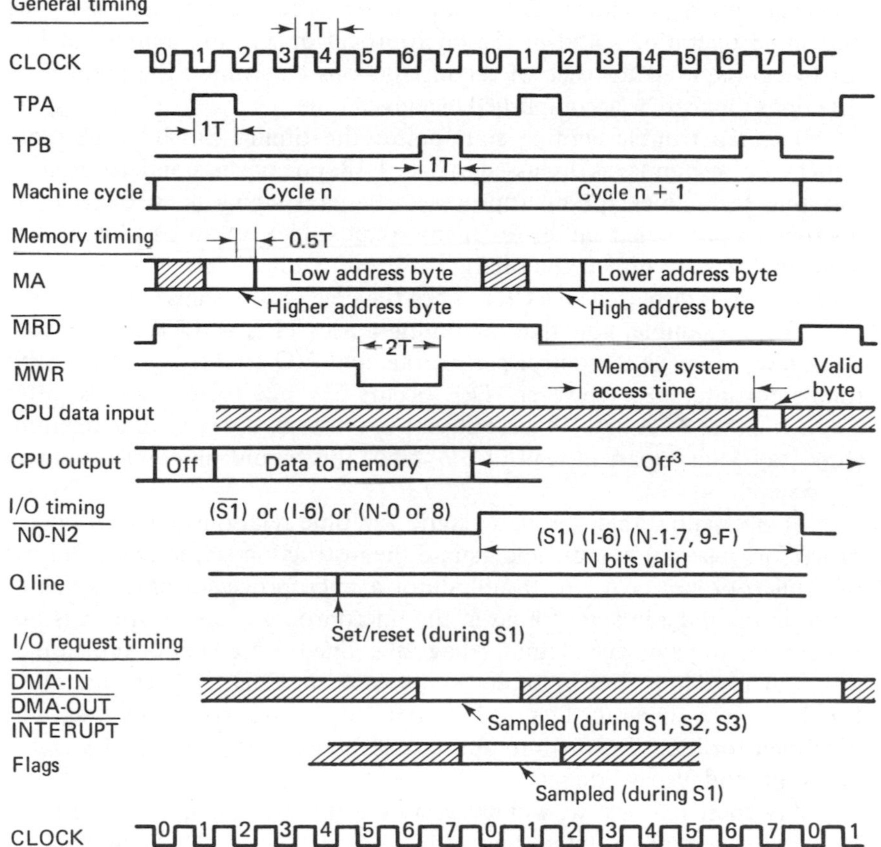

Figure 1-26 Timing diagram for basic RCA COSMAC microcomputer system.

clock pulse represents one bit in an 8-bit byte. Some functions are accomplished within the first byte; other functions require two bytes. Note that there is no reference to operating speed on the clock pulse, but that one clock cycle is shown as a time interval 1T (at clock pulse 3 on the top line). This is known as a *clock period.* If the clock frequency (set by the crystal or other external clock pulse source) is 1 MHz, the time interval or clock period 1T is approximately 1 μs.

From a programming standpoint, the timing intervals and relationships are not that critical. It is generally more important that the programmer know that it takes one or two bytes to accomplish a given function or instruction. However, from a design or troubleshooting standpoint, timing synchronization is critical. For example, when considering a design, the maximum operating speed of the microprocessor and the number of bits (or bytes) required for each of the instructions determines the number of functions that can be accomplished in a given time.

From a troubleshooting standpoint, the timing can be even more critical. For example, as discussed in Sec. 1-18, one of the standard troubleshooting techniques for microprocessor-based systems is to display the microprocessor signal pulses (as many as possible) on an oscilloscope or logic analyzer. In effect, the timing diagram of Fig. 1-26 (or a significant portion of it) is displayed on a CRT. Then the time relationships are compared.

As an example, note that the timing pulses TPA and TPB (sent from the microprocessor to control peripherals and I/O circuits) occur at 8-bit (one-byte) intervals. However, TPB occurs 5½ bits (or 5½ cycles) after TPA. If either TPA or TPB were absent or abnormal (wrong time relationship—say 3 bits apart instead of 5½ bits), this would pinpoint a fault in the system.

It is essential that you understand the time relationships of a microprocessor, just as you must understand the instruction set, to make full use of a microprocessor (or to troubleshoot a microprocessor-based system). Such timing diagrams are found in the microprocessor literature. It is not uncommon to have several timing diagrams, one for each major function or group of functions. For example, as discussed in Chapter 3, the literature for the system shown in Figs. 1-25 and 1-26 provides six timing diagrams (one each for input instruction, output instruction, $\overline{\text{DMA-IN}}$, $\overline{\text{DMA-OUT}}$, interrupt, and instruction set).

For these reasons, we will not go into a full discussion of timing here. However, one point of interest should be noted in Fig. 1-26. Each *machine cycle* consists of eight clock pulses (or a full 8-bit byte), and each instruction or function requires two or three bytes (or two or three machine cycles, whichever term is used by the microprocessor manufacturer). This relationship among clock bits, machine cycles, and instruction or function timing is common to many microprocessors.

1-15 TYPICAL MICROCOMPUTER SYSTEM OPERATION

Before going into the microprocessors and microcomputers of specific manufacturers, discussed in Chapters 3 through 7, let us consider a microprocessor and related IC equipment operating as a typical microcomputer system. The difficulty is that there are many different types of microprocessors, and even more microcomputer system arrangements. As you will discover, there is no real standardization in hardware, software, or microcomputer system configurations.

Since it would be difficult for anyone (even experienced technicians and engineers) not already familiar with computers of some type (standard, mini, or micro) to immediately grasp the operation of any microprocessor or microcomputer described in Chapters 3 through 7, we shall consider a generalized and simplified microcomputer—one that never has nor ever will be designed. Nevertheless, this microcomputer contains the basic principles upon which all microprocessor-based systems operate. Once you understand how this simplified microcomputer operates, you will be in a better position to consider the more sophisticated and realistic systems described throughout this book. Borrowing a technique used by microcomputer manufacturers, we shall call our system the LENKMICROCOMP (LENK MICRO COMPuter).

1-15-1 Microcomputer system hardware

Our microcomputer consists of a microprocessor, a 128 × 8 RAM, a 1024 × 8 ROM, and an I/O device. The RAM, ROM, and I/O are all in IC form, and are similar to the devices shown in Figs. 1-18, 1-21, and 1-24, respectively. The microprocessor is of special design but contains the usual registers, accumulators, counters, pointer, decoders, multiplexers, buffers, drivers, latches, ALU, and control circuitry described in Sec. 1-9.

As is typical, the registers are used as temporary storage locations for data bytes or words, such as the accumulators in the ALU section, where the mathematical operations are performed. The counters are used to tally various items of information such as commands (instructions) and locations (addresses) in the memory where the information can be found. Decoders translate the instruction to electrical signals (pulses) for executing these commands and for translating addresses to electrical signals, permitting the microprocessor to locate the required information and transfer it to the approximate destinations. Interconnecting all these elements are electronic and logic circuits (buffers, drivers, latches, flip-flops) that direct the signals along the appropriate paths.

1-15-2 Peripheral equipment

In most all microcomputers there must be a means of direct human-to-machine communication. The only exceptions to this are where the microcomputer system is used for control or processing of information to and from other electronic devices (such as when a microprocessor-based system is used in industrial control). Human-to-machine communication is usually the job of peripheral equipment. As is discussed in Chapter 2, there are many peripheral devices available for use with microcomputer systems.

For simplicity, we have chosen a manually operated keyboard device. This keyboard permits the operator to enter information into any location in the memory or to insert extra instructions. Our keyboard is in the form of a typewriter (similar to a teletype or TTY instrument). With this arrangement, the typewriter can both insert and print out information. As an alternative, we can use a video terminal, where information is inserted by the keyboard and read out by the CRT video display.

The information fed to the microcomputer from the peripheral keyboard falls into two general categories. There are the *data* bytes (consisting of numbers, alphabetic letters, symbols, or combinations of all three that are to be processed), and the *instruction* bytes (the commands indicating how the data bytes are to be processed). Since the microcomputer's language is composed of binary numbers (in electrical pulse form), all information to be used must first be converted to numbers (or combinations of letters and numbers) and then the numbers must be converted to binary numbers.

In the LENKMICROCOMP keyboard, the conversion is done by means of a decoder. The keyboard decoder converts letters, numbers, and symbols from the keyboard into an ASCII code which appears at the keyboard output in the form of an 8-bit binary word or byte. This byte is in parallel form, and is applied to the microcomputer's 8-bit I/O IC. As an example, assume that the letter A on the keyboard is pressed. This is converted to a hex 41 by the keyboard decoder, and appears as binary 01000001 at the I/O terminals.

1-15-3 Microcomputer program

Microcomputers solve problems in a step-by-step manner. Since the microcomputer cannot think by itself (contrary to popular opinion), a *program* must be prepared that breaks the problem down into a series of sequential, logical, and simple steps. This is the task of the programmer. While an extended discussion of the art of programming (and it is an art, not a science) is not intended for this book, you, the reader, must have some understanding (preferably a very detailed understanding) of the program if you are to learn how a microcomputer operates. For example, as discussed in Sec. 1-18, the first step in troubleshooting a microcomputer is to operate the system through its normal program and note any abnormalities in operation, sequence, or failure to perform a given step.

Since there are many variations among microprocessors, programs must be specifically developed for a particular microprocessor. The programmer must know the microprocessor language and the manner in which the microprocessor operates. In short, you must know the instruction set! The program that we shall consider here is for our hypothetical, general-purpose microcomputer, the LENKMICROCOMP.

1-15-4 The basic program

As an example of how a program may be prepared for the microcomputer, let us consider how far a freely falling body will fall in 5 s. The equation for this problem is $d = gt^2/2$, where d is the distance in feet, t the time in seconds, and g the acceleration due to gravity (32 f/s for each second of fall).

The programmer analyzes the problem and breaks it down into a sequential series of logical steps. The programmer than draws up a *flowchart,* which diagrams the sequence of steps to be taken in solving the problem. Such a flowchart is shown in Fig. 1-27.

Although the flowchart helps the programmer analyze the problem, the microcomputer cannot use the flowchart as is. The microprocessor has its own language (machine language), which is based on binary numbers, not alphabetic letters or words. Accordingly, the flowchart must be con-

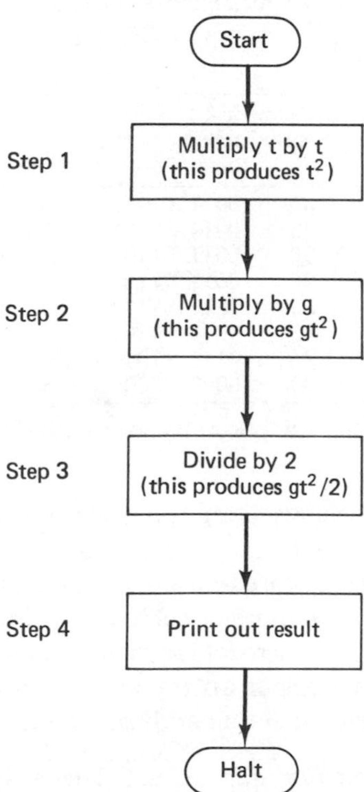

Figure 1-27 Basic flowchart for falling-body problem.

verted to a program or sequential set of instructions (in machine language) which the microprocessor can follow.

This conversion process is known as *assembly* and is discussed in Sec. 1-17. Some microprocessor manufacturers provide software programs, known as *assemblers,* that aid in the conversion process.

There are many ways in which manufacturers identify their insructions. First, some manufacturers call their instructions *operation codes* (or simply *op codes*). In some cases each op code or instruction is identified by a binary number. This is the same binary number applied to the data inputs of the microprocessor to initiate an instruction or function, as discussed in Sec. 1-8. However, as discussed in Sec. 1-17, machine-language programming (using binary numbers) is very laborious and subject to error, except for very simple, short programs.

Most microprocessor manufacturers identify the instructions by an alphabetic abbreviation or *mnemonic,* by a numeric abbreviation (usually in hex), and by an assembly code or statement. Examples of such identification for our LENKMICROCOMP are shown in Fig. 1-28. Note that the assembly code or statement is used for the convenience of the programmer when writing a program. However, only the numeric portion is used by the microprocessor (in binary form). Hex is used as shorthand for the binary number.

Alphabetic (Mnemonic) Representation	Numerical Representation Hex	Binary	Meaning of Instruction
CAD	3A	0011 1010	Clear accumulator and add
ADD	3B	0011 1011	Add
SUB	3C	0011 1100	Subtract
MUL	3D	0011 1101	Multiply
DIV	3E	0011 1110	Divide
STO	3F	0011 1111	Store
PRT	7A	0111 1010	Print
HLT	00	0000 0000	Halt

Figure 1-28 Examples of typical op codes for the LENKMICROCOMP.

Both the numbers representing the instructions and the numbers that constitute data are stored in the memory at particular addresses. Each instruction or data byte is stored at a separate address. The programmer must keep a record of the address or each instruction or data byte. Then, if the programmer wishes the microcomputer to obtain any specific instruction or data byte, the address is put on the address bus by the program, and the instruction or data stored at that address appear on the data bus.

Arrangement of instruction addresses. There are several methods for arranging the instruction addresses in the memory. Since the instructions follow in sequence, the address of the instructions, too, may be in sequential order. Thus, instruction 1 may be stored, say, at address 0001. Then, instruction 2 can be stored at address 0002, instruction 3 at address 0003, and so forth.

Before the start of operations, the address of instruction 1 (0001) is placed in a *program counter* register within the microprocessor. Then, as the microprocessor executes instruction 1, a signal is sent to the program counter, advancing the count by 1. The number in the program counter is now 0002, which is the address of instruction 2. The microprocessor obtains the address of the second instruction from the program counter (that is, the number in the program counter appears on the address bus). As the microprocessor executes instruction 2, the program counter advances to 0003, which is the address of instruction 3. This process continues as long as there are instructions to be carried out. The final instruction directs the microprocessor to stop.

Keep in mind that the instructions are *permanently* programmed into the ROM at the indicated addresses. Neither the instructions nor the order in which they appear can be altered (unless the ROM is erasable). An erasable or alterable ROM is used during development of the program. When the program is debugged and the desired order of instructions is determined, a ROM is permanently programmed to that order.

Arrangement of data adddresses. There are several methods for arranging the data bytes in memory. One method is to store both the instruction and data bytes in each address. Then, when the microprocessor is directed to that address (that is, when that address word appears on the address bus), the microprocessor will find both the op code indicating an instruction and the data to be acted upon. Another method is to store each data byte at any address that is unoccupied and available. Using this system, each step of the program requires two machine cycles, one for instructions and one for data. Some microprocessors require three machine cycles for each program step. Usually, the first cycle is for the op code or instruction, with the remaining two cycles for data. Keep in mind that data bytes are *temporarily programmed* into the RAM at the desired addresses. In our case, the data bytes are entered at the peripheral typewriter keyboard.

Note that with any of the systems for instruction and data addressing, the program does not contain the actual data but the address at which the data bytes are stored. For example, if the programmer wishes the microprocessor to add a certain number, the programmer indicates to the microprocessor the instruction for addition (the addition instruction word appears on the data bus) and gives the address of the data byte number to be added (the data byte address word appears on the address bus). The microprocessor will then obtain the data byte at the selected address and add it to whatever number appears in the microprocessor arithmetic register or accumulator.

Example of programming. As an example, let us program the falling-body problem (using the flowchart of Fig. 1-27 and the instructions or op codes of Fig. 1-28). The data values involved are:

1. t, the time (in seconds) that the body is falling.
2. g, the acceleration (in feet per second of fall) due to gravity.
3. 2, the number by which gt^2 is divided.

As previously indicated, $t = 5$ and $g = 32$.

These data bytes may be stored at any unoccupied address in the memory. For example, the data byte for t (5) can be stored at address 1001, data byte g (32) at address 1030, and data byte 2 at address 1201. The program listing will then appear as shown in Fig. 1-29.

This method of listing the program is often called an *assembly listing* since it shows the program in assembly language (hex op codes, mnemonics,

	Program Stored in Computer		
Instruction Address	Operation Code	Data Address	Explanation
0001	3A	1001	CAD (clear and add). Erase any number remaining in the accumulator from a previous operation. Bring the contents of address 1001 (t) to the accumulator.
0002	3D	1001	MUL (multiply). Multiply the number in the accumulator by the number at address 1001. (The result is t^2).
0003	3D	1030	MUL (multiply). Multiply the number in the accumulator by the number at address 1030 (g). (The result is gt^2).
0004	3E	1201	DIV (divide). Divide the number in the accumulator by the number at address 1201 (2). (The result is $gt^2/2$).
0005	3F	2001	STO (Store). Store the number in the accumulator at address 2001.
0006	7A	2001	PRT (print). Print out data stored at address 2001.
0007	00		HLT. The microcomputer is directed to halt.

Figure 1-29 LENKMICROCOMP program for falling-body problem.

explanations, etc.) rather than in machine language (binary numbers). The differences in program listing methods are discussed further in Secs. 1-16 and 1-17.

Initially, the program counter is set to instruction address 0001 by a signal from the peripheral typewriter keyboard (via the keyboard decoder, I/O IC, and the data bus and/or control lines). The instruction at that address (which happens to be op code 3A) tells the microprocessor to clear the accumulator to zero and then add the number found at data address 1001 (which is decimal 5, or t).

In some microprocessors, this operation can be accomplished in one machine cycle, since part of the byte at address 0001 is the op code (3A) and part is the address (1001) at which the data to be addressed reside. This second part of the byte is described as the *operand* in some microprocessor literature (since the second part is to be operated on by the instruction or op code).

In our microcomputer, the operation is accomplished in two machine cycles (one for the op code, one for the data or operand address). However, the program counter in our microprocessor advances only one step (to instruction address 0002), even though two machine cycles are required.

The instruction at address 0002 (which is op code 3D) tells the microprocessor to multiply the number in the accumulator by the number found at data address 1001. This is the same data address used in the previous step and contains a data byte equal to decimal 5. The result in the accumulator is now 5×5, or 25, or t^2. Again, two machine cycles are used (one for instruction and one for data), and the program counter advances to instruction address 0003.

The instruction at address 0003 (again op code 3D) tells the microprocessor to multiply the number in the accumulator by the number found at data address 1030 (which is decimal 32 or g). The result in the accumulator is now 25×32, or decimal 800, or gt^2, and the program counter advances to instruction address 0004.

The instruction at address 0004 (now op code 3E) tells the microprocessor to divide the number in the accumulator by the number found at data address 1201 (which is decimal 2). The result is now $gt^2/2$, or decimal 400, which is the answer to our problem (the body will fall 400 feet in 5 s). The program counter advances to instruction address 0005.

The instruction at address 0005 (now op code 3F) tells the microprocessor to store the number appearing in the accumulator at address 2001. The program counter advances to instruction address 0006, which tells the microprocessor to print out the result at address 2001 on the peripheral typewriter (via the data bus, I/O IC, and keyboard decoder). The operator thus has a permanent record of the answer. In the case of a video terminal, the answer appears on the CRT display. After the printout, the program counter advances to instruction address 0007, which directs the microprocessor to halt.

1-15-5 Special program instructions

In addition to the routine instructions for our LENKMICROCOMP system, typical examples of which are shown in Fig. 1-28, there are a number of instructions that help make the microcomputer a flexible, decision-making machine. These are the *branch* instructions (also known as jump, skip, or transfer instructions) shown in Fig. 1-30. These instructions direct the microcomputer to leave the main program at some designated point and, under proper conditions, branch or jump to some other designated point in the program. This is sometimes known as a branch or subroutine *call.*

Alphabetic (Mnemonic) Representation	Numerical Representation Hex	Binary	Meaning of Instruction
BRA	20	0010 0000	Branch, unconditionally
BRN	21	0010 0001	Branch, on negative
BRP	22	0010 0010	Branch, on positive

Figure 1-30 Examples of branch op codes for the LENKMICROCOMP.

For example, assume that op code 20 and address 0033 appears at a certain point of the program, say at instruction address 0011. The instruction (op code 20) tells the microprocessor to leave the main program at this point and branch or jump to address 0033. However, the program counter first increments by 1 to address 0012. The contents of the program counter (0012) are then put into an address in an unoccupied area of memory, usually called the *stack.* The stack thus saves the address of the instruction to be executed after the branch routine is completed.

With the address of the next step in the main program safely stored in memory, the program counter goes to the address specified by the branch instruction (0033 in our case). After the instruction at 0033 is performed, the microprocessor follows, in sequence, instructions at addresses 0034, 0035, and so on until the last address of the branch instruction is reached. This last address usually contains an instruction to return to the main program. Such an instruction need specify no address. When the microprocessor receives a return instruction, the microprocessor replaces the current contents of the program counter with the address stored in the stack (0012). This causes the microprocessor to resume execution of the original program at the point immediately following the original branch instruction.

Conditional and unconditional branches. We have described above an example of an *unconditional branch* instruction. The other two branch instructions shown in Fig. 1-30, BRN (op code 21) and BRP (op code 22), are examples of *conditional branch* instructions. If, for example, op code 21 and address 0033 appear in the program, it means that if the number in a certain counter or register is negative, the microprocessor must branch to address 0033, perform the instruction, and proceed (in sequence) from there. If the number is not negative, the microprocessor is to ignore the branch instruction and proceed with the original program. The BRP instruction is the same as the BRN except that branching is to occur if the number is positive. Otherwise, the branch instruction is ignored.

1-15-6 Microcomputer operation cycle

Once the program has been entered (or *loaded*) into memory (that is, with instructions permanently programmed into the ROM, and data bytes temporarily entered into the RAM via the peripheral typewriter), the microcomputer is ready to go automatically through the program cycle. Each cycle has two alternate phases: the *instruction* phase (or instruction *fetch* as it may be called), and the *execution* phase. After these two phases have been completed, the cycle is repeated. The duration of each phase is determined by a fixed number of clock pulses. Typically, there are eight clock pulses per machine cycle. Each phase may require one or more machine cycles.

The combined fetch and execution of a signal instruction is referred to as an *instruction cycle.* The portion of a cycle identified with a clearly defined activity is called a *state.* The interval between clock pulses is referred to as a *clock period,* as discussed in Sec. 1-14. Typically, one or more clock periods are necessary for the completion of a state, and there are several states in a cycle. The flow diagram of the LENKMICROCOMP operation cycle is shown in Fig. 1-31.

Instruction or fetch phase. The first instruction fetch is initiated by a start command. In our case, this command is initiated by the peripheral typewriter. The start command sets the first instruction address (0001) into the *program counter.* The instruction phase of the operation cycle starts when this address is transferred to the *address register.*

Note that as information is transferred from one storage location to another, the information is not erased from the original location unless specifically so ordered. Thus, in our example, the address of the first instruction word appears in both the program counter and the address register. On the other hand, when new information is placed in a storage location, any previous information stored at that location is first erased.

The output of the address register is applied to memory via the address bus. The word at the selected address in memory is transferred to the *storage register* via the data bus. From the storage register, the op-code portion of the word is transferred to the *instruction register.* Here, the word is decoded by the operation decoder, and the microprocessor circuits perform the indicated instruction. Also from the storage register, the portion of the

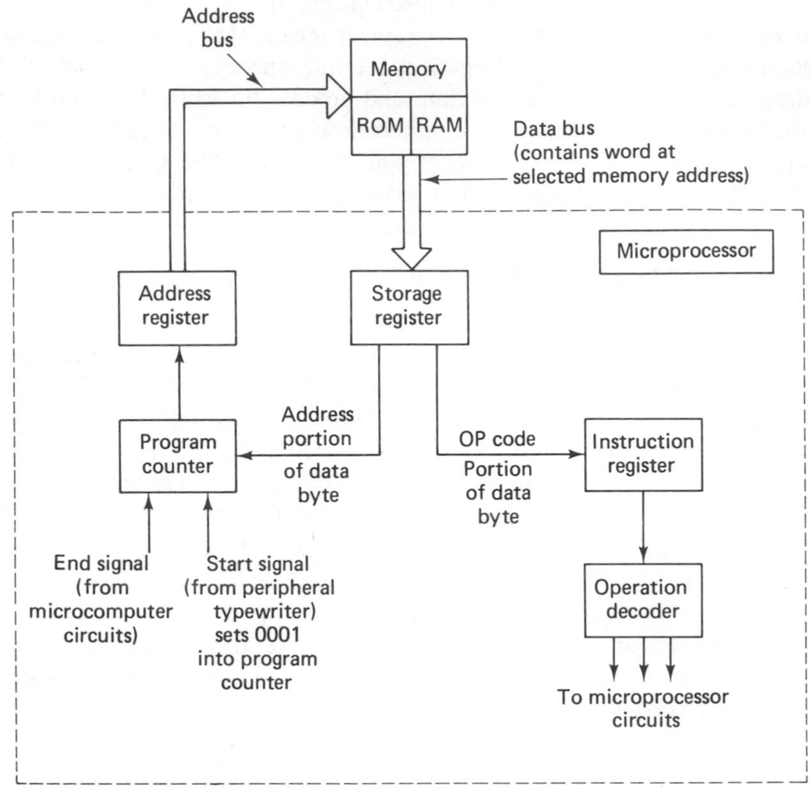

Figure 1-31 Flow diagram of LENKMICROCOMP operation cycle.

word that contains the address of the data to be used is transferred to the address register, first erasing the information previously stored there. This completes the instruction phase of the cycle.

Execution phase. The execution phase starts when the data address placed in the address register during the instruction phase is applied to memory via the address bus. The data word at the selected address in memory is transferred to the storage register via the data bus. The data byte is then processed in accordance with the instruction (still in the instruction register). When the processing is finished, an *end signal* or *processing complete* signal advances the program counter by 1 (to 0002 in our case). The program counter now contains the address of the next instruction, and the instruction fetch or phase can start.

This completes the execution phase of the operation cycle. The cycle is repeated over and over again, the instruction phase alternating with the execution phase for each cycle, until the entire program is complete.

In the case of a branch operation, the op-code portion of the instruction word is that of the branch instruction, and the operand portion is the address of the next instruction to be followed if branching is to take place. Under such conditions, this address is placed in the program counter, replacing the address already there, as described in Sec. 1-15-5. The microcomputer will then follow the branch program until a return to the original program is instructed.

We have just described the complete operation cycle of the LENK-MICROCOMP. Different microcomputers may have different methods for going through the cycle, but the basic principles of operation are essentially the same for all microcomputers.

1-15-7 Subroutines, libraries, and nesting

Practically every instruction to the microprocessor involves a routine series of steps. Thus, to add to 8-bit numbers, for example, the LSD must be added first. If there is a carry, the carry must be added to the next-significant bits. Then these bits must be added. If there is another carry, this carry must also be added to the MSD, and then they must be added. Although this series of calculations is complete within itself, the series may only be part of a larger program.

Since the microprocessor can only follow instructions, this routine series of steps must be included in the program. However, to save the user's time, this series of steps is listed in the microprocessor literature. Such listings or general-purpose set of instructions are called *libraries, routines,* or *subroutines.* Often, the term "libraries" is given to a group of routines.

A typical subroutine might include all the steps necessary to find square root, sines, cosines, logarithms, and so on. If these types of calculations are repeated throughout the program, the programmer may prepare a special program for each of them and store the program in memory. Usually, subroutines are handled as a branch or jump. Then, when the programmer calls for a routine, the microprocessor is given the branch op code and the address of the first branch instruction, as discussed in Sec. 1-15-5.

Subroutines are often *nested.* That is, one subroutine calls a second subroutine. The second may call a third, and so on. This is acceptable as long as the microcomputer has enough capacity to store the necessary return addresses and the microprocessor is capable of doing so. The maximum depth of nesting is determined by the depth of the stack (or reserve memory). If the stack has a space for storing three return addresses, then three levels of subroutines may be accommodated.

1-15-8 Interrupts

Most microprocessors have some provision for interrupts. Generally, interrupts are used for communications with peripheral equipment. For example, assume that the LENKMICROCOMP is processing a large volume of data, portions of which are to be printed on the peripheral typewriter. The microcomputer can produce one 8-bit data byte output (or one alphabet character) for each machine cycle, but it may take the typewriter the equivalent of several machine cycles (or several dozen) to actually print out the character specified by the data byte. The microprocessor could then remain idle, waiting until the typewriter can accept the next data byte.

If the microprocessor is capable of interrupts, the microprocessor can output a data byte, then return to data processing. When the typewriter is again ready to accept the next data byte, the typewriter can request an interrupt. When the microprocessor acknowledges the interrupt, the main program is suspended, and the microprocessor automatically branches to a routine that will output the next data byte. (This is known as *servicing* the peripheral device, or servicing the interrupt.) After the data byte is delivered to the typewriter and the corresponding character is printed, the microprocessor continues with main program execution. Note that this is, in principle, quite similar to a branch or subroutine call, except that the jump is initiated externally (by the typewriter) rather than by the program.

There are more complex interrupt schemes, particularly where several peripherals must share the same microprocessor. Usually, such interrupts involve assigning priority levels (*prioritizing*) the peripherals. One approach (called the *polled method*) is for the microprocessor to check each peripheral, in turn, on a given priority basis, for a service request. The polled method is generally wasteful, since part of the main program is used up whether the peripherals need service or not. It is generally more effective for the microprocessor to stop only when the peripheral sends an interrupt. The peripherals can still be assigned priorities. For example, if peripheral A is first priority and B is second priority, A will be serviced before B if both peripherals make a service request simultaneously. B will be serviced first only if A is not making a request.

1-16 MACHINE LANGUAGE VERSUS ASSEMBLY LANGUAGE PROGRAMMING

A microprocessor may be programmed by writing a sequence of instructions in binary code which the microprocessor can interpret directly. For example, referring back to Fig. 1-28, the instruction for addition is binary 00111011. If this byte is programmed into memory and then appears on the data bus when the microprocessor data port is open, the microprocessor will add (probably the contents of one register to another). This is *machine language programming* and is useful only where the program to be written is small.

At best, writing a program in machine language is a tedious task, subject to many errors. The task of writing a program can be speeded up, and errors minimized, when hex is used instead of binary (both hex and binary are shown in Fig. 1-28). However, hex coding has two major limitations.

First, hex coding is not self-documenting. That is, the code itself does not give any indication in human terms of the operation to be performed. The user must learn each code, or constantly use a *program reference card* or *sheet* to convert.

Second, hex coding is *absolute.* That is, the program will work only when stored at a specific location in memory. This is because branch or jump instructions in the program reference specific addresses elsewhere in the program. Consider the example shown in Fig. 1-32, which is the listing of an eight-step program written in machine code (but in hex format).

Step Number	Machine Code	Explanation
0 1	1011 1000 0010 0000	Load decimal 32 in register R0
2 3	1011 1010 0000 0101	Load decimal 5 in register R2
4	0000 1001	Load port 1 to accumulator
5	1111 0000	Transfer contents of accumulator to register addressed by register 0
6	0001 1000	Increment R0 by 1
7 8	1110 1010 0000 0100	Decrement register 2 by 1; if result is zero, continue to step 9; if not, go to step 4
9	—	
10	—	

Figure 1-32 Basic eight-step program written in machine code arranged in hex format.

Steps 0007 and 0008 of Fig. 1-32 make reference to step (or address) 0004. If the program is moved, step 0008 must be changed to refer to the new address of step 0004.

1-16-1 Assembly language

The problems just discussed can be overcome by writing the program in *assembly language* where alphanumeric symbols are used to represent machine language codes, branch addresses, and so on. For example, the instruction to increment the contents of register 0 becomes INC R0 instead of hex 18, giving the user the meaning of the instruction at a glance. Our example program of Fig. 1-32 can then be written in assembly language as shown in Fig. 1-33.

Step Number	Hex Code		Assembly Code
0	B8		MOV RO, #32
1	20		
2	BA		MOV R2, #05
3	05		
4	09	INP:	IN A, P1
5	FO		MOV @RO, A
6	18		INC RO
7	EA		DJNZ R2, INP
8	04		

Figure 1-33 Basic eight-step program written in assembly language, but including hex code.

The use of assembly language makes it much easier to write a program, but it results in a program that is useless to the microprocessor (which operates only with binary numbers). One way to overcome this problem is to write the program in assembly language but to include the hex code (as shown in Fig. 1-33). Then when you enter the program into the microcomputer, it is relatively easy to convert from hex to binary. Of course, this requires that you *remember both the hex code and the assembly code* for each instruction of the microprocessor. Although it is not a bad idea for you to learn all of the hex codes, it does require more remembering (or looking up) on your part, and thus increases the chance for error.

A more convenient method is to *assemble* programs using an *assembler,* which is a program that converts from one code to another. In our case, the assembler converts from a verbal-type assembly code to binary numbers. In practice, the assembler program is entered into another microcomputer (or any computer or computerlike device), you write the program for your microcomputer on paper (known as the *source program*), and you enter your microcomputer program into the other computer (known as a *host* computer), which prints out a program (usually on paper tape or disks) in binary form. This program is known as the *object program* and can be entered directly into your microcomputer from the paper-tape reader or disk.

When a different computer is used for assembly, the program is known as a *cross-assembler.* It is also possible to use *time-sharing* services for assembly, and there are special devices and equipment developed by manufacturers for assembly of their microcomputer programs. Such devices and procedures are discussed throughout Chapters 3 through 7. For now, let us consider the assembly code shown in Fig. 1-33.

1-16-2 Typical assembly or source code

The first statement in Fig. 1-33 can be verbalized as follows: Move to register 0 the decimal number 32. Move instructions should always be structured such that the destination is first and the source is second. The sign "#" indicates that the source is comprised of "immediate" data (or data contained in the following byte of memory). In this case, the data byte is specified as decimal 32. Some assemblers will accept hex (or even binary) notation. Note that the assembly code of Fig. 1-33 is based on the INTEL MCS-48 system described in Chapter 5. It is essential that you learn the assembly codes and language of your particular microprocessor system just as you must learn the instruction set.

The input instruction IN A, P1 has the same form as a MOV instruction, indicating that the contents of port 1 are to be transferred to the accumulator. In front of the input instruction is an *address label* INP. This label allows the program to be written in a form independent of its final location in program memory since the branch instruction at the end of the program can refer to this label rather than to a specific address. This is a very important advantage of assembly language programs over machine language, since instructions can be added or deleted throughout the program during debugging without requiring that any jump address be changed.

The next instruction, MOV @ R0, A, can be verbalized as "Move to the data memory location addressed by R0 the contents of the accumulator." The @ sign indicates an indirect operation whereby the contents of either register 0 or register 1 acts as a pointer to the data memory location to be operated on.

The last instruction is a Decrement and Jump If Not Zero instruction, which acts in combination with the specified register as a *loop counter.* (A loop is a sequence of instructions in which the last instruction is a jump or return back to the first instruction.) In this case, register 2 is loaded with 5 initially, then decremented by 1 each time the loop is executed. If the result of the decrement is not zero, the program jumps to INP and executes another input operation. The fifth time through the loop the result is zero, and execution goes to whatever routine follows the DJNZ instruction.

Advanced assemblers. In addition to the normal features provided by assemblers, more advanced assemblers offer such advantages as *evaluation of expressions* at assembly time, *conditional assembly,* and *macro* capability.

Evaluation of expressions. Certain assemblers allow the use of arithmetic expressions and multiple symbols in the operand portion of the instructions. For example, the assembler for the INTEL MCS-48 system described in Chapter 5 accepts such an instruction as ADD A, # ALFA*BETA/2.

ALFA and BETA are two previously defined symbols. At assembly time, the expression ALFA*BETA/2 will be evaluated and the resulting number (which is the average of ALFA and BETA) treated as immediate data and designated as the second byte of the ADD immediate instruction. This expression allows the immediate data of this instruction to be defined in a single statement and eliminates the need for a third symbol equal to ALFA*BETA/2.

Conditional assembly. Conditional assembly allows the programmer to select only certain portions of the assembly language (source) program for conversion to machine (object) code at assembly time. This allows the inclusion of various debugging routines to be included in the program during development. Using conditional assembly, these routines can be left out when the final assembly is done. Conditional assembly also allows several versions of one basic program to be generated, by selecting various portions of a larger program at assembly time.

Macro assembly. A macro instruction is essentially a symbol that is recognized by the assembler to represent a specific sequence of several standard instructions. A macro is a shorthand way of generating the same sequence of instructions at several locations in a program without having to rewrite the sequence each time it is used. For example, a typical macro instruction might be one that performs a subtract operation. Some microprocessors do not have a single instruction that performs subtraction, but require several instructions, such as

COMP A (complement the accumulator).

ADD A REG (add the contents of register to accumulator).

COMP A (complement the accumulator).

This routine subtracts a register from the accumulator and leaves the result in the accumulator. The sequence can be defined as a macro with the name SUB, and can specify a register by number (such as register 1, 2, 3, etc.). To subtract register 3 from the accumulator, the programmer writes SUB R3, and the assembler will automatically insert the three instructions, with R3 substituted for REG.

Once the assembly language source code is written, it can be converted to a machine-executable object code (in binary form) by passing the source code through the assembler program.

1-17 DEVELOPMENT OF A MICROPROCESSOR-BASED SYSTEM

The exact procedures for development of a microprocessor-based system (such as a microcomputer) are different for each type of microprocessor, and depend on such factors as what support equipment and design aids (simulators, emulators, etc.) and support software (assembler programs, debug programs, etc.) are available from the manufacturer of the microprocessor. [Those systems that include a very complete line of hardware, software, design aids, and so on, are said to be *pervasive*. When a particular item of hardware or software is very effective (for assembly, debugging, testing, troubleshooting, etc.), it is said to be a *powerful* tool]. The support equipment and design aids for several microprocessor systems are described in Chapters 3 through 7. A more comprehensive discussion of the microprocessor development cycle is given in Chapter 8. Here, we will consider a typical microprocessor-based-system development approach.

1-17-1 Learning the microprocessor and system components

The first step in developing any microprocessor-based system is to become familiar with the microprocessor and all of the system components. Most microprocessor manufacturers also produce a line of compatible system components such as RAMs, ROMs, and I/O units. The microprocessor is the most important component, so the learning process should start there. As a minimum, you must learn all the microprocessor instructions, since the entire system compatibility is based on what the microprocessor can and cannot do. Next, learn the capabilities and limitations of the other system components (how many bits and addresses in the ROM and RAM, how many data and control lines available in the I/O IC). This sort of information is given in the manufacturers' user manuals and/or data sheets.

1-17-2 Hardware characteristics

Do not overlook the hardware aspect of the microprocessor and other components. For example, what power supplies are required? What is the power dissipation for each IC in the system? What are the operating and storage temperature ranges? How many ROMs, RAMs, and I/Os can be driven by one microprocessor? How long does it take to process each instruction? (This will tell you how long it will take to process an entire program.) This sort of information is given in design manuals and/or data sheets.

1-17-3 Manufacturers' training courses

Some microprocessor manufacturers sponsor training courses or programs for their systems. Generally, these are 2- or 3-day sessions held at the manufacturers' facilities or at selected cities (or at customers' facilities for large groups). If you have access to such programs, you should take advantage of them, since they will provide hands-on experience. Also, you will have all information and literature for a particular microprocessor system at your fingertips. These training courses are especially helpful for those who have had no previous computer experience.

1-17-4 Writing sample programs

Once you are familiar with the microprocessor and related system components (either through self-instruction or manufacturers' training), the next step is to gain a better "feel" for what a microprocessor can do in your own applications by writing several exercise programs that perform basic functions. For example, in a typical microprocessor program, you may require such things as I/O routines, delays, counting functions, look-up tables, arithmetic functions, and logical operations.

Once you have made up routines to solve these functions, you can retain the programs to serve as a set of "building blocks" for future applications programs. For example, when you have developed a routine for subtraction that is compatible with your particular microprocessor, you can use the same routine for all future programs. Several sample programs are included in the remaining chapters of this book.

1-17-5 Defining system functions with a flowchart

A flowchart similar to that shown in Fig. 1-27 is probably the simplest method of defining the functions to be accomplished by a program. Thus, when you think you thoroughly understand your microprocessor, the system functions to be implemented by a program can be defined using the flowchart method. Of course, the flowchart must include all the functions to be accomplished and the sequence in which the microprocessor must execute these functions. Once the system application is flowcharted, you can identify and analyze all the critical time-related functions and then write a sample program to verify that performance requirements can be met.

Keep in mind that there are usually many, many ways to accomplish the same overall system function, using the same microprocessor, but with different programs. Of course, each program will have a different number of steps. Generally, the shortest program is the most desirable, for obvious reasons. The shortest program requires the least amount of memory (and thus requires a minimum of ROM/RAM ICs), results in the fastest system, and keeps the chance for error at a minimum.

1-17-6 Defining hardware configuration

When you have defined the system function with a flowchart, and written a sample or trial program, the next step involves defining the hardware required to implement the function. For example, input/output capability must be defined in terms of number of inputs, number of outputs, bidirectional lines, latching or nonlatching I/O, output drive capabilities, and so on. Likewise, the number of words of RAM storage required for intermediate results and data storage must be determined. (Some systems require a battery backup to maintain the RAM data in case of power failure.)

Amount of program memory. Typically, the most difficult hardware parameter to define is the amount of program memory needed to store the applications program. (Program memory is stored in the ROM.) Although previously written exercise programs will make this "guestimate" more accurate, a generous amount of breathing room should be allowed in program memory until coding is complete and the exact requirements are known.

Keep in mind that it may be possible to eliminate a few program steps (develop a new, shorter program) to match available memory hardware. Also, there may be hardware to replace programs. For example, many special functions such as serial communications or keyboard/display interfaces may be implemented with programs. However, there may be a compatible I/O IC that will do the same job. As a trade-off, it may be more advantageous to use these ICs rather than the programs, particularly where such functions place a severe load on the microprocessor in terms of time or program memory. In simple terms, it may be more advantageous to use a special-purpose I/O IC rather than a longer program (that slows down system performance and requires a larger memory). Such factors should always be considered when defining microprocessor hardware.

1-17-7 Writing the program code

Once the system function and hardware have been defined, the next step is to convert the program to a machine code that is suitable for the microprocessor. (This is sometimes known as *generating the code.*) An experienced programmer/designer is often able to generate the code during the same time that the hardware is being defined and assembled (printed-circuit-card layout, power supply, etc.). Then the trial program can be entered in memory and immediately tested for bugs.

There are several options available when it is time to write the program machine code. Unfortunately, not everyone has all these options available. Obviously, the designer/programmer with a complete set of manufacturer's design aids (both hardware and software) has an advantage over the student/hobbyist who has nothing but minimum hardware and possibly some data sheets. Of course, designer/programmers need every advantage, since they do not have the luxury of making many mistakes, over an infinite period of time, as does the student/hobbyist.

There are two basic approaches for writing the program code: hardware and software.

1-17-8 Basic hardware approach

The most primitive approach to program codes is to write each step in machine language (binary code) and enter each step in memory using machine language. (This is the approach most common for the student/hobbyist.) As an example, once a trial program has been written and the binary code for each step determined (possibly using hex as shorthand), the program can be entered (programmed) into an erasable or alterable PROM using a basic circuit similar to that of Fig. 1-22. Then the hardware (microprocessor, ROM, RAM, I/O keyboard/display, etc.) is interconnected in "breadboard" (experimental) form, power is applied, and the program is tested for bugs.

The PROM can be erased and reprogrammed as necessary until the program is free of bugs. Then the erasable PROM can be replaced by a permanent PROM that is programmed using the desired (bug-free) program. The final ROM is connected in the system, and the program is given a final test. At this point, you have a complete, functioning, microprocessor-based system.

1-17-9 Sophisticated hardware approach

The basic hardware approach described in Sec. 1-17-8 is slow, tedious, and generally inefficient, except for very simple programs (and is the system followed by the average student/hobbyist). Most major microprocessor manufacturers provide design aid hardware to simplify and speed up development of a microprocessor-based system. Such hardware includes *simulators, emulators,* and *evaluation kits.* Some of these design aids also include software or are a combination of software and hardware. Specific hardware design aids for the various system are described in Chapters 3 through 7. Here we concentrate on a typical system.

A typical hardware design aid includes a microprocessor, ROM, RAM, and I/O as well as some form of keyboard/display to enter and read out programs. All these devices are interconnected on a board or chassis, possibly using plug-in PC (printed circuit) boards and ICs. In effect, a complete microprocessor-based system (including a keyboard/display), interconnecting wiring, and power supply are provided, using compatible ICs of the same manufacturer. The hardware is supplied with a users' manual which includes operating instructions and sample programs. The advantage of such a system is obvious. You can develop a complete, functioning system (including the programs to meet your application needs) without having to assemble various hardware components on a trial-and-error basis. Once you have the designed system and the debugged programs, you can order the exact hardware from the manufacturer, including how you want the ROM programmed.

The PROMPT 48, which is part of the Intel system described in Chapter 5, is a typical design aid using the sophisticated hardware approach. The system is described further in Chapter 5 and will not be duplicated here. However, the following is included to help you understand the basic element of the hardware approach. Keep in mind that the Intel system of Chapter 5 is a complete, microprocessor-based system, or microcomputer, all contained within a single IC.

The PROMPT 48 is a low-cost design aid consisting of an 8748 processor (which is the Intel designation for their single IC microcomputer with erasable PROM) to execute programs; control circuitry to provide the debugging function, such as *single step* and *breakpoints*; a monitor program stored in a ROM; an EPROM programmer; and a hex keyboard and display. (The operating controls of the PROMPT 48 are shown in Chapter 5.)

There are two processor sockets on the PROMPT 48 panel. The PROGRAMMING SOCKET is for programming the 8748, and the EXECUTION SOCKET is one in which a programmed 8748 executes its program while under control of the monitor routine.

Use of the PROMPT 48 involves the following basic steps:

1. Loading an application program into the RAM memory via the hex keyboard. As an option, the program can be loaded into memory via an external TTY.
2. Inserting an erased 8748 in the PROGRAMMING SOCKET and transferring the applications program to an EPROM within the 8748.
3. Transferring the programmed 8748 to the EXECUTION SOCKET, where the program is executed and debugged under control of the monitor.

The monitor routine allows the user to single-step the 8748 through each step of the program. The contents of the memory and/or internal registers can be examined (using the panel readout) and modified at each step. Although single stepping is slow, the process makes sure that each program step is bug-free.

The monitor routine also allows the user to run the 8748 through steps at full speed, but to stop at predetermined breakpoints. Such breakpoints could be at the beginning or end of significant subroutines, or at any desired point in the program.

The PROMPT 48 also includes 1000 bytes of writable program memory which may be used to debug user programs. Thus, if you discover that part of the program is incorrect, the undesired part can be replaced by another program, temporarily written into this memory. A *multiple single-step* feature is also provided, in which the 8748 steps through its program, dumping all internal contents to an external RAM, where the contents can later be displayed or typed out on an external terminal. Paper-tape input and output in hex format is also available through the external TTY. Thus, once a satisfactory program is reached, it can be retained on paper in a format that is suitable for programming in the 8748.

The advantages of single stepping, and the ability to stop at breakpoints in the program, are discussed further in Sec. 1-18.

1-17-10 Software design-aid approach

There are about as many software design aids for microprocessor systems as there are microprocessor manufacturers. All these design aids use some form of assembler (or possibly a macroassembler), described in Sec. 1-16-1. In some cases, the assembler is used in conjunction with manufacturers' design-aid hardware. That is, you can write the program in assembly language, enter the program in the design-aid hardware, and end up with a machine language program (usually on paper tape or magnetic disks). In other cases, the software is designed for use with in-house computers. (The assembler is actually a cross-assembler used with a host computer; Sec. 1-16-1.) In other cases, the assembler is used with time-sharing computer systems. Some typical software design aids are described in Chapters 3 through 8.

1-17-11 Production of a microprocessor-based system

Once a working program has been achieved, a preproduction phase usually follows wherein several prototype systems (possibly with microprocessors of different manufacturers) are evaluated in simulated situations or in actual field operation. During this period, the use of an erasable ROM allows quick alteration of the program when problems (bugs) or suggested changes arise. Depending upon the magnitude and number of future changes anticipated, the first production units may be shipped with an erasable PROM. However, for maximum cost-reduction potential in high-volume applications, a custom ROM (programmed at the factory by the manufacturer) is usually necessary. This is an easy transition if two conditions are met: (1) the custom ROM must be compatible in electrical terminal configuration (pin for pin) and in machine code, and (2) you must have retained a paper tape of the program in machine code (as you will if you follow hardware and/or software approaches of Secs. 1-17-9 and 1-17-10). Generally, you can ship the paper tape to the ROM manufacturer along with your order.

1-18 TROUBLESHOOTING MICROPROCESSOR-BASED SYSTEMS

A microprocessor is a solid-state, digital-programmed device. Thus, all the troubleshooting techniques that apply to such devices also apply to the microprocessor. For example, most microprocessor-based system failures can be solved using multitrace oscilloscopes, as well as logic clips, probes, and pulsers. Such troubleshooting basics are described in the author's *Handbook of Practical Solid-State Troubleshooting* (Englewood Cliffs, N.J.: Prentice-Hall, Inc., 1971) and will not be repeated here.

However, there is one instrument that can be used very effectively in microprocessor systems. This instrument is called the *logic analyzer* or *logic-state analyzer.* The following paragraphs describe the basics involved when the logic analyzer is used with microprocessor systems.

1-18-1 The basic microprocessor troubleshooting approach

The classic approach for troubleshooting any programmed device is to monitor a significant system function (such as the data and address buses), go through each step in the program, and compare the results with the program listing for each address and step. (This is sometimes known as a *program trace* or, more simply, a *trace* function.) One technique for this procedure is called *single stepping* (discussed in Sec. 1-17-9). With the single-stepping approach, you remove the normal clock pulses and replace them with single, one-at-a-time pulses obtained from a switch or pushbutton. This permits you to examine and compare the data at each address with that shown in the program.

For example, assume that each of the eight lines on the data bus are connected to a multitrace oscilloscope so that the bit on each line appears as a pulse on a corresponding trace. A pulse on the trace indicates a binary 1, whereas the absence of a pulse indicates a binary 0 on that line. A simplified version of such a test setup is shown in Fig. 1-34.

The test is started by applying a single pulse to the reset or clear line. Then sufficient single pulses are applied to the clock line until address number 1 (0001) appears on the address bus. Now assume that the program listing shows that a hex 7F (binary 0111–1111) data byte should be on the data bus at address 0001 but that the oscilloscope traces show binary 0011–1111. Obviously, the wrong instruction will be applied to the microprocessor and the system will malfunction. This could be caused by a broken line on the data bus, by a defect in the memory, by the absence of a memory-read pulse or a memory-read pulse that appears at the wrong time (opens the memory data buffer too soon or too late), or by several other possible causes. However, you have isolated the problem and determined where it occurs in the program.

1-18-2 Timing problems

If the problem appears to be one of timing, the oscilloscope can be used to check the time relationship of the related pulses. For example, the oscilloscope can be connected to the data bus, address bus, and read line as shown in Fig. 1-35. The oscilloscope then shows the *time relationships* among the pulses on these lines.

In this simplified example, the read pulse must hold the memory data buffer closed until the selected address pulses appear on the address bus (sometimes known as the *valid address* point), must hold the buffer open just long enough for all 8 data bits to appear on the data bus, and then must close the buffer until the next address is applied. In a practical case, the entire timing diagram (discussed in Sec. 1-14 and shown in Fig. 1-26) can be duplicated on a multitrace oscilloscope.

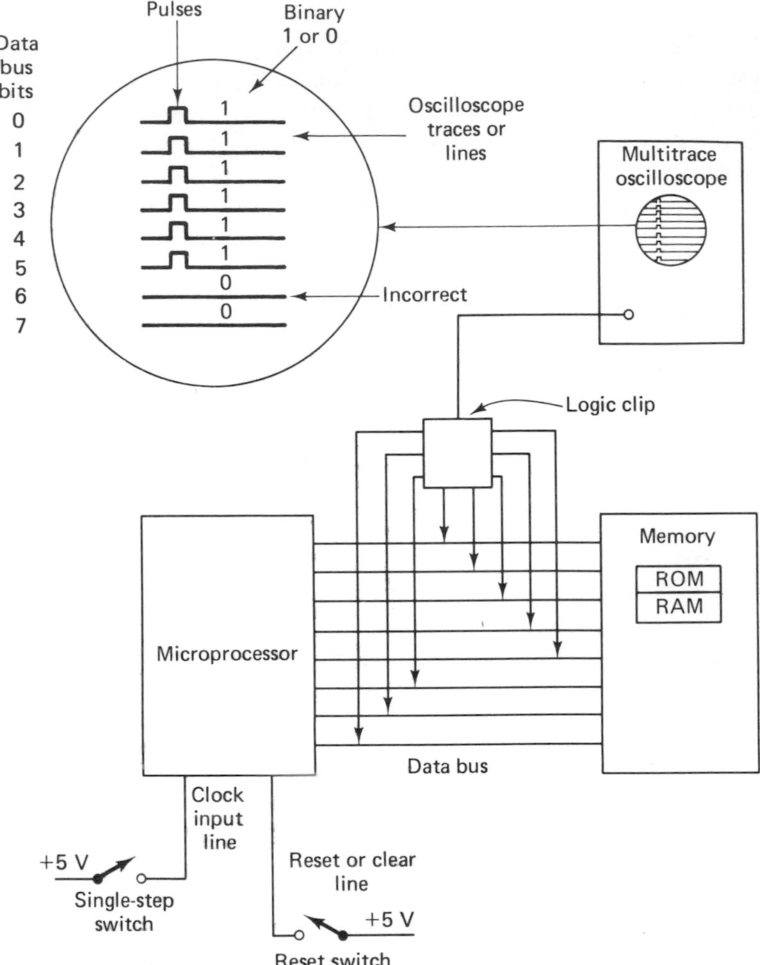

Figure 1-34 Basic microprocessor troubleshooting approach using multitrace oscilloscope and single stepping.

1-18-3 The logic analyzer

While single stepping and a check of system timing can pinpoint most microprocessor problems, there is an obvious drawback. Typically, a data byte is 8 bits and thus requires 8 clock pulses, or 8 one-at-a-time pushes of the single-step button. Since all program steps require at least one byte (and often two or three bytes, possibly 24 bits), you must, for example, push that button many times if the malfunction occurs at step 0333 of the program. This means that you must spend endless hours comparing program listings against binary readouts at addresses. (If you are already familiar with the

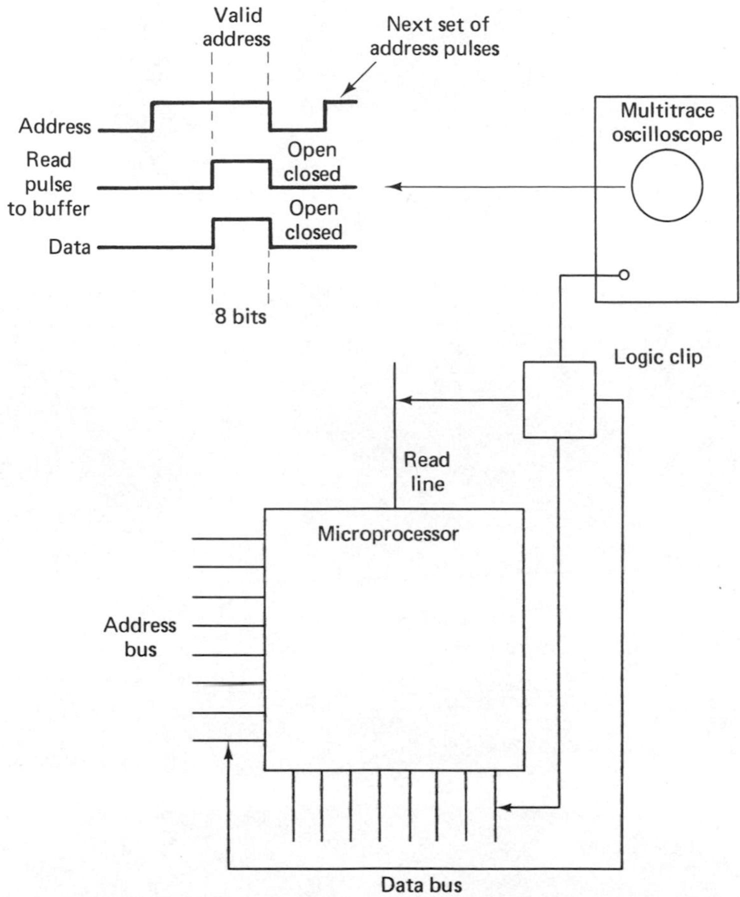

Figure 1-35 Basic microprocessor troubleshooting approach for timing problems.

troubleshooting of programmed devices, you know that the most time-consuming part of the task is in making such comparisons).

The logic analyzer overcomes this basic problem by permitting you to select for display the data at a particular address. The logic analyzer will then run through the program near the normal system speed (a fraction of a second) and display the selected data at the desirable breakpoints (as discussed in Sec. 1-17-9).

Figure 1-36 shows a typical logic analyzer and some related displays. A logic analyzer is essentially a multitrace oscilloscope combined with electronic circuits to produce special displays. The electronic circuits that produce these displays are sometimes known as *formatters.* The logic analyzer shown in Fig. 1-36 is operated by a keyboard. Other logic analyzers

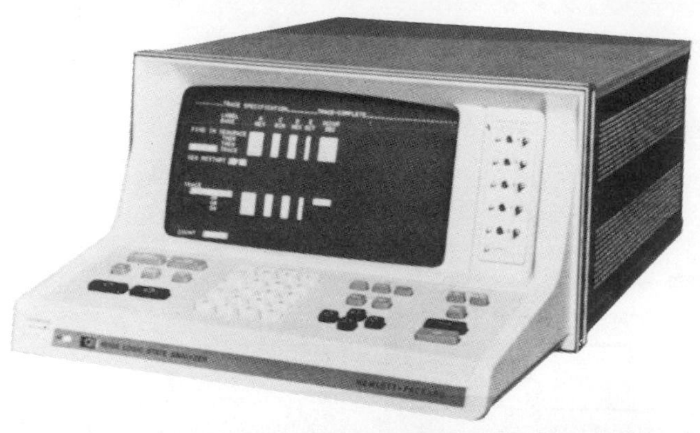

TRACE LIST .... TRACE COMPLETE

LABEL	A	B	C	D	E	F	TIME	
BASE	HEX	HEX	HEX	OCT	BIN	DEC	DEC (FEL)	
SEQUENCE	Ø1	A	A	7	1Ø	1		
START	Ø1	A	A	7	1Ø	Ø	21.8	US
+Ø1	Ø1	B	Ø	2	11	1	3.7	US
+Ø2	Ø1	B	1	6	1Ø	1	3.5	US
+Ø3	Ø1	B	2	3	1Ø	1	4.7	US
+Ø4	Ø1	B	3	Ø	ØØ	1	3.5	US
+Ø5	Ø1	B	4	7	1Ø	1	3.5	US
+Ø6	Ø1	B	5	2	Ø1	1	4.7	US
+Ø7	Ø1	B	6	6	1Ø	1	3.5	US
+Ø8	Ø1	B	7	3	Ø1	1	4.7	US
+Ø9	Ø1	B	8	Ø	ØØ	1	3.5	US
+1Ø	ØØ	7	D	Ø	ØØ	1	3.5	US
+11	ØØ	7	E	Ø	ØØ	1	4.7	US
+12	ØØ	7	F	Ø	ØØ	1	4.7	US
+13	ØØ	8	Ø	6	Ø1	1	4.7	US
+14	ØØ	8	1	6	1Ø	1	5.8	US
+15	ØØ	8	2	Ø	ØØ	1	3.6	US
+16	ØØ	D	2	7	Ø1	1	1Ø.6	US
+17	ØØ	D	3	1	1Ø	1	12.5	US
+18	ØØ	D	4	1	1Ø	1	4.7	US

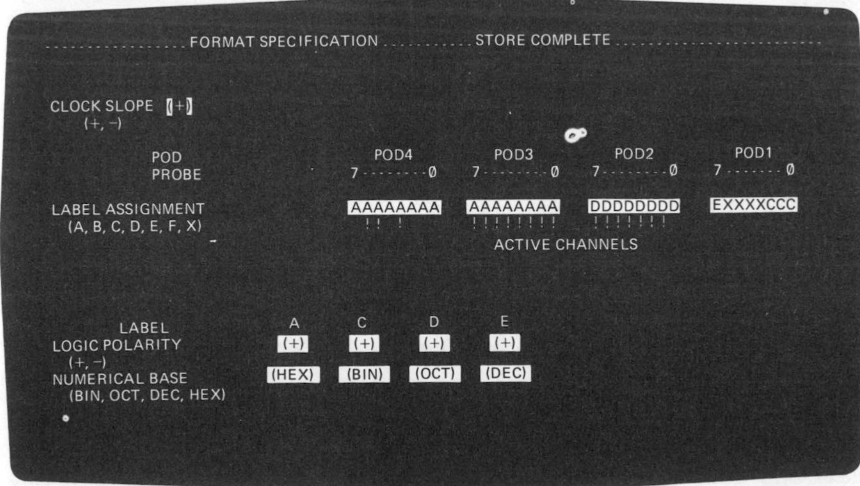

Figure 1-36 Hewlett-Packard 1610A logic analyzer and some related displays.

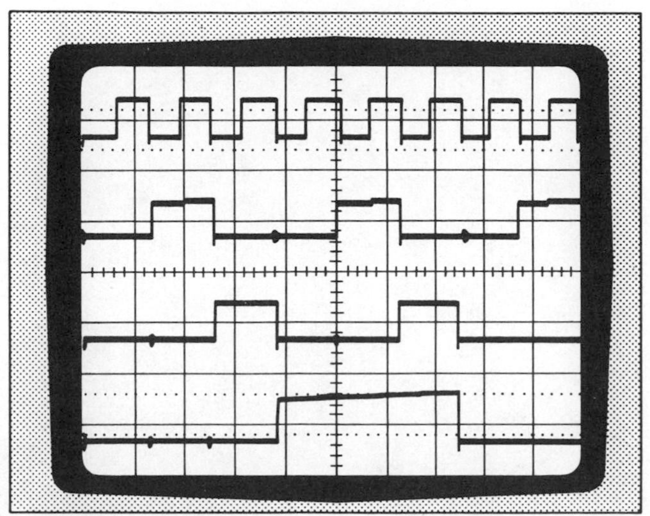

Figure 1-37 Typical timing diagram (time-domain) display as produced on a logic analyzer.

use switches and controls. No matter what control system is used, the logic analyzer is capable of three basic displays.

1-18-4 Timing display

The multitrace feature of the logic analyzer can be used to reproduce *timing diagrams,* in a manner similar to that of a conventional multitrace oscilloscope. Figure 1-37 shows a typical timing diagram display as produced on a logic analyzer. (This is sometimes known as a *time-domain* display.)

1-18-5 Tabular data display

The data display format of the logic analyzer (sometimes called the *data domain* format or display) is used to display data bytes (as they appear on the data and/or address buses) in binary form. In effect, the bytes appear as they would on paper (1s and 0s rather than the presence or absence of pulses). Figure 1-38 shows that several data bytes can be displayed simultaneously. This makes it possible to check the data words before and after a selected point in the program. With some logic analyzers, the selected data word is indicated by extra brightness of the display. In Fig. 1-38 the top data word is the selected word (the breakpoint starts at this word and continues for 16 steps or words).

To use the tabular data format, you connect the logic analyzer to the data and/or address buses by means of logic probes supplied with the analyzer. Then you select a particular data word and/or address breakpoint from the program listing by means of the logic analyzer controls (keyboard or switches) and start the program. The microprocessor system then runs

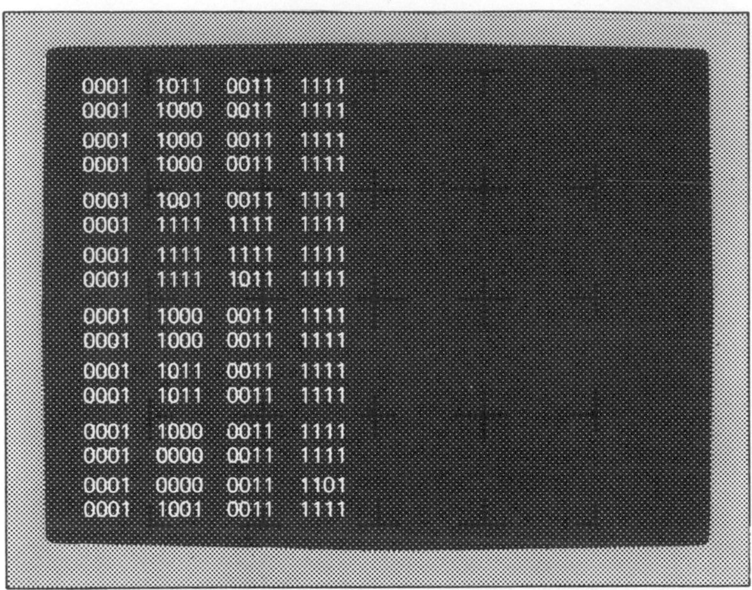

Figure 1-38 Typical tabular data (data-domain) display as produced on a logic analyzer.

through the complete program, but only the desired portion of the program is displayed.

Figure 1-39 shows a comparison of a typical program listing versus a logic analyzer display. In this example, note that both the address and data bytes are shown for 16 steps of the program. However, only the first nine addresses are of interest, with address 0004 being of special interest. Compare this tabular display with that of the timing display (Fig. 1-37). Even those readers not familiar with troubleshooting will quickly realize the advantages of a tabular display for microprocessor troubleshooting and for debugging. Keep in mind that the program can be operated at near its normal speed, and can be examined on a line-by-line basis, 16 lines at a time. The next 16 lines can be selected by the simple setting of a switch or touch of a key. Compare this with single stepping through the entire program.

1-18-6 Mapping display

Another display unique to logic analyzers is the mapping display or mapping "signature." A mapping display is formed by connecting the MSB bits of a data word to the vertical deflection circuits of the logic analyzer (those circuits that cause vertical deflection of the oscilloscope trace), while the LSB bits are connected to the horizontal deflection circuits. This produces a series of dots as shown in Fig. 1-40. In the mapping mode, the display is an array of 256 dots instead of a table of 1s and 0s. Each dot represents one possible combination of the 16 input lines so that any input is represented

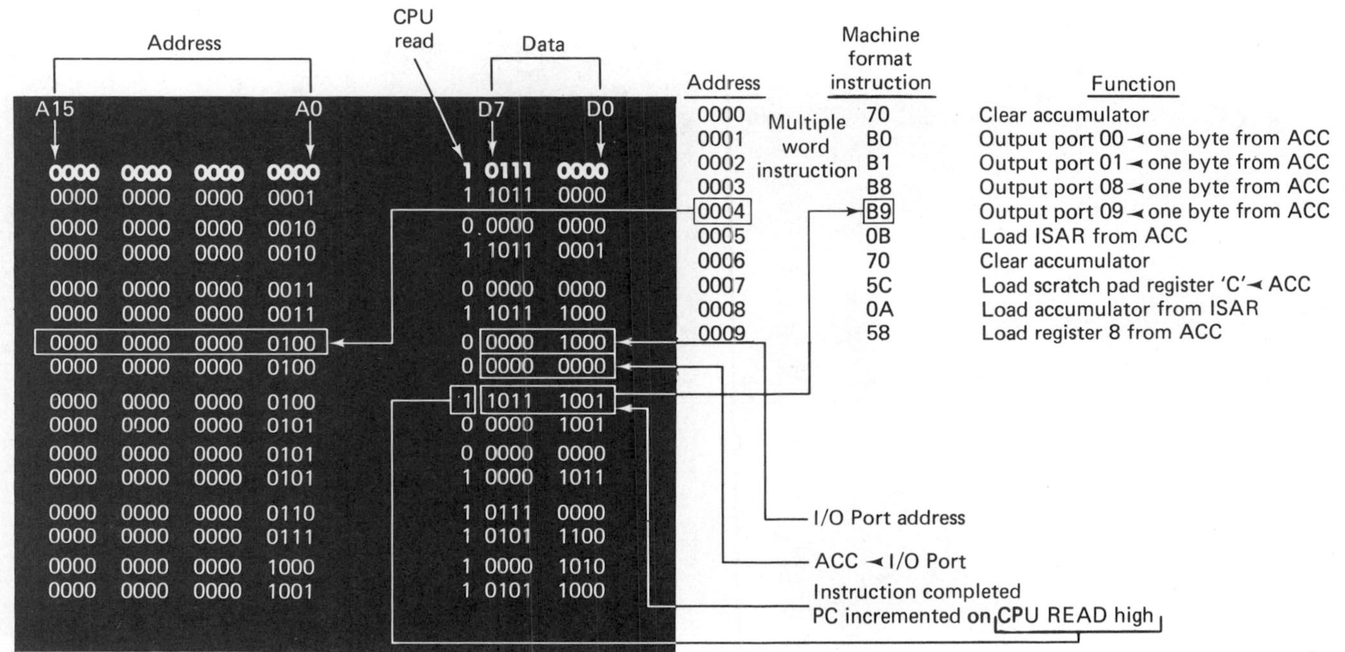

Figure 1-39 Comparison of a typical program listing versus a logic analyzer tabular data display.

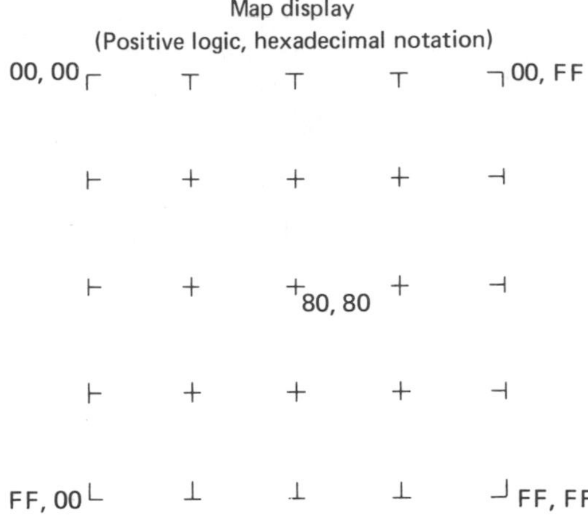

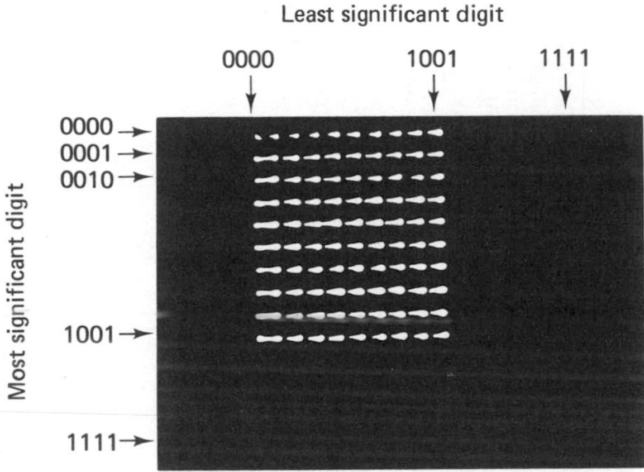

Figure 1-40 Typical mapping display as produced on a logic analyzer.

by an illuminated dot. An input of all 0s (or 00 00 in hex) is at the upper left corner of the display, whereas an input of all 1s (or FF FF in hex) is at the lower right. The dots are interconnected so that the sequence of data changes can be observed. The interconnecting line gets brighter as it moves toward a new point, thereby showing the direction of data flow.

When the mapping display is used to monitor a microprocessor program, or a portion of a program, the display assumes a unique pattern or signature. Once you have learned to recognize the patterns, it is relatively easy to tell at a glance if the program is proceeding normally. Compare the table and map display of Fig. 1-41. The same data bytes (16 words, 16 bits per word) are in tabular form in Fig. 1-41a, and plotted in a map format in Fig. 1-41b.

```
0010 0110 0001 1010
0000 0000 0001 1010

0000 0000 0001 0000
0000 0000 0000 0000

0000 0101 0001 1010
0010 0101 0001 1101
0010 0101 0001 1111
0010 0101 0001 1000

0010 0101 0001 1111
0000 0000 0001 1111
0000 0000 0001 0001
0000 0000 0000 0000

0000 0110 0001 1001
0010 0110 0001 1101
0010 0110 0001 1111
0010 0110 0001 1101
```

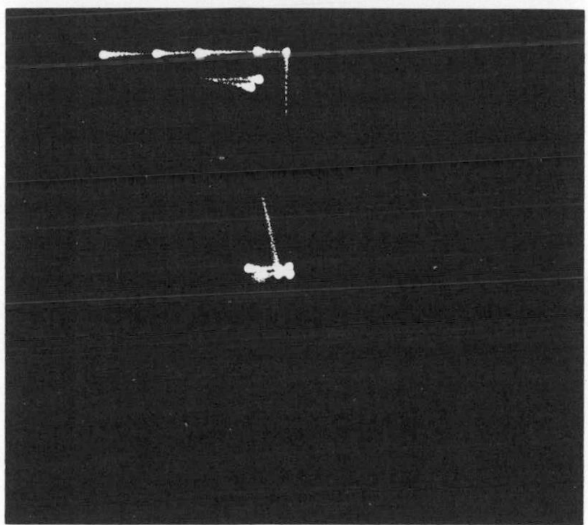

Figure 1-41 Comparison of tabular display and mapping display as produced on a logic analyzer.

Some logic analyzers are provided with a *cursor* function to help locate specific points in the mapping display. Generally, the cursor is a bright circle that can be manipulated over the display by the analyzer controls. In use, the cursor is positioned over an area of interest on the map and the address or data word is read out on the analyzer controls. For example, as shown in Fig. 1-42, there is a gap between the sixth and seventh lines of the display. By positioning the cursor over the last dot in the sixth line and reading the corresponding word on the controls, you know the exact address or data word at which the malfunction occurs.

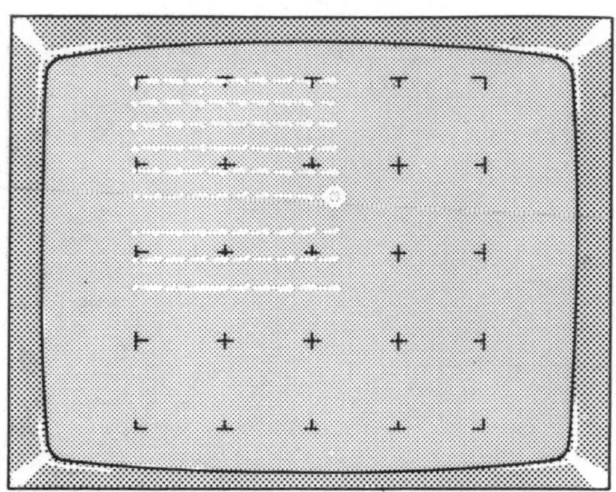

Figure 1-42 Using the cursor function of a logic analyzer mapping display to locate a malfunction in a program.

Keep in mind that the examples given here are very elementary. Logic analyzers, in the hands of experienced operators, are very powerful tools for testing, debugging, troubleshooting, and analyzing *all forms* of data-manipulating equipment, not just microprocessors.

2 Peripheral and Support Equipment

The *peripheral* equipment used with microcomputers and microprocessor-based systems is essentially the same as for larger, conventional computers and minicomputers. As one example, a typical microcomputer can be operated with a video terminal (keyboard and display CRT) or with an electric typewriter or TTY. Likewise, a microcomputer can be used with the console-type magnetic tape recorders (or with magnetic drums and/or disks) for high-volume storage of data. Of course, this requires suitable I/O devices, or software programs (or a combination of both) that match the peripheral characteristics to those of the microcomputer system.

The story is not quite the same for *support* equipment used with microprocessor-based systems. Such support equipment (simulators, emulators, system evaluators or analyzers, PROM programmers, component testers, software, etc.) is designed for use with microcomputer equipment. Going further, such equipment is generally supplied by the microprocessor manufacturer, for use only with their line of products. An exception is the Tektronix 8002 Microprocessor Lab (described in Chapter 8), which is designed as a support or design aid for several major microprocessor systems.

It should be noted that peripheral and support equipment are sometimes interchangeable. For example, a keyboard/display used during design or development of a microprocessor system can also be used to enter and display data once the system has been developed. For these reasons, we shall concentrate mostly on the basics of peripheral/support equipment in this chapter, and describe the details of specific manufacturers' support equipment in the related chapters.

2-1 THE NEED FOR PERIPHERAL EQUIPMENT

The primary function of peripheral equipment is to translate human instructions and data into microprocessor language (binary data bytes) and from microprocessor language into a form suitable for readout. In effect, the peripheral equipment (in conjunction with the microcomputer I/O IC) reconciles the "outer world" with the microcomputer.

There are two major reasons for this reconciliation or translation. First, the outer world rarely expresses anything in binary data bytes. (Generally, the outer world uses numbers, letters, words, etc.) However, the microprocessor always uses binary data bytes. Second, the microprocessor operates at extremely high speeds when compared to the outer world. For example, in the fraction of a second that it takes to strike a key of an input typewriter, a microprocessor can perform hundreds or thousands of operations.

2-1-1 Peripherals in data processing

To take advantage of available microprocessor speed when used in data-processing applications, the information to be processed is prepared in advance and stored. Common storage forms include paper tape, punch cards, and magnetic tape, drums, or disks. The basic relationship between a data-processing microcomputer and peripheral devices is shown in Fig. 2-1.

Note that the terms *on-line* and *off-line* are used to indicate *direct* and *indirect* connection to the microcomputer. For example, a paper-tape punch that is operated by an electric typewriter is an off-line device for indirect input. The paper-tape reader that converts holes in the paper tape into pulses applied to the microcomputer is an on-line device for direct input. Information is put into the off-line devices by human operators. The on-line devices then automatically convert the information into data bytes (in pulse form) for application to the microcomputer. On-line devices require only that the human operator load the tapes or cards, and turn on the unit.

With a data-processing system such as the one shown in Fig. 2-1, the microcomputer does not have to wait for the operator to type out messages, since the microcomputer can read directly from the tapes or cards. Large

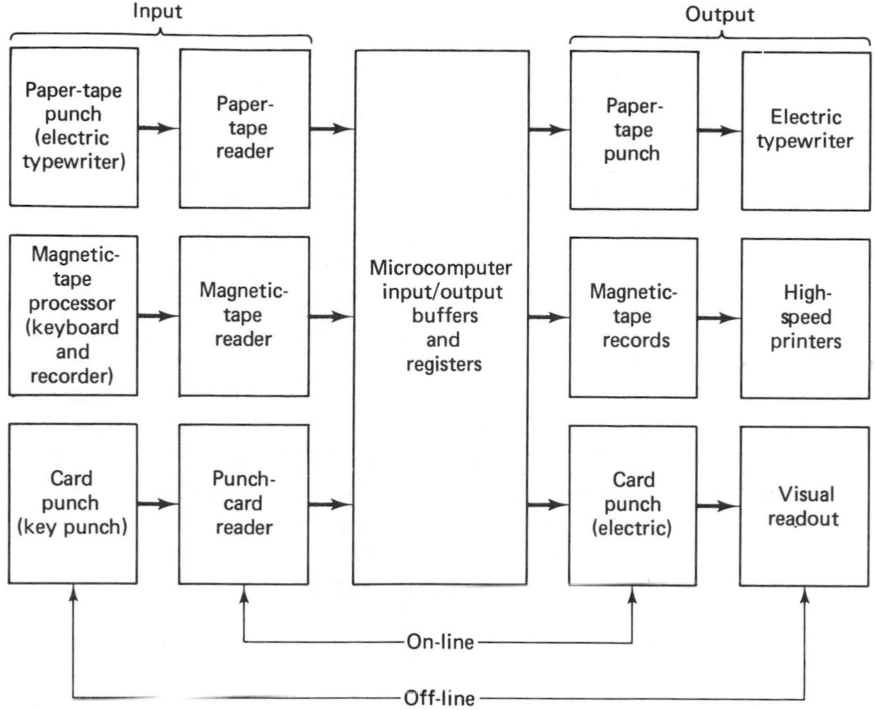

Figure 2-1 Basic relationship between the microcomputer and input/output accessories in data-processing applications.

quantities of tapes or cards can be made in advance by many operators, handling different problems on separate typewriters. The microcomputer can look at all the tapes or cards from the appropriate reader. After processing, the microcomputer directs the on-line tape or card punch (or magnetic recorder) to store the processed data. The tapes or cards containing the processed data are then read out on output printers or typewriters (or other visual display devices).

These output readout devices are not as fast as the microprocessor. However, the devices are very fast in comparison to human operators and have a chance of keeping pace, since many microprocessor calculations require repeated steps.

2-1-2 Peripherals in real-time processing

Not all microcomputers are used for data processing. In fact, most high-volume data-processing systems still use larger computers and minicomputers. Many microcomputers operate on a *real-time* basis, where the microcomputer stands ready to solve problems presented by the human operator. Where human operators must command a microcomputer, a manual keyboard (as found on an electric typewriter or TTY) is the simplest and most common form of input/output device. The commands are typed and applied directly to the microcomputer (in the form of data bytes). The processed output signals from the microcomputer then "type out" the answers on the same keyboard.

2-1-3 Peripherals in process control applications

Many microprocessor-based systems receive continuously changing inputs and produce corresponding readouts. Microprocessor-based systems used to monitor (and control) industrial processes are an example. There are generally no off-line devices with such systems. Instead, these microprocessor systems receive inputs from *transducers,* which convert such factors as process temperature, flow rate, and volume into electrical voltages. The voltages, which are *analogs* of the temperature, flow, and volume, are converted into data bytes by an *analog-to-digital* circuit (which is a form of decoder). The automatic readout from the microprocessor system, in addition to supplying a permanent record on a typewriter or printer, is also used to control the industrial process. At the microcomputer output, the data bytes are converted to a corresponding electrical voltage by a *digital-to-analog* circuit (another form of decoder). The output electrical voltages are then applied to control voltages, switches, and so on, as needed to control the industrial process.

2-2 ELECTRIC TYPEWRITER OR TTY TERMINALS

Electrical typewriters and TTYs provide both input and output for a microcomputer. Generally, the same I/O IC is used for both input and output functions.

2-2-1 Basic input circuit

Figure 2-2 shows the input relationship between a peripheral typewriter or TTY and a typical microcomputer. With any peripheral typewriter system, there must be circuits between the keyboard and the microcomputer input that (1) convert the data instructions into bytes that are compatible with the microcomputer circuits, and (2) store the bytes until they can be entered into the microcomputer circuits without disrupting normal operation. This procedure is sometimes referred to as a *service routine.*

The conversion is done by a decoder circuit, while the storage and timing is done by registers and buffers, as discussed in Chapter 1. The present design trend is to include the register and buffer functions in the I/O IC of the microcomputer with the decoder function in the typewriter.

Note that the data bytes are transmitted in both parallel and serial form from the peripheral to the microcomputer. The parallel method is the

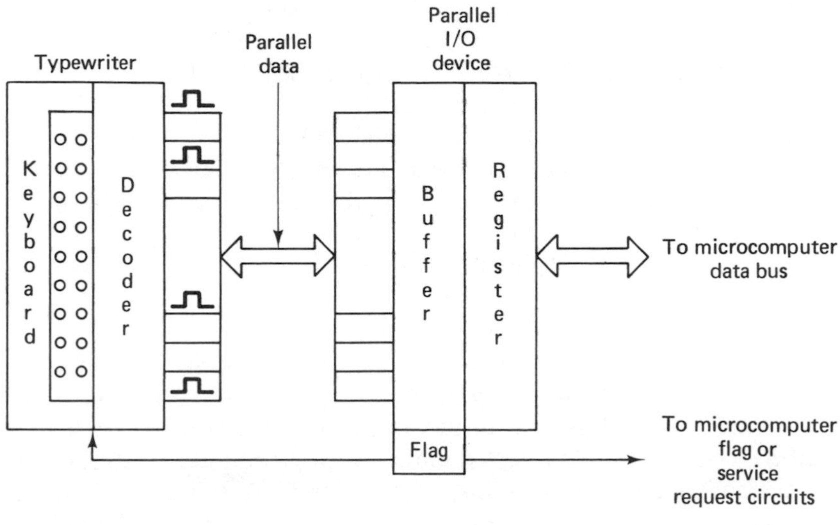

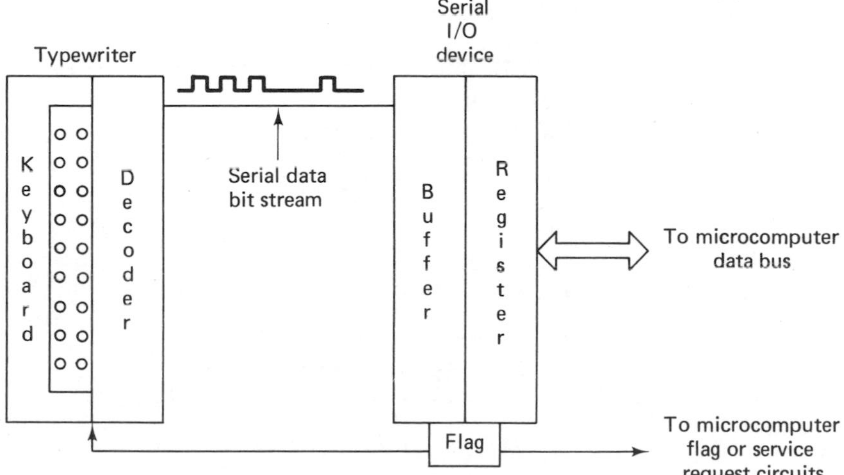

Figure 2-2 Input relationship between a peripheral typewriter and a microcomputer for both serial and parallel operation.

fastest and requires the simplest I/O circuit in the microcomputer. However, TTY terminals generally transmit their data bytes over a *single* telephone line (or a pair of lines). (Eight lines, plus any control, flag, service request, or interrupt lines, are required for an 8-bit parallel system.) Thus, TTYs (and all serial data transmission devices) require a special serial I/O IC (often called an *asynchronous* or *universal* I/O). Most major microprocessor manufacturers produce at least one serial I/O, as discussed in the related chapters.

TTY serial data transmission. While on the subject of TTY operation, it is conventional to transmit serial data in a fixed format similar to that shown in Fig. 2-3. When a user strikes a key on the TTY keyboard (an "M," for example) the information denoting that character is converted to its ASCII code (4D in hex) and appears at the TTY output as a *serial data bit stream.* Note that each of the character data bits (b_0 through b_6) is identified on Fig. 2-3. The character (the letter M in this case) is framed by a start bit B, and two stop bits FF. By convention (or *protocol*), 2 stop bits are used for data transmitted at 10 characters per second, and 1 stop bit for higher data-transmission rates.

A parity bit P is also shown in Fig. 2-3. (Parity, and its relation to the ASCII code, is discussed in Sec. 1-8-8.) The parity bit is a 1 only if the seven data bits contain an odd number of 1s. Hence, the total number of 1s in the 8 intelligence bits (7 data bits plus 1 parity bit) is always an even number. This convention is called the *even-parity* option for ASCII-coded data transmission (which is, in general, used for TTYs and most of the serial data-transmission devices). Since there are 4 bits (an even number) in the ASCII code for the letter M, the parity bit is a 0 in Fig. 2-3.

Input timing sequence. With either serial or parallel transmission, the data/instructions must pass from the typewriter to the microcomputer circuit in a precisely timed sequence. As shown in Fig. 2-2, the decoder

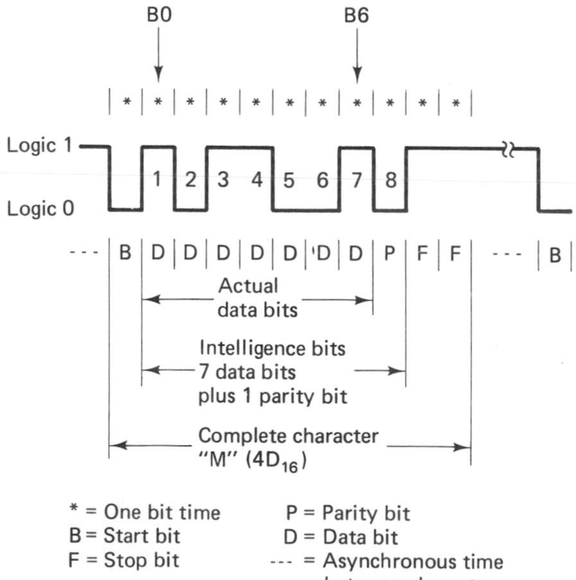

Figure 2-3 TTY serial data transmission format (showing character "M").

output is applied to a register/buffer combination. The buffer is opened and closed by pulses or controls signals from the microcomputer, in response to *service requests* (also called flags, interrupts, etc.) from the typewriter. This reconciles the high speed of the microcomputer with the slow speed of the typewriter. For example, assume that the buffer can be opened and closed 10,000 times per second and that it takes 1 s for the typewriter key to be pressed and released. No matter what time the data byte from the keyboard starts and stops, the buffer/register has thousands of times to read in, store, and read out the data byte to the microcomputer.

This combination of service request signals, and timing signals, is necessary to prevent undesired conflict between the typewriter and microcomputer circuits. Assume, for example, that the microcomputer is performing a series of mathematical calculations on data bytes previously entered by the keyboard and that the operator starts to enter more data. In the normal sequence, a service request is sent by the typewriter. In practice, a service request is sent for each data byte, or each time a typewriter key is struck. The service request indicates to the microprocessor that there is new information to be entered into the buffer. If old information in the buffer has been read out to the microcomputer, the buffer is reset to zero, and the new data are entered and read out to the microcomputer.

Now assume that the microcomputer is not ready to accept new information (previous data bytes are still being processed). Then the buffer accepts the new data, but does not pass them to the microcomputer until the circuits are ready. Keep in mind that since the microcomputer operates at such a high speed, the operator does not have to "wait" until the computer is finished before striking the next key.

2-2-2 Basic output circuit

Microcomputer output circuits are essentially the reverse of input circuits. The output circuits to an electric typewriter or TTY must (1) convert the processed data bytes into a form (usually numbers, letters, words, etc.) that is compatible with the typewriter keys and (2) synchronize the high-speed microprocessor output with that of the lower-speed typewriter.

As in the case of input, the conversion is done by a decoder circuit (usually within the typewriter), whereas the synchronization is done by the I/O buffer/register, which operates in response to a combination of microcomputer and typewriter signals.

Figure 2-4 shows the output relationship between a peripheral typewriter or TTY and a typical microcomputer. In the readout mode, the keys are operated by electrical voltages from the decoder. When the buffer/register is opened, the data byte is applied to the decoder, which, in turn, applies the operating voltage to the appropriate typewriter key. This causes the appropriate key to strike and print out the corresponding character (number, letter, symbol, etc.).

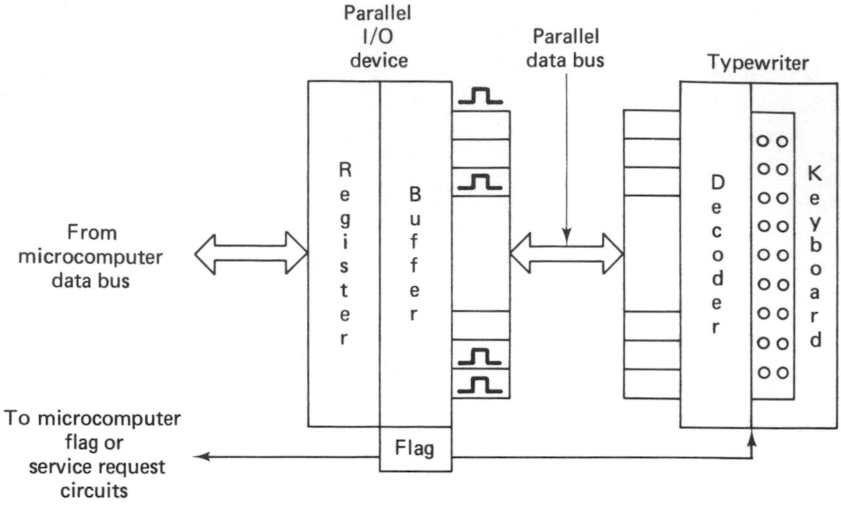

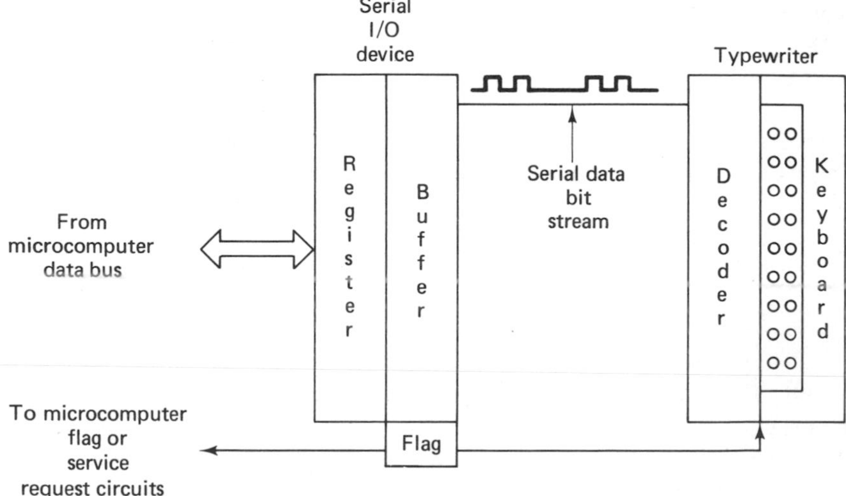

Figure 2-4 Output relationship between a peripheral typewriter and a microcomputer for both serial and parallel operation.

In the normal sequence, a service request is sent by the typewriter. This indicates to the microcomputer that the keyboard is ready to receive data from the buffer. The register is set to zero, the new data byte is entered from the microcomputer, the buffer is opened, and the data byte is passed to the decoder. In turn, the decoder operates the corresponding key.

It is obvious that the microcomputer can solve problems faster than the keyboard can type them out. This means that two conditions must occur. First, the output buffer must be held in the existing state long enough for the key to be struck. Second, the normal routine of the computer must be interrupted so that the answers to several problems are not computed while the output buffer is held open. In actual practice, the interruption occurs at some convenient point in the microcomputer operation (usually at the end of a timing cycle). This problem is discussed further in related chapters.

2-3 VIDEO TERMINAL (KEYBOARD/CRT)

The video terminal can be used as an input/output device for microprocessor-based systems, particularly in inquiry/response situations, where information is required for immediate use. Unless the CRT portion of the video terminal is attached to a printing device, no permanent record of displayed data is kept.

As shown in Fig. 2-5, the video terminal is essentially a cathode-ray tube or CRT (complete with vertical and horizontal sweep circuits similar to those used in TV sets and oscilloscopes) plus a keyboard. Information is displayed on the face of the CRT immediately after it is received from the microcomputer or entered from the keyboard.

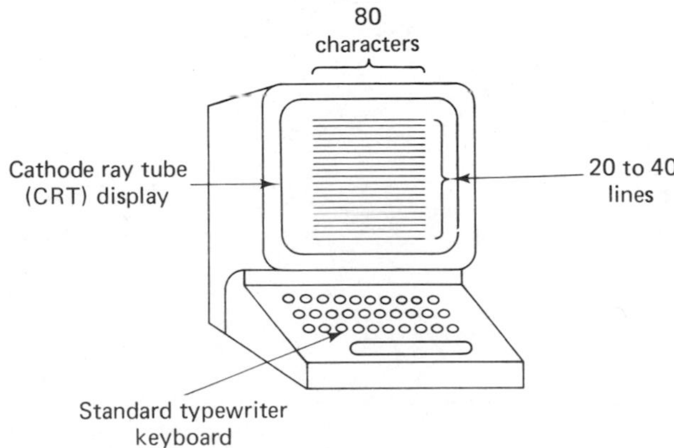

Figure 2-5 Typical video terminal (CRT display/keyboard).

The input function of the video terminal is accomplished by the keyboard in a manner similar to that described for the basic input circuit (Sec. 2-2-1). That is, the keyboard output is converted into data bytes (in machine language suitable for the microcomputer) by a decoder (which is generally part of the video terminal).

The output function is performed by the CRT. The horizontal and vertical sweep deflection circuits of the CRT are standard. The electron beam is swept across the CRT face several hundred (or thousand) times per second. Typically, the deflecting circuits sweep out 20 or 40 rows or horizontal lines of characters (letters, numbers, or symbols), with each line divided into 80 spaces (for 80 characters).

There are many systems used to produce the characters. Most video terminals use some type of *character generator,* usually in IC form. Such character generators are a form of decoder and convert binary data bytes into electrical voltages that alter or manipulate the CRT electron beam as necessary to trace out characters on the screen.

2-3-1 Typical character-generator operation

Figure 2-6 shows how one character generator operates. With this system, the characters are produced by modulating the CRT electron beam intensity with timing pulses that occur at precise intervals as the beam passes

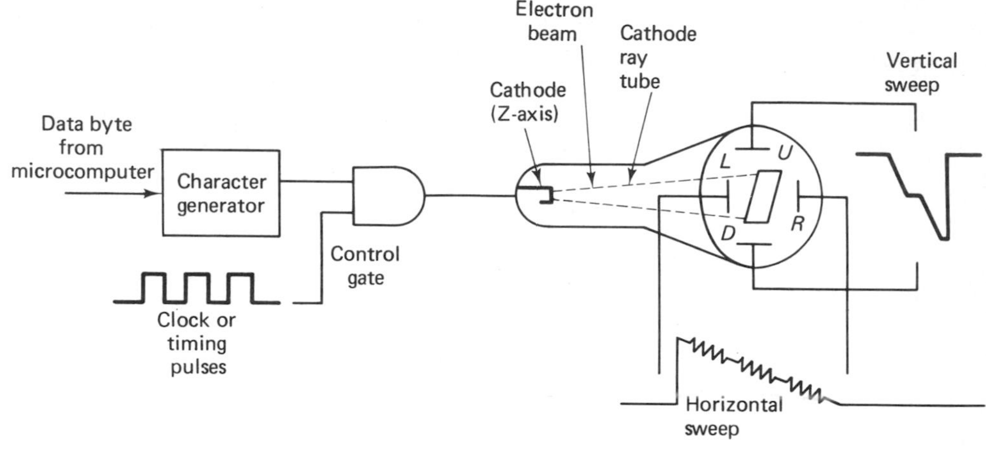

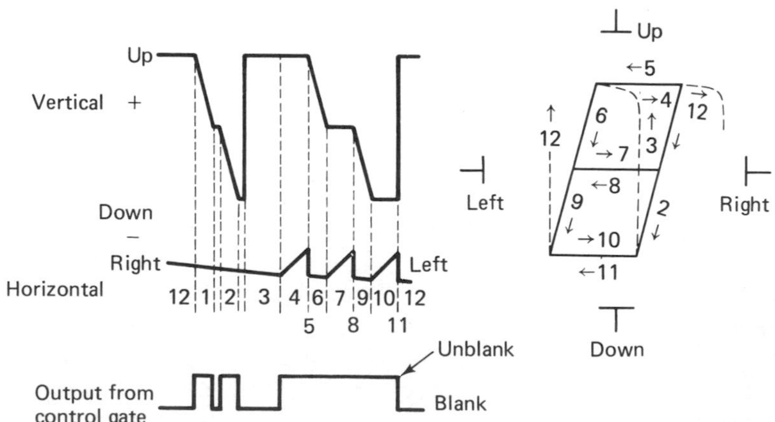

Figure 2-6 How visual display is formed on video terminal.

a given point on the CRT face. Pulse timing is controlled by outputs from the character generator.

The relationship of timing pulses to the horizontal and vertical deflection voltages is synchronized by master timing pulses. In the example shown, two vertical sweeps are required for each character. Thus, to produce 80 characters across one line, the master pulses must trigger 160 vertical sweeps for each horizontal sweep.

The master pulses are applied to a gate that is controlled (to modulate the electron beam) by operation of the character generator. In turn, the character generator receives input from the microcomputer's output (usually from the I/O IC). In the absence of output from the character generator, no pulses pass to the CRT, the screen is blanked, and no characters appear, even though the vertical and horizontal deflection voltages are available. When there is a data byte at the microcomputer output, this data byte is applied to the character generator, unblanking the screen at appropriate points on the vertical and horizontal sweeps.

The relationships of the vertical and horizontal deflection voltages, together with the blanking and unblanking (modulation), are shown in Fig. 2-6b. The heavy lines on the vertical and horizontal sweeps indicate when the CRT is unblanked and producing a character (the numeral 8 in this case). For example, to form the upper right-hand side of the numeral 8 (arbitrarily labeled as time interval 1), the upper vertical deflection plate goes negative, causing the beam to move down. During the same time interval 1, the right-hand horizontal plate also goes slightly negative, causing the beam to move slightly to the left. The beam is unblanked during time interval 1, so the upper right-hand portion of the 8 is traced out.

The remaining segments of the numerical 8 can be traced out by comparing the status of the horizontal and vertical sweep voltages and the blanking condition for all time intervals during a complete character cycle (two vertical sweeps). Note that neither the vertical nor the horizontal sweeps are perfectly linear.

In all video terminal systems, the persistance of the CRT screen is fairly short. This is necessary so that the readout is removed in a reasonable period of time (to permit new data bytes to be read in). Some video terminals contain storage registers that permit the displayed characters to be retained (or *refreshed*) on the screen until the operator clears the readout.

2-4 PAPER-TAPE READER AND PUNCH

A paper-tape reader provides for direct input to a microcomputer by reading prepunched data in paper (or thin metallic) tape. A paper-tape punch provides a permanently recorded output from a microcomputer by punching output information in the paper. Often, the two functions are combined in a single instrument. One common use for a paper-tape instrument is to convert a microcomputer program into machine language. For example, a program can be entered into a computer (host computer, time-sharing computer, support simulator, etc.) using assembly language and an assembler. The output from this computer is a program in machine language which is punched into paper tape. The punched paper-tape program is then read into the microcomputer in machine language.

It should also be noted that paper-tape machines are generally useful in computer/data-processing applications, and were in use long before microprocessor-based equipment. For example, recording on paper tape is often done with machines that punch data received directly from a typewriter or keypunch, or over telephone lines. Paper-tape reader outputs can sometimes be used to drive typewriters directly, or over telephone lines.

2-4-1 Paper-tape reader

As shown in Fig. 2-7, information stored on paper tape is recorded in patterns of round punched holes located in parallel tracks (or channels) along the length of the tape. A character is represented by a combination of punches across the width of the tape. Paper tapes vary in width according to the number of channels they contain. Typically, paper tapes have either five or eight channels.

Paper-tape systems are ideally suited to the binary (or two-state) system used in microcomputers, since the basic indication of paper tape is either "hole" or "no hole." Two methods of sensing the binary bits are shown in Fig. 2-7.

In the system of Fig. 2-7a, wire brushes complete a circuit through the tape holes to a metal plate underneath the tape. As the tape is drawn across the plate, the brushes either complete the circuit through a hole (producing an output pulse) or fail to complete the circuit where there is no hole (producing no output pulse). Generally, an output pulse (hole) represents a binary 1, whereas no output pulse (no hole) represents a 0. Note that one brush is used for each track or channel of holes.

In the system of Fig. 2-7b, a light source is placed on one side of the paper tape, with photocells located on the opposite side. One photocell is used for each track or channel of holes. As the tape moves, the light strikes a photocell wherever there is a hole, producing an output or binary 1. No output (binary 0) is produced when there is no hole, since the light cannot pass to the corresponding photocell.

The holes in the paper tape can be located only at predetermined sites, as shown in Fig. 2-7c. Each set of holes across the tape represents one character. A series of characters makes up a word. Location holes guide the tape through the reader and hold the tape in proper position for reading. At each character, the tape is stopped momentarily for reading, after which

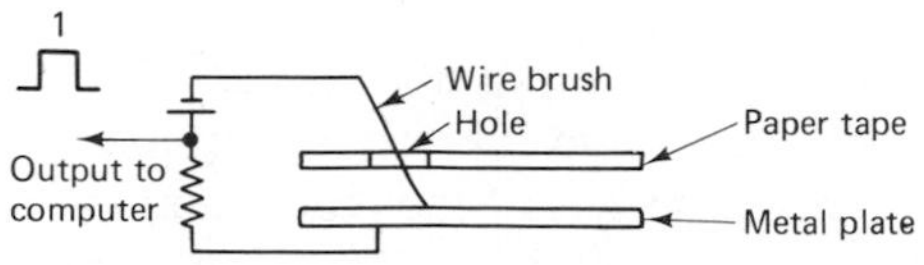

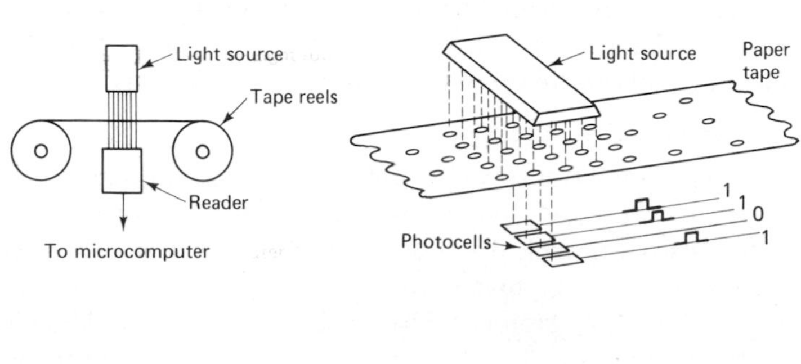

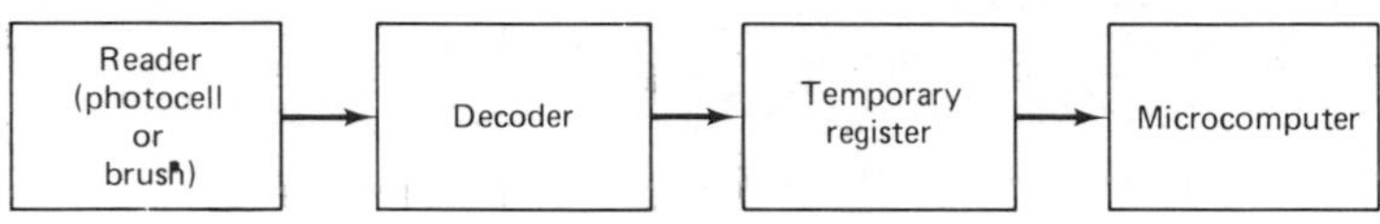

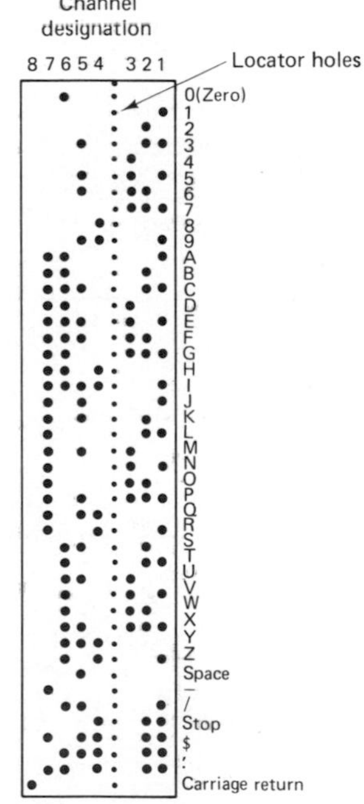

Eight-channel 44-code tape

Figure 2-7 Basic paper-tape reader circuits.

the character is stored in a temporary register. The use of this temporary register between the reader and the microcomputer input buffer compensates for the difference in speeds of the reader and microcomputer. In some systems, the temporary register is part of the microcomputer I/O IC. If the paper tape is not punched in machine language (typically an 8-bit binary data byte), a decoder is required between the tape reader and microcomputer input. The decoder converts the five- or eight-channel output from the reader into a format (machine language) suitable for the microcomputer.

2-4-2 Paper-tape punch

When paper tape is used at the microcomputer output, the holes are produced by solenoid-operated metal punches on the paper-tape punch. One punch is used for each track or channel, as shown in Fig. 2-8. The output from the microcomputer is applied through a decoder to the punch solenoids. (If the paper tape is to be punched in machine language, the decoder can be omitted.) The decoder converts the processed information from machine language into a five- or eight-channel code, as applicable.

The paper tape is driven past the punches by the same gear mechanism used in reading the tape. There is one locator hole on the tape for each frame (set of holes across the width). As the frame is pulled into position

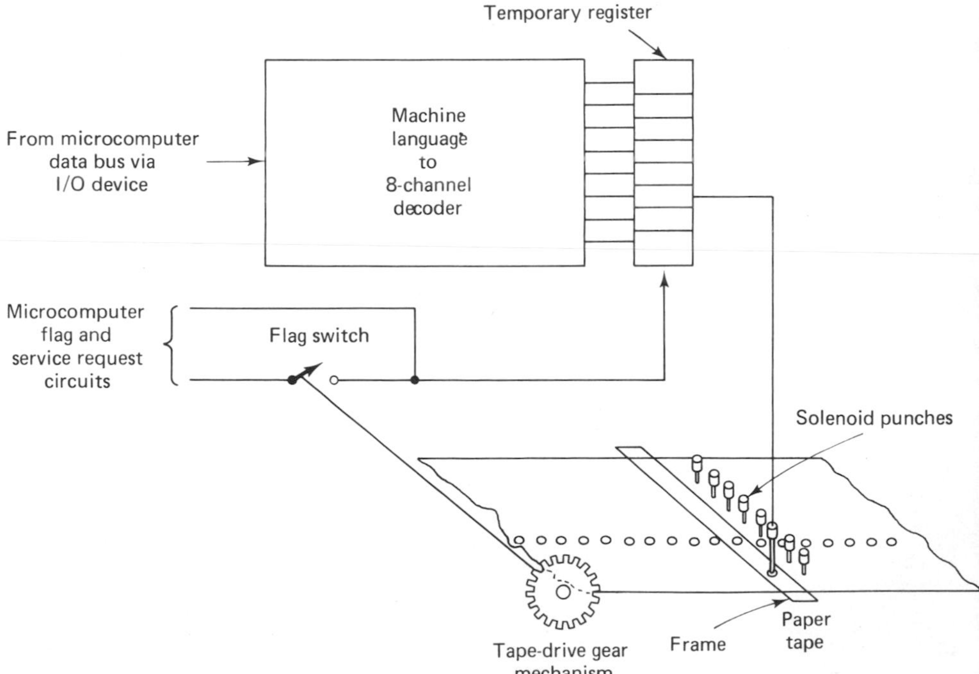

Figure 2-8 Basic paper-tape punch circuits.

below the punches, a service request signal is sent to the microcomputer. If a data byte is available at the microcomputer output, the service request permits the I/O buffer to be opened so that the data byte is passed to the punch solenoids. If there is no data byte available, the tape drive is stopped until new information is available. Thus, the microcomputer output is synchronized with the timing of the tape punch. Of course, under normal circumstances, the microcomputer will produce outputs faster than can be punched by the tape unit. For this reason, a temporary register is often used between the microcomputer and tape unit. In some cases, the temporary register is part of the I/O IC.

2-5 OUTPUT PRINTERS

When there is a limited amount of information to be read out of a microcomputer, the standard electric typewriter is the most convenient and in most common use. Such printers are sometimes known as console, message, or supervisory printers. Long rolls of paper are put into the typewriter carriage to record both the entry of data (by the operator at the keyboard) and the readout of processed data.

When high-speed readout is required or a large quantity of information is to be read out, various forms of printers are used. Note that many of these printers were used with electromechanical data-processing equipment long before computers of any kind were invented. With a standard typewriter, only one letter can be typed at a time. Likewise, the up-and-down movement of type bars in a typewriter is far too slow for computers. Output printers overcome these problems.

There are two basic types of printers:

1. *Line-at-a-time* printers, which print all characters on a given line simultaneously.
2. *Character-at-a-time printers,* which print each character serially, a position at a time, similar to the way a typewriter prints (but at much higher speeds).

No matter what printer is used, the printer receives signals from a decoder, or character generator, which converts data from the microcomputer into a form that is compatible with the printer. In some printers, a character generator similar to that described for the video terminal (Sec. 2-3) is used to convert machine language to characters. No matter what system is used, the microcomputer output buffer is synchronized with the output printer by service request signals, as discussed in Secs. 2-2, 2-3, and 2-4. That is, the printer sends a service request signal to the microcomputer when it is ready to accept the next data byte (or character).

2-5-1 Line-at-a-time printers

Line-at-a-time printers include *bar* or *gang printers,* as well as *wheel, drum,* or *chain printers,* and *electrostatic printers.* None of these are in general use with microprocessor-based systems. However, any of the printers could be used. For example, the design data for the Motorola microprocessor system described in Chapter 4 recommends a Seiko drum printer for use with a commercial (point-of-sale) transaction terminal. For that reason, we shall discuss the basics of a drum printer here.

A drum printer uses a solid cylindrical drum, around which characters are embossed as shown in Fig. 2-9. The drum rotates at a constant speed. As the A row passes the line to be printed, hammers behind the paper strike the paper against the drum, causing one or more As to be printed. As the B row moves into place, any print position requiring the letter B is printed in the same manner. One complete revolution of the drum is required to print each line.

The Seiko printer, shown in Fig. 2-10, has a continually rotating print drum mechanism which uses what is referred to as the *flying printer* technique.

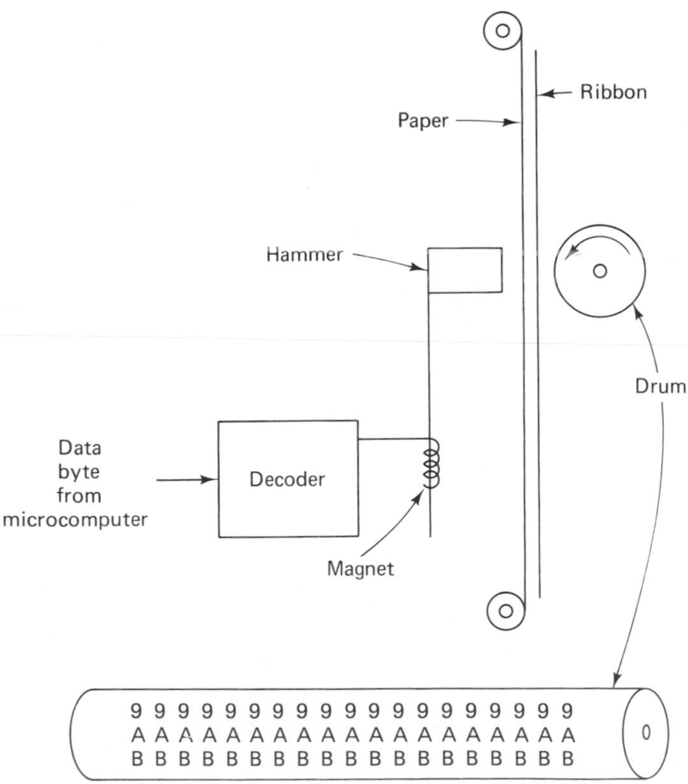

Figure 2-9 Basic drum printer.

The print drum and the ratchet shaft are geared together and rotate continuously in the direction shown. During a nonprint condition, the right end of the trigger level is held away from the ratchet by the trigger lever spring. In the nonprinting condition, the trigger magnet is not actuated and the hammers are lifted upward to a neutral position by the hammer lever springs.

When actuated, the trigger magnet actuating lever forces the opposite end of the trigger lever against the ratchet. During its next rotation, the ratchet engages the right end of the trigger lever, causing a downward motion to the right-hand end of the hammer. The hammer thus strikes through the inked ribbon paper, causing the character then under the hammer to be printed.

Any of 42 characters (alphanumeric plus special characters, such as $, *, etc.) are printed in a 21-column format. Each column position has a complete character set spaced evenly around the drum. Because of a 42:1 gear ratio, the ratchet rotates 42 times for each complete drum rotation. Thus, each character of the set is positioned under a print hammer once during every rotation of the drum.

The decoders and control circuitry actuate the hammers at just the right time in response to timing signals generated electromagnctically by means of ferrite chips or magnets and detecting heads as shown. The timing signals or pulses are generated each time a ferrite magnet passes a detecting head (the basics of magnetics are discussed in Sec. 2-6). Rotation of the ratchet shaft generates signals TP and TL for each of the 42 characters. TP provides timing for energizing the trigger magnets, TL for deenergizing. A reset signal R is generated by each complete rotation of the drum. The resulting waveform for a complete drum rotation is shown in Fig. 2-10.

2-5-2 Character-at-a-time printers

The *teletype printer* prints one character at a time in a manner similar to that of an electric typewriter. However, all the type is placed on a square block rather than on individual hammers. The type block moves from left to right, positioning the proper character at each print position. As the block stops at each position, a hammer strikes the proper character from behind. The character is depressed against an inked ribbon, which, in turn, imprints the character on the paper. Typical teletype-printer speed is about eight lines per minute.

The *matrix printer* consists of pins placed in a 5×7 matrix, as shown in Fig. 2-11. The characters are formed when the appropriate pins strike against the paper. (In some matrix printers, the pins burn spots onto the paper. However, this burning technique is not in general use.) The pins are selected by pulses from the decoder. Some matrix printers are capable of printing about 700 to 800 lines per minute, making the unit comparable in speed to most line-at-a-time printers.

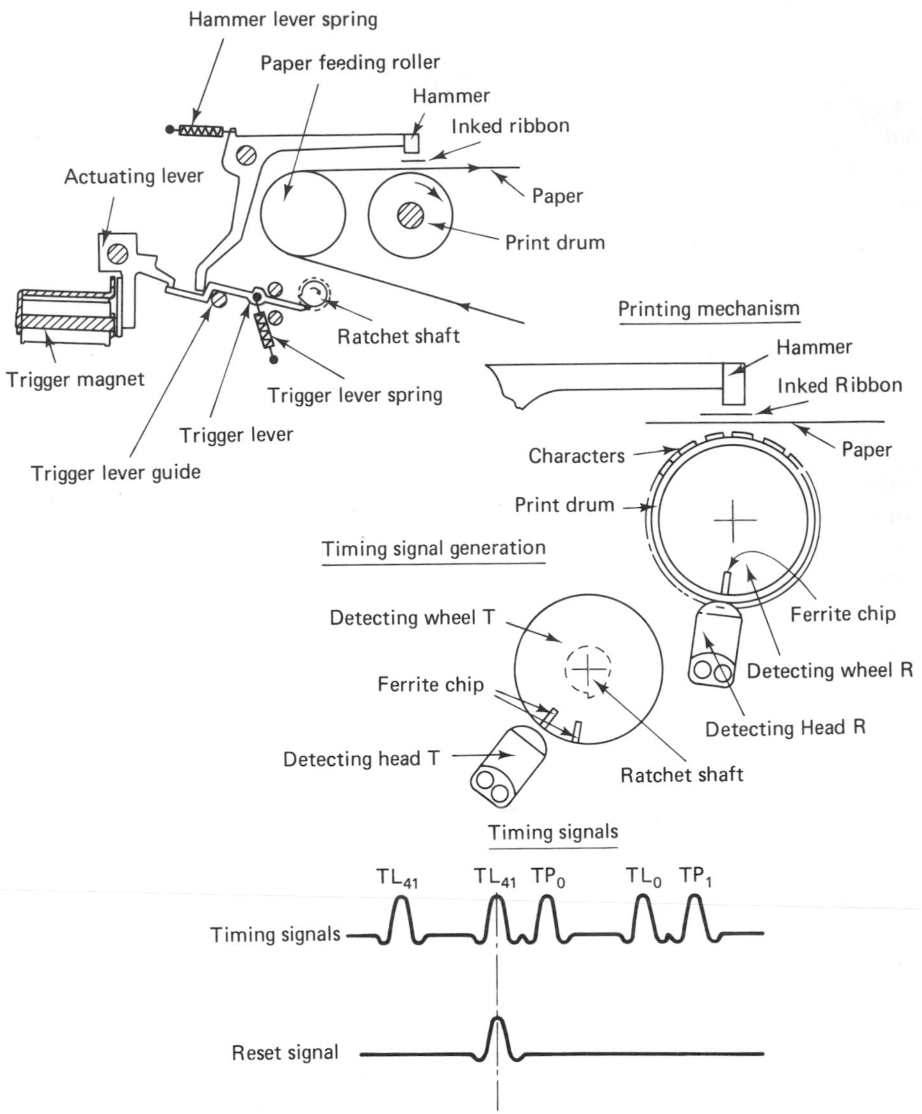

Figure 2-10 Seiko printing mechanism, timing signal generation, and timing signals.

The Motorola EXORprint shown in Fig. 2-12 is an example of the character-at-a-time matrix printers. This unit is part of the Motorola microprocessor system described in Chapter 4. The EXORprint is an economical tabletop impact printer for use in system development or as a communications terminal component. The EXORprint is a completely self-contained printing system that produces lines of eighty 5 × 7 dot matrix characters at

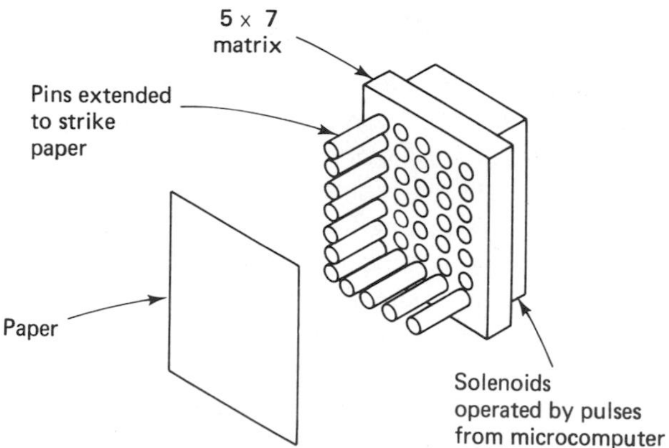

Figure 2-11 Basic matrix printer.

a maximum rate of 110 per second. This is equivalent to about 65 lines per minute. The impact head prints on 8½-in-wide roll paper using a conventional teletypewriter ribbon. Optoelectronic sensing is used to accurately position each dot and permit characters to be printed "on the fly." Circuitry within the printer cabinet is contained on an electronics board and a parallel buffered interface board. In addition to control functions, these boards contain an 80-character by 8-bit MOS static shift register and an MOS character generator that is ROM-programmed with a 64-character ASCII code subset.

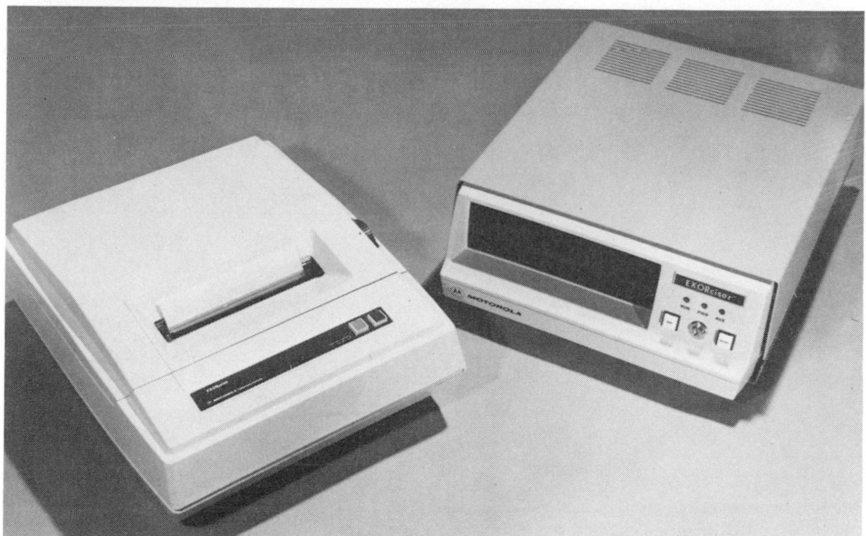

Figure 2-12 Motorola EXORprint tabletop impact printer. (Courtesy Motorola Semiconductor Products, Inc.)

2-6 MAGNETIC RECORDING BASICS

Magnetic tape, drums, disks, and ferrite-core memories all operate on the principle of *electromagnetism.* Therefore, we shall review electromagnetism as it applies to microprocessor memory or data storage.

As shown in Fig. 2-13, current through a coil creates a magnetic field. If a metal capable of being magnetized is placed in this field, the metal will become magnetized in one direction. If current flow is reversed, the metal will be magnetized in the opposite direction. As shown in Fig. 2-14, if metal is magnetized in one direction and an opposite magnetizing current is applied to change the direction of magnetism, the changing magnetic field produces (or induces) a current in another conductor (in or near the field). However, if the magnetizing current is applied so as not to change the direction of magnetism, there is no change in the magnetic field and no induced voltage. Thus, the magnetized metal has a "memory" and is ideally suited to the two-state binary logic (1 or 0) used in microprocessors and microcomputers.

There are two ways in which this magnetic principle can be used. In the case of magnetic tapes, drums, and disks, the *presence* or *absence* of magnetism is used to indicate the binary state. Generally, the presence of magnetism indicates a binary 1, whereas a binary 0 is indicated by the absence of magnetism.

In the case of ferrite cores, the *direction* of magnetism is used to indicate the state (1 or 0). Note that ferrite-core memories are not generally

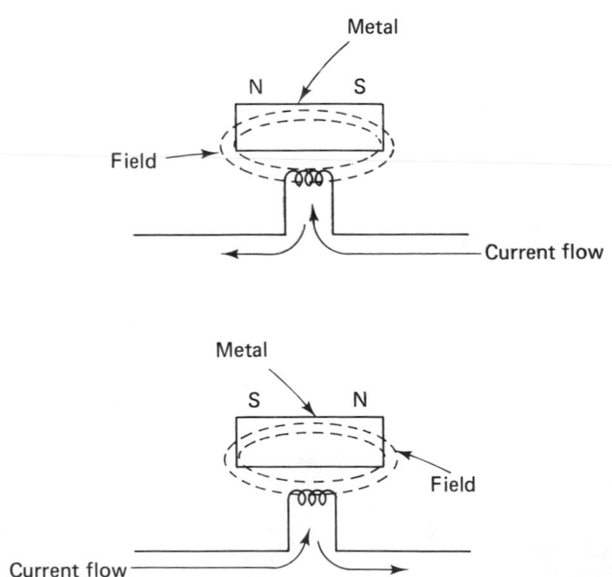

Figure 2-13 Basic principles of magnetic storage, showing metal magnetized in opposite directions by opposite currents.

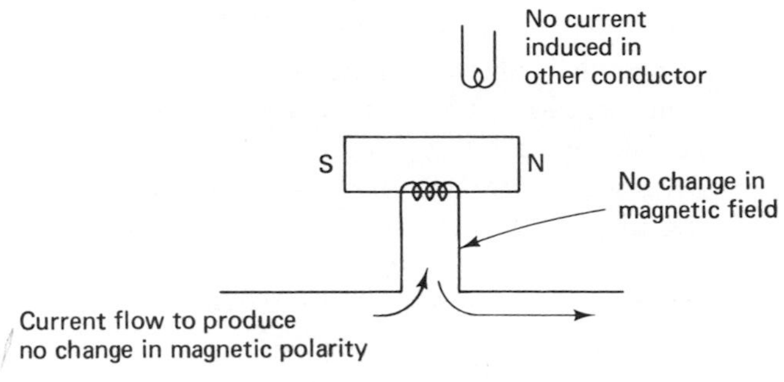

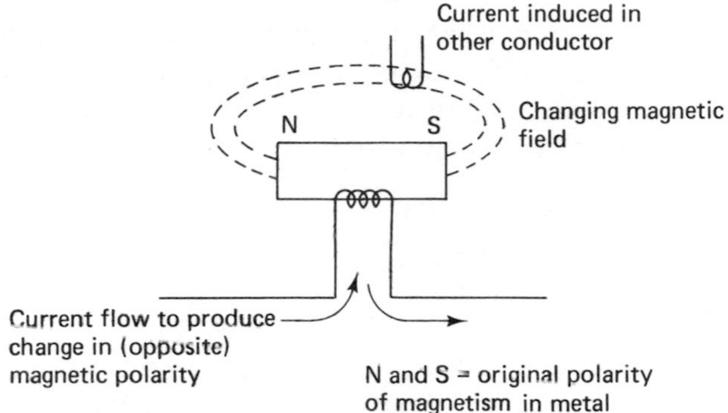

Figure 2-14 Basic principles of magnetic storage or memory, showing the effect of currents on previously magnetized metal storage elements.

used with microprocessor systems, but are often used with larger, conventional computers.

2-7 TAPE RECORDING BASICS

Magnetic-tape recorders are often used with microcomputers as an external data storage device. These recorders provide high-speed read-in and read-out of data. The most common type of magnetic-tape recorder used with microprocessor-based systems is the *cassette* recorder. However, microprocessors can also be used with the reel-to-reel tape recorders associated with larger, conventional computers. Both the cassette and reel-to-reel recorders used with microprocessor systems are similar to those used in home entertainment units. That is, both computer and home entertainment units have tape transports, record and playback heads (called *write* and *read heads*), and amplifiers. However, the detailed characteristics of the two systems are quite different.

2-7-1 Tape recorder amplifier characteristics

The amplifiers used in microcomputer recorders do not require the high fidelity of entertainment units, because microcomputer recorders operate with binary information (bits and bytes of data) rather than voice or music. Data bytes are recorded (written) and played back (read) on a *present* or *absent* basis (in most cases). Often, a binary 1 is represented by the presence of a magnetic field on the tape (sometimes known as a *magnetic spot*), while the absence of a field represents 0. In other systems, the direction of the magnetic field (north or south, + or −, etc.) represents a 1 or 0.

Because of the on–off method of recording, microcomputer tape recorders generally do not have the supersonic bias signal applied to the tape for linearity, as is the case in other recorders, where high fidelity is required. However, microcomputer recording systems often use a fixed dc bias to place the tape in a condition to be magnetized by the data bytes.

2-7-2 Tape characteristics

The tapes used in microcomputer reel-to-reel recorders are generally longer than those of home units; 2400 or 3600 ft is standard. The cassette tapes used with microcomputers are generally the same as for entertainment units. Although early magnetic tapes were made of metal, all popular tapes are now made of plastic, coated on one side with metal oxide. The oxide can easily be magnetized and retains its magnetism indefinitely. The data bits are placed across the width of the tape on parallel tracks running along the entire length. Figure 2-15 shows the recording format for a typical cassette tape used with microprocessor-based systems.

2-7-3 Tape-coding systems

The pattern of the magnetized spots across the width and along the length of the tape is a coded representation of the data stored on it. Several codes are used, as is the case with paper tape. If some code other than machine language has been used to record data on the tape, a decoder is required between the tape reader and the microcomputer input. Likewise, the output from the microcomputer is applied through a decoder to the tape recorder during "record" or "write" operation (unless the data bytes are to be recorded in machine language).

Figure 2-16 shows a tape recording format using the ASCII code. Note that there are eight channels on one track. Seven of the channels are used for the 7-bit ASCII code, and the eighth channel is used for a parity bit (discussed in Sec. 1-7). Thus, the eight channels provide for one character (letter, number, or symbol) across the width of the tape. In Fig. 2-16, each dash or short line represents a binary 1. The absence of a dash represents a binary 0.

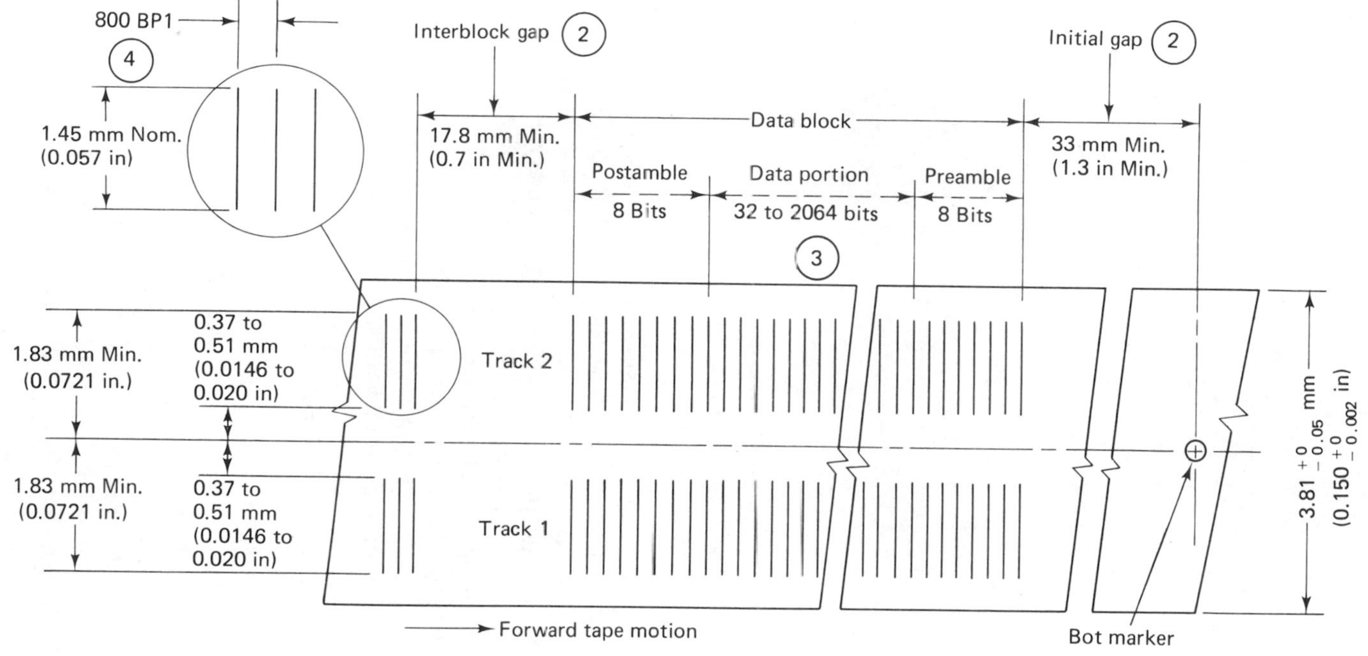

1 Tape is shown with oxide side out.

(2) Tape is fully saturated in the erase direction in the interblock gap and the initial gap.

(3) The last two characters (16 bits) of the data portion is the Cyclic Redundancy Check (CRC).

(4) Shown without phase flux reversals that may exist between data bits.

Figure 2-15 Recording format fcr 800 BPI (bytes per inch) cassette tape.

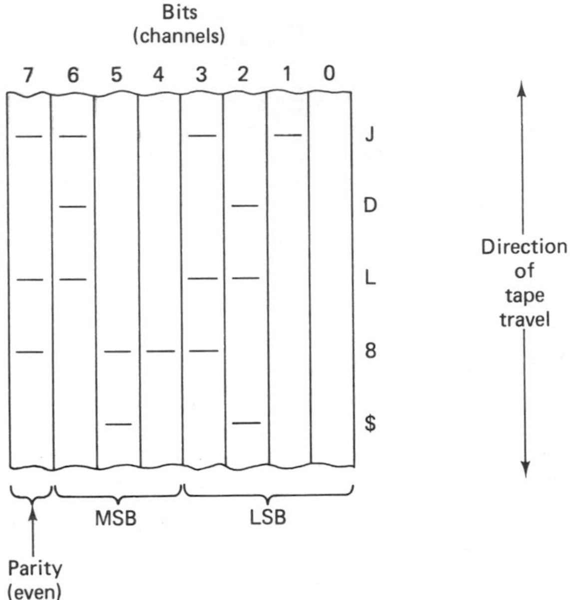

Figure 2-16 Typical tape recording format for ASCII code with eight channels on one track.

The data bytes (representing characters) are recorded serially, as the tape passes by the read/write heads. This is shown in Fig. 2-17, which illustrates one bit (on one channel) of four successive data bytes. A magnetic field (or spot) is impressed on the tape (representing a binary 1 bit) as current (in the form of pulses) passes through the "write" winding. (In some systems, one head is used for both read and write. In other recording systems, separate read and write heads are used.) In the absence of current, no spot is impressed on the tape. During the read operation, as the tape is passed across the head by the tape transport, the presence of a moving magnetic spot produces current in the read head (for a binary 1 bit). No current is produced when there is no spot on the tape passing the head (binary 0 bit).

The system shown in Fig. 2-17 uses the return-to-zero (RZ) format. Although there are many ways in which pulses can be used to represent the 1 and 0 bits, there are only three ways in common use. There are the RZ, NRZL (non-return-to-zero-level), and NRZM (non-return-to-zero-mark) formats. Figure 2-18 shows the relationship of the three formats.

In the RZ format, a 1 bit is represented by a pulse of some definite width (usually a ½-bit width) that returns to the zero signal level. A 0 bit is represented by a zero-level signal.

In the NRZL format, a 1 bit is one signal level, while a 0 bit is another

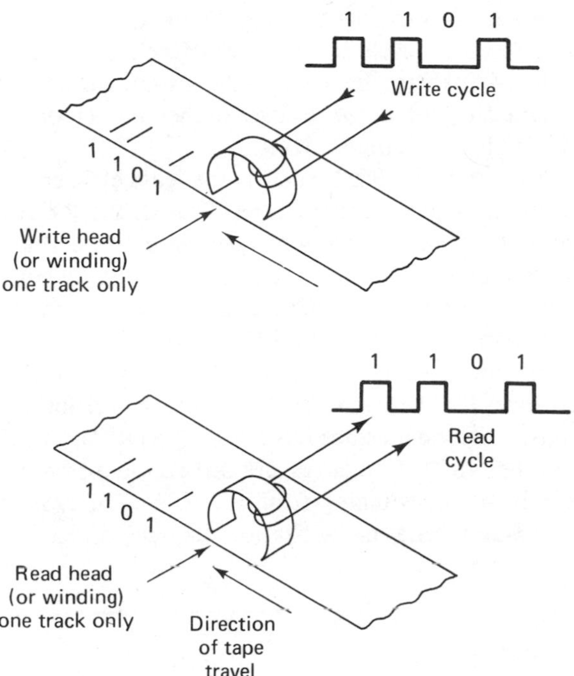

Figure 2-17 Read and write cycles of magnetic tape, showing one bit (on one channel) of four successive data bytes.

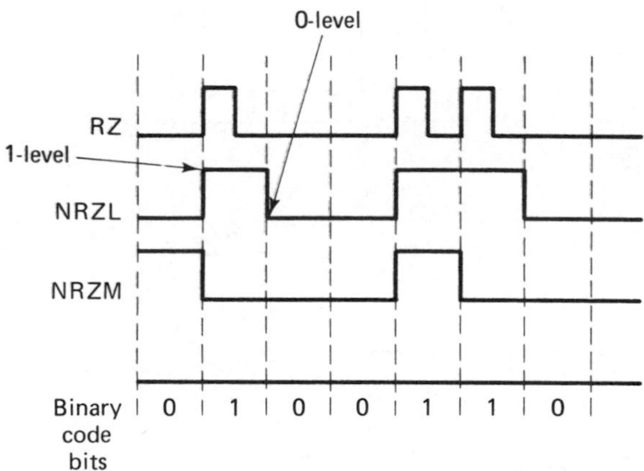

Figure 2-18 Relationship of RZ, NRZL, and NRZM data bit recording formats.

signal level. These levels can be 5 V, 10 V, or any other selected values, provided that the 1 and 0 levels are entirely different and predetermined.

In the NRZM format, the level of the waveform has no meaning. A 1 bit is represented by a *change in level* (either higher or lower), while a 0 bit is represented by no change in level.

In tape recording, the RZ format is the least efficient for storing the most information on a given area of tape. That is, the RZ format provides the lowest amount of *pulse packing* or *packing density*. Pulse packing is a measure of how dense the pulse recording is (how close together the information is recorded). The higher the pulse density, the less amount of tape will be needed for storing data. With the RZ method, the pulse current returns to 0 between bits and remains at 0 for a 0 bit. (In some RZ systems, the pulse current returns to 0 between bits, but changes direction for a 1 or 0 bit.)

Pulse density can be increased by use of the NRZL or NRZM formats of Fig. 2-19. In the NRZL format (Figure 2-19c), the direction of magnetization changes only when switching from a 0 to a 1, or from a 1 to a 0. In NRZM (Figure 2-19b), the magnetization changes direction only when it is necessary to store a 1.

2-7-4 Tape control systems

Another difference between home entertainment and computer tape systems is the method of starting and stopping. Unlike an audio tape that moves slowly and need not be stopped, computer tape moves at fast speeds. For a cassette using the format of Fig. 2-15, the tape moves at a speed of 100 in/s when searching for data, and 15 in/s when reading or writing data.

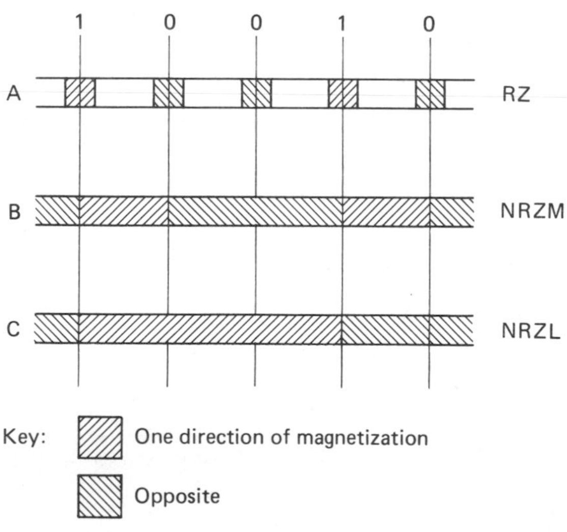

Figure 2-19 Changes in directions of magnetization for RZ, NRZL, and NRZM data bit recording formats.

Because the microcomputer must pinpoint specific data (at a selected address or block on the tape), the tape control system must be able to stop the tape at the proper point with no lost motion.

Reading and writing on tape is performed on the tape unit at a constant speed. The *transfer rate* of information to and from tape depends largely on two factors: (1) the actual movement of tape across the read/write heads and (2) the number of characters or data bytes that can be stored on 1 in of tape (packing density). For example, assume a tape movement speed of 15 in/s and a density of 800 bytes/in. At these rates, the character (or byte) transfer rate is 12,000 per second.

2-7-5 Storing data records on tape

Information is usually written on tape in groups (called *data blocks*), as shown in Fig. 2-15. In normal operation, information continues to be written on the tape until a flag or control signal is received from the microcomputer. This stops the tape drive. Some tape systems use a fixed number of characters in each block, but variable-length blocks are more common. Actual length is determined primarily by the storage capacity of the microcomputer.

As shown in Fig. 2-15, there are *interblock gaps* between data blocks. (In some systems, the gaps are known as *interrecord gaps* or IRGs.) These interblock gaps are produced when the tape continues to be driven, but no information is written on the tape. The use of interblock gaps permits the tape drive to accelerate and decelerate when starting or stopping without failing to read or write the desired information. In some tape systems, when an interblock gap is encountered during the read operation, the tape drive stops at about the center of the gap. The remaining half of the gap is used upon acceleration before the next record is read. A new read command from the microcomputer starts the tape drive again.

2-7-6 Safety and accuracy of tape records

Many safeguards must be taken to preserve data stored on microcomputer tapes. Obviously, the information can be destroyed if an erase signal is accidentally applied to the tape unit heads or if new information is written on top of old information.

A common safeguard on large reel-to-reel tape transport systems to prevent accidental overwriting of tape is a safety indicator in the form of a plastic ring. When installed on a groove around the hub of a tape reel, the ring indicates that the tape may be used to store new information. The ring is removed when the writing of new information is to be prevented. This accounts for the term *no-ring, no-write* used by many computer operators and programmers.

The tape transport of a typical cassette recorder contains two microswitches, one to sense the presence of a tape cassette in place, and the other to see if the *write protect tab* (sometimes called the *file protect tab*) is removed. If the cassette tab is removed, the tape is "write-protected" and circuits within the cassette disable the write circuits. Signals from these switches or sensors are available at the interface, and the microcomputer must check them prior to issuing any "motion" commands to the tape transport.

Just as important, but perhaps not as obvious, there must be some system to ensure that the data bytes are recorded accurately. There are three main concerns in recording data bytes. First, *all the bits* must be recorded. Second, the bits must be *readable.* Third, the bits must be recorded in correct order, both horizontally and vertically on the tape. Several systems are used to ensure these conditions.

Dual recording. Where reliability is particularly important (such as when real-time data bytes are being recorded on a one-time-only basis), dual recording systems can be used. In such systems, each data byte is written twice in each frame across the width of the tape by two sets of heads, amplifiers, and so on. Of course, this requires twice the number of channels and tracks. Note that there are two eight-channel tracks on the format of Fig. 2-15.

Constant-check read/write. Some systems provide a constant check (for readability) of data bytes being recorded. (These systems are sometimes known as *dual-gap* read/write arrangements.) All characters or data bytes written on tape are immediately read by a separate head (or winding) adjacent to the write head. Both readability and accuracy can be checked in this way.

A basic constant-check system is shown in Fig. 2-20. In this system, information in the microcomputer output register is amplified and written onto the tape by a write head. Only one bit is shown in Fig. 2-20. The circuit is repeated (amplifiers, heads, etc.) for each bit in the register. As the tape moves, the bit is read out immediately, amplified, and applied to another readout register. Each bit in the readout register is compared against the corresponding bits in the output register, using a comparator circuit.

The recording operation continues as long as the recorded bits are readable and in agreement with the bits in the output register. If there is any inequality between the two registers, the comparison circuit stops the tape drive and sends a flag to the microcomputer. In some systems, the tape drive is reversed, and the bit is rewritten at the appropriate location on the tape.

Parity and cyclic redundancy check (CRC) circuits. When dual recording and constant-check systems are not practical, parity and CRC circuits can be used to check the accuracy of bits on the tape.

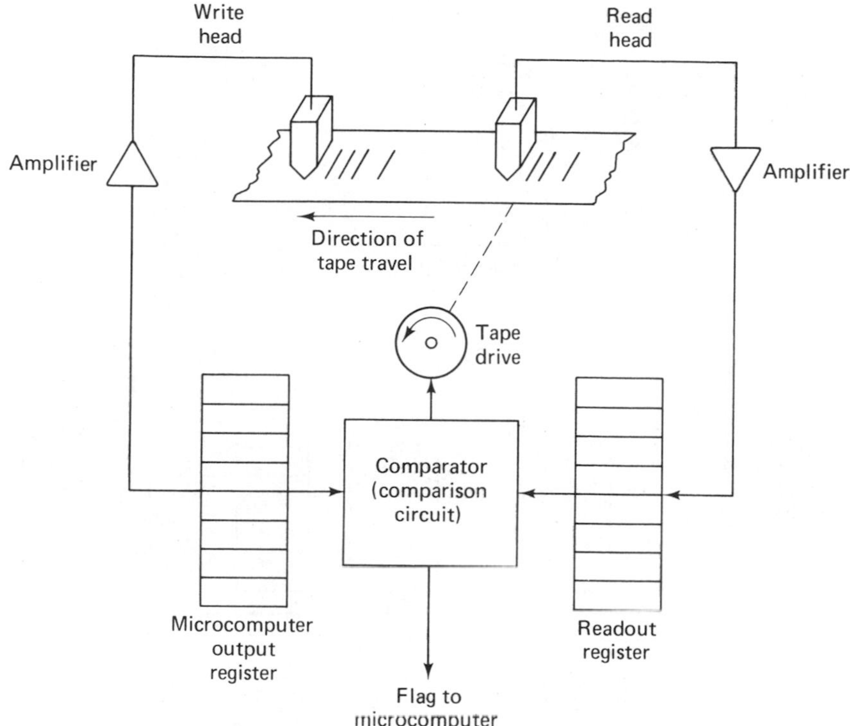

Figure 2-20 Basic constant-check (dual-gap) read/write magnetic-tape recording system.

Parity circuits use the parity system described in Sec. 1-8-8 and provide a check of individual characters (data bytes) across the track. Such systems are sometimes known as *vertical check* or *vertical parity* schemes. A basic vertical parity system is shown in Fig. 2-21. In this system, one channel of an eight-channel track is reserved for vertical even-parity check. A 1 bit is added to make an even number of 1 bits across the width of the tape. In the case of data bytes 2 and 3, both normally use an even number of 1 bits. Thus, no parity bit is added. Data bytes 1 and 4 use an odd number of 1s (three 1s). Thus, a parity bit is added to both data bytes 1 and 4. The amplified output of the read heads applied to the microcomputer is also applied to the parity-checking circuit. If the input to the parity-checking circuit is even, operation continues as normal. If the parity checker receives an old number of bits (due to recording failure, tape failure, etc.) a flag is sent to the microcomputer.

CRC circuits provide a check of a complete data block, and are thus sometimes referred to as a *horizontal parity* or *horizontal check system.* As shown in Fig. 2-15, the last two bytes or characters of the data portion

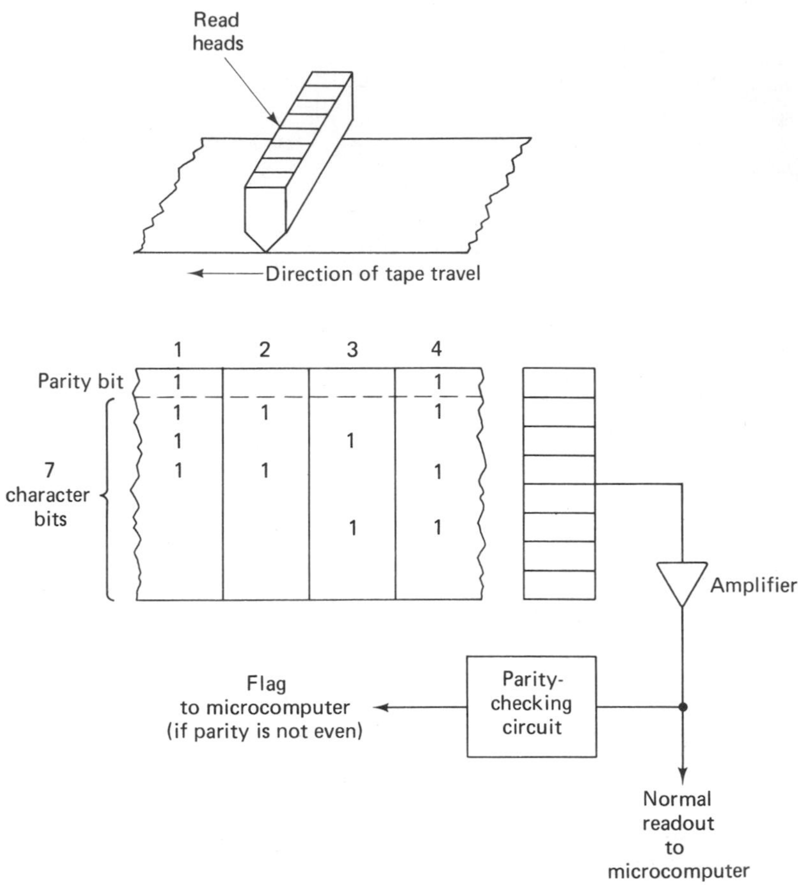

Figure 2-21 Basic vertical parity system for magnetic-tape recording control.

in the data block are called the CRC bytes. These two CRC bytes are generated by circuits that count all the data bits, starting with bit zero of the first data byte in the block (sometimes known as the address byte) ending with the last bit of the last data byte (excluding the CRC bytes). When the data block is read back from the tape, the data bits (from bit zero of the address or first data byte to the last bit of the second CRC byte) are divided by the CRC number. The remainder should be zero if all the data bits have been properly recorded and played back. A nonzero remainder indicates an error within the data read back. This nonzero remainder can be used to stop the tape drive, send a flag to the microprocessor, and so on.

Preamble and postamble bits. As shown in Fig. 2-15, there are eight preamble and postamble bits at opposite ends of the data portion of each data block. These are 8-bit patterns or bytes of alternating 1s and 0s. (This is sometimes known as a *checkerboard.*) In some systems, the preamble and postamble bits are used to establish the data rate during data recovery or read operation. In such systems, the tape drive operates at high speeds during gaps, and then slows to a fixed rate when data bytes are recorded or read. The preamble and postamble bits permit the system to lock onto or synchronize with the desired rate during read operation.

2-7-7 Locating data on tape records

Since tape has no physical markings, some means must be used to locate data at a specific point on the tape. This is true for both read and write.

In the system of Fig. 2-15, reflective markers (usually silver-coated foil) are attached to the tape at the beginning and end of tape. These are the beginning-of-tape (BOT) and end-of-tape (EOT) markers. Only the BOT marker is shown in Fig. 2-15. A photocell is mounted near the tape and picks up light from the reflective marker. A change in light on the photocell stops the tape drive at the marker until a new read or write command is given to the tape transport.

Although physical markings can be used for the beginning and end of a tape, specific information at any point between the markings must be identified by means of an *electronic address,* similar to the addresses in ROMs and RAMs. Several addressing systems are used. In one of the most common, the first character or data byte in the data portion of the data block represents the address for that block. A very simplified version of such a system is illustrated in Fig. 2-22.

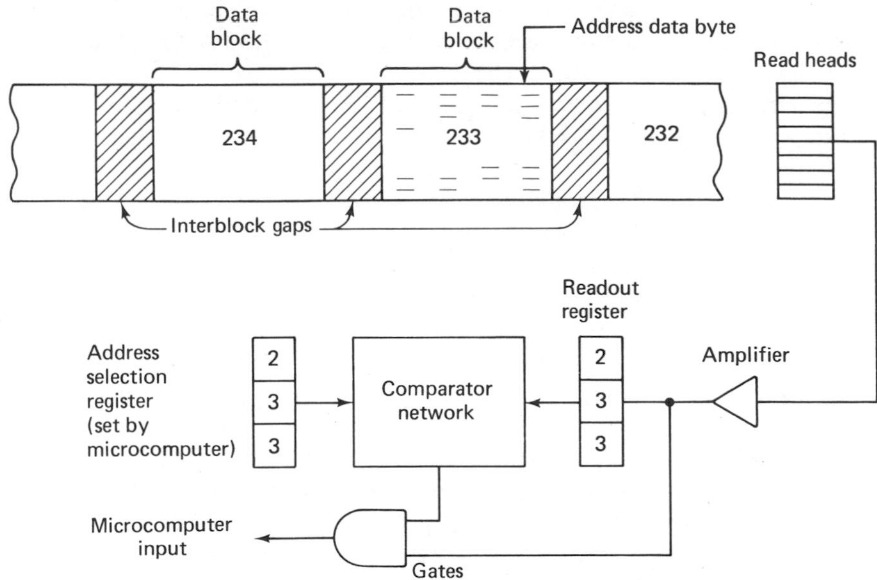

Figure 2-22 Basic circuit for locating data on magnetic-tape records.

As shown, each data block is identified by a three-digit decimal number (from 000 to 255). The read heads are connected through amplifiers and gates to the microcomputer input. When the gates are opened, the information being read is fed into the microcomputer. The gates are opened upon command from a comparator circuit. This comparator compares the data in address selection register with data in the readout register. The address selection register is set to the desired address (data block 233 in the illustration) by the microcomputer, and the tape drive is started at high speed (or search speed). When the tape is at the desired address (data block 233) the readout register indicates 233, and the comparator opens the gates. As the tape continues to move, the information in the 233 data block is read into the microcomputer. The tape stops at the end of the block, or goes to a new address, as determined by the address selection register.

Of course, the circuit of Fig. 2-22 is oversimplified for illustration purposes. In practice, the tape drive and address selection circuits move the tape from address to address, stopping, reversing, and again moving forward at high speeds.

2-8 DISKETTE (FLOPPY DISK) RECORDING BASICS

The floppy disk is the most commonly used magnetic storage device for microprocessor-based systems. The floppy disk itself (often referred to as a *diskette*) is a removable magnetic storage media which is permanently contained in a paper envelope. A *diskette drive* is a low-cost peripheral that performs the electromechanical and read/write functions necessary to record and recover data on the diskette. Figure 2-23 shows a typical diskette and diskette drive mechanism. The diskette is similar to the 45-rpm record. However, the diskette rotates at a speed of 360 rpm (typical), and the data bytes are stored magnetically on concentric tracks over the face of the diskette.

Data are recorded serially on the diskette. Usually, because of the high serial data rates, it is necessary to use special circuits for the serial/parallel conversion, data recovery, and data error checking when interfacing a diskette and a microprocessor system. The hardware that performs this function is often called a *formatter.* The formatter also serves as a buffer between the microprocessor system and the diskette, as shown in Fig. 2-24. The formatter combines with the microprocessor system to control the diskette drive, and sometimes the combination is called a *floppy disk controller.* As used here, the term "controller" includes not only the system hardware, but also those microprocessor programs which directly or indirectly control the diskette drive. The program routines for the diskette are often referred to as floppy disk (or diskette) *drivers* or *control modules.*

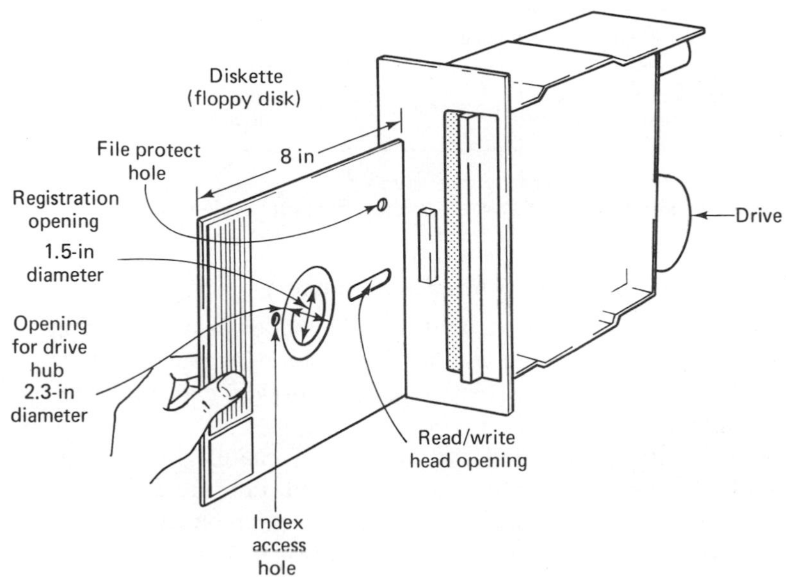

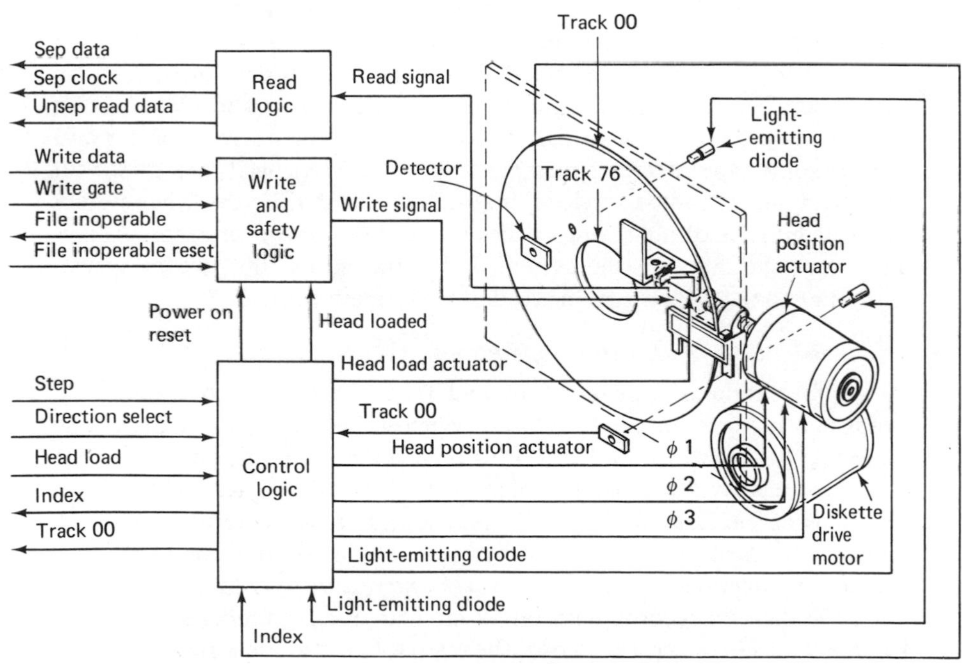

Figure 2-23 Typical diskette (floppy disk) and drive.

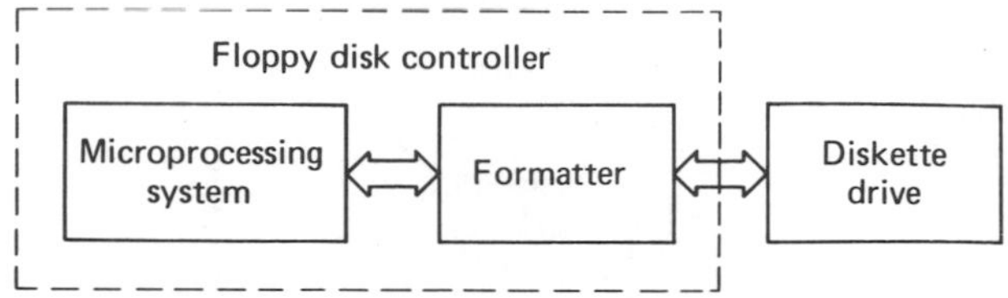

Figure 2-24 Relationship between microprocessor system and diskette.

2-8-1 Interfacing diskettes with microprocessors

There are several considerations that must be made when interfacing diskettes with microprocessors. We will not discuss all of them, since they are essentially the problem of the system designer. However, two considerations are worth mentioning here.

Some diskette drives are designed for "daisy-chain" interfacing, where some of the interconnecting lines are shared and some are dedicated. Other drives use the "radial" interface, where all the interconnecting lines are dedicated. Both interfacing techniques are shown in Fig. 2-25. Each technique has its advantages. The radial interface isolates (or buffers) each drive, whereas the daisy-chain interface requires less system hardware.

No matter what interfacing system is used, the microprocessor is, in effect, busy all the time when used with a diskette. This is due to the high data rates involved. It also means that no other microprocessor peripherals can be serviced while in a diskette read or write operation. This is true provided that the transfer of data is controlled by the microprocessor and not via some type of direct memory address (DMA) hardware. Since no other peripherals can be serviced, interrupts generated by the other system elements must be disabled during diskette read or write operations. Allowances must be made in the system design to permit 100 percent system dedication to the diskette during read or write operations.

2-8-2 Seek and restore operations

Information is transferred to and from the diskette by read/write heads in a manner similar to that described in Sec. 2-7 for magnetic tape recording. (However, data bytes are stored serially on a diskette, whereas most tape cassettes use parallel recording of the data bytes.) One of the functions of the diskette drive is to position the read/write head over the appropriate track where the data bytes are to be recorded or read. This function is sometimes referred to as a *seek and restore* operation.

The diskette records data on 77 circular tracks numbered 00 to 76. In order to access a certain record, the read/write head must first be locked in position at the track which contains that record. The operation that per-

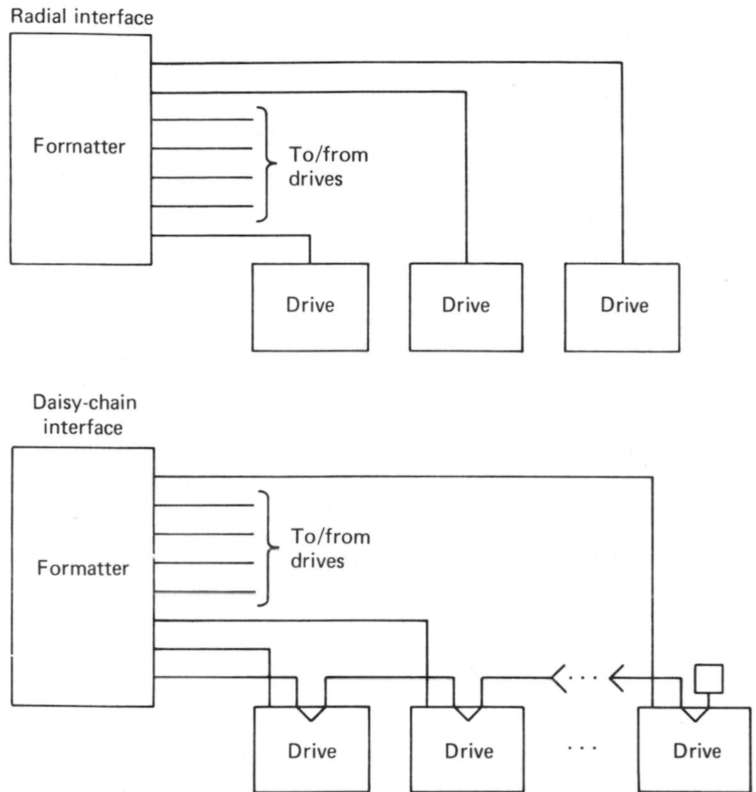

Figure 2-25 Basic arrangements for radial and daisy-chain interfacing formats.

forms the head movement function is called a *seek operation.* For the diskette, a seek is executed by stopping the head one track at a time. The timing between steps is controlled from an inverval timer.

The *restore operation* is similar to the seek operation. The main difference between seek and restore is that a restore operation always moves the read/write head to track 00. After the seek operation is completed, the only way to verify that the proper track has been accessed is to read the track address magnetically recorded on the track (in a manner similar to that for tape, as described in Sec. 2-7-7). When track 00 is accessed, the diskette drive usually generates a "track 00" status signal or flag. As shown in Fig. 2-23, the track 00 signal is often developed by an electromechanical sensor (such as a light-emitting diode, or LED, and a photocell). In some drives, a similar sensor detects when the diskette is at an "index" or start position.

2-8-3 *Data access time*

One of the primary reasons to use a diskette for storage instead of another type of magnetic device, such as a tape cassette, is improved data access time. By definition, access time includes:

1. *Seek time,* or the time for the read/write head positioner to move from its present location to the newly specified location (typically 10 ms/track).
2. *Settle time,* or the time for the positioner to settle onto a new track (typically 10 ms from the last step pulse).
3. *Latency time,* or the time required for the diskette to rotate to the desired position (typically 83.3 ms, average).

The diskette spins at a fixed rate of 167 ms per revolution. On the average, the data will be one-half of a revolution, or 83.3 ms, away from the head. This is known as *average latency time.*

2-8-4 *Typical diskette specifications*

A typical diskette system records and reads data at 250K bits/s or 4 μs/bit. When used with a typical 8-bit parallel microprocessor system, the data rate is 250 ÷ 8 = 31.25K bytes/s, or 32 μs/byte.

A single (typical) diskette has a capacity of 2,050,048 bits, or 256,256 bytes on the 77 tracks. There are 26 sectors on each track and 128 bytes on each sector. Track recording formats are discussed further in Sec. 2-8-6.

2-8-5 *Functional description of a typical diskette drive*

The diskette drive shown in Fig. 2-23 consists of read/write and control electronics, drive mechanism, read/write head, track positioning mechanism, and the removable diskette. These components perform the following functions: interpret and generate control signals, move read/write head to the selected track, read and write data. The relationship and interface signals for the internal functions of the drive are shown in Fig. 2-23.

General operation. The head-positioning actuator positions the read/write head to the desired track on the diskette. The head load actuator loads the diskette against the read/write head and data may then be recorded or read from the diskette. The head position actuator, which consists of an electrical stepping motor and lead screw, positions the lead screw clockwise or counterclockwise in 15° increments. A 15° rotation of the lead screw moves the read/write head one track position. The microprocessor system increments the stepping motor to the desired track.

The diskette drive motor rotates the spindle at 360 rpm through a belt-drive system. Fifty or 60 Hz power is accommodated by changing the drive pulley. A registration hub, centered on the face of the spindle, positions the diskette. A clamp that moves in conjunction with the latch handle fixes the diskette to the registration hub.

The read/write head is in direct contact with the diskette. The head surface has been designed to obtain maximum signal transfer to and from the magnetic surface of the diskette with minimum head/diskette wear. The read/write head is mounted on a carriage that is located on the head position actuator lead screw, as shown in Fig. 2-26. The diskette is held in a plane perpendicular to the read/write head by a platen located on the base casting. The precise registration assures perfect compliance with the read/write head. The diskette is loaded against the head with a load pad actuated by the head load solenoid.

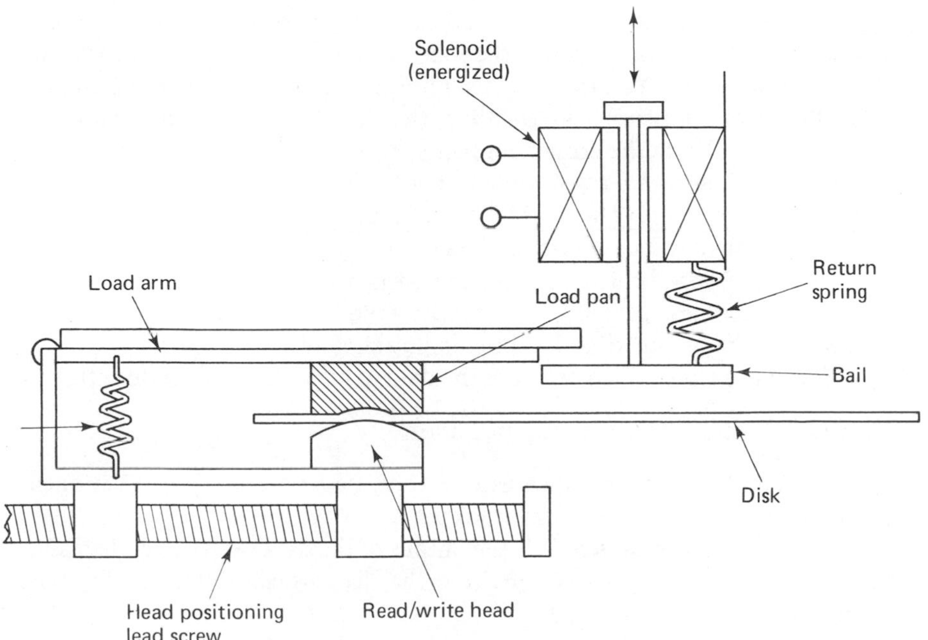

Figure 2-26 Head load and carriage assembly.

Signal interface. The signal interface between the diskette drive and the microprocessor system consist of lines required to control the drive, and to transfer data to and from the drive. All lines in the signal interface are digital in nature (the signals are in pulse form) and either provide signals to the drive (input) or provide signals to the microprocessor (output).

Input. There are six input signal lines:

1. *Direction select,* which defines the direction of motion of the read/write head when the *step* line is pulsed. An open circuit or binary 1 defines

the direction as out, and if a pulse is applied to the step line, the read/write head will move away from the center of the diskette (toward track 00). Conversely, if the direction select input is shorted to ground, or a binary 0 is applied, the direction of motion is defined as in, and if a pulse is applied to the step line, the read/write head will move toward the center of the diskette (toward track 76).

2. *Step input,* which is a control signal that causes the read/write head to move with the direction of motion defined by the direction select line. The access motion is initiated on each binary 0 to binary 1 transition of the step input signal.

3. *Load head,* which is a control signal to an actuator that allows the diskette to be moved into contact with the read/write head. A binary 1 deactivates the head load actuator and causes a bail to lift the pressure pad from the diskette. This removes the load from the diskette and read/write head. A binary 0 level on the load head line activates the head load actuator and allows the pressure pad to bring the diskette into contact with the read/write head with the proper contact pressure.

4. *File inoperable reset,* which provides a direct reset for the file inoperable output signal. The file inoperable condition is reset when a binary 0 is applied to the file inoperable reset line.

5. *Write gate,* which controls the writing of data on the diskette. A binary 1 on the write gate line turns off the write function. A binary 0 enables the write function, and disables the stepping circuitry.

6. *Write data,* which provides the data to be written on the diskette.

Output. There are six output signal lines:

1. *Track 00,* which indicates when the read/write head is positioned at track zero (the outermost data track).

2. *File inoperable,* which is the output of the data safety circuitry, and is at a binary 0 level when a condition that jeopardizes data integrity has occurred.

3. *Index,* which is a signal provided by the diskette drive once each revolution (166.67 ms) to indicate the beginning of the track. Normally, the index signal is at binary 1 and makes the transition to 0 level for a period of 1.7 ms once each revolution.

4. *Separated data,* which comprises the interface line over which read data are sent to the microprocessor system. The signals written on the diskette (using a frequency-modulation system) are demodulated by the drive electronics and are converted to data pulses. The data pulses (representing the data bytes on the diskette) are sent over the separated data line. Normally, the separated data signal is at binary 1, and each data bit recorded on the diskette causes the signal to make the transition to a 0 level for 200 ns.

5. *Separated clock,* which provides the microprocessor system the

clock bits recorded on the diskette. The levels and timing are identical to the separated data line except that a separated clock pulse occurs each 4 us. The recording formats are discussed in Sec. 2-8-6.

6. *Unseparated read data,* which provides raw data (clock and data bits together) to the microprocessor.

2-8-6 Diskette recording formats

The format of the data recorded on the diskette is totally a function of the microprocessor system. Data bytes are recorded on the diskette using frequency modulation as the recording mode. Each data bit recorded has an associated clock bit recorded with it. Data bits written on and read back from the diskette take the form as shown in Fig. 2-27. As shown, the clock bits and data bits (if present) are interleaved in the form of *bit cells.* By definition, a bit cell is the period between the leading edge of one clock bit and the leading edge of the next clock bit.

A *data byte,* when referring to serial data being written onto or read from the diskette drive, is defined as eight consecutive bit cells. The MSB cell is defined as bit cell 0 and the LSB cell is defined as bit cell 7. When reference is made to a specific data bit (such as data bit 3), it is with respect to the corresponding bit cell (bit cell 3).

During a write operation, bit cell 0 of each byte is transferred to the diskette drive first, with bit cell 7 being transferred last. Correspondingly, the most significant byte of data is transferred to the diskette first, and the least significant byte last. When data bytes are being read back from the

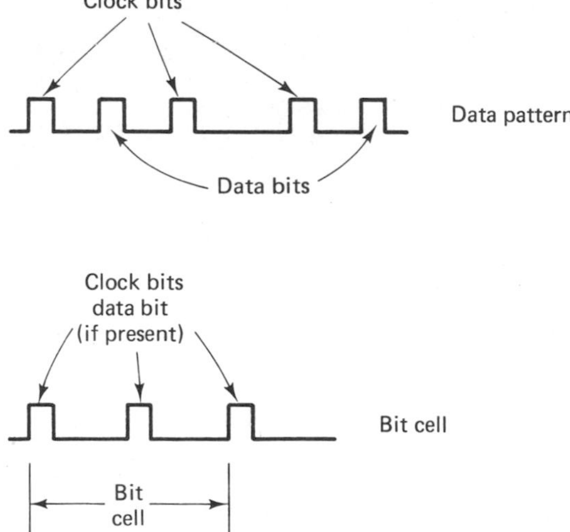

Figure 2-27 Basic diskette data bit recording format, showing formation of a bit cell.

drive, bit cell 0 of each byte is transferred first, with bit cell 7 last. As with reading, the most significant byte is transferred first from the drive to the microprocessor. Figure 2-28 illustrates the relationship of the bits within a byte. Figure 2-29 illustrates the relationship of bytes for read and write data.

Track formats. Each of the 77 tracks (00 through 76) may be formatted in numerous ways, dependent upon the microprocessor system. The diskette drive shown in Fig. 2-23 uses either *index recording* or *sector recording.*

Index recording format. With index recording, the microprocessor may record one long record or several smaller records. Each track is started by a physical index pulse, and then each record is preceded by a unique recorded identifier. This type of recording is called *soft sectoring.* Figure 2-30 shows a typical index recording format.

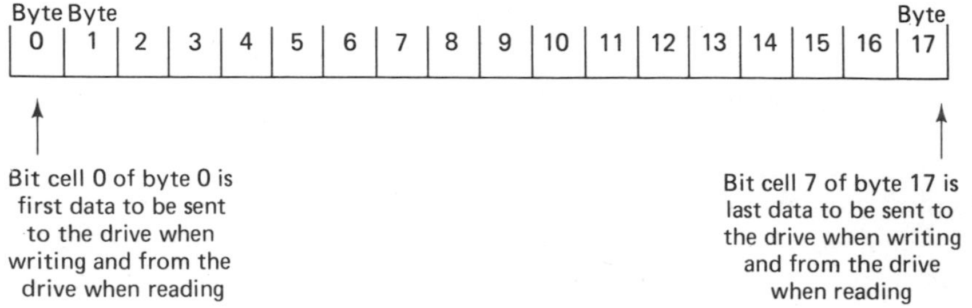

Figure 2-28 Relationship of bits within a data byte as recorded on a diskette (floppy disk).

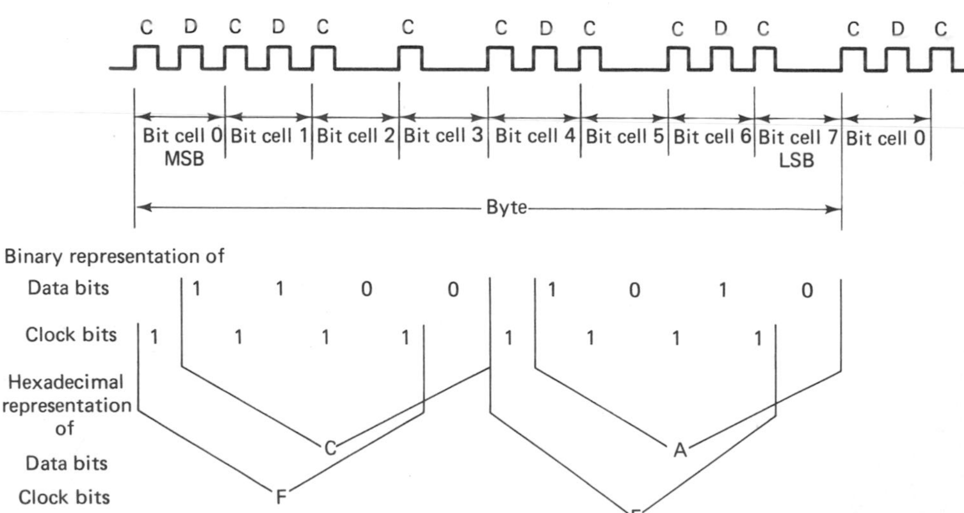

Figure 2-29 Relationship of bytes for read and write data as recorded on a diskette (floppy disk).

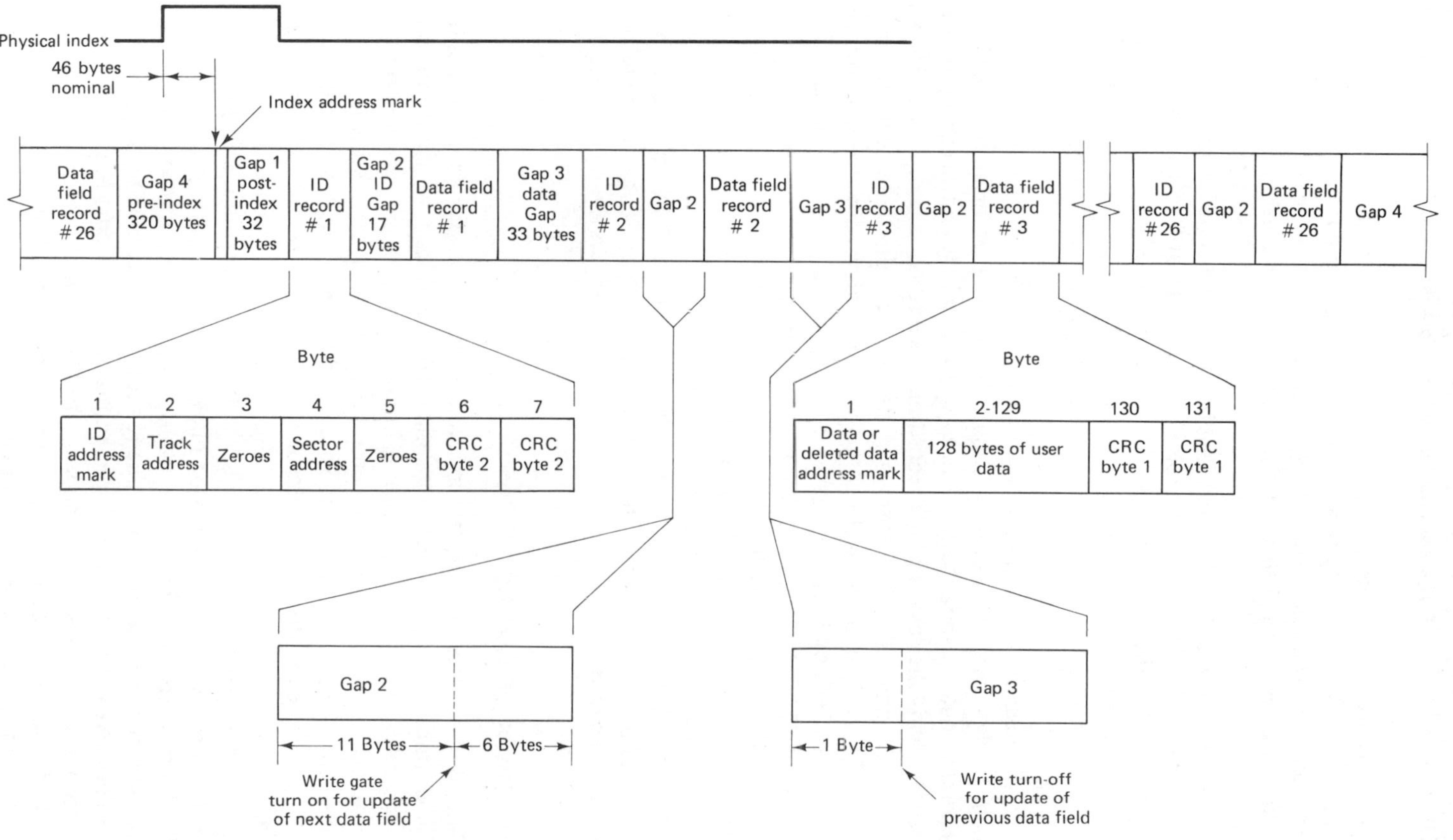

Figure 2-30 Diskette index recording format with soft sectoring.

Sector recording format. With sector recording, the microprocessor may record up to 32 sectors (or records) per track. (Some systems use 26 sectors per track.) Each track is started by a physical index pulse, and each sector is started by a physical sector pulse. This type of recording is called *hard sectoring.*

Keep in mind that the recording format is controlled primarily by the microprocessor. However, the choice between hard and soft sectoring is set by the diskette drive. For soft sectoring (index recording) only one index hole is required in the diskette, as shown in Fig. 2-23. For hard sectoring (sector recording) one hole is required for each sector (typically 32 or 26 holes).

Because of the great variety of formats available, we will not discuss them further here. However, it should be noted that diskette recordings generally include some feature to ensure the safety and accuracy of the records. As is the case for tape recordings, described in Sec. 2-7-6, diskette recordings generally use a form of CRC (cyclic redundancy check). Each field (Fig. 2-30) written on the diskette is appended with two CRC bytes. These two CRC bytes are generated by circuits that count all the data bits, starting with bit 0 of the address mark and ending with bit 7 of the last byte within a field (excluding the CRC bytes). When a field is read back from the diskette, the data bits (from bit 0 of the address mark to bit 7 of the second CRC byte) are divided by the CRC number. A nonzero remainder indicates an error bit in the data read back, while a remainder of zero indicates that the data bytes have been read back correctly. The nonzero (error) indication can be used to stop the drive, send a flag to the microprocessor, and so on.

2-9 DATA COMMUNICATIONS

Data communications is the transmission of data from one point to another. For example, the data from one microcomputer can be transmitted to another microcomputer in the same building, in the same city, or to a city across the country. Likewise, a central computer can serve several users on a *time-sharing* basis, each with the users at different remote locations.

At present, most data-transmission systems use the telephone and teletype lines already available. This requires the translation of microcomputer information (generally in the form of pulses) into a form suitable for transmission across telephone lines. A *data set* and/or a *modem* are the devices used to perform the translation. In most modems, the pulses are used to modulate an audio tone (or tones) that can be transmitted over the lines. At the receiving end, the audio tones are demodulated and converted back to pulses by the modem. Both serial and parallel transmission methods can be used. However, serial is the most popular, since only a single line (or pair of lines) is required.

Many data communications systems in present use include a standard telephone, in addition to the circuits for modulation and demodulation of the pulses. This permits operators to communicate before and after the transmission of data. In a typical situation, the operator will dial a number, putting the operator in touch with operators at the opposite end of the line. After making the necessary arrangements, data can be transmitted back and forth between the locations via the modems and lines.

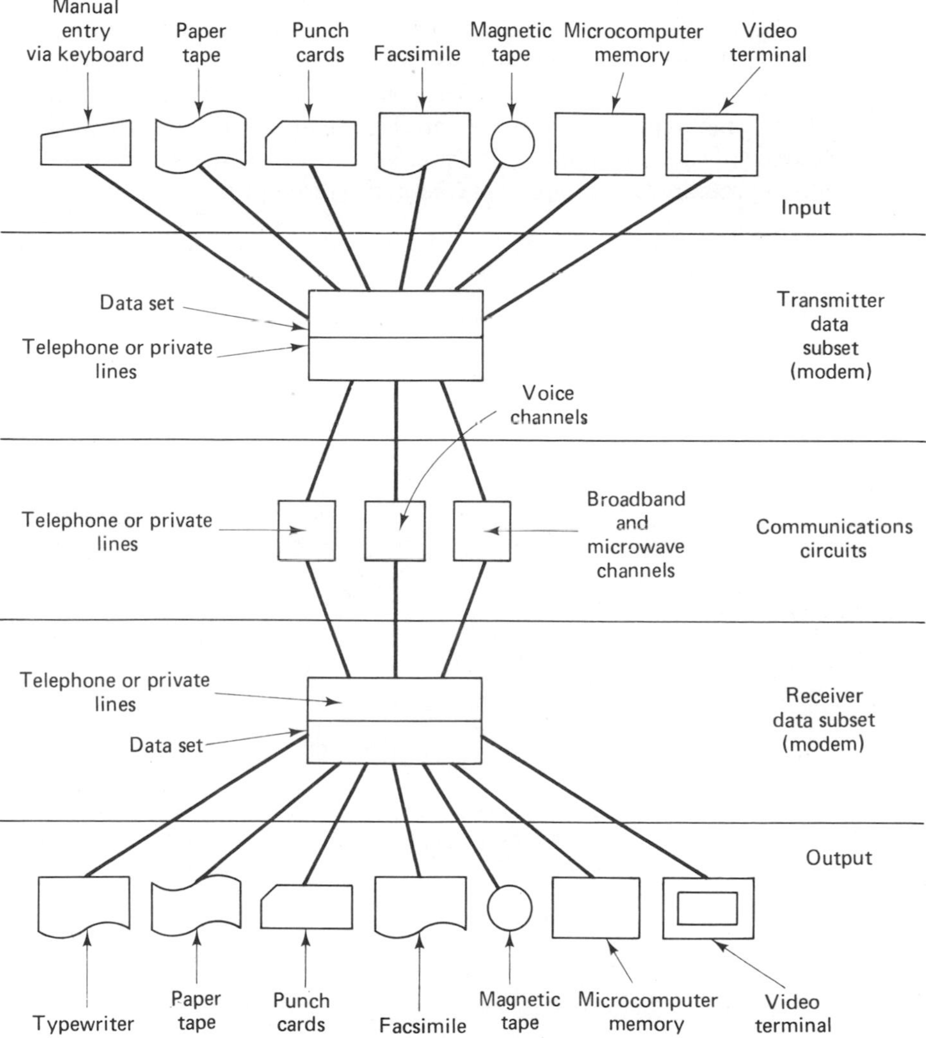

Figure 2-31 Data transmission (communication) systems in common use.

Any of the input/output units described thus far can be used as terminal devices, in association with the data set or modem. The video terminal described in Sec. 2-3 is one of the most popular terminal devices. For example, a time-sharing user can have a visual display unit and a data set or modem at an office location connected by telephone lines to a computer at some remote point. The input and output of the visual display unit is connected through the data set or modem to the telephone lines. With this arrangement, the video terminal is (in effect) connected directly to the computer.

Figure 2-31 summarizes the data transmission systems in common use. Because these systems are essentially the same for microcomputers and conventional (larger) computers, we will not discuss them in any detail. The only major difference between microcomputer and conventional computer data communications is in the interface adaptors (or I/O circuits) used between the microcomputer and the communications system. Interface devices and programs are discussed in Chapters 3 through 7.

3 RCA COSMAC 1800 Microprocessors

This chapter is devoted entirely to the COSMAC 1800 microprocessor system manufactured by the Solid State Division of RCA Corporation. The chapter starts with a discussion of basic system hardware and system interfacing, then proceeds on with basic programming techniques. The discussion on programming is supplemented with a sample program. Next, the development aids are described.

The details presented in this chapter represent only a small fraction of the data taken from the manufacturer's literature (manuals and data sheets). However, the information presented is sufficient for a reader of any level to evaluate the system. The chapter also provides a realistic view of actual state-of-the-art microprocessor-based systems. This supplements the theoretical and typical descriptions of Chapters 1 and 2.

The system includes a complete set of hardware for microprocessor-based systems and microcomputers (microprocessor, ROMs, RAMs, I/Os, and miscellaneous latches, decoders, ports, etc.). The manufacturer also makes available a variety of aids for design, development, test, debugging, and troubleshooting of system components. The basic system relationships of the ICs are discussed in Sec. 1-13 and shown in Fig. 1-25. Readers should study Sec. 1-13 before proceeding with this chapter.

3-1 MICROPROCESSOR ARCHITECTURE AND NOTATION

Figure 3-1 illustrates the internal structure of the COSMAC microprocessor CDP1802. The architecture is based on a register array of 16 general-purpose, 16-bit *scratch-pad* registers. (The term "scratch pad" applies to registers used for the temporary storage of data.) Each scratch-pad register, R, is designed by a 4-bit binary code. Hex notation is used for the 4-bit code.

Using hex notation, R(3) refers to the 16-bit scratch-pad register designated or selected by the binary code 0011. R(3).0 refers to the low-order (less-significant) 8 bits (or byte) of R(3). R(3).1 refers to the high-order (more-significant) byte of R(3).

Three 4-bit registers labeled N, P, and X hold the 4-bit binary codes (hex digits) that are used to select individual 16-bit scratch-pad registers. The 16 bits contained in a selected scratch-pad can be used in several ways.

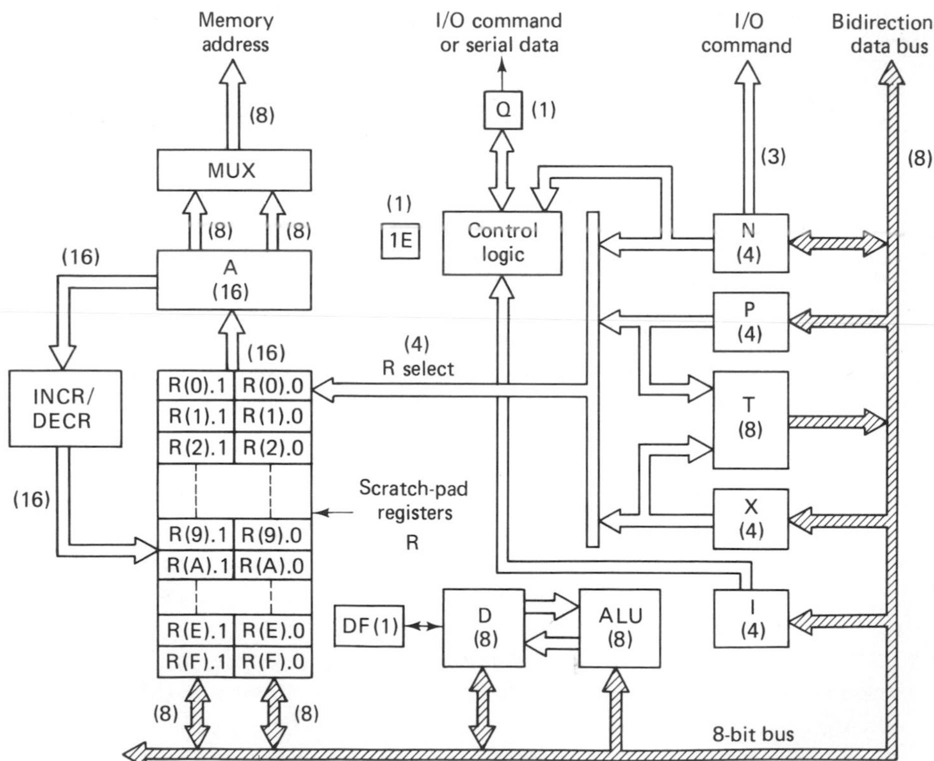

Figure 3-1 Internal structure of COSMAC microprocessor CDP1802.

Considered as two bytes, the 16 bits may be sequentially placed on the eight external memory address lines (address bus) for memory read/write operations. Either byte can also be gated to the 8-bit data bus for subsequent transfer to the D register. The 16-bit value in the A register can also be incremented or decremented by 1 and returned to the selected scratch-pad register to permit a scratch-pad register to be used as a counter.

The notation R(X), R(N), or R(P) is used to refer to a scratch-pad register selected by the 4-bit code in X, N, or P, respectively. Figure 3-2 illustrates the transfer of a scratch-pad register byte, designed by N, to D. The left half of Fig. 3-2 illustrates the initial contents of various registers (in hex). The operation performed can be written as

$$R(N),0 \longrightarrow D$$

This expression indicates that the low-order 8 bits contained in the scratch-pad register designated by the hex digit in N are to be placed into the 8-bit D register. The designated scratch-pad register is left unchanged.

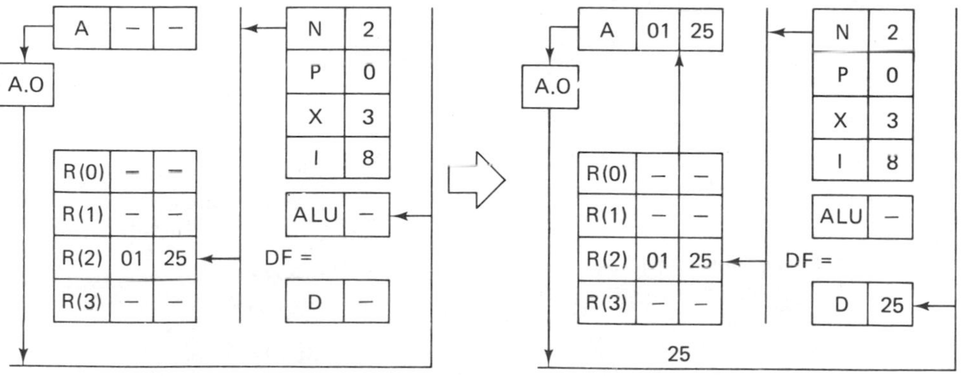

Figure 3-2 Use of N designator to transfer data from scratch-pad register R(2) to the D register.

The right half of Fig. 3-2 illustrates the contents of the CDP1802 registers after this operation is completed. The following sequence of steps is required to perform this operation:

1. N is used to select R. (left half of Fig. 3-2)
2. R(n) is copied into A.
3. A.0 is gated into the bus. (right half of Fig. 3-2)
4. The bus is gated to D.

Memory or I/O data used in various COSMAC operations are transferred by means of the common data bus. Memory cycles involve both an address and the data byte itself. Memory addresses are provided by the contents of scratch-pad registers. An example of a memory operation is

$$M(R(X)) \longrightarrow D$$

This expression indicates that the memory byte addressed by R(X) is copied into the D register. Figure 3-3 illustrates this operation. The following steps are required:

1. X is used to select R.
2. R(X) is copied into A.
3. A addresses a memory byte.

(left side of Fig. 3-3)

4. The addressed memory byte is gated to the bus.
5. The bus is gated to D.

(right side of Fig. 3-3)

Reading a byte from memory does not change the contents of memory.

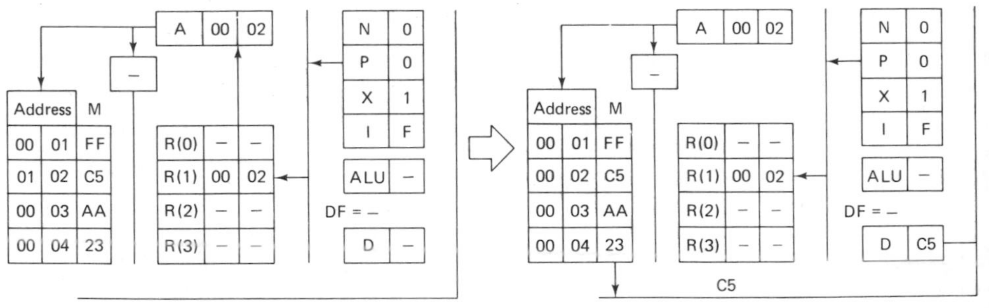

Figure 3-3 Transfer of data from memory to the D register.

The 8-bit arithmetic-logic unit (the ALU shown in Fig. 3-1) performs arithmetic and logical operations. The byte stored in the D register is one operand, and the byte on the bus (obtained from memory) is the second operand. The resultant byte replaced the operand in D. A single-bit register data flag (DF in Fig. 3-1) is set at 0 if no carry results from an add or shift operation. DF is set to 1 if a carry does occur. During subtraction, DF = 0 if the subtrahend is larger than the minuend, indicating that a borrow has occurred. The 8-bit D register is similar to the accumulator found in many computers.

The internal flip-flop Q can be set or reset by instructions, and can be sensed by conditional branch instructions. The state of Q is also available as a microprocessor output and is often used as an I/O command or with serial data transmission.

3-1-1 Microprocessor instruction format

As discussed in Chapter 1, all microprocessor operations or functions are specified by a sequence of instruction codes stored in external memory. A one-byte instruction format is applicable for most instructions. Two 4-bit hex digits contained in each instruction byte are designated as I and N, as shown in Fig. 3-4.

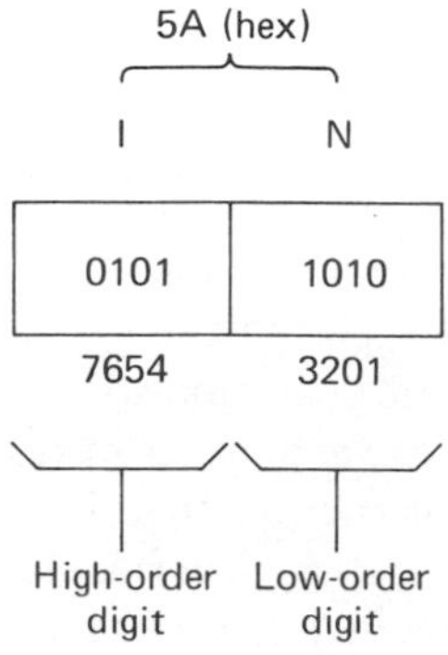

Figure 3-4 One-byte instruction format.

For most instructions, the execution requires two machine cycles. The first cycle fetches or reads the appropriate instruction byte from memory and stores the two hex instruction digits in registers I and N. The values in I and N specify the operation to be performed during the second machine cycle. I specifies the instruction type. Depending upon the instruction, N either designates a scratch-pad register, as shown in Fig. 3-2, or acts as a special code, as described in the following paragraphs.

As in the case of any microprocessor, instructions are normally executed in sequence. A program counter is used to address successively the memory bytes representing instructions (as discussed in Chapter 1). However, in the COSMAC architecture, *any one* of the 16-bit scratch-pad registers can be used as a program counter. The value of the hex digit contained in register P determines which scratch-pad register is currently being used as the program counter. The operations performed by the instruction fetch cycle are:

$$M(R(P)) \longrightarrow I,N;R(P) + 1$$

Instruction fetch cycle. Figure 3-5 illustrates a typical instruction fetch cycle. Register P has been previously set to 1, designating R(1) as the current program counter. During the instruction fetch cycle, the "0298" contained in R(P) is placed in A and used to address the memory. (As shown in Fig. 3-1, register A is connected to the memory address bus through a multiplexer.) The F4 instruction byte at M (or at memory address 0298) is

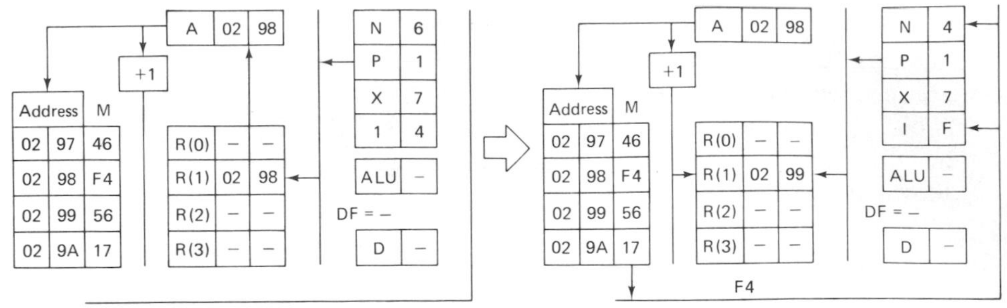

Figure 3-5 Typical instruction fetch cycle.

read into the data bus and then gated into I and N. The value in A is incremented by 1 (to 0299) and replaced the original value in R(P). The next machine cycle will perform the operation specified by the values in I and N.

Following the execute cycle, another instruction fetch cycle will occur. R(P) designates the next instruction byte in sequence (or instruction 56, which is located at address 0299). Alternately repeating instruction fetch and execute cycles in this manner causes sequences of instructions that are stored in memory to be executed.

Branch and skip instructions. Although most of the program instructions have a one-byte format, some are two or three bytes long.

The *immediate* and *short-branch* instructions have a two-byte format, as shown in Fig. 3-6. For example, the instruction "30" followed by "45" will execute an unconditional branch to address 45. Instruction "FC" followed by "22" will execute an immediate add operation in which the operand 22 is added to the second operand from the D register.

The *long-branch* instructions have a three-byte format, as shown in Fig. 3-7. When the instruction C32F9A is encountered, a conditional long-branch operation is performed. In this case, if the DF flag is set, a long branch to the address 2F9A is executed. If DF is not set, the next instruction in sequence is executed (the instruction following 9A).

The *long-skip* instructions are one byte and require no address bytes (as the long-branch instructions do). However, the unconditional long-skip and long-skips with test conditions met will, in effect, have the instruction format shown in Fig. 3-8. If the test conditions are met, the two bytes are

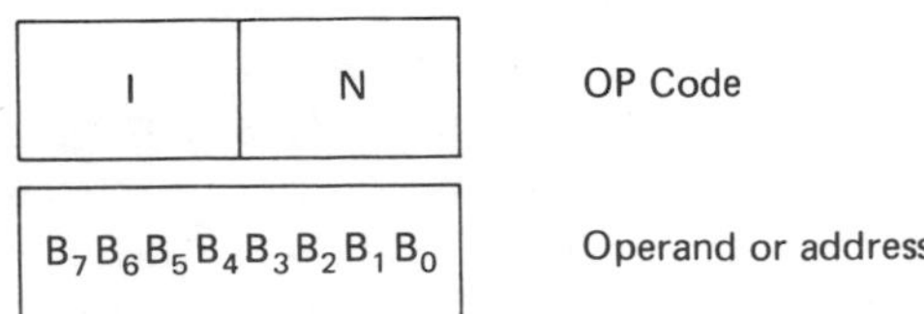

Figure 3-6 Two-byte instruction format.

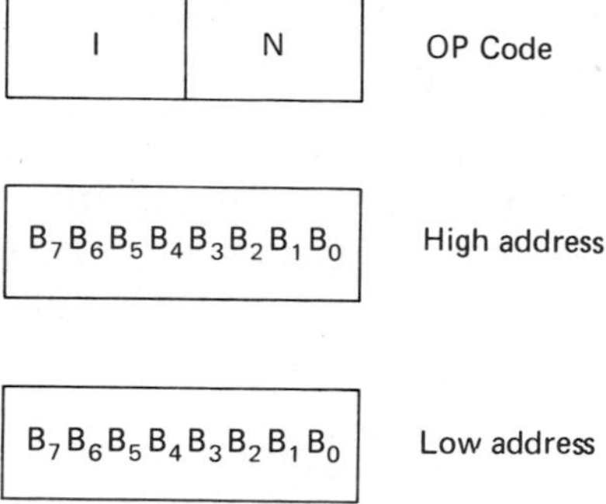

Figure 3-7 Three-byte format for long-branch instructions.

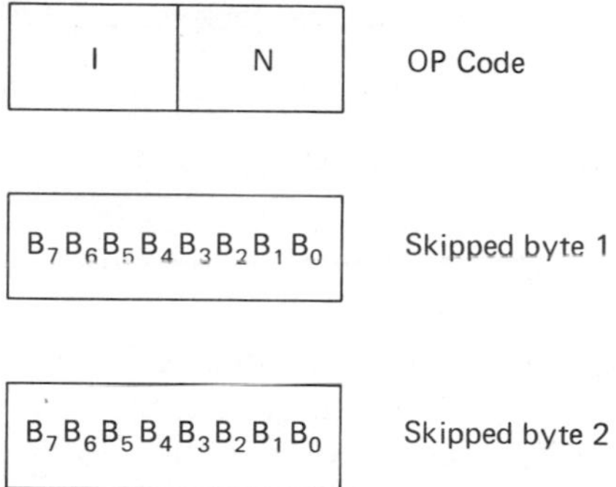

Figure 3-8 Three-byte format for long-skip instructions.

skipped. If the test condition is not satisfied, execution continues at the first byte following the operation code.

3-1-2 Microprocessor timing

The microprocessor machine cycle, during which an instruction byte is fetch from memory, is called *state 0* (S0). The machine cycle during which the instruction is executed is called *state 1* (S1). During execution of a program, the CDP1802 generally alternates between S0 and S1, as shown in Fig. 3-9. Each machine cycle (S0 or S1) is internally divided into eight time intervals, as shown in Fig. 1-26. Each time interval is equivalent to one cycle (T). The rate at which machine cycles occur is, therefore, one

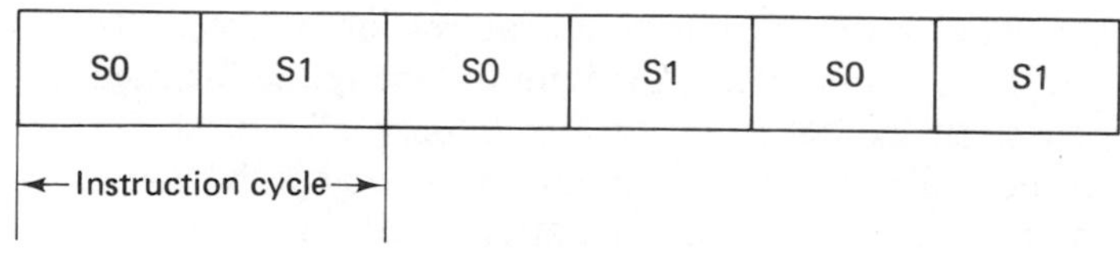

Figure 3-9 Sequence of machine states for normal instruction cycles.

eighth of the clock frequency. The *instruction time* is 16T for two machine cycles, and 24T for three machine cycles.

The majority of instructions require the same fetch/execute time. The only exceptions are the long-branch and long-skip instructions. These instructions require two machine cycles for execution. The instruction cycle in these cases contains three machine cycles (one fetch and two execute). The state sequencing will then be as shown in Fig. 3-10.

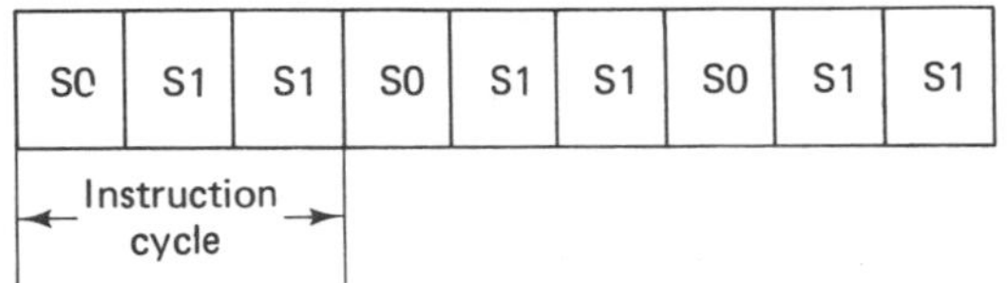

Figure 3-10 Sequence of machine states for long-branch and long-skip instruction cycles.

3-1-3 Microprocessor addressing modes

There are four basic modes of addressing in the COSMAC architecture: *register, register-indirect, immediate,* and *stack.*

Register. In register addressing, the address of the operand is contained in the four lower-order bits (the N-field of the instruction byte, as shown in Fig. 3-4). This addressing mode allows the user to directly address any of the 16 scratch-pad registers for the purpose of counting or moving data in or out of registers. Typical instructions in this category are DECREMENT (2N) and GET LOW (8N).

Register-indirect. Register-indirect addressing is a variation of indirect addressing which uses microprocessor registers as pointers to memory. In this mode, the selected register *contains no data, but the address of data.* A 4-bit address in register N will specify one of the 16 scratch-pad registers whose contents are the address of data in memory.

It should be noted that this form of indirect addressing is the dominant mode in the COSMAC microprocessor system. Indirect addressing allows the user to address up to 65 kilobytes of memory with a single one-byte instruction.

Immediate addressing. In immediate addressing, register R(P) addresses memory so that the operand is the byte following the instruction. R(P) is incremented after its use. Immediate addressing allows the user to extract data from the program stream without setting up special constant areas in memory and a pointer to them. Operations ADD IMMEDIATE (FC) and LOAD IMMEDIATE (F8) are examples of immediate instructions.

Stack. In stack addressing, one specific microprocessor register is *implied* as the pointer to memory. Often, R(X) is used, and in one case R(2) is used. [As discussed in Chapter 1, a stack is a last-in/first-out (LIFO) working area in memory used to store immediate calculations and to keep track of transfers of control between parts of a program.]

Addressing mode advantages. The strength of the COSMAC architecture, and its ability to optimize program size and efficiency as compared with more conventional minicomputer architectures, lies in these four addressing modes and the liberal number of registers. By using stacks for working space, immediate addressing for all constants, register pointers for tabular and vector arrays, and the registers themselves for miscellaneous counters and switches, it is possible to make the best use of program space. This subject is discussed further in Sec. 3-4.

3-1-4 Multiple program counters

As discussed in Chapter 1, a program counter is a register that points to the next instruction to be fetched and executed. COSMAC provides the unique capability to specify, in a single instruction, any one of the 16 registers as the program counter. This feature makes it possible to maintain pointers to several different programs simultaneously and to transfer control quickly from one to another. A point to a program that services an interrupt request is a special and important example of this feature.

3-1-5 Instruction repertoire or set

The microprocessor is capable of performing 91 operations in response to the corresponding instruction. The operations include register operations, memory reference, logic, arithmetic, branching, skip, control, and I/O byte transfer. For obvious reasons, we will not duplicate the entire instruction set (or instruction repertoire as it is called by the manufacturer) here. However, we will discuss examples of the instruction set to illustrate how microprocessors work and to provide a basis for comparison with other microprocessors.

Instruction identification. Each instruction is designated by its 2-bit hex code and by a name. A description of the operation is provided using symbolic notation. A two- to four-letter abbreviated name is also given and is used as a mnemonic for assembly language programming. This is illustrated in Fig. 3-11, which illustrates a typical register operation or instruction as it appears in the user manual. The instruction of Fig. 3-11 is to "increment register N by 1." The letters INC represent the mnemonic, INCREMENT REG N is the verbal description of the operation, R(N) + 1 is the symbolic description, and 1N is the 2-bit hex code. When I = 1, the scratch-pad

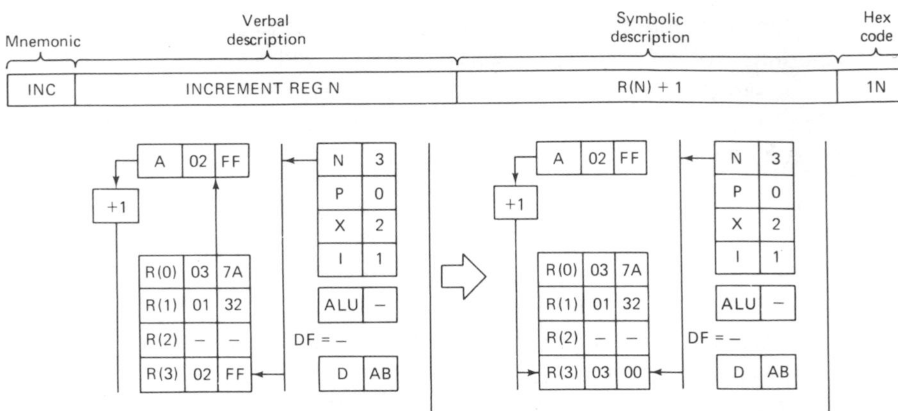

Figure 3-11 Example of instruction 1N—INCREMENT R(N).

register specified by the hex digit in N [which happens to be register R(3) in this example] is incremented by 1. Note that FFFF + 1 = 0000.

Arithmetic operations. This group of instructions provides the operations ADD, SUBTRACT, and REVERSE SUBTRACT. The three basic instructions are augmented with instructions to handle immediate data, data with carry or borrow, and immediate data with carry or borrow. In general, R(X) is the pointer to one operand in memory. The other operand is found in D. For immediate data, R(P) is used as the pointer and addresses the byte in memory after the instruction, called the *immediate byte.*

An example of arithmetic operations is shown in Fig. 3-12, which illustrates an "Add with carry" function. As shown, when I = 7 and N = 4, the specified byte plus the content of DF are added to the contents

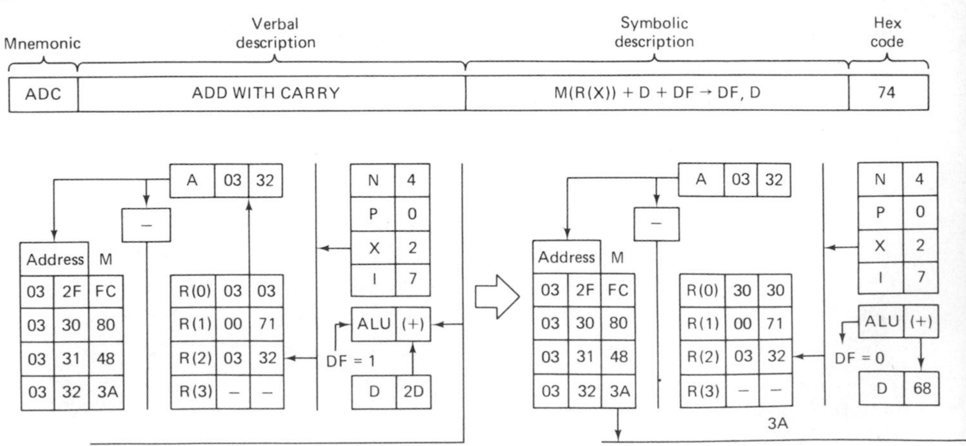

Figure 3-12 Example of instruction 74—ADD WITH CARRY.

of the D register. The 8-bit result of the binary addition replaces the D operand. DF will indicate if the addition generated a carry. Using the values shown in Fig. 3-12:

Byte in memory:	3A	= 00111010
D register contents:	2D	= 00101101
DF contains		1
Result:	68	= 01101000
After addition:		
D contains:		01101000
DF contains:		0

The ADD WITH CARRY instruction is useful when multibyte words are to be added. In the sample, two 8-bit words are first added, and generate a carry that must be included in the next-higher-order byte addition, as shown below. For example, add:

```
                 3AF0
               + 2D20
               ------

                    1

                   3A                   F0
                 + 2D                 + 20
                 ----                 ----
DF = 0             68     DF = 1        10

Final result: DF = 0                  6810
```

Branching. In short-branch operation, the current program counter R(P) normally steps sequentially through a list of instructions, skipping over immediate data bytes. When I = 3, a short-branch instruction is executed. The N-code specifies which condition is tested. If the test is satisfied, a branch is effected by changing R(P).

When a branch condition is satisfied, the byte immediately following the branch instruction replaces the low-order byte of R(P). The next instruction byte will be fetched from the memory location specified by the byte following the branch instruction. If the test condition is not satisfied, execution continues with the instruction following the immediate byte. This ability to branch to a new instruction sequence (or back to the beginning of the same sequence to form a *loop*) is fundamental to stored-program computer usefulness.

Because with this instruction only the low-order byte of R(P) can be modified, the range of memory locations that can be branched is limited. Since only the low-order 8 bits can be modified, a short branching is limited to 2^8, or 256 bytes. Each 256-byte memory segment is called a *page.* This same system (or a similar one) of dividing memory into pages is common to many microprocessor-based systems, as it is with larger, conventional computers.

An example of short-branch operation is shown in Fig. 3-13, which illustrates a "conditional branch" function. As shown, when I = 3 and N = 2, a conditional short-branch operation dependent on the value of D is performed. The byte in D is examined and if it is equal to zero, a branch operation is performed. If the value of D is not zero, R(P) is incremented by 1. This increment causes the branch address byte following the 32 instruction to be skipped so that the next instruction in sequence is fetched and executed.

This instruction is often used following an arithmetic logic unit (ALU) operation. For example, an EXCLUSIVE-OR operation (F3 or FB) might be used to compare an input byte with a byte representing a constant. A zero-result byte in D would represent equality. The 32 instruction could then be used to branch to a location in the program for handling this value

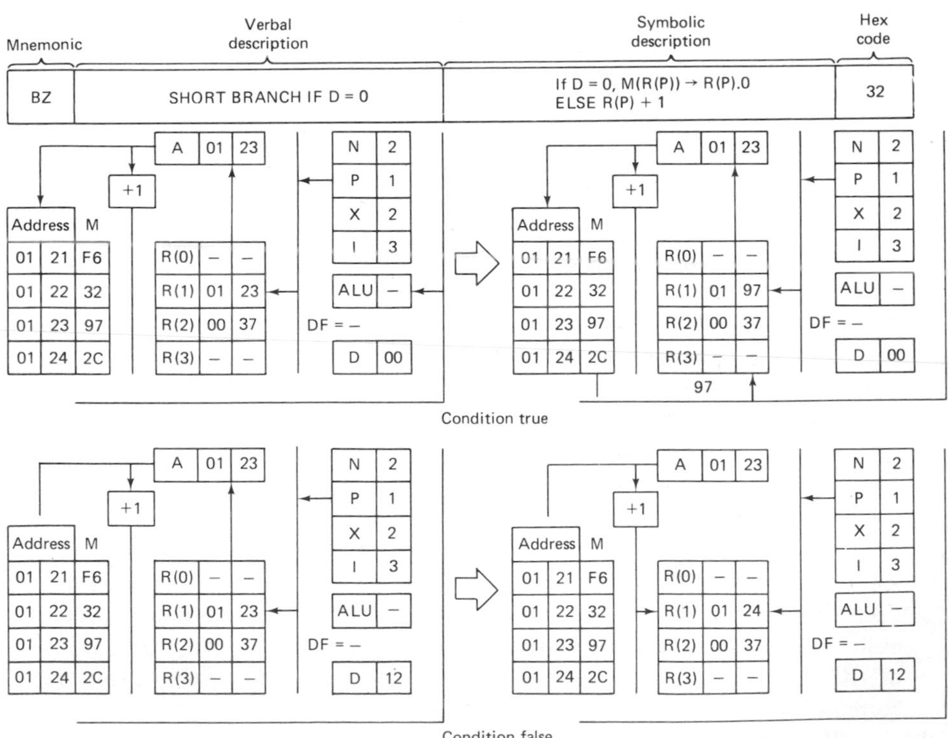

Figure 3-13 Example of instruction 32—SHORT BRANCH IF D = 0 for both false and true conditions.

of the input byte when D = 00, or to proceed to the next instruction in sequence if D ≠ 00, possibly to look for equality with other constants.

The *long-branch* instructions have a two-byte address and allow branching to any location within the full memory space during three machine cycles (one fetch plus two execute). An example of long-branch operation is shown in Fig. 3-14, which illustrates a "conditional branch" function (the same condition as for the short-branch function shown in Fig. 3-13.

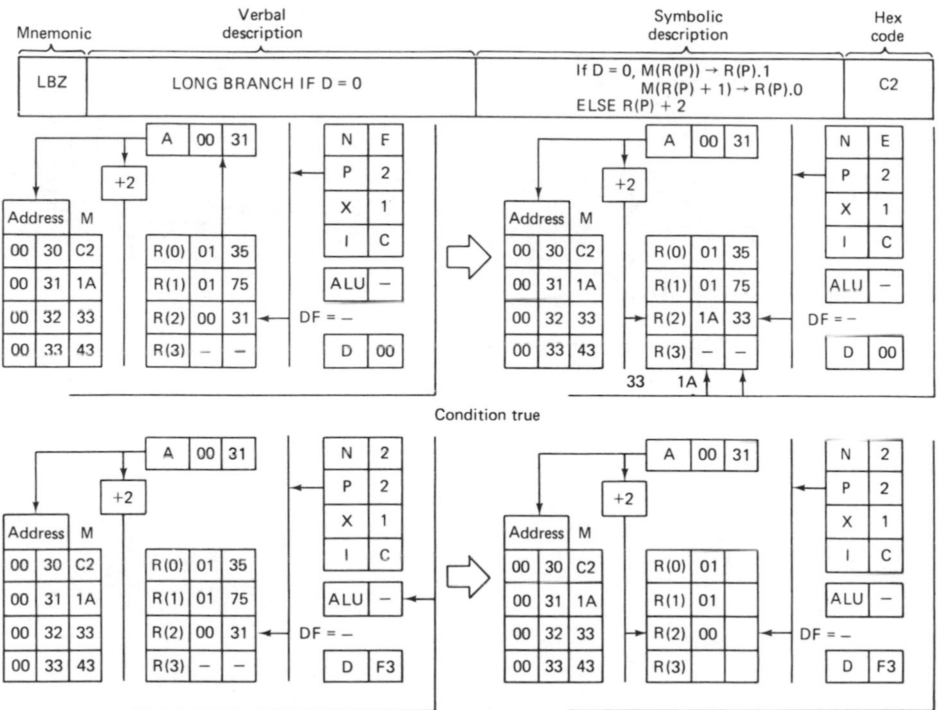

Figure 3-14 Example of instruction C2—LONG BRANCH IF D = 0 for both true and false conditions.

As shown in Fig. 3-14, when I = C and N = 2, a conditional long branch is performed. If D = 0, the contents of the program counter R(P) will be replaced with a specified two-byte address. If D ≠ 0, the program counter is incremented twice. As an example, when C2 is fetched from the instruction sequence C21A3343, the next instruction to be fetched is at memory address 1A if D = 0. If D ≠ 0, execution continues with 43.

Skip instructions. The *short-skip* operation is unconditional and skips the byte following the operation code. The *long skip* is also unconditional, but skips two bytes following the operation code. The other skip instructions are long skips if test conditions for D, DF, or Q are satisfied. The long-skip instructions require three machine cycles, one fetch and two execute, as do the long-branch instructions.

An example of long-skip operation is shown in Fig. 3-15, which illustrates a "conditional long-skip" function (the same condition as for the branch functions shown in Figs. 3-13 and 3-14).

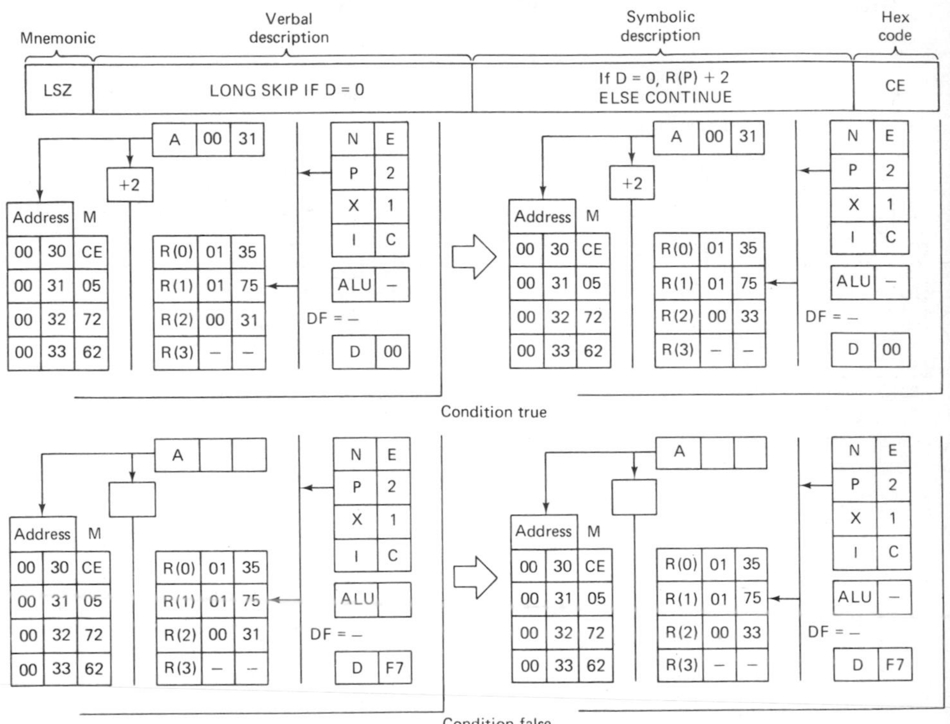

Figure 3-15 Example of instruction CE—LONG SKIP IF D = 0 for both true and false conditions.

Interrupt and subroutine handling. The special interrupt servicing instructions can best be understood by examining the COSMAC response to an interrupt. When an interrupt occurs, it is necessary to save the current configuration of the machine by storing the values of X and P, and to set X and P to new values for the interrupt service program. The interrupt forces X and P to be automatically transferred into a temporary register T (P goes to the lower 4 bits, while X goes into the higher 4 bits), and forces a value of 1 into P and 2 into X. In addition, further interrupts are disabled by resetting the interrupt enable flip-flop (E) to 0. Also, a specific code is provided on the COSMAC state code line. Details of the interrupt servicing are discussed further in Sec. 3-3. The microprocessor functions during a basic interrupt are shown in Fig. 3-16.

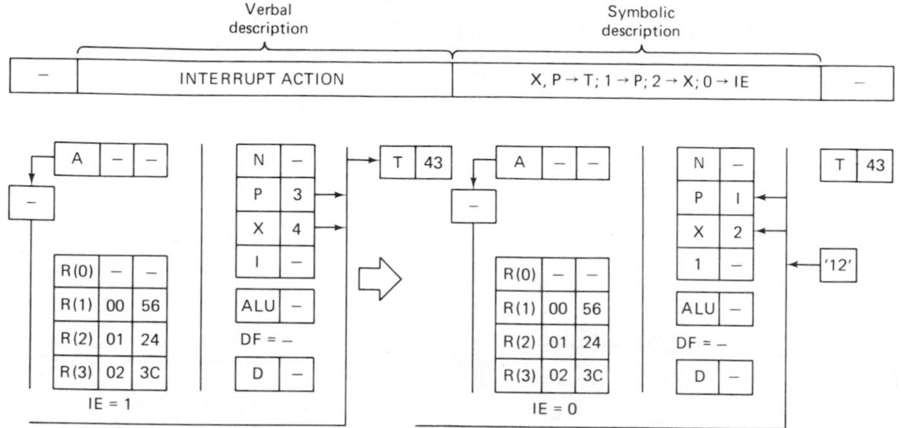

Figure 3-16 Example of INTERRUPT ACTION.

3-2 COSMAC SYSTEM HARDWARE

In addition to the CDP1802 microprocessor, the COSMAC system includes ROMs, RAMs, I/Os, and miscellaneous ICs. The following paragraphs describe these components. Keep in mind that system components are subject to change. For example, certain items can be changed, deleted, or replaced.

3-2-1 ROM ICs

Figure 3-17 illustrates the functional diagrams of system ROMs. The CDP1831 and CDP1833 are static, mask-programmable ROMs. Both units will interface directly with the CDP102 microprocessor without additional components. The CDP1831 contains 4096 bits, organized as 512 words by 8 bits. The CDP1833 contains 8192 bits, organized as 1024 words by 8 bits. Both units respond to 16-bit address, multiplexed on 8 address lines. Address latches are provided on-chip to store the 8 most-significant bits of the 16-bit address.

By mask option, the CDP1831 can be programmed to operate in any 512-word byte of 64-kilobyte memory space. Three chip select signals, CS1, CS2, and $\overline{\text{MRD}}$, are provided. The polarity of the clock (TPA) and CSL/CS2 are user mask-programmable. The chip enable output signal (CEO) goes high when the device is selected. This signal is intended for use as an output disable control for small memory systems.

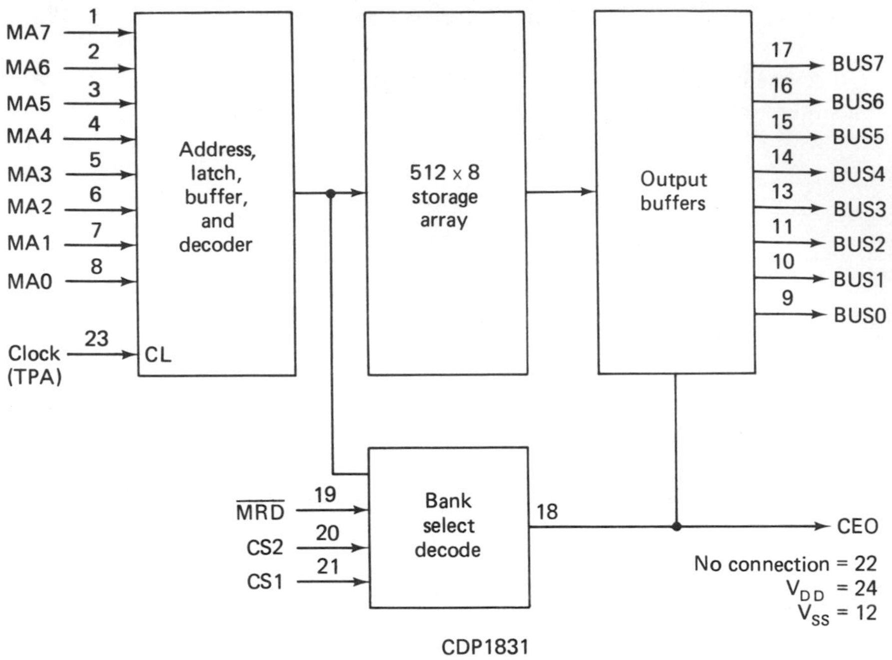

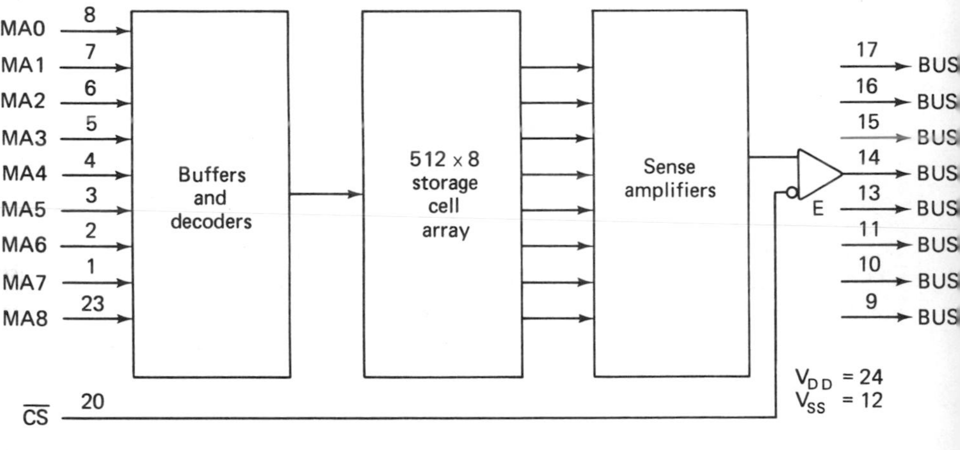

Figure 3-17 RCA static ROM functional diagrams.

By mask option, the CDP1833 can be programmed to operate in any 1024-word byte of 64-kilobyte memory space. Two chip select signals are also provided. The polarity of MUX(TPA), CEI, $\overline{\text{MRD}}$, CS1/CS2 are user mask-programmable. The chip enable output signal (CEO) is high when either CEI is high or the chip is selected. CEO and CEI can be con-

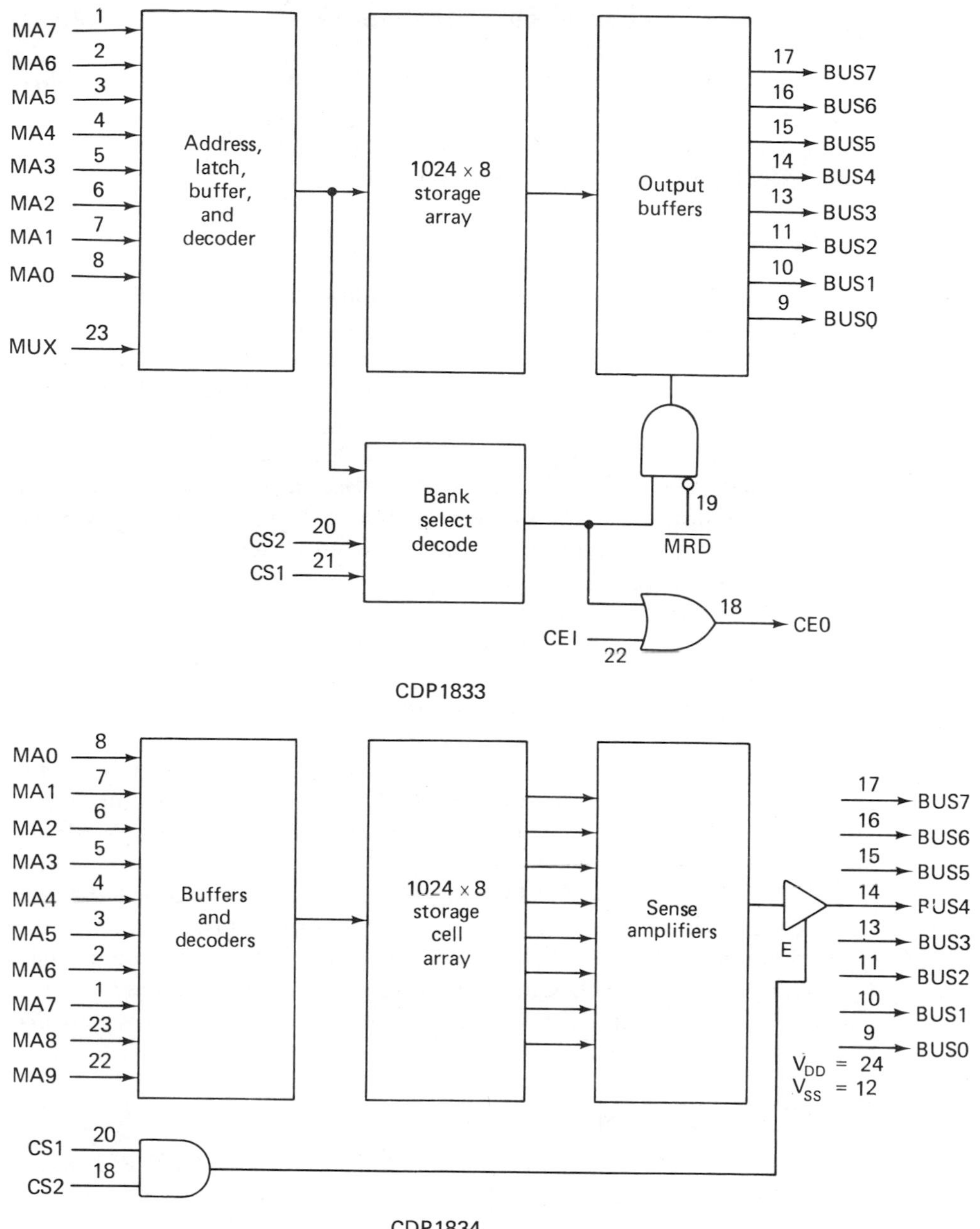

Figure 3-17 (continued)

nected in a daisy chain (Chapter 2) to control selection of RAM chips in a microprocessor system without additional components.

Two versions of the ROMs are available. The CDP1831/33D has a recommended operating voltage range of 3 to 12 V. The CDP1831/33CD voltage range is 4 to 6 V.

The CDP1832 and CDP1834 are static, mask-programmable ROMs. These ROMs are completely static; no clocks are required. Two chip select inputs CS1/CS2 are provided for memory expansion. The polarity of each chip select input is user-mask-programmable.

3-2-2 RAM ICs

Figure 3-18 illustrates the functional diagrams of system RAMs. The output state of the CDP1821S (1024-word by 1-bit) is a function of the input address and chip select states only. Valid data will appear at the output in one access time following the latest address change to a selected chip. After valid data appears, the address may then be changed immediately. It is not necessary to clock the chip select input or any other input terminal for fully static operation. Thus, the chip select input may be used as an additional address input. With the device in an unselected state ($\overline{CS} = 1$), the internal write circuitry and output sense amplifiers are disabled. This feature allows the three-state data outputs from many arrays to be OR-tied to a common bus for ease of memory expansion.

The CDP1822S (256-word by 4-bit) has separate inputs and data outputs and is operated from a single voltage supply. Two chip select inputs, of opposite polarity, are provided to simplify system expansion. The $\overline{MRD}$ signal (output disable control) provides wire-OR capability and is also useful in common input/output systems. After valid data appears at the output, the address inputs may be changed immediately. These output data will be valid until either the $\overline{MRD}$ signal goes high or the device is de-selected ($\overline{CS1}$ = high or CS2 = low).

The CDP1824 (32-word by 8-bit) (Fig. 1-20) is fully decoded and does not require a precharge or clocking signal for proper operation. The unit has common (bidirectional) input and output and is operated from a single voltage supply. The $\overline{MRD}$ signal (output disable control) enables the three-state output drivers and overrides the $\overline{MWR}$ signal. A $\overline{CS}$ input is provided for memory expansion.

3-2-3 Eight-bit input/output port

Figure 1-24 illustrates the functional diagram of the CDP1852, which is an 8-bit input/output port. Operation of the CDP1852 is described in Sec. 1-12-1.

3-2-4 Universal asynchronous receiver/ transmitter (UART)

Figure 3-19 illustrates the functional diagrams of the CDP1854 UART. UARTs are I/O devices that provide the necessary formatting and control

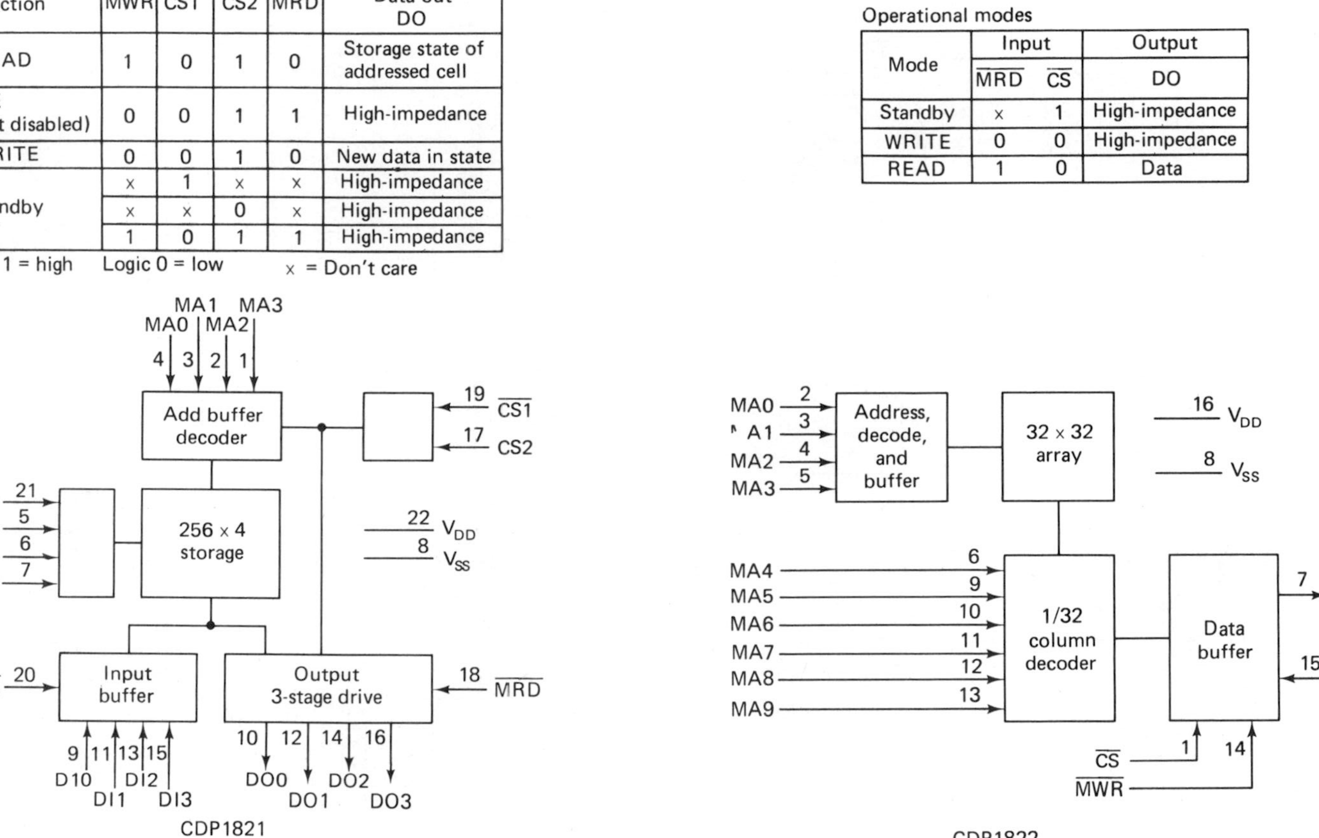

Operational modes

Function	$\overline{MWR}$	$\overline{CS1}$	CS2	$\overline{MRD}$	Data out DO
READ	1	0	1	0	Storage state of addressed cell
WRITE (output disabled)	0	0	1	1	High-impedance
WRITE	0	0	1	0	New data in state
Standby	x	1	x	x	High-impedance
	x	x	0	x	High-impedance
	1	0	1	1	High-impedance

Logic 1 = high   Logic 0 = low   x = Don't care

Operational modes

Mode	Input		Output
	$\overline{MRD}$	$\overline{CS}$	DO
Standby	x	1	High-impedance
WRITE	0	0	High-impedance
READ	1	0	Data

Figure 3-18 RCA RAM functional diagrams.

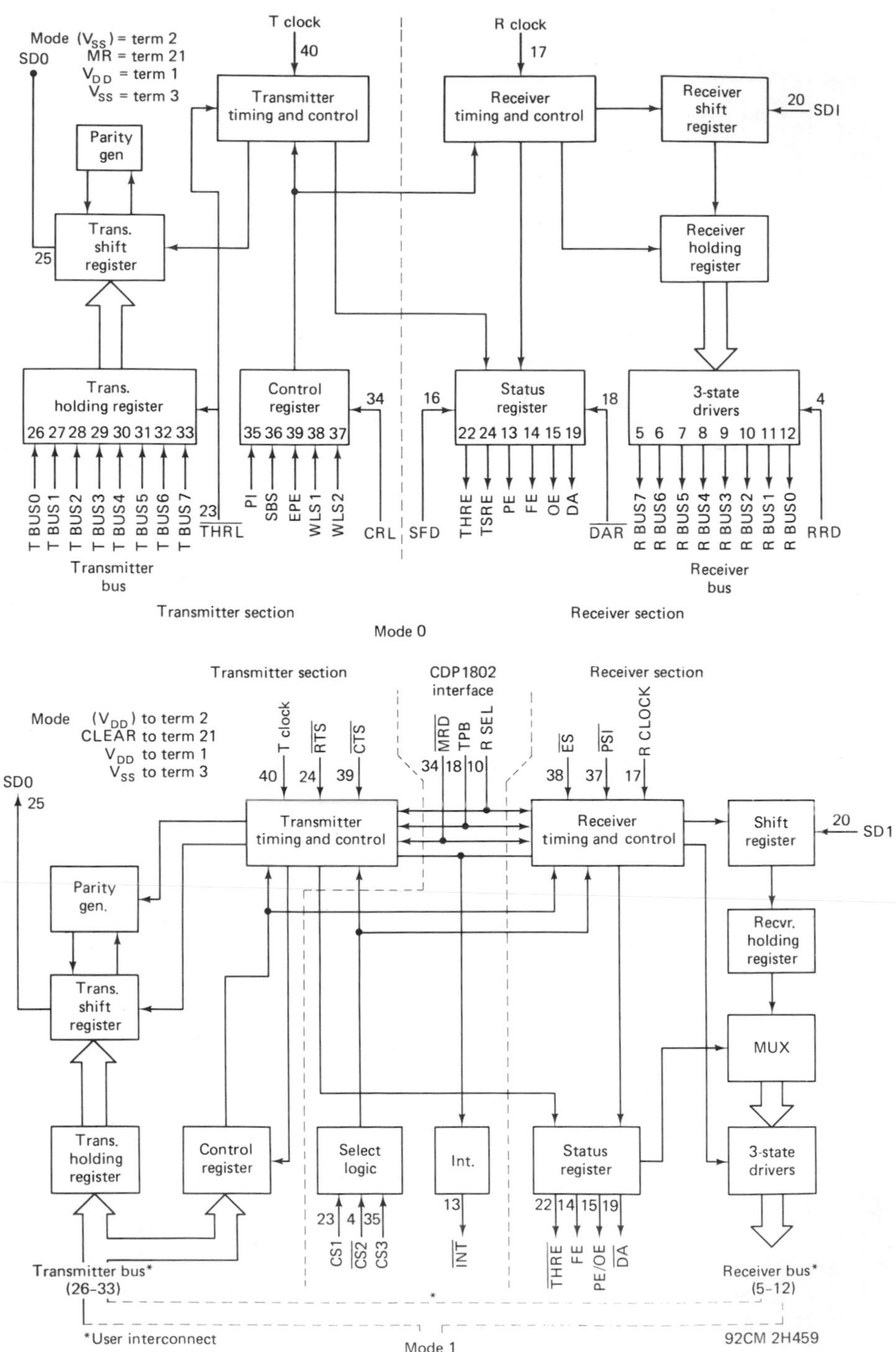

Figure 3-19 RCA UART functional diagrams.

for interfacing between serial and parallel data. For example, a UART can be used to interface between a peripheral with serial I/O ports and the 8-bit CDP1802 microprocessor parallel data system. The CDP1854 is capable of *full duplex operation* (that is, simultaneous conversion of serial input data to parallel output data, and parallel input data to serial output data), as well as half-duplex (where only one half of the capability is used).

The UART can be programmed to operate in one of two modes by using the mode control input. When the mode input is high (MODE = 1, Fig. 3-19), the CDP1854 is directly compatible with the CDP1802 microprocessor system without additional interface circuitry. When the mode input is low (MODE = 0), the device is functionally compatible with industry standard UARTs. The UART is also pin-compatible with these types, except that pin 2 is used for the mode control input instead of a $V_{GG} = -12$ V supply connection.

The following is a description of the industry standard (MODE = 0) operation of the UART. Both models are described fully in the UART data sheet.

Initialization and controls in Mode = 0. The MASTER RESET (MR) input is pulsed, resetting the control, status, and receiver holding registers, and setting the SERIAL DATA OUTPUT (SDO) signal high. Timing is generated from the clock inputs, transmitter clock (TCLOCK), and receiver clock (RCLOCK), at a frequency equal to 16 times the serial data bit rate. When the receiver data input rate and the transmitter data output rate are the same, the TCLOCK and RCLOCK inputs may be connected together. The CONTROL REGISTER LOAD (CRL) input is pulsed to store the control inputs PARITY INHIBIT (PI), EVEN PARITY ENABLE (EPE), STOP BIT SELECT (SBS), and WORD LENGTH SELECTs (WLS1 and WLS2). These inputs may be wired to the proper voltage levels (V_{SS} or V_{DD}) instead of being dynamically set, and CRL may be wired to V_{DD}. The CDP1854 is then ready for transmitter and/or receiver operation.

Transmitter operation in Mode = 0. Figure 3-20 is the timing diagram for transmitter operation in Mode = 0. At the beginning of a typical transmitting sequence, the transmitter hold register is empty (THRE is HIGH). A character is transferred from the transmitter bus to the transmitter holding register by applying a low pulse to the TRANSMITTER HOLDING REGISTER LOAD ($\overline{\text{THRL}}$) input, causing THRE to go low. If the transmitter shift register is empty (TSRE is HIGH) and the clock is low, on the next high-to-low transition of the clock, the character is loaded into the transmitter shift register, preceded by a start bit. (Serial data transmission is discussed further in Sec. 2-2-1 and illustrated in Fig. 2-3).

Serial data transmission begins one-half clock period later with a start bit, and 5 to 8 data bits, followed by the parity bit (if programmed) and

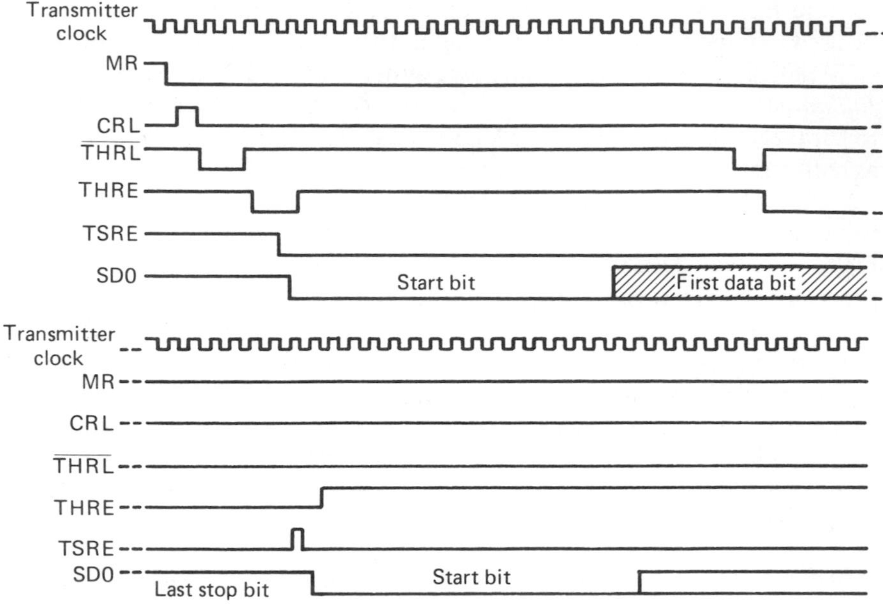

Figure 3-20 Transmitter timing diagram.

stop bits. The THRE output signal goes high one-half clock period later on the high-to-low transition of the clock. When THRE goes high, another character can be loaded into the transmitter holding register for transmission, beginning with a start bit immediately following the last stop bit of the previous character. This process is repeated until all characters have been transmitted. When transmission is complete, THRE and transmitter shift register empty (TSRE) will both be high. The format of serial data is shown in Fig. 3-21 (compare this with Fig. 2-3). Duration of each serial output data bit is determined by the transmitter clock frequency (f_{CLOCK}) and will be $16/f_{CLOCK}$.

Receiver operation in Mode = 0. Figure 3-22 is the timing diagram for receiver operation in Mode = 0. The receive operation begins when a start bit is selected at the SERIAL DATA IN (SDI) input. After detection of a high-to-low transition on the SDI line, a divide-by-16 counter is enabled and a valid start bit is verified by checking for a low-level input 6½ receiver clock periods later. When a valid start bit has been verified, the following data bits, parity bit (if programmed), and stop bit(s) are shifted into the receiver shift register at clock pulse 6½ in each bit time. If so programmed, the parity bit is checked and receipt of a valid stop bit is verified. On count 6½ of the first stop bit, the received data are loaded into the receiver holding register. If the word length is less than 8 bits, zeros (low output voltage

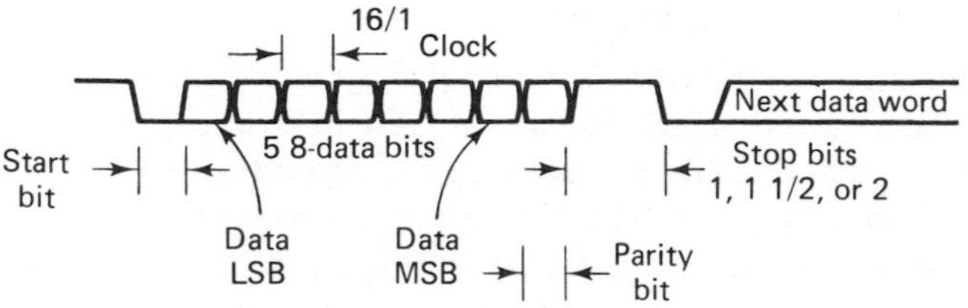

Figure 3-21 Serial data word format.

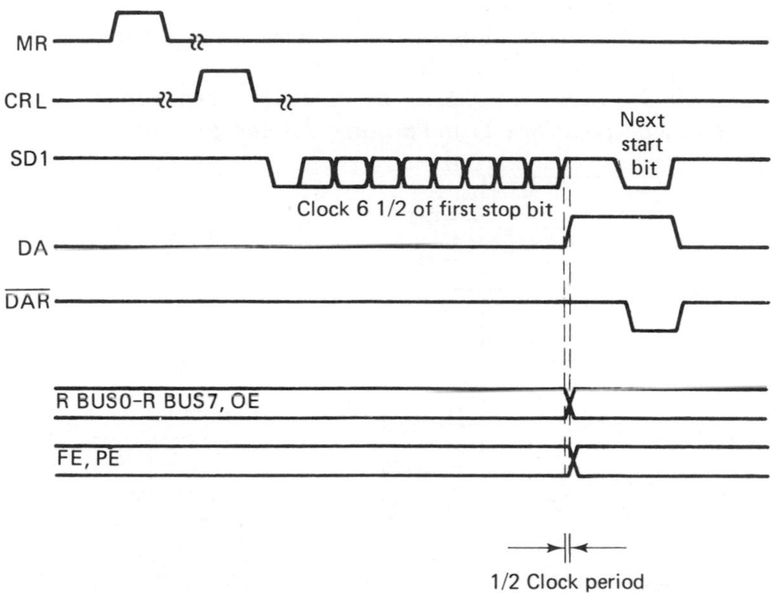

Figure 3-22 Receiver timing diagram.

level) are loaded into the unused leftmost bits. If DATA AVAILABLE (DA) has not been reset by the time the receiver holding register is loaded, the OVERRUN ERROR (OE) signal is raised. One-half clock period later, the PARITY ERROR (PE) and FRAMING ERROR (FE) signals become valid for the character in the receiver holding register. The DA signal is also raised at this time.

The three-state output drivers for DA, OE, PE, and FE are enabled when STATUS FLAG DISCONNECT (SFD) is low. When RECEIVER REGISTER DISCONNECT (RRD) goes low, the receiver bus three-state output drivers are enabled and the data bus is available at the RECEIVER BUS (R BUS O-R BUS 7) outputs. Applying a negative pulse to the DATA AVAILABLE RESET (DAR) resets DA. The preceding sequence of operations is repeated for each serial character received.

3-2-5 N-bit 1 of 8 decoder

Figure 3-23 illustrates the functional diagram of the CDP1853 decoder. These decoders are designed for use in CDP1800 microprocessor systems. Only one of eight outputs is true or high, depending on the status of the inputs (EN, N0, N1, and N2). For example, when EN, N0, and N1 are high (binary 1) and N2 is low (binary 0), bit 3 is selected. The status of the EN input is determined by two factors, the chip enable (CE) line and two clock inputs (clocks A and B, TPA and TPB). When CE is high, the selected output will be true (high, binary 1) from the trailing edge of CLOCK A (high-to-low transition) to the trailing edge of CLOCK B (high-to-low transition). All outputs are low when the device is not selected (CE = 0) and during conditions of CLOCK A and CLOCK B. Although designed for use with the CDP1800 system, the CDP1853 can also be used as a general 1-of-8 decoder for I/O and memory system applications.

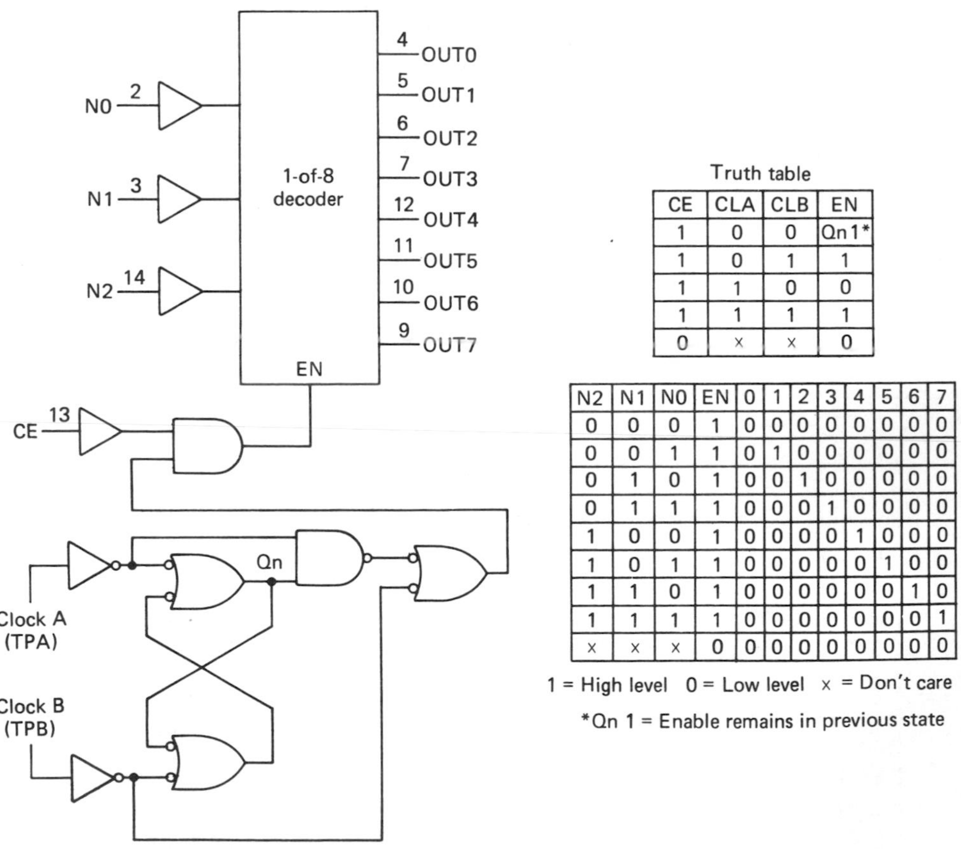

Truth table

CE	CLA	CLB	EN
1	0	0	Qn 1*
1	0	1	1
1	1	0	0
1	1	1	1
0	x	x	0

N2	N1	N0	EN	0	1	2	3	4	5	6	7
0	0	0	1	0	0	0	0	0	0	0	0
0	0	1	1	0	1	0	0	0	0	0	0
0	1	0	1	0	0	1	0	0	0	0	0
0	1	1	1	0	0	0	1	0	0	0	0
1	0	0	1	0	0	0	0	1	0	0	0
1	0	1	1	0	0	0	0	0	1	0	0
1	1	0	1	0	0	0	0	0	0	1	0
1	1	1	1	0	0	0	0	0	0	0	1
x	x	x	0	0	0	0	0	0	0	0	0

1 = High level 0 = Low level x = Don't care

*Qn 1 = Enable remains in previous state

Figure 3-23 RCA N-bit 1-of-8 decoder functional diagram and truth tables.

3-2-6 Four-bit bus buffers/separators

Figure 3-24 illustrates the functional diagrams of the CDP1856 and CDP1857 buffers/separators. These units are 4-bit noninverting bus separators designed for use in the CDP1800 microprocessor systems. Both units can be controlled directly by the CDP1802 microprocessor without the use of additional components.

The CDP1856 is designed for use as a bus buffer or separator between the CDP1802 data bus and memories. When the $\overline{\text{MRD}}$ signal = 0 (low), it enables the three-state bus drivers (DB0–DB3) and outputs data from the DATA-IN terminals to the data bus. When $\overline{\text{MRD}}$ = 1 (high), it disables the three-state bus drivers and enables the three-state data output drivers (D00–D03), thus transferring data from the data bus to the DATA-OUT terminals.

The CDP1857 is designed for use as a bus buffer or separator between the CDP data bus and I/O devices. When $\overline{\text{MRD}}$ = 1, it enables the three-state bus drivers (DB0–DB3) and transfers data from the DATA-IN lines onto the data bus. When $\overline{\text{MRD}}$ = 0, it disables the three-state bus drivers (DB0–DB3) and enables the three-state data output drivers (D00–D03), thus transferring data from the data bus to the DATA-OUT terminals.

Both CDP1856 and CDP1857 provide a chip select (CS) input signal which, when high (1), enables the bus-separator three-state output drivers. The direction of data flow, when enabled, is controlled by the MRD input signal. Both units can be used as bidirection bus buffers when the corresponding data-in (DI) and data-out (DO) terminals are connected to each other.

3-2-7 Four-bit latch with decode

Figure 3-25 illustrates the functional diagrams of the CDP1858 and CDP1859 latch decoders. These units are 4-bit latch decoders designed for use in the CDP1800 microprocessor systems. Both units are specifically designed for use as memory-system decoders and interface directly with the CDP1802 microprocessor multiplexed address bus at maximum clock frequency.

The CDP1858 interfaces the CDP1802 address bus and up to 32 CDP1822 256 × 4 RAMs (Sec. 3-2-2) to provide a 4-kilobyte RAM system. No additional components are required. The CDP1856 generates the chip selects required by the CDP1822 RAM. The chip select outputs are a function of the address bits connected to inputs MA0 through MA3. The MA0–MA3 address bits are latched at the trailing edge of TPA (generated by the CDP1802). When ENABLE = 1 (V_{DD}), the CS outputs = 0 (V_{SS}), and the CE outputs = 1. When ENABLE = 0, the outputs are enabled and correspond to the binary decode of the inputs. The ENABLE input can be used for memory system expansion.

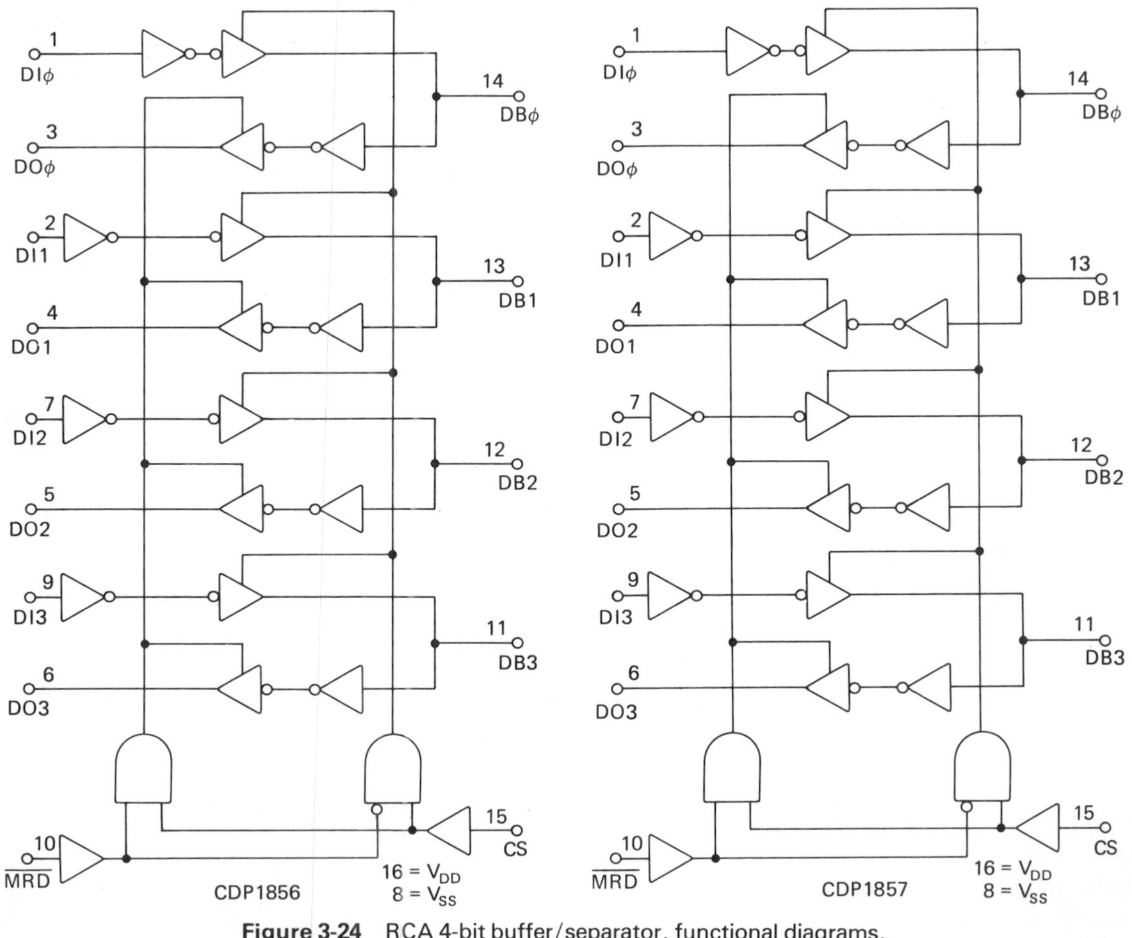

Figure 3-24 RCA 4-bit buffer/separator, functional diagrams.

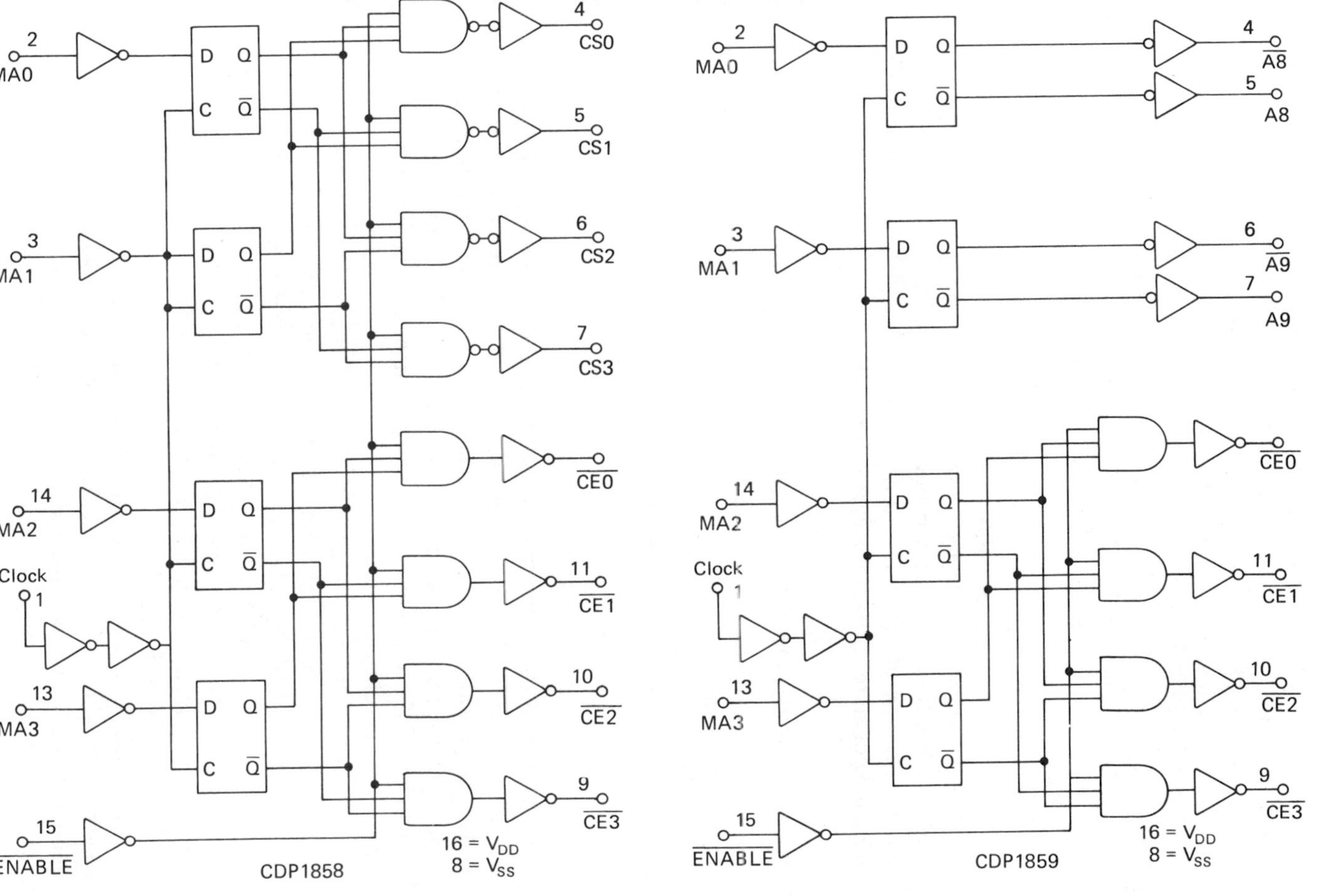

Figure 3-25 RCA 4-bit latch decoder, functional diagrams.

The CDP1858 is also compatible with nonmultiplexed address bus microprocessors. By connecting the CLOCK input to 1 (V_{DD}), the latches are in the data-following mode, and the decoded output can be used in general-purpose memory-system applications.

The CDP1859 interfaces the CDP1802 address bus and up to 32 CDP1821 1024 × 1 RAMs (Sec. 3-2-2) to provide a 4-kilobyte RAM system. The CDP1859 generates the chip selects required by the CDP1821 RAM. The chip select outputs are a function of the address bits connected to inputs MA2 and MA3. The address bits connected to inputs MA0 and MA1 are latched by the trailing edge of TPA (generated by the CDP1802) to provide the two additional address lines required by the CDP1821 when used in a CDP1802-based system. When ENABLE = 1, the CE outputs are 1s; when ENABLE = 0, the CE outputs are enabled and correspond to the binary decode of the MA2 and MA3 inputs. ENABLE does not affect the latching or state of outputs $\overline{A8}$, A8, $\overline{A9}$, or A9.

3-3 BASIC SYSTEM INTERFACING

The CDP1802 microprocessor user manual describes many system interfacing techniques and operations in some detail. The following paragraphs describe selected portions of this data.

3-3-1 Memory interface and timing

Figure 3-26 shows the interfacing required for a mixed ROM/RAM system, using the hardware described in Sec. 3-2. No external parts, except the data and address buses as shown, are required for interfacing between memory and the microprocessor. (However, additional circuits are required for interface from the microprocessor to control and/or I/O devices, as discussed in the following paragraphs.)

The state of the $\overline{MWR}$ and $\overline{MRD}$ lines determines whether a byte is to be read from the addressed memory location, written into it, or neither operation performed. Note that the $\overline{MRD}$ and $\overline{MWR}$ lines are active low. The microprocessor controls the destination of the memory output byte when it appears on the data bus. The byte may be strobed into an internal microprocessor register or into an external I/O register.

During a WRITE cycle, the memory output is in a high-impedance state. The microprocessor or I/O circuits can then place a byte to be stored in memory on the bus. A negative-going $\overline{MWR}$ pulse will then cause the data byte to be written into the addressed memory location. Eight bus pull-up resistors should be provided to place the bus in a known state when it is not being driven.

Note that ROMs are connected in the same manner as RAMs, but

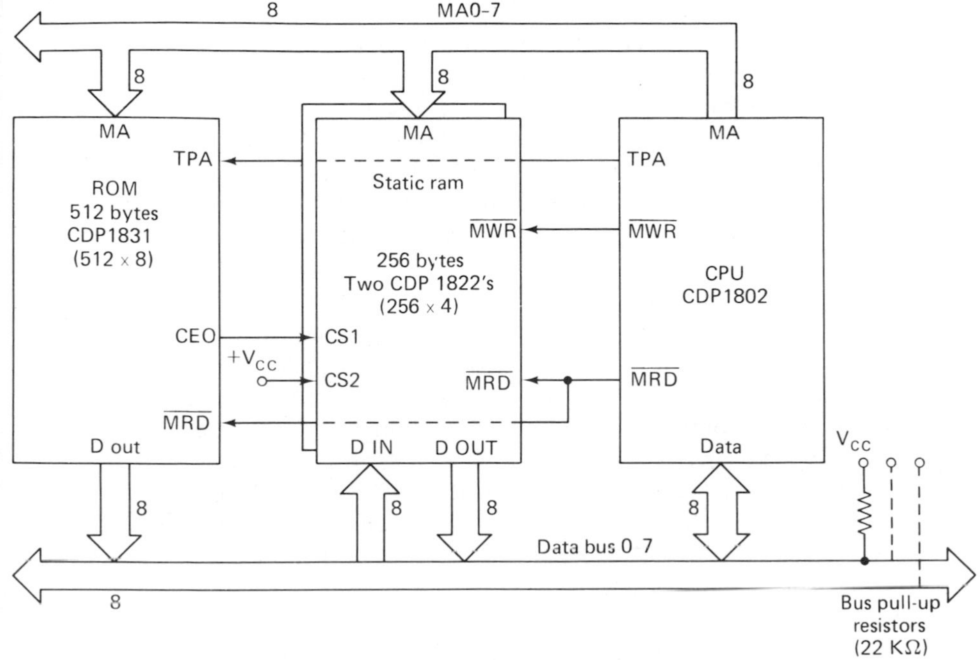

Figure 3-26 Interface for a mixed ROM/RAM system.

with the write controls omitted. The CDP1831 ROM (Sec. 3-2-1) is especially easy to use because address latching is provided on-chip to latch the eight most significant bits of a 16-bit address. The on-chip decoder is mask-programmable, which enables placement of a 512-byte memory block anywhere within 65 kilobytes of memory space. Note that the chip enable output (CEO) signal goes high when the device is selected. It is intended as a chip-select control for small (up to 256-byte) RAM systems.

Also note that the CDP1802 microprocessor can be used with other industry standard ROMs and RAMs, including dynamic RAMs. However, this requires special circuitry, as discussed in the user manual.

3-3-2 Control interface

The CDP1802 microprocessor has an internal oscillator that works with a crystal connected between the CLOCK and $\overline{\text{XTAL}}$ terminals. If desired, however, an external oscillator may be used and fed into the CLOCK input. If an external oscillator is used, no connection is required at the $\overline{\text{XTAL}}$ terminal. (Note that care must be taken not to load the $\overline{\text{XTAL}}$ line.)

Any type of clock may be used as long as the rise and fall times of the clock pulse are less than 15 μs. Each machine cycle consists of 8 clock pulses, and each instruction requires two or three machine cycles. Thus, with a

6.4-MHz clock frequency, a machine cycle of 1.25 μs can be achieved, and instructions are executed in 2.5 to 3.75 μs, depending on the instruction.

During normal operation, the CLEAR and WAIT lines are both held high. A low level on the CLEAR lines puts the machine into the reset mode with registers I, N, X, P, Q, and Data bus = 0, and IE = 1. Actually, registers X, P, and R(0) are reset during a special S1 cycle (not available to the programmer), immediately following transition from the reset mode to any of the other modes (load, run, or pause). The clock must be running to effect this cycle.

If the $\overline{\text{CLEAR}}$ and $\overline{\text{WAIT}}$ lines are both held low, the machine enters the *load mode.* This mode allows input bytes to be sequentially loaded into memory, beginning at M(0000). Input bytes can be supplied from a keyboard, tape reader, and so on, by way of the DMA function (Sec. 3-3-5). This feature permits direct program loading without the use of external "bootstrap" programs in the ROMs.

If the $\overline{\text{WAIT}}$ line is brought low (with CLEAR high), the microprocessor stops operations on the next negatively going transition of the clock. (This is called the *pause* mode.) Output signals are held at their values indefinitely. This state is useful for several purposes. Using the $\overline{\text{WAIT}}$ line, the microprocessor can be easily single-stepped for debugging purposes or, if stopped early in the machine cycle, the microprocessor can be held off the data bus to allow for other microprocessor systems (multiprocessor systems). Also, the $\overline{\text{WAIT}}$ line can be used as a data-ready signal from a slow memory or peripheral, or signals TPA and TPB can be stretched. When the $\overline{\text{WAIT}}$ line is returned high, the machine resumes running on the next negative-going transition of the clock input. The $\overline{\text{WAIT}}$ signal does not inhibit the on-chip crystal oscillator DMAs (Sec. 3-3-5) and interrupts (3-3-6) are not acknowledged in the pause mode.

Simplified control interface. Figure 3-27 shows one circuit using standard devices from the RCA Corporation (Solid State Division) CD4000 series for controlling the run and load modes of the CDP1802. Note the power-on reset feature. To load and start a program using the circuit of Fig. 3-27, the sequence of operation is as follows.

First, depress the reset and then the load buttons. The microprocessor is now ready to load by means of the DMA channel. When loading is completed, depressing the reset and then the run buttons will start program execution at M(0000) with R(0) as the program counter (after one machine cycle).

If a DMA request is present when the run switch is turned on, the machine will go to the DMA state immediately with R(0) as the program counter. The user should therefore inhibit DMA externally until the program has changed to a program counter different from R(0). Interrupts, however, are disabled until the first instruction or DMA request is executed. This

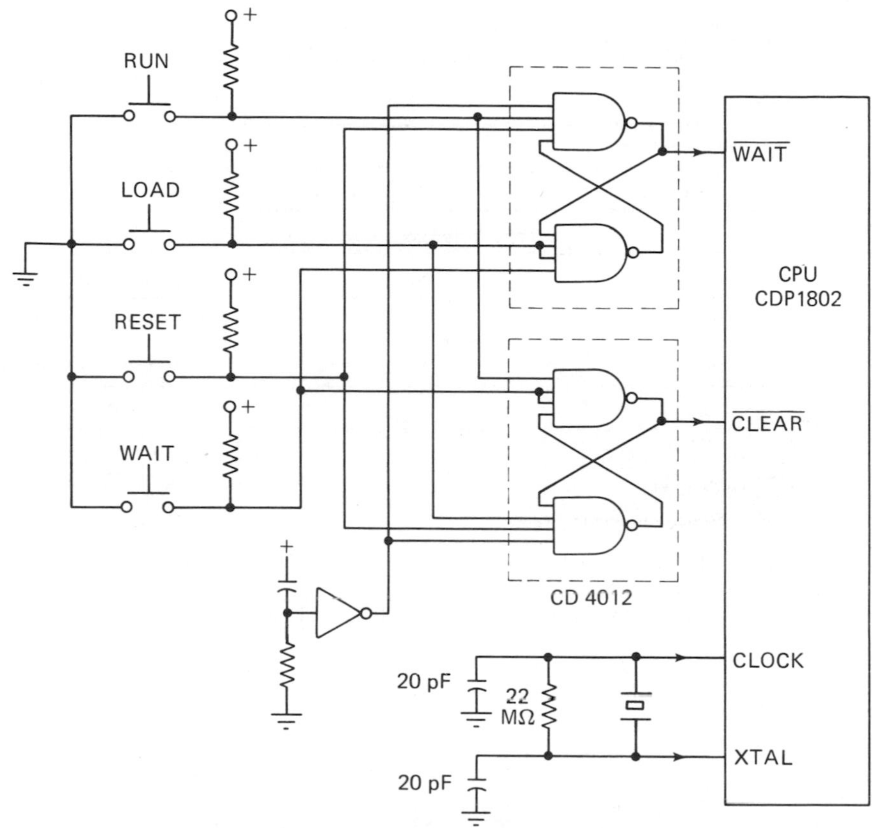

Figure 3-27 Simple control interface for CDP1802.

delay allows the programmer to place instruction 71 (disable) and 00 (idle) in the first two memory bytes to inhibit interrupts until ready for them. The combined effect of the two instructions is to set IE = 0. Interrupts must not occur, however, when the machine is in the load mode because interrupts will force the machine into an unknown running state. Figure 3-28 shows the sequence of events and states involved in loading and running a program.

Single stepping. A circuit that can be used for a form of single stepping is shown in Fig. 3-29. When this circuit is used, the microprocessor is single-stepped, *one machine cycle per switch depression.* Such a circuit can speed up the debugging and/or troubleshooting process.

3-3-3 I/O interface

The three basic ways in which the CDP1802 can communicate with I/O devices are programmed I/O, interrupt I/O, and direct memory access

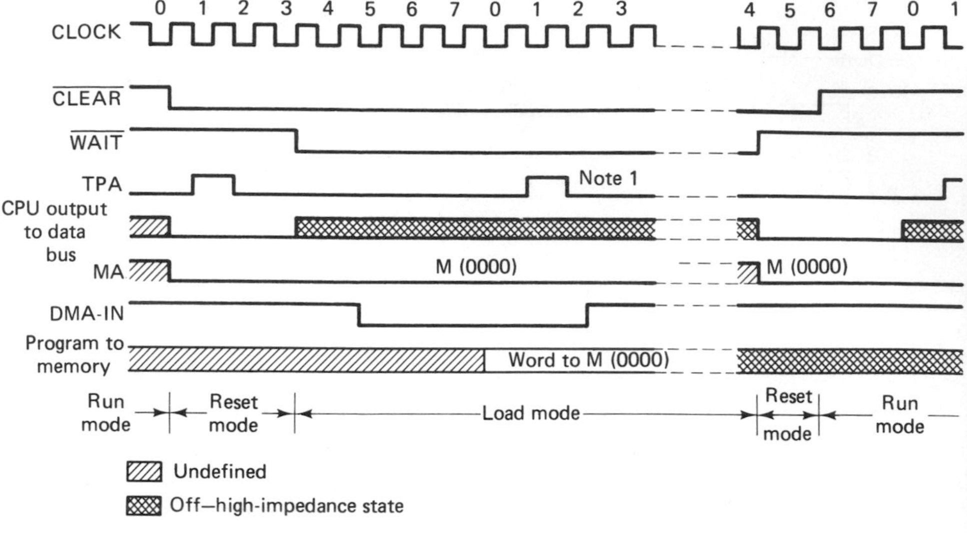

Figure 3-28 Timing diagram for load and run sequence.

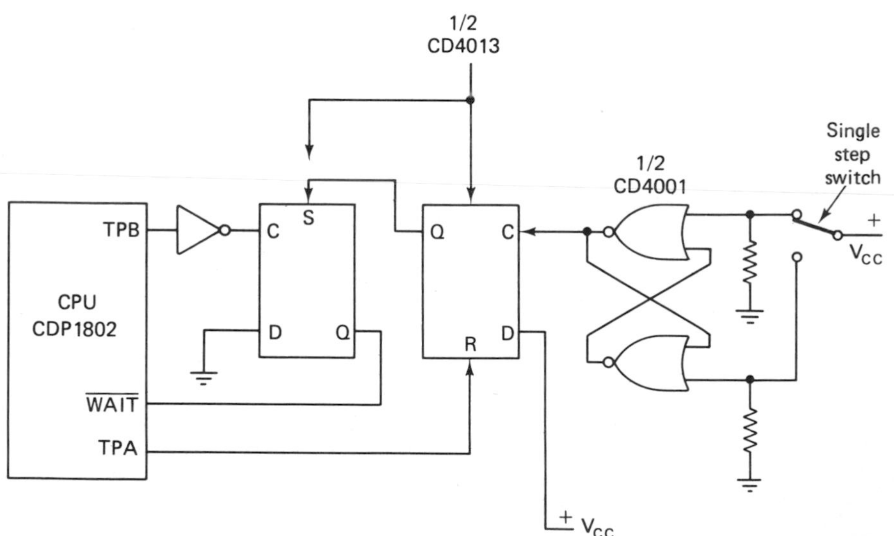

Figure 3-29 Circuit for single stepping the CDP1802 microprocessor.

(DMA). In the programmed I/O mode, all data transfer is controlled and timed by the program. In the interrupt I/O mode, the microprocessor responds to an I/O-generated signal. In the DMA mode, a direct high-speed data channel is established between memory and I/O device. In effect, the I/O device "steals" execution cycles from the microprocessor and transfers data during these time slots. The following paragraphs describe a few of the I/O interface techniques.

3-3-4 Programmed I/O

Figure 3-30 illustrates how the CDP1802 can be used with multiple input/output ports. Such a circuit is controlled by the program. Although only two ports (one input and one output) are shown in Fig. 3-30, other ports can be selected by means of a decoder. The circuit is particularly useful where more than two or three ports are required. If more than three I/O devices are required, the N lines can be decoded to specify up to 1 of 7 different I/O ports.

As an example, if line 1 is selected from the decoder by executing instruction 69 (input 1), the input register is enabled to the bus because $\overline{MRD}$ is high during the memory-write cycle. Decode line 1 will also be active-high during an output instruction 61 (output 1), but $\overline{MRD}$ is low during the memory-write cycle. Decode line 1 will also be active-high during an output instruction 61 (output 1), but $\overline{MRD}$ is low during the memory-read cycle, disabling the input register from the bus. At TPB (Fig. 1-26), the valid byte from memory is strobed into the output register.

The user's strobe or write signal can be used to activate an EF flag or the interrupt line. An I/O request can be acknowledged by a signal from

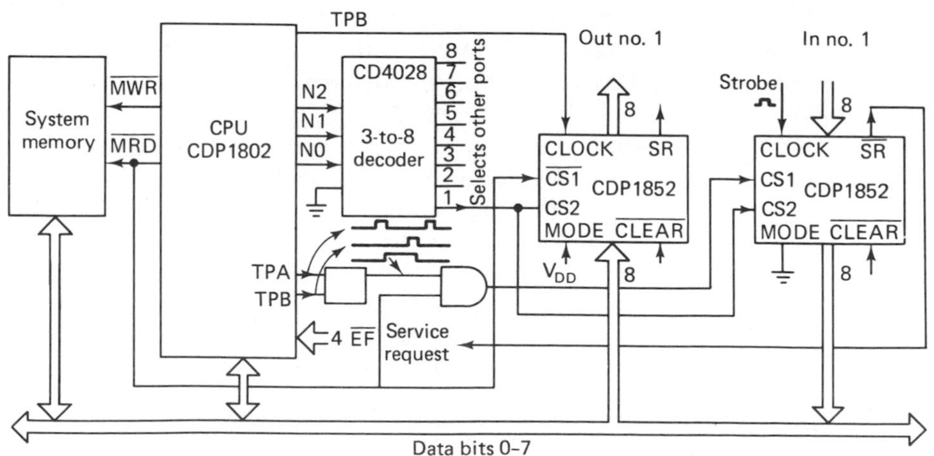

Figure 3-30 Selection of I/O devices by one-level decoding—1-of-7 input ports or 1-of-7 output ports.

the N lines. If the interrupt is asserted, the two-state code lines SC0 and SC1 are both high, acknowledging an interrupt (S3) cycle.

3-3-5 DMA operation

The I/O example of Sec. 3-3-4 requires that a program periodically sample I/O device status. If more than one I/O device is used, each must be *polled* in turn, using up part of the program for each polling. Also, the programmed I/O approach requires several instruction executions for each I/O byte transfer. In many cases it is desirable to have I/O byte transfers occur without burdening the program, or to transfer data at higher rates than possible with programmed I/O. A built-in DMA (direct memory access) feature permits high-speed I/O byte-transfer operations independent of normal program execution.

During DMA operation, register R(0) is used as the memory address register and should not be used for other purposes. Two lines, $\overline{\text{DMA-IN}}$ and $\overline{\text{DMA-OUT}}$, are used to request DMA byte transfer to and from the memory. Also, specific code is provided on the state code lines (SC0, SC1) to indicate a DMA cycle (S2).

DMA-IN. Figure 3-31 illustrates a typical DMA-IN circuit. The leading edge of an enter pulse will clock an input byte into the register and activate the $\overline{\text{DMA-IN}}$ request.

A low $\overline{\text{DMA-IN}}$ line automatically modifies the normal fetch–execute sequences. If the $\overline{\text{DMA-IN}}$ line goes low during an instruction fetch cycle (S0), the normally following execute cycle (S1) will still be performed. Following this execute cycle (S1), a special DMA cycle (S2) occurs. If the $\overline{\text{DMA-IN}}$ line goes low during an instruction execute cycle (S1), the DMA cycle (S2) will follow immediately after S1. If the $\overline{\text{DMA-IN}}$ line is reset to its high state during the DMA cycle (S2) the deferred next instruction fetch cycle (S0) will be performed following the S2 cycle, as shown in Fig. 3-31.

An S2 cycle is indicated by a low SC0 line and a high SC1 line. This condition is used to place a DMA input byte onto the bus as shown. (A full set of timing diagrams is given in the user manual.) The S2 cycle stores the input byte in memory at the location addressed by R(0). Register R(0) is then incremented by 1 so that subsequent S2 cycles will store input bytes in sequential memory locations. S2 cycles do not alter the sequence of program execution. The program will, however, be slowed down by the S2 cycles that are "stolen." The concurrent program must, of course, properly use R(0).

Thus far, single byte transfer per enter request has been discussed. If the $\overline{\text{DMA-IN}}$ remains low, S2 cycles will be performed until the $\overline{\text{DMA-IN}}$ goes high. In this mode of block transfer, the reset logic in Fig. 3-31 must be modified. The DMA mode permits a maximum I/O byte transfer rate of

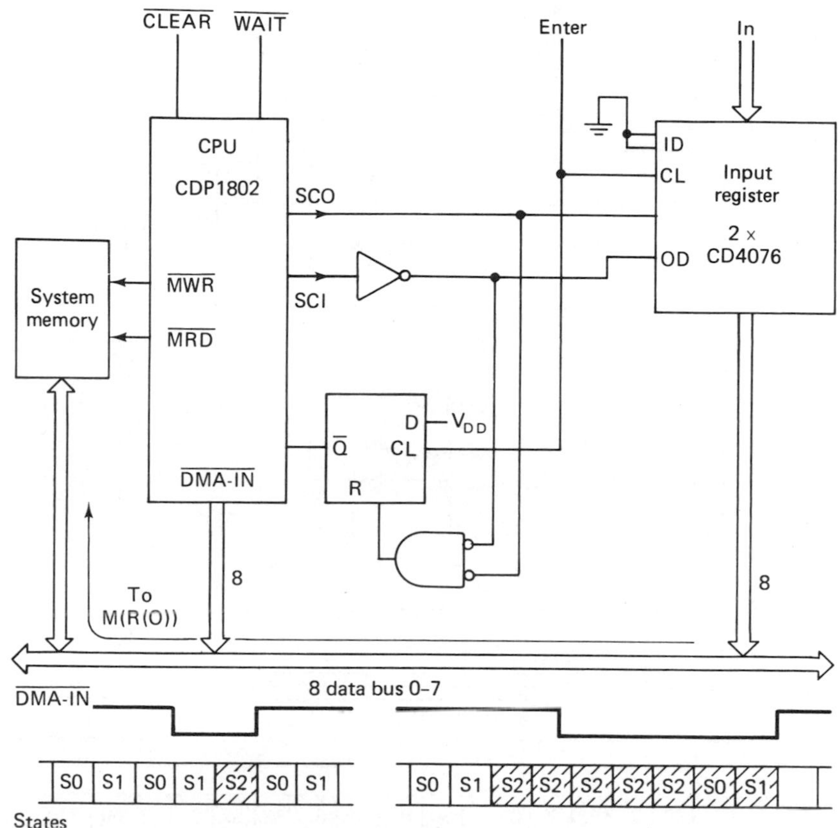

Figure 3-31 Implementation of DMA-IN operation.

one byte per machine cycle, which, with 2 μs per instruction cycle time, amounts to a transfer rate of 1 megabyte/s.

The DMA-IN feature, in conjunction with $\overline{\text{CLEAR}}$ and $\overline{\text{WAIT}}$ signals, provides a built-in *program load mechanism.* A low on $\overline{\text{CLEAR}}$ and high on $\overline{\text{WAIT}}$ puts the microprocessor in the *reset* mode. The microprocessor then idles (S1) state with R(0) = 0000. The *load* mode is next entered by bringing the $\overline{\text{WAIT}}$ line low (now both $\overline{\text{CLEAR}}$ and $\overline{\text{WAIT}}$ are low). This mode allows input bytes to be sequentially loaded into memory beginning at M(0000). Input bytes can be supplied from a keyboard, tape, and so on, via the DMA-IN function and circuitry similar to Fig. 3-31.

DMA-OUT. DMA output bytes can be strobed into an output device by TPB, as shown in Fig. 3-32. A low on the $\overline{\text{DMA-OUT}}$ line causes 32 cycles to occur in a similar manner as a low on the $\overline{\text{DMA-IN}}$ line. The S2 cycle caused by a low on the $\overline{\text{DMA-OUT}}$ line places the memory byte addressed by R(0) on the bus, and increments R(0) by 1. The program must set R(0)

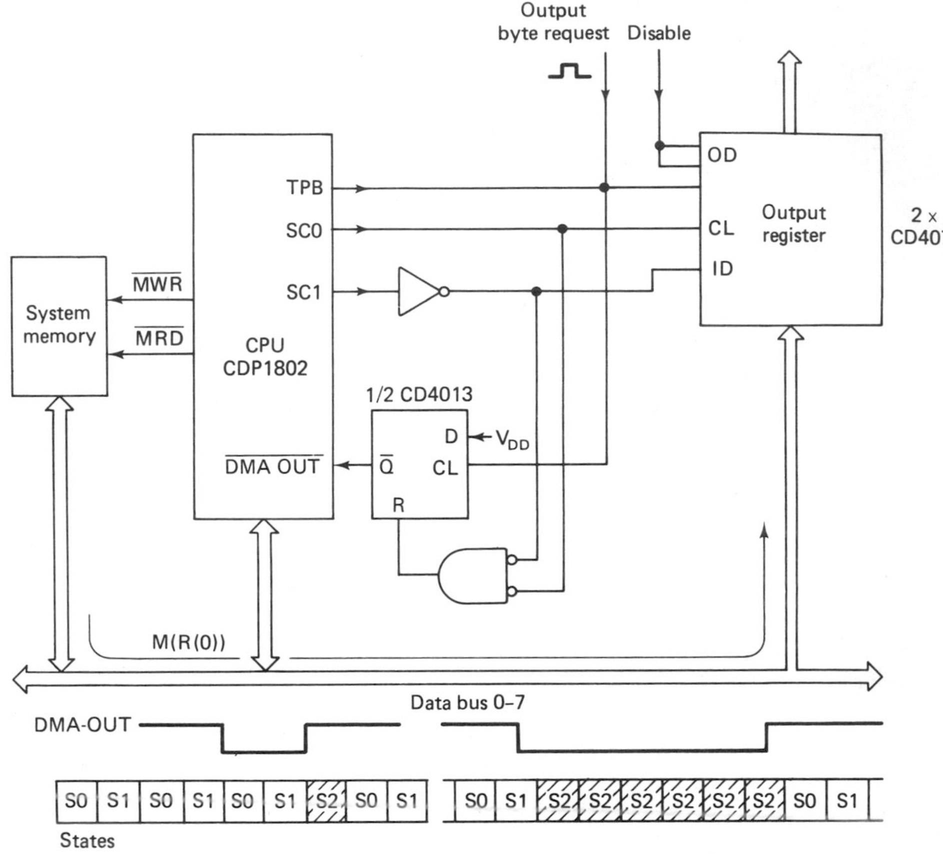

Figure 3-32 Implementation of DMA-OUT operation.

to the address of the first output byte of the desired memory sequence before the DMA transfer request occurs.

It should be noted that there is a definite priority system for DMA and interrupt functions of the CDP1802 microprocessor. In the event of concurrent DMA and interrupt requests, DMA-IN has first priority, followed by DMA-OUT and then interrupt.

3-3-6 Interrupt I/O

The interrupt mechanism permits an external signal to interrupt program execution and transfer control to a program designed to handle the interrupt condition. This function is useful for responding to system alarm conditions, initializing the DMA memory pointer, or, in general, responding to real-time events less urgent than those handled by DMA, but more urgent than those which can be handled by sensing external flags.

A low on the INTERRUPT line causes an *interrupt response* cycle

(S3) to occur following the next S1 cycle, provided that the IE flip-flop is set. Execution of an S3 cycle is indicated by a high on both the SC0 and the SC1 lines.

Figure 3-33 shows a typical interrupt circuit. The flip-flop is reset during the S3 cycle. The current values of the X and P registers are stored in the T register during the S3 cycle. P is then set to 1, X to 2, and IE to 0. Following S3, a normal instruction fetch cycle (S0) is performed. The S3 cycle, however, changes P to 1 so that, next, the sequence of instructions starting at the memory location addressed by R(1) will be executed. This sequence of instructions is called the *interrupt service program.* The sequence saves the current state of registers such as T, D, and possibly some of the scratch-pad registers, by storing them in reserved memory locations. DF must also be saved if the interrupt service program will disturb it. The service program then performs the desired functions, restores the saved registers to their original states, and returns control to execution of the original program. Special instructions RETURN, DISABLE, and SAVE (70, 71, 78) facilitate interrupt handling.

The CDP1802 also provides a special 1-bit register called interrupt enable (IE). When IE is set to 0, the state of the interrupt line is ignored. IE is set to 1 in the reset mode. IE can be set to 1 or 0 by RETURN and DISABLE instructions, respectively. IE is automatically set to 0 by an S3 cycle, preventing subsequent interrupt cycles even if the $\overline{\text{INTERRUPT}}$ line stays low. The program must set IE to 1 to permit subsequent interrupts. Setting IE to 1 takes place automatically when the program executes the

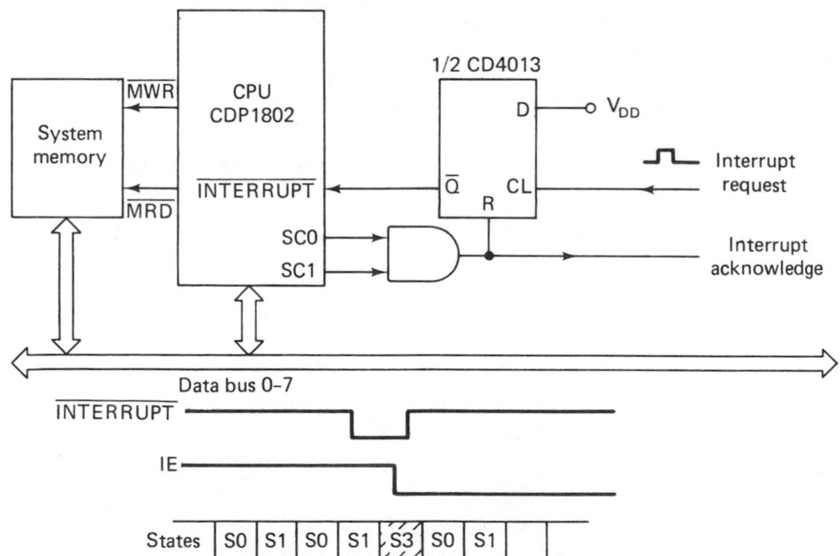

Figure 3-33 Typical circuit for implementation of interrupt operation.

RETURN instruction. Sharing the $\overline{\text{INTERRUPT}}$ line with a number of interrupt signal sources is possible.

When the interrupt is used in a system, R(1) must be reserved for use as the interrupt service program counter, and R(2) is normally used as a pointer to the storage area.

3-3-7 Parallel I/O interface

Figure 3-34 shows the microprocessor interfaced to other components in the 1800 system for parallel I/O interface. Only five components plus a crystal are required to interface directly in a simple and efficient system configuration. The *RC* network connected to $\overline{\text{CLEAR}}$ is optional and provides power-on reset. This basic system implementation can easily be expanded for larger memory capacity, and/or more I/O ports, by following the techniques of the user manual.

3-3-8 Serial I/O interface with the UART

Figure 3-35 shows the microprocessor interfaced to a telephone line for serial data communications using the UART described in Sec. 3-2-4. As shown in Fig. 3-19, there are four registers under program control in the UART. One is loaded from the bus in the transmit mode, one is read to the bus in the receive mode, a control register is loaded from the bus at initialization, and a status register is read in the receive mode. The 2-bit code on $\overline{\text{MRD}}$ and RSEL determines which register is selected and the direction of data flow. The UART is enabled to the data bus when the three chip selects (CS1, CS2, CS3) are asserted. Thus, by decoding, a large number of UARTs can operate in a system on the same bus.

3-4 BASIC PROGRAMMING TECHNIQUES

The purpose of this section is to discuss basic programming concepts especially as they relate to the writing of COSMAC programs. Although intended for those readers new to programming, experienced programmers are encouraged to read this section and get a feeling for microprocessor programming.

3-4-1 Allocation of resources

Before detailed programming can begin, decisions must be made as to which functions are to be executed by software and which are to be implemented in this I/O hardware. The layout of data in memory must be planned, and the use of registers worked out.

The hardware/software trade-off is often the most difficult but rewarding phase of designing a microprocessor-based product. On the basis of previous familiarity, engineers may tend to favor the use of hardware

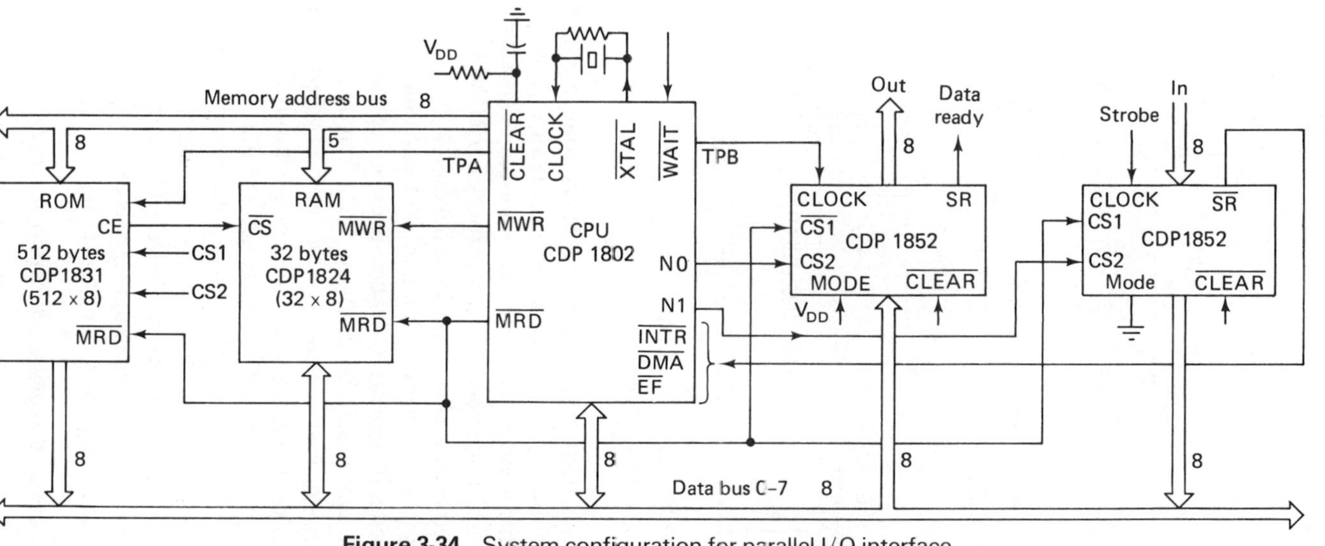

Figure 3-34 System configuration for parallel I/O interface.

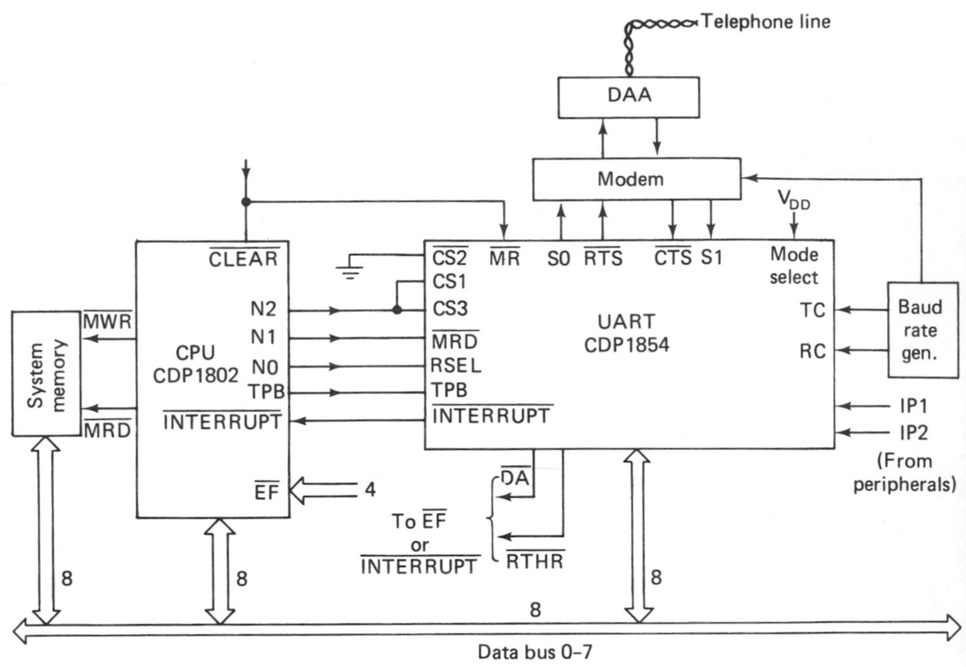

Figure 3-35 System configuration for asynchronous serial data communication interface.

when similar functions may be done more economically in software. As a guideline, try initially to do everything in software (except jobs requiring submicrosecond response). Use I/O hardware only when the microprocessor can not keep up. Even then, a microprocessor/ROM subsystem may be more cost-effective than special-purpose hardware.

Allocation of the various built-in I/O capabilities of COSMAC is difficult to discuss in general terms because applications are so varied. The DMA channel can clearly be used for such functions as block transfers between a floppy disk and memory. The decision whether to use the DMA or the interrupt channels for a slow communications line is more difficult, and depends on what other I/O interfacing is required.

Often, the most basic system design issue is deciding what functions to carry out in response to one or more interrupt signals. Generally, the less done in servicing interrupts, the better. This minimizes the problems of contention among multiple interrupt signals and makes the system easier to design, debug, and more likely to be error-free.

3-4-2 RAM and register allocation for data

Registers must be allocated among program counter usage, data pointing, storage usage, and general utility usage. This allocation may vary dynamically as a program executes, but generally it is more efficient to assign fixed functions to most registers. Likewise, certain data bytes should always be stored in RAM. The following points should be considered when deciding where a particular type of data byte should be placed in the program.

For programming purposes, data bytes may be handled in the four following ways.

Isolated variables in registers. Some data bytes represent isolated variables or parameters referred to at many different parts of a program. In COSMAC, such data bytes are best handled by direct use of registers to hold the random isolated variables. The advantage of using register storage directly is that simple 1-byte instructions can be used to bring data to and from the data register (D register of Fig. 3-1), saving time and program space when compared with storing the data bytes in RAM. Further, a variable that needs to be incremented or decremented can be stored in the low half of a register, and incremented or decremented in place, without using the D register.

Constants in memory. In COSMAC, data bytes that represent constants are best placed in memory and addressed by the data *immediate* mode (Sec. 3-1-3). In most cases, the immediate mode provides the best economy of resources, since there is no need for a special pointer to memory, and a 1-byte instruction is sufficient to address the mode. Also, the immediate mode is easy to "read" because each constant used is found at the point in the program where it is needed, and its value is immediately obvious. Constants can readily be located and changed during the programming process. With immediate addressing, a constant that is used at several different places in a program will, of course, be stored several different times. Thus, in extreme cases where the same constant is used extensively, it may be better to set up a pointer to such a constant.

Temporary or intermediate results in the stack. In COSMAC, data bytes that represent temporary, intermediate results obtained in the process of a computation and then thrown away are best placed in the stack (Sec. 3-1-3). The stack is implemented by dedicating a block of RAM and using one register R(2) to point at the "top" of the stack (the space or address where the next byte should be put). The programmer "pushes" intermediate results onto the stack for storing, using R(2) as the pointer and then decrementing the pointer (so that the block of RAM used starts at the *highest address*). Later, the programmer "pops" the results off when ready for use by the ALU or other function, incrementing the pointer before so doing. (Users of certain Hewlett-Packard calculators will be familiar with the idea that a stack can be used to organize a very complicated calculation.)

Sometimes, it is necessary to use a data byte pushed into the stack soon, with no intervening further use of the stack. In such cases, the programmer can omit the decrement of the pointer after pushing data, and omit the increment before using data, thus saving one or two instructions. Such deviations from standard usage should be *well marked by comments in the program* to avoid problems in case the code is changed later.

There are many advantages to the stack. The main reason is efficient use of resources (amount of memory and register space). For example, only one register pointer R(2) is required to work with a potentially large number of data bytes. Also, RAM is used efficiently because the allocation of space required must match the maximum number of intermediate bytes stored at any given time rather than the total required over the duration of the program. (The maximum "depth" of a stack is generally very small.) Finally, the stack is efficiently addressed by 1-byte COSMAC instructions, thus saving program space.

Blocks of data in memory with register pointers. Data bytes that appear in strings or groups are best stored in RAM and addressed by setting up a register pointer to the beginning (or end) of the string. Multiple strings usually should have multiple address pointers. The COSMAC instructions are designed to work efficiently with such data, allowing the pointer to be incremented or decremented as the data bytes are accessed. Sometimes, the programmer will share a few pointers between several different strings of data not being simuntaneously accessed. In this case, it is good practice to allocate all strings to one 256-byte page of memory so that a pointer can be moved from one data item to another simply by loading the lower byte of the pointer register. If ROM tables are used frequently, the use of a dedicated pointer may also be justified.

3-4-3 Writing a program

There are three basic structures in any program, including the programs of microprocessor-based equipment, that are of particular importance. These include *loops, conditional branches,* and *subroutines.* The following paragraphs describe how these structures are handled in COSMAC.

Loops. As discussed in Chapter 1, a loop consists of an initialization section, the main body of steps to be executed, and a test section to determine whether and how often to loop through the main body. As a simple example, consider a routine that implements a delay. Figure 3-36 shows such a routine in three forms: *flowchart, symbolic,* and *numeric.*

The flowchart (Fig. 3-36a) shows the program structure explicitly, and says in words what happens at each point in the structure.

The symbolic form (Fig. 3-36b) specifies the instructions to be executed, and includes the movement of data among the various COSMAC registers. The delay constant, which is assumed to be stored in a memory location, is loaded into D and then moved to the lower half of a utility register UTIL.

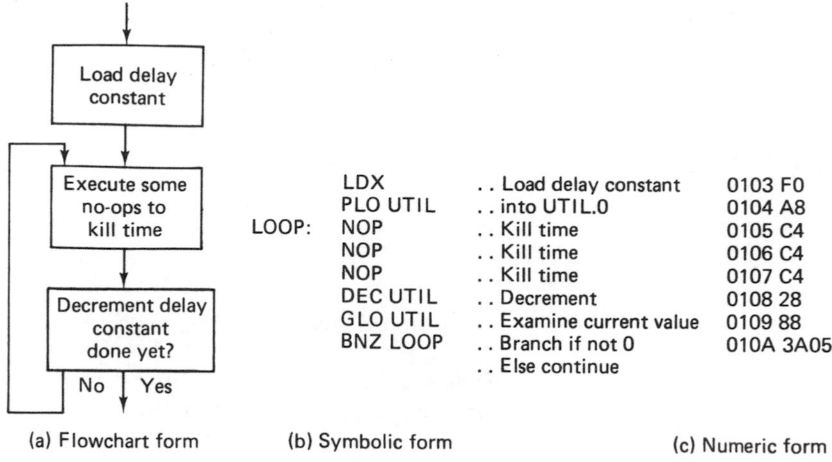

(a) Flowchart form (b) Symbolic form (c) Numeric form

Figure 3-36 Simple loop example; delay function.

The expression "LOOP" labels the next part of the program for future use. Three NOP instructions are specified. These instructions are the *main body* of the loop. At the end of the NOP instructions, the utility register is decremented. Finally, the lower half of UTIL is loaded into the D register and a conventional branch instruction is executed. Control keeps going back to the "LOOP" until the count goes to zero.

The numeric form (Fig. 3-36c) shows the program as it might appear in hex code. Note that UTIL is assumed to be register R(8).

Conditional branches. In the conditional branch, a comparison or test of some kind is made, and one of two different bodies of code is executed, depending on the outcome. Figure 3-37 shows a simple example of a conditional branch where variable Z is to have a lower limit. Z is compared to 03. If Z is greater than 03, the value of Z is passed on. If Z is equal to or below 03, then 03 is substituted in the program. Note that once the appropriate action is carried out by operation, the two branches of the program come back together.

Any function can be programmed by defining steps in a loop to be loops themselves, and by building up a group of nested loops and conditionals (sometimes known as a *hierarchy* of nested loops or conditionals). Structures of this type are the most efficient to generate, the most efficient to check out, and the least likely to contain undetected bugs. More complicated structures are very common (they appear in COSMAC utility programs, for example) because programmers like to play "tricks" such as branching from one part of a program into another, sharing a common part for a while, and then branching back to the original part conditionally on some obscure characteristic that distinguishes the two program parts.

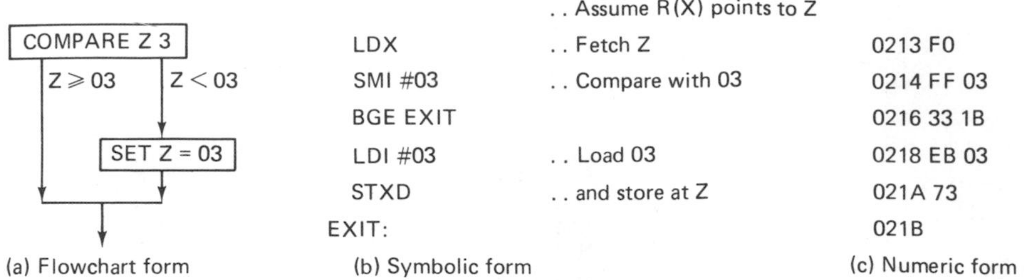

Figure 3-37 Simple conditional branch example: limiting a variable.

Such practices can lead to problems. For example, a simple change in one part of code may have unfortunate consequence for another part which is "borrowing" a piece of the branch. Generally, the best flowchart is one without odd-looking branches from one part to another. There are exceptions, of course.

Subroutines. Subroutines can be used when a piece of program is useful in many different places throughout the overall program, but you want to avoid the problems discussed for conditional branches. The subroutine technique permits the programmer to put the routine into only one place in memory but use the routine as many times as needed throughout the program. When properly applied, a subroutine becomes a substitute "instruction" which does something that might have been implemented in the microprocessor as a true instruction.

To be effective, a subroutine must be exactly defined as to the function it performs, where it gets the data, where it puts the results, and what resources (register and/or RAM) are used. Subroutines may have the structure of a loop or of a conditional branch. In either case, subroutines may use other subroutines within the body of their code. The main design effort in a large program is in the building up of a set of subroutines suitable for a given application.

COSMAC offers many different ways to handle subroutine structure, representing different trade-offs among efficiency in execute time, efficiency in program size, and efficiency in use of register resources. COSMAC also offers more direct mechanisms for treating subroutines as extensions of the basic instruction set (*interpretive techniques*), as described in Sec. 3-4-6.

3-4-4 Typical COSMAC subroutine techniques

In large programs, a particular sequence of instructions is often used many times. For example, a code conversion from one data format to another might be required several places in a communications program. You could simply insert the proper sequence of instructions each place in the program where needed. However, this duplication of instructions will consume much memory storage space, especially if the sequence is long and used frequently.

An alternative method is to write the sequence only once and reuse it each time where needed. This shared use of the same code is done by writing the function as a subroutine that can be *called each time* when needed. When the subroutine has completed its function, it *returns* to the program that called it. A subroutine may be called many times from different places in the main program. Most programs will contain several subroutines. The COSMAC architecture provides several techniques for calling and returning from subroutines, many of which are described in the user manual. The following paragraphs discuss the SEP register technique, which is the fastest and yet the most basic subroutine call and return used in COSMAC. The SEP register technique involves three basic steps.

Step 1. Point one of the 16 registers to the subroutine that the program will call. This step is typically done by executing the following code:

```
LDI A.0(sub) . . . replace ''sub'' with subroutine name
PLO Rn       . . . replace ''n'' with a register number
LDI A.1(sub) . . . ''sub'' is the entry point to the subroutine
PHI Rn       . . . ''n'' is the register to point to ''sub''
```

This four-instruction sequence will load the address of the first instruction in the subroutine into a register. Thus, the register ''n'' will *point* to the *entry point* of the subroutine. If the programmer does not use this register for any other purpose than to point to the subroutine, the initialization procedure need be done only once. If, however, the same register is to be used variously in the program to point to another subroutine or to hold data, the register must be reinitialized before additional calls. As a shorthand notation, the four-instruction sequence is represented by a statement such as: LOAD 'RN', 'SUB'.

Step 2. A call to the subroutine is performed by making R(n) the program counter. This change is done by executing the instruction SEP to register ''n''. Execution of the subroutine will then begin with R(n) as the program counter. Because the initial value of P is 0 at program startup, this technique is also used to change program counters from R(0) to any other register.

Step 3. A return from the subroutine is performed by making R(p) the program counter, where p was the register used as the program counter *by the calling program at the time of the call* to the subroutine. This change is done by executing the instruction SEP to register ''p''. The execution of the calling program will resume with R(p) as the program counter.

Example of main program calling a subroutine. In this example, a subroutine is called by loading its address into a register and using ''SEP register'' to do the call. The subroutine is called from two places in the main program. When it has performed its function, the subroutine does a return by doing a SEP back to the register of the main program. This returning SEP instruction is performed just in front of the entry point to the subroutine. This step leaves the subroutine's program counter as it was originally (that is, pointing to the same location as at initialization). Thus, the initialization need be done only once in this example. In this example, execution starts with R(0) as the program counter, then R(3) becomes the program counter, with R(7) as the subroutine entry pointer. Figure 3-38 shows the steps involved for the SEP register technique when the subroutine is called from two places in the main program.

3-4-5 Interrupt service

The use of the COSMAC interrupt line involves special programming instructions, in that an interrupt may occur between any two instructions in a program. Thus, the sequence of instructions initiated by the interrupt routine must save the values of any machine registers it shares with the original program, and restore these values before resuming execution of the interrupted program.

R(1) must always be initialized to the address of the interrupt service program before an interrupt is allowed. Figure 3-39 illustrates a hypothetical interrupt service routine. R(1) is initialized to 0055 before permitting interrupt. R(2) is a stack pointer (that is, it addressed the free topmost byte in a variable-size data storage area). This stack area grows in size as the pointer moves upward (lower memory addresses), much like a stack of dishes on a table. Also like the dish stack, it shrinks as bytes are removed from the top. In the interrupt service example of Fig. 3-39, the stack grows by two bytes as registers X, P, and D are stored on it, and then decreased to its original size when X, P, and D are restored. Such a stack is sometimes referred to as a LIFO (last in, first out) because the first item removed from the stack is the last one placed on it.

When bytes are to be stored onto the stack by the interrupt routine, the pointer R(2) is first decremented to assure that it is pointing to a free space. In the example of Fig. 3-39, location 00F0 may have been in use when the interrupt occurred, so the pointer decrements to 00EF to store X and P. When bytes are no longer needed, they are removed from the stack and the pointer is incremented.

The stack in Fig. 3-39 is used to store the values of X, P, and D associated with the interrupted program. If the interrupt will modify any other registers (scratchpad or DF), their contents must also be saved.

After these "housekeeping" steps have been completed, the "real work" requested by the interrupt signal can be performed. This work may involve such tasks as transferring I/O bytes, initializing the DMA pointer R(0), checking the status of peripheral devices, incrementing or decrementing an internal timer/counter register, and branching to an emergency power-shut-down sequence.

Upon completion of the real work, return housekeeping must be

Register assignment table		
Register	Function	Comment
R(3)	The "MAIN" program counter	Arbitrary
R(7)	"Subroutine" entry pointer	Arbitrary

Programming Technique:

. . Execution starts with R(0) as the program counter.
. . Load the address of "MAIN" program into R(3):

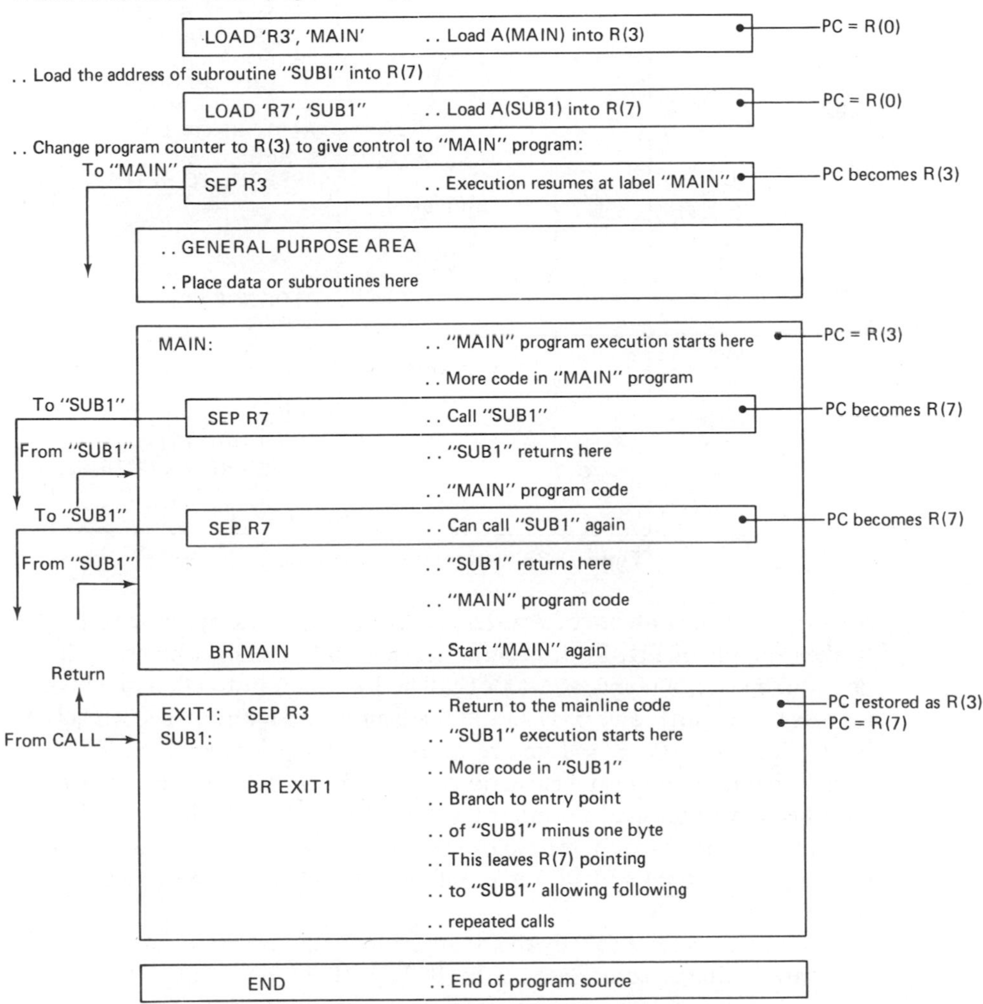

Figure 3-38 Steps involved for the SEP register technique when the subroutine is called from two places in the main program.

START HERE

ADDRESS	BYTE	OPERATION	COMMENTS
0053	42	EXIT: LDA R2	RESTORE D
0054	70	RET	RESTORE X, P AND R(2); ENABLE INTERRUPTS
0055	22	DEC R2	DEC STACK POINTER
0056	78	SAV	OLD X, P ONTO STACK
0057	22	DEC R2	DEC STACK POINTER
0058	52	STR R2	OLD D ONTO STACK
		–	SAVE OTHER REGIS–TERS IF REQUIRED
		–	PERFORM "REAL WORK" REQUESTED BY INTERRUPT
		–	RESTORE OTHER REGS.
		–	PREPARE TO RETURN
	30	BR EXIT	
	53		
–			
–			
–			STORAGE FOR OTHER REG.
00EE			STORAGE FOR D
00EF		STACK	STORAGE FOR T, i.e. OLD X, P
00F0			STACK TOP WHEN INTERRUPTED
–			OTHER STACK ENTRIES
–			
–			

Figure 3-39 Interrupt service routine.

performed. The contents of registers saved on the stack are now restored. In the example of Fig. 3-39, program execution branches to memory location M(0053). R(2) points at M(00EE). The LDA (42) instruction at M(0053) restores the original value of D and R(2) advances to M(00EF). The RETURN instruction (70) sets IE = 1 and restores the original, interrupted X and P register values. The next instruction executed will be the one that would have been executed had no interrupt occurred (unless the interrupt is still present, in which case the whole process is repeated). Note that R(1) is left pointing at M(0055) and R(2) is pointing at M(00F0), as they were before the interrupt.

When IE is reset to 0 by the S3 interrupt response cycle, further interrupts are inhibited regardless of the $\overline{\text{INTERRUPT}}$ line state. This setting prevents a second interrupt response from occurring while an interrupt is being processed. The RETURN instruction (70) that restores original program execution at the end of the interrupt routine sets IE = 1 so that subsequent interrupts are permitted.

Sometimes the programmer needs to control IE directly. For example, you may want to permit new interrupts to interrupt the servicing of old interrupts. Or, you may want to shut off interrupts during a critical part of the main program.

The RETURN and DISABLE instructions can be set or reset to IE without changing P and performing a branch. A convenient method is to set X equal to the current P value and then perform the RETURN (70) or DISABLE (71) instruction, using the desired X, P for the immediate byte. For example, if IE = 0, X = 5, and P = 3, the sequence

```
E3   SEX R3     . . . set X = 3
70   RET        . . . return X to 5, P to 3, 1   IE, R(3) + 1
53   ,#53       . . . immediate byte
```

would have no effect other than setting the interrupt enable IE. A similar sequence with a DISABLE (71) instruction can be used to disable interrupts during a critical instruction sequence.

3-4-6 Interpretive techniques

An interpretive system offers the advantages of a higher-level language without the disadvantages of complex translation programs. The idea is to define a set of *pseudo instructions* that are more powerful than basic microprocessor instructions and, consequently, easier to use in programs. Each pseudo instruction is implemented by a corresponding subroutine. In the simplest interpretive system, each subroutine ends with a mechanism that passes control on to the next subroutine (that is, pseudo instruction) to be executed.

The sequence of pseudo instruction is defined by a *pseudo program,* in somewhat the same way that a program defines a sequence of instructions. A *pseudo program counter* is a register that is generally pointing at the next pseudo instruction to be executed. Just as with a real program counter, pseudo branch instructions may affect the normal sequencing of the pseudo program counter.

As an example of interpretive techniques, let one of the registers be PPC, the pseudo program counter. Then let PC be the normal program counter. Suppose that all subroutines begin and end on the same page in memory. Subroutines may branch to other pages, but they eventually come back. Then, a pseudo program is nothing more than a series of addresses—the low-byte address of each successive subroutine to be executed. Each subroutine ends with the same two instructions:

```
LDA PPC     . . . fetch next address
PLO PC      . . . into PC low
```

These instructions give control over to the next subroutine.

An example of a (long) branch pseudo instruction would be:

```
LBR:  LDA PPC      . . . put first address byte
      STR STACK    . . . into the stack.
      LDA PPC      . . . put second byte
      PLO PPC      . . . into PPC low.
      LDN STACK    . . . put first byte
      PHI PPC      . . . into PPC high.
      LDA PPC      . . . Go
      PLO PC       . . . to next pseudo instruction.
```

A typical set of pseudo instructions might include multiple-precision or floating-point arithmetic functions, I/O handling instructions, multiway branches on arithmetic comparisons, subroutine linkage routines, and a mechanism to drop into standard COSMAC instructions whenever necessary. More details and a discussion of alternative interpretive systems are found in COSMAC literature.

3-5 SAMPLE PROGRAMS

The following sample program illustrates how COSMAC architecture and instructions can be used to implement a basic program. Full details on more complex programs are described in COSMAC literature.

Processing two input bytes. This program inputs two bytes from two different devices. Compare this with the sample program of Sec. 5-5. These devices might be the outputs from two analog-to-digital converters or mechanical position resolvers. The program compares the digital inputs and, if they are equal, sets the Q flag to 1. In the event the two bytes are unequal, the Q flag is set to 0 and the larger of the two values is outputted to a third device. A minor change to this program could be in outputting the difference between the two bytes, an indication perhaps of the degree of mechanical position or error.

The overview operation of this program is given in the flowchart of Fig. 3-40. A more detailed flowchart corresponding to the actual implementation is given in Fig. 3-41, which more closely corresponds to the assembly program listing shown in Fig. 3-42. A few programming techniques used in this program warrant special attention.

First, the INITIALIZATION block in Fig. 3-40 becomes two blocks in Fig. 3-41. A portion of the original initialization block is done only once during the execution of the program. The other part is done every time the program loops back to the label GO. This arrangement was done to save memory at the expense of execution time, a common trade-off. The output instruction increments R(X) each time it is executed. To maintain R(X) pointing to the same memory location, it could be followed by a DEC R2.

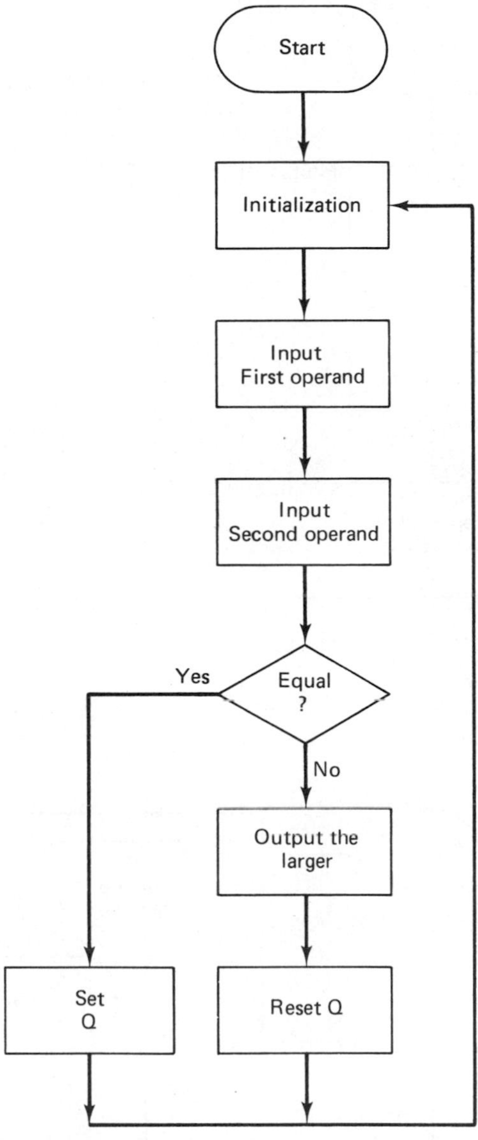

Figure 3-40 Program flowchart for processing two input bytes; inputting two bytes, comparing them, outputting the larger, and setting Q to 1 if equal.

However, the execution of the LDI and PLO lines (lines 4 and 5), which are already in the program, serves the same purpose. The decrement instruction, therefore, is purposely omitted.

Second, lines 8 through 10 use the characteristics of the input instruc-

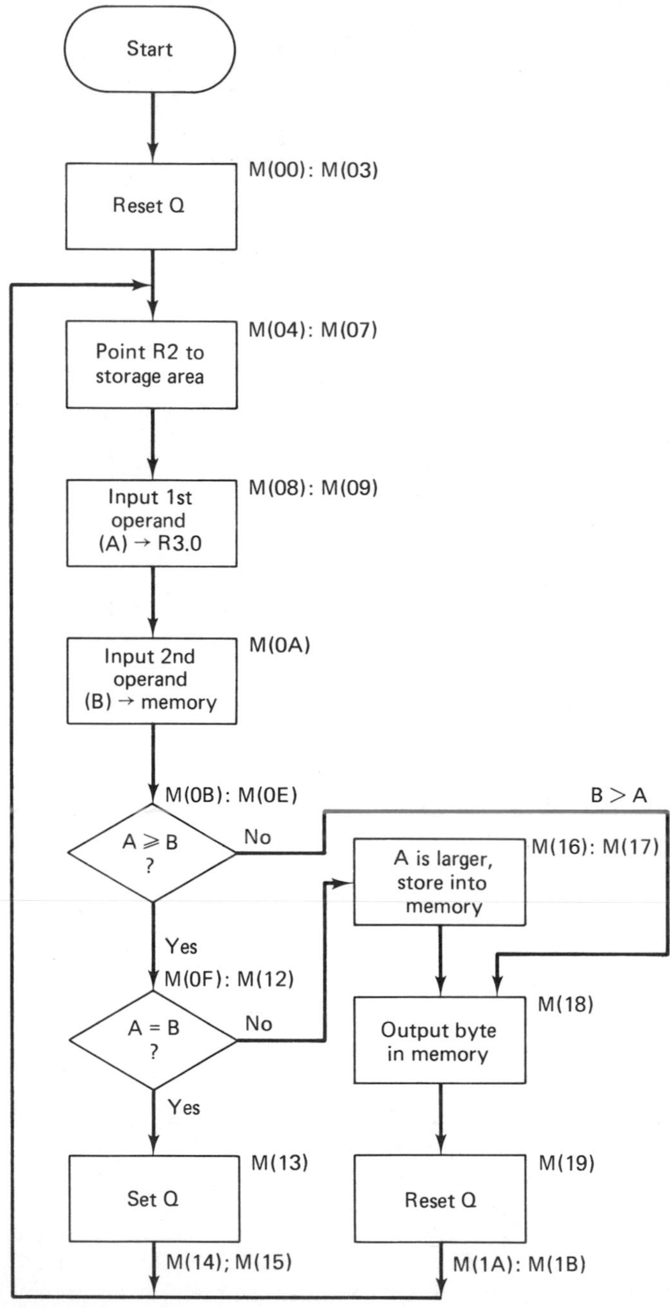

Figure 3-41 Detailed program flowchart for processing two input bytes.

```
0000  7A;               REQ               .. RESET Q TO "0"
0001  F800;             LDI A.1 (STORE)   .. SET STORAGE POINTER R(2)
0003  B2;               PHI R2            .... TO POINT AT A FREE LOCATION
0004  F81C;   GO:       LDI A.0 (STORE)   .... IN RAM M(STORE)
0006  A2;               PLO R2            .... "  "
0007  E2;               SEX R2
0008  69;               INP 1             .. READ 1ST INPUT BYTE INTO D
0009  A3;               PLO R3            .. SAVE THE 1ST INPUT
000A  6A;               INP 2             .. READ 2ND INPUT BYTE INTO
000B  ;                                   .... MEMORY
000B  83                GLO R3            .. LOAD THE 1ST INPUT INTO D
000C  F7;               SM                .. 1ST INPUT MINUS 2ND INPUT
000D  3B18;             BNF RES2          .. BRANCH TO RES2 IF 2ND INPUT
000F  ;                                   .... IS GREATER THAN 1ST INPUT;
000F  ;                                   .... OTHERWISE;
000F  83;               GLO R3            .. LOAD THE 1ST INPUT INTO D
0010  F3;               XOR               .. M(R(2)).X OR D. TO CHECK IF THE
0011  ;                                   .... TWO INPUTS ARE EQUAL
0011  3A16;             BNZ RES1          .. BRANCH TO RES1 IF NOT EQUAL
0013  ;                                   .... (1ST INPUT IS GREATER THAN
0013  ;                                   .... 2ND INPUT); OTHERWISE;
0013  7B;               SEQ               .. EQUAL; SET Q FLAG
0014  3004;             BR GO             .. GO BACK TO BEGINNING
0016  ;
0016  83;     RES1:     GLO R3            .. LOAD 1ST INPUT INTO D
0017  52;               STR R2            .. STORE IT AT M(STORE)
0018  ;
0018  61;     RES2:     OUT1              .. OUTPUT LARGER VALUE
0019  7A;               REQ               .. RESET Q FLAG
001A  3004;             BR GO             .. GO BACK TO BEGINNING
001C  ;
001C  ;       STORE     ORG  *            .. STORAGE AREA
001C  ;
001C  ;
001C  ;
001C  ;
001C  ;                 END               .. END OF PROGRAM SOURCE
0000
```

Figure 3-42 Assembly listing for two-byte processing program.

tion to advantage. Because the data byte goes into both memory and D, the first input instruction is followed by the storing of the data from D into a scratch-pad register. The second input instruction uses the feature that the data byte also goes into memory. After the retrieval of the first byte from the scratch pad, the contents of D and memory are ready for comparison.

3-6 COSMAC DEVELOPMENT AIDS

The following paragraphs describe development aids available to COSMAC users. Full details are given in the instruction manuals.

3-6-1 Microtutor II, CDP18S012

Figure 3-43 shows the Microtutor II, which is a complete basic microcomputer system intended for engineers, students, or hobbyists who wish to understand and use microprocessors. Preassembled and containing its own regulated power supply, Microtutor II provides quick and easy hands-on microprocessor experience.

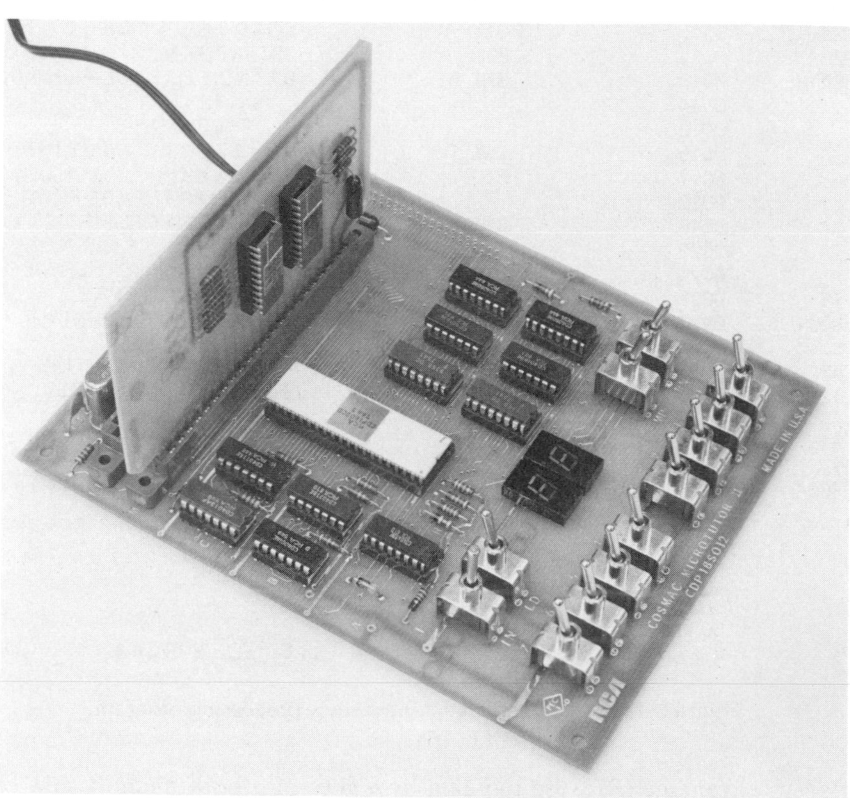

Figure 3-43 RCA Microtutor II, CDP182012. (Courtesy RCA Corporation, Solid State Division.)

Microtutor II is designed around the RCA CDP1802 COSMAC microprocessor, as shown by the block diagram of Fig. 3-44. Inputs are provided via eight binary toggle switches; hex outputs are displayed on two seven-segment LED (hex-digit) displays along with the Q light output. Additional toggle switches are provided for all the required controls to examine and alter memory locations and to initiate program execution. A memory protect switch inhibits the memory write operation to prevent an improperly running program from writing into itself. Programs are loaded via the on-chip

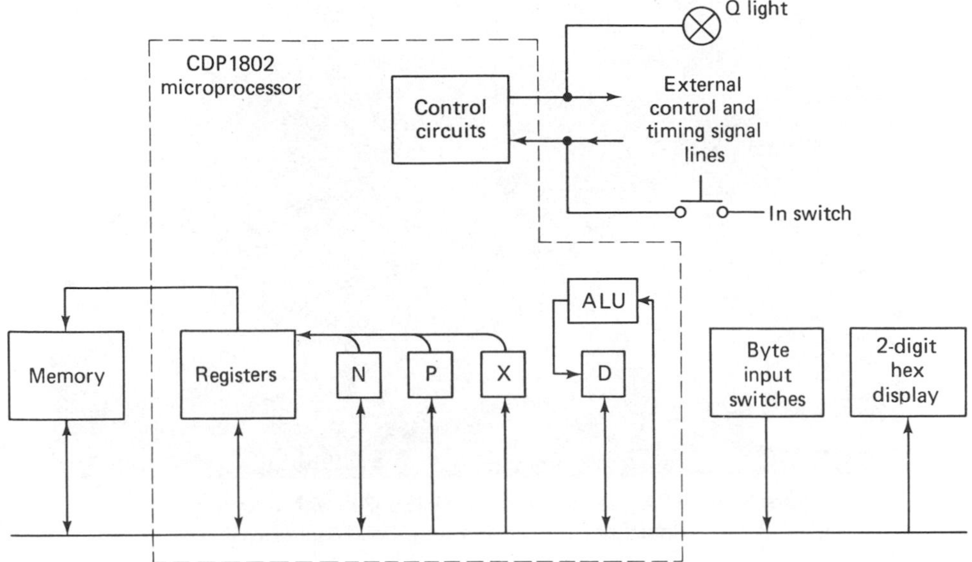

Figure 3-44 RCA Microtutor II, block diagram.

DMA facility, which eliminates the need for a bootstrap loading routine. A crystal clock is used for stable timing applications. A regulated power supply is also provided.

Microtutor II is provided with 256 bytes of CMOS RAM mounted on a memory card which attaches to the base through a standard 44-pin connector. An additional prewired socket (E1 in Fig. 3-43) and a set of connector holes (E2) are provided through which all the COSMAC Microtutor II signals are available for system expansion. Additional RAM and user I/O interfaces can be connected to this extra socket, and an operating system described in the user manual can be loaded into the additional RAM to provide a utility memory. The operating system greatly expands the Microtutor II capability, and the memory and I/O extendibility allows the use of Microtutor II in an almost unlimited spectrum of experimental applications.

3-6-2 Evaluation kit CDP18S020

Figure 3-45 shows the evaluation kit, which is a system designed for three principal uses:

1. To evaluate the RCA1800 CMOS microprocessor series circuits.
2. To learn about basic microprocessor-based system design, hardware interfacing, and programming.
3. To breadboard and prototype a COSMAC-based microcomputer system.

Figure 3-45 RCA evaluation kit, CDP18S020, with microterminal, CDP18S021. (Courtesy RCA Corporation, Solid State Division.)

The evaluation kit includes a 5-V 600-mA power supply and either a standard ASCII terminal or an RCA microterminal (as described in Sec. 3-6-3). The heart of the kit is the CDP-1802D 8-bit microprocessor, surrounded by RAMs, ROMs, and I/O ports. The microterminal or direct terminal interfacing complete the kit. The system can be divided into three functional areas: *control and communications, RAM memory,* and *user I/O.*

The control and communications area contains the microprocessor, the utility ROM and RAM, the I/O ports, the control logic and switches, the terminal interface, and the display. The RAM memory and the user I/O areas are available to the user for expansion and customizing the performance of the kit. A standard 44-pin connector is used for all required system communications and power; a separate connector makes all 40 pins of the microprocessor available to the user; and a third 44-pin connector is provided for the user I/O area.

3-6-3 Microterminal CDP18S021

Figure 3-46 shows the microterminal, which is a fully assembled, compact, hand-held terminal designed for interfacing with CDP1802-based microcomputer systems. Combined with its utility program, designated by the manufacturer as UT5 and supplied as firmware, the microterminal:

1. Is specifically suited for use with the evaluation kit (Sec. 3-6-2) or comparable user-designed systems.
2. Can be easily used in portable or battery-operated applications (requires less than 375 mA at 5V).

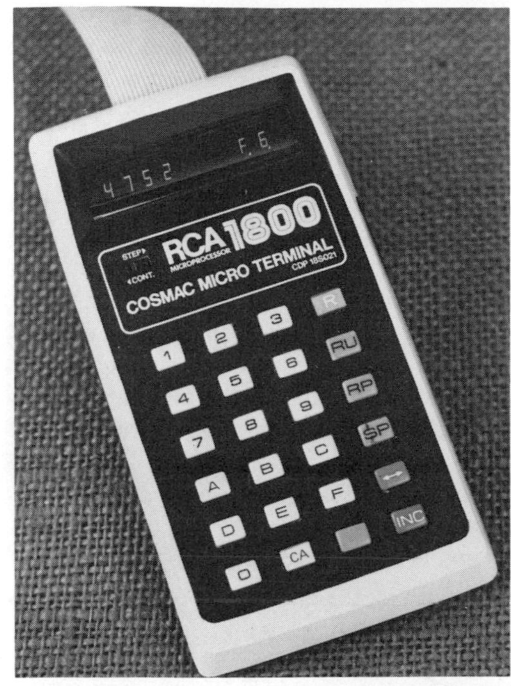

Figure 3-46 RCA Microterminal, CDP18S021. (Courtesy RCA Corporation, Solid State Division.)

3. Performs standard control, communications, and debug functions.

4. Is a low-cost, convenient non-hard-copy alternative to more expensive conventional terminals (such as a video terminal).

Data and memory addresses, as well as the control functions, are entered through the keyboard. Both the address and data are displayed in hex. The microterminal directly interfaces with the evaluation kit without the need for additional hardware or software. The combination of the two provides a low-cost microcomputer development system.

The display is a field of eight seven-segment LEDs for full hex display. The left four digits normally display the memory address (4752 in Fig. 3-46), and the two right-hand digits show the data (F6 in Fig. 3-46). The decimal points in the appropriate field are lit to indicate the addressing mode being used at the time (data entry or address entry). A 20-wire ribbon cable is supplied for all necessary interfacing signals.

The utility program UT5, supplied as firmware, is the controller for the microterminal. The program contains a series of useful subroutined linked together to run the system and to perform custom functions as organized by the programmer. The UT5 routines include display formatting and control, keyboard scan, debounce and decode, register initialization for the CDP1802 call-and-return subroutine linkage, independent control of all eight display digits and decimal points, readout control of microprocessor registers R1 through RF, consecutive readout of memory locations at 1-Hz rate, display of registers RA and RB in a user program, and read and modify of the RAM.

3-6-4 Micromonitor CDP18S030

Figure 3-47 shows the micromonitor, which is a self-contained, powerful debugging tool for use with any CDP1802 microprocessor system. The micromonitor permits in-circuit debugging in real time (single step) of both hardware and software. The micromonitor includes a built-in keyboard and display, status indicator lights, and software debugging routine. The primary use of the micromonitor is for prototype-system software and hardware debugging. However, because of its easy portability, the micromonitor is also useful as a field service tool. In addition, the micromonitor can be used as a versatile production tester.

By means of a single cable connection, the micromonitor can be interposed between the microprocessor of a system under test and all the interfaces of the microprocessor, giving the user control of both hardware

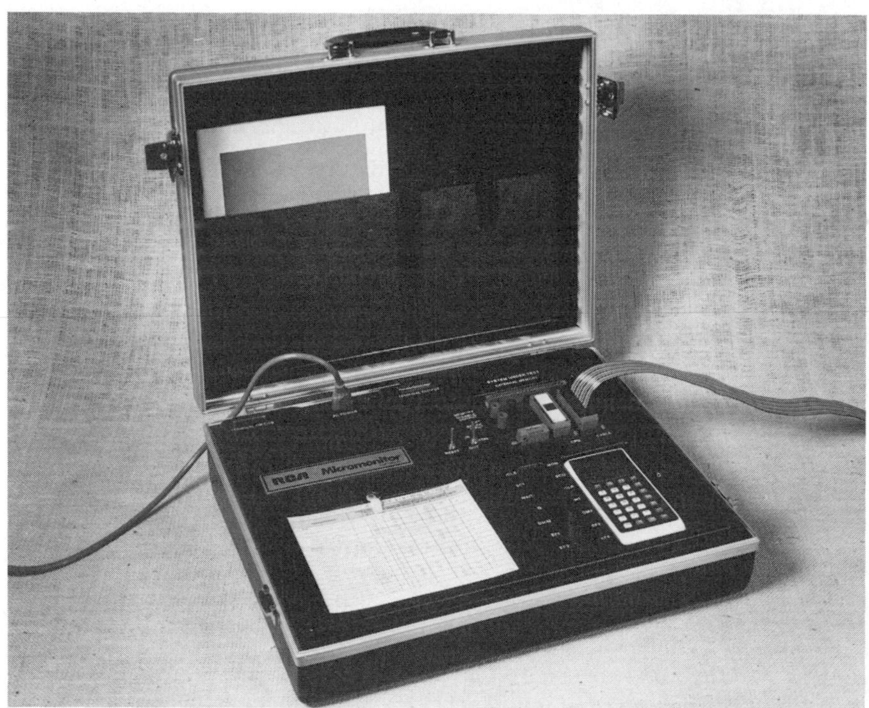

Figure 3-47 RCA micromonitor, CDP18S030. (Courtesy RCA Corporation, Solid State Division.)

interfaces and program execution. The micromonitor is controlled by its own internal microprocessor, but uses the microprocessor, power supply, clock, memory, and so on, *of the system under test to run a user program.* In this way, the micromonitor does not "emulate" the system but provides a reliable measure of true system performance.

The micromonitor can be operated from its own keyboard or, if a hard-copy record is desired, from an external terminal. Remote operation from a floppy disk file of commands is also possible when the micromonitor is used with development system II, CDP18S005 (described in Sec. 3-6-5).

System features. The micromonitor provides an extensive set of debugging capabilities. The 43 commands permit the user to examine or modify memory and all microprocessor registers and flags. The micromonitor also provides read/write capability to any I/O device and can generate signals to all microprocessor control, request, and flag inputs, and can either inhibit or allow system-generated requests to the DMA and interrupt lines.

Break conditions can be programmed for all of the following: external flag lines, auxiliary break input, idle, interrupt response, or memory read/write. When a break occurs, the values of D, X, P, and R(P) are recorded, providing a trace function. A log of the last 16 values of these registers is available to the user.

Three modes for running programs are available. One mode provides for real-time running, starting at a specified address or continuing from a break. The number of break conditions to be encountered before the micromonitor takes control can be specified in this mode. Another mode provides for single or a specified number of instruction cycles. Data are logged after each instruction cycle in this mode. The third mode provides for a single or a specified number of machine cycles to be executed.

3-6-5 Development system II CDP18S005

Figures 3-48 and 3-49 show the development system II, which is an interactive software and hardware prototyping system for the development of the products based on the RCA1800 family of microprocessor parts. The system uses the CDP1802 as the microprocessor and includes a RAM-based resident editor and assembler. The system has space for additional I/O devices so that it can be used for hardware prototyping as well as program development. In small-volume applications, the system can be used as the major building block for dedicated microcomputers.

System features. The system is designed for flexibility and expansion, providing seven spare memory PC module positions and ten spare I/O positions. Extra memory or operational I/O modules are available, or users may design and add their own. Interfacing for both standard 20-mA current loop and EIA RS232C terminals are available, so a wide variety of

Figure 3-48 RCA Development System II, CDP18S005. (Courtesy RCA Corporation, Solid State Division.)

terminals can be used with the system. Interfacing for the hand-held microterminal (Sec. 3-6-3) is also available.

System software. The system comes with a resident system utility program in firmware (ROM/RAM module) and with both paper tape and magnetic cassette versions of resident editor and resident assembler programs. These programs permit the user to do program development on the system. The *system utility program* allows the user to imspect and modify memory and start program execution at any location. The *resident editor program* permits standard text editing, such as adding or deleting characters, words, or lines. The *resident assembler* converts instruction mnemonics into machine code. Both the resident editor and resident assembler programs are available on floppy disks (Sec. 3-6-6).

3-6-6 Floppy disk system II, CDP18S805V2

The floppy disk system (FDS) is a mass-memory storage unit designed to work with the development system II (Sec. 3-6-5) to facilitate rapid program development. Use of the FDS reduces program development time significantly in comparison with systems using other media. For example, assembly of a 1-kilobyte program takes approximately 10 minutes when the FDS is used, as compared to approximately 1 hour with a 10-character-per-second paper-tape system.

The floppy disk system consists of the following elements:

1. A dual-disk drive mechanism with cable.
2. An interface module.

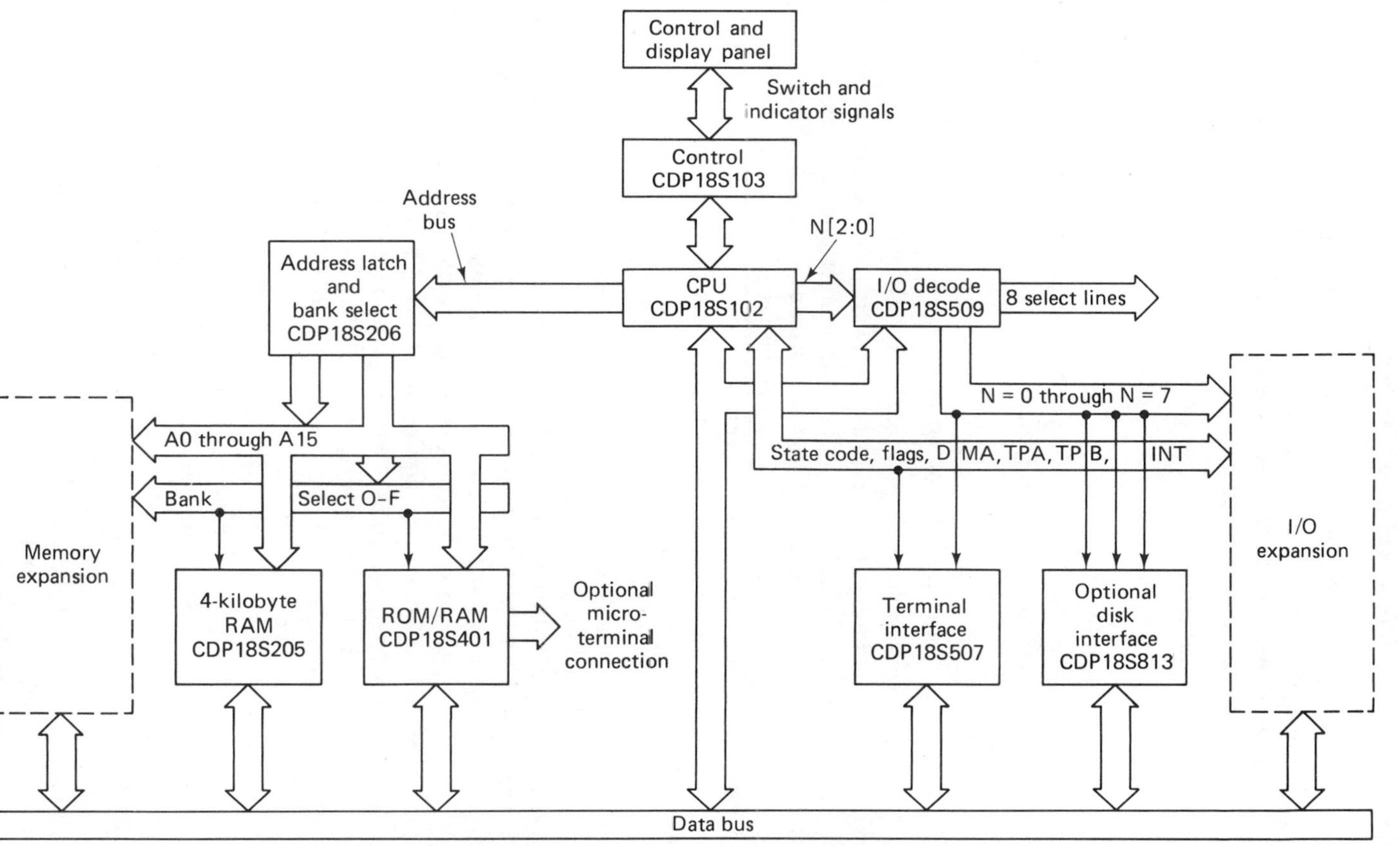

Figure 3-49 RCA Development System II, CDP18S005, block diagram.

3. A system diskette containing the following programs: assembler, editor, diagnostic, tape-to-diskette transfer, diskette copy, memory save, ROM save, printer, diskette file examination, change notice, and demonstration program.
4. A blank diskette.
5. An instruction manual.

Installation of the FDS requires nothing more than plugging the interface module into the development system and the interfacing cable into the module. Disk loader and utility programs are already contained in the ROM and development system.

3-6-7 Software development package CSDP

The software development package is a versatile interactive integrated program for developing and checking software for COSMAC microprocessor systems. The CSDP includes an assembler and combined simulator/debugger. The assembler program translates symbolic source statements into machine language. That is, the assembler produces microprocessor machine code directly in simulated memory. If requested, the assembler can generate a source listing and diagnostic messages that can be directed to a disk file or the data terminal.

The simulator mimics the actions of all instructions and interrupts and maintains simulated copies of the microprocessor memory, flags, and all registers. The *debugger,* through a set of debug commands, allows the programmer to perform a number of functions, including the following: set breakpoints, set read or write guards for any memory address, set interrupts, inspect and modify any memory address, inspect and modify any register or flag, save the machines state at any point during simulation, restore the machine state from any previous saved state, single-step and trace-through program execution, trace jumps, and simulate ROM.

The simulator also halts a program and gives diagnostic messages for invalid instruction codes or for attempted execution of data reads or writes outside simulated memory.

To operate the CSDP, the user first creates a source file containing the program. This file is written in assembly language. (There are two assembly languages, designated as Level I and Level II.) At the user's option, the file may also contain debug-mode commands. The editor program of the host computer may be used to create or modify this file.

The debugger may then be used to call in the assembler to create the object code from the source code. The debugger can also be used to monitor program simulation by saving, restoring, modifying, or inquiring about the simulation conditions.

3-6-8 Video interface processor

Figures 3-50 and 3-51 show the COSMAC video interface processor, or VIP, which is a low-cost, hobbyist computer kit. The VIP kit permits hobbyists to assemble a microcomputer with which they can create and play video games, generate graphics, and develop microprocessor control functions. The VIP is a complete computer on a PC card, and outputs directly with a monochrome CRT display. When used with an FCC-approved modulator, the VIP can output to a TV receiver. Programs can be generated and then stored in an audio cassette tape recorder for easy retrieval and use.

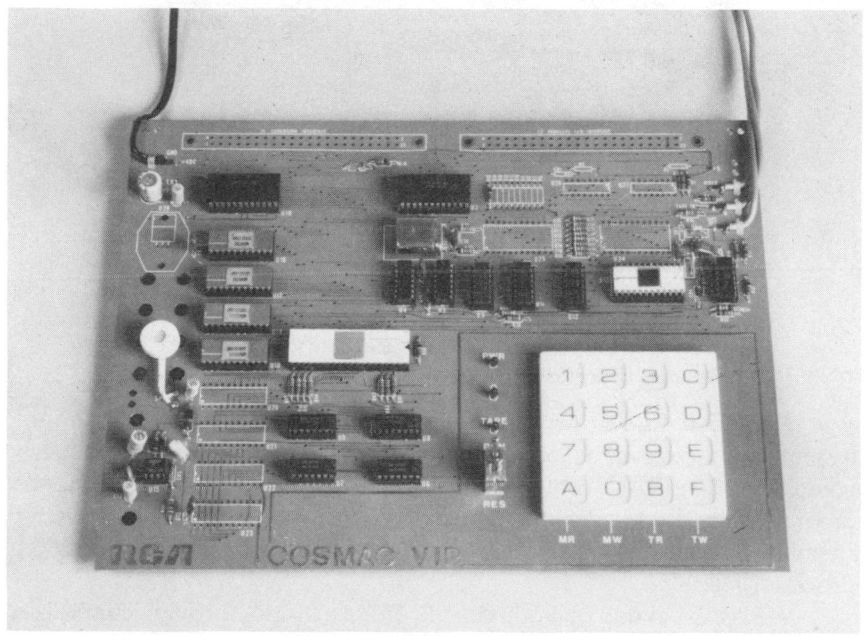

Figure 3-50 RCA video interface processor (VIP). Courtesy RCA Corporation, Solid State Division.)

The VIP uses the CDP1802 microprocessor, and includes RAMs, single-chip graphic video display interface, built-in hex keyboard, 100-byte per second audio tape cassette interface, simple wall-plug regulated power supply, and easy expandability for both memory and I/O.

The VIP uses a special language designated as CHIP-8, which has 31 instructions in a two-byte format. This interpretive programming language simplifies the hobbyist's efforts in programming by using hex code. Although simple, the instructions permit such programming tasks as displaying a pattern on the CRT, generating a random byte, sounding a tone, providing 16 one-byte variables, and permitting a subroutine nesting.

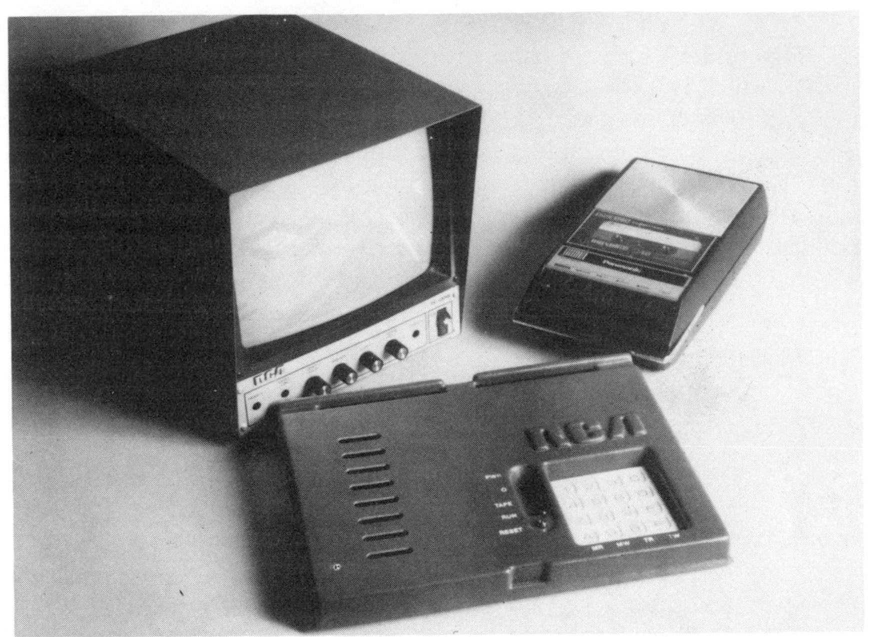

Figure 3-51 RCA video interface processor (VIP) with CRT display and cassette. (Courtesy RCA Corporation, Solid State Division.)

A 512-byte ROM operating system offers the hobbyist benefits in that it simplifies such tasks as loading a program into the RAM via the hex keyboard, recording RAM contents on cassette tapes, transferring tape-recorded programs into RAM, displaying memory bytes in hex format on a CRT, stepping through RAM contents, and examining contents of the microprocessor registers.

VIP is expandable, both on the PC card and through connectors. RAM capacity can be doubled from a nominal 2K to 4K bytes by adding additional RAM devices, and can be expanded to a total of 32K bytes by adding further memory capacity through a 44-pin connector socket in the card. Parallel I/O expansion to 19 lines can be achieved on the PC card for such purposes as music synthesizers, relays, a low-cost printer, or an ASCII keyboard. The 44-pin connector socket on the board also permits the addition of other circuitry for applications.

A hobbyist manual is included with the VIP. The manual contains detailed information on kit assembly, operating procedures, CHIP-8 language, machine language programming, logic descriptions, test programs, and troubleshooting guides. The manual also includes program lists for 20 video games, offering simple instructions on using the hex keyboard so that a novice can enter the programs for the 20 games and use the games immediately without having to learn programming.

4 Motorola M6800 Microcomputer System

This chapter is devoted entirely to the M6800 microcomputer system manufactured by Motorola Semiconductor Products, Inc. The chapter starts with a discussion of basic system components and system interfacing, then proceeds on with discussions of minimum system requirements, addressing modes, microprocessor control signals, and basic programming techniques. The discussion on programming is supplemented with a sample program. Next, the development aids are described.

The details presented in this chapter represent only a small fraction of the data taken from the manufacturer's literature (manuals and data sheets). However, the information presented is sufficient for a reader of any level to evaluate the system. The chapter also provides a realistic view of actual state-of-the-art microprocessor-based systems. This supplements the theoretical and typical descriptions of Chapters 1 and 2.

The system includes a complete set of hardware (microprocessor, serial and parallel interface adapters, ROMs, RAMs, alterable ROMs, clocks, modem, modulator, buffers, and bus extenders). The manufacturer also makes available a variety of aids for design, development, test, debugging, and troubleshooting of system components.

4-1 BASIC MICROCOMPUTER FAMILY

The basic M6800 microcomputer family, shown in Fig. 4-1, includes the microprocessor, ROM, RAM, peripheral interface adapter (PIA), asynchronous communications interface adapter (ACIA), and system clock. The following paragraphs of this section provide a brief description of these basic elements.

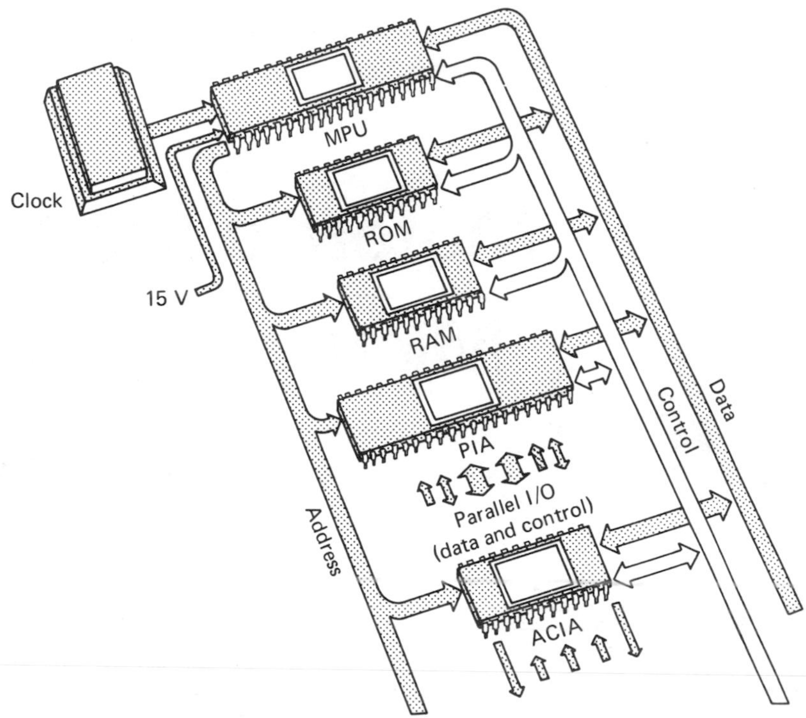

Figure 4-1 Basic Motorola M6800 microcomputer family.

4-1-1 Microprocessor M6800

Figure 4-2 shows the symbolic diagram and programming model of the M6800 microprocessor. (Note that this IC is referred to by the manufacturer as a microprocessing unit, or MPU.) Figure 4-3 shows the relationship of the microprocessor to the system, as well as a simplified block diagram. A more detailed block diagram is given in Fig. 1-15.

The microprocessor is a bidirectional, bus-oriented, 8-bit parallel machine with 16 bits of address. For most systems, depending on interconnection capacitance, the microprocessor is capable of directly interfacing with eight peripheral parts and one TTL load on the same bus at a 1-MHz clock rate. For systems requiring additional peripheral parts, a data bus extender (BEX) is available.

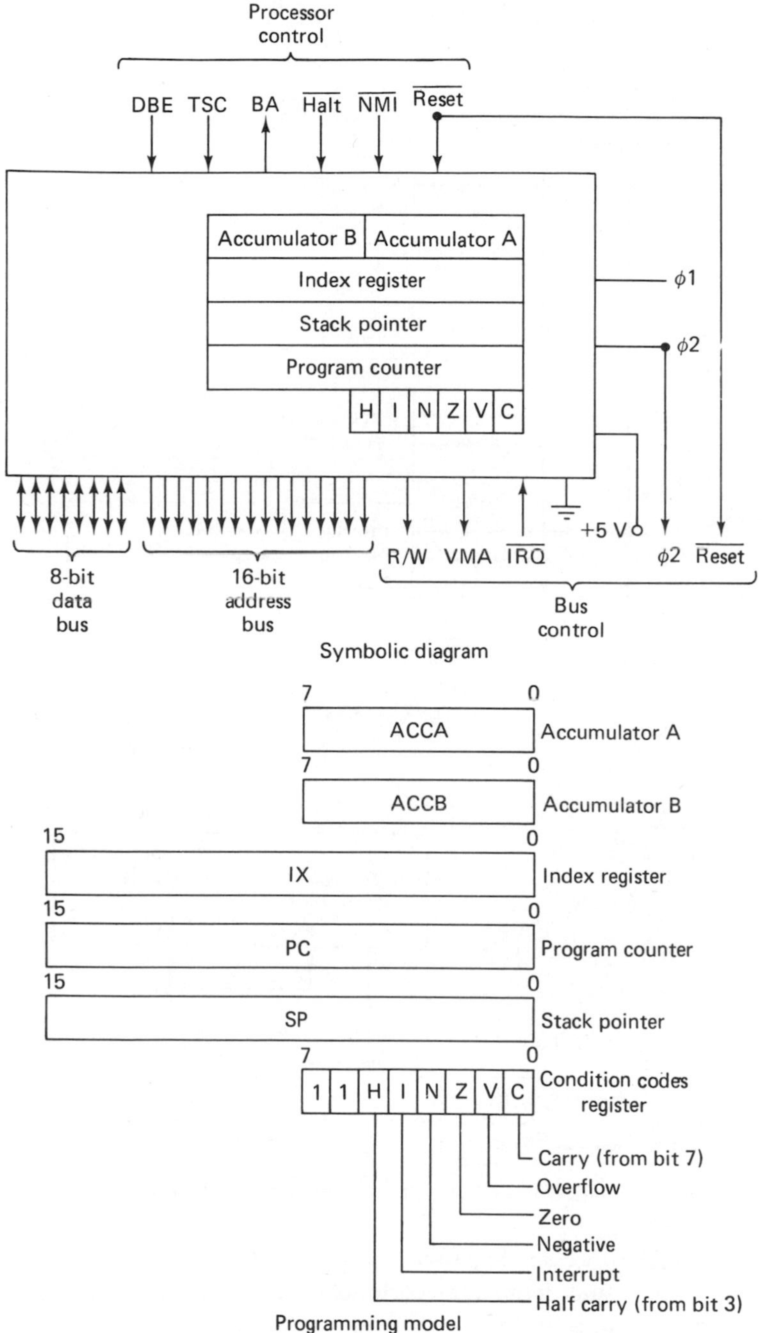

Figure 4-2 M6800 microprocessor, symbolic diagram and programming model.

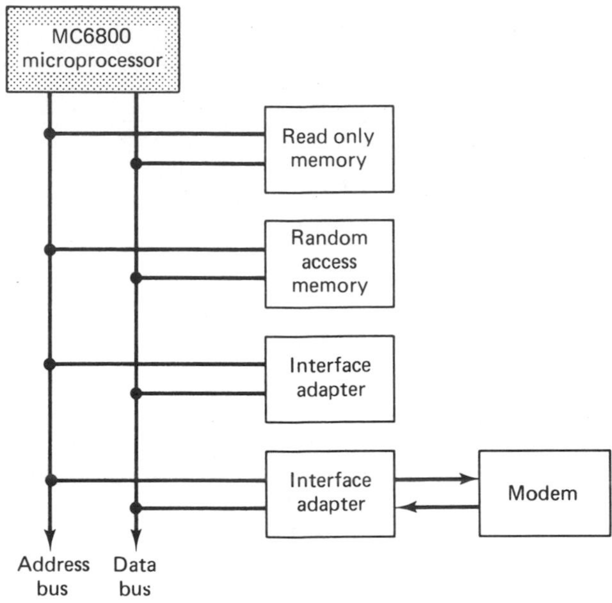

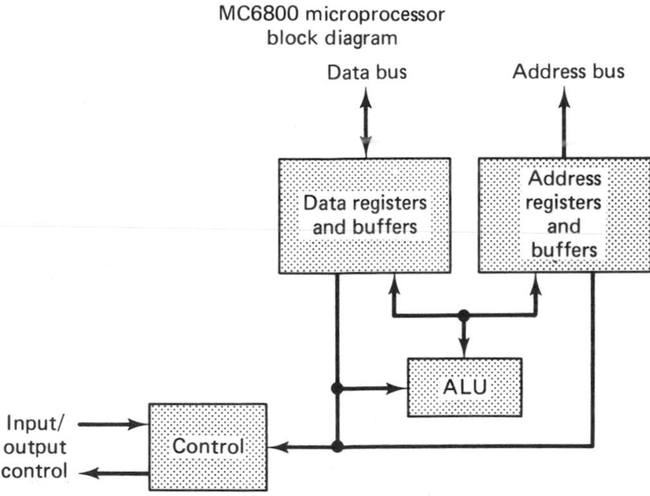

Figure 4-3 M6800 system relationships and microprocessor block diagram.

The microprocessor has two 8-bit *accumulators* that are used to hold operands and results from the Arithmetic Logic Unit (ALU). The 16-bit *index register* stores 16 bits of memory address for the *index mode* of memory addressing (Sec. 4-3). The *stack pointer* is a two-byte (8 bits/byte) register that contains the address of the next available location in an external push-down/pop-up stack (Sec. 4-5). This stack is normally a random access read/write memory that may have any location (address) that is convenient. In those applications that require storage of information in the stack when power is lost, the stack must be nonvolatile.

The *program counter* is a 16-bit register that contains the program address. A *condition code register* (or flag register) contains 6 bits of condition codes. The condition codes indicate the results of an ALU operation: Negative (N), Zero (Z), Overflow (V), Carry from bit 7(C), and Half carry from bit 3 (H). These bits of the condition code register are used as testable conditions for the conditional branch instructions. Bit 4 is the interrupt mask bit (I). The unused bits of the condition code register (B6, B7) are always 1s.

The minimum instruction execution time is 2 μs. Microprocessor control lines include Reset, which automatically restarts the microprocessor, as well as Interrupt Request and Non-Maskable Interrupt to monitor peripheral status. Also, there is a Three-State Control, Data Bus Enable, and a Halt control line which can be used for direct memory access (DMA), or multiprocessing. Microprocessor controls are discussed further in Sec. 4-4.

4-1-2 128-character × 8-bit RAM MCM6810A

Figure 4-4 shows the interfacing, relationship to the system and basic block diagram of the MCM6810A RAM. A more detailed block diagram is shown in Fig. 1-18.

The RAM is a static memory that interfaces directly to the microprocessor and is organized in an 8-bit byte fashion. The RAM has six chip select (CS) inputs, four active low and two active high, that interface directly to the address bus. The interface shown in Fig. 4-4 demonstrates the simplicity of interface in the M6800 system. Since all M6800 components operate at the same TTL levels and with the same drive capability, the data, address, and control lines can be interconnected without adding external TTL buffers. Memory timing of the RAM is set to permit simple operation at full speed with the microprocessor.

Four of the chip selects are used to decode the system address lines. In small and medium-sized systems, this address decoding will be sufficient to distinguish all packages in the system without using any additional address decoding packages.

4-1-3 1024 × 8-bit ROM MCM6830A

Figure 4-5 shows the interfacing, relationship to the system, and basic block diagram of the MCM6830A ROM. A more detailed block diagram is shown in Fig. 1-21.

The ROM is a static memory that also interfaces directly to the microprocessor. The output drivers are level compatible with the M6800 family.

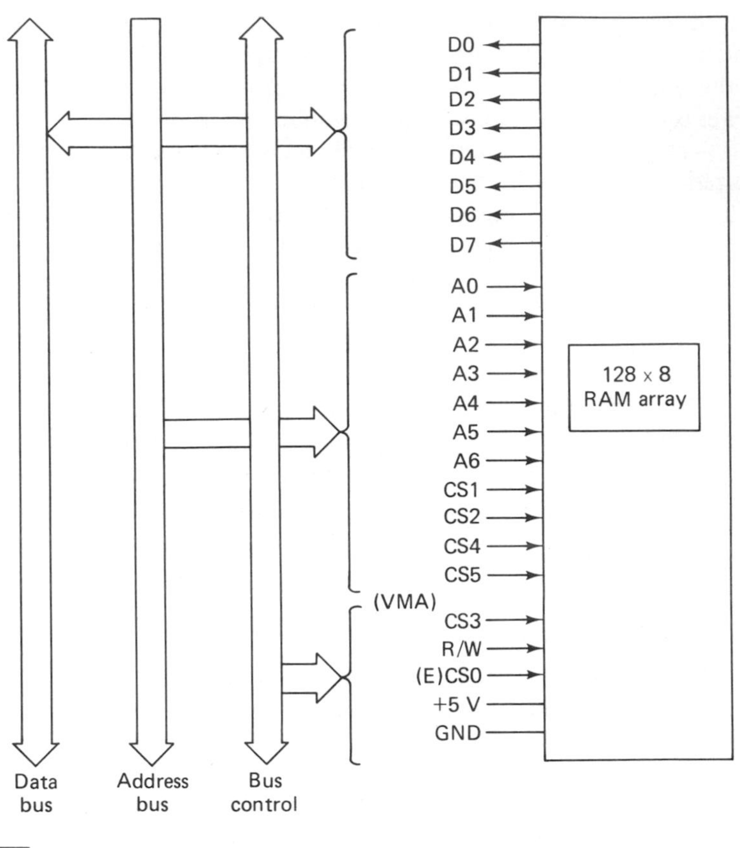

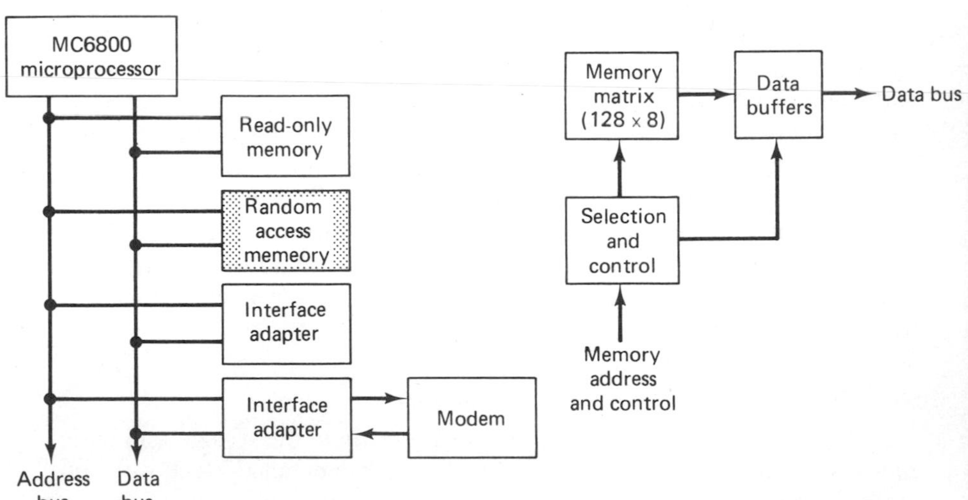

Figure 4-4 MCM6810A RAM, interfacing, relationship to system, and basic block diagram.

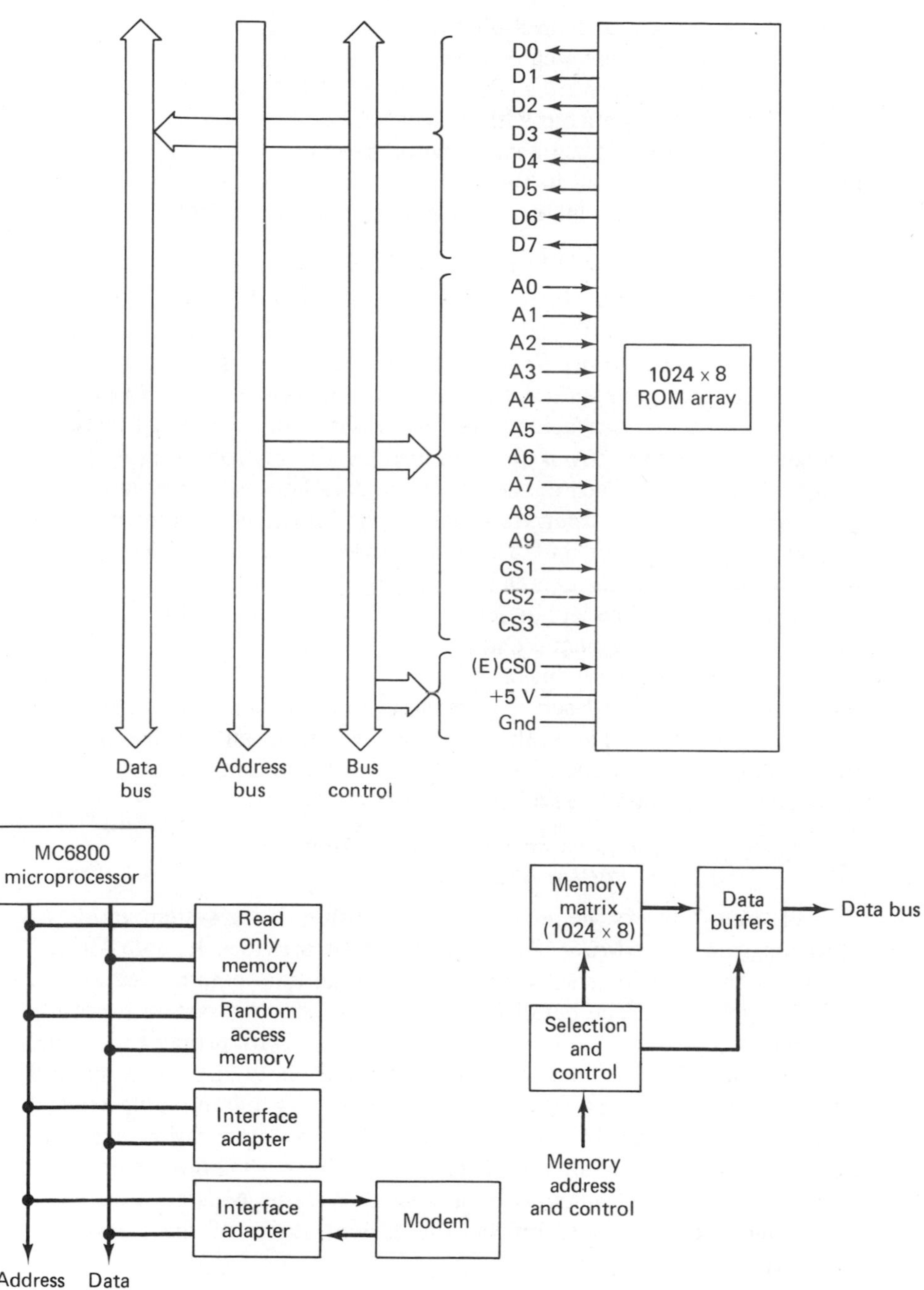

Figure 4-5 MCM6830A ROM, interfacing, relationship to system, and basic block diagram.

The ROM is organized in an 8-bit byte fashion similar to the RAM, and has 10 address lines plus 4 chip selects. The ROM bus interface shown in Fig. 4-5 is as straightforward as that of the RAM. All outputs may be connected directly to the data bus without drivers.

The three chip selects (mask-programmable) on the ROM are used to provide address decoding in the system. In many systems, the decoding possible with these lines will be sufficient to distinguish the ROM.

4-1-4 Peripheral interface adapter (PIA) MC6820

Figure 4-6 shows the interfacing, relationship to the system, and basic block diagram of the MC6820 PIA. The PIA provides a universal means of interfacing peripheral equipment to the microprocessor through two 8-bit bidirectional peripheral data buses and four control lines. No external logic is required for interfacing to many peripheral devices. The functional configuration of the PIA is programmed by the microprocessor during system initialization. Each of the peripheral data lines can be programmed to act as an input or output, and each of the four control/interrupt lines may be programmed for one of several control modes. This allows a high degree of flexibility in the overall operation of the interface.

The data bus lines, chip selects, read/write, and enable lines have the same static and dynamic characteristics as the other elements in the M6800 system. The reset line is used to initialize the PIA. The register select lines RS0 and RS1 serve the same purpose in the PIA as addressed lines do in memory. That is, they address the control and status registers, thus making the PIA look like memory to the microprocessor. A full description of the interface lines is given in Sec. 4-2.

4-1-5 Asynchronous communications interface adapter (ACIA) MC6850

Figure 4-7 shows the interfacing relationship to the system and basic block diagram of the MC6850 ACIA. The ACIA provides the data formatting and control to interface asynchronous serial data communications to the microprocessor. The parallel data of the M6800 bus system is serially transmitted and received (full-duplex) by the ACIA, with proper formatting and error checking. The functional configuration of the ACIA is programmed via the data bus during system initialization. A programmable control register provides variable word lengths, clock division ratios, transmit control, receive control, and interrupt control. Three I/O lines are provided to control external peripherals or modems. A status register is available to the microprocessor and reflects the current status of the transmitter and receiver.

4-1-6 Synchronous serial data adapter (SSDA) MC6852

Figure 4-8 shows the relationship to the system, and the basic block diagram of the MC6852. The SSDA provides a bidirectional serial interface

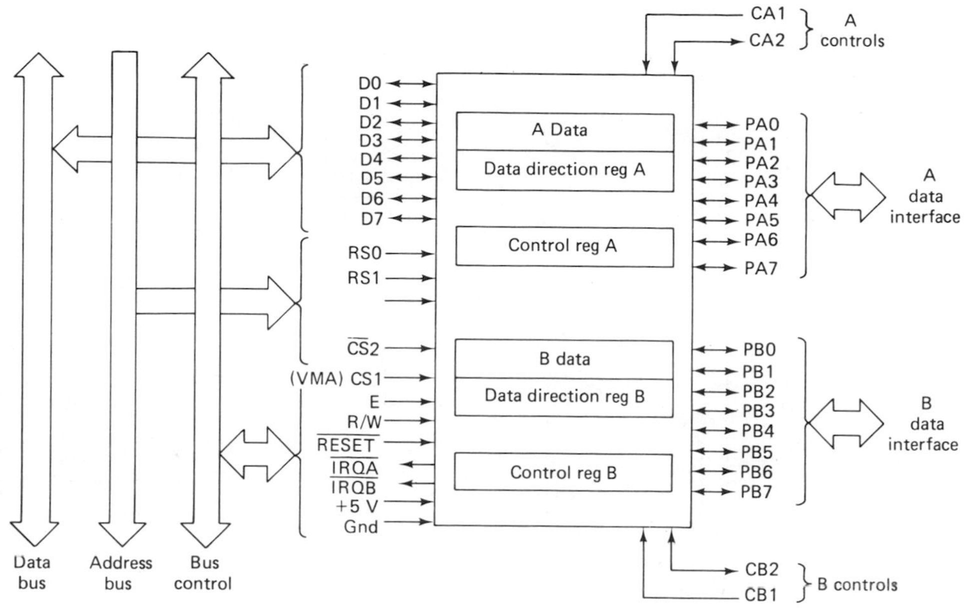

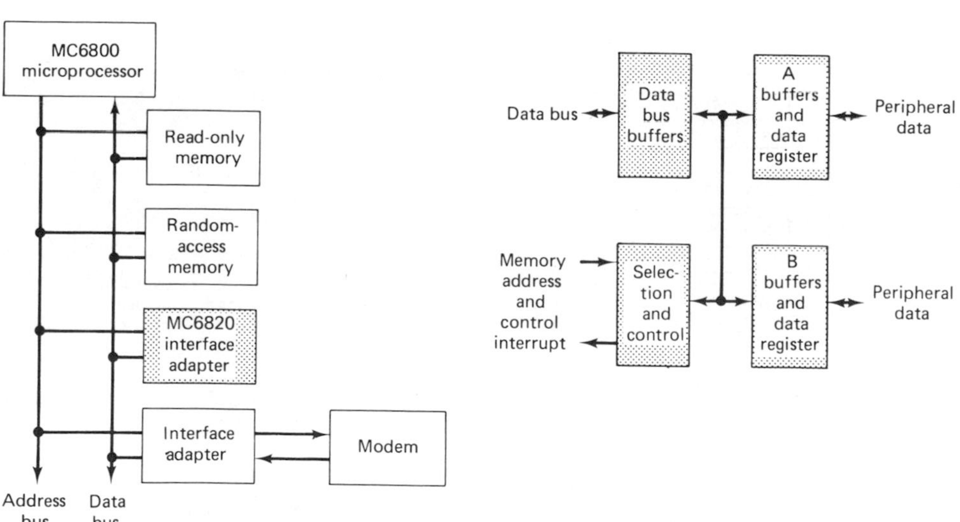

Figure 4-6 MC6820 PIA, interfacing, relationship to system, and basic block diagram.

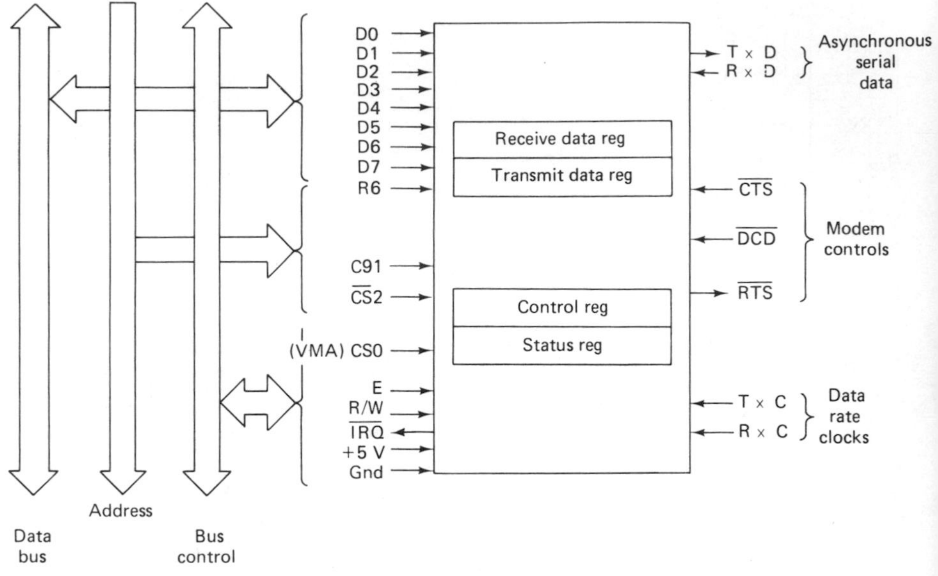

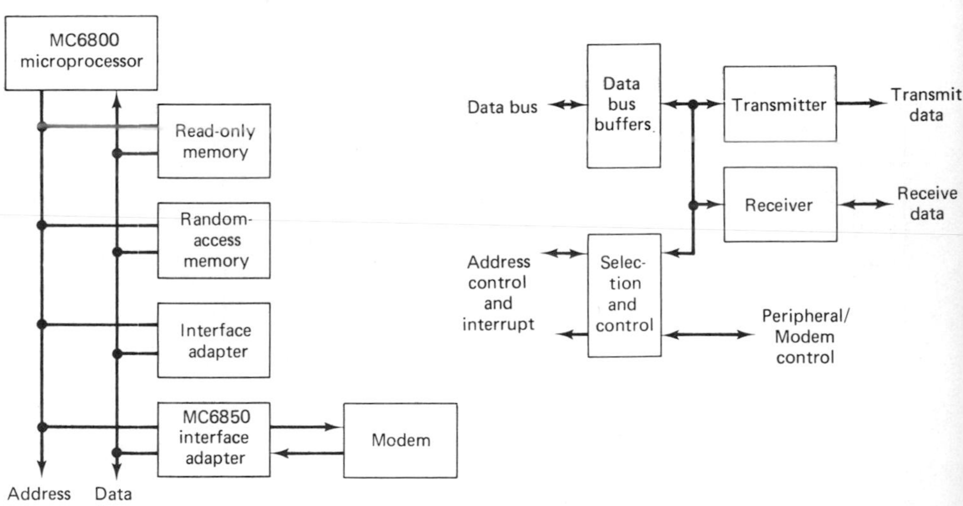

Figure 4-7 MC6850 ACIA, interfacing, relationship to system, and basic block diagram.

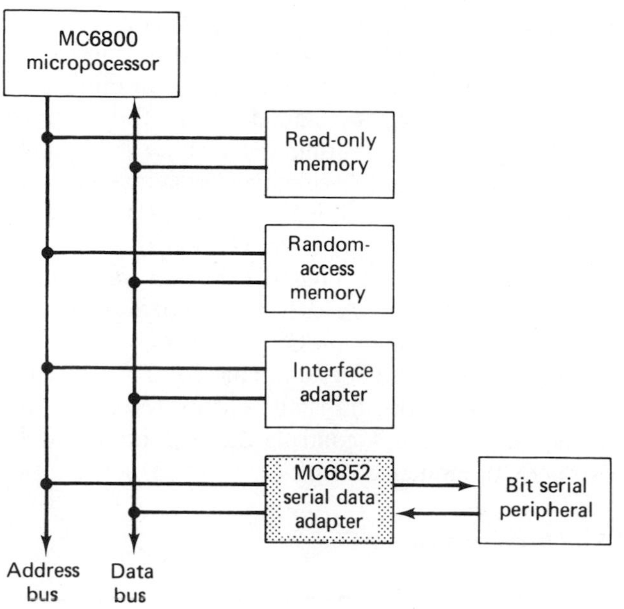

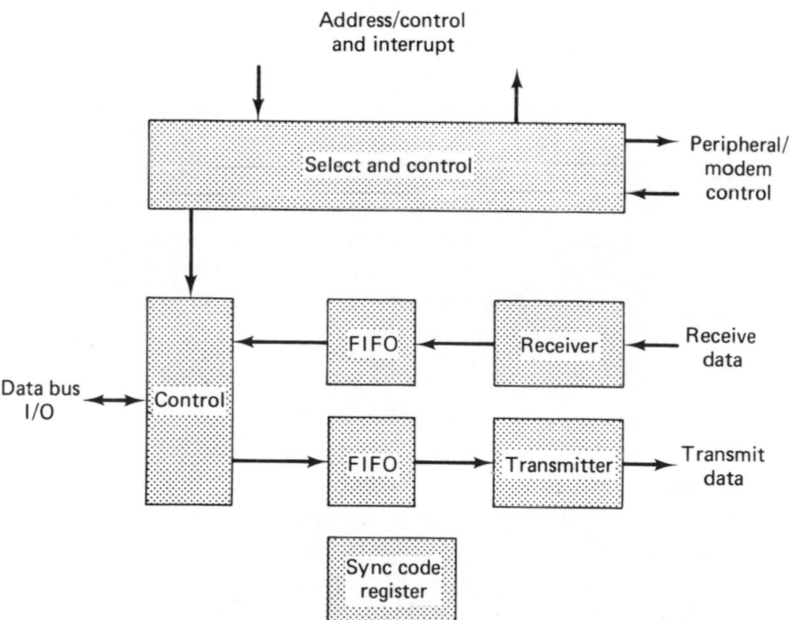

Figure 4-8 MC6852 SSDA, relationship to system and basic block diagram.

for synchronous data information interchange. Synchronous serial data are the type used by such peripherals as floppy disk controllers, cassette or cartridge tape controllers, data communication terminals, and numerical control systems, as discussed in Chapter 2. The SSDA contains interface logic for simultaneously transmitting and receiving standard synchronous communications characters in bus-organized systems such as the M6800.

The bus interface of the SSDA includes select, enable, read/write, interrupt, and bus interface logic to allow data transfer over an 8-bit bidirectional data bus. The parallel data of the bus system are serially transmitted and received by the SSDA with synchronization and error checking. The functional configuration of the SSDA is programmed via the data bus during system initialization. Programmable control registers provide control for variable word lengths, transmit control, receive control, synchronization control, and interrupt control. Status, timing, and control lines provide peripheral or modem control.

4-1-7 Digital modem MC6860

Figure 4-9 shows the relationship to the system, the basic block diagram, and a typical system configuration of the MC6860.

The digital modem is a MOS subsystem designed to be integrated into a wide range of equipment (not just the M6800) using serial data communications. The modem provides the necessary modulation, demodulation, and supervisory control functions to implement a serial data communications link, over a voice-grade channel, using frequency shift keying (FSK) at bit rates up to 600 bits/s. The M6800 can be implemented into a wide range of data storage devices, remote data communication terminals, and I/O interfaces. The modem operates from a single voltage supply and is fully TTL-compatible, as well as compatible with the M6800 family. As shown in Fig. 4-9, the modem interfaces directly with the ACIA (Sec. 4-1-5).

4-1-8 Digital modulator MC6862

Figure 4-10 shows the relationship to the system, the block diagram, and a typical system interface for the MC6862. The digital modulator is an MOS subsystem designed to be integrated into a wide range of equipment (not just the M6800) using serial data communication. The modulator provides the necessary modulation and control functions to implement a serial data communication link over a voice-grade channel, using differential phase shift keying (DPSK) at bit rates of 1200 or 2400 bits/s. Phase options are provided for both the U.S. and international markets. The MC6862 can be implemented into a wide range of data-handling systems, including stand-alone modems, data storage devices, remote data communication terminals, and I/O interfaces for counters.

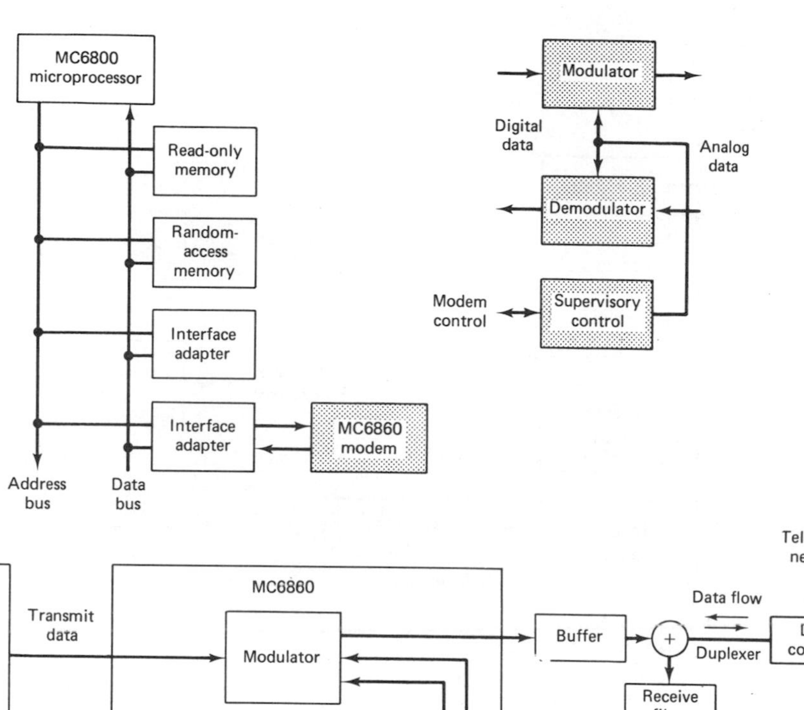

Figure 4-9 MC6860 digital modem, relationship to system, basic block diagram, and typical system configuration.

4-1-9 Two-phase microprocessor clocks MC6870 and MC6871

Figure 4-11 shows the block diagrams of two clocks required for the basic M6800 system (Fig. 4-1). The MC6870 provides two clock phases, plus one TTL clock signal. The MC6871 also provides separate clock signals for the memory.

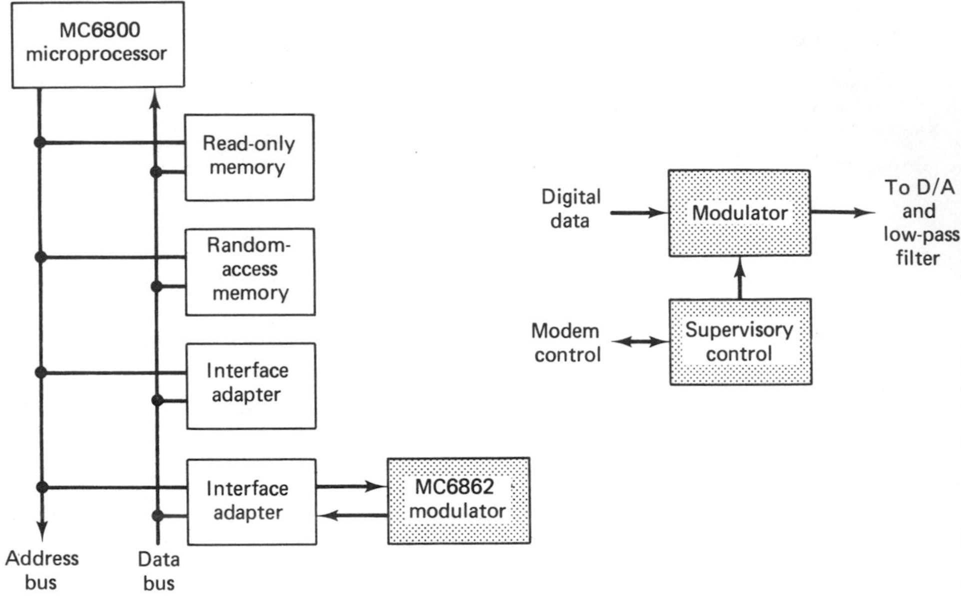

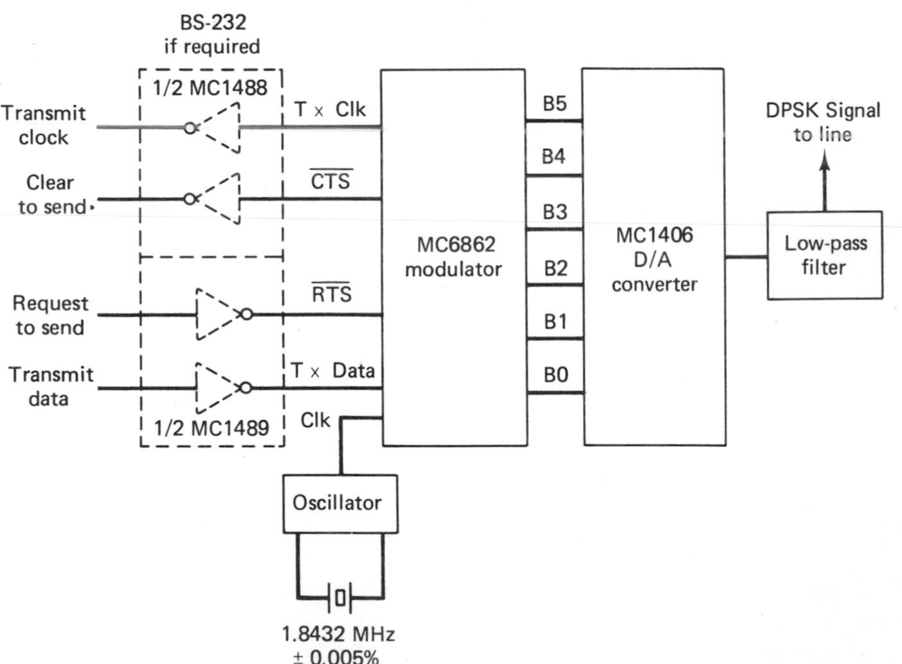

Figure 4-10 MC6862 digital modulator, relationship to system, block diagram, and typical system interface.

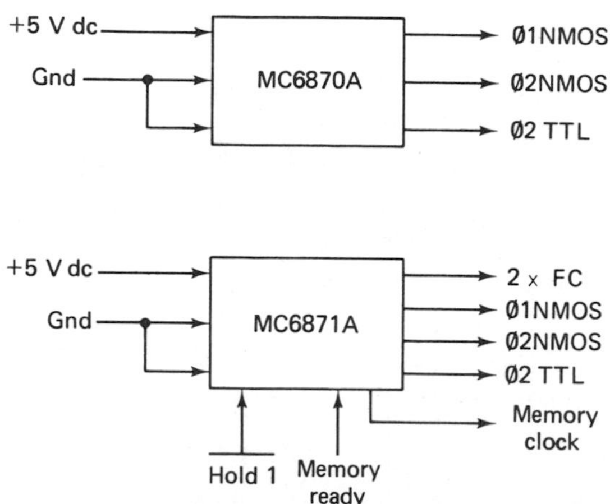

Figure 4-11 MC6870 and MC6871 two-phase microprocessor clocks.

Each clock module requires a single 5-V supply. The NMOS outputs can drive highly capacitive loads ranging from 80 to 160 pF and meet all microprocessor input waveshape and timing requirements. Each TTL output signal leads the phase-2 NMOS so that additional system device delays can be accommodated. All TTL outputs are buffered so they can drive five TTL devices and maintain all output specifications. Each clock is crystal-controlled and is compensated for variations in temperature, voltage, and load. The standard frequency of each model is 1 MHz. However, other frequencies between 250 kHz and 2.5 MHz can be ordered.

4-1-10 Quad three-state bus transceiver MC6880

Figure 4-12 shows the relationship to the system and the pin-connection diagram of the MC6880. The device is essentially a bus extender for the M6800 family. Both the 40-mA driver and 16-mA receiver outputs are short-circuit-protected and use three-state enabling inputs. The maximum input current of 200 μA at any of the device input pins assures proper operation despite the limited drive capability of the microprocessor. The inputs are also protected to suppress excessive undershoot voltages.

4-1-11 Triple bidirectional bus switch XC6881

Figure 4-13 shows the relationship to the system and the functional diagram of the XC6881. The XC6881 is a three-channel, noninverting, bidirectional bus extender designed to allow bidirectional exchange of TTL-level digital information between a selected pair of ports in a three-port network. All three ports of each channel may be forced to a high-impedance condition through that channel's enable input. Port pair selection and listener/talker status for the three channels is determined through the control and select inputs. All inputs are M6800-family-compatible.

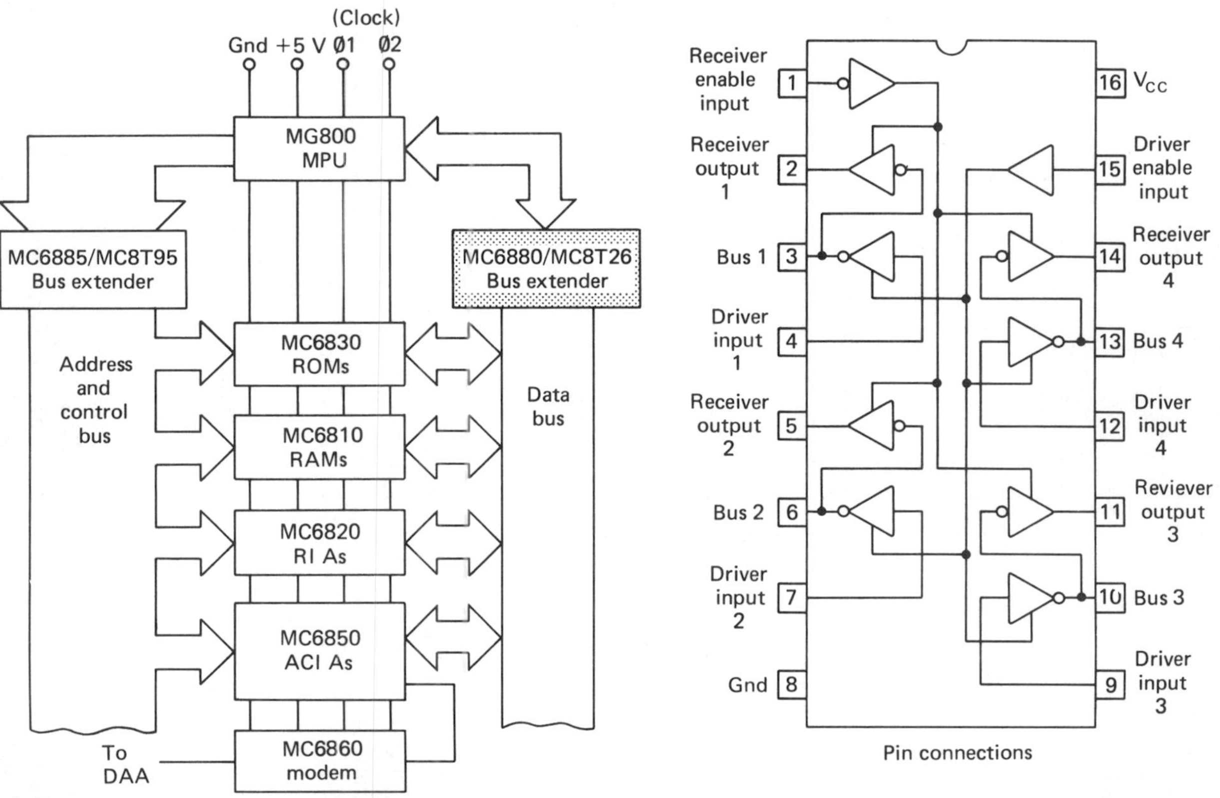

Figure 4-12 MC6880 quad three-state bus transceiver, relationship to system and pin-connection diagram.

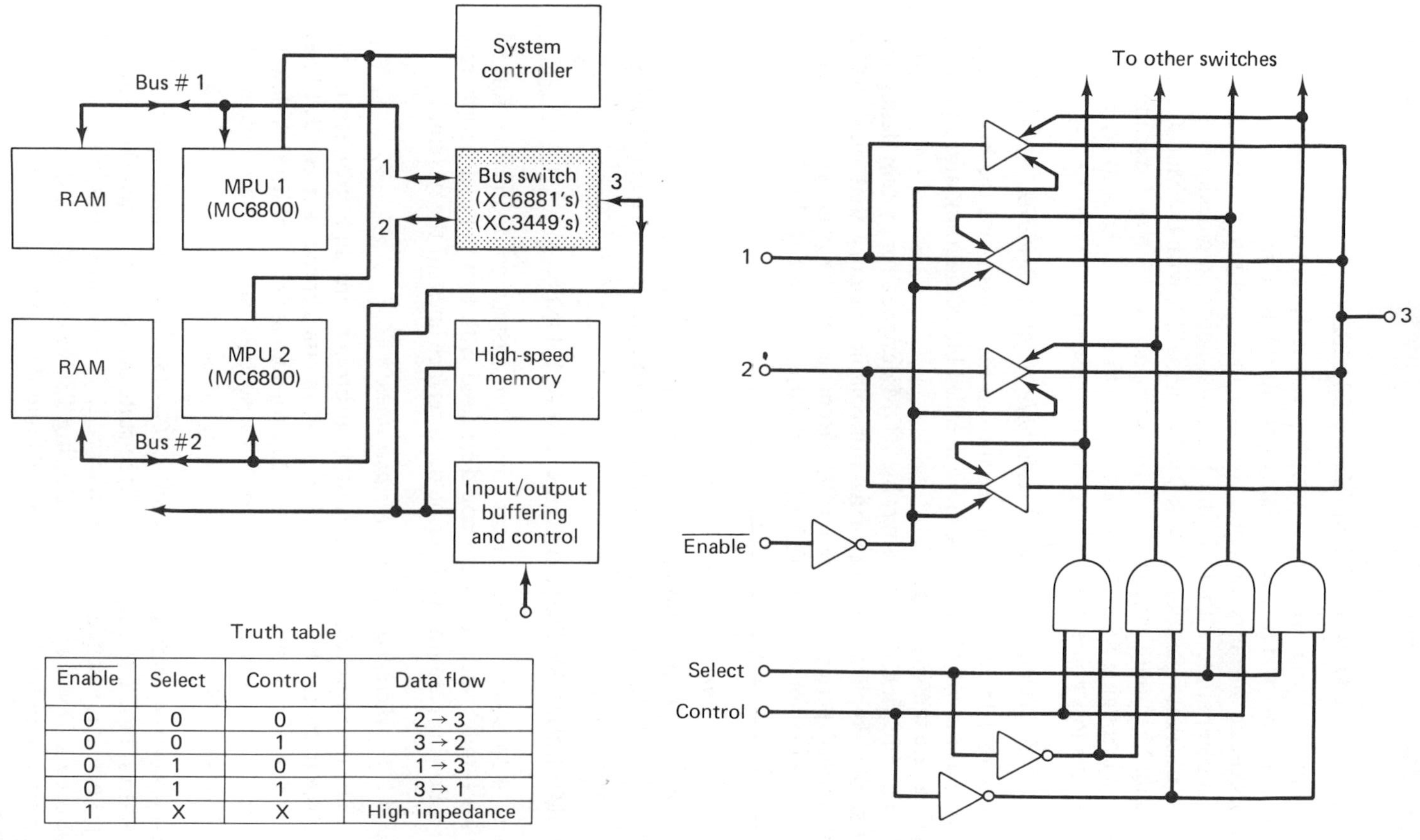

Truth table

$\overline{\text{Enable}}$	Select	Control	Data flow
0	0	0	2 → 3
0	0	1	3 → 2
0	1	0	1 → 3
0	1	1	3 → 1
1	X	X	High impedance

X - Don't care

Figure 4-13 MC6881 triple bidirectional bus switch, relationship to system and functional diagram.

4-1-12 2048-word × 8-bit ROM MCM6832

Figure 4-14 shows the relationship to the system and the functional block diagram of the MCM6832. The ROM is a mask-programmable byte-organized memory designed for use in bus-organized systems. The device is compatible with TTL and DTL and needs no clocks or refreshing because of static operation. The ROM is compatible with the M6800 family, providing read-only storage in byte increments. Memory expansion is provided through a chip select input. The active level of the chip select input and the memory content are defined by the customer.

4-1-13 1024-word × 8-bit alterable ROM MCM6870L

Figure 4-15 shows the relationship to the system and the basic block diagram of the MCM6870L. A more detailed block diagram, and a package drawing, are shown in Fig. 1-23.

The MCM6870L is an alterable ROM designed for system debug use, and similar applications requiring nonvolatile memory that must be reprogrammed periodically. The transparent lid on the package (Fig. 1-23) allows the memory content to be erased with ultraviolet light. The memory can then be electrically reprogrammed.

4-1-14 Other system components

Other system components include such devices as dynamic RAMs and clock buffers. Additional M6800 family components are being developed.

4-2 MINIMUM SYSTEM AND INTERFACE LINES

Figure 4-16 shows a theoretical minimum system configuration for the M6800 family. Such a system could be used with two parallel peripherals. The following paragraphs describe the interface lines for the system.

4-2-1 Microprocessor interface lines

The microprocessor input/output is broken into three groups: the bus interface lines, the bus control lines, and the microprocessor control lines. Description of bus interface and bus control lines are covered here. A description of the microprocessor control lines, such as halt and data bus enable, is presented in Sec. 4-4.

Microprocessor address bus lines (A0–A15). Sixteen pins are used for the address bus. The outputs are three-state bus drivers. When the output is turned off, it is essentially an open circuit. This permits the microprocessor to be used in DMA applications. Putting TSC (three-state control, Sec. 4-4) in its high state forces the address bus and R/W lines to go into the three-state mode.

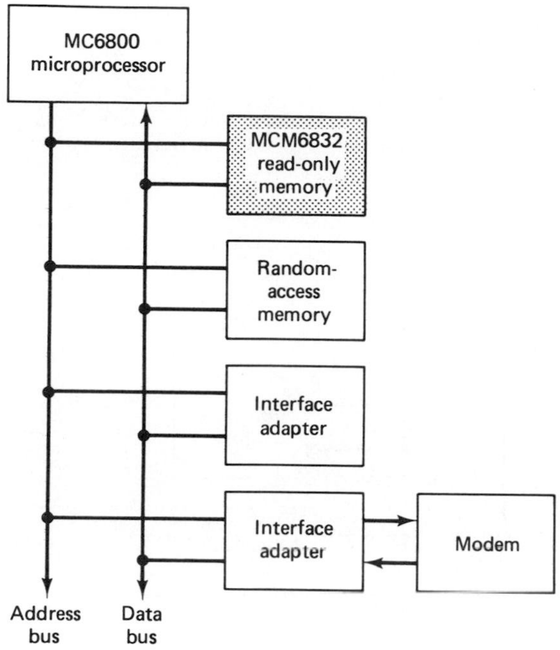

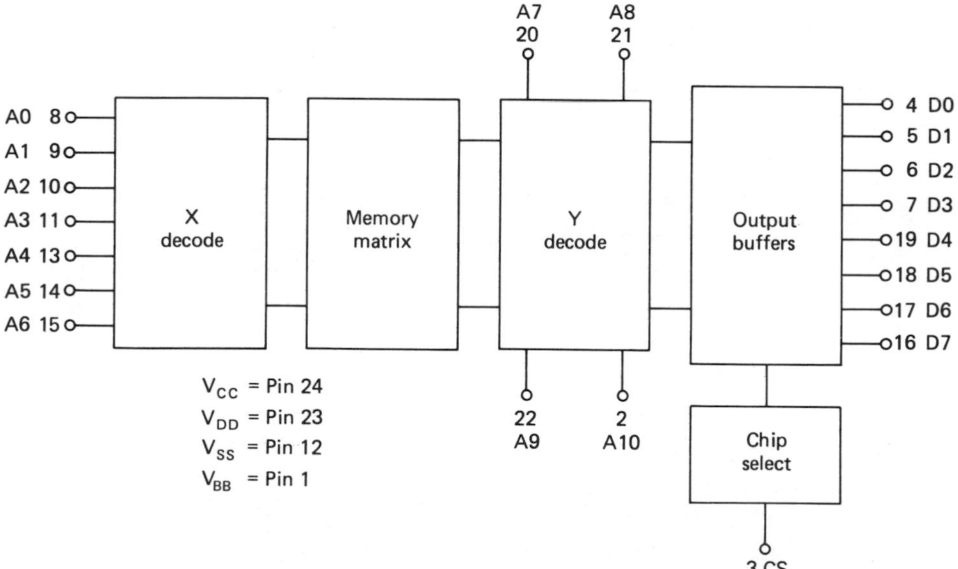

Figure 4-14 MCM6832 ROM, relationship to system and functional block diagram.

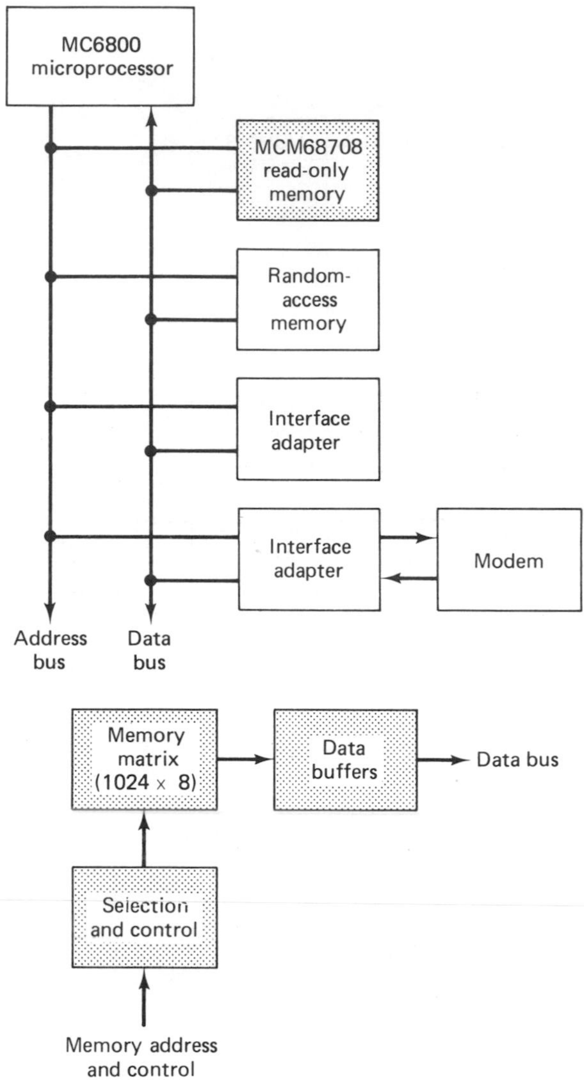

Figure 4-15 MCM6870L alterable ROM, relationship to system and basic block diagram.

Microprocessor data bus lines (D0–D7). Eight pins are used for the data bus, which is bidirectional, and transfers data to and from the memory and peripheral devices. The three-state drivers can be put into the three-state mode by forcing DBE (data bus enable, Sec. 4-4) low.

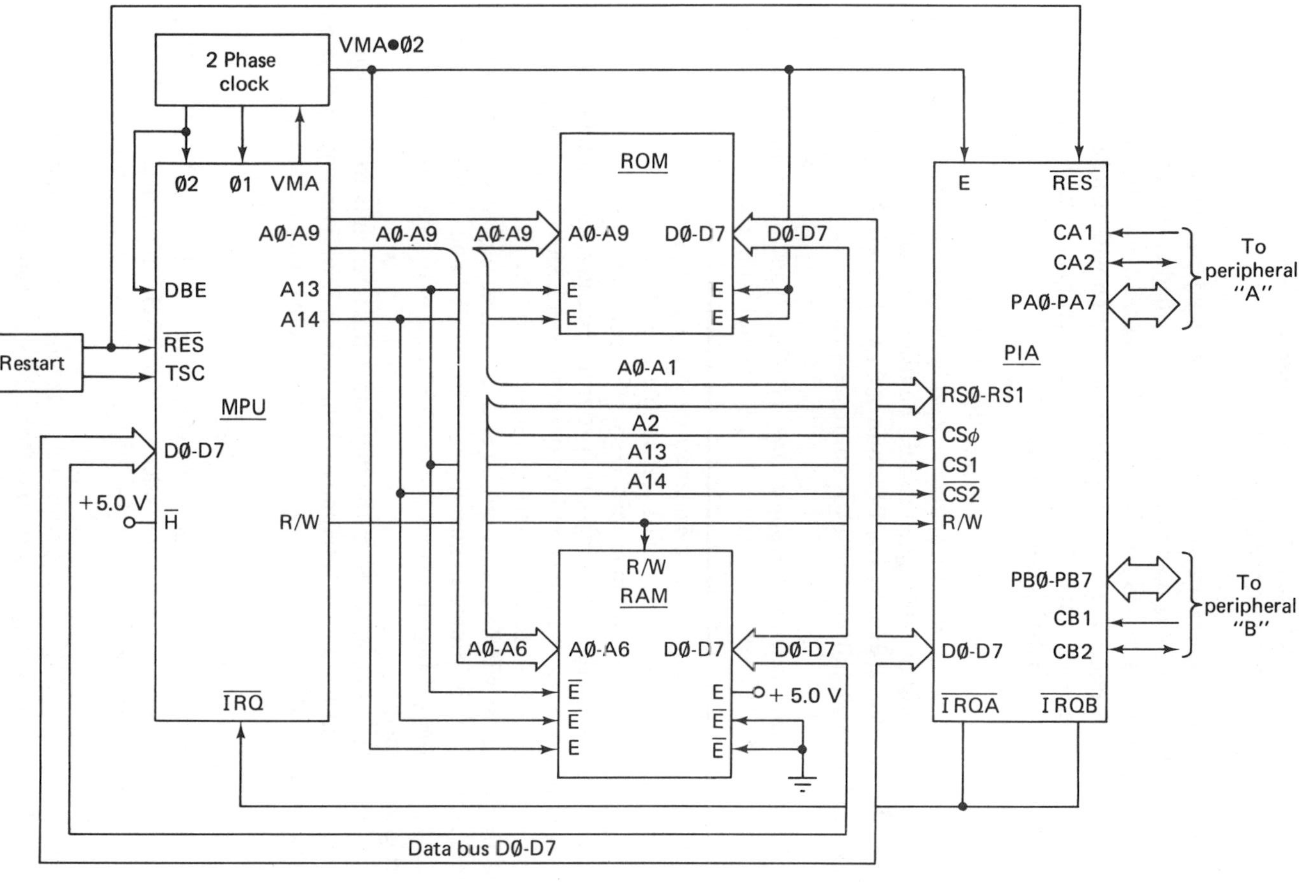

Figure 4-16 Theoretical minimum system configuration for M6800 family.

Microprocessor clock inputs, phases 1 and 2. Two pins are used for a two-phase nonoverlapping clock.

Microprocessor read/write line (R/W). The read/write line is an output that signals the peripheral and memory devices whether the microprocessor is in a read (high) or write (low) state. The normal standby state of this signal is read (high). Three-state control going high will turn read/write to the high-impedance state. Also, when the microprocessor is halted, the R/W line will be in the high-impedance state.

Microprocessor valid memory address line (VMA). This output indicates to the peripheral devices that there is a valid address on the address bus. In normal operation, this signal should be used for enabling the RAM and peripheral devices such as the PIA and ACIA. The VMA signal is active high. The output buffer of VMA is not three-state.

Microprocessor interrupt request line ($\overline{IRQ}$). This level-sensitive input requests that an interrupt sequence be generated within the microprocessor when $\overline{IRQ}$ is low. The microprocessor will wait until it completes the current instruction that is being executed before it recognizes the request. At that time, if the interrupt mask bit in the condition code register (bit I, Fig. 4-2) is not set, the microprocessor will begin an interrupt sequence. The contents of the index register, program counter, accumulators, and condition code register are stored away on the stack and the interrupt mask bit is set so that no further interrupts may occur. At the end of the cycle, a 16-bit address will be placed on the address bus that points to a vectoring address, which is located in memory locations FFF8 and FFF9. An address located at these locations causes the microprocessor to jump to an interrupt routine in memory.

The $\overline{Halt}$ line must be in the high state for interrupts to be serviced; interrupts will be latched internally while Halt is low. The wired-OR capability of the IRQ input requires a 3-R minimum external resistor to V_{CC}.

4-2-2 PIA and memory interface lines

The peripheral and memory interface lines are the data bus (D0–D7), the address inputs, the register selects (RS0–RS1), chip selects, R/W, the enable E, and interrupt request ($\overline{IRQ}$). A description of these follows.

Data bus (D0–D7). The peripheral data bus lines are bidirectional and capable of transferring data to and from the microprocessor and memory. The drivers are three-state input/output buffers.

Address inputs (A0–A15). Sixteen address lines are available for addressing peripherals and memories. Seven are used for addressing the internal locations of the RAM and 10 are used for addressing internal locations of the ROM. The address inputs are high-impedance.

Register selects (RS0–RS1). Register select inputs on the PIA (and the ACIA) are essentially the same as address inputs to the RAM and ROM. Bus address lines are tied directly to the register select inputs, in a minimum system configuration.

There are six locations within the PIA (Fig. 4-6) accessible to the microprocessor data bus: two peripheral registers (A and B), two data direction registers (A and B), and two control registers (A and B). Selection of these locations is controlled by the RS0 and RS1 inputs, together with CRA-2/CRB-2 in the control register, as follows:

		Control Register Bit		
RS1	*RS0*	*CRA-2*	*CRB-2*	*Location Selected*
0	0	1	×	peripheral register A
0	0	0	×	data direction register A
0	1	×	×	control register A
1	0	×	1	peripheral register B
1	0	×	0	data direction register B
1	1	×	×	control register B

× = don't care.

The register select input (RS) performs a somewhat different function when the ACIA (Fig. 4-7) is used instead of the PIA. The state of RS in the ACIA in conjunction with R/W determines which of four registers will be read by the microprocessor, or written into by the microprocessor, as follows:

RS	*R/W*	*Register*
0	0	control register
0	1	status register
1	1	receive data register
1	0	transmit data register

Chip selects (CS0–CS5). Chip selects on the PIA and memory devices are used to distinguish one device from another. The number of chip selects available varies from three on the PIA to six on the RAM. The chip selects may tie directly to the microprocessor address bus and VMA line in a minimum system configuration. Chip select lines are high-impedance inputs. The PIA and memory are enabled by various combinations of "true" and "not true" chip selects.

Read/write (R/W). The read/write is a high-impedance input that is used to control the direction of data flow through the microprocessor data bus interface. When R/W is high (microprocessor read cycle), the PIA and memory data bus drivers are turned on and the selected location is read. When R/W is low, the data bus drivers are turned off and the microprocessor writes into the selected location.

Enable (E). The enable input E is the PIA and memory enable signal. The E input is a high-impedance input which enables the PIA and memory output data buffers. One of the chip selects is used for the E enable on the RAM and ROM.

Peripheral interrupt request ($\overline{IRQA}$ and $\overline{IRQB}$). The only difference between the special function I/O devices (PIA and ACIA) and memories from a system consideration is that the I/O devices have interrupt outputs that are used as a request for servicing.

$\overline{\text{IRQA}}$ and $\overline{\text{IRQB}}$ from the PIA are ORed to the system $\overline{\text{IRQ}}$ line. Since the PIA may be used to detect incoming interrupt signals on any of its control lines, this connection must be made to initiate the interrupt sequence at the microprocessor. The IRQ will be pulled down by the PIA following detection of a pulse on any control line that has been enabled as a system interrupt. IRQ will be held low until the interrupt is serviced. Thus, no interrupts will be lost to the system even if the interrupt mask is set at the microprocessor.

The ACIA interrupts the microprocessor under conditions that differ from those described for the PIA. Assuming that the ACIA transmitter and receiver interrupts are enabled by bits in the control register, the ACIA will interrupt the microprocessor if the transmitter data register is empty, or the receiver data register if the transmitter data register is full or if the data carrier detect (DCD) input goes high, indicating a loss of the modem carrier.

4-2-3 PIA to peripheral interface lines

The PIA provides two 8-bit bidirectional data buses and four interrupt/control lines for interfacing to peripheral devices (see Figs. 4-6 and 4-16).

Section A peripheral data (PA0–PA7). Each of the peripheral data lines can be programmed to act as an input or output. This is done by setting a 1 in the corresponding data direction register bit for those lines that are to be outputs. A 0 in the bit of the data direction register causes the corresponding peripheral data line to act as an input. During a microprocessor "read peripheral data operation," the data on peripheral lines programmed to act as inputs appear directly on the corresponding microprocessor data bus lines. In the input mode, the internal pullup resistor on these lines represents a maximum of one standard TTL load.

The data in output register A will appear on the data lines that are programmed to be outputs. A 1 written into the register will cause a high on the corresponding data line, while a 0 results in a low. Data in output register may be read by a microprocessor "read peripheral data A" operation when the corresponding lines are programmed as outputs. These data will be read properly if the voltage on the peripheral data lines is greater than 2 V for a 1 output and less than 0.8 V for a 0 output. Loading the output lines such that the voltage on these lines does not reach full voltage causes the data transferred to the microprocessor on a read operation to differ from that contained in the respective bit of output register A.

Section B peripheral data (PB0–PB7). The peripheral data lines in the B section of the PIA can be programmed to act as either inputs or outputs in a similar manner to PA0–PA7. However, the output buffers driving these lines differ from those driving lines PA0–PA7. The PB lines have three-state capability, allowing them to enter a high-impedance state when the peripheral data line is used as an input. In addition, data on the peripheral data lines PB0–PB7 will be read properly from those lines programmed as outputs even if the voltages are below 2 V (for a high). As outputs, the PB lines are compatible with standard TTL and may also be used as a source of up to 1 mA at 1.5 V to directly drive the base of a transistor switch.

Interrupt input (CA1–CB1). Peripheral input lines CA1 and CB1 are input-only lines that set the interrupt flags of the control registers. The active transition for these signals is also programmed by the two control registers.

Peripheral control (CA2). The peripheral control line CA2 can be programmed to act as an interrupt control or as a peripheral control output. As an output, this line is compatible with standard TTL. As an input, the internal pull-up resistor on this line represents one standard TTL load. The function of this signal line is programmed with control register A.

Peripheral control (CB2). Peripheral control line CB2 may also be programmed to act as an interrupt input or peripheral control input. As an input, this line has high input impedance and is compatible with standard TTL. As output, CB2 is compatible with standard TTL and may also be used as a source of up to 1 mA at 1.5 V to directly drive the base of a transistor switch. This line is programmed by control register B.

4-3 MICROPROCESSOR INSTRUCTIONS AND ADDRESSING MODES

The microprocessor is capable of 72 instructions. In source language or code, each of the instructions is identified by a three-letter combination, such as ABA (add accumulator B to accumulator A), ADC (add with carry), and so on. Each of the instructions assembles into one to three bytes of machine code (object code). The number of bytes depends on the particular instruction and on the addressing mode. The coding of the first (or possibly the only) byte corresponding to an executable instruction is sufficient to identify the instruction and the addressing mode. When an instruction translates into two or three bytes of code, the second byte or the second and third bytes contain(s) an operand, an address, or information from which an address is obtained during execution.

The hex, octal, and decimal equivalents for all 72 instructions, together with full descriptions of the instructions, are given in the system literature and will not be duplicated here. Instead, we shall concentrate on the addressing modes, of which there are seven.

4-3-1 Dual addressing

Eleven of the instructions require addressing of *two operands,* as indicated in Fig. 4-17 by the column headed Dual Operand. For all of these, the first operand must be either accumulator A or accumulator B (Fig. 4-2). This is specified, respectively, by A or B as the first character in the operand field, with the second character being a space. For dual addressing, the specification of the first operand (either A or B) is separated from that of the second operand by one or more space characters. The second operand is specified in accordance with the rules for *immediate, direct, extended,* or *indexed* addressing (as subsequently defined), depending on which modes of addressing are valid.

As an example, the instruction ADC requires dual addressing. Instruction ADC adds the contents of the C bit to the sum of the contents of ACCX and M, and places the result in ACCX. (C is the contents of the C condition code register; ACCX is either accumulator A or B; M is the contents of memory at the address where the instruction occurs.) The symbol for ADC is ACCX ⟵ (ACCX) + (M) + (C). C is set if there was a carry from the most-significant bit of the result and is cleared (or zero) otherwise. The available addressing modes, execution time, and machine code for instruction ADC are as follows:

Addressing Modes	*Execution Time (Number of Cycles)*	*Number of Bytes of Machine Code*	*Hex Code*
A IMM	2	2	89
A DIR	3	2	99
A EXT	4	3	B9
A IND	5	2	A9
B IMM	2	2	C9
B DIR	3	2	D9
B EXT	4	3	F9
B IND	5	2	E9

	(Dual operand)	ACCX	Immediate	Direct	Extended	Indexed	Implied	Relative
ABA		•	•	•	•	•	2	•
ADC	x	•	2	3	4	5	•	•
ADD	x	•	2	3	4	5	•	•
AND	x	•	2	3	4	5	•	•
ASL		2	•	•	6	7	•	•
ASR		2	•	•	6	7	•	•
BCC		•	•	•	•	•	•	4
BCS		•	•	•	•	•	•	4
BEA		•	•	•	•	•	•	4
BGE		•	•	•	•	•	•	4
BGT		•	•	•	•	•	•	4
BHI		•	•	•	•	•	•	4
BIT	x	•	2	3	4	5	•	•
BLE		•	•	•	•	•	•	4
BLS		•	•	•	•	•	•	4
BLT		•	•	•	•	•	•	4
BMI		•	•	•	•	•	•	4
BNE		•	•	•	•	•	•	4
BPL		•	•	•	•	•	•	4
BRA		•	•	•	•	•	•	4
BSR		•	•	•	•	•	•	8
BVC		•	•	•	•	•	•	4
BVS		•	•	•	•	•	•	4
CBA		•	•	•	•	•	2	•
CLC		•	•	•	•	•	2	•
CLI		•	•	•	•	•	2	•
CLR		2	•	•	6	7	•	•
CLV		•	•	•	•	•	2	•
CMP	x	•	2	3	4	5	•	•
COM		2	•	•	6	7	•	•
CPX		•	3	4	5	6	•	•
DAA		•	•	•	•	•	2	•
DEC		2	•	•	6	7	•	•
DES		•	•	•	•	•	4	•
DEX		•	•	•	•	•	4	•
EOR	x	•	2	3	4	5	•	•

	(Dual Operand)	ACCX	Immediate	Direct	Extended	Indexed	Implied
INC		2	•	•	6	7	•
INS		•	•	•	•	•	4
INX		•	•	•	•	•	4
JMP		•	•	•	3	4	•
JSR		•	•	•	9	8	•
LDA	x	•	2	3	4	5	•
LDS		•	3	4	5	6	•
LDX		•	3	4	5	6	•
LSR		2	•	•	6	7	•
NEG		2	•	•	6	7	•
NOP		•	•	•	•	•	2
ORA	x	•	2	3	4	5	•
PSH		•	•	•	•	•	4
PUL		•	•	•	•	•	4
ROL		2	•	•	6	7	•
ROR		2	•	•	6	7	•
RTI		•	•	•	•	•	10
RTS		•	•	•	•	•	5
SBA		•	•	•	•	•	2
SBC	x	•	2	3	4	5	•
SEC		•	•	•	•	•	2
SEI		•	•	•	•	•	2
SEV		•	•	•	•	•	2
STA	x	•	•	4	5	6	•
STS		•	•	5	6	7	•
STX		•	•	5	6	7	•
SUB	x	•	2	3	4	5	•
SWI		•	•	•	•	•	12
TAB		•	•	•	•	•	2
TAP		•	•	•	•	•	2
TBA		•	•	•	•	•	2
TPA		•	•	•	•	•	2
TST		2	•	•	6	7	•
TSX		•	•	•	•	•	4
TSX		•	•	•	•	•	4
WAI		•	•	•	•	•	9

Note: Interrupt time is 12 cycles from the end of the instruction being executed, except following a WAI instruction. Then it is 4 cycles.

Figure 4-17 Instruction addressing modes and associated execution times.

Thus, if hex 89 (binary 10001001) appears on the data bus at a given memory location, the contents of condition code register C is added to the sum of accumulator A and memory M, using the *immediate mode* (Sec. 4-3-4). If the data bus word is changed to hex F9 (binary 11111001), the same function will be performed, but using accumulator B and the indexed mode (Sec. 4-3-6).

4-3-2 Accumulator addressing (single operand)

Thirteen of the instructions address a single operand, and thus can address either accumulator A or accumulator B. These instructions are indicated by the column headed ACCX in Fig. 4-17. This mode of addressing is specified by writing a single character A or B (corresponding to accumulator A or accumulator B), omitting the space between the operator and the operand field.

4-3-3 Inherent addressing

In many cases, the mnemonic operator itself specifies one or more registers that contain operands or in which results are saves. For example, instruction ABA requires two operands that are located in accumulator A and accumulator B. Instruction ABA also determines that the result of execution will be saved in accumulator A.

For some instructions, all the information that may be required for the addressing is contained in the mnemonic operator, and no operand field is used in the source statement. There are 25 such instructions. These are indicated by the column headed Inherent in Fig. 4-17. Assembly of this type of source instruction results in only one byte of machine code. Some other instructions that contain addressing information inherently in the mnemonic code also require further addressing (immediate, direct, extended, or indexed) or operand information, which is then placed in an operand field.

4-3-4 Immediate addressing

The instructions with which the immediate mode of addressing is permissible are indicated by the column headed Immediate in Fig. 4-17. Immediate addressing is selected by beginning the specification of the corresponding operand (in the operand field of a source statement) with the number character "#."

With the immediate mode, the operand field of the source statement either contains the actual value of the operand, or it includes a symbol or an expression that has an algebraic value equal to the value of the operand. The operand may be specified in accordance with any of the following formats: #Number, #Symbol, #Expression, #'C.

In the first three of these alternative forms, the assembler will find or compute a numerical value of the operand. For any executive instruction in the immediate mode (except CPX, LDS, or LDX), the numerical value must be a whole number from 0 to 255 (decimal). For instructions CPX, LDS, or LDX, any value from 0 to 65,535 (decimal) is valid.

In the last of the alternative forms (#'C), the apostrophe instructs the assembler to translate the next character into the corresponding 7-bit ASCII code. The ASCII code so obtained is then the value of the operand. The single character "C" can be any character of the ASCII character set with a hex value from 20 through 5F.

For the immediate mode, the assembler inserts the actual value of the operand into the machine code. Except for the three operators (CPS, LDS, and LDX), an instruction in the immediate mode is assembled into two bytes of machine code, and the value of the *operand is entered as the second byte.* When it is a number, the operand is entered in the memory in unsigned 8-bit binary code. When it is an ASCII character, the corresponding 7-bit ASCII code applies, using bits 0–6, with bit 7 set to 0.

For the three instructions (CPX, LDS, or LDX) used in the immediate mode, the source statement is assembled into *three bytes of machine code.* The numerical operand (which can have any value from 0 through FFFF) will be entered in the *second and third bytes.* The second byte will contain the most-significant part of the operand, and the third byte will contain the least-significant part of the operand. Both parts are entered into the respective bytes of memory in unsigned 8-bit binary code.

The instructions (CPX, LDS, or LDX) in the immediate mode are not normally used with an operand in the format #'C. However, in such a case, the assembler would place the ASCII-coded character "C" in the third byte of the machine code.

When the immediate mode of addressing is used, the numerical address is, in effect, that of the *second byte* of machine code that results from assembly of the source instruction. Data flow for the immediate addressing mode is shown in Fig. 4-18.

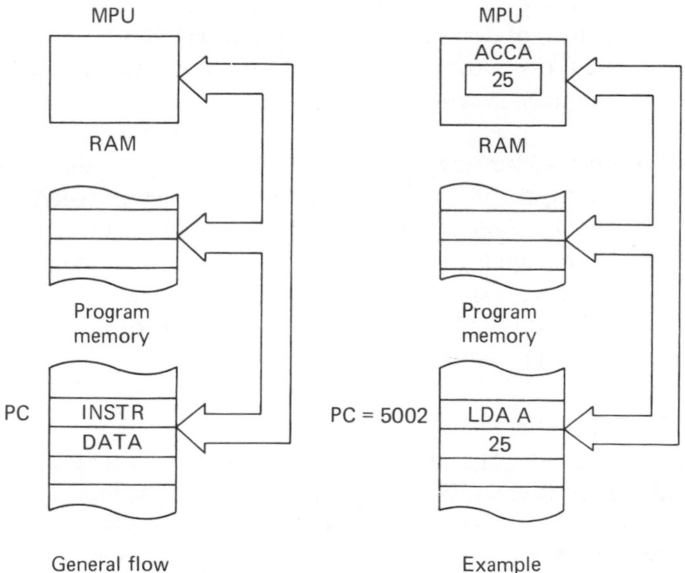

Figure 4-18 Immediate addressing mode data flow.

4-3-5 Relative addressing

For the relative addressing mode to be valid, there is a rule that limits the distance in the machine language program from the branch instruction to the destination of the branch. The rule that applies to the relative addressing mode is that the address of the destination of the branch must be within the range specified by

$$(PC + 2) - 128 \leq D \leq (PC + 2) + 127$$

where PC = address of first byte of branch instruction
D = address of destination of branch instruction

When it is desired to transfer control beyond the range of the branch instructions, this can be done by using JMP (unconditional jump) or JSR (jump to subroutine). These instructions do not use the relative mode.

The assembler translates a branch instruction into two bytes of the machine code. The second byte contains a relative address. This is stored as a number in 8-bit, two's-complement binary form, with a decimal value in the range −128 to +127. These numbers correspond to the limits of the range of a branch instruction.

The relationship between the relative address and the absolute address of the destination of a branch instruction is expressed by

$$D = (PC + 2) + R$$

where PC = address of first byte of branch instruction
D = address of destination of branch instruction
R = 8-bit, two's-complement binary number, stored in second byte of branch instruction

The relative addressing mode is available only to the conditional branch instructions, the unconditional branch instruction (BRA), and the branch to subroutine (BSR). None of these source instructions can use any other of the several modes of addressing. The three-character mnemonic instruction, therefore, is sufficient to determine when the relative mode of addressing will be used for the assembler. An example of the data flow for the relative addressing mode is shown in Fig. 4-19.

4-3-6 Indexed addressing

The indexed column of Fig. 4-17 indicates the instructions for which indexed addressing is valid. With indexed addressing, the numerical address is variable, depending on the contents of the index register. The current address is obtained whenever it is required during the execution of a program rather than being predetermined by the assembler, as it is for the

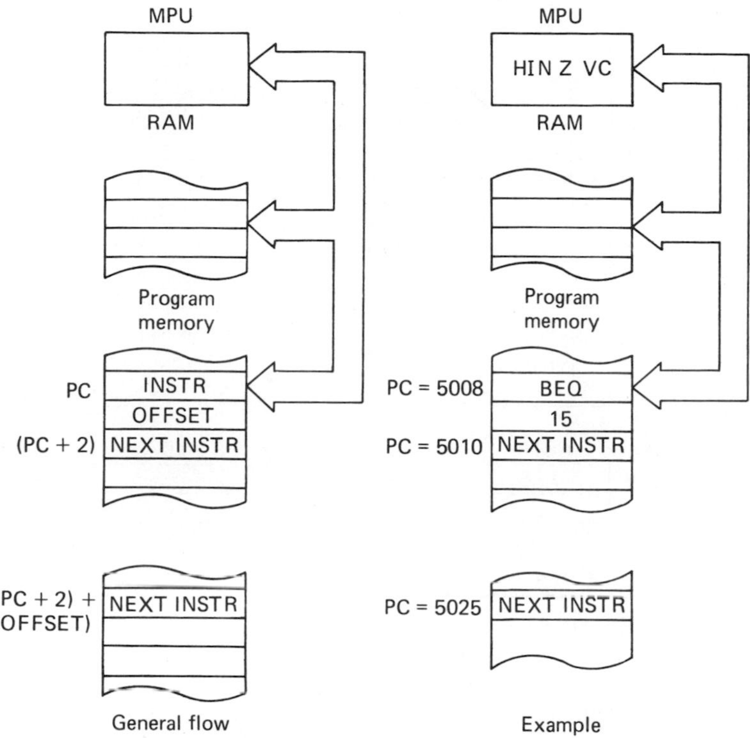

Figure 4-19 Relative addressing mode data flow.

other addressing modes. The operand of the source statement contains a numerical value which, when added to the contents of the index register during execution of a program, will provide the numerical address. Alternatively, the operand may contain a symbol or an expression which the assembler is able to replace by the value that is to be added to the contents of the index register. An example of the indexed addressing mode is shown in Fig. 4-20.

In indexed addressing, the data for obtaining the numerical address may be written in any of the formats

X
,X
Number,X
Symbol,X
Expression,X

The single character X informs the assembler that the indexed mode is to be used (the character X being reserved to denote the index register). The format X, when used alone, instructs the assembler that the address of

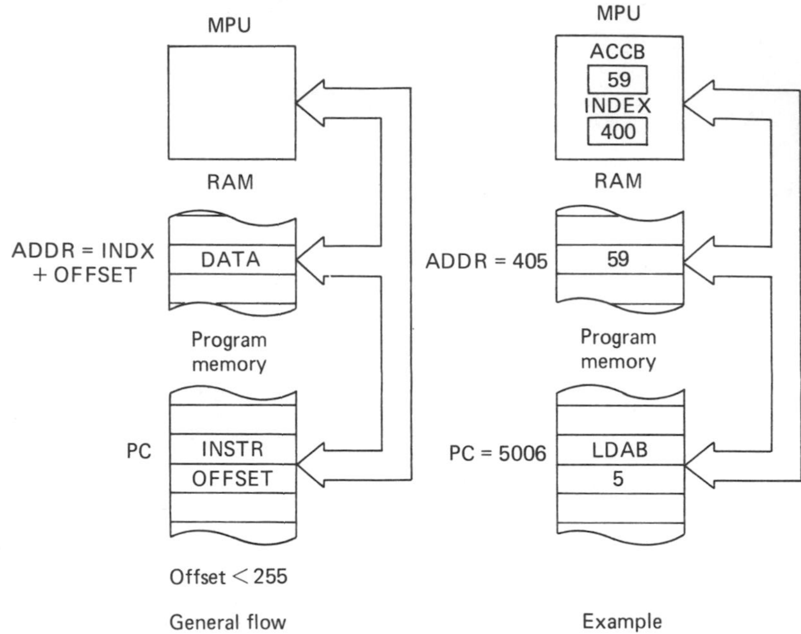

Figure 4-20 Indexed addressing mode data flow.

the operand is identical with the contents of the index register. This format has the same effect on the assembler as if 0,X had been written.

If a symbol or an expression is used rather than a number, the assembler will find or compute a numerical value of that symbol or expression. The source program must then include other statements that define a numerical value for the symbol or that enable the assembler to compute a numerical value for the symbol or expression. Only values from zero to FF (hex) are valid. This value is added to the contents of the index register during execution to obtain the numberical address as follows:

$$D = \text{numerical value} + X$$

where X = contents of index register
D = numerical address

For indexed addressing, the source instruction is translated into two bytes of the machine code. The second byte contains the number, in unsigned 8-bit binary form, which is added to the contents of the index register during execution of the instruction. The number thus obtained is the numerical address (in accordance with the previous formula).

4-3-7 Direct and extended addressing

In direct addressing, the source instruction is translated into two bytes of machine code. The second byte will contain the address in unsigned 8-bit binary form.

In extended addressing, the source instruction is translated into three bytes of machine code. The second of these bytes will contain the highest 8 bits of the address. The third byte will contain the lowest 8 bits of the address. The contents of the second and third bytes will both be coded in unsigned 8-bit binary form.

For both direct and extended addressing, the address, which is placed by the assembler into the second and third bytes of the machine code, is the absolute numerical address.

As may be seen in Fig. 4-17, there are several instructions for which the extended mode of addressing is valid and not the direct mode. For these instructions, when using any of the number, symbol, or expression formats, the assembler will select the extended mode of addressing, regardless of the value of the numerical address. The source statement will be translated into three bytes of the machine code.

For those instructions that may use the direct mode of addressing as well as the extended mode, the assembler selects the mode according to the following rule. The assembler will select direct addressing if the numerical address is in the range 0 to 255 (decimal) and will select extended addressing if the numerical address exceeds 255 (decimal). Examples of the direct and extended addressing modes are shown in Figs. 4-21 and 4-22, respectively.

4-4 MICROPROCESSOR CONTROLS

In addition to the 72 instructions entered on the data bus and the bus control lines, the microprocessor has six control lines, as shown in Fig. 4-2. Two of the control lines, $\overline{\text{Reset}}$ and DBE (data bus enable), are used for all systems. The remaining control lines, $\overline{\text{NMI}}$ (nonmaskable interrupt), $\overline{\text{Halt}}$, BA (bus available), and TSC (three-state control) can be used to increase flexibility.

4-4-1 Reset

The $\overline{\text{Reset}}$ input is used to reset and start the microprocessor from a power-down condition, resulting from power failure or initial start-up. $\overline{\text{Reset}}$ input can also be used to reinitialize the microprocessor at any time after start-up.

If a high level is detected on $\overline{\text{Reset}}$, this will signal the microprocessor to begin the reset sequence, during which the contents of the last two loca-

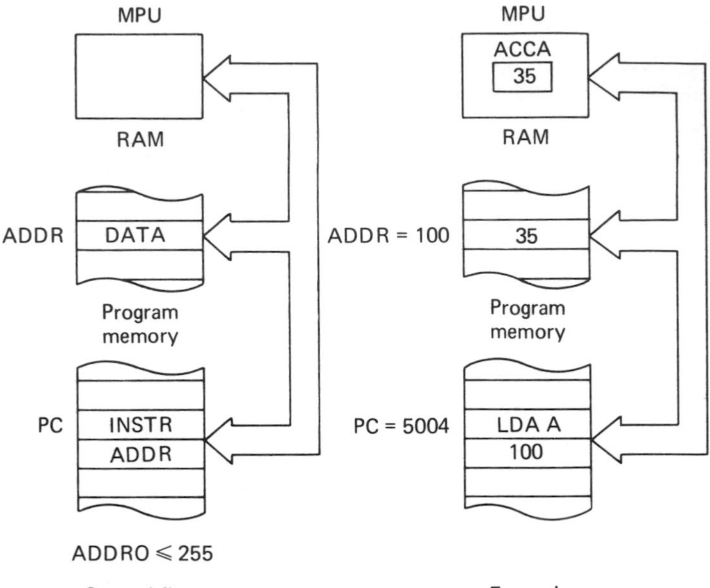

Figure 4-21 Direct addressing mode data flow.

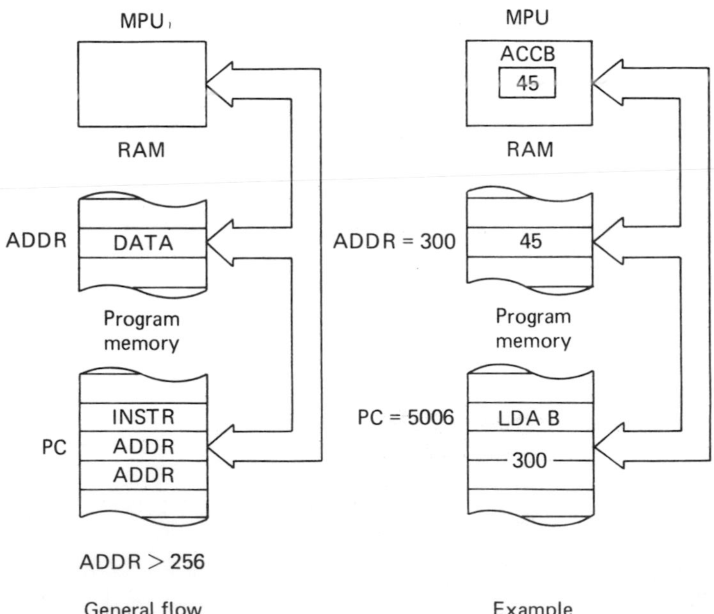

Figure 4-22 Extended addressing mode data flow.

tions (FFFE and FFFF) in memory will be loaded into the program counter to point to the beginning of the reset routine. During the reset routine, the interrupt mask bit is set and must be cleared under program control before the microprocessor can be interrupted by $\overline{\text{IRQ}}$. While $\overline{\text{Reset}}$ is low (assuming that a minimum of eight clock cycles have occurred), the microprocessor output signals will be in the following states: VMA = low, BA = low, data bus = high impedance, R/W = high (read state), and the address bus will contain the reset address FFFE.

4-4-2 Nonmaskable interrupt (NMI)

The microprocessor is capable of handling two types of interrupts: maskable ($\overline{\text{IRQ}}$), as described in Sec. 4-2-1, and nonmaskable ($\overline{\text{NMI}}$). $\overline{\text{IRQ}}$ is maskable by the interrupt mask (bit I) in the condition code register. $\overline{\text{NMI}}$ is not maskable; that is, an interrupt signal on the $\overline{\text{NMI}}$ line produces an interrupt without regard to other conditions.

4-4-3 $\overline{\text{Halt}}$ and single instruction execution

The $\overline{\text{Halt}}$ line provides an input to the microprocessor to allow control of the program execution by an outside source. If $\overline{\text{Halt}}$ is high, the microprocessor will execute the instructions. If $\overline{\text{Halt}}$ is low, the microprocessor will go to a halted or idle mode. A response signal of BA (bus available) provides an indication of the current microprocessor status. When BA is low, the microprocessor is in the process of executing the control program. If BA is high, the microprocessor has halted and all internal activity had stopped.

When BA is high, the address bus, data bus, and R/W line will be in a high-impedance state, effectively removing the microprocessor from the system bus. VMA is forced low so that the floating system bus will not activate any device on the bus which is enabled by VMA.

While the microprocessor is halted, all program activity is stopped, and if either an $\overline{\text{NMI}}$ or $\overline{\text{IRQ}}$ interrupt occurs, it will be latched into the microprocessor and acted on as soon as the microprocessor is taken out of the halted mode. If a $\overline{\text{Reset}}$ command occurs while the microprocessor is halted, the following states occur: VMA = low, BA = low, data bus = high impedance, R/W = high (read state), and the address bus will contain address FFFE as long as $\overline{\text{Reset}}$ is low. As soon as the $\overline{\text{Halt}}$ line goes high, the microprocessor will go to locations FFFE and FFFF for the address of the reset routine.

4-4-4 Three-state control (TSC)

When the TSC line is at 1, the address bus and the R/W line are placed in a high-impedance state. VMA and BA are forced low whenever TSC = 1 to prevent false reads or writes on any device enabled by VMA.

While TSC is held at 1, the phase 1 and phase 2 clocks must be held high and low, respectively, in order to delay program execution (this is required because of the bus lines being in an indeterminate state). Since the microprocessor is a dynamic device, the phase 1 clock can be stopped for a maximum time PWH without destroying data within the microprocessor. TSC can then be used in a short direct memory access (DMA) application.

4-4-5 Bus available (BA)

The BA signal will normally be in the low state. When activated, BA will go to the high state, indicating that the microprocessor has stopped and that the address bus is available. This will occur if the $\overline{\text{Halt}}$ line is in the low state or if the microprocessor is in the wait state as the result of a wait instruction. At such times, all three-state output drivers will go to their off state and other outputs will go to their normally inactive level. The microprocessor is removed from the wait state by the occurrence of a maskable interrupt (when bit I in the CCR goes to 0), or a nonmaskable interrupt (by a signal on the $\overline{\text{NMI}}$ line). Note that if TSC is high, BA will be low.

4-4-6 Data bus enable (DBE)

DBE is the three-state control signal for the microprocessor data bus and will enable the bus drivers when in the high state. This input is TTL-compatible. However, in normal operation, DBE is driven by the phase 2 clock. During a microprocessor read cycle, the data bus drivers will be disabled internally. When it is desirable that another device control the data bus, such as in DMA applications, DBE should be held low.

4-5 BASIC PROGRAMMING TECHNIQUES

The following paragraphs describe basic programming techniques for the M6800 system. Far more detailed descriptions are available in the system literature.

4-5-1 Stack and stack pointer

In the M6800 system, the stack consists of any number of locations in RAM memory. The stack provides for temporary storage and retrieval of successive bytes of information, which may include any of the following: current status of the microprocessor, return address, and data. The stack can be used for the following purposes: interrupt control, subroutine linkage, temporary storage of data (under control of the program), and a re-entrant code.

As shown in Fig. 4-2, the microprocessor includes a 16-bit stack pointer. This pointer contains an address which enables the microprocessor to find the current location of the stack. When a byte is stored in the stack, it is stored at the address contained in the stack pointer. The stack pointer is decremented (by one) immediately following the storage in the stack of each byte. Conversely, the stack pointer is incremented (by one) immediately before retrieving each byte from the stack, and the byte is then obtained from the address contained in the stack pointer. The programmer must ensure that the stack pointer is initialized to the required address before the first execution of an instruction that manipulates the stack.

Normally, the stack will consist of a single block of successive memory locations. However, some instructions in the source language change the address contained in the stack pointer without storing or retrieving information into or from the stack. The use of these instructions may result in the stack being other than one continuous sequence of memory locations. In such a case, it may alternatively be considered that there exist two or more stacks, each of which consists of a block of successive locations in the memory.

4-5-2 Saving microprocessor status

The status of the microprocessor unit is saved in the stack during the following operations:

1. In response to an external condition indicated by a negative edge on the nonmaskable interrupt control input signal to the microprocessor.
2. During execution of the machine code corresponding to either of the source language instructions SWI (software interrupt) of WAI (wait for interrupt).
3. During servicing of an interrupt from a peripheral device, in response to an interrupt request control signal, provided that the interrupt mask bit (I of the CCR) is clear.

The status is stored in the stack in accordance with the scheme shown in Fig. 4-23. Before storing the status, the stack pointer contains the address of a memory location represented in Fig. 4-23 by "m." The stack, if any, extends from location "m + 1" to higher locations. The status is stored in seven bytes of memory, beginning with the byte at location "m" and ending with the byte at location "m − 6." The stack pointer is decremented after each byte of information is entered into the stack.

The information that is saved in the stack consists of the numerical content of all registers of the programming model, shown in Fig. 4-2, except the stack pointer.

The value stored for the program counter (PCH and PCL) is in accordance with the following rules:

1. In response to a nonmaskable interrupt or to an interrupt from a peripheral device, the value saved for the program counter is the address of

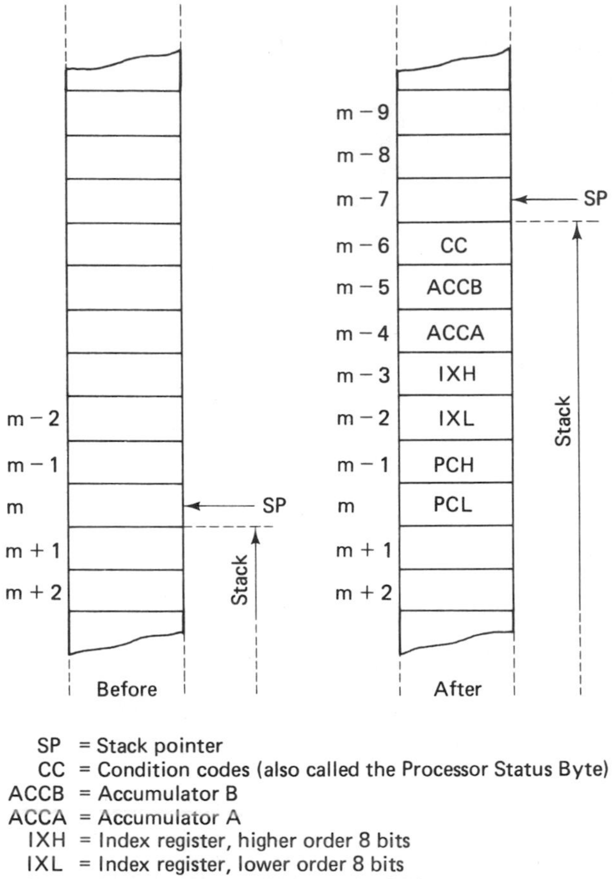

SP = Stack pointer
CC = Condition codes (also called the Processor Status Byte)
ACCB = Accumulator B
ACCA = Accumulator A
IXH = Index register, higher order 8 bits
IXL = Index register, lower order 8 bits
PCH = Program counter, higher order 8 bits
PCL = Program counter, lower order 8 bits

Figure 4-23 Saving the status of the microprocessor in the stack.

that instruction which would be executed next if the interrupt had not occurred.

2. During execution of a SWI or WAI instruction, the value saved for the program counter is the address of that SWI or WAI instruction, plus one.

The values stored for the other registers (CC, ACCB, ACCA, IXH, and IXL) are in accordance with the following rules:

1. In response to a nonmaskable interrupt, or an interrupt from a peripheral device, the values saved are those that result from the last instruction executed before the interrupt was serviced.

2. During execution of a SWI or a WAI instruction, the values saved are those that result from the last instruction executed before the SWI or WAI instruction.

3. The condition codes H, I, N, Z, V, and C, in bit positions 5 through 0 of the microprocessor condition code register, are stored in bit positions 5 through 0, respectively, of the applicable memory location in the stack. Bit positions 7 and 6 of that memory location are set (that is, they go to the 1 state).

4-5-3 Interrupt pointers

A block of memory is reserved for pointers that provide for read-only storage of the addresses of programs that are to be executed in the event of a reset (or power on), a low state of the nonmaskable interrupt control input, a software interrupt, or a response to an interrupt signal from a peripheral device. The respective pointers each occupy two bytes of memory and are disposed at locations from "n − 7" to "n," as shown in Fig. 4-24.

The location indicated in Fig. 4-24 by "n" is that location which is addressed when all the lines of the address bus are in the 1 state (high). In most systems, the location "n" will be the highest address in the memory. However, the actual numerical value of "n" depends on wiring of the address bus (if all or part of the 16 address bus lines are used).

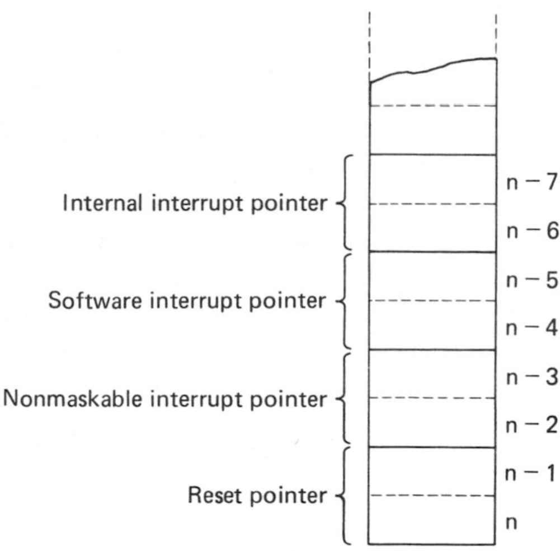

Note: n = memory location addressed when all lines of the address bus are in the high (1) state.

Figure 4-24 Reset and interrupt pointers.

Reset (or power on). The reset control input to the microprocessor is used to start execution of the program, either for initial start-up, or from a power-down condition following a power failure. When a positive pulse (or 1 state) is detected on the reset line, the program counter is loaded with the address stored in the restart pointer at locations "n − 1" and "n" of memory (Fig. 4-24). The microprocessor then proceeds with execution of a restart program, which begins with the instruction addressed by the program counter. The restart and the continued execution, however, depend on the halt control input being in the "go" condition (when the halt line is in the 1 state).

When the halt line is at 1, the microprocessor will fetch the instruction addressed by the program counter and start the execution. When the halt line changes to 0, execution will stop. The stop may become effective at the completion of execution of the current instruction. Alternatively, one more instruction may be executed before the step becomes effective, owing to the look-ahead capability (described in later paragraphs). Execution of the program will not be resumed until the "go" condition is restored (halt line at 1).

The halt line must remain in the "go" condition for the interrupt sequences to be completed. Otherwise, the microprocessor will stop execution at the end of an instruction. The following paragraphs, which describe the interrupt operations, assume that the "go" state is maintained.

NMI (nonmaskable interrupt). The sequence of operations that occurs following a nonmaskable interrupt is initiated by a 0 on the NMI control line. Execution of the current instruction is completed. The response of the microprocessor to the NMI signal may begin on completion of execution of the current instruction. Alternatively, one or more instructions in the program may first be executed, owing to the look-ahead capability.

The status of the microprocessor is then saved in the stack, as described in Sec. 4-5-2, and the program counter is loaded with the address stored in the NMI pointer at locations "n − 3" and "n − 2" of memory (Fig. 4-24). The microprocessor then starts execution of the NMI program, which begins with the instruction now addressed by the program counter.

SWI (software interrupt). During execution of the SWI instruction, the status of the microprocessor is saved in the stack, as described in Sec. 4-5-2. The value saved for the program counter is the address of the SWI instruction, plus 1.

After the status has been saved, the interrupt mask bit I is set (I = 1). The microprocessor will not respond to an interrupt request from a peripheral device while the interrupt mask is set.

The program counter is then loaded with the address stored in the software interrupt pointer at locations "n − 5" and "n − 4" of memory

(Fig. 4-24). The microprocessor then proceeds with execution of a software interrupt program, which begins with the instruction now addressed by the program counter.

The microprocessor will remain insensitive to an interrupt request from any peripheral device (signaled by a 0 state of the interrupt request control line to the microprocessor) until the interrupt mask bit has been reset by execution of the programmed instructions.

IRQ (interrupt request). A request for an interrupt by a peripheral device is signaled by a low state of the interrupt request control input to the microprocessor (IRQ). The microprocessor will not respond to an interrupt request while the interrupt mask bit is set (I = 1). Normal execution of the program continues until the interrupt mask bit is reset (I = 0), enabling the microprocessor to respond to an interrupt request.

Execution of the current instruction will always be completed before the microprocessor responds to an interrupt request. The response of the microprocessor to the interrupt request may begin on the completion of the current instruction. Alternatively, one more instruction in the program may first be executed, owing to the look-ahead capability of the microprocessor. The response of the microprocessor to the interrupt request then proceeds as follows:

1. *Saving the status.* Provided the last instruction executed was not a WAI instruction, the status of the microprocessor is saved in the stack, as described in Sec. 4-5-2. The value saved for the program counter is the address of the instruction that would be the next to be executed if the interrupt had not occurred. If the last instruction executed was a WAI instruction, the address of the next instruction is not saved, since PC and MPU status were already saved by the WAI instruction in preparation for an interrupt.

2. *Interrupt mask.* The interrupt mask bit is then set (I = 1). This prevents the microprocessor from responding to further interrupt requests until the interrupt mask bit has been cleared by execution of programmed instructions.

3. *Internal interrupt pointer and program.* The program counter is loaded with the address stored in the internal interrupt pointer at locations "n − 7" and "n − 6" of memory (Fig. 4-24). The microprocessor then proceeds with execution of an internal interrupt program, which begins with the instruction currently being addressed by the program counter. The internal interrupt pointer is selected by logic which is internal to the microprocessor. At the point when execution of the internal interrupt program begins, no distinction will have been made regarding the source of the interrupt request. In a system in which there is more than one possible source of interrupt request, the internal interrupt program must include a routine for

identifying the origin of the request. (In a system composed of the Motorola microcomputer kit, this routine would consist of a programmed interrogation of the addressable registers of the PIAs and ACIAs, to identify the peripheral device that has requested the interrupt.)

WAI (wait instruction). During execution of the WAI instruction, the status of the microprocessor is saved in the stack, as described in Sec. 4-5-2. The value saved for the program counter is the address of the WAI instruction, plus 1.

Execution of the WAI instruction does not change the interrupt mask bit. If the interrupt mask bit is set (I = 1), the microprocessor cannot respond to an interrupt request from any peripheral device. Execution stops after the microprocessor status is saved and can be resumed only via a nonmaskable interrupt or a reset request.

If the interrupt mask bit is in the reset state (I = 0), the microprocessor will service any interrupt request that may be present. If the interrupt request input is in the high state, execution will be suspended, and the microprocessor will wait for an interrupt request to be signaled. If an interrupt request is signaled by the interrupt request changing to the low state, the interrupt will be serviced as previously described, the interrupt mask bit will be set, the program counter will be loaded with the address stored in the internal interrupt pointer, and execution of the internal interrupt program will begin.

Manipulation of the interrupt mask bit. The interrupt mask bit is affected by execution of the source language instructions SWI and RTI, and by the servicing of an interrupt request from a peripheral device, as previously described. The interrupt mask may also be manipulated by the use of any of the following instructions:

CLI, clear interrupt mask bit.

SEI, set interrupt mask bit.

TAP, transfer accumulator A to condition code register.

The state of the interrupt mask bit can also be affected as a result of the following instruction:

TPA, transfer the condition code register to accumulator A.

During execution of the TPA instruction, the condition codes H, I, N, Z, V, and C, in bit positions 5 through 0 of the condition code register, are stored in bit positions 5 through 0, respectively, of accumulator A. Bit positions 7 and 6 of accumulator A are set (go to the 1 state). After execution of the TAP instruction, the state of each of the condition codes (H, I, N, X,

V, C) will be whatever is retrieved from the respective bit positions (5 through 0) of accumulator A.

Special programming requirements. A comprehensive program should make provision for the following special requirements:

1. *Pointers.* The program should place the addresses of the reset and interrupt routine in the respective pointers (see Fig. 4-24) at the high-address end of memory. The addresses would usually be placed in the pointers by use of the FDB assembler directive in the source program.

2. *Reset and interrupt sequences.* The sequences of instructions to be addressed by the reset pointer, the nonmaskable interrupt pointer, the software interrupt pointer, and the internal interrupt point should be provided in the program.

3. *Input and output.* The program will normally include provisions for inputs and outputs relating to peripheral devices. In a programmable system composed of the parts of the Motorola Microcomputer Family M6800, the input and output routines will involve reading and writing coded data from and into the addressable registers of the PIAs and ACIAs. The input and output routines will normally be reached via conditional branch instructions in the internal interrupt program. Typical input/output programs are described in Sec. 4-6.

Look-ahead feature. The microprocessor responds, at the completion of the instruction being executed, to any of the following signals: halt, nonmaskable interrupt, and interrupt request (when the interrupt mask is in the reset state). However, if the interrupt occurs during the last cycle of an instruction, the look-ahead to the next instruction feature will mask the interrupt until completion of the next instruction.

RTI (return from interrupt). The source language instruction RTI assembles into one byte of machine code. Execution of this instruction consists of restoration of the microprocessor to a state pulled from the stack. The information that is obtained from the stack provides for the numerical content of the registers of the programming model shown in Fig. 4-2. Operation is the reverse of that presented in Fig. 4-23. Seven bytes of information are pulled from the stack and stored in respective registers of the microprocessor. The address stored in the stack pointer is incremented before each byte of information is pulled from the stack. After execution of the RTI instruction, the state of each of the condition codes (H, I, N, Z, V, and C) will be whatever is retrieved from the respective bit pointers (5 through 0) of the applicable memory location in the stack. In particular, it should be noted that the interrupt mask bit (I bit) may be either set or reset by execution of the RTI instruction.

4-5-4 *Subroutine linkage*

The stack provides an orderly method of calling a subroutine and returning from the subroutine. (This is generally referred to as *linkage.*) Use of a stack also allows subroutine calls from within a subroutine (when subroutine *nesting* is used).

Call subroutine (BSR or JSR). A return address is saved in the stack during execution of the machine code corresponding to either of the source language instructions BSR (branch to subroutine) or JSR (jump to subroutine). The return address is stored in the stack in accordance with the scheme shown in Fig. 4-25. Before storing the return address, the stack pointer contains the address of a memory location represented in Fig. 4-25 by "m." The stack, if any, extends from memory location "m + 1" to higher locations. The return address is stored in two bytes of memory, at locations "m − 1" and "m." The stack pointer is decremented after each byte of the return address is pushed into the stack.

For either of the instructions (BSR or JSR), the return address saved in the stack is that of the next byte of memory following the bytes of code that correspond to the BSR or JSR instruction. Thus, for the BSR instruction, the return address is equal to the address of the BSR instruction, plus two. For the JSR instruction, the return address is equal to the address of the JSR instruction, plus three or plus two, according to whether the instruction is used with the extended or indexed mode of addressing (Sec. 4-3-7).

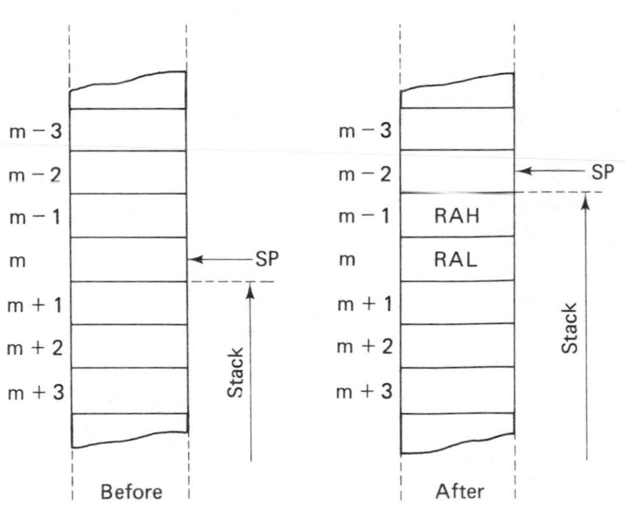

SP = Stack pointer
RAH = Return address, higher order 8-bits
RAL = Return address, lower order 8-bits

Figure 4-25 Saving a return address in the stack.

RTS (return from subroutine). During execution of the RTS instruction, the return address is obtained from the stack and loaded into the program counter. The address stored in the stack pointer is incremented before each byte of the return address is pulled from the stack. This operation is the reverse of that represented in Fig. 4-25.

4-5-5 Data storage in the stack

The source language instruction PSH is used for storing a single byte of data in the stack. This instruction addresses either register A or register B. The contents of the specified register is stored in the stack, in accordance with the scheme represented in Fig. 4-26. The address contained in the stack pointer is decremented.

Conversely, the source language instruction PUL retrieves data from the stack. This instruction addresses either register A or register B. The address contained in the stack pointer is incremented. A single byte of data is then obtained from the stack and loaded into the specified register. The operation is the reverse of that represented in Fig. 4-26.

4-5-6 Reentrant code

Reentrant code is an attribute of a program which allows the program to be interrupted during execution, entered by another user, and, subsequently, reentered at the point of interruption by the first user, thus producing the desired results for all users—a program with an intermediate state of execution that is totally restorable when it is reentered after an interruption. The instruction TSX allows data on the stack to be manipulated by the indexed mode of addressing (Sec. 4-3-6).

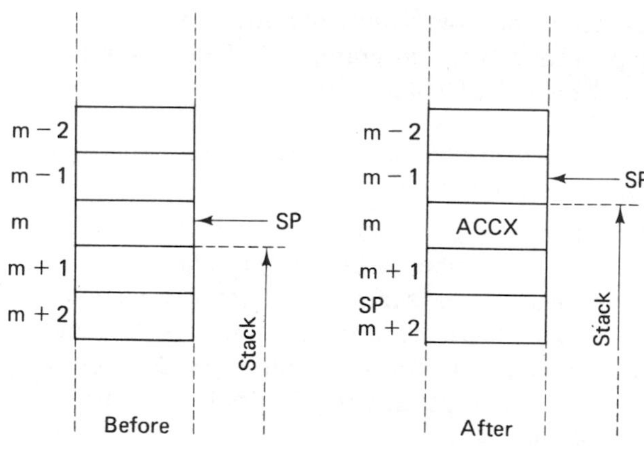

SP = Stack pointer
ACCX = Accumulator A or B

Figure 4-26 Data storage in the stack.

4-5-7 Manipulation of the stack pointer

The address saved in the stack pointer is affected by execution of the source language instructions (SWI, WAI, RTI, BSR, JSR, RTS, PSH, and PUL) and also by the servicing of a nonmaskable interrupt or an interrupt request from a peripheral device, as previously described. In these operations, the stack pointer is coordinated with the storing and retrieval of information in the stack.

The address in the stack pointer may also be manipulated without storing or retrieving information in the stack. This is carried out by the following source language instructions: DES (decrement stack pointer), INS (increment stack pointer), LDS (load the stack pointer), and TXS (transfer index register to stack pointer).

The use of any of these instructions can result in the stack being other than a block of successive locations in memory. The content of the stack pointer is also involved in execution of the following instructions: STS (store the stack pointer) and TSX (transfer stack pointer to index register).

The instruction TSX loads the index register with a value equal to the contents of the stack pointer, plus one. The instruction TXS loads the stack pointer with a value equal to the contents of the index register, minus 1. This is in accordance with operation of the stack pointer during execution of the instructions SWI, WAI, BSR, JSR, or PSH, or during servicing of an interrupt from a peripheral device, in which case the stack pointer is set to 1 less than the address of the last byte stored in the stack.

4-6 SAMPLE PROGRAMS

The following sample programs illustrate how the basic M6800 system can be used to implement a basic program. Full details on more complex programs are described in M6800 literature.

4-6-1 Interfacing a high-speed paper-tape reader without interrupts

The following paragraphs describe how a typical high-speed paper-tape reader/punch, such as described in Sec. 2-4, can be interfaced to the M6800 system. Compare this with the sample program described in Sec. 7-8. From a practical standpoint, there are several techniques that could be used for such interfacing, some of which involve interrupts. The following procedure can be done without interrupts and requires only one interface IC, the PIA discussed in Sec. 4-1-4.

Tape reader/punch characteristics. The paper-tape station incorporates a high-speed paper-tape reader and a high-speed punch mechanism. Such stations are frequently used in data-logging applications and in digital data-processing systems. The paper tape is standard 1-in-wide eight-channel (hole) tape. Of the eight channels across the tape, seven are ASCII-coded character with the eight holes used for a parity check. When paper tape is punched, a ninth, but much smaller, hole is also punched. This ninth hole is the *strobe* hole, which, when detected, indicates that the code holes are properly positioned over the reading head. This event is usually used as a timing reference for the anticipated presence of characters. The strobe hole is also used by low-speed and mechanical tape readers to control tape feed.

In higher-speed devices, a friction-feed method is used, usually involving pinch rollers. Such rollers allow a more even control of tape movement, even at very rapid tape feeding rates. The strobe hole is then detected optically by a photocell, generating a strobe signal that initiates the reading of the code pattern. This latter method is the one used by the reader under discussion here.

The paper-tape station is self-powered, and its input and output signals are all TTL-compatible. This makes connection to the microprocessor interface (PIA) straightforward without the need for buffers or additional logic. Tape movement is initiated by applying a high-level signal to the drive input of the reader. Movement continues as long as the drive signal remains high. Switching the drive input to low activates the brake and stops tape feed.

PIA interface capabilities. The tape reader/microprocessor interface is made up of 10 lines, one signal into the reader (the drive line) and nine from the reader. Eight lines are used for data channels and one for the strobe input signal. These 10 signals can be handled by *one section* of the PIA, as discussed in Sec. 4-1-4 and shown in Fig. 4-6. The PIA is connected to the microprocessor by the three main system buses, carrying data, address, and control. PIA connections to the peripheral (tape reader) consist of 16 data lines and four control signal lines. These can be considered as two separate sections, A and B, each with eight data plus two control lines. The eight data lines, PA0–PA7, correspond to the eight channels of the tape reader/punch. Control lines CA1 and CA2 can be used for the strobe and drive signals.

As shown in Fig. 4-27, the A section of the PIA is used in this application. The drive signal from the PIA to the reader is generated by control CA2. The strobe signal is an input to the PIA from CA1. As discussed in Secs. 4-1 and 4-2, the operating characteristics of CA1 and CA2 and the direction of the bidirectional data lines can be established as required by programming the PIA control and data direction registers, respectively.

Controlling tape movement. There are two alternative methods of controlling tape movement. The tape can be fed continuously by maintaining CA2, the drive input, at a high level. Or the tape can be moved incrementally,

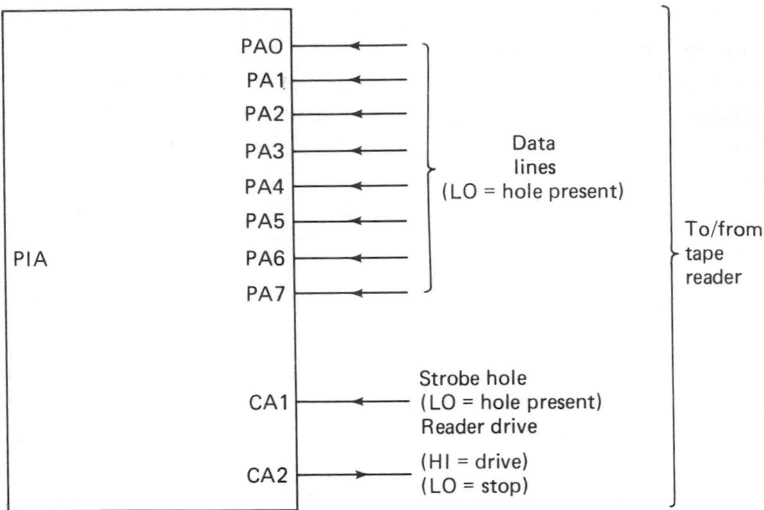

Figure 4-27 Interface to a high-speed paper-tape reader using one section of a PIA.

character by character, by taking the drive low to stop the tape whenever a fresh strobe hole is detected by the reader photocell and pulls CA1 low. This means that unless drive is taken high after a character is read, the tape will automatically stop.

However, provided that the drive signal is restored to the high level within approximately 20 μs, the motion of the tape will seem smooth and uninterrupted. In our example, the latter tape-drive method is used.

PIA flag. The PIA sets a flag in its control register when an active transition (pulse) is detected on a control line (CA1 or CA2). In this case, the flag is set by a pulse on the strobe line, CA1. The flag is cleared automatically by reading the contents of the associated data register. In our example, a flag indicates that a fresh character is ready but has not yet been read.

Flowchart. Figure 4-28 illustrates the solution to the interface problem in flowchart form. Note that there is no logic required except that of the PIA. The object of the flowchart routine is to obtain or fetch a single character from the reader. The tape is stepped, and when the next strobe hole is detected, the code-hole pattern is read into the microprocessor accumulator A via the PIA data register.

Source program solution. A source program of the interface solution is shown in Fig. 4-29. This routine used approximately 1.5 ms of microprocessor time per character read. The first few lines of the program (actually it is a subroutine) consist of comments for the benefit of the reader. The sub-

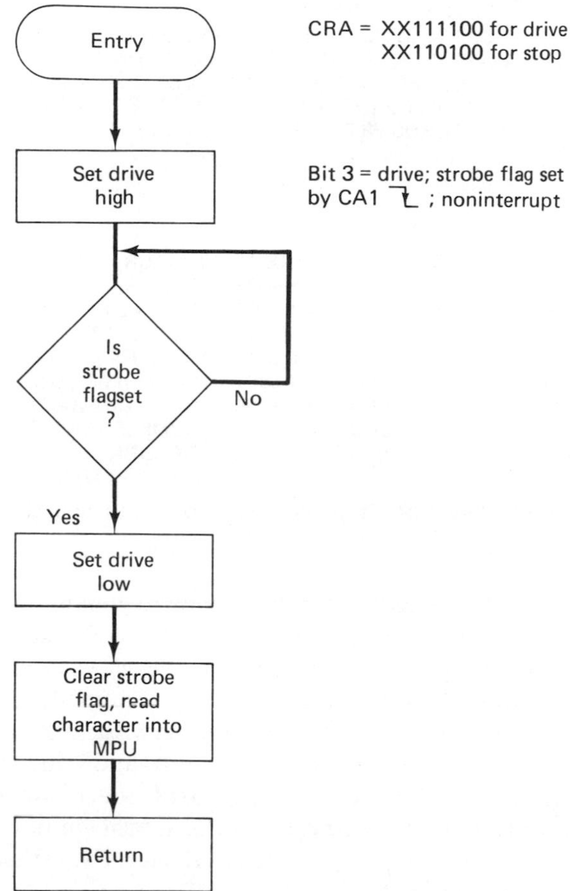

Figure 4-28 Flowchart for "read one character" routine.

routine is called FETCH1, which describes the routine's task, that of fetching (or reading) one character into the microprocessor.

The comments are optional and have been used here to describe the routine's function and some of the requirements of the system in which it is used. For example, the address of the PIA is assumed to be 8000 (in hex) for the data direction and data registers, and 8001 (in hex) for the control register. Note that there is almost a one-to-one relationship between the flowchart and the routine's instructions.

4-6-2 Interfacing a keyboard

The following paragraphs describe how a keyboard, such as that on an electric typewriter or TTY discussed in Sec. 2-2, can be interfaced to the M6800 system. Again, the interface requires only the PIA described in Sec. 4-1-4.

```
                  ♦ FETCH1 – VERSION 1
                  ♦ SUBROUTINE TO FETCH SINGLE CHAR FROM READER
                  ♦ ASSUMES NO INVERTER OPTION ON CA2
                  ♦ ASSUMES PIA DRA/DDRA AT 8000. CRA AT 8001
                  ♦ CRA BIT 3 DIRECTLY CONNECTED TO DRIVE
                  ♦ RETURNS WITH CHARACTER CODE IN ACC. A


2000  86  3C    FETCH1 LDA  A#00111100B  CRA PATTERN
2002  B7  8001         STA  A $8001     SET DRIVE HIGH
2005  B6  8001  TSTFLG LDA  A $8001     IS FLAG SET YET?
2008  2A  FB           BPL    TSTFLG    NO – TEST IT AGAIN
200A  86  37           LDA  A#00110111B  CRA PATTERN
200C  B7  8001         STA  A $8001     SET DRIVE LOW
200F  B6  8000         LDA  A $8000     READ CHARACTER, CLR FLAG
2012  43               COM  A           COMPLEMENT TO CORRECT PHASE
2013  39               RTS              RETURN
```

Figure 4-29 Assembly (source) listing for "read one character" routine.

The sample program uses a typical business keyboard with a full range of keys, such as those used for accounting computers. The keys are arranged into two groups; one group corresponds to the *alphanumeric* (so-called "QWERTY" layout) keyboard commonly found in modern electric typewriters. The second group of keys is called the *control key pad* and is used by the operator to enter mostly numerical information and to control the operation of the microcomputer. The keyboard under discussion is electronic. The basic layout and output terminals are shown in Fig. 4-30. The keys are connected to a decoder within the keyboard. (Note that the decoder may also be known as an encoder.)

A strobe signal is generated whenever a code key is depressed. The internal decoder generates an 8-bit code plus some additional control bits for every key depressed. For the purpose of this discussion it is assumed that this combination of codes and extra bits is *not suitable* for direct connection to the microcomputer. That is, the keyboard output cannot be connected directly to the data and control buses within the system.

Interface requirements. The requirements of this interface are for an 8-bit code which totally and uniquely defines each character, which may be upper- or lowercase, or a control function. The code generated must contain 7 bits, equivalent to the ASCII code of the character (less the parity bit), and an eighth bit defining whether the code is to be interpreted by the microcomputer as an ASCII character (when the key is an alphanumeric group key) or as a control function generated by the control group of keys. (Since the system ignores the parity bit, bit 7 can be used for this eighth bit.)

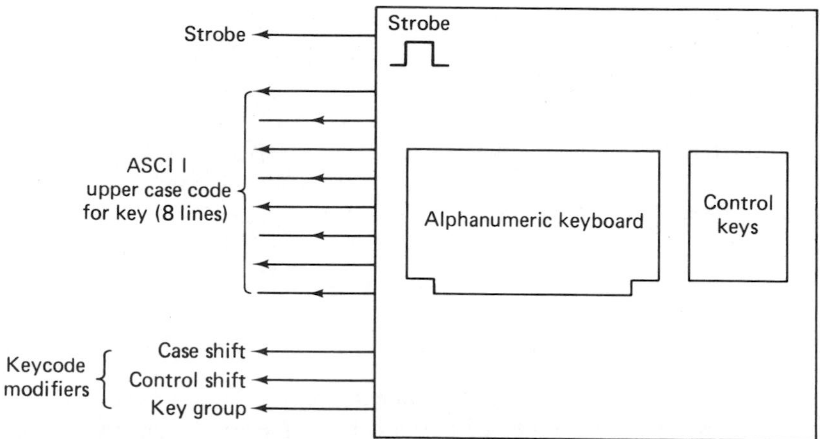

Figure 4-30 Electronic keyboard layout showing output signals.

As the operator keys in data at the keyboard, the codes generated are stored in a known location in the system memory from which they can be retrieved by the microprocessor as required. This area of store, or buffer, can be defined as being of any size.

Buffered keyboards. Most keyboards are buffered in microcomputer or other data-entry applications because this allows the operator to "get ahead" of the microprocessor without causing an error due to missed codes. There is, however, normally a limit to how many characters can be stored. When the limit is reached, this fact must be signaled to the operator. In our system, a maximum of 32 codes (or characters) are to be held in a buffer area of 32 bytes in the microcomputer memory.

Interrupt. Our system causes the interrupt function of the microprocessor and PIA because it is assumed that the microprocessor has several other peripherals to service. Whenever a character is keyed, an interrupt is requested. Upon receiving an interrupt from the keyboard, the microprocessor (having completed the current instruction) reads the character keyed, recodes the character as necessary to match the M6800 data format, and then stores the character in the next vacant location in the buffer. Whenever there are no interrupts awaiting service, the microprocessor reads the contents of the buffer and then clears the buffer.

Keyboard codes. The following chart gives details of the codes generated by the keyboard internal decoder and any modifications required for their processing by the microprocessor. All the keyboard codes contain 7 ASCII bits, plus one parity bit, and when modifying the codes, the control shift key takes precedence over a simultaneously depressed case shift key.

Key Modifiers	*Meaning*	*Required Code*
Control shift = 1	Control shift key is down	ASCII control code
Control shift = 0	No control shift	ASCII character or symbol code
Case shift = 1	Case shift key is down	ASCII code for lowercase character
Case shift = 0	No case shift	ASCII code for uppercase character
Key group = 1	Key is in alphanumeric group	Bit 7 = 1
Key group = 0	Key is in control group	Bit 7 = 0, code is correct

Keyboard signals. Twelve signals are generated by the keyboard, 11 of which are data (defining the key that has been depressed); the twelfth is the strobe timing signal, which is the only "control" input to the interface. The keyboards must therefore use both the A and B sections of the PIA.

Interconnections and flowcharts. Connections between the PIA and keyboard are shown in Fig. 4-31. Flowcharts are shown in Fig. 4-32 and 4-33. Figure 4-32 shows the keyboard routine that loads the code for the keyed character into an area of memory designated as the character buffer. Figure 4-33 shows the subroutine (RDKEYS) that generates the required code from the keyboard signals and loads this code into accumulator A.

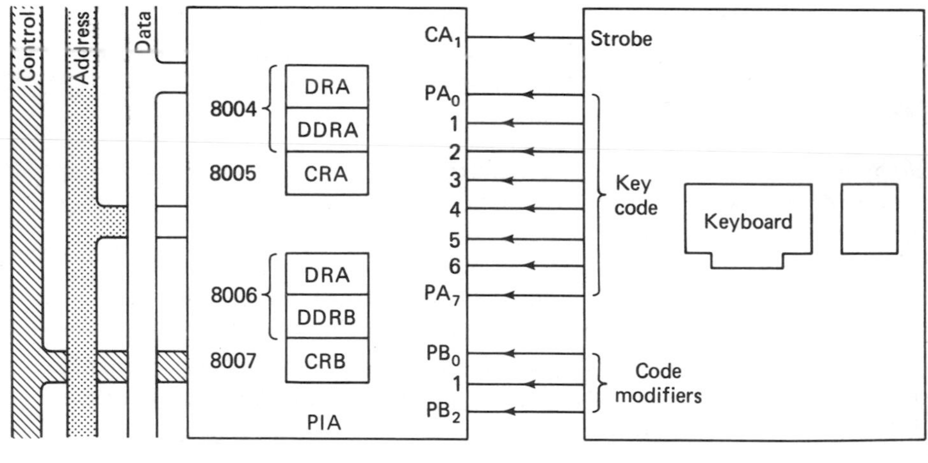

Key

DRA/B = Data register A/B } Having a shared address of
DDRA/B = Data direction register A/B } 8004_H and 8006_H respectively
CRA/B = Control register A/B } Having addresses 8005_H and 8007_H respectively

Figure 4-31 Business computer keyboard interfaced to the PIA.

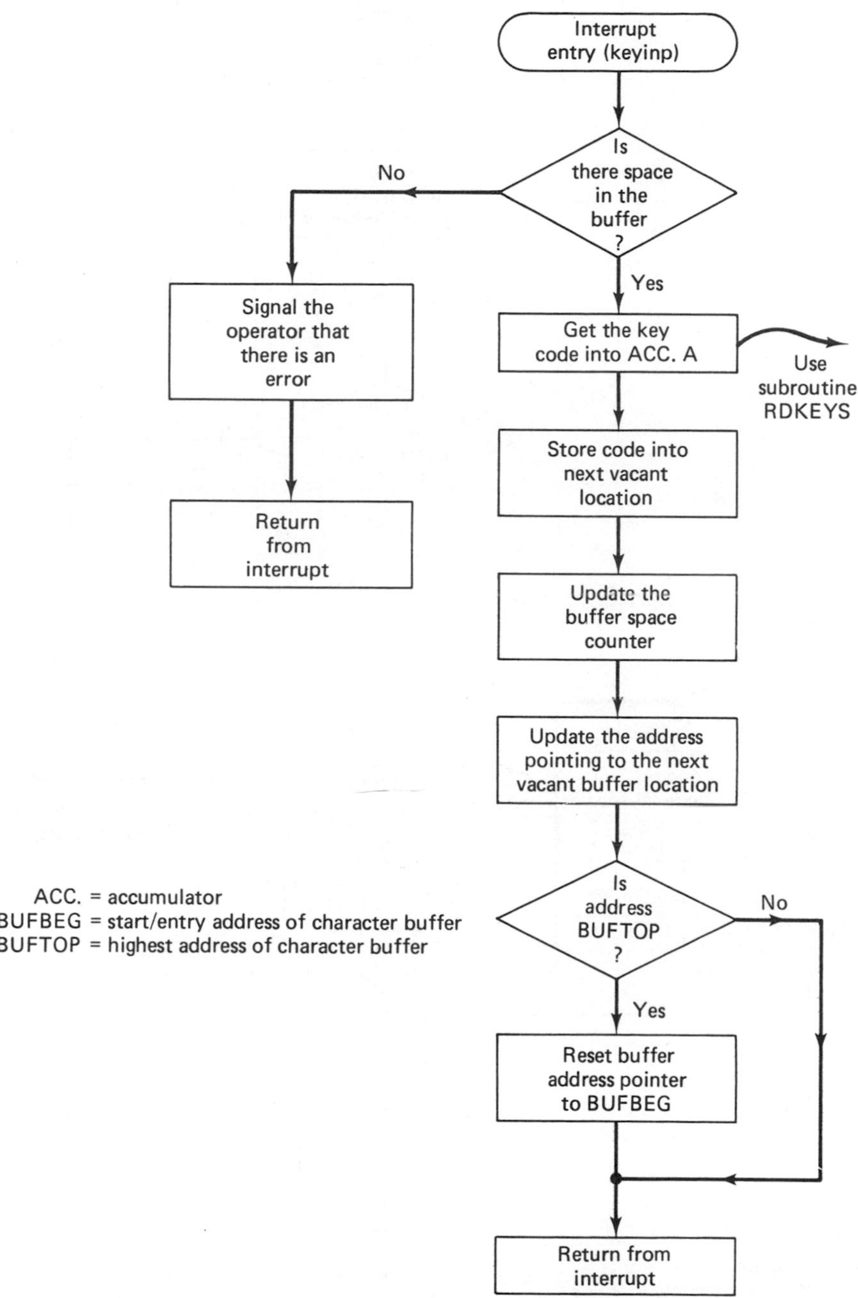

Figure 4-32 Flowchart of the keyboard routine which loads the code for the keyed character into an area of store designated as the character buffer.

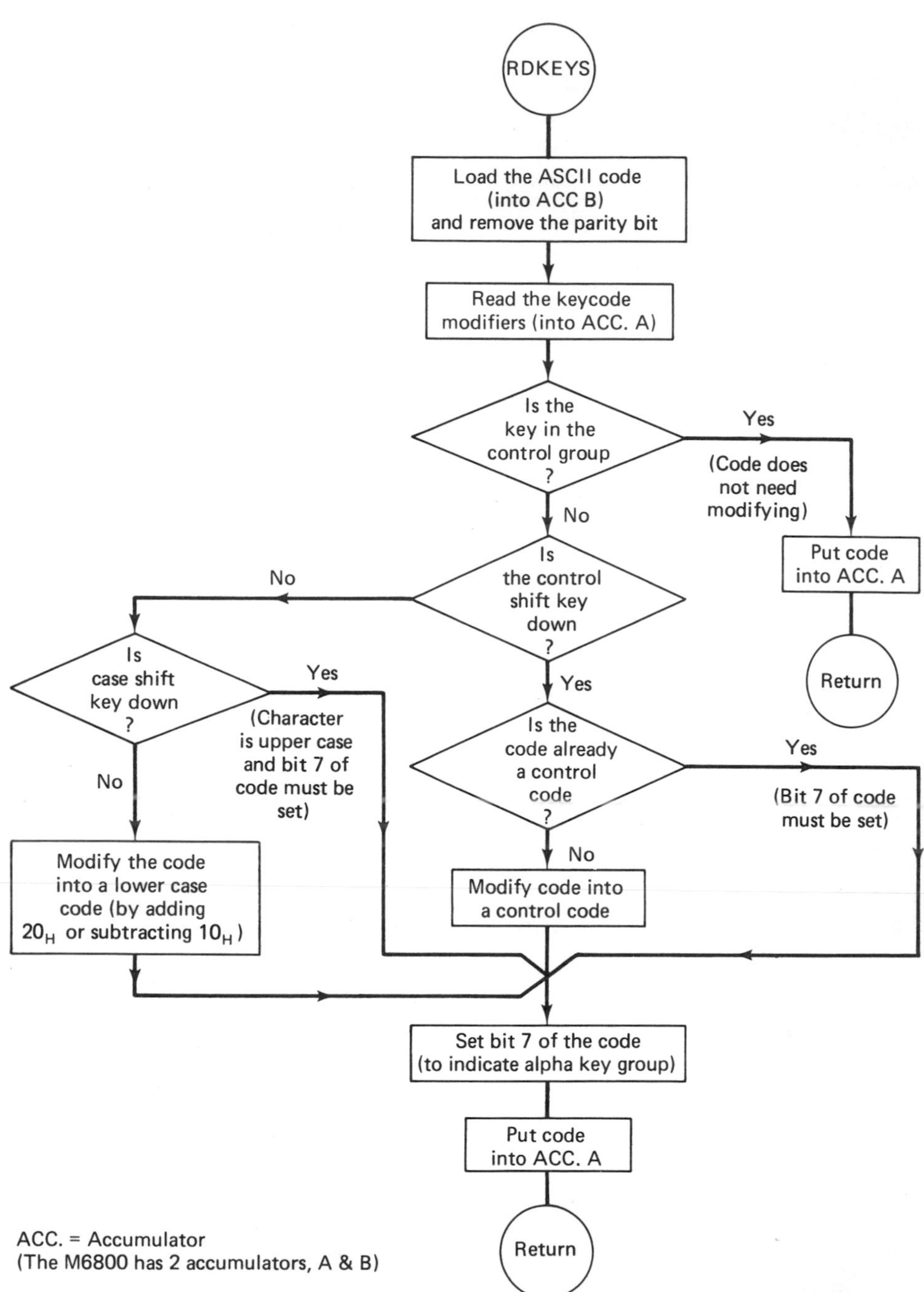

Figure 4-33 Flowchart of the subroutine (RDKEYS) which generates the required code from the keyboard signals and loads this code into accumulator A.

Code modifiers. Because the three key modifiers influence the way in which the key code is treated, it is these three signals that direct the microprocessor's passage through the subroutine which generates the special key codes (Fig. 4-33). The decisions and branches (all of which are shown in the flowcharts as diamond-shaped symbols with two exits) are needed in order to apply the correct modifications to the key code. To make these decision points in the program use as few program instructions and machine cycles as possible, the three code modifier bits are copied directly into the CCR (condition code register) of the microprocessor via the PB0–PB2 inputs of the PIA (Fig. 4-31).

Error signal. As shown in Fig. 4-32, the interrupt service routine checks that there is space in the buffer before calling up the subroutine, and signals an error to the operator. (As a practical matter, this signal can be a bell, buzzer, or flashing light on the keyboard.) The error signal is generated only if the buffer is full.

Strobe signal. The strobe signal is connected into the CA1 input of the PIA, as indicated in Fig. 4-31, and thus controls the CRA register. Control register A is loaded with a control word (XX000111) or hex 07 and, when the strobe signal is applied (keys are depressed), this word causes an interrupt and sets the flag bit (bit 7). In this way, the strobe signal controls the interrupt request to the microprocessor.

4-7 M6800 DEVELOPMENT AIDS

The following paragraphs describe development aids available to M6800 users. Full details are given in the instruction manuals.

4-7-1 EXORciser M68SDT

Figure 4-34 shows the EXORciser, which is an emulator for M6800-based systems. The EXORciser is a modularized, expandable instrument which permits instant breadboarding and evaluation of any M6800-based microcomputer system. It consists of a prewired, bus-oriented chassis and power supply, together with three basic modules: an MPU module, a Debug module, and a Baud Rate module. These provide the basic control and interface functions of a microcomputer and house the system development and diagnostic programs. A number of separately available, optional memory modules and additional interface modules (up to 12) may be added, simply by plugging them into existing prewired sockets, to convert the basic system into an exact prototype of a desired end system. Thus, the EXORciser, with its built-in EXbug firmware, enables the designer to configure, evaluate, and debug the final system hardware and software using actual M6800 components.

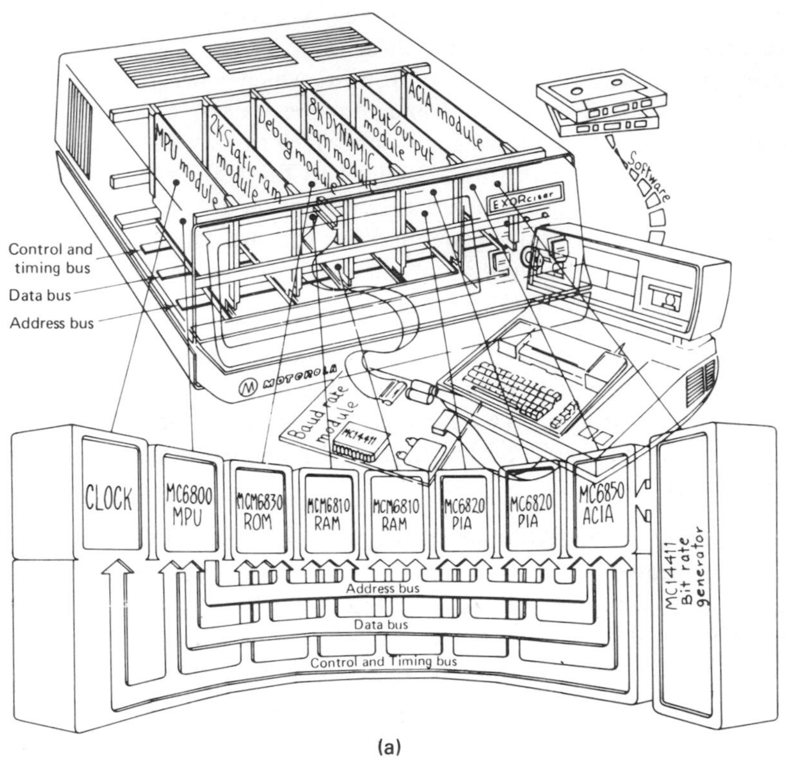

(a)

Figure 4-34 (a) EXORciser M68SDT emulator for M6800-based systems, relationship of components: (b) EXORciser M68SDT emulator for M6800-based systems, photo. (Courtesy Motorola Semiconductor Products, Inc.)

Figure 4-34 shows the major components of the basic EXORciser as well as those of several optional EXORciser modules. The built-in Baud Rate module contains, primarily, an MC14411 Bit Rate Generator, which determines the data transfer rates between an external data terminal and the EXORciser. The Baud Rate module supplies eight switch-selectable baud rates, all of which are compatible with standard data transfer rates used by terminals.

The MPU (or microprocessor unit, which is the term used by Motorola) module includes a built-in crystal-controlled 1-MHz clock, which provides the timing for the microprocessor system under development as well as for the rest of the EXORciser. In addition, the MPU module houses the M6800 microprocessor, which gives the EXORciser computation and control capabilities.

The Debug module, through its EXbug firmware stored in three ROMs, enables the user to evaluate and debug a system under development.

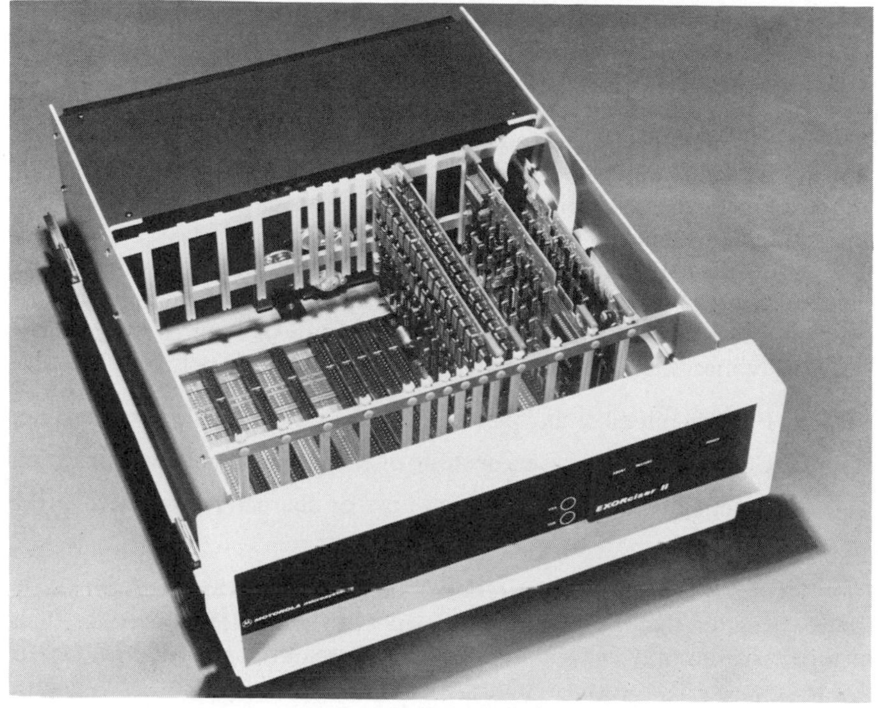

(b)

Figure 4-34 *(Continued)*

The Debug module's two RAMs provide a 256-byte scratch-pad memory for the EXbug routines.

These functional subsystems of the basic EXORciser are supplemented by a power supply and a bus-oriented distribution system. This bus system transfers the power supply voltage as well as the data, address, and control signals to the optional modules. The memory and I/O modules are available as options and thus provide more flexibility than emulator systems, where the memory and/or I/O is fixed. Overall, the EXORciser can address up to 65 kilobytes of memory and addresses the I/O modules (as well as the memory modules) as memory.

Basic design procedure. Using the EXORciser in a typical design process normally begins by defining the functions to be performed by the proposed system. In this definition phase, the designer makes the required trade-offs between the system hardware and software functions.

Next, the designer emulates the proposed system in the EXORciser using the appropriate memory and I/O modules. In most cases, the modules are simply plugged into the EXORciser. However, for those systems that require special interface circuitry and customized circuitry, provisions have been made on the I/O modules for the designer to insert 14-, 16-, and 24-pin wirewrap sockets and construct the special circuitry. Also, the designer can construct any customized circuitry on Universal Wirewrap module.

The terminal illustrated in Fig. 4-34 provides a means for communications between the designer and EXORciser. This can be done by means of the terminal keyboard, from paper tape, or from a cassette associated with the particular terminal in use.

Using the capabilities of the M6800 Resident Editor, the designer next enters a source program, either via the terminal keyboard or from the selected medium. The user can then modify and change the source program as required to meet the proposed system requirements. This includes:

1. Printing out all or any part of the program for detailed examination.
2. Changing any characters or string of characters in the source program.
3. Deleting or adding instruction lines or characters anywhere in the program.

At the end of the editing process, the Resident Editor will provide a source program that may be stored on paper tape, cassette, or diskette. This source program may be used in subsequent assembly operations on any of the compatible Motorola assemblers and cross-assemblers.

The EXORciser's M6800 Co-Resident Assembler or the Resident Macro Assembler and Linking Loader can be used to automatically translate the source program into an object program (machine language). The Co-Resident Assembler requires a minimum of 8K bytes of memory, while the Macro Assembler and Linking Loader requires a minimum of 14K bytes of memory.

The resultant object program is available from the EXORciser in three forms:

1. A printed assembly listing of the source program.
2. An object program on paper tape, cassette, or diskette.
3. A machine file, consisting of the machine-coded program stored directly into the EXORciser memory. This option permits the program to be executed immediately after assembly with no need for subsequent loading.

The Macro Assembler in its assembly process allows the assignment of the memory addresses of a program to be relocatable and assigned when loaded by the Linking Loader rather than fixed during the assembly operation. With the Co-Resident Assembler, the program address assignments are fixed in the assembly operation.

Once the designer has configured the EXORciser to emulate the hardware and has developed the programs, the system is ready for debugging. The EXORciser, with its EXbug system development firmware, permits the user to debug *both the system hardware and system software* as required until the system is up and operating.

When the USE (user system evaluator) option is installed, the EXORciser can be used to test and evaluate external equipment. By removing the M6800 microprocessor from the external user system and connecting the USE cable from the EXORciser into the microprocessor socket, the EXORciser with the EXbug firmware can be used to debug and troubleshoot microprocessor systems.

The EXORciser can also be used as a production tool. An EXORciser equipped with USE can be used in a final test area for testing the user production system. With MOTEST (Sec. 4-7-2), a component tester, the EXORciser also can be used to test the M6800 family of parts.

MPU module MEX6800. Figure 4-35 is the block diagram of the MPU module. This module is the heart of both the EXORciser Debug system and the user system under development by providing both the system clock and the microprocessor. The MPU module also automatically initiates and EXORciser restart operation when power is first applied to the EXORciser. The clock circuit generates a crystal-controlled 1-MHz signal, but the system

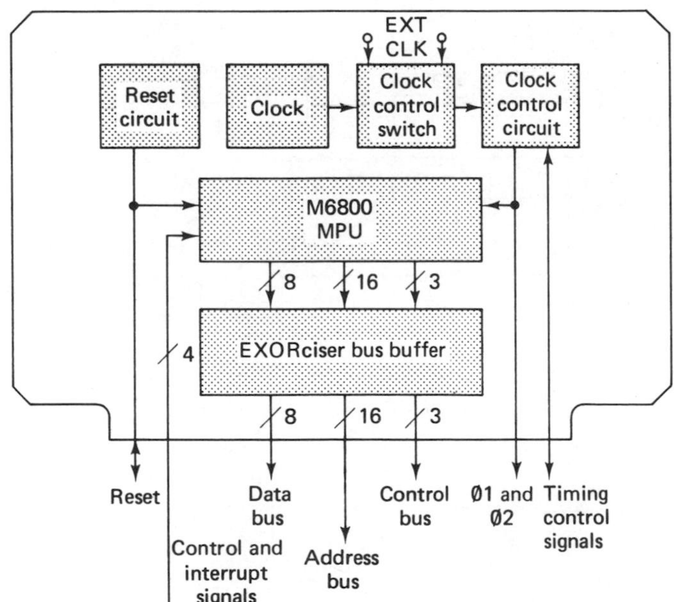

Figure 4-35 MPU module MEX6800, block diagram.

may be operated with an external clock at frequencies between 100 kHz and 1 MHz by means of a switch mounted on the MPU module.

In addition to generating the basic EXORciser timing signals, the clock circuit provides the EXORciser with the capability of refreshing dynamic memories and working with slow memories.

Debug module. Figure 4-36 is the block diagram of the Debug module. This module, through the EXbug firmware and implementation hardware, provides the EXORciser with the capability to evaluate and debug a system under development. The EXbug firmware is stored in the module's three ROMs, with the module's two RAMs serving as a scratch-pad memory for the EXbug routines.

Using the EXbug routines the designer can search the input medium for a file, load a file into the EXORciser memory, verify the contents in the EXORciser memory, print out the contents of the EXORciser memory, and record the memory contents on a selected medium. In between these I/O functions, the user can examine and, if required, change the memory contents. The user can insert and remove one hardware breakpoint and up to eight software breakpoints. The user can also run in real time or trace

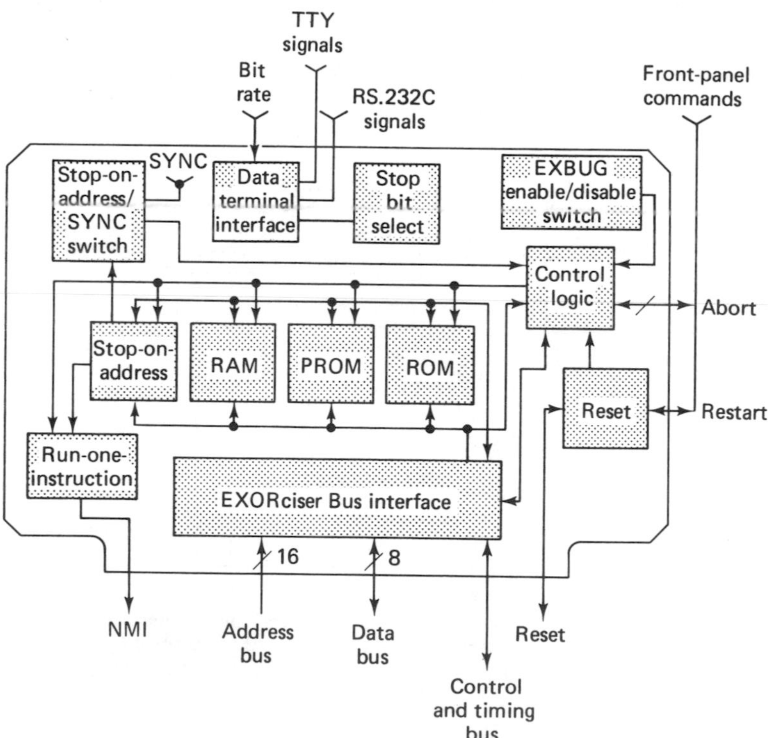

Figure 4-36 Debug module, block diagram.

through the user program or a selected portion of the user program. While using these routines, the user modifies the hardware and software as required until the system is up and running. A DISABLE switch on the module may be used to disable the EXbug routines. The user communicates with EXbug via an external terminal, working in conjunction with the Baud Rate module and the Debug module.

Baud Rate module. Figure 4-37 is the block diagram of the Baud Rate module. This module, in conjunction with the Debug module, enables the designer to communicate with EXbug via a data terminal or set (Sec. 2-9). The Baud Rate module crystal oscillator baud rate generator and baud rate switch provide the EXORciser with eight standard rates (110, 150, 300, 600, 1200, 2400, 4800, 9600). This module also interconnects the Debug module to a data terminal and with the front panel.

Memory modules. The optional memory modules include a 2K static RAM, an 8K dynamic RAM, a 16K dynamic RAM, and an EROM/RAM module.

Interface modules. The optional interface modules include an I/O module for parallel devices and an ACIA module for serial devices.

Auxiliary modules. The optional auxiliary modules include a universal wirewrap module and an extender module (which permits access to any EXORciser module from outside the EXORciser chassis.

System analyzer. The optional system analyzer is a module that can be used with the EXORciser or for field service. *In field service applications,* the system analyzer derives operating power and I/O signals directly from the system under test. The system analyzer stops the system at any point in

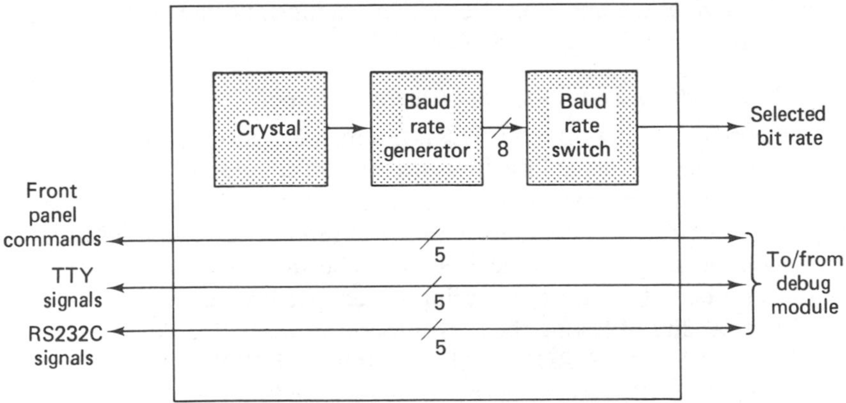

Figure 4-37 Baud Rate module, block diagram.

its program, steps through the program, changes the contents of the system memory, and monitors and records the microprocessor operation during a selected portion of the program. The system analyzer can perform these functions without shutting down operation of the system. ***In EXORciser applications,*** the system analyzer adds a variety of options to the system's inherent program development capabilities. In conjunction with the EXORciser and USE, the system analyzer offers a powerful combination of development and diagnostic tools available for microcomputer work.

PROM programmer. Once a program is designed and debugged, it is entered into a ROM, which becomes part of the system. When the end system is manufactured in large quantities, these programmed ROMs are often purchased in quantity from the component supplier. When only a few end systems are to be produced, the equipment manufacturer may elect to use an Electrically Alterable PROM (EAPROM) and do their own programming (as discussed throughout Chapter 1).

The PROM programmer, in conjunction with the EXORciser, will perform this function quickly, easily, and inexpensively. The PROM programmer operates in conjunction with the EXbug firmware to program EPROMs of the 2704 and 2708 type. In use, the PROM programmer verifies data in the EPROM, transfers data from the EPROM to the EXORciser RAM memory, and transfers blocks of data from one memory location to another. As a point of reference, programming time varies between about ½ minute (for the 2704) to 1½ minutes (for the 2708).

USE module. This optional module extends all the capabilities of the EXORciser to an existing user system. Whereas the basic EXORciser permits design of a microprocessor system through emulation, the USE module brings the diagnostic and evaluation capabilities of the EXORciser to bear on an existing system. In conjunction with the system analyzer, the USE module provides a comprehensive system diagnostic center for all M6800-based equipment.

4-7-2 MOTEST-I component tester MEX68CT

Figure 4-38 shows the MOTEST-I, which is a tester that provides the EXORciser with the capability of testing M6800 components in an environment that closely approximates end-use conditions. The MOTEST-I system requires an EXORciser containing an MPU module, Debug module, Baud Rate module, and the required memory. The memory size is determined by the number of device types being tested. At present, the MOTEST-I has the capability of testing the microprocessor unit, PIA, ACIA, 128 × 8 RAM, and 1024 × 8 ROM. Using a universal ROM card, additional TTL-compatible ROMs can also be accommodated.

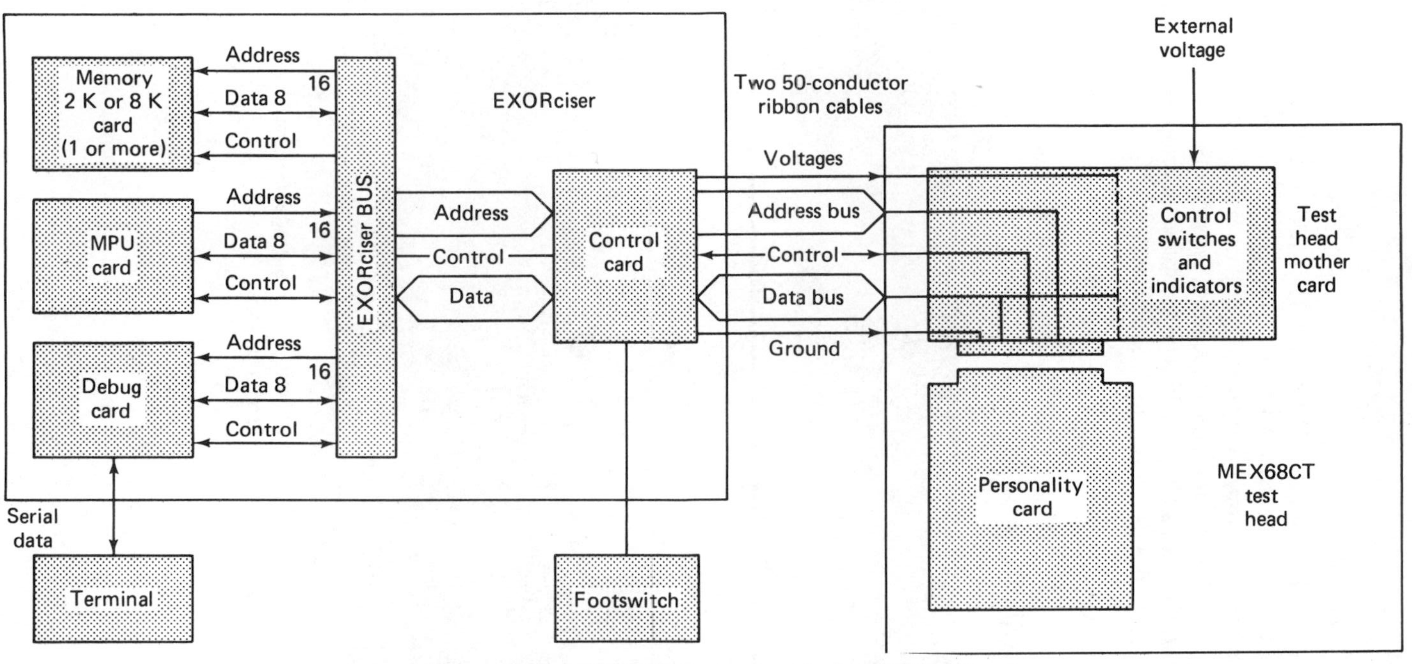

Figure 4-38 MOTEST-I component tester MEX68CT.

4-7-3 EXORdisk II

Figure 4-39 shows the EXORdisk II, which is a floppy disk storage system such as that described in Sec. 2-8. The EXORdisk II extends the EXORciser memory capacity by up to 1 million bytes of memory. Together with the EXORciser, and an associated, separately available interface module, the EXORdisk II provides a complete development system with high-speed software-development capabilities.

4-7-4 EXORprint

Figure 2-12 shows the EXORprint, which is a tabletop impact printer such as described in Sec. 2-5.

Figure 4-39 EXORdisk II floppy disk storage system. (Courtesy Motorola Semiconductor Products, Inc.)

5 Intel MCS-48 Microcomputers

This chapter is devoted entirely to the MCS-48 single-chip microcomputer manufactured by Intel Corporation. The chapter starts with a discussion of basic system hardware and architecture, then proceeds with a brief description of how the system may be expanded. This is followed by a summary of the instruction set and examples of hardware and software applications. The chapter concludes with a description of compatible system components and of development aids or support equipment.

The details presented in this chapter represent only a small fraction of the data taken from the manufacturer's literature (manuals and data sheets). However, the information presented is sufficient for a reader of any level to evaluate the system. The chapter also provides a realistic view of actual state-of-the-art microprocessor-based systems. This supplements the theoretical and typical descriptions of Chapters 1 and 2.

5-1 INTRODUCTION TO THE MCS-48 SYSTEM

The MCS-48 system is a true *single-chip microcomputer* containing all the functions required in a digital processing system. This microcomputer, its variations, and its optional peripherals are collectively called the MCS-48 microcomputer family. At present, the family consists of the following:

8048 microcomputer with ROM.

8748 microcomputer with EPROM.

8035 microcomputer without ROM.

8243 I/O expander.

8355 ROM program memory and I/O expander.

8755 EPROM program memory and I/O expander.

8155 data memory and I/O expander.

8048 microcomputer. The head of the family is the 8048 microcomputer shown in Fig. 5-1. As illustrated in Fig. 5-1a, the microcomputer contains the following functions in a single 40-pin package: 8-bit CPU (control processor unit), 1K × 8 ROM program memory, 64 × 8 RAM data memory, 27 I/O lines, 8-bit interval timer/event counter, oscillator and clock driver, reset circuit, and interrupt circuit.

A 2.5- or 5.0-μs cycle time, and a repertoire of over 90 instructions, each consisting of one or two cycles, makes the 8048 the equal in performance of many presently available multichip microprocessors. A single 5-V power supply is required for all MCS-48 components.

The 8048 is designed to be an efficient control processor, as well as an arithmetic processor. The instruction set allows the user to directly set and reset individual lines within the I/O ports, as well as test individual bits within the accumulator. A large variety of branch and table look-up instructions make the 8048 very efficient in implementing standard logic functions. Over 70 percent of the instructions are single-byte; all others are two-byte. This means that many functions requiring 1.5K to 2K bytes in other systems may very well be compressed into the 1K words resident in the 8048.

8748 microcomputer. In addition to the 8048 in which the program ROM is mask-programmed by Intel to user specifications, there is the 8748, with user-programmable and erasable EPROM program memory for prototype development. The 8748 (Fig. 5-1b) is essentially a single-chip microcomputer breadboard which can be modified over and over again during development and preproduction, then simply replaced by the low-cost 8048 ROM for volume production. The 8748 provides a very easy transition from development to production, and also provides an easy vehicle for temporary field updates while new ROMs are being made.

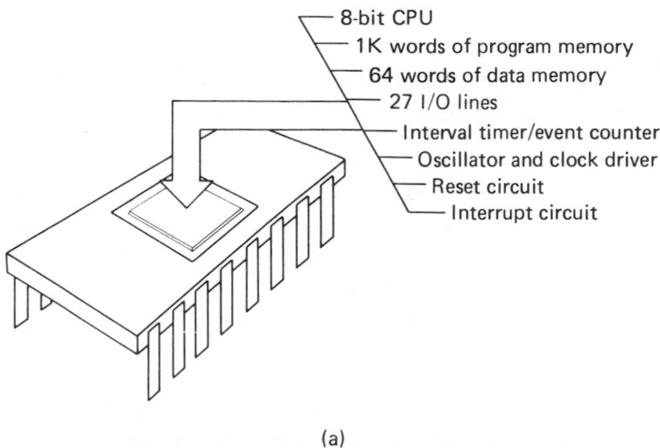

(a)

(b)

Figure 5-1 (a) Intel 8048 microcomputer functions; (b) Intel 8748 microcomputer with EPROM. (Courtesy Intel Corporation.)

8035 microcomputer. The 8035 is an 8048 without internal program memory which allows the user to match the program memory requirements exactly by using a wide variety of external memories. The 8035 allows the user to select a minimum-cost system no matter what program requirements exist.

8243 I/O expander. The 8243 I/O expander provides 16 I/O lines in a 24-pin package. For systems with large I/O requirements, multiple 8243s can be used.

8355, 8755, and 8155 expanders. Program and data memory may be expanded using standard memories, or memories in the 8355, 8755, and 8155 expanders.

For such applications as keyboards, displays, serial communication lines, and so on, the Intel MCS-80 peripheral circuits may be added to the MCS-48 system.

5-2 SINGLE-COMPONENT MCS-48 SYSTEM

This section describes the functional characteristics of the 8048, 8748, and 8035 single-component microcomputers. Unless otherwise noted, the following details apply to all three versions. This section is limited to those functions useful in single-chip implementations of the MCS-48.

5-2-1 Architecture

Figure 5-2 shows the basic MCS-48 architecture. The following paragraphs provide a brief description of the single-chip microcomputer functions.

5-2-2 Arithmetic section

The arithmetic section contains the basic data manipulation functions of the 8048, and can be divided into the following blocks: arithmetic logic unit (ALU), accumulator, carry flag, instruction decoder.

In a typical operation, data stored in the accumulator are combined in the ALU with data from another source on the internal bus (such as a register or I/O port) and the result is stored in the accumulator or other register.

Instruction decoder. The op-code portion of each program instruction is stored in the instruction decoder and converted to outputs that control the function of each of the blocks in the arithmetic section. These lines control the source of data, and the destination register, as well as the function performed in the ALU.

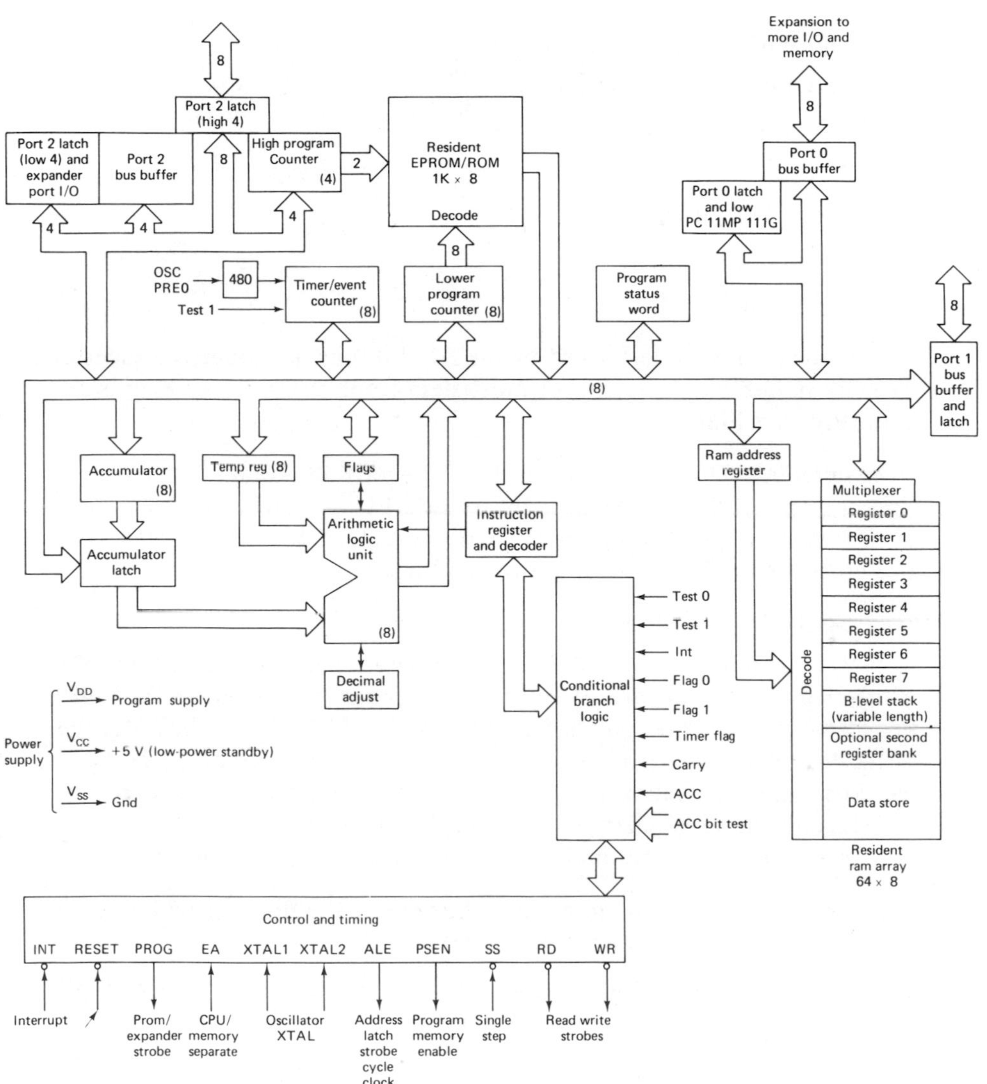

Figure 5-2 Basic MCS-48 architecture.

ALU. The ALU accepts 8-bit data words from one or two sources, and generates an 8-bit result under control of the instruction decoder. The ALU can perform the following functions:

Add With or Without Carry.

And, OR, Exclusive OR.

Increment/Decrement.

Bit Complement.

Rotate Left, Right.

Swap Nibbles.

BCD Decimal Adjust.

If the operation performed by the ALU results in a value represented by more than 8 bits (overflow of most-significant bit), a Carry Flag is set in the Program Status Word.

Accumulator. The accumulator is the single most important data register, since it is one of the sources of input to the ALU and often the destination of the result of operations performed in the ALU. Data bytes to and from I/O ports and memory also normally pass through the accumulator.

5-2-3 Program memory

As shown in Fig. 5-3, the Resident program memory consists of 1024 words, 8 bits wide, that are addressed by the program counter. In the 8748, this memory is user-programmable and -erasable EPROM. In the 8048, the memory is ROM which is mask-programmable at the factory. The 8035 has no internal program memory and is used with external devices. Program code is completely interchangeable among the three versions.

There are three locations in program memory of special importance:

Location 0. Activating the Reset line causes the first instruction to be fetched from location 0.

Location 3. Activating the Interrupt input line (if interrupt is enabled) causes a jump to subroutine.

Location 7. A timer/counter interrupt resulting from timer/counter overflow (if enabled) causes a jump to subroutine.

Therefore, the first instruction to be executed after initialization is stored in location 0, the first word of an external interrupt service subroutine is stored in location 3, and the first word of a timer/counter service routine is stored in location 7. Program memory can be used to store constants as well as program instructions. This permits easy access to data look-up tables.

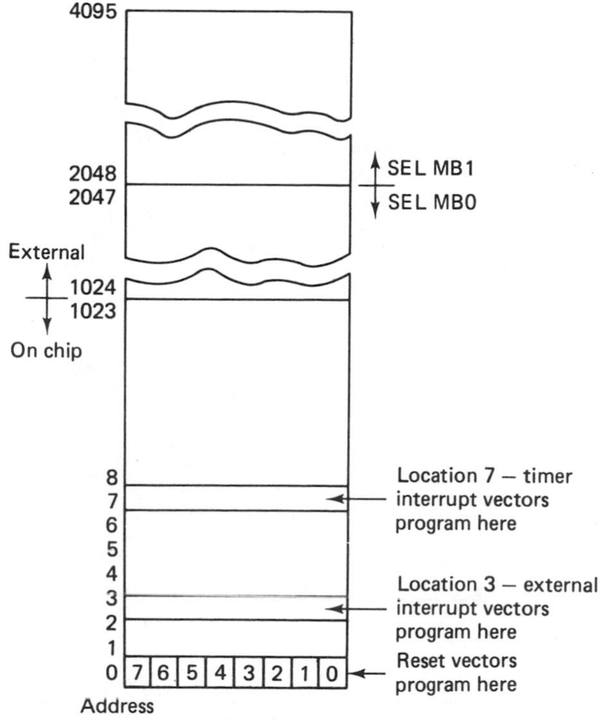

Figure 5-3 MCS-48 program memory map.

5-2-4 Data memory

As shown in Fig. 5-4, Resident data memory is organized as 64 words, 8 bits wide. All 64 locations are indirectly addressable through either of the two RAM pointer registers that reside at address 0 and 1 of the register array. In addition, the first 8 locations (0–7) of the array are designated as working registers and are directly addressable by several instructions. Since these registers are more easily addressed, they are usually used to store frequently accessed intermediate results. The DJNZ instruction makes efficient use of the working registers as *program loop counters* by allowing the programmer to decrement and test the register in a single instruction.

By executing a Register Bank Switch instruction (SEL RB), RAM locations 24–31 are designated as the working registers in place of locations 0–7, and are then directly addressable. This second bank of working registers may be used as an extension of the first bank or reserved for use during interrupt service subroutines allowing the registers of Bank 0 used in the main program to be instantly "saved" by a Bank Switch. Note that if this second bank is not used, locations 24–31 are still addressable as general-purpose RAM.

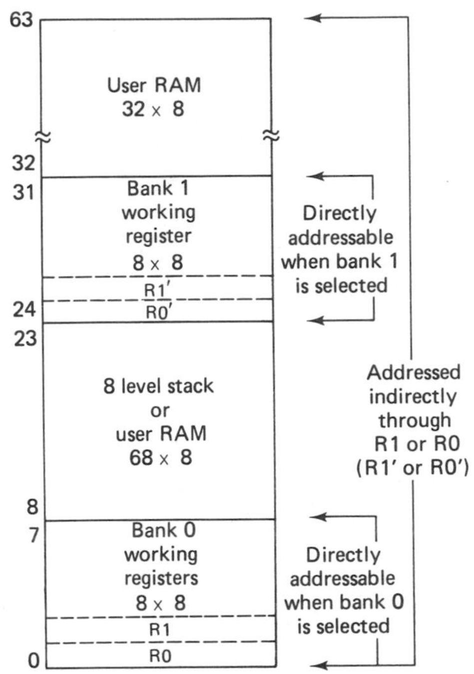

Figure 5-4 MCS-48 data memory map.

Since the two RAM Pointer Registers R0 and R1 are a part of the working register array, bank switching effectively creates two more pointer registers (R0′ and R1′), which can be used with R0 and R1 to easily access up to four separate working areas in RAM at one time. RAM locations (8–23) also serve a dual role in that they contain the program counter stack, as discussed in Sec. 5-2-7. These locations are addressed by the Stack Pointer during subroutine calls as well as by RAM Pointer Registers R0 and R1. If the level of subroutine nesting is less than eight, all stack registers are not required, and can be used as general-purpose RAM locations. Each level of subroutine nesting not used provides the user with two additional RAM locations.

5-2-5 Input/Output

The 8048 has 27 lines that can be used for input or output functions. These lines are grouped as three ports of eight lines each, which serve as either inputs, outputs, or bidirectional ports, and three "test" inputs that can alter program sequences when tested by conditional jump instructions.

Ports 1 and 2. Ports 1 and 2 are each 8 bits wide and have identical characteristics. Data bytes written to these ports are statically latched and remain unchanged until rewritten. As input ports, these lines are nonlatching (that is, inputs must be present until read by an input instruction). Inputs are fully TTL-compatible and outputs will drive one standard TTL load.

The lines of ports 1 and 2 are called quasi-bidirectional because of a special output circuit structure that allows each line to serve as an input and output or both, even though outputs are statically latched.

Bus. Bus is also an 8-bit port, which is a true bidirectional port with associated input and output strobes. If the bidirectional feature is not needed, BUS can serve as either a statically latched output port or a non-latching input port. Input and output lines on this port cannot be mixed, however.

5-2-6 Test and $\overline{INT}$ inputs

Three pins (T0, T1, and $\overline{\text{INT}}$) serve as inputs and are testable with the conditional jump instruction. These pins allow inputs to cause program branches without the necessity to load an input port into the accumulator.

5-2-7 Program counter and stack

The Program Counter is an independent counter, while the Program Counter Stack is implemented using pairs of registers in the Data Memory Array (see Fig. 5-5). Only 10 bits of the Program Counter are used to address the 1024 words of on-board program memory, while the most significant 2 bits are used for external Program Memory fetches. The Program counter is initialized to zero by activating the Reset line.

An interrupt or CALL to a subroutine causes the contents of the program counter to be stored in one of the eight register pairs of the Program Counter Stack. The pair to be used is determined by a 3-bit Stack Pointer which is part of the Program Status Word (PSW) as discussed in Sec. 5-2-8. Data RAM locations 8 through 23 (Fig. 5-4) are available as stack registers and are used to store the Program Counter and 4 bits of PSW, as shown in Fig. 5-5.

The stack pointer, when initialized to 000, points to RAM locations 8 and 9 of RAM array. The stack pointer is then incremented by one to point to locations 10 and 11, in anticipation of another CALL. *Nesting of subroutines within subroutines can continue up to eight times without overflowing the stack.* If overflow does occur, the deepest address stored (locations 8 and 9) will be overwritten and lost, since the stack point overflows from 111 to 000. The stack pointer also underflows from 000 to 111.

The end of a subroutine, which is signaled by a return instruction (RET or RETR), causes the stack pointer to be decremented and the contents of the resulting register pair to be transferred to the program counter.

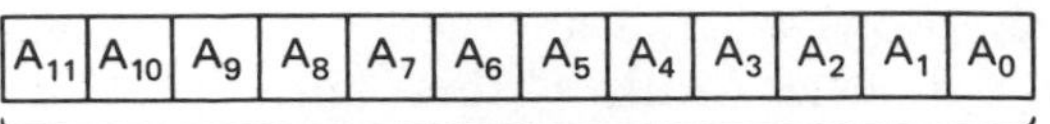

Program counter

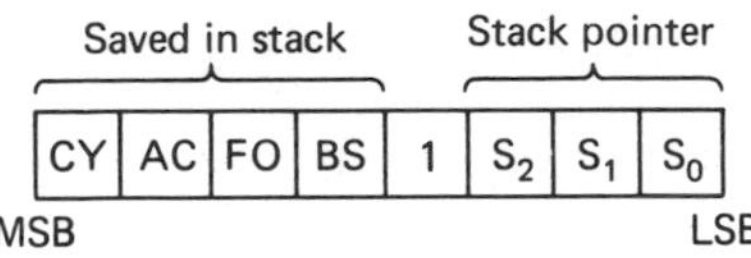

CY Carry
AC Auxillary carry
F0 Flag 0
BS Register bank select

Program status word (PSW)

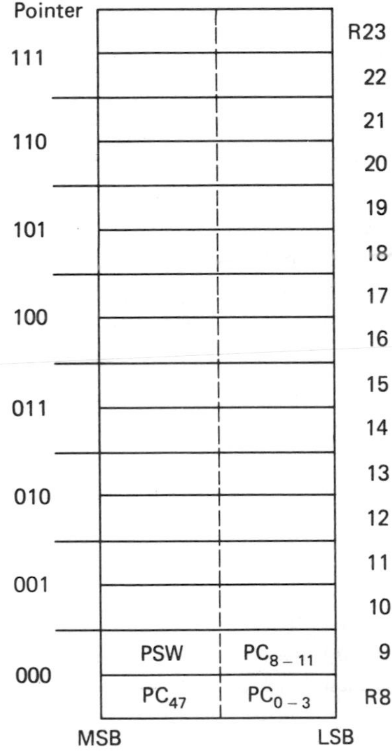

Program counter stack

Figure 5-5 MCS-48 program counter, program status word (PSW), and program counter stack.

"PROMPT stands for PROgraMming Tool. Programs can be entered via the panel keyboard, programming socket, or serial channel. Almost any terminal can be interfaced to the serial channel, including a teletypewriter, CRT, or the Intellec Microcomputer Development System (Sec. 5-6-2). Programs, first written in assembly language, *are entered in machine language,* and debugged on the panel display and keyboard. Most MCS-48 operations can be specified with only two keystrokes.

Once entered, routines can be exercised one instruction (single-step) or many instructions at a time. The principal MCS-48 register, the accumulator, is displayed while single stepping. Programs can be executed in real time or with as many as eight different breakpoints.

The PROMPT 48 is actually a complete, fully assembled and powered microcomputer system, including program memory, data memory, I/O, and system monitor beyond that available on MCS-48 single-chip microcomputers. 1K bytes of PROMPT system RAM serve as "writable program memory," which then becomes a ROM simulator for the program memory on each MCS-48 microcomputer being tested. 256 bytes of PROMPT system RAM serve as "external data memory" beyond the 64 register bytes on each MCS-48. Users may further expand program or data memory via the panel I/O ports and bus connector.

The PROGRAMMING SOCKET (Fig. 5-10) provides for programming the 8748 EPROM. Each location in memory may be individually programmed, one byte at a time. A read-before-write programming system prevents device damage by inadvertently programming unerased memory. A fail-safe interlock ensures that the device is properly inserted before programming pulses are applied.

The EXECUTION SOCKET accepts an 8035 or an 8748. Both are supplied with each PROMPT 48, and either can serve as the heart of the PROMPT system. There are no microprocessors within the PROMPT 48 mainframe, which contains, instead, monitor ROM and RAM, user RAM, peripherals, drivers, and sophisticated control circuitry.

One can select various access modes, such as program execution, from PROMPT system RAM or from on-chip PROM. Thus, programs can first be executed from PROMPT RAM with the 8035. When debugging is complete, the 8035 (execution socket) IC can program the 8748 (programming socket) IC. Finally, a programmed 8748 IC can be exercised by itself from the execution socket. The execution socket IC runs either monitor or user programs.

The I/O ports and bus CONNECTOR provide access to the executing IC. Only the EA (external access) SS (single step) and X1, X2 clock inputs are reserved for the PROMPT system. Thus, program or data memory may be expanded beyond that provided on-chip or in the PROMPT system. I/O ports can be expanded, as with the 8243 (Sec. 5-3), or peripheral con-

5-2-8 Program status word

The PSW is an 8-bit status word that can be loaded to and from the accumulator. Figure 5-5 shows the information available in the word. The PSW is actually a collection of flip-flops throughout the IC that can be read or written as a whole. The ability to write to PSW allows for easy restoration of machine status after a power-down sequence.

The upper 4 bits of the PSW are stored in the program counter stack with every jump to subroutine or interrupt, and are optionally restored upon return with the RETR instruction.

The PSW bit definitions are as follows:

Bits 0–2: Stack pointer bits (S0, S1, S2).

Bit 3: Not used (1 level when read).

Bit 4: Working Register Bank Switch Bit (BS); 0 = bank 0; 1 = bank 1.

Bit 5: Flag 9 bit (F0) User-controlled flag, which can be complemented or cleared and tested with the conditional jump instruction JFO.

Bit 6: Auxiliary Carry (AC) Carry bit generated by an ADD instruction and used by the decimal adjust instruction DA A.

Bit 7: Carry (CY) Carry flag, which indicates that the previous operation has resulted in overflow of the accumulator.

5-2-9 Conditional branch logic

The conditional branch logic within the machine enables several conditions, internal and external, to be tested by the user program. By using the conditional jump instruction, the following conditions can effect a change in the sequence of the program execution.

Device Testable	*Jump Conditions (Jump On)*	
Accumulator	All zeros	Not all zeros
Accumulator bit	—	1
Carry flag	0	1
User flags (F0, F1)	—	1
Timer overflow flag	—	1
Test inputs (T0, T1)	0	1
Interrupt input (INT)	0	—

5-2-10 Interrupt

An interrupt sequence is initiated by applying a 0 level input to the $\overline{\text{INT}}$ pin. Interrupt is level triggered and active low to allow several interrupt sources at the input pin. The interrupt line is sampled in every machine cycle and, when detected, causes a "jump to subroutine" at location 3 in program

Cycle counter. CLK is then divided by 5 in the cycle counter to provide a clock that defined a *machine cycle* consisting of five machine states. This clock is called Address Latch Enable (ALE) because of its function in MCS-48 systems with external memory. The clock is provided continuously on the ALE output pin.

5-2-13 Reset

The reset input provides a means for initializing the microprocessor. Reset performs the following functions:

Sets program counter to zero.

Sets stack pointer to zero.

Selects register bank 0.

Selects memory bank 0.

Sets BUS to high impedance state (except when EA = 5V).

Sets ports 1 and 2 to input mode.

Disables interrupts (timer and external).

Stops timer.

Clears timer flag.

Clears F0 and F1.

Disables clock output from T0.

5 2 14 Single step

The single-step feature provides the user with a debug capability in that the microprocessor can be stepped through the program one instruction at a time. While stopped, the address of the next instruction to be fetched is available concurrently on BUS and the lower half of Port 2. The user can therefore follow the program through each of the instruction steps.

5-2-15 Power-down mode (8048 ROM version only)

Extra circuitry has been added to the 8048 ROM version to allow power to be removed from all but the 64 × 8 data RAM array for low-power standby operation. In the power-down mode, the contents of the data RAM can be maintained while drawing typically 10 to 15 percent of the normal operating power. As shown in Fig. 5-2, V_{CC} serves as the 5-V supply pin for the bulk of the 8048 circuitry, while the V_{DD} pin supplies only the RAM array. In normal operation, both pins are at 5 V, while in standby V_{CC} is at ground and only V_{DD} is maintained at 5 V. Applying Reset inhibits any access to the RAM by the microprocessor and guarantees that RAM cannot be inadvertently altered as power is removed from V_{CC}.

5-2-16 External access mode

Normally, the first 1K words of program memory are automatically fetched from internal ROM or EPROM. The EA input pin, however, allows the user to effectively disable internal program memory by forcing all program memory fetches to reference external memory. The external access mode is very useful in system test and debug because it allows the user to disable the internal applications program and substitute an external program (such as a diagnostic routine).

5-2-17 Programming/verifying and erasing EPROM

The internal program memory of the 8748 may be erased and reprogrammed by the user as explained in the following paragraphs.

Programming/verification. In brief, the programming process consists of activating the program mode, applying an address, latching the address, applying data, and applying a programming pulse. Each word is programmed completely before moving on to the next and is followed by a verification step.

8748 erasure characteristics. The erasure characteristics of the 8748 are such that erasure begins to occur when exposed to light with wavelengths shorter than approximately 4000 angstroms (Å). It should be noted that sunlight and certain types of fluorescent lamps have wavelengths in the range 3000–4000 Å. However, constant exposure to room-level fluorescent lighting could erase the typical 8748 in approximately 3 weeks, whereas it would take approximately 1 week to cause erasure when exposed to direct sunlight. If the 8748 is to be exposed to these types of lighting conditions for extended periods of time, opaque labels (available from Intel) should be placed over the 8748 window to prevent unintentional erasure.

The recommended erasure procedure for the 8748 is exposure to shortwave ultraviolet light (UV), which has a wavelength of 2537 Å. The integrated dose (that is, UV light intensity times exposure time) for erasure should be a minimum of 15 W-s/cm^2. The erasure time with this dosage is approximately 15 to 20 min using an ultraviolet lamp with a 12,000 μW/cm^2 power rating. The 8748 should be placed within 1 in of the lamp tubes during erasure. Some lamps have a filter on their tubes and this filter should be removed before erasure.

5-2-18 Test and debug

Several MCS-48 features described in the previous sections are discussed in the following paragraphs to emphasize their use in testing MCS-48 components and in debugging MCS-48 based systems.

5-2-19 Single step

Single-step circuitry within the microcomputer, in combination with an external single-step switch, allows the user to execute one instruction at a time, whether the instruction is one or two cycles in length. After completion of the instruction, the microcomputer halts with the address of the next instruction to be fetched available on the eight lines of BUS and the lower 4 bits of port 2. This allows the user to step through the program and note the sequence of instructions being executed.

While the microcomputer is stopped, the I/O information on the BUS and the 4 bits of port 2 is not available. However, I/O information is valid at the leading edge of the clock pulse and can be latched externally.

5-2-20 Disabling internal program memory

Applying +5 V to the EA (external access) pin of the MCS-48 allows the user to effectively disable internal program memory by forcing all instruction fetches to occur from an external memory. This external memory can contain a diagnostic routine to exercise the microcomputer, the internal RAM, the timer, and the I/O lines. EA should be switched only when the microcomputer is in the RESET condition.

5-2-21 Reading internal program memory

Just as the microcomputer may be isolated from internal using EA, program memory can be read independent of the microcomputer using the verification mode mentioned in Sec. 5-2-17. The microprocessor is placed in the READ mode by applying a high voltage (+25 V for the 8748, +12 V for the 8048) to the EA pin and +5 V to the TO (8748 only) input pin. RESET must be at 0 V when voltage is applied to EA. The address of the location to be read is then applied to the same lines (TTL levels) of BUS and port 2 (that output the address during single step). The address is latched by a pulse on RESET, and a high level on RESET causes the contents of the program memory location addressed to appear on eight lines of BUS.

5-3 EXPANDING THE BASIC SYSTEM

If the capabilities resident on the single-chip 8048, 8748, or 8035 are not sufficient for system requirements, special on-board circuitry allows the addition of a wide variety of external memory, I/O, or special peripherals. The basic microcomputer can be directly and simply expanded in the following areas:

1. Program memory to 4K words.
2. Data memory to 320 words.
3. I/O by an unlimited amount.
4. Special functions using Intel 8080 peripherals.

By using *bank switching* techniques (Sec. 5-3-1) the maximum expansion capability is essentially unlimited. Expansion is accomplished in two ways.

Expander I/O. A special I/O expander circuit of the 8243 IC provides for the addition of four 4-bit input/output ports with the sacrifice of only the lower half (4 bits) of port 2 for interdevice communication. Multiple 8243s may be added to this 4-bit bus by generating the required chip select lines.

Standard 8080 bus. One port of the 8048 is like the 8-bit bidirectional data bus of the Intel 8080A microcomputer system. This allows interface to the numerous standard memories and peripherals of the Intel MCS-80 microcomputer family.

MCS-48 systems can be configured using either or both of these expansion features to optimize system capability. Both expander devices and standard memories and peripherals can be added in virtually any number and combination required.

The user literature describes fully both the MCS-48 components (ICs) and how they are used to expand the basic single-chip microcomputer for a wide variety of applications. Such data will not be repeated here. However, Fig. 5-6 illustrates basic system expansion, and the following paragraphs provide a brief description of the components.

8243 I/O expander. This IC consists of four 4-bit, bidirectional, static I/O ports and one 4-bit port which serves as an interface to the MCS-48 microcomputers. The 4-bit interface requires that only four I/O lines of the 8048 be used for I/O expansion to 16 lines, and also allows multiple 8243s to be added to the same bus.

8355/8755 ROM/EPROM and I/O expander. These ICs are designed to expand both the program memory and I/O capability of the basic microcomputer. These expanders increase program memory by 2K words and add 16 I/O lines without additional components. The completely interchangeable 8755 light-erasable EPROM and the 8355 mask-programmed ROM provide a simple transition from prototype to production. Both versions operate from a single 5-V supply and are totally speed-compatible with the MCS-48 microcomputers.

8155/56 RAM and I/O expander. The 8155 is designed to expand the data memory, I/O, and timer capability. This expander increases data memory by 256 words, adds 22 I/O lines, and adds a 14-bit timer/counter to the basic microcomputer without the necessity of any additional components. The 8156 is an 8155 with an active-high chip enable (CE) input.

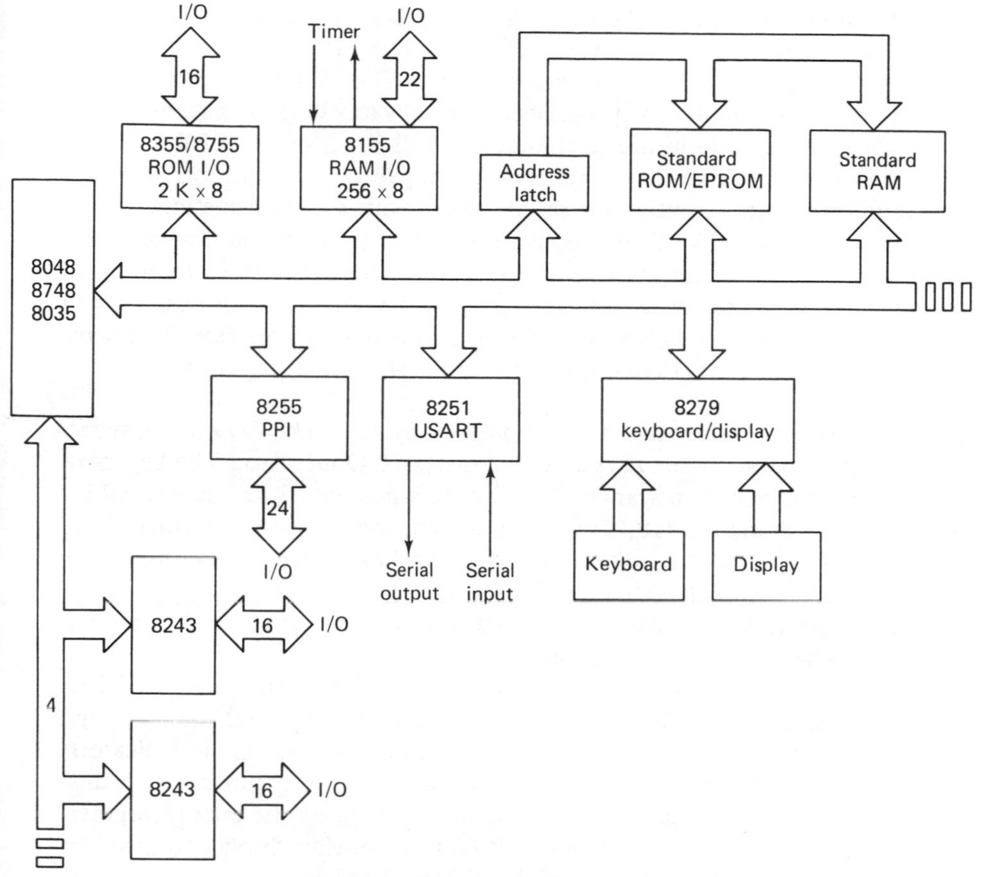

Figure 5-6 MCS-48 expansion capability.

8255A programmable peripheral interface. The 8255A is a general-purpose programmable I/O, originally designed for the 8080 but fully compatible with the MCS-48. The 8255A is used with parallel peripherals and has 24 I/O pins that may be individually programmed in two groups of 12. There are three modes of operation. In the first mode (Mode 0), each group of 12 I/O pins may be programmed in sets of 4 to be input or output. In Mode 1, the second mode, each group may be programmed to have 8 lines of I/O. Of the remaining four pins, three are used for "handshaking" and interrupt control signals. The third mode of operation (Mode 2) is a bidirectional bus mode which uses eight lines for bidirectional bus, and five lines (borrowing one from the other group) for handshaking.

8251 programmable peripheral interface. The 8251 is a universal synchronous/asynchronous receiver/transmitter (USART) designed for data communications in microcomputer systems. The USART is programmed by the microcomputer to operate using virtually any serial data transmission technique presently in use (including IBM Bi-Sync). The USART accepts data characters from the microcomputer in parallel format, and then converts them into a continuous serial data stream for transmission. Simultaneously, the USART can receive serial data streams and convert them into parallel data characters for the microcomputer. The USART will signal the microcomputer whenever it can accept a new character for transmission or whenever it has received a character for the microcomputer. The microcomputer can read the complete status of the USART at any time.

8279 programmable keyboard/display interface. The 8279 is a general-purpose programmable keyboard and display I/O interface. The keyboard portion can provide a scanned interface to a 64-contact key matrix, which can be expanded to 128. The keyboard portion will also interface to an array of sensors or a strobed interface keyboard. Keyboard entries are stored in an eight-character FIFO (first-in/first-out register). If more than eight characters are entered, overrun status is set. Key entries set the interrupt output line to the microcomputer.

The display portion provides a scanned display interface for LED, incandescent, and other popular display technologies. Both numeric and alphanumeric segment displays may be used, as well as simple indicators. The 8279 has a 16 × 8 display RAM which can be organized as a dual 16 × 4. The RAM can be loaded or interrogated by the microcomputer. Both right-entry, calculator, and left-entry typewriter display formats are possible. Both read and write of the display RAM can be done with auto-increment of the display RAM address.

5-3-1 Bank switching

Certain systems may require more than the 4K words of program memory that are directly addressable by the program counter or more than the 256 data memory and I/O locations directly addressable by the pointer registers R0 and R1. These systems can be achieved using bank switching techniques. Bank switching is the selection of various blocks or "banks" of memory using dedicated output port lines from the microcomputer. In the case of the 8048, program memory is selected in blocks of 4K words at a time while data memory and I/O are enabled 256 words at a time.

The most important consideration in implementing two or more banks is the software required to cross the bank boundries. Each crossing of the boundary requires that the microcomputer first write a control bit to an output port before accessing memory or I/O in the new bank. If program memory is being switched, programs should be organized to keep boundary crossing to a minimum. Jumping to subroutines across the boundary should be avoided when possible, since the programmer must keep track of which bank to return to after completion of the subroutine. If the subroutines are to be nested and accessed from either bank, a software "stack" should be implemented by saving the bank switch bit, just as if it were another bit of the program counter.

5-4 INSTRUCTION SET

All instructions are either one or two bytes in length, and over 70 percent are only one byte long. Also, all instructions execute in either one or two cycles (2.5 μs or 5 μs when using a 6-MHz crystal), and over 50 percent of all instructions execute in a single cycle. Double-cycle instructions include all immediate instructions and all I/O instructions.

The MCS-48 microcomputer is designed to handle arithmetic operations in both binary and BCD, as well as single-bit operations required in control applications. Special instructions have also been included to simplify loop counters, table look-up routines, and multiway branch routines.

5-4-1 Data transfers

As shown in Fig. 5-7, the 8-bit accumulator is the central point for all data transfers within the 8048. Data can be transferred directly between the eight registers of each working register bank and the accumulator. (That is, the source or destination register is specified by the instruction.) The remaining locations of the internal RAM array are referred to as data memory and are addressed indirectly via an address stored in either R0 or R1 of the active working register bank. R0 and R1 are also used to indirectly address external data memory when it is present. Transfers to and from internal RAM require one cycle, while transfers to external RAM require two. Constants stored in program memory can be loaded directly to the accumulator and to the eight working registers.

Data can also be transfered directly between the accumulator and the on-board timer/counter, or the accumulator and the program status word (PSW). Writing to the PSW alters machine status accordingly and provides a means of restoring status after an interrupt or of alternating the stack pointer if necessary.

5-4-2 Accumulator operations

Immediate data, data memory, or the working registers can be added with or without carry to the accumulator. These sources can also be ANDed, ORed, or Exclusive-ORed to the accumulator. Data may be moved to or from the accumulator and working registers or data memory. The two values can also be exchanged in a single operation.

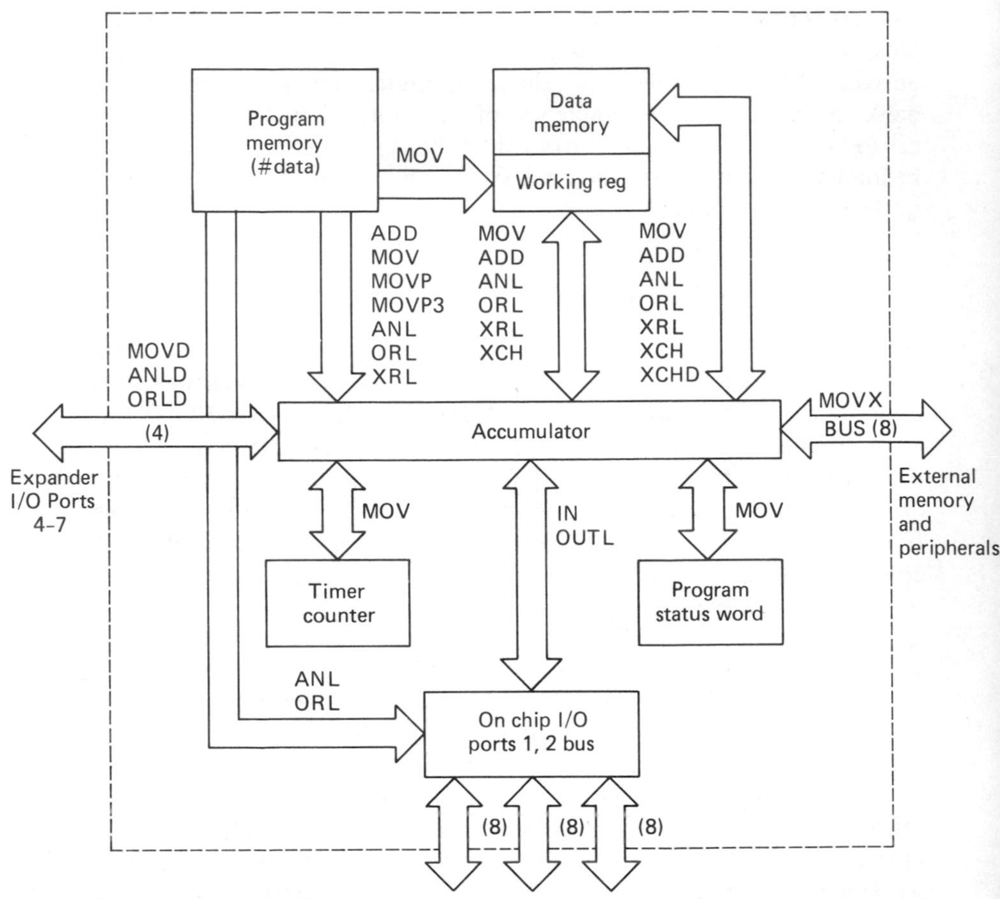

Figure 5-7 MCS-48 data-transfer instructions.

In addition, the lower 4 bits of the accumulator can be exchanged with the lower 4 bits of any of the internal RAM locations. This instruction, along with an instruction that swaps the upper and lower 4-bit halves of the accumulator (swap nibbles), provides for easy handling of 4-bit quantities, including BCD numbers. To facilitate BCD arithmetic, a decimal adjust instruction is included. This instruction is used to correct the result of the binary addition of two two-digit BCD numbers. Performing a decimal adjust on the result in the accumulator produces the required BCD result.

Finally, the accumulator can be incremented, decremented, cleared, or complemented and can be rotated left or right 1-bit at a time with or without carry. Although there is no subtract instruction in the 8048, this operation can be easily implemented with three single-byte, single-cycle instructions. A value may be subtracted from the accumulator by complementing the accumulator, adding the value to the accumulator, and then complementing the accumulator again. The result remains in the accumulator.

5-4-3 Register operations

The working registers can be accessed via the accumulator as discussed in Sec. 5-4-2, or can be loaded immediately (with some constraints) from program memory. In addition, working registers can be incremented or decremented or used as loop counters, using the "decrement and skip if not zero" instruction, as described in Sec. 5-4-5 (branch instructions). All data memory, including working registers, can be accessed with indirect instructions via R0 and R1, and can be incremented.

5-4-4 Flags

There are four user-accessible flags in the 8048: carry, auxiliary carry, F0, and F1. Carry indicates overflow of the accumulator, and auxiliary carry is used to indicate overflow between BCD digits and is used during the decimal adjust operation. Both carry and auxiliary carry are accessible as part of the program status word, and are stored on the stack during subroutines.

F0 and F1 are undedicated general-purpose flags to be used as the programmer desires. Both flags can be cleared or complemented and tested by conditional jump instructions. F0 is also accessible via the program status word and is stored on the stack with the carry flags.

5-4-5 Branch instructions

The unconditional jump instruction is two bytes and allows jumps anywhere in the first 2K words of program memory. Jumps to the second 2K of memory (4K words are directly addressable) are made by first executing a select memory bank instruction, then executing the jump instruction. The 2K boundary can only be crossed via a jump or subroutine call instruction; that is, the bank switch does not occur until a jump is executed. Once a memory bank has been selected, all subsequent jumps will be to the selected bank until another select memory bank instruction is executed. A subroutine in the opposite bank can be accessed by a select memory bank instruction, followed by a call instruction. Upon completion of the subroutine, execution will automatically return to the original bank. However, unless the original bank is reselected, the next jump instruction encountered will again transfer execution to the opposite bank.

Conditional jumps can test the following inputs and machine status: T0 input pin, T1 input pin, $\overline{\text{INT}}$ input pin, accumulator zero, any bit of accumulator, carry flag, F0 flag, and F1 flag.

Conditional jumps allow a branch to any address within the current page (256 words) of execution. The conditions tested are the instantaneous values at the time the conditional jump is executed. For instance, the "jump of accumulator zero" instruction tests the accumulator itself, not an intermediate zero flag.

The "decrement register and skip of not zero" instruction combines a decrement and a branch instruction to create an instruction very useful in implementing a loop counter. This instruction can designate any one of the eight working registers as a counter and can effect a branch to any address within the current page of execution.

A single-byte indirect jump instruction allows the program to be vectored to any one of the several different locations, based on the contents of the accumulator. The contents of the accumulator points to a location in program memory which contains the jump address. The 8-bit jump address refers to the current page of execution. This instruction could be used, for instance, to vector to any one of several routines based on an ASCII character that has been loaded in the accumulator. In this way, ASCII key inputs can be used to initiate various routines.

5-4-6 Subroutines

Subroutines are entered by executing a call instruction. Calls can be made like unconditional jumps to any address in a 2K-word bank, and jumps across the 2K boundary are executed in the same manner. Two separate return instructions determine whether or not status (upper 4-bit word of PSW) is restored upon return from the subroutine. The "return and restore status" instruction also signals the end of an interrupt service routine if one has been in progress.

5-4-7 Timer instructions

The 8-bit on-board timer/counter can be loaded or read via the accumulator while the counter is stopped or while counting. The counter can be started as a timer with an internal clock source or as an event counter or timer with an external clock applied to the T1 input pin. The instruction executed determines which clock source is used. A single instruction stops the counter whether it is operating with an internal or an external clock source. In addition, two instructions allow the timer interrupt to be enabled or disabled.

5-4-8 Control instructions

Two instructions allow the external interrupt source to be enabled or disabled. Interrupts are initially disabled and are automatically disabled while an interrupt service routine is in progress and reenabled afterward.

There are four memory bank select instructions, two to designate the active working register bank and two to control program memory banks. The operation of the program memory bank switch is explained in Sec. 5-3-1.

The working register bank switch instructions allow the programmer to immediately substitute a second eight-register working register bank for the one in use. This effectively provides 16 working registers, or the technique can be used as a means of quickly saving the contents of the registers in response to an interrupt. The user has the option to switch or not to switch banks on interrupt. However, if the banks are switched, the original bank will be automatically restored upon execution of a "return and restore status" instruction at the end of the interrupt service routine.

A special instruction enables an internal clock, which is the crystal frequency divided by three, to be output on pin T0. This clock can be used as a general-purpose clock in the user system. This instruction should be used only to initialize the system since the clock output can be disabled only by application of the system reset.

5-4-9 Input/output instructions

Ports 1 and 2 are 8-bit static I/O ports that can be loaded to and from the accumulator. Outputs are statically latched, but inputs are not latched and must be read while inputs are present. In addition, immediate data from program memory can be ANDed or ORed directly to port 1 and port 2, with the result remaining on the port. This allows "masks" stored in program memory to selectively set or reset individual bits of the I/O ports. Ports 1 and 2 are configured to allow input on a given pin by first writing a 1 out to the pin.

An 8-bit port called BUS can also be accessed via the accumulator and can have statically latched outputs as well. The BUS port can also have immediate data ANDed or ORed directly to its outputs. However, unlike ports 1 and 2, all 8 lines of the BUS must be treated as either input or output at any one time. In addition to being a static port, BUS can be used as a true synchronous bidirectional port using the "move external" instructions used to access external data memory. When these instructions are executed, a corresponding READ or WRITE pulse is generated, and data are valid only at that time. When data bytes are not being transferred, BUS is in a high-impedance state.

The basic three on-board I/O ports can be expanded via a 4-bit expander bus using half of port 2. I/O expander devices on this bus consist of four 4-bit ports which are addressed as ports 4 through 7. Like the on-board ports, these ports have their own AND and OR instructions. The ports also move instructions to transfer data in or out. The expander AND and OR instructions, however, combine the contents of the accumulator with the selected port, rather than with immediate data, as is done with the on-board ports.

I/O devices can also be added externally using the BUS port as the expansion bus. In this case, the I/O ports become "memory-mapped."

That is, the I/O ports are addressed in the same way as external data memory and exist in the external data memory address space addressed by pointer register R0 or R1.

5-4-10 Instruction set description

The user literature provides a full description of the instruction set and will not be duplicated here. However, the following paragraphs illustrate one instruction to show the format used.

A typical accumulator instruction is ADDC A,R_r or "Add Carry and Register Contents to Accumulator." The machine code is 0111 1rrr. When this machine code is applied, the contents of the carry bit are added to accumulator location 0 and the carry bit is cleared. The contents of register "rrr" (in the operand portion of the machine code) are then added to the accumulator. (For example, if the machine code is 0111 1011, the contents of register 3 are added to the accumulator.) The symbol for ADDC A,R_r is

$$(A) \longleftarrow (A) + (R_r) + (C) \qquad \text{where } r = 0\text{–}7$$

The following shows how the instruction would appear in assembly language:

LABEL	*MNEMONIC*	*OPERAND*	*DESCRIPTIVE COMMENTS*
ADDRGC:	ADDC	A,R3	;ADD CARRY AND REG 3
			;CONTENTS TO ACC

5-5 SAMPLE APPLICATIONS

The following sample applications illustrate how MCS-48 architecture and instructions can be used to implement a system or system function. One hardware application and one software application are described in brief. Full details on more complex programs are described in MCS-48 literature.

5-5-1 Hardware example

Figure 5-8 shows the detail wiring of *stand-alone, single-chip microcomputer,* using either the 8048 ROM or 8748 EPROM. Note that a 6-MHz crystal is used as a clock source. The system operates from a 5-V supply and typically draws 65 mA of current (135 mA maximum).

5-5-2 Software example

Figure 5-9 shows the flowchart and program assembly listing for a two-byte processing system. This system takes two single-byte inputs from different ports, compares them, and performs the operations, depending on the result of the comparison (see page 293).

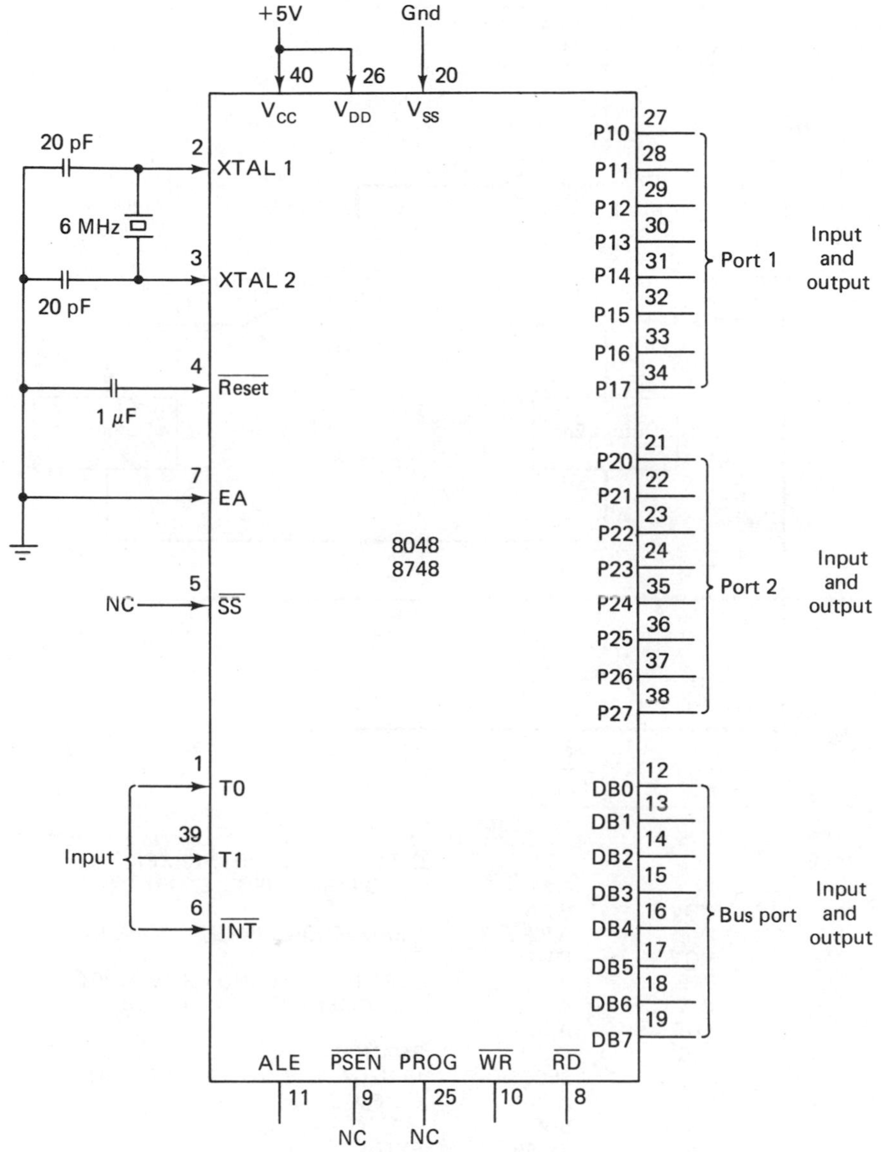

- All inputs and outputs standard TTL-compatible
- P1 and P2 outputs drive 5V CMOS directly others require 10–50K pullup for CMOS compatibility

XTAL: Series resonant
AT Cut
1 to 6 MHz

Figure 5-8 Stand-alone 8048 microcomputer.

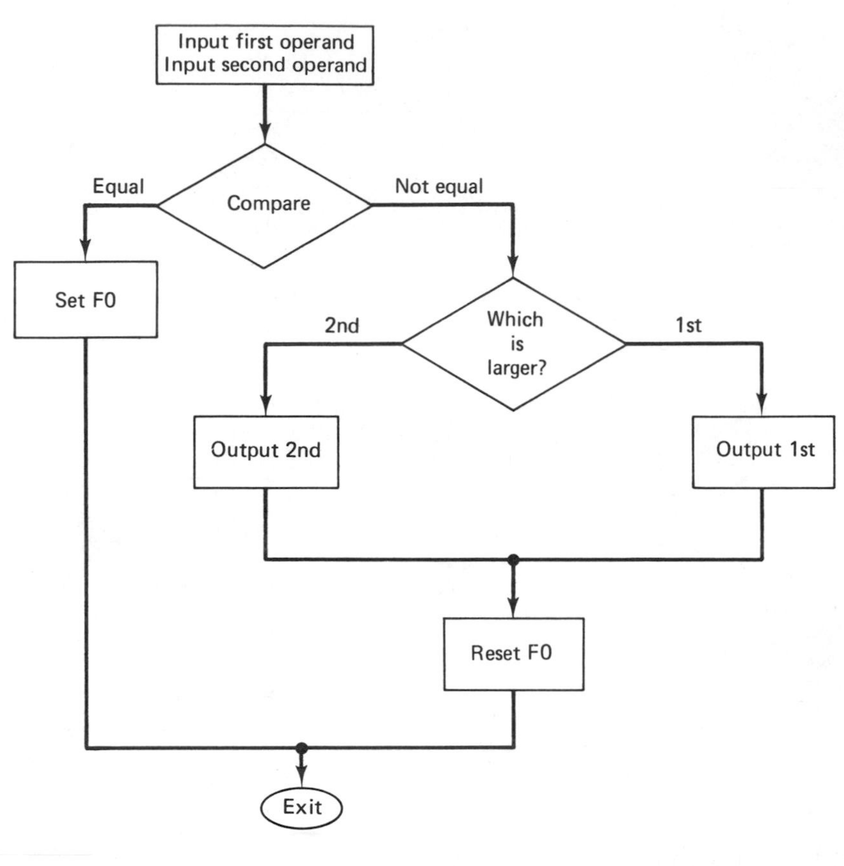


```
PROCESS:  CLR    F0        ;CLEAR F0 BIT (INITIALIZE)
          IN     A,P1      ;READ FIRST INPUT, STORE IN R0
          MOV    R0,A
          IN     A,P2      ;READ SECOND INPUT, STORE IN R1
          MOV    R1,A
          CPL    A         ;SUBTRACT SECOND FROM FIRST
          INC    A         ;(2's COMPLEMENT AND ADD)
          ADD    A,R0
          JNC    EQUL      ;BRANCH IF THEY ARE EQUAL
          JN     SECOND    ;IF NEGATIVE, SECOND WAS LARGER
          MOV    A,R0      ;ELSE, OUTPUT FIRST
          OUTL   BUS,A
          JMP    DONE      ;EXIT

SECOND:   MOV    A,R1      ;OUTPUT SECOND
          OUTL   BUS,A
          JMP    DONE      ;EXIT
  EQUL:   CPL    F0        ;SET F0
          JMP    DONE      ;EXIT
```

Figure 5-9 Flowchart and program assembly listing for a two-byte processing system.

1. (If equal) Sets flag and exits.
2. (If not equal) Resets flag and outputs the larger byte to a third port.

Compare this program with that of Sec. 3-5.

5-6 MCS-48 DEVELOPMENT AIDS

The following paragraphs describe development aids available to MCS-48 users. Full details are given in the instruction manuals.

5-6-1 PROMPT 48

Figure 5-10 shows the PROMPT 48, which is the primary development aid for the MCS-48 system. The PROMPT 48 is a low-cost, fully assembled design aid for the 8748 and is used to program, test, debug, and run MCS-48 systems. There is a special hex keyboard for data entry and a display for readout. The following paragraphs provide a brief description of the PROMPT 48 and its front-panel controls.

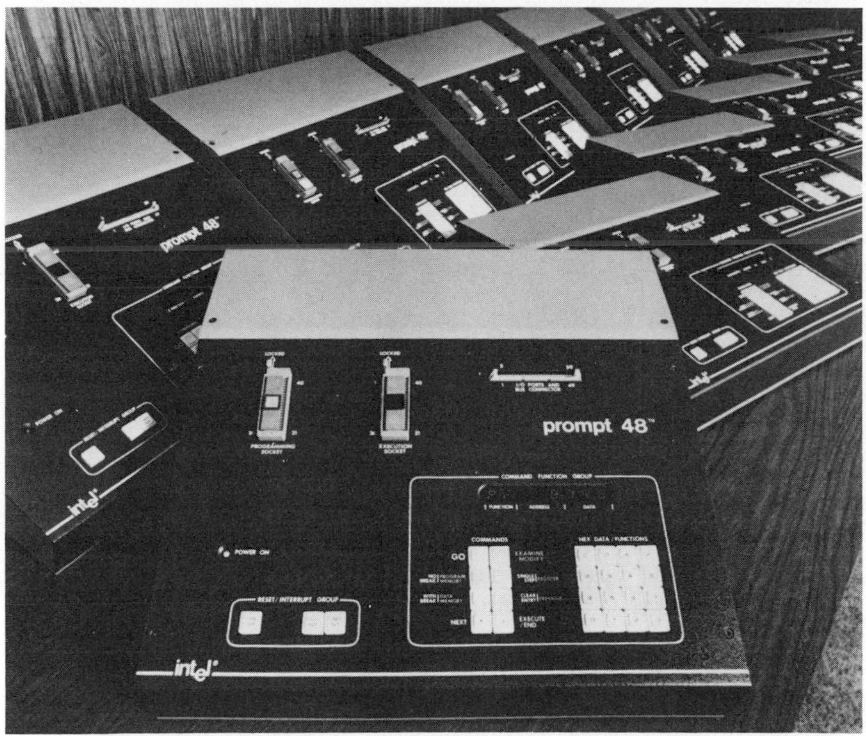

Figure 5-10 PROMPT 48 development aid for the MCS-48 system. (Courtesy Intel Corporation.)

memory as soon as all cycles of the current instruction are complete. As in any CALL to subroutine, the program counter and program status word are saved in the stack. Program memory location 3 usually contains an unconditional jump to an interrupt service subroutine elsewhere in program memory. The end of an interrupt service subroutine is signaled by the execution of a Return and Restore Status instruction RETR.

Interrupt timing. The interrupt input may be enabled or disabled under program control using the EN I and DIS I instructions. Interrupts are disabled by Reset and remain so until enabled by the user's program. An interrupt request must be removed before the RETR instruction is executed upon return from the service routine; otherwise, the microprocessor will reenter the service routine immediately. Many peripheral devices prevent this situation by resetting their interrupt request line whenever the microprocessor accesses (reads or writes) the peripheral data buffer register. If the interrupting device does not require access by the microprocessor, one output line of the 8048 may be designated as an "interrupt acknowledge," which is activated by the service subroutine to reset the interrupt request.

5-2-11 Timer/counter

The 8048 contains a counter to aid the user in counting external events and generating accurate time delays without placing a burden on the microprocessor for these functions. In both modes, the counter operation is the same, the only difference being the source of the input to the counter.

5-2-12 Clock and timing circuits

Timing generation for the 8048 is completely self-contained with the exception of a frequency reference, which can be crystal (XTAL), inductor, or external clock source. The clock and timing circuitry can be divided into the following functional blocks.

Oscillator. The on-board oscillator has a frequency range of 1 to 6 MHz. The X1 external pin is the input to the oscillator, while X2 is the output. A crystal or inductor connected between X1 and X2 provides the feedback and phase shift required for oscillation. With an inductor, the oscillator frequency can be approximately 3 to 5 MHz. For higher speed, a crystal should be used. An external clock may also be used as the frequency source.

State counter. The oscillator output is divided by 3 in the state counter to create a clock which defines the *state times* of the machine (CLK). CLK can be made available on the external pin T0 by executing an ENTO CLK instruction. The output of CLK on T0 is disabled by Reset of the microprocessor.

trollers can be memory-mapped. The socket allows the execution socket IC to be directly interfaced to the prototype system, yet be controlled from the PROMPT panel.

An optional cable, PROMPT-SER, directly connects the PROMPT system to virtually any terminal via a rear access slot. Another cable, PROMPT-SPP, allows programs and data to be downloaded from the Intellec Microcomputer Development System (Sec. 5-6-2) to the PROMPT system for debugging.

The SYSTEM RESET control initializes the PROMPT system and enters the monitor. MONITOR INTERRUPT exits a user program gracefully, preserving system status and entering the monitor. USER INTERRUPT causes an interrupt only if the PROMPT system is running a user program. A comprehensive system monitor resides in four 1K byte ROMs and drives the keyboard and displays, responding to the COMMAND/FUNCTION GROUP controls.

The COMMAND/FUNCTION GROUP panel keyboard and displays completely control the PROMPT 48. Thus, a teletypewriter or CRT is not needed (unless so desired by the user). The COMMANDS are grouped and color-coded to simplify access to the 8748 separate program and data memory. You can examine and modify registers. Memory locations can be accessed with one keystroke. Programs can be exercised in three modes. GO NO BREAK runs in real time. GO WITH BREAK is not real time. After each instruction, the MCS-48 program counter is compared against pending breakpoints. If no break is encountered, execution resumes. GO SINGLE STEP exercises one instruction at a time.

5-6-2 Intellec Microcomputer Development System (MDS)

Figure 5-11 shows the Intellec MDS, which is a modular microcomputer development system used with a number of Intel systems, including the MCS-48, MCS-85, MCS-80, and series 3000 microcomputer systems. The MDS contains all necessary hardware and software to develop and implement Intel microcomputer systems. The addition of options and peripherals provides the user with a complete in-circuit microcomputer development system, supporting product design from program development through prototype debug, to production and field test. The module contains all necessary control and data transfer circuitry to interface with the following Intellec peripherals: teletype, CRT, high-speed paper-tape reader/punch, PROM programmer, and line printer.

5-6-3 8048 In-circuit emulator (MDS-48-ICE)

Figure 5-12 shows the MDS-48-ICE, which is an Intellec system resident module. This module combines with the MDS described in Sec. 5-6-2 to interface with any user-configured 8048 system. With an ICE-48 module

Figure 5-11 Intellec Microcomputer Development System (MDS) components. (Courtesy Intel Corporation.)

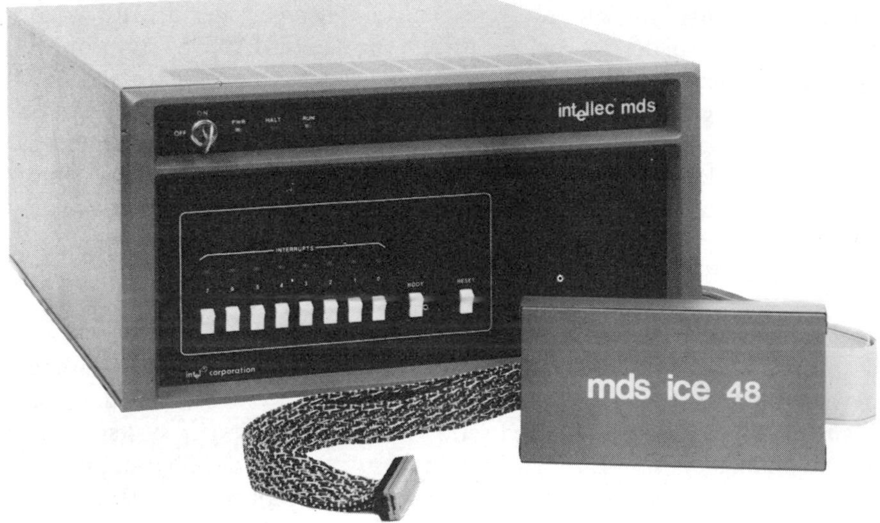

Figure 5-12 8048 in-circuit emulator (MDS-48-ICE). (Courtesy Intel Corporation.)

as a replacement for a prototype system 8048, the designer can emulate the system 8048 in real time, single-step the system program, and borrow static RAM memory for user system debugging. Powerful hardware and software debug functions are extended into the user system with minimum impact. The designer may examine and modify the system with symbolic reference instead of absolute values.

5-6-4 Universal PROM Programmer (UPP-101, UPP-102)

Figure 5-13 shows the UPP, which is an Intellec system peripheral capable of programming and verifying many Intel-programmable ROMs (PROMs). In addition, the UPP programs the PROM memory portions of the 8748 microcomputer, and the 8755 PROM and I/O chip. Programming and verification operations are initiated from the Intellec MDS console and are controlled by a Universal PROM Mapper (UPM) program.

Figure 5-13 Universal PROM programmer (UPP-101, UPP-102). (Courtesy Intel Corporation.)

5-6-5 Assemblers

In addition to the hardware described thus far, there are software support packages available for the MCS-48. These include diskette and paper-tape assemblers, PROM mappers, and a variety of program libraries.

6 Mostek Z80 Microcomputer System

This chapter is devoted entirely to the Z80 microcomputer system manufactured by Mostek Corporation. The chapter starts with a discussion of basic system hardware and architecture. This is followed by a summary of the instruction set and examples of hardware and software applications. The chapter concludes with a description of development aids or support equipment.

The details presented in this chapter represent only a small fraction of the data taken from the manufacturer's literature (manuals and data sheets). However, the information presented is sufficient for a reader of any level to evaluate the system. The chapter also provides a realistic view of actual state-of-the-art microprocessor-based systems. This supplements the theoretical and typical descriptions of Chapters 1 and 2.

The Mostek Z80 product line is a complete set of microcomputer components, development systems, and support software. The Z80 microcomputer component set includes all the circuits necessary to build high-performance microcomputer systems with virtually no other logic and a minimum number of low-cost standard memory elements.

The basic Z80 components include MK3880 CPU (central processing unit), MK3881 PIO (parallel I/O controller), MK3882 CTC (counter timer circuit), MK3883 DMA (direct memory address controller), MK3884 SIO (serial I/O controller), and SDB-80 (software development board). In addition, there are compatible add-on printed circuit boards, accessories, and support software.

6-1 MK3880 CPU

The heart of the Z80 system is a microprocessor which the manufacturer designates as the MK3880 central processing unit, or CPU. A block diagram of the internal architecture of the Z80 CPU is shown in Fig. 6-1. The CPU internal registers are shown in Fig. 6-2.

6-1-1 CPU registers

The CPU registers contain 208 bits of R/W (read/write) "memory" that are accessible to the programmer. Figure 6-2 illustrates how this "memory" is arranged into eighteen 8-bit registers and four 16-bit registers. All Z80 registers are *implemented using static RAM techniques.* The registers include two sets of six general-purpose registers that may be used individually as 8-bit registers, or in pairs as 16-bit registers. There are also two sets of accumulator and flag registers.

The special-purpose registers include:

1. The *program counter* (PC), which holds the 16-bit address of the current instruction being fetched from memory. The PC is automatically incremented after its contents have been transferred to the address lines. When a program jump occurs, the new value is automatically placed in the PC, overriding the incrementer.

2. The *stack pointer* (SP), which holds the 16-bit address of the current top of a stack located anywhere in the external system RAM memory. The external stack memory is organized as a last-in/first-out (LIFO) file. Data bytes can be pushed onto the stack from specific CPU registers or popped off the stack into specific CPU registers through execution of PUSH and POP instructions. The data popped from the stack are always the last data pushed onto it. The stack allows simple implementation of multiple-level interrupts, unlimited subroutine nesting, and simplification of many types of data manipulation.

3. The *two index registers* (IX and IY), which hold a 16-bit base address which is used in indexed addressing modes. In this mode (described in Sec. 6-1-4), an index register is used as a base to point to a region in memory from which data bytes are to be stored or retrieved. An additional byte is included in indexed instructions to specify a displacement from

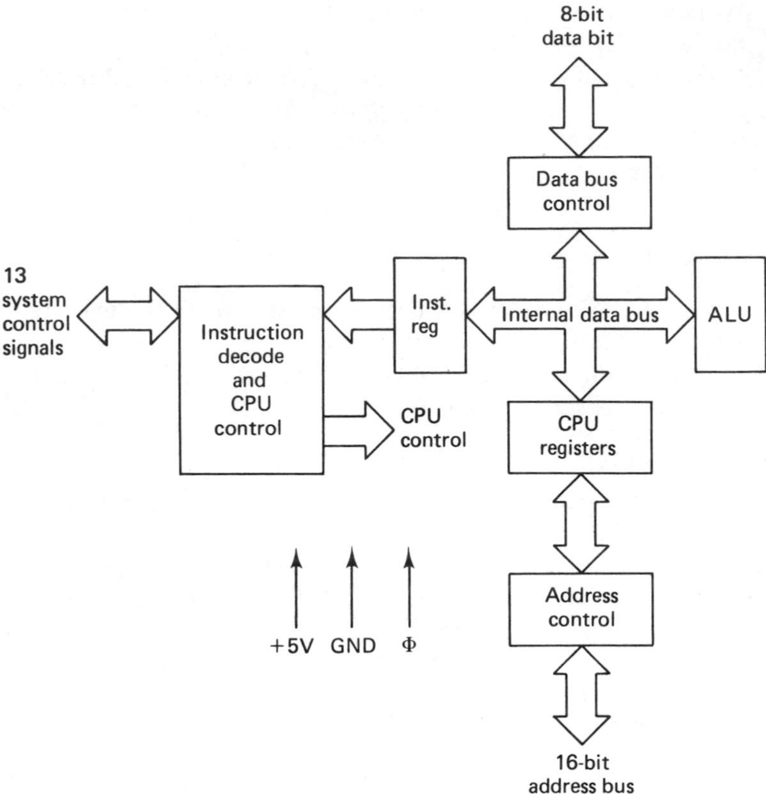

Figure 6-1 MK3880 CPU, block diagram.

Main reg set		Alternate reg set		
Accumulator	Flags	Accumulator	Flags	
A	F	A′	F′	General-purpose registers
B	C	B′	C′	
D	E	D′	E′	
H	L	H′	L′	

Interrupt vector I	Memory refresh R	Special-purpose registers
Index register IX		
Index register IY		
Stack pointer SP		
Program counter PC		

Figure 6-2 MK3880 CPU, internal registers.

this base. This displacement is specified as a two's-complement signed number (Chapter 1). This mode of addressing greatly simplifies many types of programs, especially where tables of data are used.

4. The *interrupt page address register* (I), which is used to store the high-order 8 bits of an indirect address (Sec. 6-1-4), while an interrupting device provides the lower 8 bits of the address. The Z80 CPU can be operated in a mode where an indirect call to any memory location can be achieved in response to an interrupt. This feature allows interrupt routines to be dynamically located anywhere in memory with absolute minimum access time to the routine.

5. The *memory refresh register* (R), which is automatically incremented after each instruction fetch. The Z80 CPU contains this memory refresh counter to enable dynamic memories to be used with the same ease as static memories. The data bytes in the refresh counter are sent out on the lower portion of the address bus along with a refresh control signal while the CPU is decoding and executing the fetched instruction. This mode of refresh is totally transparent to the programmer. That is, the programmer need not be concerned since the R register is not usually written into the program. Thus, the refresh operation does not slow down the program. The programmer can load the R register for testing purposes, if desired, but the R register is not normally used by the programmer.

The accumulator and flag registers. The CPU includes two independent 8-bit accumulators and associated 8-bit flag registers. The accumulator holds the results of 8-bit arithmetic or logical operations, while the flag register indicates specific conditions for 8- or 16-bit operations, such as indicating whether or not the result of an operation is equal to zero. The programmer selects the desired accumulator and flag pair with a single exchange instruction.

The general-purpose registers. There are two matched sets of general-purpose registers, each set containing six 8-bit registers that may be used individually as 8-bit registers or as 16-bit register pairs by the programmer. One set is called BC, DE, and HL, while the complementary set is called BC′, DE′, and HL′. At any one time, the programmer can select either set of registers to work with through a single exchange command for the entire set. In systems where fast interrupt response is required, one set of general-purpose registers and an accumulator/flag register may be reserved for handling this very fast routine. Only a simple exchange command need be executed to go between the routines. This greatly reduces interrupt service time by eliminating the requirement for saving and retrieving register contents in the external stack during interrupt or subroutine processing. These general-purpose registers are used for a wide range of applications by the programmer. They also simplify programming, especially in ROM-based systems, where little external read/write memory is available.

6-1-2 Arithmetic logic unit (ALU)

The 8-bit arithmetic and logic instructions of the CPU are executed in the ALU. Internally, the ALU communicates with the registers and the external data bus on the internal data bus (Fig. 6-1). The type of functions performed by the ALU include add, subtract, logical AND, logical OR, logical EXCLUSIVE OR, compare, left or right shifts or rotates (arithmetic and logical), increment, decrement, set bit, reset bit, and test bit.

6-1-3 Instruction register and CPU control

As each instruction is fetched from memory, the instruction is placed in the instruction register and decoded. The control section performs this function and then generates and supplies all the control signals necessary to read or write data from or to the registers. The control section also controls the ALU and provides all required external control signals.

6-1-4 CPU instruction set

The Z80 CPU can execute 158 different instruction types (including all 78 of the 8080A microprocessors, available from a number of manufacturers). The instructions can be broken down into the following major groups: load and exchange; block transfer and search; arithmetic and logical; rotate and shift; bit manipulation (set, reset, test); jump, call, and return; input/output (I/O); and basic CPU control.

As is the case for other systems described in this book, we will not cover full details of all instructions. However, the following paragraphs provide an introduction to the instruction types, addressing modes, mode combinations, and selected examples of instruction op codes.

Introduction to instruction types. The *load instructions* move data internally between CPU registers or between CPU registers and external memory. All these instructions must specify a source location from which the data are to be moved and a destination location. The source location is not altered by a load instruction. Examples of load group instructions include moves between any of the general-purpose registers such as "move the data to Register B from Register C." This group also includes load immediate to any CPU register or to any external memory location. Other types of load instructions allow transfer between CPU registers and memory locations. The *exchange instructions* can trade the contents of two registers.

A unique set of *block transfer instructions* is provided. With a single instruction, a block of memory of any size can be moved to any other location in memory. This set of block moves is extremely valuable when large strings of data must be processed. The Z80 *block search instructions* are also valuable for this type of processing. With a single instruction, a block of external memory of any desired length can be searched for any 8-bit character. Once the character is found, the instruction automatically terminates. Both the block transfer and the block search instructions can be interrupted during their execution so as to not occupy the CPU for long periods of time.

The *arithmetic and logic instructions* operate on data stored in the accumulator and other general-purpose CPU registers or external memory locations. The results of the operations are placed in the accumulator and the appropriate flags are set according to the result of the operation. An example of an arithmetic operation is adding the accumulator to the contents of an external memory location. The results of the addition are placed in the accumulator. This group also includes 16-bit addition and subtraction between 16-bit CPU registers.

The *bit manipulation instructions* allow any bit in the accumulator, any general-purpose register, or any external memory location to be set, reset, or tested with a single instruction. For example, the most significant bit of register H can be reset. This group is especially useful in control applications and for controlling software flags in general-purpose programming.

The *jump, call, and return instructions* are used to transfer between various locations in the user program. This group uses several different techniques for obtaining the new program counter address from specific external memory locations. A unique type of jump is the restart instruction. This instruction actually contains the new address as a part of the 8-bit op code. This is possible since only eight separate addresses located in page zero of the external memory may be specified. Program jumps may also be achieved by loading register HL, IX, or IY directly into the PC, thus allowing the jump address to be a complex function of the routine being executed.

The *input/output group of instructions* in the Z80 allows for a wide range of transfers between external memory locations or the general-purpose CPU registers and the external I/O devices. In each case, the port number is provided on the lower 8 bits of the address bus during any I/O transaction. One instruction allows this port number to be specified by the second byte of the instruction, while other Z80 instructions allow it to be specified as the content of the C register. One major advantage of using the C register as a pointer to the I/O device is that it allows different I/O ports to share common software driver routines. This is not possible when the address is part of the OP code if the routines are stored in ROM.

Another feature of these input instructions is that they set the flag register automatically so that additional operations are not required to determine the state of the input data (for example, its parity). The CPU includes single instructions that can move blocks of data (up to 256 bytes) automatically to or from any I/O port directly to any memory location. In conjunction with the dual set of general-purpose registers, these instructions provide for fast I/O block transfer rates. The value of this I/O instruction set is demonstrated by the fact that the CPU can provide all required floppy disk formatting (preamble, address, data, and enable of the CRC code) on double-density floppy disk drives on an interrupt-driven basis.

Finally, the *basic CPU control instructions* allow various options and modes. This group includes such instructions as setting or resetting the interrupt enable flip-flop or setting the mode of interrupt response.

Addressing modes. Most of the Z80 instructions operate on data stored in internal CPU registers, external memory, or in the I/O ports. Addressing refers to how the address of this data is generated in each instruction. The following gives a brief summary of the types of addressing used in the Z80, while subsequent sections detail the type of addressing available for each instruction group.

In the immediate mode of addressing, the byte following the op code in memory contains this actual operand:

op code	one or two bytes
operand	
d7 d0	

Examples of this type of instruction would be to load the accumulator with a constant, where the constant is the byte immediately following the op code.

The *immediate extended mode* is an extension of immediate addressing in that the two bytes following the op codes are the operand.

op code	one or two bytes
operand	low order
operand	high order

Examples of this type of instruction would be to load the HL register pair (16-bit register) with 16 bits (two bytes) of data.

The *modified page zero addressing instruction* (which is referred to as a *restart*) sets the PC to an effective address in page zero. This is a special single-byte call instruction to any of eight locations in page zero of memory. The value of this instruction is that it allows a single byte to specify a complete 16-bit address where commonly called subroutines are located, thus saving memory space.

op code	one byte
b7 b0	

Effective address is $(b_5b_4b_3000)_2$.

Relative addressing uses one byte of data following the op code to specify a displacement from the existing program to which a program jump can occur. This displacement is a signed two's-complement number which is added to the address of the op code of the following instruction:

op code	jump relative (one-byte op code)
operand	8-bit two's-complement displacement added to address (A + 2)

The value of relative addressing is that it allows jumps to nearby locations while only requiring two bytes of memory space. For most programs, relative jumps are by far the most prevalent type of jump, owing to the proximity of related program segments. Thus, these instructions can significantly reduce memory-space requirements. The signed displacement can range between +127 and −128 from A + 2. This allows for a total displacement of +129 to −126 from the jump-relative op code address. Another major advantage is that it allows for relocatable code.

Extended addressing provides for two bytes (16 bits) of address to be included in the instruction. These data can be an address to which a program can jump, or an address where an operand is located.

op code	one or two bytes
low-order address or low-order operand	
high-order address or high-order operand	

Extended addressing is required for a program to jump from any location in memory to any other location, or to load and store data in any memory location.

When extended addressing is used to specify the source or destination address of an operand, the notation (nn) will be used to indicate the content of memory at nn, where nn is the 16-bit address specified in the instruction. This means that the two bytes of address nn are used as a pointer to memory location. The use of the parentheses always means that the value enclosed within them is used as a pointer to a memory location. For example, (1200) refers to the contents of memory at location 1200.

In *indexed addressing* the byte of data following the op code contains a displacement which is added to one of the two index registers (the op code specifies which index register is used) to form a pointer to memory. The contents of the index register is not altered by this operation.

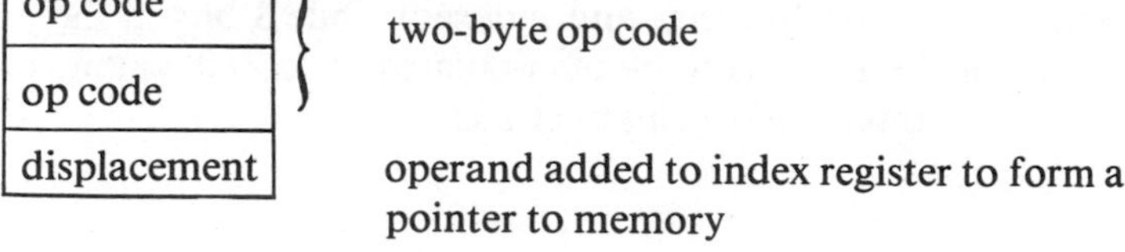

An example of an indexed instruction would be to load the contents of the memory location (index register + displacement) into the accumulator. The displacement is a signed two's-complement number. Indexed addressing greatly simplifies programs using tables of data, since the index register can point to the start of any table. Two index registers are provided, since very often operations require two or more tables. Indexed addressing also allows for relocatable code.

The two index registers in the Z80 are referred to as IX and IY. To indicate indexed addressing, the notation (IX + d) or (IY + d) is used. Here, d is the displacement specified after the op code. The parentheses indicate that this value is used as a pointer to external memory.

An example of *register addressing* would be to load the data in register B into register C. Many of the Z80 op codes contain bits of information that specify which CPU register is to be used for an operation.

Implied addressing refers to operations where the op code automatically implies one or more CPU registers as containing the operands. An example is the set of arithmetic operations where the accumulator is always implied to be the destination of the results.

Register indirect addressing specifies a 16-bit CPU register pair (such as HL) to be used as a pointer to any location in memory. This type of instruction is very powerful and is used in a wide range of applications.

op code	one or two bytes

An example of this type of instruction would be to load the accumulator with the data in memory location pointed to by the HL register contents. Indexed addressing is actually a form of register indirect addressing except that a displacement is added with indexed addressing. Register indirect addressing allows for very powerful but simple memory addressing. The block move and search commands in the Z80 are extensions of this type of addressing where automatic register incrementing, decrementing, and comparing has been added. The notation for indicating register indirect is to put parentheses around the name of the register that is to be used as the pointer. For example, the symbol (HL) specifies that the contents of the HL register is to be used as a pointer to a memory location. Often, register addressing is used to specify 16-bit operands. In this case, the register contents point to the lower-order portion of the operand while the register contents are automatically incremented to obtain the upper portion of the operand.

Bit addressing instructions allow any memory location or CPU register to be specified for a bit operation through one of three previous addressing modes (register, register indirect, and indexed) while 3 bits in the op code specify which of the 8 bits is to be manipulated. The Z80 contains a large number of bit set, reset, and test instructions.

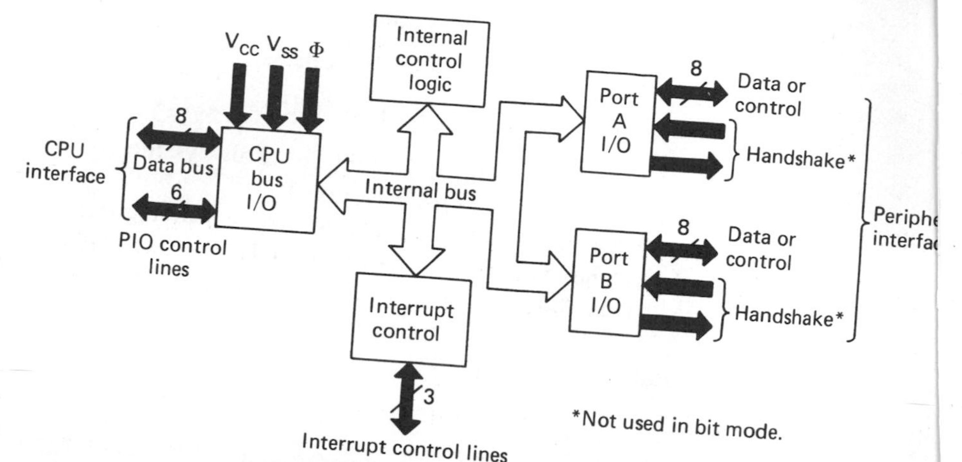

Figure 6-4 MK3881 PIO, block diagram.

3. Any one of four distinct modes of operation may be selected for a port, including byte output, byte input, byte bidirectional bus available on port A only), and bit control mode, all with interrupt-controlled "handshake."
4. Daisy-chain priority interrupt logic included to provide for automatic interrupt vectoring without external logic.
5. Eight outputs are capable of driving Darlington transistors.
6. All inputs and outputs fully TTL-compatible.
7. Single 5-V supply and single-phase clock are required.

One of the unique features of the PIO that separates it from other interface controllers is that all data transfer between the peripheral device and the CPU is accomplished under total interrupt control. Another unique feature of the PIO is that it can be programmed to interrupt the CPU on the occurrence of specified status conditions in the peripheral device. For example, the PIO can be programmed to interrupt if any specified peripheral alarm conditions should occur. This interrupt capability reduces the amount of time that the CPU must spend in polling peripheral status.

6-2-1 PIO architecture

A block diagram of the PIO is shown in Fig. 6-4. The internal structure of the PIO consists of a CPU bus interface, internal control logic, port A I/O logic, port B I/O logic, and interrupt control logic. The CPU bus interface logic allows the PIO to interface directly to the CPU with no other external logic. However, address decoders and/or line buffers may be required for large systems. The internal control logic synchronized the

Addressing mode combinations. Many instructions include more than one operand (such as arithmetic instructions or loads). In these cases, two types of addressing may be used. For example, load can use immediate addressing to specify the source and register indirect or indexed addressing to specify the destination.

Instruction op codes. We describe below one set of Z80 instructions and provide a table listing the op codes for the instructions in the set. In the table, Fig. 6-3, the shaded op codes are identical to those offered in the 8080A CPU. Also shown is the assembly language mnemonic that is used for each instruction. All instruction op codes are listed in hex notation. Single-byte op codes require two hex characters, while double-byte op codes require four hex characters.

Z80 instruction mnemonics consist of an op code and a zero, and one or two operands. Instructions in which the operand is implied have no operand. Instructions that have only one logical operand, or those in which one operand is invariant (such as the logical OR instruction) are represented by one operand mnemonic. Instructions that may have two varying operands are represented by two operand mnemonics.

Load and exchange instructions. The table of Fig. 6-3 defines the op code for all the 8-bit load instructions of the CPU. Also shown is the type of addressing used for each instruction. The source of the data is found on the top horizontal row while the destination is specified by the left-hand column. For example, load register C from register B uses the op code 48 (hex). In all the tables, the op code is specified in hex notation, and the 48 hex (0100 1000 in binary) code is fetched by the CPU from the external memory, decoded, and then the register transfer is automatically performed by the CPU.

The assembly language mnemonic for this entire group of instructions is LD, followed by the destination, followed by the source (LD DEST., SOURCE). Note that several combinations of addressing modes are possible. For example, the source may use register addressing and the destination may be register indirect, such as load the memory location pointed to by register HL with the contents of register D. The op code for this operation would be 72 (hex). The mnemonic for this load instruction would be as follows: LD (HL), D.

The parentheses around the HL indicate that the contents of HL are used as a pointer to a memory location. In all Z80 load instruction mnemonics, the destination is always listed first, with the source following. The Z80 assembly language has been defined for ease of programming. Every instruction is self-documenting.

Destination		Source: Implied		Register							Reg indirect			Indexed		Ext. addr.	Imme.
		I	R	A	B	C	D	E	H	L	(HL)	(BC)	(DE)	(IX + d)	(IY + d)	(nn)	n
Register	A	ED 57	ED 5F	7F	78	79	7A	7B	7C	7D	7E	0A	1A	DD 7E d	FD 7E d	3A n n	3E n
	B			47	40	41	42	43	44	45	46			DD 46 d	FD 46 d		08 n
	C			4F	48	49	4A	4B	4C	4D	4E			DD 4E d	FD 4E d		0E n
	D			57	50	51	52	53	54	55	56			DD 56 d	FD 56 d		16 n
	E			5F	58	59	5A	5B	5C	5D	5E			DD 5E d	FD 5E d		18 n
	H			67	60	61	62	63	64	65	66			DD 66 d	FD 66 d		20 n
	L			6F	68	69	6A	6B	6C	6D	6E			DD 6E d	FD 6E d		21 n
Reg indirect	(HL)			77	70	71	72	73	74	75							26 n
	(BC)			62													
	(DE)			12													
Indexed	(IX + d)			DD 77 d	DD 70 d	DD 71 d	DD 72 d	DD 73 d	DD 74 d	DD 75 d							DD 36 d n
	(IY + d)			FD 77 d	FD 70 d	FD 71 d	FD 72 d	FD 73 d	FD 74 d	FD 75 d							FD 36 d n
Ext. addr	(nn)			32 n n													
Implied	I			ED 47													
	R			ED 4F													

Figure 6-3 Sample of Z80 instruction op codes.

All load instructions using indexed addressing for either the source or destination location actually use three bytes of memory, with the third byte being the displacement, d. For example, a "load register E with the operand pointed to by IX with an offset of +8" would be written LD E, (IX + 8).

The instruction sequence for this in memory would be

address	A	DD	op code
	A + 1	5F	
	A + 2	08	displacement operand

The two extended addressing instructions are also three-byte instructions. For example, the instruction to "load the accumulator with the operand in memory location 6F32H" would be written: LD A, (6F 32H), and the instruction sequence would be

address	A	3A	op code
	A + 1	32	low-order address
	A + 2	6F	high-order address

Notice that the low-order portion of the address is always the first operand. (The letter H used here indicates hex notation.)

The load immediate instructions for the general-purpose 8-bit registers are two-byte instructions. The instruction "load register H with the value 36H" would be written LD H, 36H, and the instruction sequence would be

address	A	26	op code
	A + 1	36	operand

Loading a memory location using indexed addressing for the destination and immediate addressing for the source requires three bytes. For example; LD (IX − 15), 21H would appear in program sequence as

address	A	DD	op code
	A + 1	36	
	A + 2	F1	displacement (−15 in signed two's complement)
	A + 3	21	operand to load

Notice that with any indexed addressing the displacement always follows directly after the op code.

6-2 MK3881 PIO

The parallel I/O interface controller (PIO) is a programmable, two-port device that provides TTL-compatible interfacing between peripheral devices and the Z80 CPU (see Figs. 6-4 and 6-5). The CPU can configure the PIO to interface with a wide range of peripheral devices with no other external logic required. Typical peripheral devices that are fully compatible with the PIO include most keyboards, paper-tape readers and punches, printers, and PROM programmers.

Major features of the PIO include:

1. Two independent 8-bit bidirectional peripheral interface ports with "handshake" data-transfer control.
2. Interrupt-driven "handshake" for fast response.

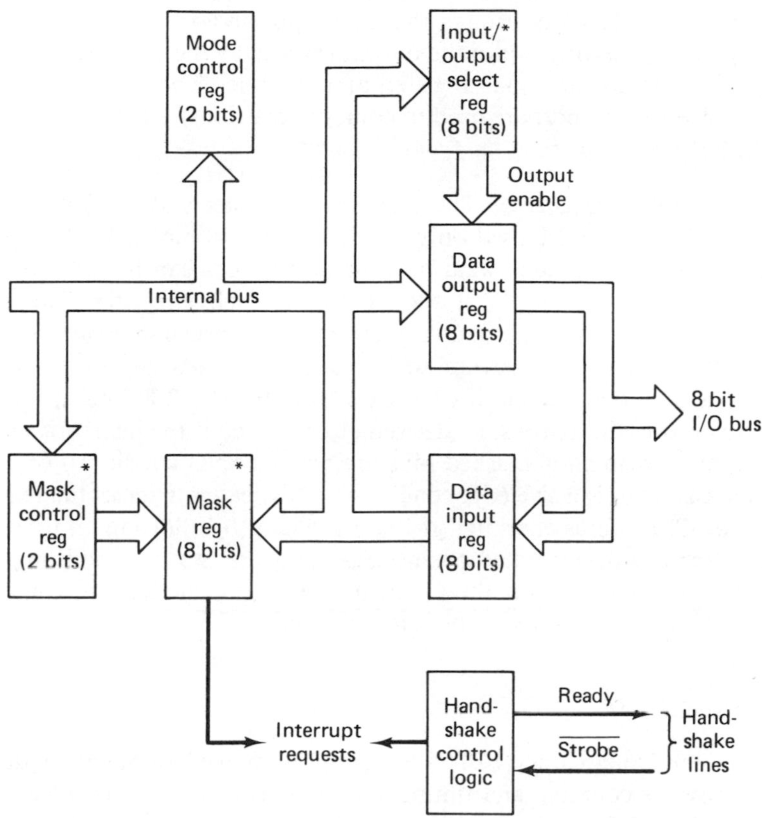

* Used in the bit mode only to allow generation of an interrupt if the peripheral I/O pins go to the specified state.

Figure 6-5 Port I/O block diagram.

CPU data bus to the peripheral device interfaces (port A and port B). The two I/O ports (A and B) are virtually identical and are used to interface directly to peripheral devices.

The port I/O logic is composed of six registers with "handshake" control logic as shown in Fig. 6-5. The registers include an 8-bit data input register, an 8-bit data output register, a 2-bit mode control register, an 8-bit mask register, an 8-bit input/output select register, and a 2-bit mask control register.

Mode control. The 2-bit mode control register is loaded by the CPU to select the desired operating mode (byte output, byte input, byte bidirectional bus, or bit control mode). All data transfer between the peripheral device and the CPU is achieved through the data input and data output registers. Data bytes may be written into the output register by the CPU or read back to the CPU from the input register at any time. The handshake lines associated with each port are used to control data transfer between the PIO and the peripheral device.

Mask and select registers. The 8-bit mask register and the 8-bit input/output select register are used only in the bit control mode. In this mode, any of the eight peripheral data or control bus pins can be programmed to be an input or an output, as specified by the select register. The mask register is used in this mode, in conjunction with a special interrupt feature. This feature allows an interrupt to be generated when any or all of the unmasked pins reach a specified state (1 or 0). The 2-bit mask control register specifies the active state desired (1 or 0), and if the interrupt should be generated when *all* unmasked pins are active (AND condition) or when *any* unmasked pin is active (OR condition). This feature reduces the requirements for CPU status checking of the peripheral by allowing an interrupt to be automatically generated on specific peripheral status conditions. For example, in a system with three alarm conditions, an interrupt may be generated if any one occurs, or if all three occur.

6-3 MK3882 CTC

The Counter Timer Circuit (CTC) is a programmable, four-channel device which provides counting and timing functions for the CPU (see Figs. 6-6 and 6-7). The CPU configures the four independent channels of the CTC to operate under various modes and conditions as required. Major features of the CTC include:

1. Each channel may be selected to operate in either a counter mode or a timer mode.
2. Programmable interrupts on counter or timer states.
3. Readable down-counter indicates the number of counts to go until zero.
4. Selectable 16 or 256 clock prescaler for each timer channel.
5. Selectable positive or negative trigger may initiate timer operation.
6. Three channels have zero count/timeout outputs capable of driving Darlington transistors.
7. All inputs and outputs are fully TTL-compatible.

Addressing mode combinations. Many instructions include more than one operand (such as arithmetic instructions or loads). In these cases, two types of addressing may be used. For example, load can use immediate addressing to specify the source and register indirect or indexed addressing to specify the destination.

Instruction op codes. We describe below one set of Z80 instructions and provide a table listing the op codes for the instructions in the set. In the table, Fig. 6-3, the shaded op codes are identical to those offered in the 8080A CPU. Also shown is the assembly language mnemonic that is used for each instruction. All instruction op codes are listed in hex notation. Single-byte op codes require two hex characters, while double-byte op codes require four hex characters.

Z80 instruction mnemonics consist of an op code and a zero, and one or two operands. Instructions in which the operand is implied have no operand. Instructions that have only one logical operand, or those in which one operand is invariant (such as the logical OR instruction) are represented by one operand mnemonic. Instructions that may have two varying operands are represented by two operand mnemonics.

Load and exchange instructions. The table of Fig. 6-3 defines the op code for all the 8-bit load instructions of the CPU. Also shown is the type of addressing used for each instruction. The source of the data is found on the top horizontal row while the destination is specified by the left-hand column. For example, load register C from register B uses the op code 48 (hex). In all the tables, the op code is specified in hex notation, and the 48 hex (0100 1000 in binary) code is fetched by the CPU from the external memory, decoded, and then the register transfer is automatically performed by the CPU.

The assembly language mnemonic for this entire group of instructions is LD, followed by the destination, followed by the source (LD DEST., SOURCE). Note that several combinations of addressing modes are possible. For example, the source may use register addressing and the destination may be register indirect, such as load the memory location pointed to by register HL with the contents of register D. The op code for this operation would be 72 (hex). The mnemonic for this load instruction would be as follows: LD (HL), D.

The parentheses around the HL indicate that the contents of HL are used as a pointer to a memory location. In all Z80 load instruction mnemonics, the destination is always listed first, with the source following. The Z80 assembly language has been defined for ease of programming. Every instruction is self-documenting.

Destination		Source: Implied		Register							Reg indirect			Indexed		Ext. addr.	Imme.
		I	R	A	B	C	D	E	H	L	(HL)	(BC)	(DE)	(IX + d)	(IY + d)	(nn)	n
Register	A	ED 57	ED 5F	7F	78	79	7A	7B	7C	7D	7E	0A	1A	DD 7E d	FD 7E d	3A n n	3E n
	B			47	40	41	42	43	44	45	46			DD 46 d	FD 46 d		08 n
	C			4F	48	49	4A	4B	4C	4D	4E			DD 4E d	FD 4E d		0E n
	D			57	50	51	52	53	54	55	56			DD 56 d	FD 56 d		16 n
	E			5F	58	59	5A	5B	5C	5D	5E			DD 5E d	FD 5E d		18 n
	H			67	60	61	62	63	64	65	66			DD 66 d	FD 66 d		20 n
	L			6F	68	69	6A	6B	6C	6D	6E			DD 6E d	FD 6E d		21 n
Reg indirect	(HL)			77	70	71	72	73	74	75							26 n
	(BC)			62													
	(DE)			12													
Indexed	(IX + d)			DD 77 d	DD 70 d	DD 71 d	DD 72 d	DD 73 d	DD 74 d	DD 75 d							DD 36 d n
	(IY + d)			FD 77 d	FD 70 d	FD 71 d	FD 72 d	FD 73 d	FD 74 d	FD 75 d							FD 36 d n
Ext. addr	(nn)			32 n n													
Implied	I			ED 47													
	R			ED 4F													

Figure 6-3 Sample of Z80 instruction op codes.

All load instructions using indexed addressing for either the source or destination location actually use three bytes of memory, with the third byte being the displacement, d. For example, a "load register E with the operand pointed to by IX with an offset of +8" would be written LD E, (IX + 8).

The instruction sequence for this in memory would be

address A	DD	op code
A+1	5F	
A+2	08	displacement operand

The two extended addressing instructions are also three-byte instructions. For example, the instruction to "load the accumulator with the operand in memory location 6F32H" would be written: LD A, (6F 32H), and the instruction sequence would be

address	A	3A	op code
	A + 1	32	low-order address
	A + 2	6F	high-order address

Notice that the low-order portion of the address is always the first operand. (The letter H used here indicates hex notation.)

The load immediate instructions for the general-purpose 8-bit registers are two-byte instructions. The instruction "load register H with the value 36H" would be written LD H, 36H, and the instruction sequence would be

address	A	26	op code
	A + 1	36	operand

Loading a memory location using indexed addressing for the destination and immediate addressing for the source requires three bytes. For example; LD (IX − 15), 21H would appear in program sequence as

address	A	DD	op code
	A + 1	36	
	A + 2	F1	displacement (− 15 in signed two's complement)
	A + 3	21	operand to load

Notice that with any indexed addressing the displacement always follows directly after the op code.

6-2 MK3881 PIO

The parallel I/O interface controller (PIO) is a programmable, two-port device that provides TTL-compatible interfacing between peripheral devices and the Z80 CPU (see Figs. 6-4 and 6-5). The CPU can configure the PIO to interface with a wide range of peripheral devices with no other external logic required. Typical peripheral devices that are fully compatible with the PIO include most keyboards, paper-tape readers and punches, printers, and PROM programmers.

Major features of the PIO include:

1. Two independent 8-bit bidirectional peripheral interface ports with "handshake" data-transfer control.
2. Interrupt-driven "handshake" for fast response.

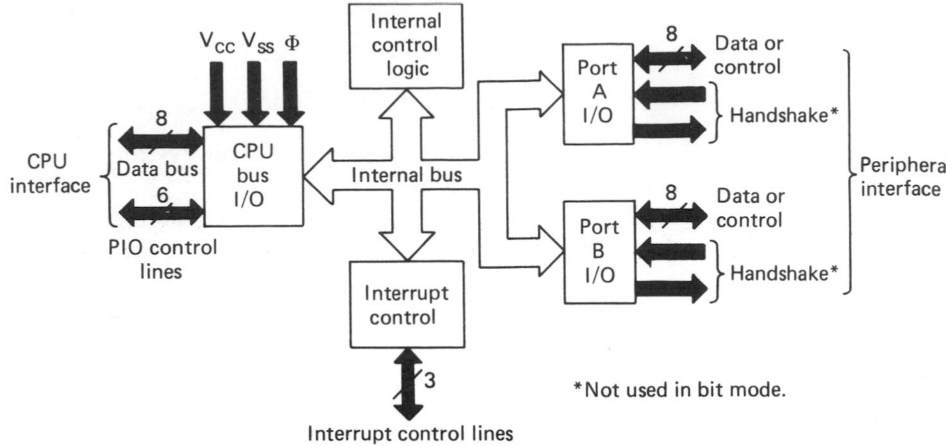

Figure 6-4 MK3881 PIO, block diagram.

3. Any one of four distinct modes of operation may be selected for a port, including byte output, byte input, byte bidirectional bus available on port A only), and bit control mode, all with interrupt-controlled "handshake."
4. Daisy-chain priority interrupt logic included to provide for automatic interrupt vectoring without external logic.
5. Eight outputs are capable of driving Darlington transistors.
6. All inputs and outputs fully TTL-compatible.
7. Single 5-V supply and single-phase clock are required.

One of the unique features of the PIO that separates it from other interface controllers is that all data transfer between the peripheral device and the CPU is accomplished under total interrupt control. Another unique feature of the PIO is that it can be programmed to interrupt the CPU on the occurrence of specified status conditions in the peripheral device. For example, the PIO can be programmed to interrupt if any specified peripheral alarm conditions should occur. This interrupt capability reduces the amount of time that the CPU must spend in polling peripheral status.

6-2-1 PIO architecture

A block diagram of the PIO is shown in Fig. 6-4. The internal structure of the PIO consists of a CPU bus interface, internal control logic, port A I/O logic, port B I/O logic, and interrupt control logic. The CPU bus interface logic allows the PIO to interface directly to the CPU with no other external logic. However, address decoders and/or line buffers may be required for large systems. The internal control logic synchronized the

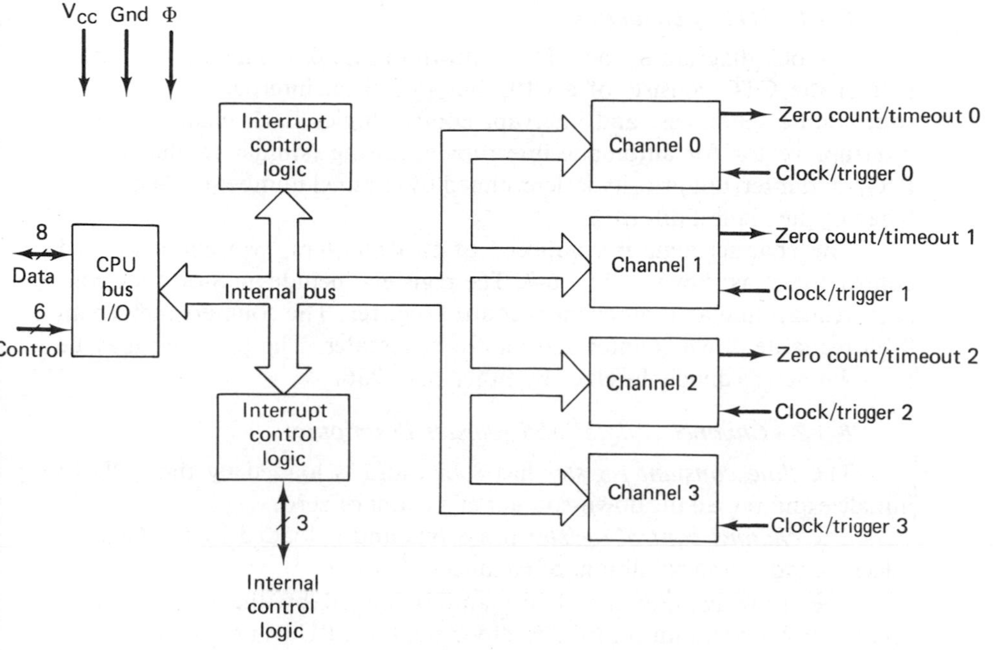

Figure 6-6 MK3883 CTC, functional diagram.

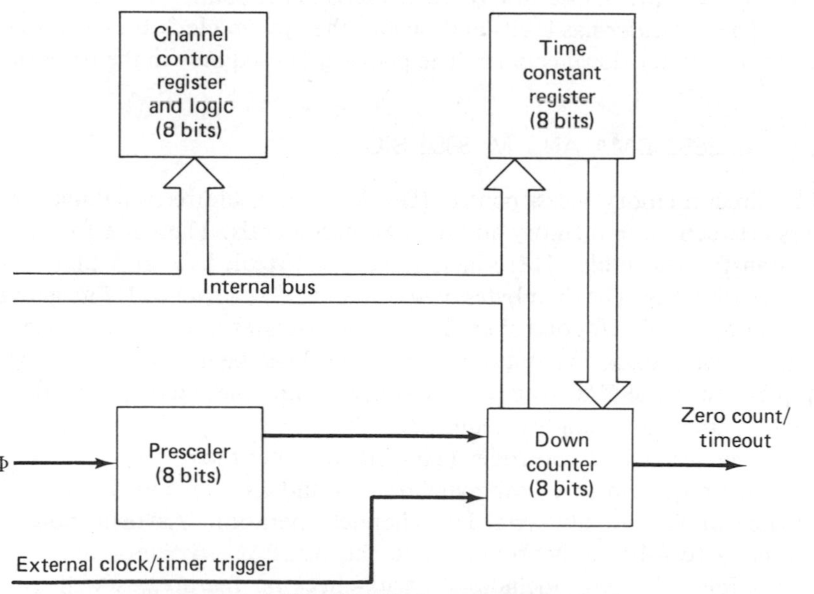

Figure 6-7 MK3882 CTC channel, block diagram.

6-3-1 CTC architecture

A block diagram of the CTC is shown in Fig. 6-6. The internal structure of the CTC consists of a CPU bus interface, internal control logic, four counter channels, and interrupt control logic. Each channel has an interrupt vector for automatic interrupt vectoring (similar to that of the PIO), and interrupt priority is determined by channel number (with channel 0 having the highest priority).

The channel logic is composed of two registers, two counters, and control logic, as shown in Fig. 6-7. The registers include an 8-bit time constant register and an 8-bit channel control register. The counters include an 8-bit readable down-counter and an 8-bit prescaler. The prescaler may be programmed to divide the clock by either 16 or 256.

6-3-2 Channel counter and register description

The *time constant register* has 8 bits and is loaded by the CPU to initialize and reload the down-counter at a count of zero.

The *channel control register* has 8 bits and is loaded by the CPU to select the mode and conditions of channel operation.

The *down-counter* has 8 bits and is loaded by the time constant register under program control. At any time, the CPU can read the number of counts to go until a zero count. This counter is decremented by the prescaler tin timer mode and by CLK/TRIG in the counter mode.

The *prescaler* has 8 bits and divides the system clock by 16 or 256 for decrementing the down-counter. The prescaler is used only in the timer mode.

6-4 MK3883 DMA AND MK3884 SIO

The direct memory access control (DMA) handles bidirectional data transfers between main memory and the Z80 peripherals. There are four modes of transfer selectable. These include no cycle steal, byte at a time, burst, and continuous. The data bytes may be handled at a rate of 1.2 megabytes/second by the DMA controller. The DMA operates in two modes: transfer data or search data. The status of each channel can be monitored by program request. Like the CTC, the DMA has programmable interrupt and priority logic. A single 5-V supply is required.

The serial I/O controller (SIO) handles peripherals with serial data interface requirements, both synchronous and asynchronous. The SIO is capable of full duplex serial I/O channel operation. Asynchronous data can be 5- to 8-bit. Synchronous data can be IBM-, BySync-, and SDLC-compatible. The SIO includes a parity-checking feature, as well as programmable interrupt and priority logic.

The user manuals contain full details of the DMA and SIO devices.

6-5 SOFTWARE DEVELOPMENT BOARD (SDB-80)

The SDB is a stand-alone microcomputer designed around the Z80 microprocessor family. Figure 6-8 shows the board mounted in a card cage and interconnected to such peripherals as a video terminal, line printer, and tape reader. Figure 6-9 shows a block diagram of the board.

The SDB-80 uses Mostek 16K dynamic RAM memories and offers a complete package of software development aids in ROM. A 10K-byte firmware package is included with the SDB-80 and provides the ability to generate, edit, assemble, load, execute, and debug Z80 programs for all types of applications.

6-5-1 Using the SDB-80

In addition to functioning as a stand-alone development aid, the SDB-80 is fully expandable through the addition of optional add-on circuit boards. The SDB-80 may also be used directly in OEM (original equipment manufacture) applications by inserting custom-programmed ROM or PROM memories into the sockets provided on the board. For these OEM applications, partially populated versions of the SDB-80 (designated OEM-80) are available without the standard system firmware, and with quantity discounts.

6-5-2 System firmware

A standard feature of the SDB-80 is a complete package of development software aids which are resident in the five MK34000 2K × 8 ROM memories located on the board. The firmware includes a sophisticated operating system, a debug package, an assembler, and a text editor. Among the many features provided are execute and breakpoint commands, console routines for examining and/or modifying memory and port locations,

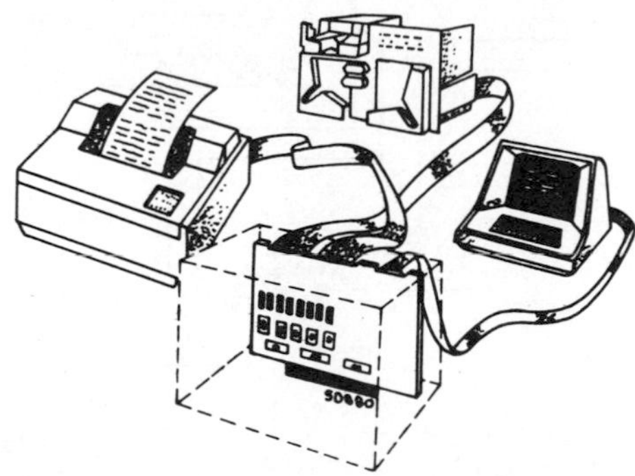

Figure 6-8 Software development board SDB-80 mounted in a card cage.

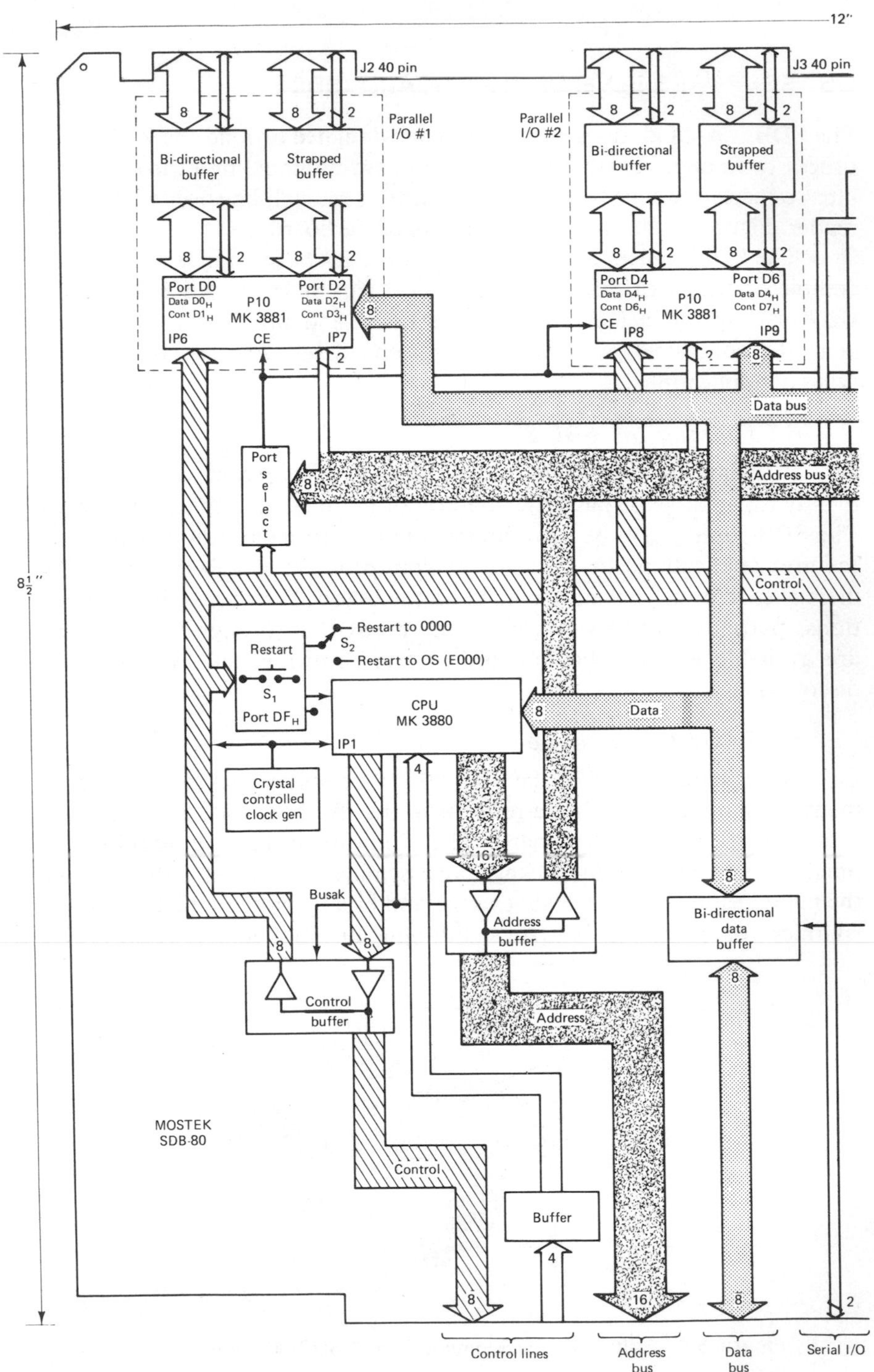

Figure 6-9 SDB-80, block diagram.

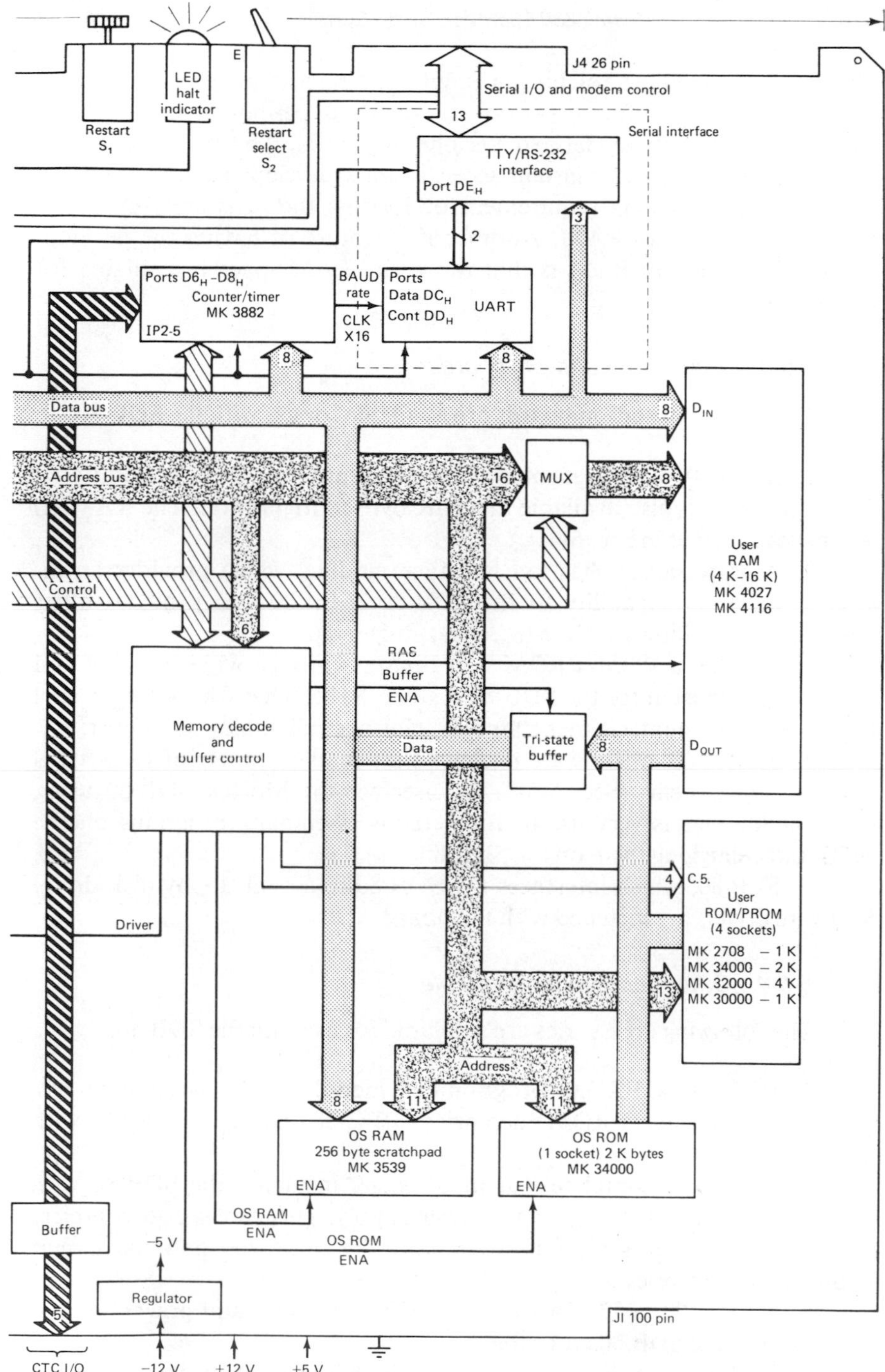

Figure 6-9 *(Continued)*

object load capabilities for both absolute and relocatable object modules, I/O driver routines for a variety of standard peripheral devices, and channeled I/O for user-defined peripheral drivers. The presence of this software in ROM provides instant access to these development aids, eliminating the time-consuming requirement of loading the software from some peripheral device into RAM. Another key feature of having the development aid software in ROM is that the entire RAM space is available for user programs.

6-5-3 Compatible add-on boards

The following add-on boards are available for use with the SDB-80:

1. RAM-80, a RAM memory board that provides bytes of additional RAM. RAM-80 is also available in a 65K byte configuration. The RAM-80 is discussed further in Sec. 6-6.
2. AIM-80, an application interface module, which provides an in-circuit emulation capability to the SDB-80. AIM-80 also provides other debugging capabilities, such as trace and single step.
3. RIO-80, a ROM/PROM I/O board, which provides parallel and serial port expansion for the SDB-80 system. RIO-80 has four 8-bit parallel I/O ports, four counter/timer channels, plus one full duplex serial port.
4. MDSX-80, a firmware package that enables owners of Intel MDS development systems (Sec. 5-6-2) to interface the Mostek SDB-80 using the RIO-80. This is very useful for persons assembling programs on the MDS and debugging them on the SDB-80.
5. FLP-80, which interfaces the SDB-80 to a dual floppy disk drive. Software drivers are included with the board.

6-5-4 Other accessories available

The following accessories are available for use with the SDB-80:

1. PPG-80, a PROM programmer module for programming UV (ultraviolet) erasable PROM memories. PPG-08 interfaces directly with the SDB-80.
2. AID-80, a complete system package, including the SDB-80 with 13-slot card cage, enclosure, and power supply, plus cables and complete documentation. The system is expandable by using the optional circuit boards and accessories.
3. XAID-100, a 13-slot card cage with enclosure and power supply. Does not include SDB-80 and cables.
4. XAID-102, a three-slot card cage without the enclosure and power supply.
5. XAID-103, a wire-wrap card, and XAID-104, an extender card.

6-5-5 Assembler/editor/loader (ASMB-80)

The ASMB-80 is a software package that consists of a text editor, Z80 assembler, and relocating linking loader. The software is supplied in ROM for the SDB-80. The programs make extensive use of the DDT-80 (Sec. 6-5-6), which is also supplied in ROM for the SDB-80 to provide the user with state-of-the-art software for developing Z80 programs. All I/O is done via the SDB-80 channels that can be directed to any software driver. The DDT-80 contains drivers for paper tape, Silent 700, TTY, CRT, and line printer devices. The ASMB-80 contains drivers for Silent 700 digital cassette and for RAM-based operation. Such RAM-based operation allows editing, assembling, and loading of programs using RAM instead of external media for intermediate storage.

6-5-6 DDT-80 operating system

The DDT-80 is the operating system for the SDB-80, and resides in a 2K ROM on the SDB-80. The DDT-80 provides the necessary tools and techniques to operate the system (that is, to efficiently and conveniently perform the tasks necessary to develop microcomputer software). DDT-80 is designed to support the user from initial design through production testing. The DDT-80 allows the user to display and update memory, registers, and ports, load and dump object files, set breakpoints, copy blocks of memory, and execute programs.

6-5-7 Nonresident software available

The following nonresident software packages are available for use with the SDB-80:

1. XFOR-80, which is a Fortran IV cross-assembler. XFOR-80 is written in Fortran IV, but assembles Z80 programs and is useful for persons desiring to perform Z80 assembly on minicomputers such as the PDP-11. XFOR-80 is furnished as a Fortran IV source deck.
2. XMDS-80, which is an 8080A cross-assembler and performs the same function as the Fortran IV cross assembler (XFOR-80) except that XMDS-80 is designed to be used with an Intel MDS system. XMDS-80 is furnished as an object tape in Intel hex format (Chapter 5).
3. XMDS-80D, which is identical to the XMDS-80 except that it is compatible with Intel MDS systems that use floppy disks. XMDS-80D is furnished as an object code on an MDS-compatible floppy diskette.

6-6 RANDOM-ACCESS MEMORY BOARD (RAM-80)

The RAM-80 is designed to provide RAM expansion capability for the Z80-based SDB-80 microcomputer (described in Sec. 6-5). For user flexibility, it is offered in two basic configurations, designated RAM-80A and RAM-80B.

Figure 6-10 shows the board mounted in a card cage and interconnected to the SDB-80. Figures 6-11 and 6-12 show block diagrams of the RAM-80A and RAM-80B, respectively.

The RAM-80A is the basic 16K-byte RAM board for users, requiring the most economical means for adding RAM to an SDB-80 microcomputer. RAM-80A is designed using the high-performance MK4027-4 4096 × 1 dynamic RAM, and includes address strapping options for positioning the decoded memory space to start on any 4K incremental address boundary.

The RAM-80B is a combination memory and I/O expansion board. The memory may be configurated to have a memory expansion of 16K, 32K, 48K, or 65K bytes of RAM. The RAM-80B provides strapping options for positioning the decoded memory space to start on any 16K address boundary. In addition to the add-on memory, the RAM-80B provides four 8-bit I/O ports from the two on-board Z80 PIO (Sec. 6-2) circuits. Each I/O port is fully TTL-buffered and has two handshake lines per I/O port. The RAM-80B also includes logic for a "page mode operation," which permits up to 1 megabyte of memory (sixteen 65K × 8 RAM 80Bs) to be used in a single SDB-80 system.

6-7 SYSTEM FLAGS

Each of the two Z80 CPU flag registers (Fig. 6-2) contains 6 bits of information that are set or reset by various CPU operations. Four of these bits are testable; that is, they are used as conditions for jump, call, or return instructions. For example, a jump may be desired only if a specific bit in the flag register is set. The four testable flag bits are:

1. *Carry flag (C).* This flag is the carry from the highest-order bit of the accumulator. For example, the carry flag will be set during an add instruction where a carry from the highest bit of the accumulator is gen-

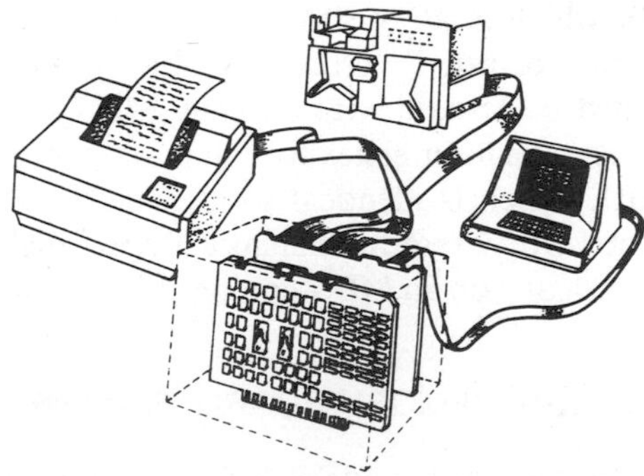

Figure 6-10 Random-access memory board RAM-80 mounted in a card cage.

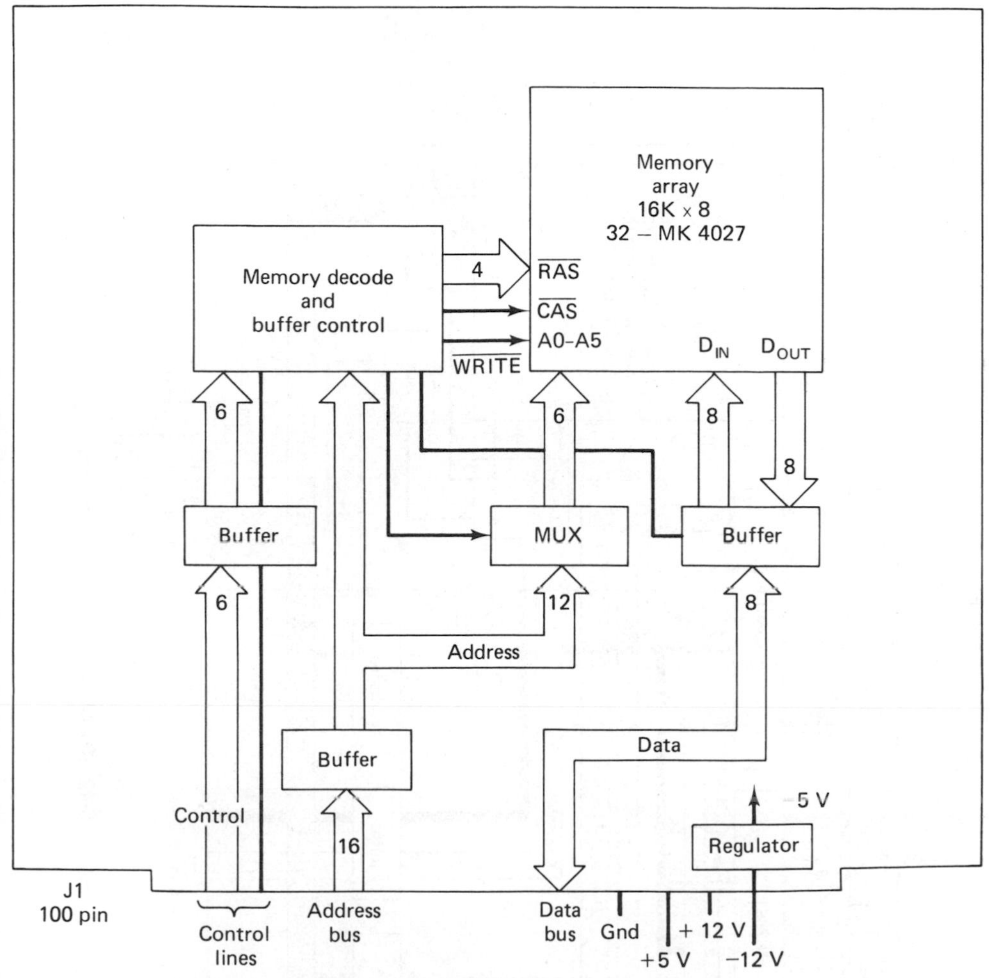

Figure 6-11 RAM-80A, functional diagram.

erated. This flag is also set if a borrow is generated during a subtraction instruction. The shift and rotate instructions also affect this bit.

2. *Zero flag (Z).* This flag is set if the result of the operation loaded a zero into the accumulator. Otherwise, the flag is reset.

3. *Sign flag (S).* This flag is intended to be used with signed numbers and is set if the result of the operation was negative. Since bit 7 (MSB) represents the sign of the number (a negative number has a 1 in bit 7), this flag stores the state of bit 7 in the accumulator.

4. *Parity/Overflow flag (P/V).* This dual-purpose flag indicates the parity of the result in the accumulator when logical operations are performed (such as AND A,B), and it represents overflow when signed two's-comple-

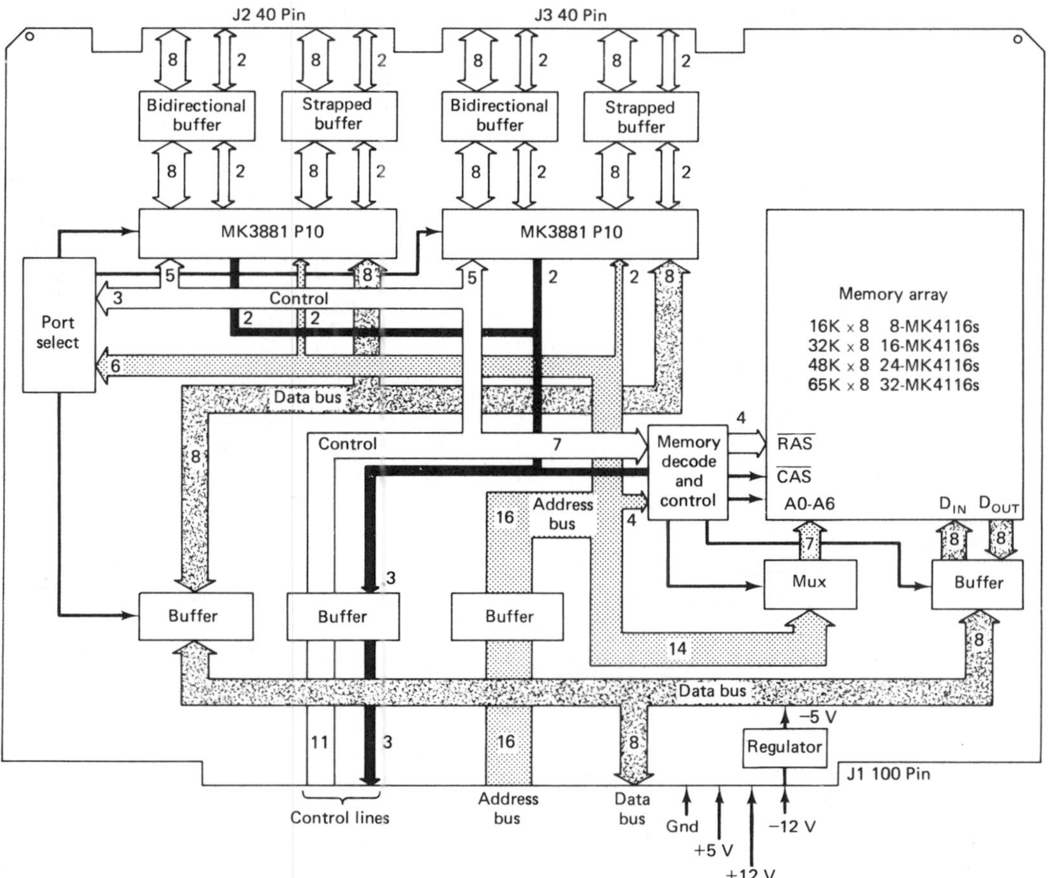

Figure 6-12 RAM-80B, functional diagram.

ment arithmetic operations are performed. The Z80 overflow flag indicates that the two's-complement number in the accumulator is in error since it has exceeded the maximum possible (+127) or is less than the minimum possible (−128) number that can be represented in two's-complement notation. For example, consider adding:

```
   +120 =  0111 1000
   +105 =  0110 1001
   -----   ---------
      C = 01110 0001 = -95 (wrong)     overflow has occurred
```

Here, the result is incorrect. Overflow has occurred, and yet there is no carry to indicate an error. For this case, the overflow flag would be set. Also, consider the addition of two negative numbers:

```
     -5 =      1111 1011
    -16 =      1111 0000
    ---        ---------
      C = 1    1110 1011 = -21 (correct)
```

Notice that the answer is correct, but the carry is set so that this flag cannot be used as an overflow indicator. In this case, the overflow would not be set.

For logical operations (AND, OR, EXCLUSIVE OR) this flag (P/V) is set if the parity of the result is even and is reset if parity is odd.

There are also two nontestable bits in the flag register. Both of these are used for BCD arithmetic. They are:

1. *Half carry flag (H).* This is the BCD carry or borrow result from the least-significant 4 bits of operation. When using a DAA (decimal adjust instruction) this flag is used to correct the result of a previous packed decimal add or subtract.
2. *Add/Subtract flag (N).* Since the algorithm for correcting BCD operations is different for addition or subtraction, this flag is used to specify what type of instruction was executed last so that the DAA operation will be correct for either addition or subtraction.

The flag register can be accessed by the programmer, and its format is as follows:

D7							D0
S	Z	X	H	X	P/V	N	C

X means that the flag is indeterminate (don't care).

6-8 SYSTEM INTERRUPT RESPONSE

The Z80 CPU has two interrupt inputs, a software maskable interrupt (an interrupt that can be programmed), and a nonmaskable interrupt (over which the program has no control). The nonmaskable interrupt ($\overline{NMI}$) *cannot* be disabled by the programmer, and will be accepted whenever a peripheral device requests the interrupt (a 0 on the $\overline{NMI}$ line). The nonmaskable interrupt is generally reserved for very important functions that must be serviced whenever they occur, such as an impending power failure. The maskable interrupt ($\overline{INT}$) can be selectively enabled or disabled by the programmer (as discussed in Sec. 6-2). This allows the programmer to disable the interrupt during periods where the program has timing constraints that do not allow it to be interrupted.

6-8-1 Nonmaskable interrupt

A nonmaskable interrupt will be accepted at all times by the CPU. When this occurs, the CPU ignores the next instruction that it fetches and, instead, does a restart to location 0066 (hex). Thus, the CPU acts exactly as if it had received a restart instruction, but it is to a location that is not one of the eight software restart locations. (A restart is a call to a specific address in page 0 of memory.)

6-8-2 Maskable interrupt

The CPU can be programmed to respond to the maskable interrupt in any one of three possible modes.

Mode 0. This mode is identical to the 8080A interrupt response mode. With mode 0, the interrupting device can place any instruction on the data bus and the CPU will execute it. Thus, the interrupting device provides the next instruction to be executed instead of the memory. Often, this will be a restart instruction, since the interrupting device only need supply a single-byte instruction. As an alternative, any other instruction, such as a three-byte call to any location in memory, could be executed.

The number of clock cycles necessary to execute this instruction is two more than the normal number for the instruction. This occurs since the CPU automatically adds two wait states to an interrupt response cycle to allow sufficient time to implement a peripheral priority control (if any is used).

Mode 1. In mode 1, the CPU will respond to an interrupt by executing a restart to location 0038 (hex). Thus, the response is identical to that for a nonmaskable interrupt except that the call location is 0038 instead of 0066. Another difference is that the number of cycles required to complete the restart instruction is two more than normal, owing to the two added wait states.

Mode 2. This mode is the most powerful interrupt response mode. With a single 8-bit byte from the user, an indirect call can be made to any memory location. With mode 2, the programmer maintains a table of 16-bit starting addresses for every interrupt service routine (see Fig. 6-13). This table may be located anywhere in memory. When an interrupt is accepted, a 16-bit pointer must be formed to obtain the desired interrupt service routine starting address from the table. The upper 8 bits of this pointer are formed from the contents of the I register, which must have been previously loaded with the desired value by the programmer. Note that a CPU reset clears the I register so that it is initialized to zero. The lower 8 bits of the pointer must be supplied by the interrupting device. Actually, only 7 bits are required from the interrupting device, as the least-significant bit must be a zero. This is required since the pointer is used to get two adjacent bytes to form a complete 16-bit service routine starting address, and the address must always start in even locations. This is illustrated in Fig. 6-13.

The first byte of the table is the least-significant (low-order) portion of the address. The programmer must obviously fill in this table with the desired address before any interrupts are to be accepted.

Note that the table can be changed at any time by the programmer (if it is stored in read/write memory) to allow different peripherals to be serviced by different service routines. Once the interrupting device supplies the lower portion of the pointer, the CPU automatically pushes the program counter onto the stack, obtains the starting address from the table, and does a jump to this address. This mode of response requires 19 clock periods to complete (7 to fetch the lower 8 bits from the interrupting device, 6 to save the program counter, and 6 to obtain the jump address).

6-9 HARDWARE EXAMPLES

This section describes a minimum Z80 system as well as the basics of adding RAM. Many additional examples are to be found in user literature.

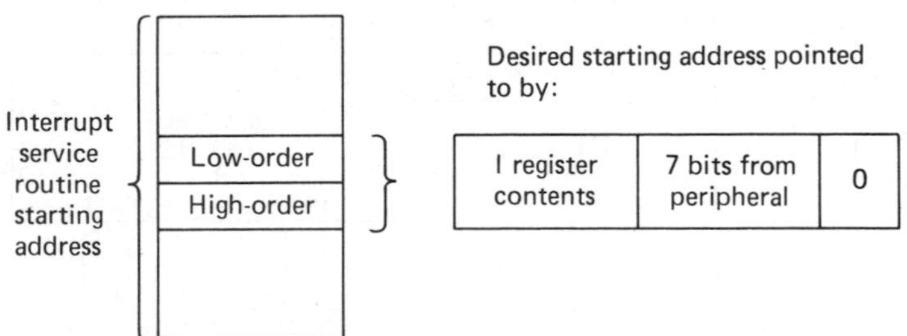

Figure 6-13 Table of 16-bit starting addresses for each interrupt service routine.

6-9-1 Minimum Z80 System

Figure 6-14 is a diagram of a very simple Z80 system. Any Z80 system must include the following: 5-V power supply, oscillator (clock), memory devices, I/O circuits, and CPU.

Power supply. Since the Z80 CPU requires a single 5-V supply, most small systems can be implemented using only this power supply.

Oscillator. The oscillator can be very simple since the only requirement is that it produce a 5-V *square-wave pulse.* For systems not running at full speed, a simple *RC* oscillator can be used. When the CPU is operated near the highest possible frequency, a crystal oscillator is generally required because the system timing will not tolerate the drift or jitter that an *RC* network will generate. A crystal oscillator can be made from inverters, and a few discrete components or monolithic circuits are widely available.

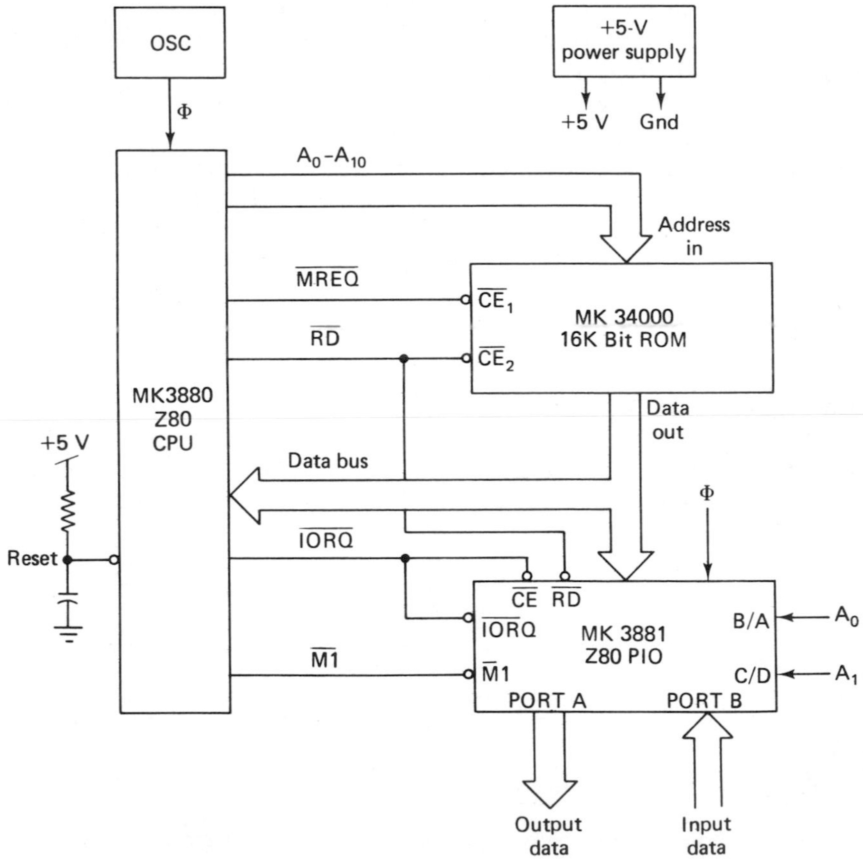

Figure 6-14 Minimum Z80 microcomputer system.

External memory. The external memory can be any mixture of standard RAM, ROM, or PROM. In this simple example, a single 16K ROM is used as the entire memory. The example assumes that the Z80 internal register configuration contains sufficient read/write storage so that external RAM memory is not required.

I/O circuits. In this simple example, it is assumed that the output is an 8-bit control word, and the input is an 8-bit status word. For example, the output could be a control word to an industrial process control (say that opens or closes a valve), with the input a word indicating the status of the process control system (say from a transducer that indicates the flow controlled by the valve). In a practical application, the input could be gated onto the data bus using any standard three-state driver. The output could be latched with any type of standard TTL latch. As shown in Fig. 6-14, the minimum system uses the PIO (Sec. 6-2) for the I/O circuit. The PIO attaches to the data bus as shown and provides the required 16 bits of I/O.

6-9-2 Adding RAM to the system

Most computer systems require some amount of external RAM for data storage and to implement a stack. Figure 6-15 illustrates how 256 bytes of static memory can be added to the basic circuit of 6-14. In the circuit of Fig. 6-15, memory space is organized as follows:

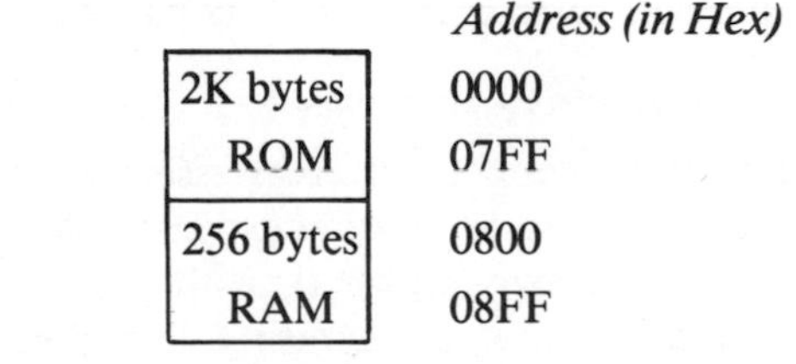

Memory	*Address (in Hex)*
2K bytes ROM	0000 – 07FF
256 bytes RAM	0800 – 08FF

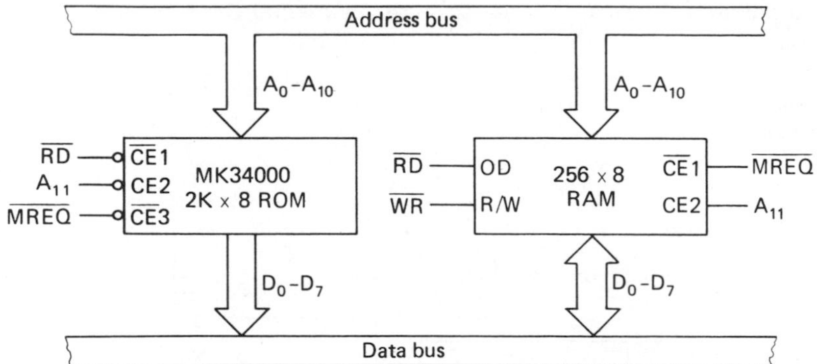

Figure 6-15 Adding 256 bytes of static memory to basic circuit.

6-10 SOFTWARE EXAMPLES

Several different approaches are possible in developing software for the Z80, as shown in Fig. 6-16. First, the assembly language (from the instruction set) can be used as the source language. Then the assembly language can be translated into machine language on a commercial time-sharing facility using a cross-assembler (Sec. 6-5-7), or the translation can be accomplished on the Z80 development system using a resident assembler (Sec. 6-5-5). Second, a high-level computer language such as PL/Z can be used as the source, and then translated into machine language on a cross-compiler. No matter what source language is used, the machine language program must be tested and debugged. This can be done on a time-sharing facility using the Z80 simulator or on a Z80 development system that uses a Z80 CPU directly.

6-10-1 Selecting a source language

The primary factors to be considered in selecting a source language are clarity and ease of programming versus code efficiency. Most high-level languages such as PL/Z are independent of machine language and are better for formulating and maintaining algorithms, but the resulting machine code is somewhat less efficient than what can be written directly in assembly language. These trade-offs can often be balanced by combining PL/Z and assembly language routines, identifying those portions of a task that must be optimized, and writing them as assembly language subroutines.

6-10-2 Resident versus cross-assembler

Deciding whether to use a resident or cross-assembler is a matter of availability and short-term versus long-term expense. While the initial expense for a development system is higher than that for a time-sharing terminal, the cost of an individual assembly using a resident assembler is negligible, while the same operation on a time-sharing system is relatively expensive, and, in a short time, this cost can equal the total cost of a development system.

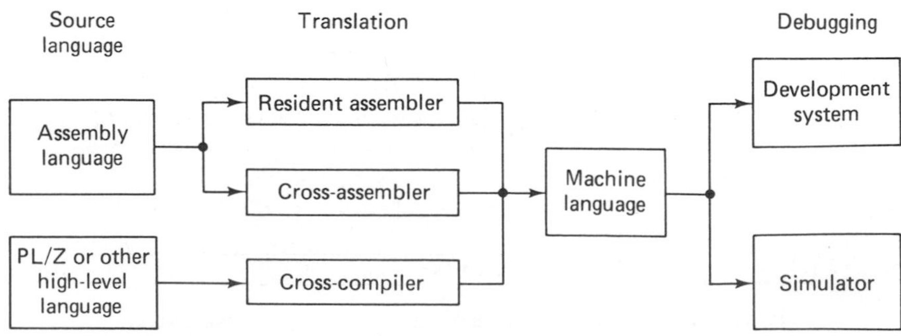

Figure 6-16 Different approaches in developing Z80 software.

6-10-3 Development system versus a simulator (for debugging)

Debugging on a development system versus a simulator is also a matter of availability and expense, combined with operational fidelity and flexibility. As with the assembly process, debugging is less expensive on a development system than on a simulator available through time sharing. Also, when the development system is used, the fidelity of the operating environment is preserved through real-time execution on a Z80 CPU, and by connecting the I/O and memory components that will actually be used in the production system.

The only advantage to the use of a simulator is the range of criteria that may be selected for such debugging procedures as program tracing and the setting of breakpoints. This flexibility exists because a software simulation can have any degree of complexity in its interpretation of machine instructions. On the other hand, development system procedures have hardware limitations such as the capacity of the real-time storage module, the number of breakpoint registers, and the pin configuration of the CPU. Despite such hardware limitations, debugging on a development system is typically more productive than on a simulator because of the direct interaction that is possible between the programmer and authentic execution of the program. In effect, if the program works on a development system using production-type components, the same program will work with actual production components.

6-10-4 Software features offered by the Z80 CPU

The Z80 instruction set provides the user with a large and flexible repertoire of operations with which to formulate control of the CPU. The following are some examples.

The primary, auxiliary, and index registers can be used to hold the arguments of the arithmetic and logical operations, or to form memory addresses, or as fast-acting storage of frequently used data.

Information can be moved directly from register to register, from memory to memory, from memory to registers, or from registers to memory. Also, register contents and register/memory contents can be exchanged without using temporary storage. In particular, the contents of primary and auxiliary registers can be completely exchanged by executing only two instructions, EX and EXX. This register exchange procedure can be used to separate the set of working registers between different logical procedures or to expand the set of available registers in a single procedure.

Storage and retrieval of data between pairs registers and memory can be controlled on a last-in/first-out basis through PUSH and POP instructions that use a special stack pointer register SP (Fig. 6-2). This stack register is available both to manipulate data and to automatically store and retrieve addresses for subroutine linkage. When a subroutine is called, for example, the address following the CALL instruction is placed on the top of the push-down stack pointed to by SP. When a subroutine returns to the calling routine, the address on the top of the stack is used to set the program counter for the address of the next instruction. The stack pointer is adjusted automatically to reflect the current "top" stack position during PUSH, POP, CALL, and RET instructions. This stack mechanism allows push-down data stacks and subroutine calls to be nested to any practical depth because the stack area can potentially be as large as memory space.

The sequence of instruction execution can be controlled by six different flags [carry, zero, sign, parity/overflow, add-subtract, half-carry (Sec. 6-7)] that reflect the results of arithmetic, logical, shift, and compare instructions. After the execution of an instruction that sets a flag, the flag can be used to control a conditional jump or return instruction. These instructions provide logical control following the manipulation of single-bit, 8-bit, or 16-bit data quantities.

A full set of logical operations, including AND, OR, XOR (EXCLUSIVE OR), CPL (NOR), and NEG (two's complement) are available for Boolean operations between the accumulator and (1) all other 8-bit registers, (2) memory locations, or (3) immediate operands.

In addition, a full set of arithmetic and logical shifts in both directions is available. These shifts operate on the contents of all 8-bit primary registers or directly on any memory location. The carry flag can be included or simply set by these shift instructions to provide both the testing or shift results and to link register/register or register/memory shift operations.

6-10-5 Examples of using special Z80 instructions

Let us assume that a string of data in memory starting at location "DATA" is to be moved into another area of memory starting at location "BUFFER," and that the string length (length of program bytes) is 737 bytes. This operation can be accomplished as follows:

```
LD    HL  ,DATA    ;START ADDRESS OF DATA STRING
LD    DE  ,BUFFER  ;START ADDRESS OF TARGET BUFFER
LD    BC  ,737     ;LENGTH OF DATA STRING
LDIR               ;MOVE STRING—TRANSFER MEMORY
                    POINTED TO
                   ;BY HL INTO MEMORY LOCATION
                    POINTED TO BY DE
                   ;INCREMENT HL AND DE,
                    DECREMENT BC
                   ;PROCESS UNTIL BC = 0.
```

Eleven bytes are required for this operation, and each byte of data is moved in 21 clock cycles.

Now let us assume that a string in memory starting at location "DATA" is to be moved into another area of memory starting at location "BUFFER" until an ASCII $ character is found. (In this case the ASCII $ character is known as a *string delimiter,* which is a symbol, character, and so on, used to set the limits of a string of program bytes.) Also, assume that the maximum string length is 132 characters. The operation can be performed as follows:

```
       LD   HL,DATA     ;STARTING ADDRESS OF DATA
                         STRING
       LD   DE,BUFFER   ;STARTING ADDRESS OF TARGET
                         BUFFER
       LD   BC,132      ;MAXIMUM STRING LENGTH
       LD   A,"$"       ;STRING DELIMITER CODE
  LOOP:CP   (HL)        ;COMPARE MEMORY CONTENTS
                         WITH DELIMITER
       JR   Z,END—$     ;GO TO END IF CHARACTERS EQUAL
       LDI              ;MOVE CHARACTER (HL) TO (DE)
                        ;INCREMENT HL AND DE,
                         DECREMENT BC
       JP   PE,LOOP     ;GO TO "LOOP" IF MORE
                         CHARACTERS
  END:                  ;OTHERWISE, FALL THROUGH
                        ;NOTE: P/V FLAG IS USED
                        ;TO INDICATE THAT REGISTER BC
                         WAS
                        ;DECREMENTED TO ZERO.
```

Nineteen bytes are required for this operation.

7 Texas Instruments TMS 9900 16-Bit Microprocessor Family

This chapter is devoted entirely to the TMS9900 16-bit microprocessor family, manufactured by Texas Instruments Incorporated. The chapter starts with a discussion of basic microprocessor architecture and the instruction set, then proceeds to a brief description of support circuits and hardware. This is followed by a summary of the prototyping system and available software. The chapter concludes with a description of system hardware design examples (minimum and maximum systems), and an input/output interface example (including hardware program listing).

The details presented in this chapter represent only a small fraction of the data taken from the manufacturer's literature (manuals and data sheets). However, the information presented is sufficient for a reader of any level to evaluate the system. The chapter also provides a realistic view of actual state-of-the-art microprocessor-based systems. This supplements the theoretical and typical descriptions of Chapters 1 and 2.

7-1 16-BIT WORD LENGTH

The TMS9900 microprocessor is a 16-bit central processing unit (CPU) mounted within a 64-pin IC. Thus, unlike all the microprocessors described previously the TMS9900 is capable of working with 16-bit instruction words on a 16-bit data bus. Typically, the other microprocessors use up to 16 bits in the address bus and memory address, but the memory word length and data bus is 8 bits. In addition to the 16-bit instruction word length, the TMS9900 has the following key features:

1. Full minicomputer instruction set capability, including multiply and divide.
2. Up to 65,536 bytes of memory.
3. 3.3-MHz speed.
4. Advanced memory-to-memory architecture.
5. Separate memory, I/O, and interrupt-bus structures.
6. Sixteen general registers.
7. Sixteen prioritized interrupts.
8. Programmed and DMA I/O capability.

7-2 TMS9900 ARCHITECTURE

Figure 7-1 is a block diagram of the TMS9900 microprocessor. Figure 7-2 shows the relationship of 16-bit memory words and byte operands.

Each of the 16-bit memory words can also be defined as two bytes of 8 bits each. The instruction set for the TMS9900 allows both word and byte operands. Thus, all memory locations are on even-address boundaries, and byte instructions can address either the even or the odd byte. The memory space is 65,536 bytes, or 32,768 words, as shown in Fig. 7-2.

7-2-1 Registers and memory

The TMS9900 uses an advanced memory-to-memory architecture. Blocks of memory, designed as *workspace,* replace internal-hardware registers with program-data registers. The TMS9900 memory map is shown in Fig. 7-3. The first 32 words are used for interrupt vectors. The next contiguous block of 32 memory words is used by an extended operation (XOP) instruction for software trap vectors. The last two memory words, $FFFC_{16}$ and $FFFE_{16}$, are used for the vector of the LOAD signal. The remaining memory is then available for programs, data, and workspace

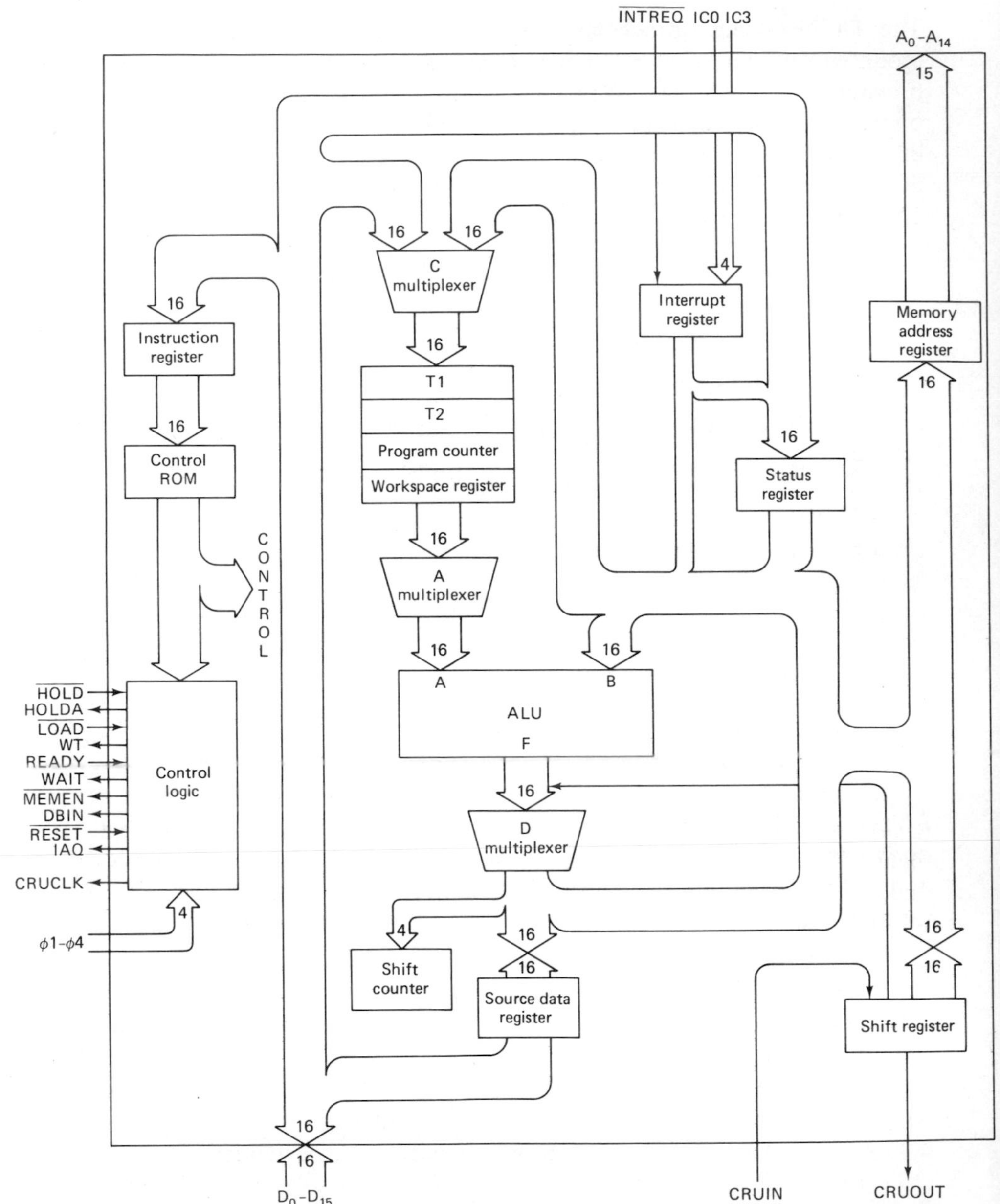

Figure 7-1 TMS9900 microprocessor, block diagram.

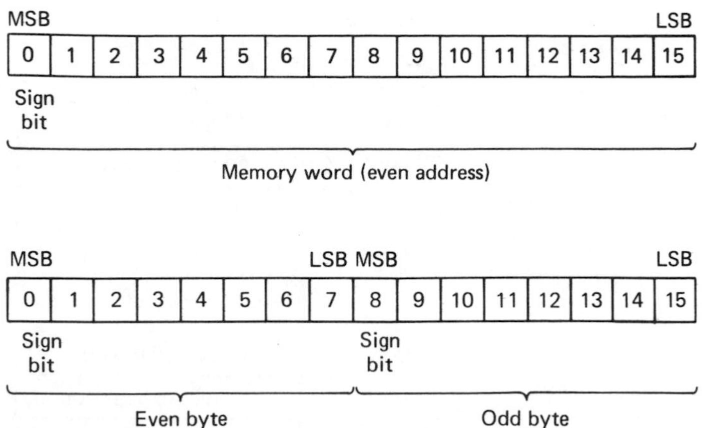

Figure 7-2 Relationship of 16-bit memory words and byte operands.

registers. If desired, any of the special areas may also be used as general memory.

Three internal registers are accessible to the user. The program counter (PC) contains the address of the instruction following the current instruction being executed. This address is referenced by the microprocessor to fetch the next instruction from memory and is then automatically incremented. The status register (ST) contains the present state of the microprocessor (and is discussed further in Sec. 7-3). The workspace pointer (WP) contains the address of the first word in the currently active set of workspace registers.

A workspace-register file can be set up to occupy 16 contiguous memory words in the general memory area (Fig. 7-3). Each workspace register may hold data or addresses and function as operand registers, accumulators, address registers, or index registers. During instruction execution, the microprocessor addresses any register in the workspace by adding the register number to the contents of the workspace pointer and initiating a memory request for the word. The relationship between the workspace pointer and its corresponding workspace is shown in Fig. 7-4.

Workspace concept. This workspace concept is particularly valuable during operations that require a *context switch,* which is a change from one program environment to another (as in the case of an interrupt) or to a subroutine. Such an operation, using a conventional multiregister arrangement, requires that at least part of the contents of the register file be stored and reloaded. A memory cycle is required to store or fetch each word. By exchanging the program counter, status register, and workspace pointer,

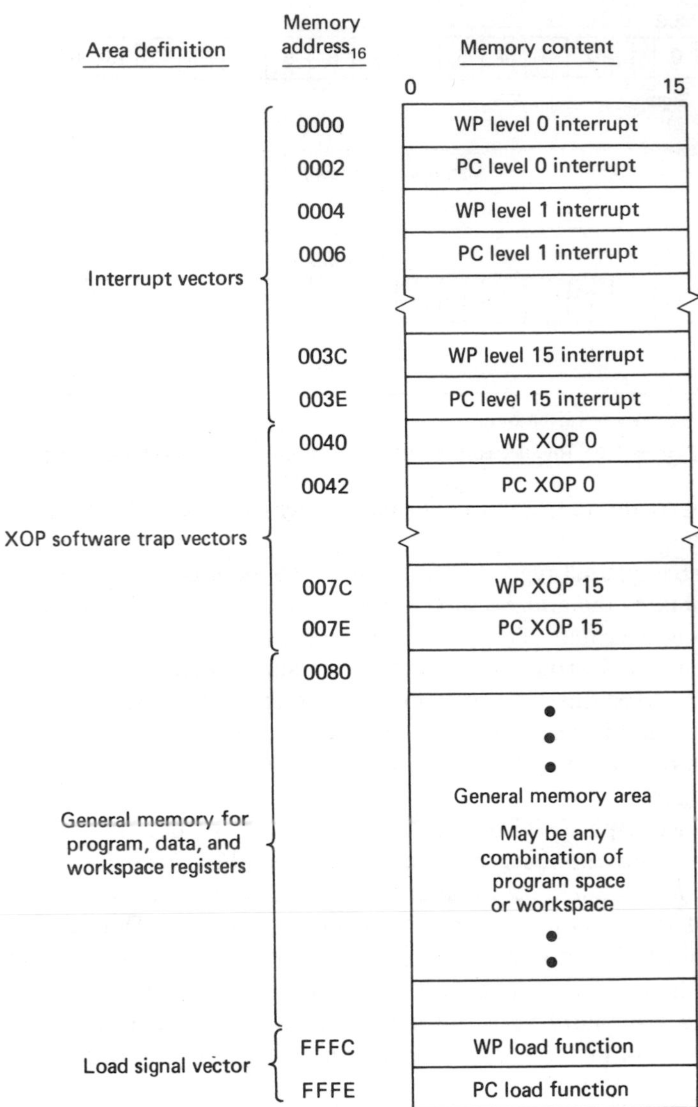

Figure 7-3 TMS9900 microprocessor, memory map.

the TMS9900 accomplishes a complete context switch with only three store cycles and three fetch cycles. After the switch, the workspace pointer contains the starting address of a new 16-word workspace in memory for use in the new routine. A corresponding time saving occurs when the original context is restored. Instructions in the TMS9900 that result in a context switch include:

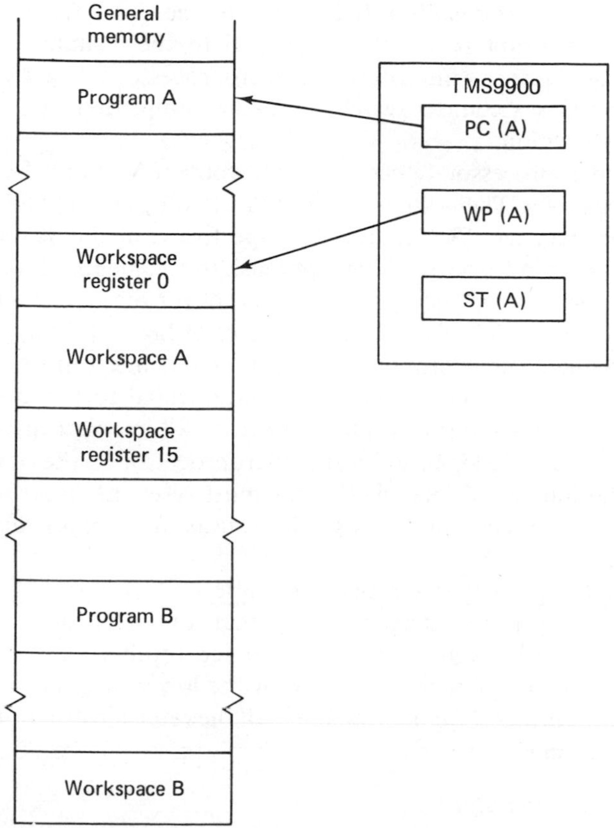

Figure 7-4 Relationship between the workspace pointer and the corresponding workspace.

1. Branch and load workspace pointer (BLWP).
2. Return from subroutine (RTWP).
3. Extended operation (XOP).

Device interrupts, $\overline{\text{RESET}}$, and $\overline{\text{LOAD}}$ also cause a context switch.

7-2-2 Interrupts

The TMS9900 uses 16 interrupt levels, with the highest priority level 0 and the lowest level 15 (see Fig. 7-4). Level 0 is reserved for the $\overline{\text{RESET}}$ function, and all other levels may be used for external devices. The external levels may also be shared by several device interrupts, depending upon system requirements.

The TMS9900 continuously compares the interrupt code (IC0 through IC3) with the interrupt mask contained in status register bits 12 through

15. (The status register is discussed further in Sec. 7-3.) When the level of the pending interrupt is less than or equal to the enabling masks level (higher or equal priority interrupt), the microprocessor recognizes the interrupt and initiates a context switch following completion of the currently executing instruction.

The microprocessor fetches the new context WP and PC from the interrupt locations. Then, the previous context WP, PC, and ST are stored in workspace registers 13, 14, and 15, respectively, of the new workspace. The TMS9900 then forces the interrupt mask to a value that is *one less* than the level of the interrupt being serviced, except for the zero-level interrupt, which loads a zero. This allows only interrupts of higher priority to interrupt a service routine. The microprocessor also inhibits interrupts until the first instruction of the service routine has been executed to preserve program linkage should a higher-priority interrupt occur. All interrupt requests should remain active until recognized by the microprocessor in the device-service routine. The individual service routines must reset the interrupt requests before the routine is complete. (A service routine for a paper-tape interface is discussed in Sec. 7-8.)

If a higher-priority interrupt occurs, a second context switch occurs to serve the higher-priority interrupt. When that routine is complete, a return instruction (RTWP) restores the first service routine parameters to the microprocessor to complete processing of the lower-priority interrupt. All interrupt subroutines should terminate with the return instruction to restore original program parameters.

7-2-3 Input/output

The TMS9900 uses a versatile direct command-driver I/O interface designed as the communications-register unit (CRU). The paper-tape interface discussed in Sec. 7-8 uses the CRU. Up to 4096 directly addressable input bits and 4096 directly addressable output bits are provided by the CRU. Both input and output bits can be addressed individually or in fields of from 1 to 16 bits. The TMS9900 uses three dedicated I/O pins (CRUIN, CRUOUT, and CRUCLK) and 12 bits (A3 through A14) of the address bus to interface with the CRU system. The processor instructions that drive the CRU interface can set, reset, or test any bit in the CRU array or move between memory and CRU data fields.

7-2-4 Single-bit CRU operations

The TMS9900 performs three single-bit CRU functions: test bit (TB), set bit to 1 (SBO), and set bit to 0 (SBZ). To identify the bit to be operated upon, the TMS9900 develops a CRU-bit address and places it on the address bus, A3 to A14. Figure 7-5 illustrates development of a single-bit CRU address.

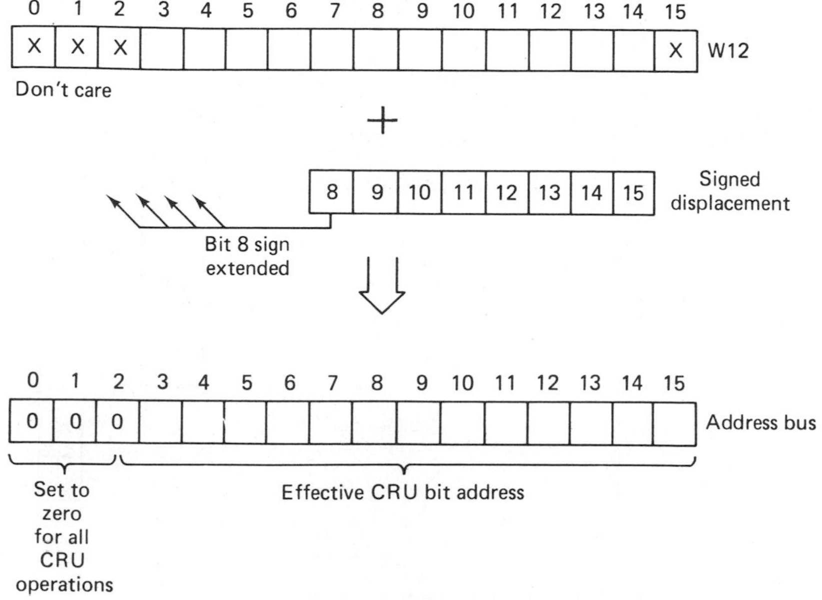

Figure 7-5 TMS9900 single-bit CPU address development.

For the two output operations (SBO and SBZ), the microprocessor also generates a CRUCLK pulse, indicating an output operation to the CRU device, and places bit 7 of the instruction word on the CRUOUT line to accomplish the specified operation (bit 7 is a 1 for SBO and a 0 for SBZ). A test-bit instruction transfers the addressed CRU bit from the CRUIN input line to bit 2 of the status register (EQUAL).

The TMS9900 develops a CRU-bit address for the single-bit operations from the CRU-base address contained in workspace register 12 (as shown in Fig. 7-5) and the signed displacement count contained in bits 8 through 15 of the instruction. The displacement allows two's-complement addressing from base minus 128 bits through base plus 127 bits. The base address from W 12 is added to the signed displacement specified in the instruction and the result loaded onto the address bus.

7-2-5 Multiple-bit CRU operations

The TMS9900 performs two multiple-bit CRU operations: store communications register (STCR) and load communications register (LDRC). Both operations perform a data transfer from the CRU to memory or from memory to CRU, as shown in Fig. 7-6. Although the figure illustrates a full 16-bit transfer operation, any number of bits from 1 through 16 may be involved. The LDCR instruction fetches a word from memory and right-shifts it to serially transfer it to CRU output bits. If the LDCR involves 8

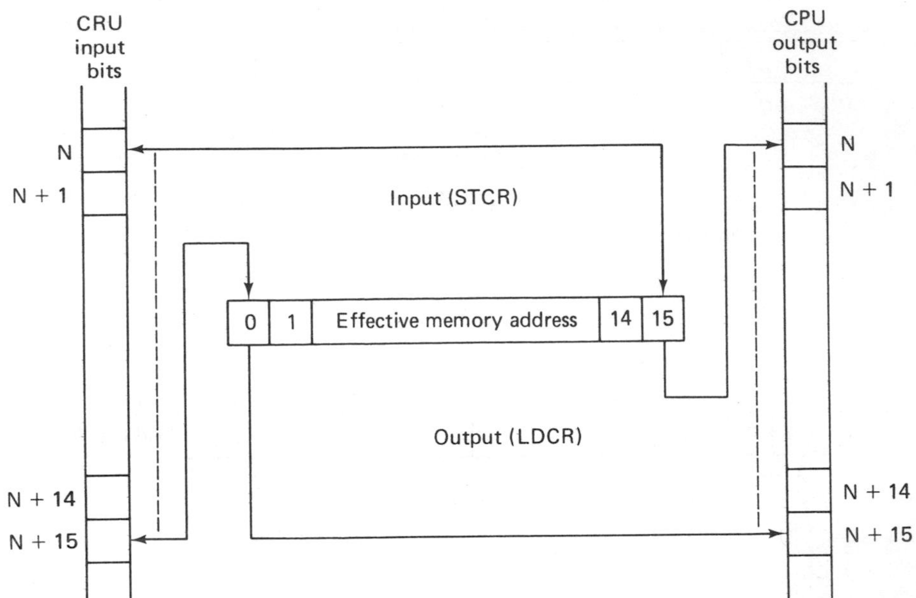

Figure 7-6 TMS9900 LDCR/STCR data transfers.

or fewer bits, those bits come from the right-hand field within the *addressed byte* of the memory word. If the LDCR involves 9 or more bits, those bits come from the right-hand field within the whole memory word. When transferred to the CRU interface, each successive bit receives an address that is sequentially greater than the address for the previous bit. This addressing mechanism results in an order reversal of the bits; that is, bit 15 of the memory word (or bit 7) becomes the lowest addressed bit in the CRU and bit 0 becomes the highest addressed bit in the CRU field.

An STCR instruction transfers data from the CRU to memory. If the operation involves a byte (or less) transfer, the transferred data will be stored on the right-hand side of the *memory byte,* with the leading bits set to zero. If the operation involves from 9 to 16 bits, the transferred data are stored in the *memory word,* with the leading bits set to zero. When the input from the CRU device is complete, the first bit from the CRU is the least-significant-bit position in the memory word or byte.

7-2-6 Flowchart

The flowchart showing the sequence of TMS9900 functions is illustrated in Fig. 7-7.

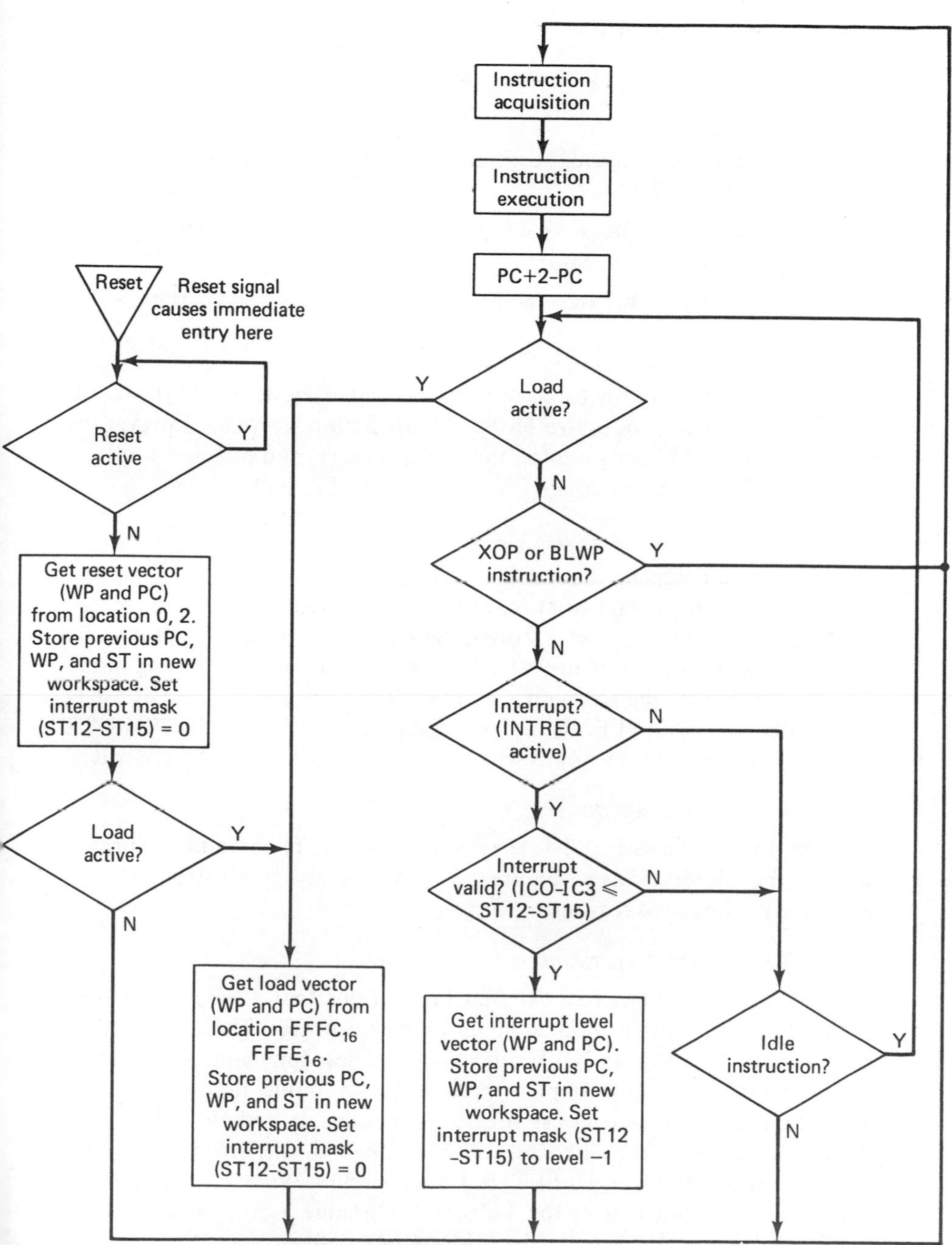

Figure 7-7 TMS9900 microprocessor, flowchart.

7-3 INSTRUCTION SET

Each of the 69 TMS9900 instructions performs one of the following operations:

1. Arithmetic, logical, comparison, or manipulation operations on data.
2. Loading or storage of internal registers (program counter, workspace pointer, or status).
3. Data transfer between memory and external devices via the CRU.
4. Control functions.

As in the case of other microprocessor systems described in this book, we will not duplicate the entire TMS9900 instruction set here. However, we will discuss the addressing modes, the status register, and one set of instructions (the external instructions).

7-3-1 Addressing modes

TMS9900 instructions contain a variety of available modes for addressing random-memory data (that is, program parameters and flags), or formatted memory data (character strings, data lists, etc.). Figure 7-8 graphically describes the derivation of the effective address for each addressing mode. The symbols following the names of the addressing modes (R, *R, *R+, @LABEL, or @TABLE R) are the general forms used by TMS9900 assemblers (Secs. 7-5 and 7-6) to select the addressing mode for register R.

7-3-2 Status register

As discussed in Sec. 7-2-1, the status register (ST) contains the present state of the microprocessor. Figure 7-9 shows the specific instruction state indicated by the status register.

7-3-3 External instructions

The TMS9900 has five external instructions that allow user-defined external functions to be initiated under program control. These instructions are CKN, CKOF, RSET, IDLE, and LREX. These mnemonics, except for IDLE, relate to functions implemented in the 990 minicomputer (Secs. 7-5 and 7-6) and do not restrict use of the instructions to initiate various user-defined functions. IDLE also causes the TMS9900 to enter the idle state and remain until an interrupt, $\overline{\text{RESET}}$, or $\overline{\text{LOAD}}$ occurs. When any of these five instructions are executed by the TMS9900, a unique 3-bit code appears on the most-significant 3 bits of the address bus (A0 through A2), together with a CRUCLK pulse. When the TMS9900 is in an idle state, the 3-bit code and CRUCLK pulses occur repeatedly until the idle state is terminated. Figure 7-10 shows the mnemonic, op code, meaning, status bits affected, description, and address bus code for each of the external instructions.

Workspace register addressing R

Workspace register R contains the operand

Workspace register indirect addressing *R

Workspace register R contrins the address of the operand.

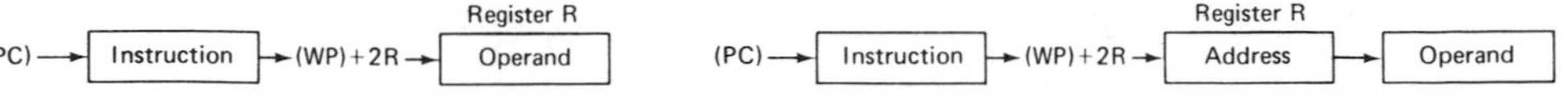

Workspace register indirect auto increment addressing *R+

Workspace register R contains the address of the operand. After acquiring the operand, the contents of workspace register R are incremented.

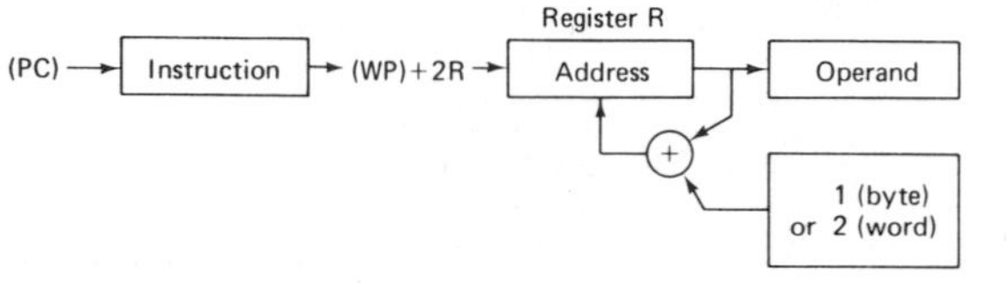

Symbolic (direct) addressing @ label

The word following the instruction contains the address of the operand.

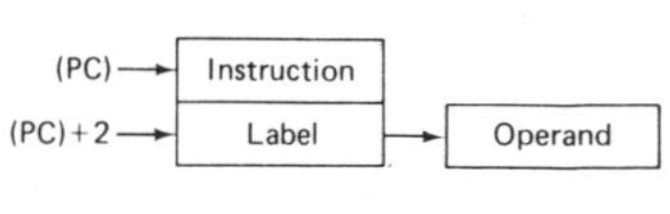

Indexed addressing @ table (R)

The word following the instruction contains the base address. Workspace register R contains the index value. The sum of the base address and the index value results in the effective address of the operand.

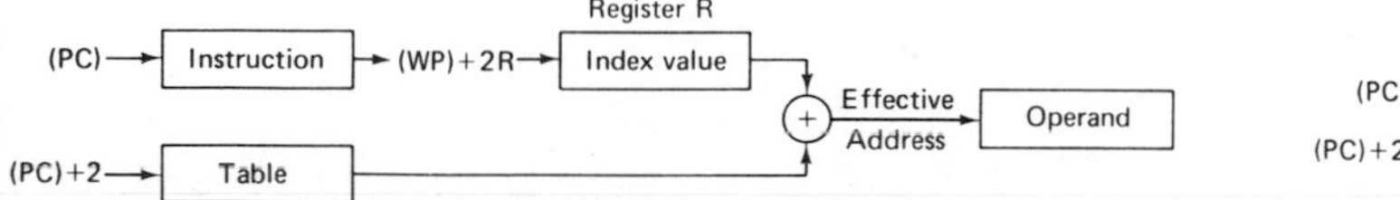

Immediate addressing

The word following the instruction contains the operand.

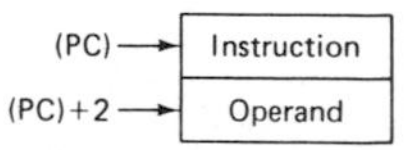

Program counter relative addressing

The 8-bit signed displacement in the right byte (bits 8 through 15) of the instruction is multiplied by 2 and added to the updated contents of the program counter. The result is placed in the PC'

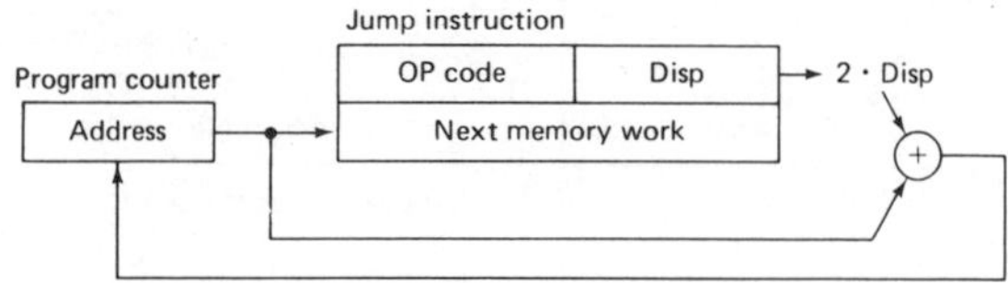

CRU relative addressing

The 8-bit signed displacement in the right byte of the instruction is added to the CRU base address (bits 3 through 14 of the workspace register 12). The result is the CRU address of the selected CRU bit.

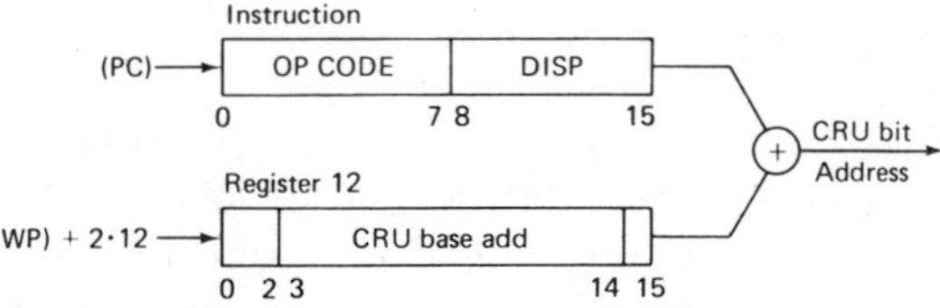

Figure 7-8 Derivation of the effective address for each addressing mode.

0	1	2	3	4	5	6	7	8	9	10	11	12	13	14	15
ST0 L>	ST1 A>	ST2 =	ST3 C	ST4 O	ST5 P	ST6 X	Not used (=0)					ST12 ST13 ST14 ST15 Interrupt Mask			

BIT	NAME	INSTRUCTION	CONDITION TO SET BIT TO 1
ST0	LOGICAL GREATER THAN	C,CB C1 ABS All others	If MSB(SA) = 1 and MSB(DA) = 0, or if MSB(SA) = MSB(DA) and MSB of [(DA)-(SA)] = 1 If MSB(W) = 1 and MSB of IOP = 0, or if MSB(W) = MSB of IOP and MSB of [IOP-(W)] = 1 If (SA) ≠ 0 If result ≠ 0
ST1	ARITHMETIC GREATER THAN	C,CB C1 ABS All others	If MSB(SA) = 0 and MSB(DA) = 1, or if MSB(SA) = MSB(DA) and MSB of [(DA)-(SA)] = 1 If MSB(W) = 0 and MSB of IOP = 1, or if MSB(W) = MSB of IOP and MSB of [IOP-(W)] = 1 If MSB(SA) = 0 and (SA) ≠ 0 If MSB of result = 0 and result ≠ 0

ST2	EQUAL	C,CB
		C1
		COC
		CZC
		TB
		ABS
		All others
			If (SA) = (DA)
			If (W) = IOP
			If (SA) and $\overline{(DA)}$ = 0
			If (SA) and (DA) = 0
			If CRUIN = 1
			If (SA) = 0
			If result = 0

ST3	CARRY	A, AB, ABS, A1, DEC DECT, INC, INCT, NEG, S, SB SLA, SRA, SRC, SRL	If CARRY OUT = 1 If last bit shifted out = 1
ST4	OVERFLOW	A, AB A1 S, SB DEC, DECT INC, INCT SLA DIV ABS, NEG	If MSB(SA) = MSB(DA) and MSB of result ≠ MSB(DA) If MSB(W) = MSB of IOP and MSB of result ≠ MSB(W) If MSB(SA) ≠ MSB(DA) and MSB of result ≠ MSB(DA) If MSB(SA) = 1 and MSB of result = 0 If MSB(SA) = 0 and MSB of result = 1 If MSB changes during shift If MSB(SA) = 0 and MSB(DA) = 1, or if MSB(SA) = MSB(DA) and MSB of [(DA)-(SA)] = 0 If (SA) = 8000_{16}
ST5	PARITY	CB, MOVB LDCR, STCR AB, SB, SOCB, SZCB	If (SA) has odd number of 1's If 1 < C < 8 and (SA) has odd number of 1's If result has odd number of 1's
ST6	XOP	XOP	If XOP instruction is executed
ST12-ST15	INTERRUPT MASK	LIMI RTWP	If corresponding bit of IOP is 1 If corresponding bit of WR15 is 1

Figure 7-9 Specific instruction state indicated by the status register.

7-4 SUPPORT CIRCUITS

The TMS9900 is provided with a wide variety of support circuits and devices, including RAMs, ROMs, PROMs, and peripherals. The peripherals include a programmable system interface (PSI), asynchronous communication controller (ACC), synchronous communications controller (SCC), clock generator, data multiplexer, addressable latch, priority encoder,

	0	1	2	3	4	5	6	7	8	9	10	11	12	13	14	15
General format:	OP CODE											N				

External instructions cause the three most-significant address lines (A0 through A2) to be set to the below-described levels and the CRUCLK line to be pulsed, allowing external control functions to be initiated.

MNEMONIC	OP CODE 0 1 2 3 4 5 6 7 8 9 10	MEANING	STATUS BITS AFFECTED	DESCRIPTION	ADDRESS BUS A0	A1	A2
IDLE	0 0 0 0 0 0 0 1 1 0 1 0	Idle		Suspend TMS 9900 instruction execution until an interrupt, $\overline{\text{LOAD}}$, or $\overline{\text{RESET}}$ occurs	L	H	L
RSET	0 0 0 0 0 0 0 1 1 0 1 1	Reset	12–15	0 → ST12 thru ST15	L	H	H
CKOF	0 0 0 0 0 0 0 1 1 1 1 0	User defined		---	H	H	L
CKON	0 0 0 0 0 0 0 1 1 1 0 1	User defined		---	H	L	H
LREX	0 0 0 0 0 0 0 1 1 1 1 1	User defined		---	H	H	H

Figure 7-10 TMS9900 external instructions.

80-bit I/O port 3 to 8 decoder, and bidirectional bus driver. These circuits and devices are described fully in the user literature. The following paragraphs provide a brief description of the three most-significant peripherals.

7-4-1 TMS9901 Programmable Systems Interface (PSI)

Figure 7-11 shows the PSI, which is a multifunctioned component designed to provide low-cost interrupts and I/O ports in a 9900 microprocessor system. The PSI interfaces to the TMS9900 CPU though the CRU circuits (that are part of the PSI), and the interrupt control lines, as shown in Fig. 7-12. The CRU interface consists of five address select lines (S0–S4), chip enable ($\overline{\text{CE}}$), and three CRU lines (CRUIN, CRUOUT, CRUCLK). When $\overline{\text{CE}}$ becomes active (low or 0), the five select lines point to the CRU bit being accessed. In the case of a write, the data bit is strobed off the CRUOUT line by the CRUCLK signal. For a read, the data bit is sent to the CPU on the CRUIN line.

The interrupt control lines consist of an interrupt request line ($\overline{\text{INTREQ}}$) and four code lines (IC0–IC3). The interrupt section of the TMS9901 prioritizes and encodes the highest priority active interrupt into the proper code to present to the CPU, and outputs this code on the IC0–IC3 code lines together with an active INTREQ. Several TMS9901s can be used with the CPU by connecting all CRU and address lines in parallel and providing a unique chip select to each device.

The system interface consists of 22 pins, divided into three groups. The six pins in group 1 ($\overline{\text{INT1}}$–$\overline{\text{INT6}}$) are normally dedicated to interrupt inputs (active low or 0) but may also be used as input ports (true data in). Group 2 ($\overline{\text{INT7}}$/P15–$\overline{\text{INT15}}$/P7) consists of nine pins which can be individually programmed as interrupt ports (active low or 0), input ports (true data in), or output ports (true data out). The remaining seven pins that comprise group 3 (P0–P6) are dedicated as individually programmable I/O ports (true data).

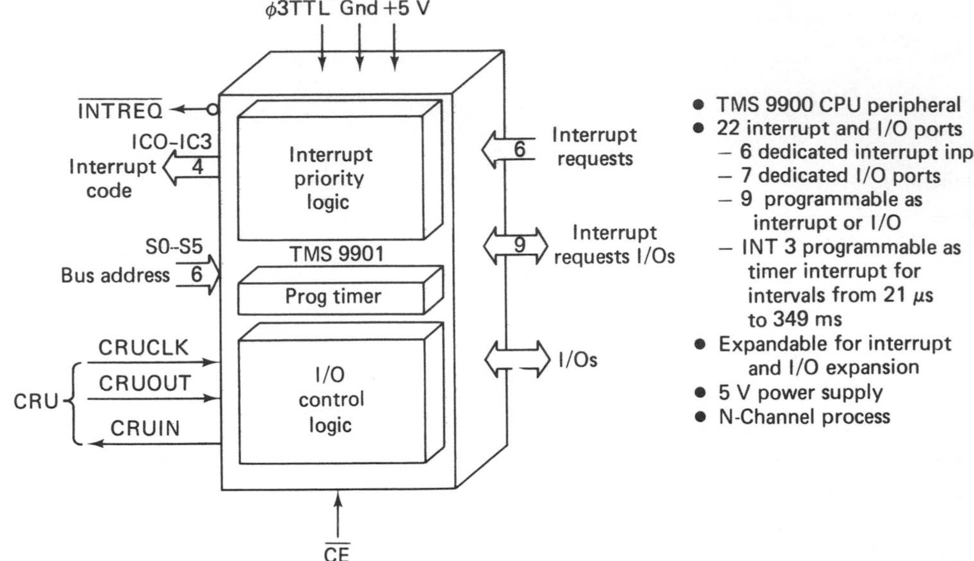

Figure 7-11 TMS9901 programmable systems interface (PSI).

7-4-2 TMS9902 Asynchronous Communication Controller (ACC)

Figure 7-13 shows the ACC, which is a peripheral device for the TMS9900 family of microprocessors. (The TMS9902 is sometimes referred to as a UART, or universal asynchronous receiver transmitter, in the manufacturer's literature.) The ACC provides an interface between the microprocessor and a serial asynchronous communication channel, performing the timing and data serialization and deserialization, thus facilitating control of the asynchronous channel by the microprocessor.

The relationship of the ACC to other components in the system is shown in Fig. 7-14. The ACC is connected to the asynchronous channel through level shifters that translate the TTL inputs and outputs to the appropriate levels. The microprocessor transfers data to and from the ACC via the CRU circuits that are part of the ACC. The CRU interface consists of five address-select lines (S0-S4), chip enable ($\overline{CE}$), and three CRU control lines (CRUIN, CRUOUT, and CRUCLK). When $\overline{CE}$ becomes active (low or 0), the five select lines address the CRU bit being accessed. When data bytes are being transferred to the ACC from the CPU, CRUOUT contains the valid data bit which is strobed by CRUCLK. When ACC data bytes are being read, CRUIN is the data bit output by the ACC.

The interface to the asynchronous communication channel consists of an output control line ($\overline{RTS}$), two input status lines ($\overline{DSR}$ and $\overline{CTS}$), and serial transmit (XOUT) and receive (RIN) data lines. The request-to-send

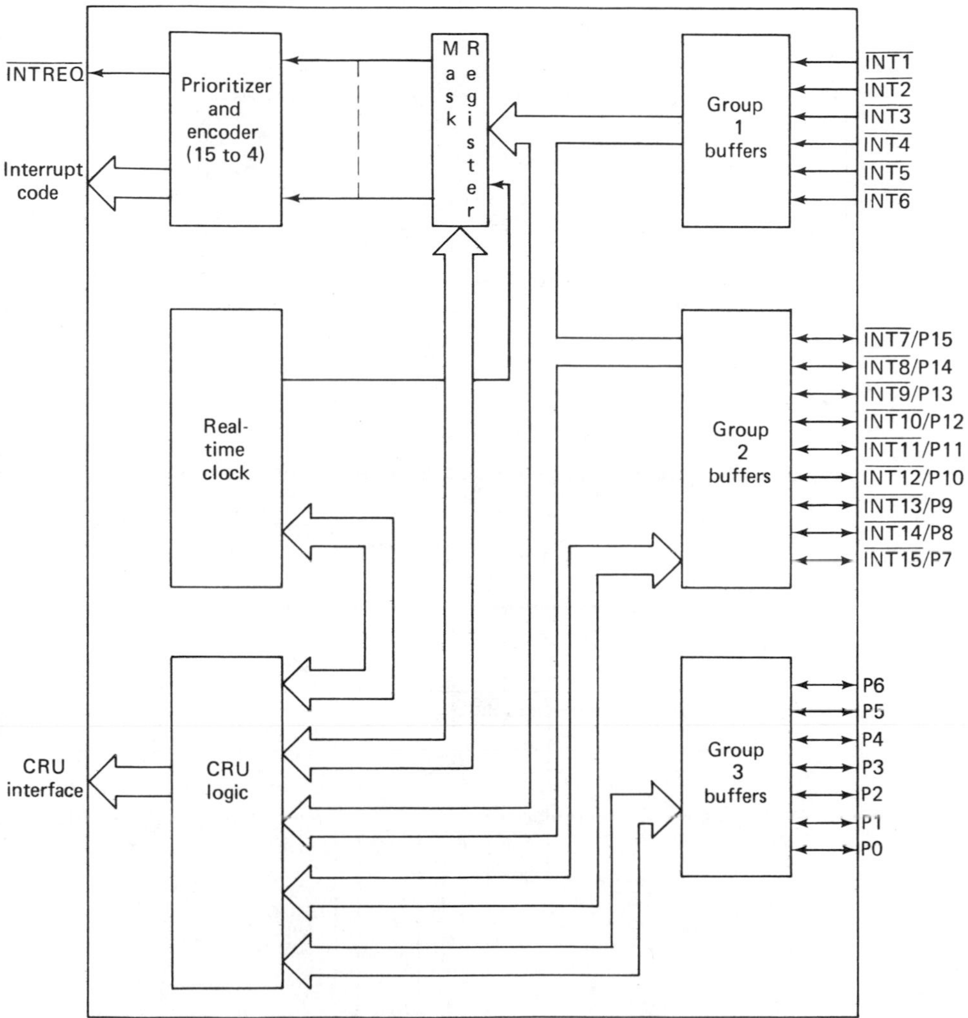

Figure 7-12 TMS9901 PSI, block diagram.

line (RTS) is active (low or 0) whenever the transmitter is activated. However, before data transmission begins, the clear-to-send ($\overline{\text{CTS}}$) input must be active. The data set ready ($\overline{\text{DSR}}$) input does not affect the receiver or transmitter. When $\overline{\text{DSR}}$ or $\overline{\text{CTS}}$ changes level, an interrupt is generated.

7-4-3 TMS9903 Synchronous Communication Controller (SCC)

Figure 7-15 shows the SCC, which is a peripheral device for the TMS9900 family of microprocessors. (The TMS9903 is sometimes referred to as a USRT, or universal synchronous receiver transmitter, in the manu-

- TMS 9900 CPU peripheral
- Programmable data rates
  110 to 76,800 baud
- Programmable character length
  5–8 bits
  –1–1½–2 stop bits
  –odd-even-no parity
- On chip interval timer
  64 μs to 16,384 μs
- Single 5-V supply
- N-channel silicon gate process
- 18-pin 0.3 in dip

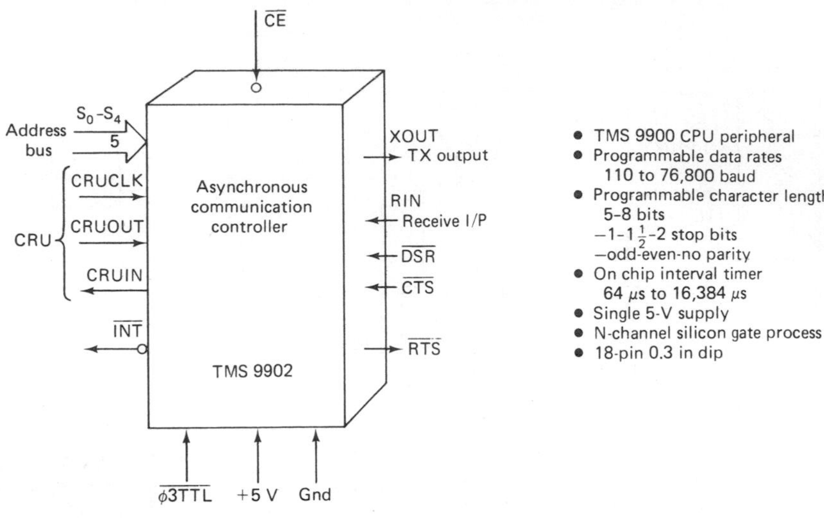

Figure 7-13 TMS9902 asynchronous communcations controller (ACC).

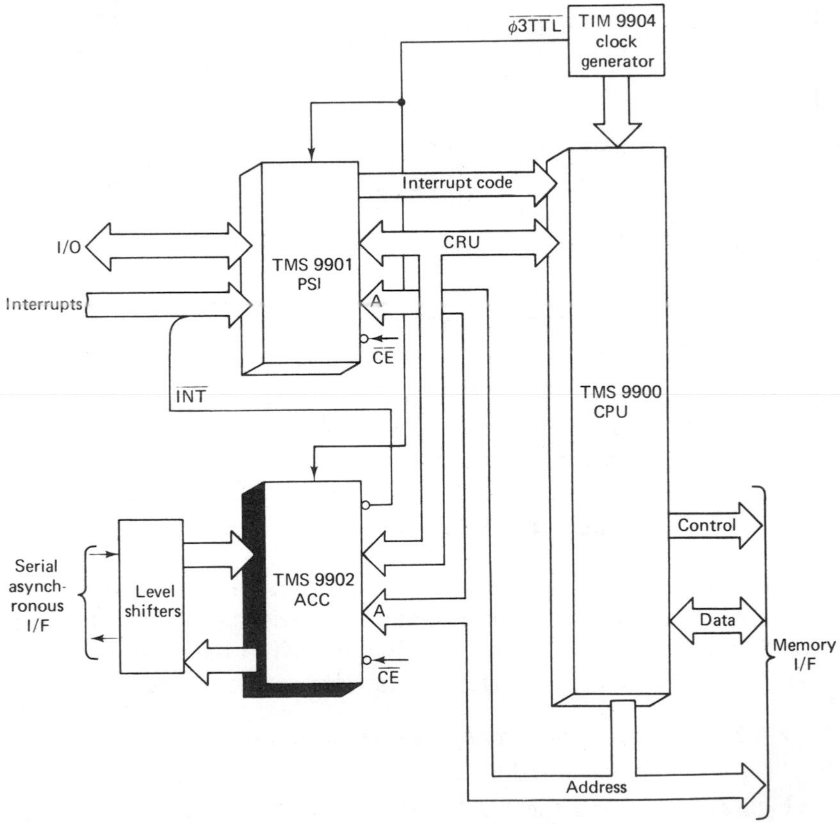

Figure 7-14 RMS9902 ACC in a TMS9900 system.

- TMS 9900 CRU peripheral
- DC to 250 K bits/sec
- Programmable sync. register and character length
- Bi-sync and SDLC compatible
- On chip interval timer 64 μs to 16,384 μs
- Single 5-V supply
- N channel silicon-gate process
- 20 pin 0.3 in dip

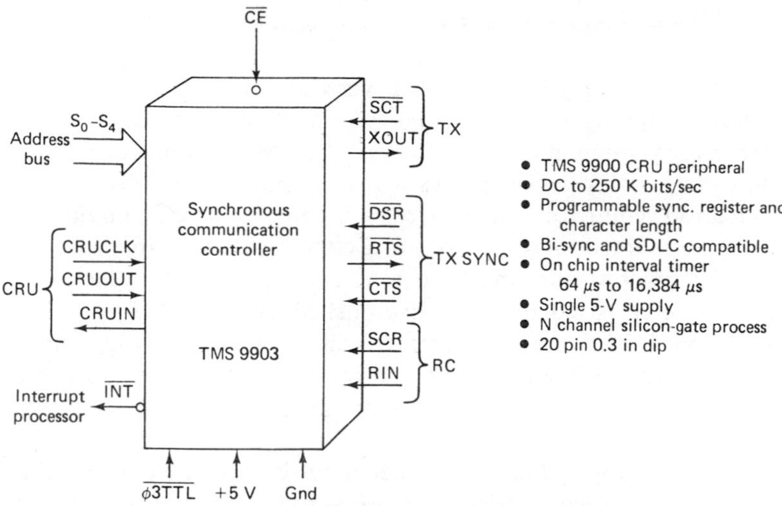

Figure 7-15 TMS9903 synchronous communications controller (SCC).

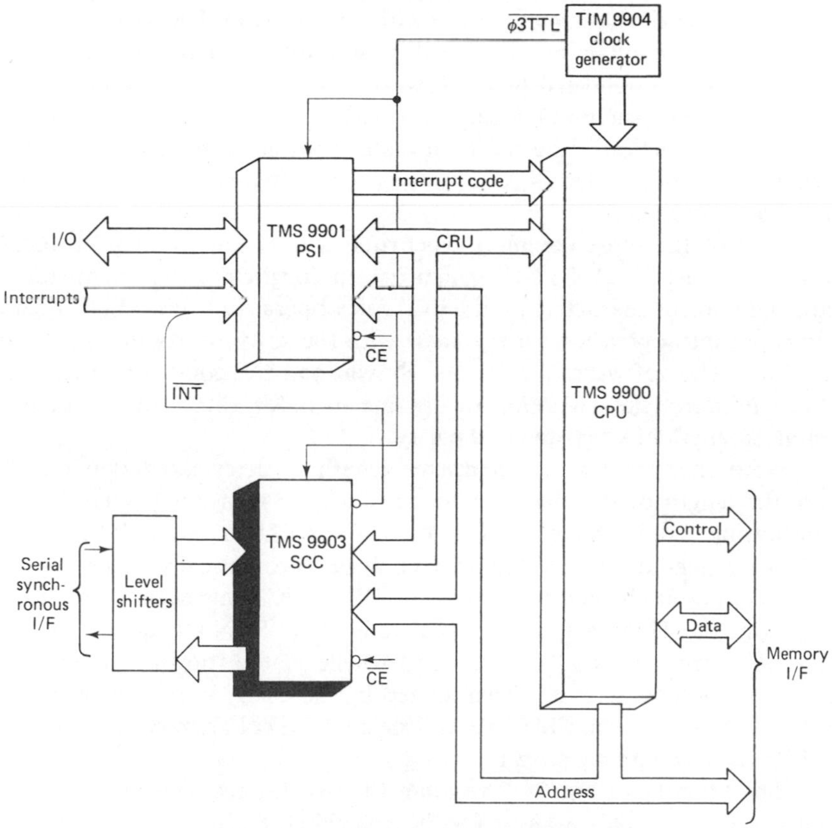

Figure 7-16 TMS9903 SCC in a TMS9900 system.

facturer's literature.) The SCC is a versatile device which provides the system designer with a wide range of capabilities in synchronous and asynchronous communications control. The TMS9903 operates in a multimode configuration which allows a broad range in the degree of active participation required in the control of high-speed serial communications. Most synchronous data-link control systems can be supported through software control of sync and fill characters, timing, CRC generation, and detection (refer to Chapter 2). Established systems such as BI-SYNC, SDLC, and HDLC are implemented directly in hardware, and others implemented through various combinations of hardware and software. The relationship of the SCC to other components in the system is shown in Fig. 7-16.

Universal applicability is further assured through the capability for dynamic character-length selection from 5- to 9-bit data words, plus parity. Definition and operation of all communications control is under software control and, as such, make upgrading to another data-link control system simply a matter of changing software with no hardware changes required.

The user manuals provide a full description of TMS9903 operation and will not be duplicated here. However, the following example should give a better appreciation of some of the TMS9903 capabilities. The example represents the actions required to initially configure the TMS9903 for a specific synchronous data-link control system (often referred to as a data-link control *protocol*).

One of the most common synchronous data-link control protocols presently in use is BY-SYNC, which uses a fixed-character-length set of data and control characters (and half-duplex operation). BY-SYNC operation is put into operation (or *invoked*) with the software routine shown in Fig. 7-17. The software instructions shown load the control register with bits to initialize the TMS9903 to operate in mode three with a received character length of seven and odd parity.

Note that transmitted character length is determined dynamically from the length of the character loaded into the transmit buffer. Hence, transmitting fixed 7-bit characters from the CPU to the TMS9903 with odd-parity generation selected and enabled automatically generates the fixed-length 8-bit characters required for BY-SYNC transmission. In normal operation, the TMS9903 will automatically insert SYN characters into the bit stream (from the SYNC 1 register) whenever the transmitter buffer is empty and no character has been loaded by the CPU. In receive operation with RYSNDL set, the TMS9903 will delete all SYN characters embedded in the received character stream.

The example of Fig. 7-17 assumes that workspace register 12 (WR12) contains the CRU base address for the TMS9903, RESET is the address of the control bit to reset the TMS9903, and the routines will be a part of the system power-up and reset routines.

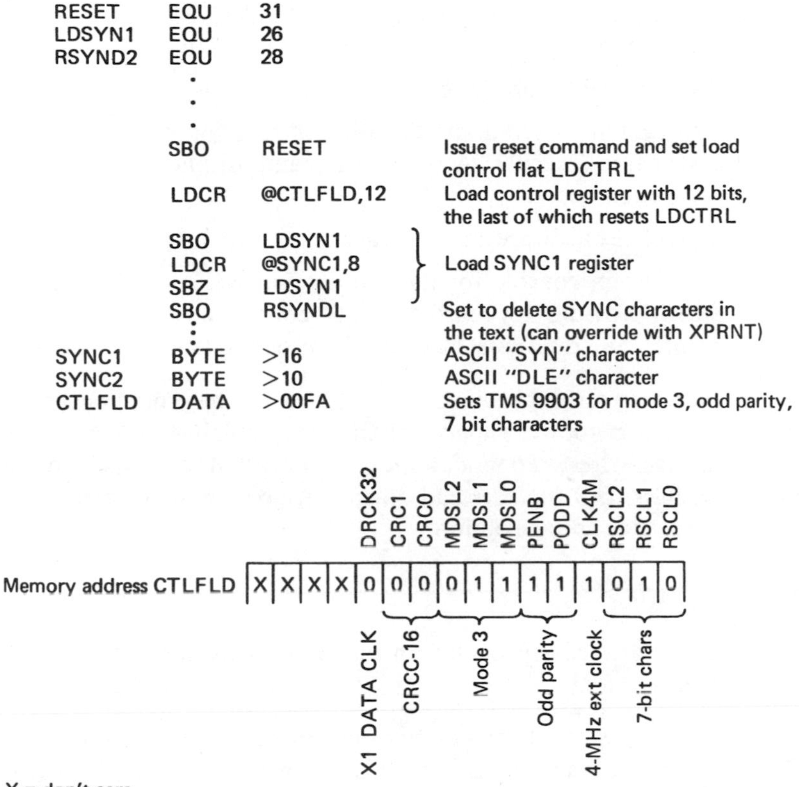

```
RESET    EQU    31
LDSYN1   EQU    26
RSYND2   EQU    28
         .
         .
         .
         SBO    RESET          Issue reset command and set load
                               control flat LDCTRL
         LDCR   @CTLFLD,12     Load control register with 12 bits,
                               the last of which resets LDCTRL
         SBO    LDSYN1       }
         LDCR   @SYNC1,8     } Load SYNC1 register
         SBZ    LDSYN1       }
         SBO    RSYNDL         Set to delete SYNC characters in
         .                     the text (can override with XPRNT)
         .
SYNC1    BYTE   >16            ASCII "SYN" character
SYNC2    BYTE   >10            ASCII "DLE" character
CTLFLD   DATA   >00FA          Sets TMS 9903 for mode 3, odd parity,
                               7 bit characters
```


Figure 7-17 Software routine for BY-SYNC operation.

7-5 PROTOTYPING SYSTEM

The TMS9900 prototyping system enables the user to generate and debug software and to debut I/O controller interfaces. The prototyping system consists of:

1. 990/4 computer with TMS9900 microprocessor.
2. 1024 bytes of ROM containing a loader for loading prototyping system software, a front-panel and maintenance utility, and a CPU self-testing feature.
3. 16,896 bytes of RAM with provisions for expansion up to 57,334 bytes of RAM.
4. Programmable-write-protect feature for RAM.
5. Interface for Texas Instruments Model 733 ASR electronic data terminal with provisions for up to five additional interface modules.

6. Available with Texas Instruments Model 733 ASR electronic data terminal.
7. 7-in-high table-top chassis.
8. Programmer's front panel with controls for run, halt, single-instruction execute, and entering and displaying memory or register contents.
9. Complete hardware and software.
10. The system console for the prototyping system is the 733 ASR, which provides keyboard entry, 30-character-per-second thermal printer, and dual cassette drives for program loading and storage.

The following optional equipment is offered for the prototyping system: battery-pack/standby-power supply, PROM programming unit and adapter boards, universal wire-wrap modules, expansion RAM modules, expansion EPROM modules, I/O modules and other interfaces, rack-mounted version, and international ac voltage option.

7-6 SOFTWARE

The following software is provided on cassettes for loading into the prototyping system:

1. *Debug monitor.* Provides full control of the prototyping system during program development and includes single instruction, multiple breakpoints, and entry and display capability for register and memory contents for debugging user software under 733 ASR console control.
2. *One-pass assembler.* Converts source code stored on cassette to relocatable object on cassette and generates program listing. (Object is compatible with other 990 series assemblers.)
3. *Linking loader.* Allows loading of absolute and relocatable object modules and links object modules as they are loaded.
4. *Source editor.* Enables user modification of both source and object from cassette with resultant storage on cassette.
5. *Trace routine.* Allows user to monitor status of computer at completion of each instruction.
6. *PROM programming/documentation facility.* Provides documentation for ROM mask generation, or communicates directly with the optional PROM programmer unit.

7-6-1 Overall software system flow and data files

The overall software system flow is shown in Fig. 7-18. The software data file system used is shown in Fig. 7-19.

The TMS9900 computer cross-support system consists of the cross-assembler and the TMS9900 simulator, which is designed to permit simulation of TMS9900 microprocessor programs. Both the simulator and cross-assembler are available on several separate nationwide commercial time-sharing services. The procedure to access the programs can be obtained from the various time-sharing services.

The *simulator loader* accepts as input one or more object modules produced by the cross-assembler. The object modules may contain relocatable and/or absolute object codes. Loader commands allow the user to specify an origin, to specify an entry point, to include an object module from the object library, or to create a file to be used by the manufacturing output utility program.

The *simulator control language* is used to control operation of the simulator. The user can specify at what memory location simulation is to begin and how many instructions are to be executed. The user can also display contents of register and memory, control and trace output, set breakpoints, and request other output to aid in debugging.

The job control language desk is used on an IBM System/370 at Texas Instruments for batch execution. Once the system has been implemented at the user's installation and a satisfactory job control deck has been created, only the source program deck and the control language deck need be changed.

As shown in Fig. 7-18, the user prepares a source program for the TMS9900 microprocessor in symbolic assembler language. The assembler

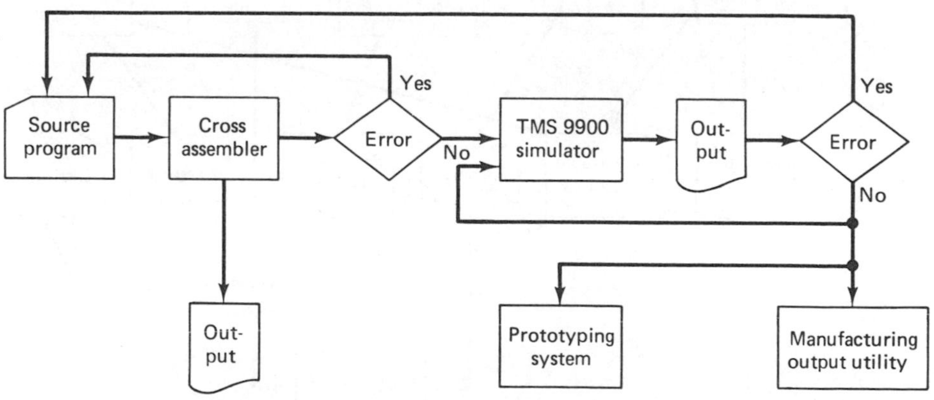

Figure 7-18 TMS9900 overall software system flow.

processes one or more source modules and produces one or more object modules. After the errors indicated by the assembler are corrected, the microprocessor program can be executed on the simulator. The simulator reads the object programs and control program and produces an instruction level trace and other outputs as directed by the control language program. After this output is analyzed by the user for possible program errors, any errors discovered are corrected by altering the assembler source program.

This cycle is repeated until the user is satisfied with the simulation results. When the program is satisfactory, the manufacturing output utility program is directed to punch card decks or write files on cassettes that are used for manufacturing ROMs or programming PROMs (as shown in Fig. 7-19).

The prototyping system may be used to complete development of programs assembled, or assembled and simulated, by the cross-support system. The prototyping system debug program allows debugging with a Model 990/4 computer. As portions of the program are validated, the user may specify those areas to be directly executed by the computer, eliminating the effects of simulation and overhead. Real-time programs may be directly executed to locate timing problems. When debugging is complete, the resulting object module is processed by the PROM programmer to produce a

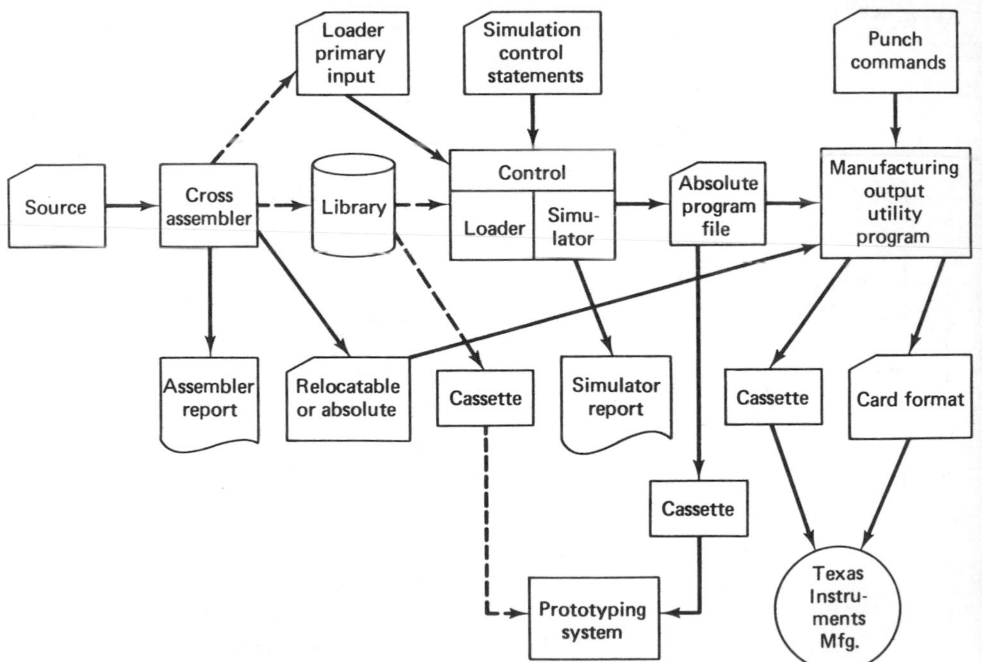

Figure 7-19 TMS 9900 software data file system.

PROM that is programmed with the object program. This PROM may be installed in the Model 990/4 computer for further testing.

Interface between the cross-support system and the prototyping system consists of object modules on cassettes. These may be the relocated and linked (absolute) object modules supplied by the loader, or may be object modules from the library as supplied by the cross-assembler.

7-7 SYSTEM DESIGN EXAMPLES

Figure 7-20 illustrates a typical minimum TMS9900 system. Eight bits of input and output interface are implemented. The memory system contains 1024 × 16 ROM and 256 × 16 RAM memory blocks. The total package count for this system is 13 packages.

A maximum TMS9900 system is illustrated in Fig. 7-21. ROM and RAM are both shown for a total of 65,536 bytes of memory. The I/O interface supports 4096 output bits and 4096 input bits. Fifteen external interrupts are implemented in the interrupt interface. The clock generator and control sections contain memory decode logic, synchronization logic,

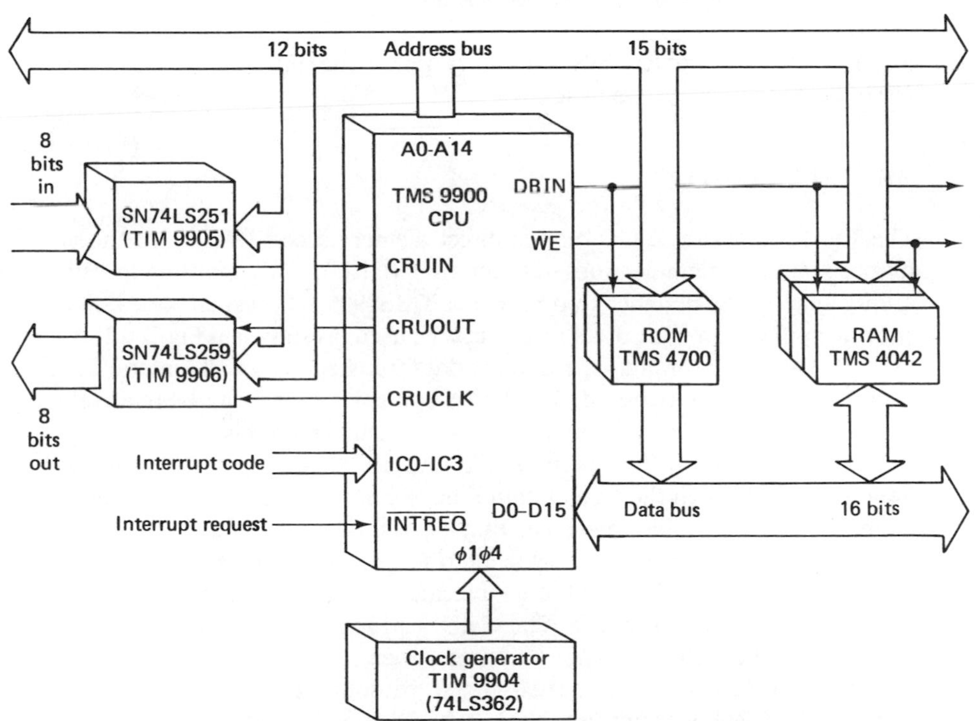

Figure 7-20 Typical minimum TMS9900 system.

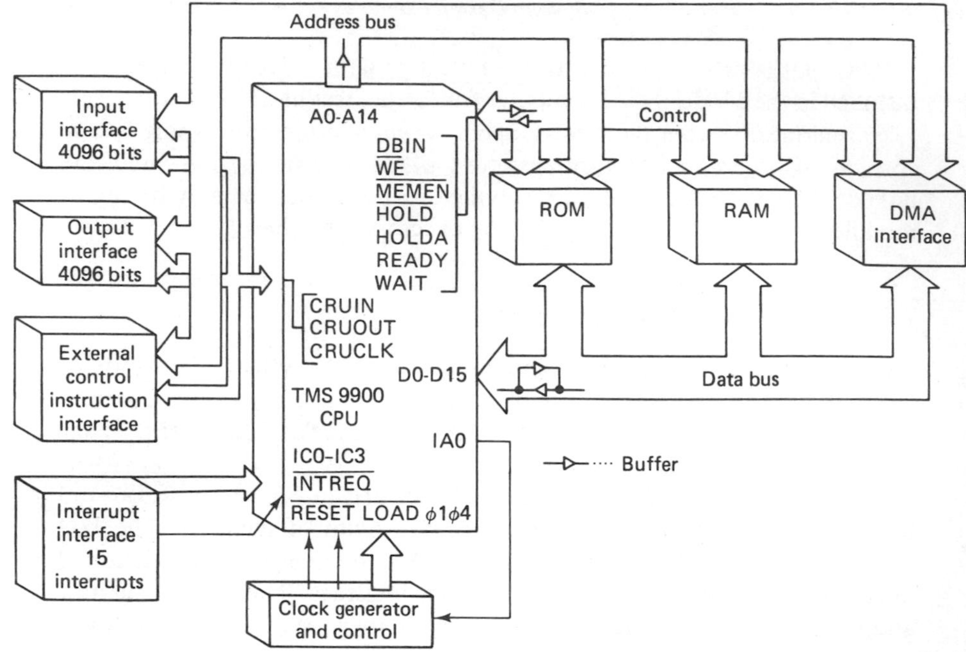

Figure 7-21 Typical maximum TMS9900 system.

and the clock electronics. Bus buffers, required for this maximum system, are indicated on the system buses.

7-8 I/O EXAMPLE

The TMS9900 has three I/O modes: direct memory access (DMA), memory-mapped, and communications register unit (CRU). This multimode capability enables the designer to optimize a TMS9900 I/O system to match a specific application. One or all modes can be used, as shown in Fig. 7-22.

DMA is used for high-speed block data transfer when CPU interaction is undesirable or not required. The DMA control circuitry can be relatively complex and expensive when compared to other I/O methods.

Memory-mapped I/O permits I/O data to be addressed with parallel data transfer through the system data bus. Memory-mapped I/O requires a memory-bus-compatible interface; that is, the device is addressed in the same manner as a memory. Thus, the interface is identical to that of memory.

CRU I/O uses a dedicated serial interface (such as one of the peripherals described in Sec. 7-4) for I/O. The CRU instructions permit transfer of 1 to 16 bits. The CRU interface requires fewer interface signals than the memory interface and can be expanded without affecting the memory system. The CRU does not use the data bus, which is used only for system memory. The following paragraphs describe a typical CRU interface.

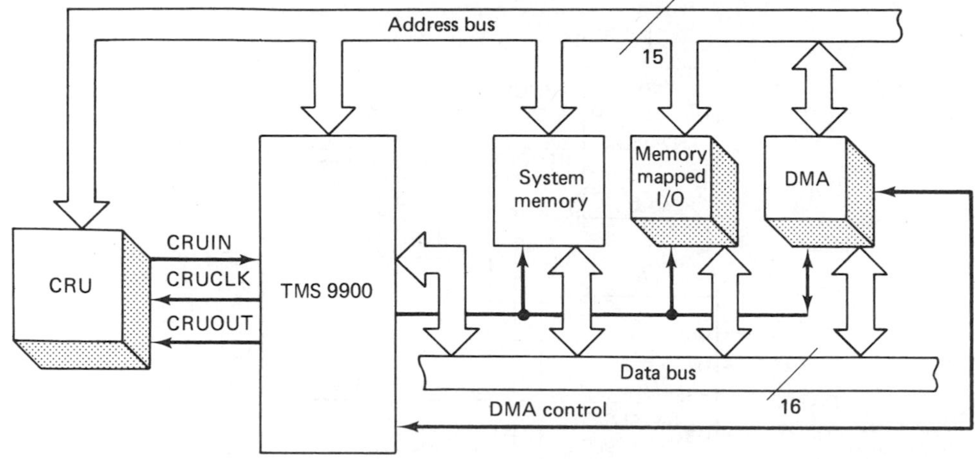

- Communications register unit CRU
- MEMORY MAPPED I/O
- DIRECT MEMORY ACCESS DMA

Figure 7-22 TMS9900 input/output capability.

7-8-1 CRU paper-tape reader interface

Figure 7-23 shows the interface circuits that connect between a paper-tape reader and the TMS9900 microprocessor. Compare this with the sample program described in Sec. 4-6. Note that a TIM9905 data multiplexer (mentioned in Sec. 7-4) contains the CRU circuits in this case. The paper-tape reader is assumed to have the following characteristics:

1. The reader generates a TTL-level active-high signal (SPROCKET HOLE) on detection of a sprocket hole on the paper tape.
2. The reader generates an 8-bit TTL active-low data byte that stays valid during SPROCKET HOLE = 1.
3. The reader responds to a TTL-level active-high command (Paper Tape RUN) signal by turning on when PTRUN = 1 and turning off when PTRUN = 0.

Operation. The interface is selected when $\overline{\text{PTRSEL}}$ = 0; $\overline{\text{PTRSEL}}$ is decoded from the A0–A11 address outputs from the TMS9900. Thus, the output of the TIM9905 is active only when $\overline{\text{PTRSEL}}$ = 0. Otherwise, the output is in high impedance and other devices may drive CRUIN.

The data inputs are selected by A12–A14 and inverted, resulting in active-high data input on CRUIN. The positive transition of SPROCKET HOLE causes PTRINT to go low. PTRINT is the active-low interrupt from the interface. PTRINT is set high, clearing the interrupt, whenever a CRU output machine cycle is executed and the address causes PRTSEL to be active. When a 1 is output to the reader on the PTRUN line, PTRUN is set, thus enabling the reader. The reader is disabled when a 0 is output to the

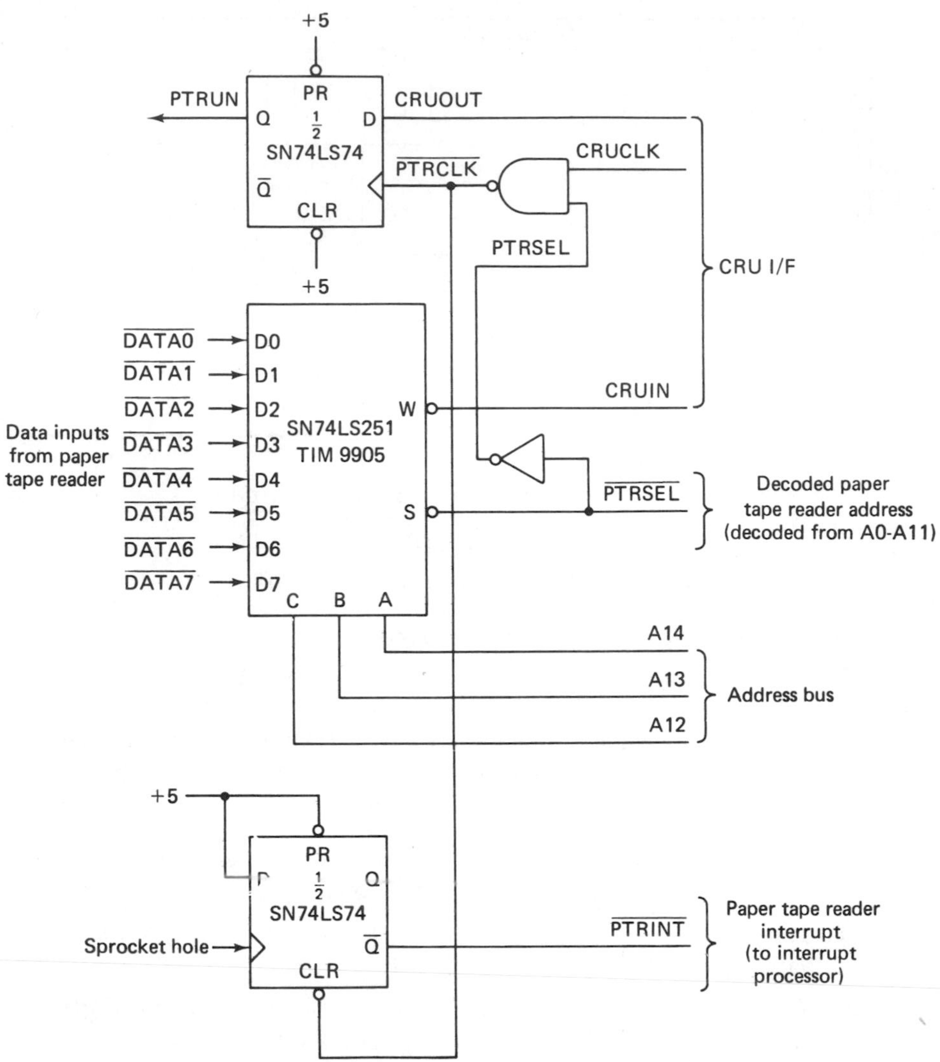

Figure 7-23 Paper-tape-reader interface.

reader on the PTRUN line. Thus, any time PTRUN is set or reset, the interrupt is automatically cleared.

Software control. The software routine for paper-tape reader control is as follows:

PTRINT	STCR (store communications register)	*R11,8
	CB (compare bytes)	*R11+,R9
	JEQ (jump equal)	PTREND
	DEC (decrement)	R10
	JEQ (jump equal)	PTREND

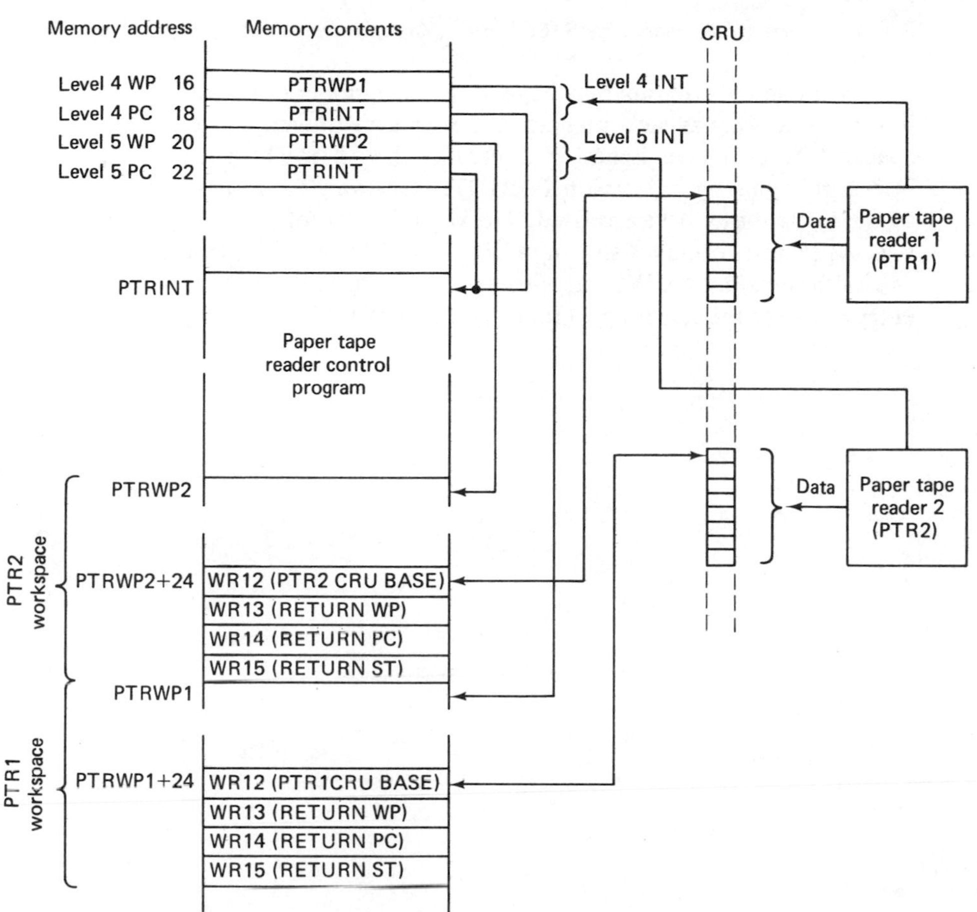

Figure 7-24 Software configuration for two paper-tape readers with common control program.

```
PTRBEG   SBO (set bit to one)                PTRUN
         RTWP (return workspace pointer)
PTREND   SBZ (set bit to zero)               PTRUN
         CLR                                 R8
         RTWP
```

The software routine assumes that the reader has its own workspace and that the workspace registers (R8–R11) are allocated as indicated. It is also assumed that the CRU input bits 0–7 (relative to CRU base) are reader data (Fig. 7-23). CRU output bit 0 controls PTRUN and clears the interrupt.

The procedure has two entry points. One entry is made by a calling routine at PTRBEG to start the reader, and the procedure returns to control that routine. Another entry is made at PTRINT via the interrupt to read a character. The return in this case is to the interrupted program.

The control program may be used by any number of paper-tape reader interfaces, as long as each interface has a separate interrupt level and workspace. As each reader issues an interrupt, the TMS9900 will process the interrupt beginning at location PTRINT. However, the workspace unique to the interrupting device is used. The organization of memory to control two paper-tape readers is shown in Fig. 7-24. The interrupt-transfer vector causes the appropriate WP value to be loaded. In both cases PTRINT, the entry point for the control program, is loaded into PC.

8 Tektronix 8002 Microprocessor Lab

This chapter is devoted entirely to the 8002 Microprocessor Lab manufactured by Tektronix, Inc. The 8002 is not a microprocessor or a microcomputer but a microprocessor development aid (MDA) which can be used with the microprocessors and microcomputers of many different manufacturers. This contrasts with the development aids described in Chapters 3 through 7, which apply only to the microprocessors of one manufacturer. The obvious advantage of the 8002 is that it can be used to compare microprocessors of different manufacturers quickly and simply, without having to invest in the complete development aid system of each manufacturer.

Tektronix provides elaborate instruction manuals for the 8002 (and the 8001 which is a similar, but slightly different, system). These instructions will not be duplicated here. Instead, this chapter provides an introduction to the 8002 and represents only a small fraction of the data taken from the manufacturer's literature.

The chapter starts with a discussion of the features most desirable in an MDA system and shows how the 8002 provides these features. Next, the microprocessor development cycle is discussed, pointing out typical microprocessor design problems and how these problems are avoided by using the 8002. The chapter concludes with a discussion of individual hardware and software modules within the 8002 system.

Figure 8-1 shows the 8002 system with optional CRT (video) terminal and prototype control probe. Figure 8-2 shows the microprocessor development cycle with the 8002. Figures 8-3 and 8-4 are simplified and comprehensive block diagrams, respectively, of the 8002 system.

8-1 PURPOSE, KINDS, AND IMPORTANT FEATURES OF AN MDA

An MDA, when functioning as a design tool, is used to develop microprocessor software programs and to design microprocessor hardware circuits. The MDA then helps to integrate the software and the hardware into a complete stand-alone microprocessor-based product.

A variety of MDAs are available on the market today. They range from simple one-circuit board learning aids to sophisticated multicabinet work stations. Most MDAs are tailored to support only one commercial microprocessor, and only a few can support the design activity for more than one. The 8002 supports several microprocessor systems from the same or different vendors.

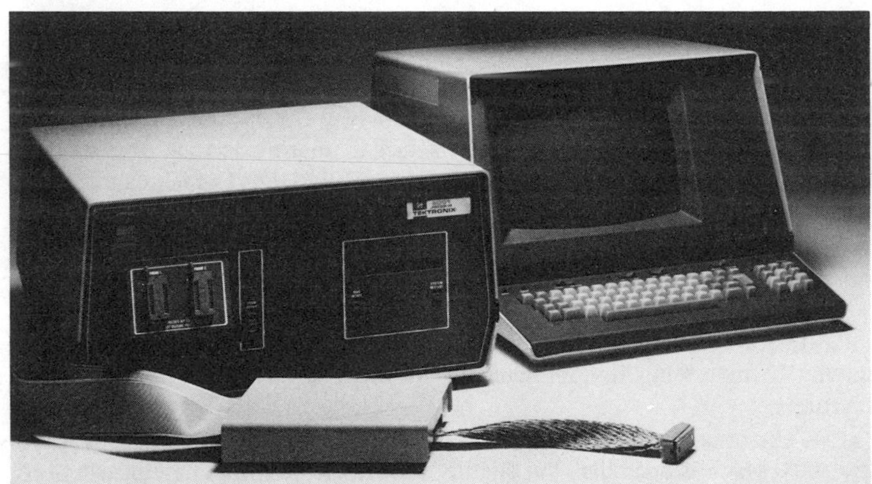

Figure 8-1 Tektronix 8002 microprocessor lab with optional CRT (video) terminal and prototype control probe. (Courtesy Tektronix, Inc., © 1977.)

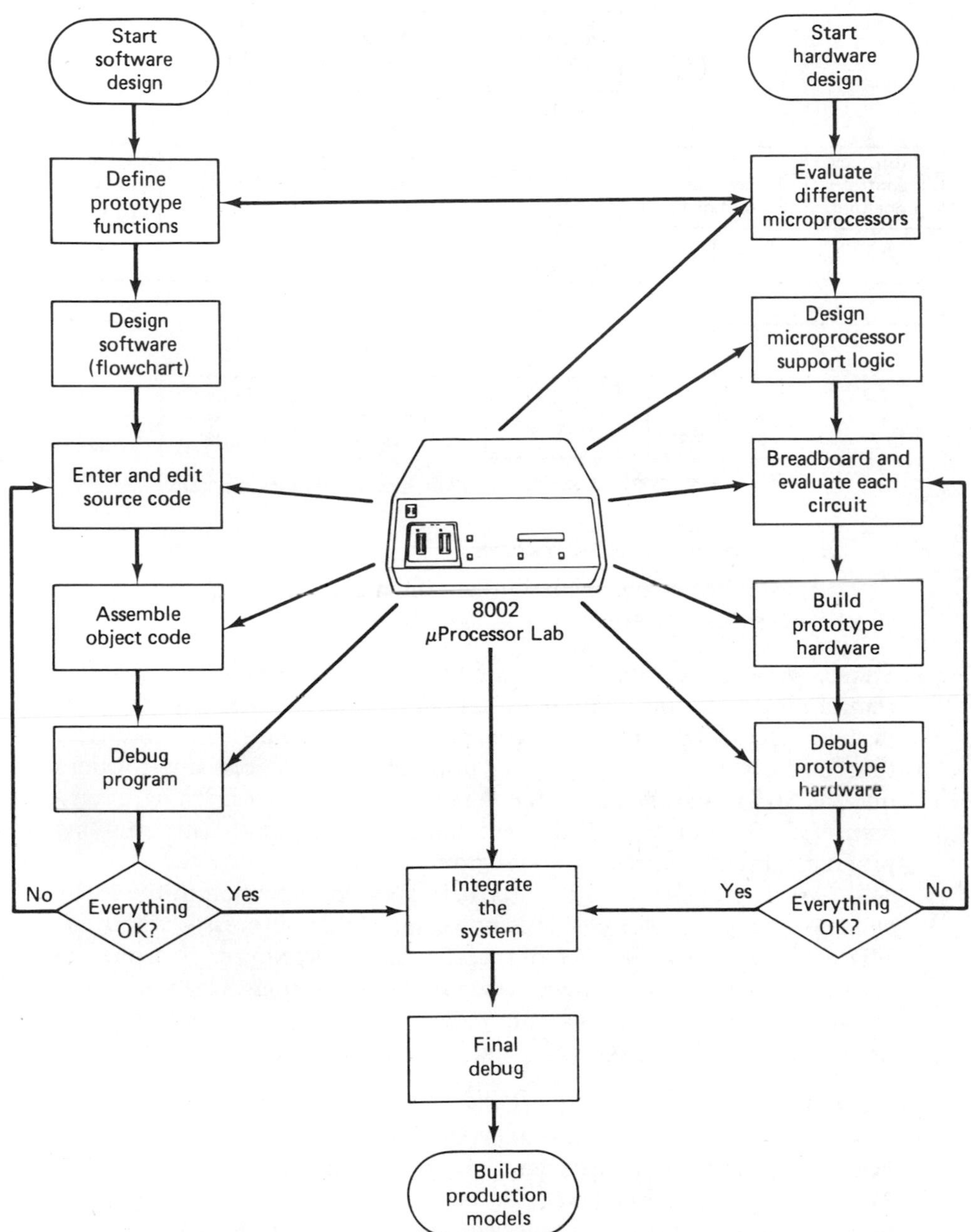

Figure 8-2 Microprocessor development cycle with the 8002 microprocessor lab.

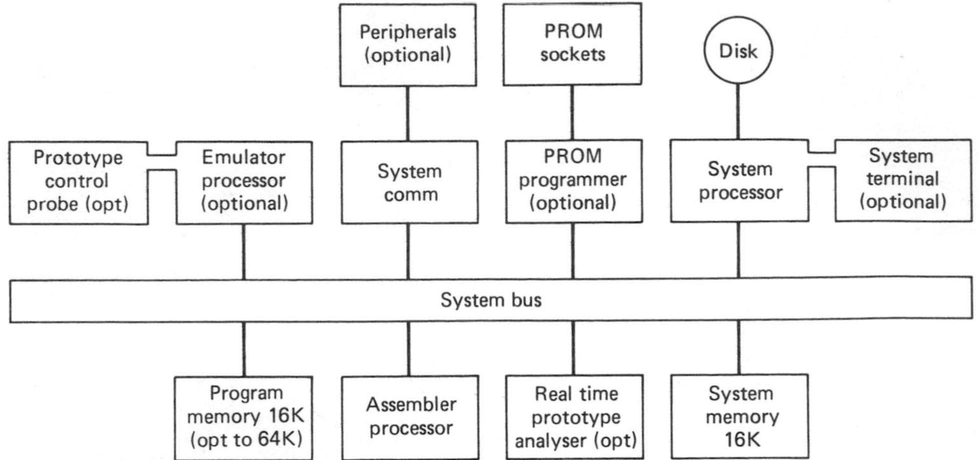

Figure 8-3 8002 microprocessor lab, simplified block diagram.

8-1-1 Important MDA features

Some of the many features that can make one MDA better than another are listed in the following paragraphs.

System programs. Most MDAs are made up of three basic elements: a central processing unit (typically a microprocessor), a memory, and I/O facilities. Most MDAs also contain support programs to perform supervisory functions. These "system programs" help enter microprocessor instructions into the MDA, and then assemble the instructions into a meaningful program for the prototype instrument under development. This resulting program is usually called a "user program."

System programs also monitor user program execution in the MDA *emulator processor.* The emulator processor, a microprocessor within the MDA, is identical to the microprocessor in the prototype. If errors are discovered, the system programs help make the corrections. One measure of an MDAs worth is the ease with which system programs perform user program entry, editing, assembly, and program debugging.

Memory and I/O capability. Other differentiating MDA features are memory and I/O capability. The MDA with fast and convenient data-handling capabilities can develop a program in minutes instead of hours. The MDA, with resident RAM and on-line disk storage, allows information to be stored on disk until needed, then quickly transferred into RAM work space for processing. Efficient memory and I/O capability can decrease the development cycle turnaround time. The 8002 uses a floppy disk operating system with 64K bytes of dynamic RAM storage in program memory. Approximately 630K bytes of on-line storage are available in the floppy disk system.

Simulation versus emulation. MDAs can use either simulation or emulation to locate run-time errors and errors in program logic. When the *simulation method* is used, the MDA software program "acts" like the prototype microprocessor. The program interpreter reads a microprocessor user program instruction, then executes the instruction like the microprocessor in the prototype. Program logic flow can be checked in this manner. However, the simulation program often runs slower than the real microprocessor, and critical timing relationships between hardware and software are impossible to verify.

An *emulation-method* MDA contains a hardware model of the prototype microprocessor. The model may be centered around discrete logic, another type of microprocessor, or a microprocessor identical to the prototype microprocessor. When the processor is identical to the prototype microprocessor, the method is called "substitution emulation." The 8002 uses the substitutive emulation method. All user programs executed on the system can be checked for critical timing relationships between the software and the prototype hardware.

Value of in-prototype testing. Typically, the simplest MDAs do not have facilities for hardware development and testing. More complete MDAs provide limited signal monitoring functions, but most of these functions could be handled by conventional hardware test equipment. The most advanced MDAs have the ability to swap known-good hardware elements into the prototype hardware, and can also swap known-good software programs. By connecting portions of the MDA circuitry to the prototype hardware in the early stages of development, the two parts can be exercised together as one complete microcomputer. The combined unit then runs under the control of the developmental software while being supervised by the MDA's debug system program. This technique, in-prototype testing, allows both hardware and software subcomponents to be tested, debugged, and verified immediately. The entire prototype system is developed from the ground up, on known-good building blocks. The chance of total system failure at the end of the development cycle is eliminated. The 8002 supports in-prototype testing to the fullest extent.

8-2 MICROPROCESSOR DEVELOPMENT CYCLE

Unified hardware/software effort from conception to completion eliminates many problems, and hard-to-find system integration bugs can usually be avoided. A commonly beneficial environment is available to all design team members throughout the microprocessor product development cycle (shown in Fig. 8-2). The following paragraphs describe a typical development cycle, using the 8002.

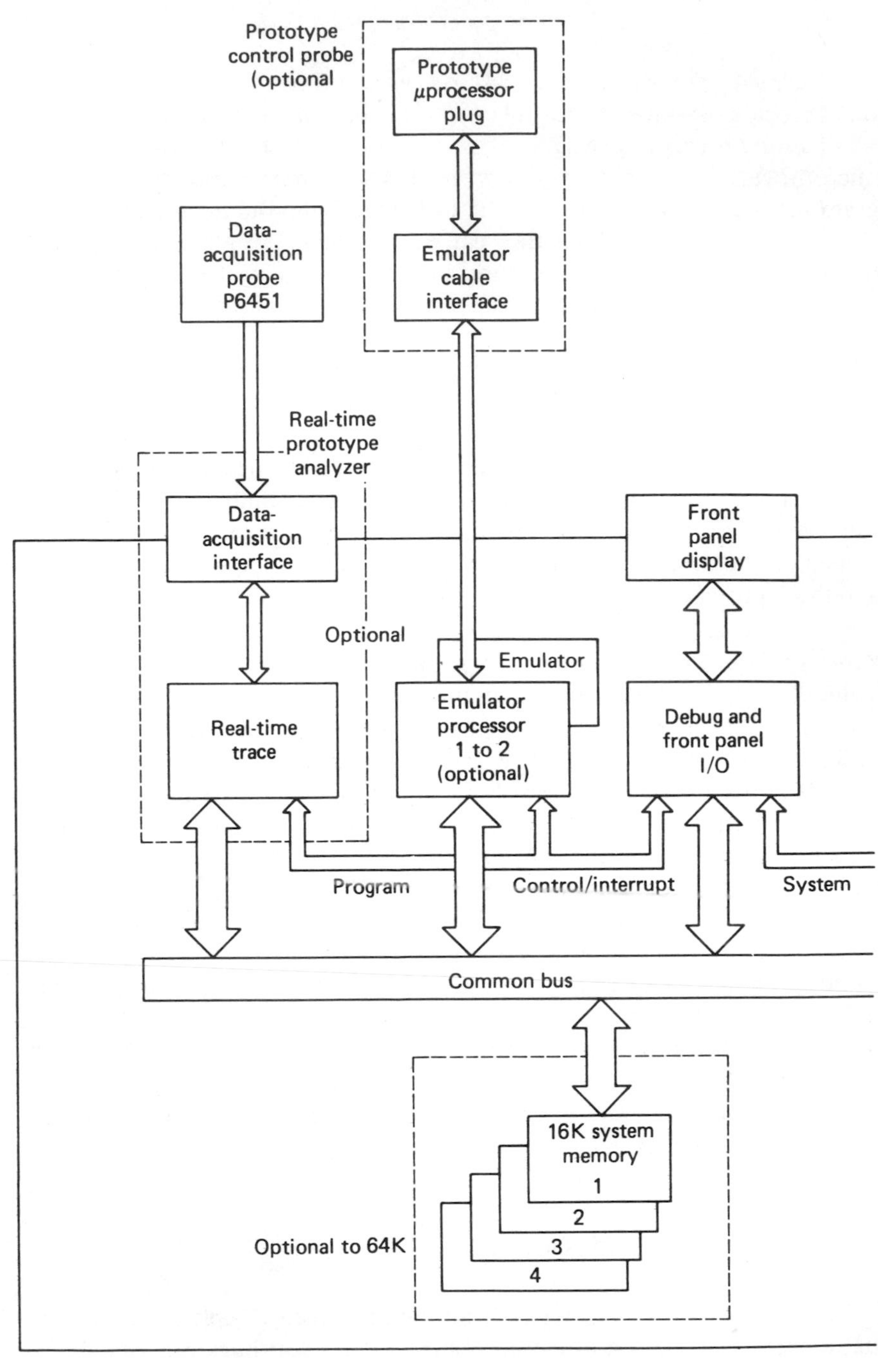

Figure 8-4 8002 microprocessor lab, comprehensive block diagram.

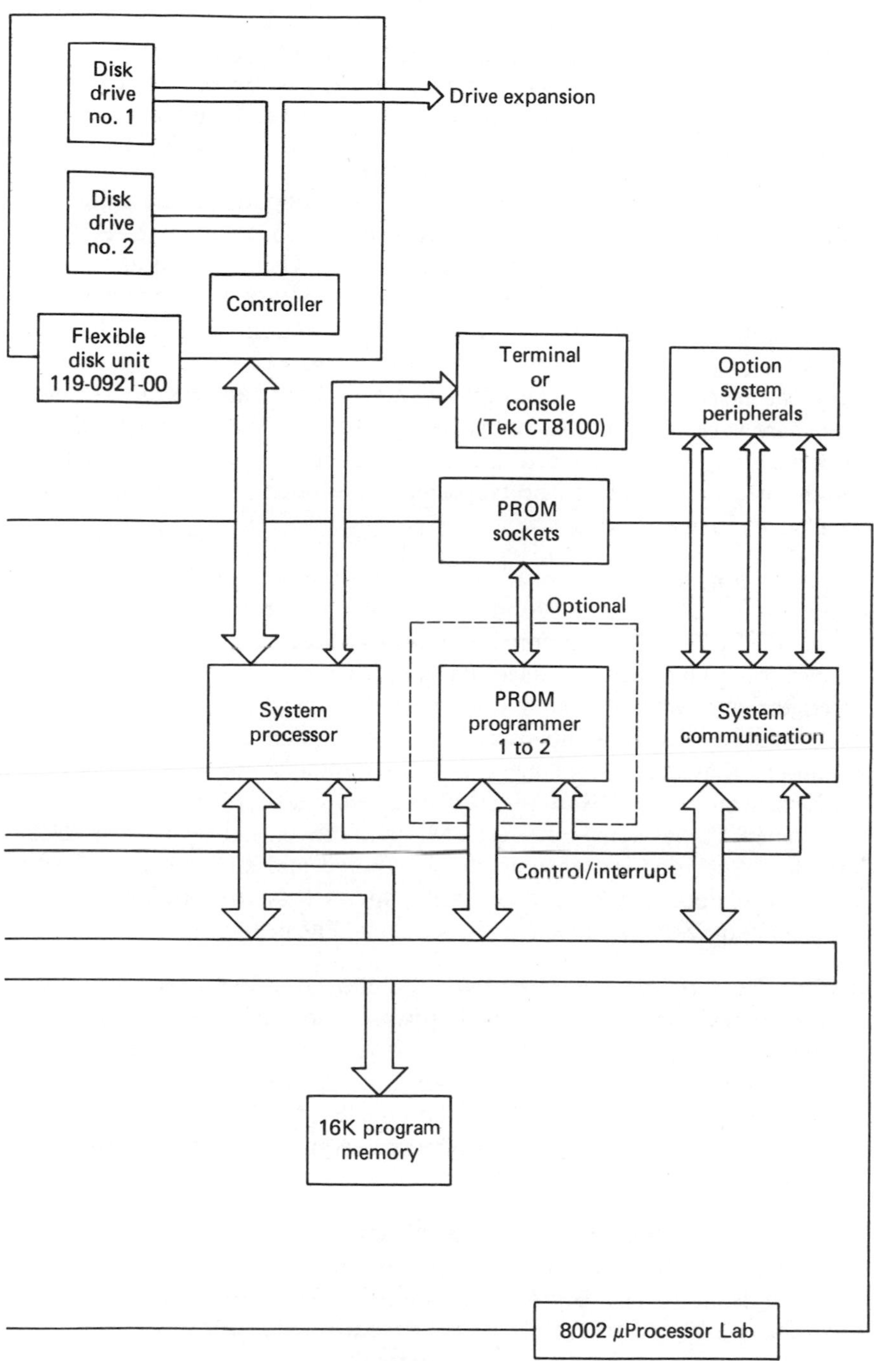

Figure 8-4 *(Continued)*

New product. Management determines the need for a new product based on microprocessor technology. The hardware and software design teams are organized, time schedules are defined, and the funds are appropriated. The purchase of an 8002 is included.

Evaluating microprocessors. Because the 8002 supports several commercial microprocessors, the performance of each microprocessor can be evaluated and compared before a final selection is made. Using the emulator processors available in the 8002, the performance of each microprocessor can be evaluated and compared before a final selection is made. Using the emulator processors available in the 8002, the software team evaluates the different microprocessor instruction sets and software architectural facilities. The hardware team evaluates hardware feature, execution speeds, and I/O handling facilities. Hardware/software trade-offs are discussed over much coffee, and a microprocessor selection is based on the overall requirements for the new product.

Defining prototype functions. Both teams are now ready to define each function in the new product and to determine whether the function should be handled by the software or the hardware. Software flowcharts are then drawn for each function. Since the design team is now familiar with the strengths and weaknesses of the selected microprocessor, the software architecture is structured appropriately. Specification documents are written to ensure that every team member clearly understands the definition of each hardware and software function and their relationships.

The 8002 has a powerful text editor and convenient flexible disk storage facilities. Specification documents are entered and stored on the flexible disks. The documents are then easily updated as the product matures. Copies are quickly available from an optional line printer.

Schematics and breadboard circuits. While the software team is working on the software specifications, the hardware team designs the support logic circuits for the prototype microprocessor. As each circuit is built, it is connected to the emulator processor via the prototype microprocessor (Fig. 8-4). Using their own test programs, stored on the flexible disk unit, the engineers test each circuit. Circuits are modified as required to improve their performance.

Software team starts coding. Using assembly language, the software engineers code the prototype microprocessor program. Because the total program is large and complex, *submodules* are created. One software engineer is assigned to the software keyboard drive, another to the math routines, and so on. Each engineer enters the assembly language program via the system console and uses the *text editor* to add, delete, or change code lines. After editing, the updated program is automatically stored on a flexible disk.

Assembly of the source code. As each program submodule becomes ready, the software engineer invokes the Tektronix assembler, which transforms the source code into machine-executable object code (machine language). Source code errors are then corrected by the engineer with the text editor. The source program is then reassembled. This process is repeated until an error-free assembler listing is obtained. The program submodule is then executed on the emulator processor.

Debugging the software. Programs loaded into program memory are executed under supervision of the debug system. Each program can be single-stepped through execution, or executed in multiple-step sequences, or executed continuously to completion. At any point, the debug system allows program execution to be suspended. Stack pointers, program counters, or general registers can be modified to correct errors. Execution can then continue.

Software and hardware subsystems debugged together. As each software module and its associated hardware module become error-free, they are tested together. All design personnel are able to observe realistic results without the need to "second-guess" actual conditions.

The software is loaded into the emulator processor; the emulator processor is connected to the prototype hardware; and testing begins. Under the supervision of the debug software and an optional real-time prototype analyzer, prototype functions are brought to life. Logic errors are immediately detected and can be corrected quickly. System integration continues until all prototype components are joined. After all hardware circuits have been tested with their software components, the prototype instruments are built.

Total system integration. When all prototype hardware is assembled, the emulator processor is connected to the prototype microprocessor socket via the optional prototype control probe. The total software program is loaded into program memory from the flexible disk files. Prototype hardware is activated; the emulator is turned on; and final system integration begins. Again, the debug system and the real-time prototype analyzer are used to monitor software/hardware activities. System integration proceeds rapidly and smoothly because each subsystem has already been debugged individually.

PROM programming. When final tests are completed, the prototype program is transferred to PROM ICs, using an optional PROM programmer. After being programmed, the PROMs are plugged into the prototype memory slots. The prototype control probe is removed from the prototype microprocessor socket and is replaced by the actual microprocessor. The prototype has now become a complete, thoroughly tested, stand-alone unit. Production can begin.

Using the 8002 as a manufacturing test device. After the new product is in production, the 8002 is used to test production models before shipment to customers. If trouble exists, the 8002 quickly isolates the problems. Troubleshooting time and troubleshooting costs are sharply reduced.

8-3 8002 MICROPROCESSOR LAB HARDWARE COMPONENTS

The 8002 internal architecture centers around a system microprocessor which uses other microprocessors to perform different software and hardware support functions. The system contains 16K bytes of system RAM and up to 64K bytes of RAM program memory (depending upon the options selected). The system also supports two flexible disk drives with approximately 315K bytes on each disk.

Figures 8-3 and 8-4 show simplified and full block diagrams, respectively, of the 8002 architecture and hardware. The system contains three microprocessors: the system processor, assembler processor, and the emulator proessor. Each microprocessor resides on a separate plug-in circuit card in the system mainframe. These cards are connected to each other through a common system bus. Also residing in the mainframe are the optional PROM programmer, the RS-232-C interface (for system communication) with three I/O ports, the 16K-byte system memory, and the standard 16K-byte program memory (expandable to 64K).

The flexible disk unit is housed in a separate chassis and communicates with the other system components through the system processor. Other optional system peripherals such as the CRT terminal and a line printer communicate with the system through the RS-232-C interface. The following is a brief description of each component in the system.

8-3-1 System processor

The system processor performs the following supervisory functions:

1. *System input/output* which directs all I/O activity for the system peripherals, such as the flexible disk, the console, and the line printer.
2. *File management,* which organizes, stores, and retrieves user programs and system programs from the disk drives.
3. *Text editing,* which executes the text editor program and maintains text files on the flexible disk unit.

4. *Debugging,* which executes the debug program and controls the emulator processor through separate debug hardware.
5. *System utility,* which performs all system utility functions such as processing the messages between system peripheral devices.
6. *PROM programming,* which monitors and controls all PROM activity.

8-3-2 Assembler processor

The assembler processor runs the Tektronix Assembler program when the TEKDOS ASM command is executed. (TEKDOS is described in Sec. 8-4.) All assembler I/O activity to and from the flexible disk drive unit is handled by the system processor.

8-3-3 Emulator processor

The emulator processor, a system option, runs and debugs user programs written for a particular commercial microprocessor. A separate processor is available for each commercial microprocessor you wish to emulate. Emulator processors available at the time of this writing are the 8080, 6800, Z80, 8085 and 9900. More are planned for the near future.

The emulator processor serves two purposes. First, the emulator processor runs the user program while the system debugger program is active. This detects program *run-time errors* (such as not allowing the correct number of machine cycles to complete a given instruction) and *program logic errors* (such as issuing an invalid instruction or a valid instruction at the wrong point or sequence in the program). Second, with the addition of an optional prototype control probe, the emulator processor takes the place of the actual microprocessor in the prototype under development. The user program can then drive and test the prototype hardware while under the supervision of the debug system.

8-3-4 System memory

The system memory is a 16K-byte dynamic RAM located on a separate module within the main chassis. The system memory is accessed only by the system processor and is used to store TEKDOS programs while they are executing. The system memory also provides buffer space for all I/O activities.

8-3-5 Program memory

The standard 16K-byte program memory is located on a separate module within the main chassis. Additional 16K-byte memory modules can be added to increase the total capacity to 64K bytes. The primary purpose of program memory is to store a user program while the program is being executed by the emulator processor. The system processor also uses program memory as a text buffer during next editing sessions.

8-3-6 Prototype control probe

The optional prototype control probe consists of cables, interface circuits, and a 40-pin connector (Fig. 8-1). The connector plugs into the empty microprocessor socket on the prototype circuit board. The prototype control probe allows the emulator processor and program memory to take the place of the actual microprocessor and its associated memory in the prototype. Thus, the user program can be run, tested, and debugged in the prototype while under the supervision of the debug system.

The following three emulator operational modes are available with the prototype control probe plugged into the prototype:

1. *System mode (Mode 0),* where the emulator processor runs the program residing in program memory.
2. *Partial emulation mode (Mode 1),* where the emulator processor runs the program residing in the program memory and prototype memory (all I/O signals and data are supplied by the external prototype hardware).
3. *Full emulation mode (Mode 2),* where the emulator processor runs the program resident in the external prototype memory (all I/O signals and data are also supplied by the prototype hardware).

8-3-7 Real-time prototype analyzer

The optional real-time prototype analyzer enables you to dynamically monitor the prototype address bus, data bus, and up to eight other locations of your choice on the prototype circuit board. The analyzer's main function is to locate critical timing problems, and hardware/software sequence problems in the prototyping during the last stages of system integration and debugging. The analyzer monitors prototype activity while the prototype is running at full speed. The test results are printed on either the system console or the optional line printer.

During real-time trace, the last 128 bus transactions are continuously stored in a real-time trace buffer located in the analyzer module. Buffer contents are normally displayed in the pretrigger mode, but they may also be set for variable center or posttrigger by using the capabilities of the real-time prototype analyzer command set. As an example, by combining EVT (event), BIF (break if), and CNT (count) commands, the analyzer may be set to count 64 real-time trace stores from the designated breakpoint, and so to provide a center-trigger display. Such a display, as it might appear on the system console, is shown in Fig. 8-5. Note that the display is centered on the line at address 1E9D.

ADDR	DATA	MNEMONIC	EXTERNAL	BUS
F8BF	FE	OPI	00000001	M R F
F8C0	DA		00001000	M R
F8C1	08	RZ	10101010	M R F
1E90	BA		01100000	M R
1E90	30		00100100	M R
30BA	D3	OUT	00001000	M R F
30BB	F3		10000000	M R
F3F3	0A		00111000	I W
30BC	00	NOP	00000000	M R F
30BD	76	HLT	01001001	M R F

Figure 8-5 Example of real-time trace display. (Courtesy Tektronix, Inc., © 1977.)

8-3-8 PROM programmer

The PROM programmer option allows user programs to be transferred from program memory into PROM ICs. These PROMs are then plugged into the prototype memory sockets and provide permanent program instructions for the prototype microprocessor. Not only can user programs be transferred from program memory into PROMs, but the reverse action can also take place; the contents of PROMs can be read into program memory. In addition, the user program residing in a PROM can be compared with the user program residing in program memory. The differences are displayed on the system console. This comparison technique (called CPROM) is used to verify the contents of a PROM.

The CPROM compare function allows the user to make an address-by-address comparison of the PROM and the developmental program. An inequality between designated PROM bytes and memory bytes causes the memory address, memory byte content, and PROM byte content to be displayed on the system console. Figure 8-6 shows such a display as it might appear on the console. Note that at memory address 0000, the PROM shows a contents of FF, whereas the memory shows a contents of 1F.

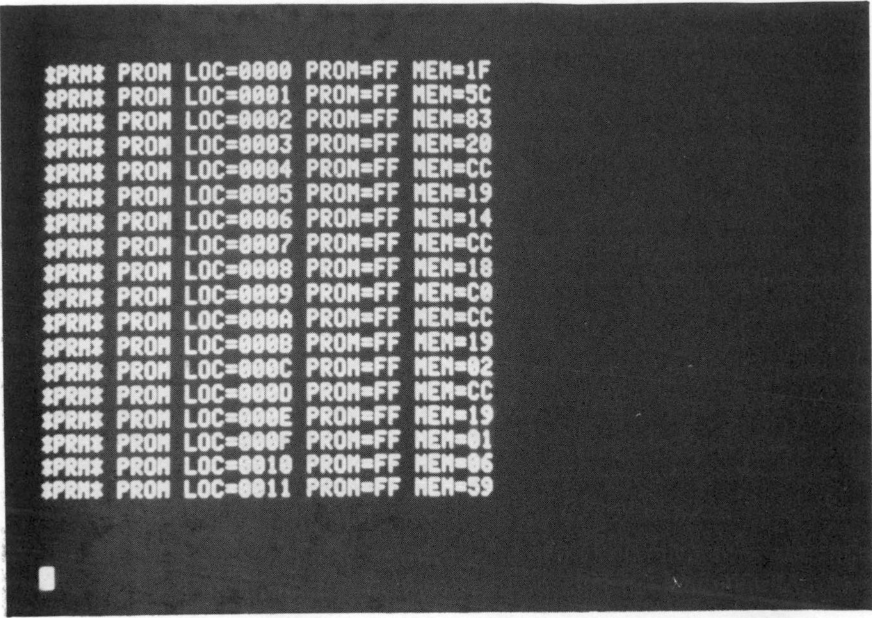

Figure 8-6 Example of PROM comparison display. (Courtesy Tektronix, Inc., © 1977.)

8-3-9 System communications

The system communications board provides three I/O ports for connecting optional peripheral devices to the system. Any device that conforms to the EIA (Electronic Industries Association) standard RS-232-C can be connected to the interface board. Typically, devices such as an optional line printer are connected to the interface. A larger host computer can also be connected to the 8002. User programs can be transferred from the host and down-loaded into the program memory for execution.

8-3-10 Flexible disk unit

A flexible disk (floppy disk) is the on-line mass storage device for the 8002. The flexible disk unit consists of two separate disk drive assemblies, a microprocessor controller, a power suppy, and a cabinet (Fig. 8-1). The flexible disk unit communicates directly with the system processor module through an interconnecting cable. Another flexible disk unit can be connected into the system to provide a four-disk drive option.

8-3-11 System terminal

The 8002 system terminal, also referred to as the system console, serves as the main communication channel between the system and the operator (Fig. 8-1). (Any terminal-like device can be used as the system terminal if the device has a keyboard, a display, and an RS-232-C communication port.) The terminal cable is connected directly to the system processor board in the mainframe.

The CRT terminal shown in Fig. 8-1 features a 9-in refresh alphanumeric display. Another printing terminal (not shown) features a printout display (instead of a refresh CRT) and keyboard.

8-4 8002 SOFTWARE COMPONENTS

The following paragraphs provide a brief description of software available with the 8002 and its options.

8-4-1 TEKDOS (TEKTRONIX Disk Operating System)

TEKDOS, the operating system for the 8002, is loaded from the system disk in the flexible disk unit each time the system is powered up. TEKDOS contains the supervisory software programs for the system. The TEKDOS operation commands are described fully in the user manuals and will not be duplicated here. Instead, we will concentrate on what is available in software.

Text editor. The text editor, invoked by the EDIT command, is used to (1) enter new user programs into memory, then store the programs on disk; and (2) correct user programs for errors detected during assembly. The text editor can also be used to store and update the support documentation for the prototype under development.

Figure 8-7 illustrates the INSERT command, which is part of the text editor functions. As shown, MOV B,A is being inserted into the program at the desired sequence.

TEKTRONIX assembler. After a source program has been entered and stored on a flexible disk unit by the text editor, the user program must be translated into machine-executable object code (machine language). This function is performed by the TEKTRONIX assembler. The assembler then stores the assembled object code on disk in another file.

The assembler is loaded from disk into program memory and runs on the assembler processor. The assembler uses free space in program memory for I/O buffers and symbol tables. Versions of the TEKTRONIX assembler exist for each microprocessor supported by the 8002. A separate disk is used for each version.

Linker. The linker software is considered a submodule of the assembler software and is provided with each system disk. The linker is used to join several smaller user program modules into one large program. This feature allows several software engineers to work on program segments independently, and then join the segments into a large workable program.

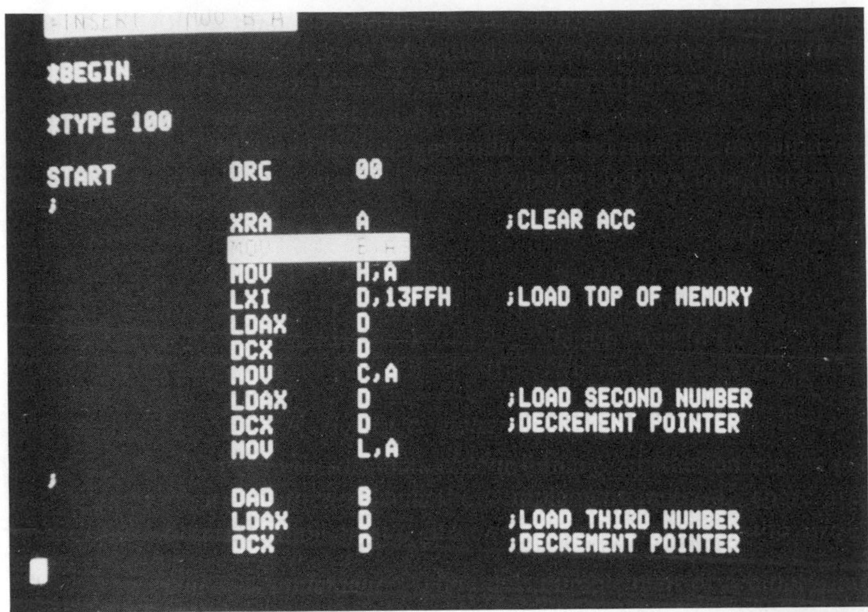

*BEGIN
*TYPE 100
START ORG 00
;
XRA A ;CLEAR ACC
MOV H,A
LXI D,13FFH ;LOAD TOP OF MEMORY
LDAX D
DCX D
MOV C,A
LDAX D ;LOAD SECOND NUMBER
DCX D ;DECREMENT POINTER
MOV L,A
;
DAD B
LDAX D ;LOAD THIRD NUMBER
DCX D ;DECREMENT POINTER

Figure 8-7 Example of INSERT command part of the text editor function.) (Courtesy Tektronix, Inc., © 1977.)

Emulator. The emulator software allows user programs to be loaded into the optional emulator processor for operation, testing, and debugging.

Debug system. When the TEKDOS DEBUG command is invoked, the debugging system is loaded from disk into system memory. With the user program under debug control, every program instruction may be traced; and program memory, emulator processor registers, and prototype memory may all be examined (and altered if necessary). Two software breakpoints may be set to suspend program execution, thus enabling the user to view the effects of memory accesses at specified addresses in program memory. (This is sometimes known as taking a *snapshot* of the program.) Although debugging system operation is basically the same for every microprocessor supported by the 8002, display formatting reflects the individual characteristics of each IC.

Figure 8-8 shows a typical console display during the DEBUG command. Note that the memory location, instruction, mnemonic, operand, pointer, and eight registers are displayed (simultaneously) for each line of the program.

Figure 8-9 shows a "memory mapping," which also serves as a debugging tool. With memory mapping, the user may assign portions of the program to 8002 program memory, or to prototype. The assignments may be made by single addresses or in 512 blocks of 128 bytes each. Memory

```
>TRACE ALL
>GO 0

LOC   INST    MNEM OPER    SP    RF RA RB RC RD RE RH RL

0000  AF      XRA  A       0000  46 00 00 00 00 00 00 00
0001  47      MOV  B,A     0000  46 00 00 00 00 00 00 00
0002  67      MOV  H,A     0000  46 00 00 00 00 00 00 00
0003  11FF13  LXI  D,13FF  0000  46 00 00 00 13 FF 00 00
0006  1A      LDAX D       0000  46 12 00 00 13 FF 00 00
0007  1D      DCX  D       0000  92 12 00 00 13 FE 00 00
0008  4F      MOV  C,A     0000  92 12 00 12 13 FE 00 00
0009  1A      LDAX D       0000  92 0C 00 12 13 FE 00 00
000A  1D      DCX  D       0000  92 0C 00 12 13 FD 00 00
000B  6F      MOV  L,A     0000  92 0C 00 12 13 FD 00 0C
000C  09      DAD  B       0000  92 0C 00 12 13 FD 00 1E
000D  1A      LDAX D       0000  92 B1 00 12 13 FD 00 1E
000E  1D      DCX  D       0000  96 B1 00 12 13 FC 00 1E
000F  4F      MOV  C,A     0000  96 B1 00 B1 13 FC 00 1E
0010  09      DAD  B       0000  96 B1 00 B1 13 FC 00 CF
0011  1A      LDAX D       0000  96 54 00 B1 13 FC 00 CF

>>
```

Figure 8-8 Typical console display during the DEBUG command. (Courtesy Tektronix, Inc., © 1977.)

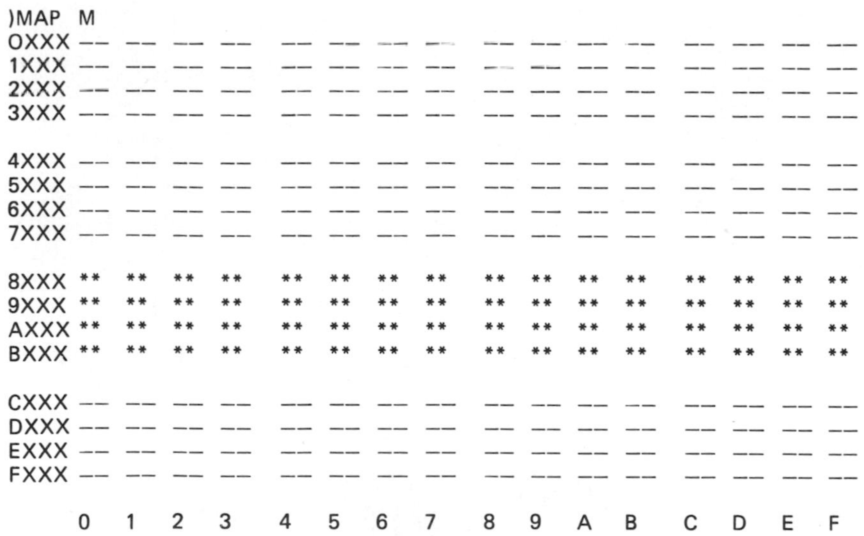

```
)MAP  M
0XXX -- -- -- --  -- -- -- --  -- -- -- --  -- -- -- --
1XXX -- -- -- --  -- -- -- --  -- -- -- --  -- -- -- --
2XXX -- -- -- --  -- -- -- --  -- -- -- --  -- -- -- --
3XXX -- -- -- --  -- -- -- --  -- -- -- --  -- -- -- --

4XXX -- -- -- --  -- -- -- --  -- -- -- --  -- -- -- --
5XXX -- -- -- --  -- -- -- --  -- -- -- --  -- -- -- --
6XXX -- -- -- --  -- -- -- --  -- -- -- --  -- -- -- --
7XXX -- -- -- --  -- -- -- --  -- -- -- --  -- -- -- --

8XXX ** ** ** **  ** ** ** **  ** ** ** **  ** ** ** **
9XXX ** ** ** **  ** ** ** **  ** ** ** **  ** ** ** **
AXXX ** ** ** **  ** ** ** **  ** ** ** **  ** ** ** **
BXXX ** ** ** **  ** ** ** **  ** ** ** **  ** ** ** **

CXXX -- -- -- --  -- -- -- --  -- -- -- --  -- -- -- --
DXXX -- -- -- --  -- -- -- --  -- -- -- --  -- -- -- --
EXXX -- -- -- --  -- -- -- --  -- -- -- --  -- -- -- --
FXXX -- -- -- --  -- -- -- --  -- -- -- --  -- -- -- --

     0  1  2  3   4  5  6  7   8  9  A  B   C  D  E  F
```

Figure 8-9 Graphic display of memory-mapping function.

mapping is operable during partial or full emulation, and allows the designer to map *known good* portions of program memory over to the prototype but, at the same time, to maintain the ability to examine, alter, or move the contents of either memory.

The graphic display (Fig. 8-9) is a matrix in which each element represents 128 bytes of prototype or program memory. An asterisk (*) indicates that those 128 bytes have been mapped to user prototype memory. A hyphen (-) indicates each 128-byte block assigned to program memory.

PROM programmer. The PROM programmer software supervises and controls the transfer to user programs between memory and the PROM IC plugged into the front panel. The PROM programmer hardware is discussed in Sec. 8-3-8.

Glossary

absolute: Pertaining to an address fully defined by a memory address number or to a program that contains such addresses (as opposed to one containing symbolic addresses).

access time: The time required to extract information from or store information into memory. *Read time* is access time required to extract information. *Write time* is time required to store information. Since the access time to different locations (addresses) of memory may be different, access time in a memory is the path that takes the longest time.

accumulator: See *register.* A register in which numbers are totaled or manipulated or temporarily stored for transfers to and from memory or external devices. Generally, an accumulator is a register used in arithmetic circuits, such as the totalizing circuit of an adder, or as a place to hold one operand for arithmetic and logical operations.

adder: Circuit used to perform addition in arithmetic section of microprocessor. Generally, the output of an adder represents the sum of the inputs.

address: A number (noun) that identifies one location in memory. Also (verb), the process of directing the microprocessor to read a specified memory location. "Address" can also refer to a specific channel of information.

address modification: A programming technique of changing the address referred to by a memory reference instruction so that each time a particular instruction is executed it will affect a different memory.

address word: A microprocessor word that contains only the address of a memory location.

addressing modes: See *memory addressing modes.*

ALGOL: Algorithmic-oriented language; a computer language similar to Fortran, but with modifications.

algorithm: Any system of computation in arithmetic. In microprocessors, algorithm is the routine by which arithmetic functions (addition, subtraction, etc.) are accomplished.

alter: A modification of the contents of an accumulator or extend bit (for example, clear, complement, or increment).

ALU (Arithmetic-Logic Unit): That part of a microprocessor which executes adds, subtracts, shifts, ANDs, ORs, and so on.

analog: Pertaining to information that can have continuously variable values, as opposed to digital information, which can be varied in degrees no smaller than the value of the least-significant digit.

analog computer: A computer that solves problems by translating physical conditions (position, flow, temperature, etc.) into electrical quantities, manipulating the electrical values (by addition, subtraction, integration, differentiation, etc.) and then translating the electrical quantities into a readout or display. Analog computers do not use digital techniques. However, there are "hybrid" microcomputers using both analog and digital methods.

AND: A logical operation in which the resultant quantity (or signal) is true if all the input values are true, and is false if at least one of the input values is false.

assemble: A procedure used by progammers to convert programs drawn up in symbolic form (generally flowcharts) into a microcomputer language.

assembler: Software that converts an assembly language program into machine language. The assembler assigns locations in storage to successive instructions and replaces symbolic addresses by machine language equivalents. If the assembler runs on a computer other than that for which it creates the machine language, it is a cross-assembler.

assembly language: An english-like programming language which saves the programmer the trouble of remembering the bit patterns in each instruction; also relieves the programmer of having to keep track of data locations and instructions in the program. The assembler operates on a "one-for-one" basis in that each phrase of the language translates directly into a specific machine language word, as contrasted with *high-level language.*

assembly listing: A printed listing made by the assembler to document an assembly. It shows, line for line, how the assembler interpreted the assembly language program.

asynchronous operation: Circuit operations without reliance upon a common timing source. Each circuit operation is terminated (and the next operation initiated) by a return signal from the destination denoting completion of an operation. (Contrast with *synchronous operation.*)

automatic code: A technique used by programmers wherein the microcomputer itself is used to code programs (such as using the microcomputer to translate a program in flowchart form into a machine language program).

automation: With regard to computers, automation is any system in which many or all of the processes of production, movement, and inspection of parts and materials are automatically performed or controlled by a computer.

auxiliary storage: Any storage system that supplements another storage system. For example, external cassette tapes and floppy disks can be used as auxiliary (or secondary) storage to supplement a microcomputer's ROMs and RAMs.

bar printer: A microcomputer readout device using multiple type bars positioned side by side across a single line. Converts computer electrical readout into type printed on paper sheets or rolls.

base page: The lowest numbered page of a memory. The base page can be directly addressed from any other page.

BASIC: A computer language based upon common English language terms.

batch processing: A technique used by programmers where all information to be processed is coded and collected into groups before processing.

baud: A communications measure of serial data transmission rate; loosely, *bits per second,* but includes characteristic framing start and stop bits.

benchmark program: A sample program used to evaluate and compare microcomputers. In general, two microcomputers will not use the same number of instructions, memory words, or machine cycles to solve the same problem.

binary: In microcomputers, "binary" refers to a number system involving only two possibilities (typically high or low, positive or negative, present or absence of pulses). In mathematics, "binary" refers to a number system with a base of 2. Any system of numbers or codes involving only two states (typically 1 or 0).

binary-coded decimal (BCD): A number system or form of notation where individual decimal digits are represented by a group of binary digits. Typically, each decimal digit is represented by four binary digits arranged in an 8421 order. For example, the decimal number 38 is represented in BCD form as 0011 (a pure binary 3) followed by 1000 (a pure binary 8).

binary counter: A circuit using a group of flip-flops to convert a series of pulses into binary form. See *counter.*

binary point: The fractional dividing point of a binary numeral; equivalent to *decimal point* in the decimal numbering system.

binary program: A program (or its recorded form) in which all information is in binary microcomputer language. See *machine language.*

bistable: A device or circuit with two opposite stable states (such as a bistable flip-flop).

bit: An abbreviation for *bi*nary digi*t*. In number systems, a bit is a single character in a group. Thus, the pure binary number 1001 has 4 bits. In microcomputers, a bit is generally the presence (or absence) of a pulse in a group of pulses representing a binary number. The term "bit" is also used to classify the storage capacity of a memory (such as 50 words of 8 bits each).

bit density: A physical specification referring to the number of bits that can be recorded per unit or length or area (1000 bits per inch of tape, and so on).

bit-serial: One bit at a time, as opposed to bit-parallel, in which all bits of a character can be handled simultaneously.

bootstrap (bootstrap loader): A technique or device for loading first instructions (usually only a few words) of a routine into memory; then using these instructions to bring in the rest of the routine. See *load facility.*

branch instructions: Instructions that direct the microcomputer to leave the basic program at some point and branch to another point in the same program. Also known as *jump, skip,* and *transfer* instructions. Usually, branch instructions are carried out between two decision instructions. A branch is a decision-making instruction which, on appropriate condition, forms a new address into the program counter. The conditions may be zero result, overflow on add, an external flag raised, and so on. One of two alternative program segments in memory are chosen, depending on the results obtained.

breakpoint: A location specified by the user at which program execution (real or simulated) is to terminate. Used to aid in locating program errors.

buffer: Loosely, any electronic device or circuit used between two other devices or circuits. Generally, buffers do not translate information into another form (such as an encoder or decoder) but act to hold the information. In specialized applications, a buffer is a storage device used to compensate for a difference in time of occurrence of events or a different rate of flow. For example, a paper-tape punch can be considered as a buffer, since it permits data to be stored slowly (on a manual keyboard) and then provides for fast read-in to the microcomputer (when the paper tape is played at high speeds).

buffer register: A register used for intermediate storage of information in the transfer sequence between the microcomputer and a peripheral (I/O) device. The buffer can be located in either the microprocessor or the peripheral. RAMs and ROMs often contain buffer registers.

bus: A major electrical path connecting two or more electrical circuits. Typically, a bus is a group of wires that allow memory, microprocessor, and I/O devices to exchange words. The *data bus* and *memory bus* are commonly found in most all microcomputer systems.

byte: A group of bits, possibly (but not necessarily) making up a complete character or word. The most frequent byte size is 8 bits.

call routine: See *subroutine.*

carry: A digit, or equivalent signal, resulting from an arithmetic operation which causes a positional digit to equal or exceed the base of the numbering system.

chain printer: A computer readout device using a chain of several links, each of which contain alphabetic and numeric characters. The characters are printed on paper by means of electrically operated hammers. Converts microcomputer electrical readout into type printed on paper sheets or rolls.

character: The general term to include all symbols, such as alphabetic letters, numerals, punctuation marks, and mathematical operators (+, −, %). Also, the coded representation of such symbols.

checkerboard: An alternating pattern of 0s and 1s stored in a microcomputer for testing purposes.

chip: Specifically, chip refers to the chip of semiconductor material on which integrated circuits are printed. The term can be used in place of integrated circuit or IC.

clear: Reset; typically, when used as a verb, clear means to reset all cells or elements of a device (register, buffer, etc.) to 0.

clock: A device that sends out timing pulses to synchronize the actions of the microcomputer. Typically, common clock signals are sent to all elements of a microcomputer system.

COBOL (Common Business Oriented Language): A computer language developed for business data processing.

code: A system of symbols that can be used by the microcomputer and that in specific arrangements has a special external meaning.

coding: When used by programmers, ''coding'' refers to the translation of a flow diagram into a microcomputer language.

comb printer: A computer readout device using a set of characters mounted so as to face a paper sheet or roll. The characters are printed on paper by means of electronically operated hammers. Converts microcomputer electrical readout into type printed on paper sheets or rolls.

communication system: A microcomputer system having facilities (data sets, modems) for long-distance transfers of information between remote and central locations.

comparator: A circuit for comparing quantities (such as microcomputer words) against presetable upper and lower limits (or against another word) and giving an indication of the comparison results (such as comparing the number of bits in two registers).

compile: When used by programmers, ''compile'' refers to the preparation of a microcomputer language program from a program written in another programming language.

compiler: A language translation program used to transform symbols meaningful to a human operator into codes meaningful to a microcomputer. More restrictively, a program that translates a machine-independent source language into machine language of a specific microcomputer, thus excluding assemblers. Any software used to convert a program in a high-level language such as Fortran into an assembly language or machine language program.

configuration: The arrangement of either hardware or software when combined to operate as a system.

console: Same as *control panel.*

console printer: A computer output printer used primarily for relaying information to the operator. Console printers can be part of the microcomputer, but are usually an auxiliary printer.

contents: The information stored in a register or a memory location.

control: When used by programmers, "control" refers to programming instructions that determine branch instructions.

control bit: A signal, or the stored indication of this signal, which controls the transfer of information to and from peripheral devices. See *flag bit.*

control panel: That part of the microcomputer which contains the operating controls, indicators, and readouts.

control statement: When used by programmers, "control statement" refers to a form of branch instructions that transfers control of the instruction sequence to a statement elsewhere in the program.

counter: A device or circuit used to tally items of information. Microcomputers often include a *program counter.*

CPU (Central Processing Unit): (Same as microprocessor; that part of a microcomputer system which controls the interpretation and execution of instructions. In general, a CPU will contain an arithmetic logic unit (ALU), timing and control, an accumulator, scratch-pad memory, program counters and address stack, instruction register and decode, parallel data and I/O bus, memory, and I/O control.

cross-assembler: A symbolic language translator that runs on one type of microcomputer to produce machine code for another type of microcomputer. See *assembler.*

cycle stealing: A memory cycle stolen from the normal microprocessor operation for a DMA. See *DMA.*

cycle time: Time interval at which any set of operations is repeated regularly in the same sequence.

cycling tape: When used by programmers, "cycling tape" refers to making a new magnetic tape file by updating old magnetic tapes.

data byte: See *byte.*

data pointer: A register holding the memory address of the data (operand) to be used by an instruction. Thus, the register "points" to the memory location of the data.

data register: Any register that holds data.

data set: A device used for translation of microcomputer language (pulses) into a form suitable for transmission over communications lines (telephone, telegraph, etc.) and for translation back to microcomputer language.

data string: A series of data bytes stored in a given sequence in memory.

data word: A microcomputer word consisting of a number, a fact, or other information that is to be processed by the microcomputer.

Often used in place of *data byte.* However, a data word can contain more than one byte.

debug: To eliminate programming mistakes, including omissions, from a program. Similar to *troubleshooting,* but correctly means to locate mistakes in software rather than hardware.

debug programs: Debug programs help the programmer to find errors in the program while they are running on the microcomputer and to replace or patch instructions into (or out of) the program.

decoder: A circuit or device used to translate electrical signals from one form to another (binary to BCD, BCD to hexadecimal, etc.).

decrement: To change the value of a number in the negative direction. If not otherwise stated, a decrement of 1 is usually assumed.

diagnostic programs: These programs check the various hardware parts of a system for proper operation, microprocessor diagnostics check the microprocessor, memory diagnostics check the memory, and so on.

disk storage: A means of storing binary digits in the form of magnetic spots on a rotating circular plate coated with a magnetic material. The information is stored and retrieved by read/write heads positioned over the surface of the disk. Most microcomputer systems use *floppy disk* drives.

direct addressing: The address of an instruction or operand is completely specified in an instruction without reference to a base register or index register.

DMA (Direct Memory Access): A means of transferring a block of information words directly between an external device and the microcomputer memory, bypassing the need for repeating a service routine for each word. This method greatly speeds the transfer process. With DMA, an I/O device takes control of the microprocessor for one or more memory cycles, in order to write to or read from memory. The order of executing the program steps (instructions) remains unchanged.

double-length word: A word that, due to its length, requires two words to represent it. Double-length words are normally stored in two adjacent memory locations.

drum printer: A microcomputer readout device using a drum embossed with letters and numbers. The characters are printed on paper by means of electrically operated hammers. Converts microcomputer electrical readout into type printed on paper sheets or rolls.

dump: To record memory contents on an external medium (such as magnetic tape cassettes).

editor: As an aid in preparing source programs, certain programs have been developed that manipulate text material. These programs, called *editors, text editors,* or *paper-tape editors,* make it possible to compose assembly language programs on-line, or on a stand-alone system.

electrostatic printer: A microcomputer readout device using electrostatic printing (magnetized powdered ink, followed by a heat treatment).

enable: A signal condition that permits some specific event to proceed, whenever it is ready to do so. Used synonymously with *strobe.*

EXCLUSIVE OR: A logical operation in which the resultant quantity (or signal) is true if at least one (but not all) of the input values is true and is false if the input values are all true or all false.

execute: The process of interpreting an instruction and performing the indicated operation(s).

execute phase: A predetermined state of the microcomputer logic which causes the microprocessor to *interpret as data* the information read out of the memory during a memory cycle.

exit sequence: A series of instructions to conclude operation in one area of a program and to move to another area.

extend: A register (usually one or two bits) which extends the effective length of other registers (usually for addition or rotation of bits).

fetch: A process of addressing the memory and reading into the microprocessor the information word, or byte, stored at the addressed location. Most often, fetch refers to the reading out of an instruction from memory.

fetch phase: A predetermined state of the internal microcomputer logic which causes the microcomputer to *interpret as an instruction* the information read out of memory during a memory cycle.

field: When used by programmers, the term represents an area of an instruction, word, or byte assigned to a particular class of data (such as the address portion of a microcomputer word).

fixed-instruction computer (stored-instruction computer): A computer where the sequence of the instruction set is fixed by the manufacturer. The user must design application programs using this instruction set sequence (in contrast to the *micro-programmable computer,* for which the users must design their own instruction set sequence and thus customize the computer for their needs).

fixed memory: See *ROM.*

fixed point: A numeric notation in which the fractional point (whether decimal, hex, binary, or octal) appears at a constant, predetermined position. Compare with *floating point.*

flag bit: A signal, or the stored indication of this signal, which indicates the readiness of a peripheral device to transfer information. See *control bit.*

flag lines: Inputs to a microprocessors controlled by I/O devices and tested by branch instructions.

flip-flop: An electronic circuit (usually a multivibrator) having two stable states and thus capable of storing a binary digit. The states are controlled by signal levels at the input and are sensed by signal levels at the output.

floating point: A numeric notation in which the integer and the exponent of a number are separately represented (frequently by two computer words), so that the implied position of the fractional point can be freely varied with respect to the integer digits. Compare with *fixed point.*

flowchart: A chart (usually in symbolic form) used by programmers to show steps of a program. Generally, a flowchart is drawn on the basis of the particular program requirements and then converted to a language that is compatible with the microcomputer.

format: A predetermined arrangement of bits, language symbols, or characters.

FORTRAN (formula translations or translator): A computer language, or group of languages (Fortran I, II, III, IV), developed primarily for scientific and mathematical data processing. Fortran programs are written in a form resembling algebra rather than in step-by-step instructions.

four-bit system: A basic microcomputer logic code capable of handling information in groups of 4 bits or pulses.

gate: An electronic switch or circuit which passes or stops the flow of current, signals, or pulses. Gates produce an output on condition of certain rules governing input conditions. For example, a two-input AND gate produces a true output only when input 1 *and* input 2 are true (both at binary 1).

guard: A mechanism (usually a certain arrangement of bits in a register or memory location) to terminate program execution (real or simulated) upon access to data at a specified memory location. Used in debugging.

hardware: Physical equipment (electronic or electromechanical components, instruments, or systems) forming a system (such as a microprocessor, ROM, RAM, I/O, etc.).

hexadecimal: Number system using 0, 1, . . ., A, B, C, D, E, F to represent all the possible values of a 4-bit digit. The decimal equivalent is 0 to 15. The hexadecimal digits can be used to specify a byte.

high-level language: Programming language that generates machine codes from problem- or function-oriented statements. Fortran, Cobol, and Basic are three commonly used high-level languages. A single functional statement may translate into a series of instructions or subroutines in machine language, in contrast to a low-level (assembly) language, in which statements translate on a one-for-one basis.

IC (Integrated Circuit): A collection of circuits all fabricated on a single semiconductor chip. Typical microcomputer ICs include the microprocessor, RAM, ROM, I/O, etc.

immediate addressing: The method of addressing an instruction in which the operand is located in the instruction itself or in the memory location immediately following the instruction.

immediate data: Data that immediately follow an instruction in memory, used as an operand by that instruction.

INCLUSIVE OR: A logical operation in which the resultant quantity (or signal) is true if at least one of the input values is true and is false if the input values are all false.

increment: To change the value of a number in the positive direction. If not otherwise stated, an increment of 1 is usually assumed.

incremental magnetic tape: A form of magnetic tape recording in which the recording transport advances by small increments, stopping the tape advancement long enough to record or read one character at the spot located under the read/record head.

indexed addressing: An addressing mode in which the address part of an instruction is modified by the contents in an auxiliary (index) register during the execution of that instruction.

index register: A register which contains a quantity that may be used to modify memory address.

indirect address: The address initially specified by an instruction when it is desired to use that location to redirect the microcomputer to some other location to find the effective address or the instruction.

indirect addressing: A means of addressing in which the address of the operand is specified by an auxiliary register or memory location specified by the instruction rather than by bits in the instruction itself.

indirect phase: A predetermined state of the microcomputer logic which causes the microprocessor to *interpret* as an address the information read out of memory during a memory cycle.

inhibit: To prevent a specific event from occurring.

initialize: The procedure of setting various parts of a stored program to starting values so that the program will behave the same way each time it is repeated. The procedures are often included as part of the program itself.

input: Information or instructions to be processed, usually transferred from a peripheral device into the microcomputer. Can also apply to the transfer process itself.

input/output (I/O): Relating to the equipment or method used for transmitting information into or out of the microcomputer.

input/output channel: The complete input or output facility for one individual device or function, including its assigned position in the microcomputer, the interface circuitry, and the external device.

input/output system: The circuitry involved in transferring information between the accumulators and the peripheral devices.

instruction: A set of bits that defines microcomputer operation and is a basic command understood by the microprocessor. Instructions may move data, do arithmetic and logic functions, control I/O devices, or make decisions as to which instruction to execute next.

instruction code: The arrangement of bits which tells the microcomputer to execute a particular instruction.

instruction cycle: The process of fetching an instruction from memory and executing it.

instruction length: The number of words needed to store an instruction. One-word instructions are used in most microcomputers, but some use multiple words to form one instruction. Multiple-word instructions have different instruction execution times, depending on the length of the instruction.

instruction register: A register that forms part of the instruction logic. The instruction register generally receives bits from the transfer register when each new instruction is read out of memory and retains these bits for instruction identification. Often, the instruction register is not a "working register."

instruction repertoire: See *instruction set.*

instruction set: The set of general-purpose instructions available with a given microprocessor. In general, different machines have different instruction sets. The number of instructions only partially indicates the quality of an instruction set. Some instructions may only be slightly different from another; others may rarely be used. Instruction sets should be compared using *benchmark programs* typical of the application, to determine execution times and memory requirements.

instruction time: The time required to fetch an instruction from memory and execute it.

instruction word: A microcomputer word containing an instruction code. The code bits may occupy all or part of the word.

interface: The connecting circuitry that links the microcomputer system to peripheral devices.

interpreter: A program that fetches and executes "instructions" (*pseudo instructions*) written in a higher-level language. The higher-level language program is a *pseudo program.* Contrast with *compiler.*

intercord gap (IRG): An interval of space or time deliberately left between recording portions of data or records. Such spacing is used to prevent errors through loss of data or overwriting and permits magnetic tape start–stop operations.

interrupt: The process, generally initiated by an external device, which causes the microcomputer to interrupt a program in process, generally for the purpose of transferring information between that device and the microcomputer.

interrupt mask (interrupt enable): A mechanism (often an arrangement of bits in a register) which allows the program to specify whether or not interrupt requests will be accepted.

interrupt request: A signal to the microcomputer that temporarily suspends the normal sequence of a routine and transfers control to a special routine. Operation can be resumed from this point later. Ability to handle interrupts is very useful in communications applications, where it allows the microprocessor to service many channels.

interrupt service routine: A routine (program) to properly store away to the stack the present status of the machine in order to respond to an interrupt request; perform the "real word" required by the interrupt; restore the saved status of the machine; and then resume operation of the interrupted program.

I/O control electronics (I/O controller): The control electronics required to interface an I/O device to a microprocessor.

I/O interface: See *I/O control electronics.*

I/O port: A connection to a microprocessor which is configured (or programmed) to provide a data path between the microprocessor and the external devices, such as keyboard, display, reader, etc. An I/O port of a microprocessor may be an input port or an output port, or may be bidirectional.

jump: A departure from the normal one-step incrementing of the program counter. By forcing a new value (address) into the program counter the next instruction can be fetched from an arbitrary location (either farther ahead or back). For example, a program jump can be used to go from the main program to a subroutine, from a subroutine back to the main program, or from the end of a short routine back to the beginning of the same routine to form a loop. See also *branch instruction.* If you reached this point in the glossary from *branch,* you have executed a *jump.* Now Return.

label: Any arrangement of symbols, usually alphanumeric, used in place of an absolute memory address in microcomputer programming.

library routine: A routine designed to accomplish some commonly used mathematical function and kept permanently available on a library program tape, floppy disk, and so on.

linkage: See *subroutine.*

loader: A program to read a program from an input device into RAM. May be part of a package of utility programs.

load facility: A hardware facility to allow program loading using DMA. It makes bootstrap unnecessary.

logical operation: A mathematical process based on the principles of truth tables (such as AND, OR, NAND, etc., operations).

loop: A self-contained series of instructions in which the last instruction can cause repetition of the series until a terminal condition is reached. Branch instructions are used to test the conditions in the loop to determine if the loop should be continued or terminated.

low-level language: See *machine language.*

machine: A term for a microprocessor or microcomputer (of historical origin).

machine code: See *machine language.*

machine cycle: The basic microprocessor cycle. In one machine cycle an address may be sent to memory and one word (data or instruction) read or written, or in one machine cycle, a fetched instruction can be executed. One machine cycle typically consists of eight clock pulses.

machine language: The numeric form of specifying instructions, ready for loading into memory and execution by the machine. This is the lowest-level language in which to write programs. The value of every bit in every instruction in the program must be specified (by giving a string of binary, octal, or hex digits for the contents of each word in memory).

machine state: See *state code.*

machine timing: The regular cycle of events in the operation of internal microprocessor circuitry. The actual events will differ for various processes, but the timing is constant through each recurring cycle.

macroinstruction: A symbolic source language statement which is expanded by the assembler into one or more machine language instructions, relieving the programmer of having to write out frequently occurring instruction sequences.

memory: That part of a microcomputer which holds data and instructions. Each instruction or data byte is assigned a unique address which is used by the microprocessor when fetching or storing the information.

memory addressing modes: The method of specifying the memory location of an operand. Common addressing modes are direct, immediate, relative, indexed, and indirect. These modes are important factors in program efficiency.

memory address register: The microprocessor register that holds the address of the memory location being accessed.

memory cycle: That portion of the microcomputer timing during which the contents of one location of memory is read out (into a register) and written back into that location.

memory protect: A means of preventing inadvertent alteration of a selected segment of a memory.

microprogrammable computer: A computer in which the internal microprocessor control signal sequence for performing instructions is generated from a ROM. By changing the ROM contents, the instruction set sequence can be changed. This contrasts with a *fixed-instruction computer,* in which the instruction set sequence cannot be readily changed.

mnemonic: An abbreviation or arrangement of symbols used to assist human mnemonics. For example, in one microprocessor, CLE stands for "clear the E register." This is easier to remember than, say, "perform instruction 33."

multiple precision: Referring to arithmetic in which the microcomputer, for greater accuracy, uses two or more words to represent one number (the more bits used, the greater the precision in microcomputer arithmetic).

multiple processing: Using two or more microprocessors in a single system, operating out of a common memory. This arrangement permits execution of as many programs as there are microprocessors.

nesting: Subroutines that are called by subroutines are said to be nested. The *nesting level* is the number of times nesting can be repeated.

nibble: A sequence of 4 bits operated upon as a unit. Also see *byte.*

object program: Program that is the output of an automatic coding system, such as an assembler. Often the object program is a machine language program ready for execution.

on-line system: A system of I/O devices in which operation of such devices is under control of the microprocessor, and in which information reflecting current activity is introduced into the data processing or controlling system as soon as it occurs.

OP code (operation code): A code that represents specific operations of an instruction.

operand: That which is operated on. An operand is usually identified by an address part of an instruction.

operating system: System software controlling the overall operation of a multipurpose computer system, including such tasks as memory allocation, input and output distribution, interrupt processing, and job scheduling.

overflow: A register (usually 1 or 2 bits) which indicates that the result of an addition has exceeded the maximum permitted value. The addition result will thus be missing one or more significant bits. Also, a signal or alarm which indicates that the capacity of the microprocessor circuit (usually a register) has been exceeded.

page: A natural grouping of memory locations by higher-order address bits. In an 8-bit microprocessor, $2^8 = 256$ consecutive bytes often may constitute a page. Then words on the same page only differ in the low-order 8 address bits.

page zero: The memory page that includes the lowest-numbered memory addresses.

parity: An equality checking scheme to ensure accuracy of transferred or transmitted data.

pass: The complete process of reading a set of recorded information (one tape, one disk, etc.) through an input device, from beginning to end.

PLA (Programmable Logic Array): A PLA is an array of logic elements that can be programmed to perform a specific function. In this case, the array of logic elements can be as simple as a gate or as complex as a ROM. The array can be programmed (normally mask-programmable during manufacture) so that a given input combination produces a known output function.

pointer: Registers in the microprocessor that contain memory addresses. See *program counter* and *data pointer.*

program: A collection of instructions properly ordered to perform a particular task.

program counter: A microprocessor register which specifies the address of the next instruction to be fetched and executed. Normally, it is incremented automatically each time an instruction is fetched.

PROM (Programmable ROM): An IC memory array that is manufactured with a pattern of either all 0s or 1s and has a specific pattern written into it by the user using a special hardware programmer. Some PROMs, called EAROMs (electrically alterable ROMs), can be erased and reprogrammed. The erasure is generally done with ultraviolet light.

protocol: The standard or accepted format for transmission of data over a communications system.

prototyping system: A hardware system used to breadboard a microprocessor-based product. Contains microprocessor, memory, basic I/O, power supply, switches and lamps, provisions for custom I/O controllers, memory expansion, and often a utility program in fixed memory (ROM).

pseudo instruction: See *interpreter.*

pseudo program: See *interpreter.*

RAM (Random-Access Memory): Any type of memory that has both read and write capability. It is randomly accessible in the sense that the time required to read from or to write into memory is independent of the memory location where data were most recently read from or written into. In contrast, in a *serial memory,* this time is variable. RAM memory is generally not permanent.

real time: The time elapsed between events occurring externally to the microcomputer. A microcomputer that accepts and processes information from one such event and is ready for new information before the next event occurs is said to operate in a real-time environment.

register: A fast-access circuit used to store bits or words in a microprocessor. Registers play a key role in microprocessor operation. In most applications, the efficiency of programs is related to the number of registers.

relative addressing: The address of the data referred to is the address given in the instructions, plus some other number. The "other number" can be the address of the instruction, the address of the first location of the current memory page, or a number stored in a register. Relative addressing permits the machine to relocate a program or a block of data by changing only one number.

relocatable: Pertains to programs where instructions can be loaded into any stated area of memory.

resident software: Assembler and editor programs incorporated with a prototyping system to aid in user program writing and development. See *software.*

return routine: See *subroutine.*

ROM (Read-Only Memory): A fixed memory that cannot be readily rewritten. ROM requires a masking operation during production to permanently record program or data patterns in it. The information is stored on a permanent basis and used repetitively. Such storage is useful for programs or tables of data that remain fixed, and is usually randomly accessible.

routine: Usually refers to a subprogram or task which is less complex than the main program. A program may contain many routines. See *program.*

scratch-pad memory: RAM or registers that are used to store temporary intermediate results (data) or memory addresses (pointers).

select code: A number assigned to I/O channels for the purpose of identification in information transfers between the microcomputer and external devices.

serial memory (serial access memory): Any type of memory in which the time required to read from or write into the memory is dependent on the location in memory. This type of memory must wait while nondesired memory locations are accessed. Examples are paper tape, disk, and magnetic tape.

service routine: A sequence of instructions (or program) designed to accomplish the transfer of information between a particular device and the microcomputer.

sign: The algebraic plus or minus (+ or −) indicator for a mathematical quantity. Often, this is represented by a bit (usually the most-significant bit) in a word. Such bits are called *sign bits.*

simulators: Software simulators are sometimes used in the debug process to simulate the execution of machine language programs using another computer (often a time-sharing system). These simulators are especially useful if the actual computer is not available. They may facilitate the debugging by providing access to internal registers of the microprocessor that are not brought out to external pins or ports.

skip: An instruction that causes the microprocessor to omit the instruction in the immediately following location. A skip is usually arranged to occur only if certain specified conditions are sensed and found to be true, thus allowing various decisions to be made. A skip instruction is a form of *branch instruction* or *jump instruction.*

snapshots: Capture of the entire state of a machine (real or simulated), including memory contents, registers, flags, and so on. Also applies when a development tool or logic analyzer is used to capture and display a large portion of microcomputer contents.

software: Computer programs. Often used to denote general-purpose programs provided by the manufacturer, such as assembler, editor, compiler, and so on.

source program: Computer program written in a language designed for ease of expression by human beings; symbolic or algebraic. Often applied to *assembly language.*

stack: A sequence of registers and/or memory locations used in LIFO (last-in/first-out) fashion. A *stack pointer* specifies the last-in entry (or where the next-in entry will go).

stack pointer: The counter, or register, used to address a stack in memory.

stand-alone system: A microcomputer software development system that operates without connection to another computer or time-sharing system. Such a system can include an assembler, editor, debugging aids, and possibly some of the features of a prototyping system. The term also applies to certain "computer-on-a-chip" microprocessors that include ROM, RAM, and I/O within a single IC.

starting address: The address of a memory location in which is stored the first instruction of a given program. The starting address is not always the lowest-numbered address. Generally, a block of addresses are reserved for some specific purpose other than the normal program.

state code: A coded indication of the existing microprocessor state (such as responding to an interrupt, servicing a DMA request, executing an I/O instruction, etc.).

string length: The length of a data string or group, such as a number of adjacent addresses used for a given memory function.

subroutine: A subprogram (group of instructions) reached from more than one place in a main program. The process of passing control from the main program to a subroutine is a *subroutine call,* and the mechanism is a *subroutine linkage.* Often data or data addresses are made available by the main program to the subroutine. The process of returning control from subroutine to main program is *subroutine return.* The linkage automatically returns control to the original position in the main program or to another subroutine. See *nesting.*

symbolic address: A label assigned in place of asbolute numeric addresses, usually for purposes of relocation. See *relocatable.*

synchronous operation: Use of a common timing source (clock) to time circuit or data-transfer operations. (Contrast with *asynchronous operation.*)

syntax: Formal structure. The rules governing sentence structure in a language, or statement structure in a language such as assembly language or Fortran.

terminal: An I/O device at which data leaves or enters a microcomputer system (such as a CRT video terminal, electric typewriter, TTY, etc.).

test and branch: See *branch.*

time sharing: A system where a central computer is used by several operators at remote locations.

TTL (transistor–transistor logic): The most common form of digital logic circuit. Most microprocessors and microcomputers are compatible with TTL. Major TTL characteristics are a 5-V power supply, and pulses that swing from zero volts (for a 0) to slightly less than 5 V (for a 1).

unbundling: Pricing certain types of software and services separately from the hardware.

universal asynchronous receiver/transmitter (UART): A device that translates serial data bits from two-wire lines to parallel format (receive mode), or parallel data bits to serial format for transmission over two-wire lines (transmit mode).

utility program: A program providing basic conveniences, such as capability for loading and saving programs, for observing and changing values in a computer, and for initiating program execution.

waiting loop: A sequence of instructions (frequently only two) which is repeated indefinitely until a desired external event occurs, such as the receipt of a flag signal.

word: The basic group of bits that is manipulated (read in, stored, added, read out, etc.) by the microcomputer in a single step. Two types of words are used in every microcomputer: data words and instruction words. Data words contain the information to be manipulated. Instruction words cause the microcomputer to execute a particular operation.

word length: The number of bits in the microcomputer word. The longer the word length, the greater the *precision* (number of significant digits). In general, the longer the word length, the richer the instruction set, and the more varied the addressing modes.

Index

A

B

C

D

E

F

G

H

I

J

K

L

M

N

O

P

R

S

T

U

V

W